Boone County: From Mastodons to the Millennium

Written by
Jennifer S. Warner

With help from the
1998 Boone County Bicentennial Book Committee

Boone County:
From Mastodons to the Millennium

Was a community effort
involving many Boone Countians
including the Bicentennial Book Committee.

Special thanks to these people and organizations
who also contributed a great deal of time:
Asa Rouse, Katie Presnell, Margaret Stephens, Betty Roter, Ann Leake, Bruce Wess,
City of Florence, John Cobb and The *Recorder* Newspapers, Lee Thomas of the *Dixie News*,
The Boone County Library Research Staff;
Margaret Whitehead, Pat Yannarella, Michelle Foster, Lynn Gorz, Mike Corboy;
And others

Funded in part through:

1998 Boone County Judge Executive Ken Lucas
Fiscal Court Members Harold Campbell, Shirley Meihaus and Irene Patrick

Boone County Planning Commission

Cinergy, the power behind ULH&P

Scripps Howard Foundation
The E.W. Scripps Company, *The Cincinnati Post, The Kentucky Post* and WCPO-TV

Cover shows the Boone County seal
Dust jacket designed by Kay Maydak
© 1998

ISBN-0-9663536-1-7

Any proceeds from book sales will be used to begin a Boone County Historical Society

Philosophy
From
Boone County Recorder
Vol. 1, No. 1, Sept. 24, 1875

If you must form harsh judgements, form them of yourselves, not of others, and, in general begin by attending to your own deficiencies first. If every one would sweep up his own walk, we would have very clean streets.

Like most garments, like most carpets, every thing has a right side and a wrong side.
You can take any joy and by turning it around find troubles on the other side; or you may take the greatest trouble, and by turning it around find joy on the other side.
The gloomiest mountain never casts a shadow on both sides at once, nor does the greatest of life's calamities.

Give a boy a market-basket of groceries to carry home, and he will swing it across his spine, bend halfway to the ground and groan with agony, but give him that weight of baseball bats, and he will skip along as merry as a potato bug in a ten-acre lot.

Foreword From the Bicentennial Book Committee

We cannot know where we are going unless we understand where we came from.

Numerous stories have been told about the history of Boone County. Some were true, a number were fiction, and others were fables bearing labels of truth. We, the members of the Bicentennial Publication Committee, have worked for well over a year to sort through those stories and publish this volume. While that has been a daunting and time-consuming task, like our pioneers, we have worked diligently and believed in God, expecting everything to work out.

It has been a pleasure, a labor of love, and has provided each of us a sense of satisfaction. We have worked well together. We've been fortunate to have the excellent leadership of our Chairman Bruce Ferguson, the writing ability of Jennifer Warner, and the publishing services of Windmill Publications Inc.

We've been concentrating on the past, re-familiarizing ourselves with the history of this region's development, trying to understand how societal pressures and events of the past twenty decades have affected us as a community, and seen how we have become what we are in 1998. After following this historic trail, we strain to catch a glimpse of what might lie ahead, what changes our grandchildren and great grandchildren will see if they remain in Boone County.

It is our sincere desire that these books will not simply gather dust on the coffee tables and shelves of those who purchase or receive them as gifts. We hope that the contents will appeal to everyone,
- stirring the memories of those who have lived in Boone County for many years,
- capturing the imaginations of recent arrivals, and
- encouraging all to share Boone County's story with their youngsters.

Many issues loom before Boone County residents, decisions that will be made by the Class of 2000 and their offspring. We present this work, knowing full well that it is not exhaustive and not a history textbook. Nevertheless, it is the fascinating story of our people, our community – our beloved Kentucky home. We have worked many hours. We hope you enjoy this volume.

Boone County Bicentennial Book Committee

Chairman Bruce Ferguson

Martha Daugherty, Betsy & Steve Conrad, Brenda & Ritsel Sparks,
Christine & Paul Godsey, Nancy Tretter, Gail Chastang,
Virginia & Don Lainhart, Sandra Rudicill Cupps,
Barbara Bardes, Jan Garbett, and Steve Gillespie.

Hannah Baird, Boone County Bicentennial Committee Chairperson

Boone County:
From Mastodons to the Millennium

*A story of the geography, people and events
that influenced the tip of Northern Kentucky*

Table of Contents

Philosophy from 1890	1
Bicentennial Committee Forward	3
Contents	5
Preface	7
Chapter 1 Prehistoric-1775 **Salty Monsters and Men**	9
Chapter 2 1776-1809 **The Pioneer Path**	27
Chapter 3 1810-1829 **Settling In**	53
Chapter 4 1830-1849 **Steamboats and Stagecoaches**	64
Chapter 5 1850-1861 **Transporting Growth**	84
Chapter 6 1861-1869 **Civil War - Balancing On The Line**	105
Chapter 7 1870-1889 **Boone Communities Grow**	128
Chapter 8 1890-1899 **Commuting Begins, Population Declines**	164
Chapter 9 1900-1909 **Telephones, Cars & Baseball**	187
Chapter 10 1910-1919 **War Changes Women's Roles**	223
Chapter 11 1920-1939 **A Flood of Change**	251
Chapter 12 1940-1959 **Landing An Airport**	296
Chapter 13 1960-1979 **Becoming Suburbia**	335
Chapter 14 1980-1997 **Record Growth Continues**	369
Boone County Census Figures	401
Bicentennial Heroes	402
Map	405
Bibliography	406
About the Author	409
Index	410

Dear Reader,

History, like all the details of our lives, is very subjective. We are only capable of interpreting through our own eyes. I believe that in researching history, as in life generally, the more one opens one's mind and looks to diverse sources, the more one learns what is or was "real."

That is what I have attempted to do in drafting this book. Extreme time constraints have prevented the massive quantity of research that would provide more validation. The process needs several years and a league of volunteers.

No doubt, I've included too much here – I've tried to tell at least a little bit about everyone and everything I've come across.

Reviewing volumes and pages of materials, I picked out information that both reflected everyday life and was unusual. One of the most unusual – Loder's story about a whale brought down the Ohio on a barge –was confirmed in a Dinsmore diary.

While much has changed, little has changed. Crime and vice aren't new, indeed, they were common "in the good old days" – as are frustration and disappointment with day-to-day life. The number of suicides L.A. Loder recorded in the 1800s shocked me.

Reflecting Values

Individual values became very apparent, especially in the few diaries I had time to review. Every year Loder noted the anniversary of his mother's death. Frank Rouse very respectfully dealt with the illness and death of one of his charges at the county infirmary. When Tom Roberts' mother needed help after his father died, he harnessed his incredible intellect into farmwork.

I wish I'd had time to review more diaries and to follow up on the leads that began snowballing as the deadline loomed. What drove the diarists to jot down their daily thoughts and experiences? How did a busy storekeeper and justice of the peace with children, grandchildren and other responsibilities find time to document his life? What did these individuals expect to happen to their diaries?

Thanks

Special thanks to Betty Roter for sharing her stories about Beaver and giving children an idea of what women's lives were like before microwaves, dishwashers, indoor plumbing and hypermarts.

Thanks also to William Conrad who loved history enough to spend thousands of hours laboriously transcribing L.A. Loder's handwritten diaries and researching details for his other books.

Comprehensive Lists

Where conflicting information could not be confirmed, I have simply included everything – all the stories about how Rabbit Hash got its name, for instance. No one knows for sure, so take your pick.

Spelling and Language

The English language's affinity for slang and general malleability became very evident as my research progressed. As Mrs. Ann Fitzgerald said, "*They spelled words the way they sounded*" and they weren't highly educated nor concerned about enunciation. (Loder wrote corps to mean corpse.)

Direct quotes – with original spellings – from many people and sources share with you those quaint, antiquated and colloquial styles.

Using many handwritten documents and finding many variations of spelling makes it difficult to discern the "correct" name spelling. Early settler's names changed without notice (Zimmerman was German for Carpenter, for instance.) Again, if references were given using different spellings, I have included them in parentheses. While variations were found on name spellings for families who remain in Boone County, we have aligned those to current usage.

Community names changed regularly, often depending on who was the largest landholder at the time. Bruce Ferguson has helped locate buildings and towns that no longer exist and listed current place names with the antiquated names like Grant (Belleview). Where possible, I've listed current owners of historic properties.

Organization

Once communities were established, about 1870, the chapters are organized using a geographic system, beginning with Constance in the north end of the county, following the river south (through Petersburg, Belleview, McVille, Rabbit Hash, Hamilton and Big Bone), then circling up through Verona, Walton, Union, Florence and ending at Burlington.

While I've attempted to represent every community, varying amounts of information are available for different eras – and the time constraint monster was chasing me again. Logically, when Petersburg was the largest community in the county, more information is given. Conversely, as its population declined, less information was available.

Enjoy

Of course there is never enough time to "complete" a work like this. I regret I could not talk personally with more of you.

I apologize for any errors you may find, though I encourage you to read with an open mind. Several proofreaders thought they found "errors" – which when pursued were simply correct facts unknown to them.

Since much of this kind of a history relies on individual memories and stories passed down through different people the "facts" vary. The individuals sharing information believed what they were telling me was accurate.

Leave Your Own Legacy

For the benefit of your own families, I encourage all of you to pull out paper and pencil, cassette and tape player, keyboard and computer, or video camera and tape to leave a legacy for your children.

Follow Betty Roter's example. Jot down your most traumatic, most exciting, most frightening, most whatever – memories – so they will be preserved to help educate the young, who now more than ever, need guidance from the past.

And most of all, encourage your children to read and understand history – it's more fascinating, intriguing, entertaining and educational than any sitcom they can flip to on the TV.

Jennifer Warner

Chapter 1
Prehistoric – 1775 Salty Monsters and Men

Massive natural forces created unique geological characteristics in what we now know as Boone County, Kentucky. The Ohio River borders the Commonwealth's northernmost county for 40 miles on the north and west. Its 252 square miles include several creeks – Big Bone, Gunpowder, Middle, Mud Lick and Woolper.

Three glaciers bulldozed the terrain, creating a new bed for the Ohio River and leaving sand and gravel in what we now call Boone County. Marshy saline springs left behind by the forces that shaped southwestern Boone County's geology created another unique feature.[1]

Early explorers and cartographers called it Big Bone Lick. The salt and mineral laden earth and water attracted all types of living creatures through the ages, proving a death trap for many. Centuries later, American Indians, settlers and explorers came to the lick to boil away the water, leaving salt to enhance and preserve their meat.

European explorers and scouts, astounded by monstrous bones littering the springs, collected the oddities as early as the 1700s. The talk of Europe, Big Bone Lick was shown on most New World maps drawn after 1740. Some say it was better known than New York City.

By the 19th century, great minds began theorizing about the odd creatures' origins. Eventually the top scientists of the era – including Thomas Jefferson and Ben Franklin – had identified the extinct creatures. The mental paths they pursued led to the beliefs generally held today – and to the evolution

---

Boone County Prehistory Summary

1.2 million years ago
Wisconsin, Illinoisian, Kansan, Nebraskan glaciers move earth.

12,000-20,000 years ago
Pleistocene era: Mastodon, bison, giant ground sloths, woolly mammoths, giant stag moose roam the region.

10,000-8,000 BC
Paleo families use flint spear points and follow meat animals.

7,500-500 BC
Archaic barterers design spear throwers, trade nationally.

1,000 BC - AD 1,000
Woodland gatherers fish, garden, make pottery, and use bows. Adena culture creates log-lined tombs, believes in after-life.

600-300 BC
Hopewell craftsmen accumulate wealth and influence, grow tobacco, and expand trade networks.

AD 1,000-1500s
Late Prehistoric Indians or Fort Ancient people use hunting dogs, traps and bone needles as well as grind corn, weave grasses, evaporate salt, and add shells to strengthen ceramics.

1500s-1800s
American Indians, who live in tribes with a defined social structure, raise crops and hunt game animals. They greet European explorers, but soon begin fighting to retain their land and lifestyles.

---

[1] Dr. Bill Bryant

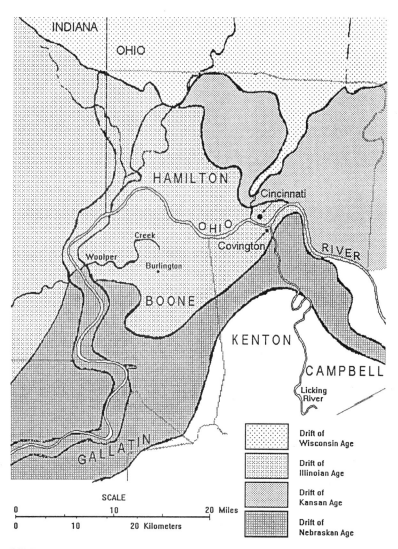

Dr. Bill Bryant's illustration shows how glaciers reached into Boone County.
Graphic courtesy of Dana Kisor

Four Glaciers

Huge ice sheets, two miles thick in places, bulldozed millions of tons of soil southward into what is now Boone County. As the glaciers receded, melting ice left stony debris carried for centuries in old stream valleys along the county's northeast edge.

Glacial activity influenced only three of Kentucky's northernmost counties – Boone, Kenton and Campbell.

While glaciers shaped and reshaped much of the nation's topography during the last 1.2 million years, three glacial periods – the Nebraskan, Kansan and Illinoisan – altered Boone County's topography and soils. A fourth, the Wisconsin glacier, stopped just north of the Ohio River.

The Nebraskan, the oldest, came through about 1.5 million years ago, covering the Ohio River valley as far south as Walton in Boone County and down into Gallatin County along the river. From 800,000 to 1 million years ago, the Kansan ice sheets rearranged the land.

The Nebraskan and Kansan glaciers created the flat, elevated site occupied by the Cincinnati/ Northern Kentucky Airport as they advanced and receded, filling valleys and leveling peaks.

The Illinoisan glacier arrived about 300,000 years ago. It formed one side of the Rabbit Hash hill, the Wisconsin the other, making it a unique place geologically as well as historically.

theories Kentuckian John Scopes would be condemned for a century later.

Well after the American Indians were driven North and West, Boone Countians would learn that they were not the first humans living in Boone County.

Archeological evidence has shown that after the mammoths died out about 10,000 BC, several fairly sophisticated human civilizations existed along the Ohio River's edge. The Paleo, Archaic, Woodland, Hopewell, and Fort Ancient people hunted and built villages here. Many sites where artifacts have been found are yet to be systematically evaluated.

The earliest information about Boone County's origin comes from geologists.

About 30,000 years ago, the Wisconsin glacier stopped just north of the Ohio River. It retreated, then returned 15,000 years ago, forming Mill Creek Valley, the path I-75 now follows through Cincinnati.[2]

As mountains of sand and gravel deposited by glaciers eroded, rocky cliffs were exposed. Ice domes crossed old river systems, impounding water for centuries until warming trends caused it to melt. Trickles grew to torrents, carving out the bed of the Ohio River.

Glacial debris is still visible at several sites in Boone County, including Boone Cliffs near Middle Creek and Bald Point near Camp Michaels by Gunpowder Creek.

The Illinois glacier carried small rocks that compressed into huge conglomerates like Split Rock near the mouth of Woolper Creek. Glaciers deposited the sand and gravel now mined along the Ohio River in western Boone County.[3]

Some geologists theorize the glacier's thick ice tied up so much of the earth's fresh water that ocean levels dropped and exposed a 50-mile wide land bridge between Asia and North America called Beringia. Mastodons, mammoths and other prehistoric animals could then migrate across the Bering Strait and down into what is now Boone County.

As game animals moved, primitive men may have followed their meat sources, unwittingly drifting south and eastward.

Other archeologists believe that explorers – the ice-age equivalents of Daniel Boone and Simon Kenton, knowingly led the human migration.[4]

In terms of physical characteristics, American Indians look more like the Asian Mongoloid peoples than Europeans or Africans, lending credibility to the ice bridge theory.

Massive Monsters

During the Pleistocene era 12,000 to 20,000 years ago, Kentucky's weather was cool and moist, probably similar to Alaska's today. Archaeological evidence indicates a profuse and varied animal population that included beaver species as big as bears. Mastodon, bison, giant ground sloths, woolly mammoths, musk ox, giant stag moose and other creatures came to what is now southern Boone County to drink from springs and lick salt and minerals.

Thick-furred mastodons, weighing from 9,000 to 11,000 pounds and more than 9' tall, were forced south by great sheets of ice. As they drank and fed at the saline springs, the mastodons' tremendous weight pushed their feet into the swampy earth. The more they struggled, the more they sank in ground that acted like quicksand. Many died there and became completely buried in the ooze.

Explorers discovered individual teeth of these huge animals that weighed nearly 10 pounds. Some mastodon teeth had a chewing surface 7" long and 4" or 5" broad. Some tusks were 11' long and 6" or 7" in diameter. Others were 7' or 8' long. Thigh bones were 4' or 5' long. Bones preserved in the ancient prehistoric layer show ribs that were 4" or 5" thick.[5]

In his 1751 journal, Col. Christopher Gist, an agent of the Ohio Land Company of Virginia, said he found *"a jaw tooth of better than four pounds weight. It appeared to be the furthest tooth in the jaw and looked like fine ivory when the outside was scraped off."*[6]

The mammoth, the mastodon and all but the modern species of bison apparently disappeared from North America about 10,000 years ago. Archaeologists aren't certain why they became extinct but they have several

---

[2] Dr. Bill Bryant
[3] Dr. Bill Bryant.
[4] K.M. Fraser, *The Prehistory of Man in Kentucky*, (The Kentucky Prehistory Curriculum Project, 1986), 22.
[5] Richard H. Collins, updated version of Lewis Collins' *History of Kentucky*, (Louisville, Ky. Richard H. Collins & Co. Publishers, Originally printed in 1874, 1877 edition), 52.
[6] Willard Rouse Jillson, *Big Bone Lick*, (The Standard Printing Co., Louisville, Ky. 1936), 6.

Boone Cliffs Nature Preserve contains large rocks created by conglomerations of glacial outwash.
Photo by Bruce Wess, Wild Walks Photography

theories. Most believe the large mammals were not able to survive the climatic changes accompanying the receding glaciers. But natural disasters or disease may have killed hundreds of thousands of them at once. Or perhaps man hunted them to extinction.

The salt licks and river no doubt attracted early humans as well as the huge mammals to Boone County. The saline springs come from seawater trapped in what are called lower Paleozoic sediments, a layer commonly called Saint Peter sandstone.

Archeological evidence shows Paleo Indians lived in this area from 10,000 to 8,000 BC. Four fluted flint spear points, distinctive of Paleo Indians, were found here.[7]

Archeologists believe that the Paleo people were nomadic. They lived in small, family-sized bands following migrating game animals. Their houses were basically windbreaks made of brush or rough-cured animal hides. Big Bone Lick may have been a "kill site" where hunters ambushed animals trapped in the saltwater spring's mud. However, none of the distinctive Paleo flint points were found near the animals' bones.[8]

Archaic Hunters - 7500 BC

By 7500 BC, the climate had warmed to be more hospitable to the Archaic people. During the 7,000 years the Archaics inhabited this corner of Northern Kentucky, tundra-like vegetation gave way to hardwood forests where deer, beaver, fox, opossum, otter, turkey and smaller game animals lived. The hunters carved fishhooks from bone and wove nets of vegetable fiber to catch fish and shellfish.[9]

Most artifacts found near Rabbit Hash and East Bend Bottoms are Archaic. These people hunted game for food, but gathered nuts and plants as well. The Archaics lived in larger and more stationary groups than the Paleo people. Archaic hunting and nut gathering camps, probably used during the fall and winter, were found in the woods farther from the river.

In the spring and summer they lived near the river bottoms. The Archaic people did not

---

[7]S.F Starr, The Archeology of Hamilton County, Ohio, (Cincinnati, Museum of Natural History, Vol. XXIII(1). 1960), 13.
[8]Fraser, 24.
[9]Fraser, 25.

plant or raise food crops, but hunted wild animals for food and clothing. They devised a spear thrower or *atlatl* to increase their hunting spears' penetrating power.

Archaic projectile points were not as finely made as those of the Paleo people, perhaps because the simple sharpening procedure was so widely known by their time. Variations in point types could indicate these early humans met with other groups of people.

Archaic tools were all of stone. Trading with people from the Lake Superior region, they obtained copper. From Atlantic coastal tribes they received marine shells. The unique materials became jewelry and ornaments in addition to whatever uses their shapes suggested. Archaic people may have bartered food, skins and flint for toolmaking or gypsum mined from salt caves.

1000 BC to AD 1000

The region's climate and terrain was hospitable enough to attract the Woodland people from 1000 BC to AD 1000. Like the Archaics, they hunted deer and other small game. They fished and gathered wild plants, but also raised squash and gourds. Since they grew some food themselves, they did not wander as much in search of game.

To store food and hold water, they made pots from local clay. They designed vessels in which they could boil water and cook soups.

Early Woodland hunters used spears and stone points, but around AD 700 they began using bows and arrows. By the time Columbus arrived, the bow and arrow had been used in North America for only 700 to 800 years.

Woodland hunters had used spears and spear throwers for 11,000 years. What many people now call arrowheads are really spear points, knives or other types of cutting or piercing tools.

The Adena people, a subgroup of Woodland Indians, lived in the Ohio Valley from 1000 BC to AD 200. The Adena may have been immigrants from the north or from Mexico. They were taller and more powerfully built than were their Archaic predecessors. No information has been found about whether they migrated or the colony simply died out. They constructed some of the

William Fitzgerald points to artifacts discovered at Big Bone Lick State Park and displayed in a kosk there in the 1960s. Contributed by Barbara Sharpe from Bob Sharpe's photo collection.

burial mounds found in northern Boone County.

Archaeological evidence shows only the most important people were buried in mounds. Log-lined tombs were covered with dirt that villagers probably carried a basketful at a time. Customs of treating individuals' bodies differently after death indicates the Adena had a social or class structure. Evidence of consistent traditions shows they believed in an afterlife.[10]

An ancient fort, probably built by the Woodland people, was discovered one-half mile upstream from Petersburg. It was slated for excavation in 1992, but the investigation has never begun.[11] Unfortunately, agricultural cultivation has destroyed many mounds and earthen structures.

In 1942, Kentucky archaeologist W.S. Webb excavated the Robbins Mound in southwestern Boone County near Union. He found mica ornaments, combs made of bone, ground stone "gorgets" (the prehistoric equivalent of the modern man's tie), copper bracelets, a cut and polished animal skull probably designed to be worn as a mask, and a spoon carved from a turtle shell. Small stone tablets incised with graphics may have been used as stamps to decorate textiles or to represent clan or village affiliations.[12]

Hopewell Craftsmen 300 BC

About 300 BC, Hopewell civilizations moved into this region. No Kentucky Hopewell sites have been systematically excavated, but evidence has been found of their existence here.[13] More common across the Ohio River, they surpassed the Adena in wealth and influence, but declined in about AD 600.

The Hopewell people built large elaborate earthworks and were excellent artists and craftsmen. They may have been invaders who pushed the Adena elsewhere into Kentucky and the east, or they could have lived side-by-side with the other culture, each learning from the other.

The Hopewells may have been business people whose economic interdependence held their widely scattered settlements together. The Ohio Valley's geography, with its confluence of rivers, was well suited to this early form of commerce.

The Hopewells may have been the first to cultivate tobacco, although the Fort Ancient Woodland people cultivated more crops. Hopewell pipes, carved in shapes of animals and birds, have been found as far west as Oklahoma and as far east as New York. Reasons for this civilization's decline are unknown. Its small, isolated settlements employed the extensive trade networks and large earthworks of the Hopewells.

When the Hopewells and Adena lived in what is now Boone County, large oak, beech, black walnut, maple, yellow poplar, ash, sycamore, hickory, and elm trees covered the land. Fruits and berries grew on vines along the forest's edge. Fires set by man as a hunting technique or by lightning opened up the forest, where bluestem, wild rye and running buffalo clover grew. Native cane, a woody-stemmed grass like bamboo grew 10 to 12' tall. Some "canebrakes" stretched for miles across the rolling hills.

In the spring, hard rains pushed creeks and rivers over their banks, flooding the land. During dry summer seasons, people could wade across the Ohio.

Late Prehistoric AD 1000

Late Prehistoric or Fort Ancient villagers moved here in about AD 1000. They may have greeted European or Viking explorers and trappers who began to visit 500 years later.

Selecting "chert" or flint from along the rivers, these hunters shaped it into arrowheads, drills, scrapers and knives. Using round, hand-sized granite hammers, the men "knapped" or chipped away glass-like flakes from the brittle rock. Deer antler or wooden tools shaped the fine points. In recreating the process, some good knappers made an arrowhead in less than 10 minutes.

Deer gut strips tied the stone point to a notch in the tip of the arrow's shaft. For antler

---

[10] Don Clare, *Ancestry- Our Ohio River Heritage*, (s.p. 1996) 29.
[11] A. Gwynn Henderson, *Prehistoric Research at Petersburg, Boone County, Ky.*, (University of Kentucky, Program for Cultural Resource Assessment, Archaeological Report 289, Dec. 1993), 13.
[12] Fraser, 28.
[13] Fraser, 28.

Chapter 1 Prehistoric-1775 Salty Monsters and Men

arrowheads, shafts were glued firmly into the hollow horn. To bring down large game, Fort Ancient people made small, thin, triangle-shaped flint tips that were attached to arrows of cane or seasoned hickory trimmed with turkey or hawk feathers.

Using only sharpened hickory shafts with fire-hardened tips, they killed beaver, bobcats and groundhogs. Traps made from logs and saplings caught small fur-bearing animals. Fish and freshwater mussels added to their diet.

Although they used dogs as hunting companions, the Fort Ancient people did not have pack animals. Wild animal trails, some worn 3' deep and 10' to 100' wide by herds of bison or their predecessors, were the roads. Trading with other tribes obtained other kinds of rock, like granite for hammers and sandstone to grind corn and sharpen sticks. A soft red stone called pipestone was carved into pipes and pendants.

Crushed mussel shells added strength to ceramic pots, jars, pans and other vessels made from local clay. Baskets, floor mats and clothing were woven from cane and grasses. Using bone needles and animal gut thread, Fort Ancient people sewed animal hides together for clothing and strung beads for jewelry. They also evaporated brine water in shallow pans to make salt.

Dinner may have included common slider and softshell water turtles and the Eastern box land turtle. Archeological evidence showed they preferred eating suckers, freshwater drum, and golden, shorthead and river redhorse; but other fish available to them included gar, buffalo, channel catfish, bass and sunfish. Elk and bear were important because just one fed many families. The Indians also ate and used thick-shelled fresh-water mussels. Of the 75 species in the Ohio, 28 could have been found near Petersburg, and archeological evidence indicates residents actually ate only half of the available varieties.

Clan Life

Perhaps as many as 500 Fort Ancient people lived in permanent villages made up of 25 huts usually located along rivers, like the ones discovered along the Ohio near Petersburg.

Stockade-type fences protected some villages. In this society, women constructed their homes, peeling bark from hickory or oak saplings then pounding them into the ground for corner posts. Elm or ash branches made the walls, woven in and out between the posts. The houses' roofs and sides were covered with flattened elm bark wedged in with poles tied to the framework.

The structures sizes varied from 50'x 18' to 70' x 30'. Between 15 and 25 related people lived in each. A hole in the roof's center vented a cooking fire that provided heat and light. Doors were large pieces of elm bark or bearskin. When rot, insects and mice overran the house, the women tore it down and rebuilt.[14]

Sleeping rooms were lined with benches covered with elk and bear skins. Shallow pits under the benches stored dried berries, nuts or corn and items used in ceremonies. Some pits were lined with grasses or bark and covered with animal skin, stretched tightly to make it harder for mice to get to the food.

In the summer, small fire pits scattered around the village were kept smoldering with corn cobs to deter mosquitoes and other biting insects.

Several clans or family groups, known by animal names, lived in each village. The village chief and his family lived in a larger house near the village center where leaders discussed politics, marriages, trade and other important matters. Ceremonies and dances packed the ground in front of the chief's house.

Rules were strict and very logical, perhaps

---

[14] A. Gwynn Henderson, *Kentuckians Before Boone*, (University Press of Kentucky, Lexington, Ky. 1992) 13-14.

Bruce Ferguson and his brother Walter Ferguson assisted with the Cleek-McCabe excavation.
Photo courtesy of Bruce Ferguson

leading into some of today's standards. Men could not marry women of their own clan. When couples married, the wife moved in with her husband. Their children belonged to the father's clan.

Practices dictated the dead were buried either in a cemetery area at the village's edge or in a small mound according to clan grouping.

Fields where corn, beans, squash, gourds, sunflowers and tobacco grew surrounded the village. Bean vines climbed three kinds of corn plants – flour or bread corn, flint or hominy corn and popcorn. Squash and gourds covered the ground at the base of the corn hills. Between the rows of corn hills, women planted sunflowers and tobacco. Dead trees too big for the men to cut with stone axes stood in the fields.[15]

Charred wood dating from the late 1200s to the 1400s was found during a 1992 Petersburg excavation. Ceramic jars which date to the 1200s and 1300s feature designs and shapes particular to the region.[16]

Designs relate more closely to a southern Ohio site along the Great Miami River than to other Kentucky sites. Researchers think the later settlement was larger and more dispersed than the earlier one, following the trend of increasing village size during that era. Many flint projectile points or "arrowheads" dating from the 1000s to 1500s were found.

The rumor placing pigmy tribes at Petersburg may have arisen from discovering some 24" x 15" stone burial vaults containing

---

[15]Clare, 30-31.
[16]Clare, 37.

human bones. Historians believe these bones – from normal-sized humans of the time – may have been carried a long distance, perhaps from a battlefield, to a sacred area or homeland. Care taken of the dead indicates a faith in a higher power or some belief that life continued in another form.

Cleek-McCabe Site

While 425 archeological sites have been identified in Boone County, the best-documented middle Fort Ancient circular village in Kentucky is the Cleek-McCabe site on Mud Lick Creek. The site's name came from property owners Anna Cleek and her husband Mr. McCabe. Under the auspices of the federal government's Works Progress Administration, the University of Kentucky investigated the site in 1939. A descriptive report of the large-scale excavation has never been published.

We do know that archeologists found two mounds located on opposite sides of a midden ring under a plowed cornfield. This center circle could be a precursor to the "town square" concept seen in historic communities like downtown Burlington.

One burial mound contained the remains of 21 people. Beneath the mound were the remains of an earlier village – several large rectangular buildings that contained fire areas, a prepared clay hearth, limestone slab platforms, and burials. A radiocarbon test of a bone sample estimated that the individual lived in AD 1010.

The rectangular structures covered the remains of yet another circular building measuring 13 meters in diameter, which may have been a charnel or burial house. The construction sequence and overlap show that the circular building's location directly influenced where the other structures, and ultimately, the mound, were built.

This suggests that each building and mound were linked together either by ritual or by association with the place covered by the mound.

It also implies that the mound marked the end of a ritual cycle that had begun decades earlier with the circular building's construction.[17]

Arrasmith Site

Not far away, in the Gunpowder Creek Valley about three miles from the Ohio River, is the Arrasmith Site. Two roughly circular Fort Ancient villages with central plazas were found there. One village measured 125 meters in diameter with a 70-meter central plaza. Radiocarbon dating showed the village was occupied in the late 1300s or early 1400s, somewhat later than the Cleek-McCabe site.

The village at the north end of the terrace measured 115 by 125 meters and had an oblong plaza. Ceramics and chipped stone tools were similar to those from the Madisonville horizon (AD 1400-1550) sites in southwestern Ohio and northern Kentucky.[18]

American Indians

The "Indians" (called so because explorers mistakenly thought they had reached India) who met Kentucky's first European explorers may have been direct descendants of these Fort Ancient people. No one knows exactly what happened between the final days of the Fort Ancients in the 1500-1600s and contact with Europeans, but the native inhabitants disappeared.

Most scholars have ruled out warfare, famine, pestilence or natural disasters and think that lack of immunity to European diseases probably wiped them out. Survivors may have moved north across the river.

About 1550, Kentucky's inhabitants began encountering British, French and Spanish explorers, trappers and settlers whose ideas as well as diseases, devastated the native cultures. The Indians, who believed no one

---

[17]R. Barry Lewis, editor, *Kentucky Archaeology*, (University Press of Kentucky, Lexington, Ky. 1966), 168-169.
[18]David Pollack, *The Archaeology of Kentucky: Past Accomplishments and Future Directions, Vol. 2*, (Kentucky Heritage Council, Frankfort, Ky. 1990), 488.

could "own" land because it belonged to all, were unprepared to deal with Europeans and their unlimited desires for property, resources and land.[19]

Explorers Reach Kentucky

In the 1600s, Indians had told French, English and Spanish explorers of a great river that flowed westward across America called "L'Oyo" or "La Belle Riviere" – both meaning beautiful river. Indians told them it flowed to the great lake of salt water.

The word Kentucky may have come from the Wyandot Indian phrase "Kah Ten Tah Te" meaning "Land of Tomorrow" or an Iroquoian word that could be translated as "place of meadows."[20] The Southern pronunciation "Cain Tuck" could also have come from the great cane fields that amazed early explorers traveling down the Ohio. Kentucky does not mean "dark and bloody ground."

While Indians helped visiting Europeans find their way and survive in America, the invaders did not repay them in kind.

A British fur trader named Abraham Woods set traps in the Ohio valley in the mid 1600s, but did not formally claim the region. By 1700, the Ohio River was fairly well known below the mouth of the Great Miami, which is just up river from Boone County.

The hunters followed the same network of solidly packed animal trails within the deep forests that their human predecessors had used. The trails connected salt licks, water holes, canebrakes and meadow land. Many of these roads or traces crossed the Ohio River, following the easiest overland path through the heavy forest to Big Bone Lick, probably the most popular gathering place in the region for mammals of all kinds. The paths were so distinctive and full of unique landmarks that long hunters (so named either because they carried long rifles or because they hunted for extended periods of time) who had been through the area could arrange meeting places and describe sites to each other.

Le Moyne's Visits

In 1729 or 1739 (sources differ), a French engineer named M. Chasegros de Lery headed an expedition to make compass surveys of the Ohio River. Jacques Nicholas Bellin, the French cartographer exhibited his map of Louisiana in Paris in 1744. Chasegros's discovery was noted as "the place where they found the elephant bones in 1739." Benjamin Franklin called the valley "the great licking place" while some pioneers called it "jelly ground."[21]

Chasegros' expedition was protected by a military entourage led by the French Canadian soldier and explorer Captain Charles Le Moyne, second Baron de Longueil, and commander at Fort Niagara.[22] (This French name is misspelled many different ways – Lemoyne, DeLongueil, etc. – in most articles about Kentucky's early history.)

Ten years later on a mission to stop hostile Chickasaw Indians on the lower Mississippi, Le Moyne first recorded discovering fossils at Big Bone Lick. He shipped a tusk, femur and molars – which he believed came from an elephant – to France where they were placed in the king's collection of curiosities, then later transferred to the National Institute of France.

France was prepared to occupy the Ohio Valley, but the steady stream of French alarmed the English, especially subjects living in Virginia and Maryland. In an effort to stop further French advancement and encourage English families to settle there, England's King George II issued a patent for 500,000 acres of Ohio Company Land. Christopher Gist, who had first explored the Ohio Valley in 1751 with his Negro slave, returned with Lawrence Washington (a brother of the first

---

[19]Fraser, 32.
[20]Lowell H. Harrison & James C. Klotter, *A New History of Kentucky*, (University Press of Kentucky, Lexington, Ky. 1997), 6.

[21] *Edwin Way Teale, Wandering Through Winter, (Dodd, Mead & Co., New York, 1957) 240-241.*
[22]Clare, 32-33.

president) to make the claim for the English.

Stopping at Portsmouth, Ohio, the explorers met French traders who gave them a jaw-tooth weighing over four pounds, several 11' long rib bones, a skull spanning 6', and several teeth they called horns, which were more than 5' long. The traders described the place where the bones were found as 20 miles below the mouth of the Big Miami River and up a small stream that flowed into the Ohio from the south.[23]

French Plates

In response to the English land claim, a French army unit marched down the Ohio, periodically making ownership proclamations for France. Leader Pierre Joseph Celoron de Bienville buried lead plates along the way, which he believed settled the ownership dispute.

Celoron went down the Ohio as far as he could (to the Great Miami River) then continued on foot, visiting Indian settlements in an attempt to convince them of France's claim to the land. The Indians couldn't understand the concept of anyone owning the river and its tributaries and they were apparently satisfied with their treatment by British traders and saw no benefit in dealing with the French.[24]

In Detroit, British Governor Henry Hamilton wanted to hold Western lands for England's colonial interests, so he began to incite hostile Indians, who were unhappy with conflicting treaties. Treaties had cost Indians land and the ever-increasing numbers of white settlers were claiming even more.

The Detroit fort supplied guns, strategies and encouragement for the disgruntled Indians to harass and terrorize incoming settlers, intending to scare them back east. What is

This photo taken in Boone Cliffs shows Boone County as it may have looked when early explorers visited. Photo by Bruce Wess, Wild Walks Photography

often described as a brutal Indian custom, scalping may have begun because the "civilized" British paid Indians by the scalp for killing settlers.

French and Indian wars fought in the Ohio Valley from 1754 to 1763 prevented settlements in this region. Whites attempting to travel down the river or settle were attacked and plundered.

Early Lick Visitors

That didn't stop European visitors with backwoods skills from exploring the curious big bones here. Indian trader Robert Smith, of the village of Pickawillany on the Big Miami River near Urbana, Ohio, frequently visited

---

[23] A.M. Yealey, *History of Boone County Kentucky*, (reprint of *Boone County Recorder* articles, s.p.,1960), 2.
[24] Clare, 33-34.

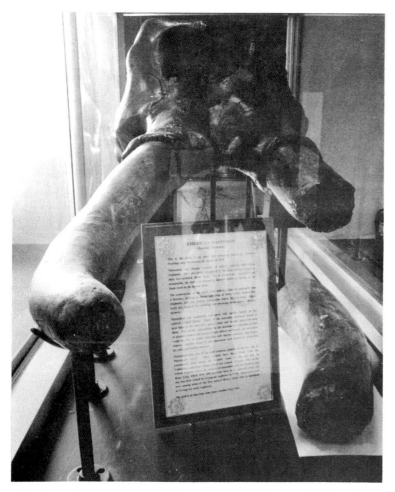
Early explorers saw mastodon skulls like this one displayed at Big Bone Lick State Park.
Photo by Bruce Wess, Wild Walks Photography

Big Bone Lick and was one of the first to realize the value of the big bones. He had taken quite a few in 1744 – no doubt the best specimens – when the French destroyed his village and stockade. The brutal invaders killed, dismembered and cooked the body of "Old Britain," a much respected Miami chief.[25]

In 1752, after a trading expedition to the Falls of the Ohio River near Louisville, John Findley stopped at Big Bone to meet with Shawnee Indians.

Seventeen years later, Findley led Daniel Boone into Kentucky, pointing out topographical features that Boone used as guideposts when leading settlers here.

Findley, like others of his time, probably traveled in a canoe or "pirogue" made of bark or of a hollowed log.

Mary Ingles' Story

Indian raids were not restricted to the wilderness fringes. In 1755, a Shawnee raid in Montgomery County, Va., captured Mary Draper Ingles, her sister-in-law, Mrs. Draper, and Mary's two young sons. Their husbands and other settlers were away from the cabins, tending their wheat crop. Although Mrs. Draper was injured and Mary was late in her third pregnancy, the women carried their toddlers as the Indians marched them away from their homes.

On the third night, Mary, who was in her early 20s, gave birth to a daughter. The march resumed in the morning. When pursuit didn't develop, the Shawnee chose to make a leisurely 29-day trip to "Indiantown" at the mouth of the Scioto River where Portsmouth, Ohio, is now located. Here, although Mrs. Draper was tortured with a painful gauntlet run, Mary was spared, but separated from her children.

She pretended indifference to her captivity. The Shawnee praised her cooking skills. Some say she was adopted as the chief's daughter.

French traders visiting from Detroit helped improve her lot. Mary sewed shirts from checked fabric the traders brought. As soon as a shirt was finished, a Frenchman ran through the village, swinging it on a staff, praising it as an ornament and Mrs. Ingles as a very fine squaw. They then made the Indians pay her at least twice the shirt's value. This profitable employment continued for about three weeks and Mrs. Ingles was more kindly treated by her

---

[25] Jillson, 27.

captors.[26]

In early autumn, Mary went with an Indian party to Big Bone Lick on a salt-making expedition. An elderly Dutch woman, Ghetel Stumf, who had been a prisoner for some time, went also.

Plotting an escape, Mary asked Ghetel to accompany her. Asking permission to gather grapes, they were allowed to leave the group. Mary had squirreled away a blanket and a knife and obtained a tomahawk from a Frenchman in the salt-making party who was "sitting on one of the big bones cracking walnuts."

Following a buffalo trace to the Ohio River, they walked for five days, coming opposite the village where they had lived with their captors. Kentucky's Route 8 (now known as the Mary Ingles Highway) is believed to be part of the path the women followed.

On familiar ground, they found an empty cabin and remained for the night. In the morning they caught a horse browsing nearby, loaded it with corn and proceeded up river – escaping observation although they were within sight of the Indian village and individual Indians for several hours.

The season was dry and the rivers low, but the Big Sandy was deep at its mouth. Non-swimmers, the women added steps to their journey by following the river until they found a crossing. When they attempted to walk across on driftwood, the horse fell among the logs and could not be extricated. The women packed what corn they could, but lived meagerly on grapes, black walnuts, pawpaws, and sometimes roots.

Starvation and constant fear of human and animal dangers drove the Dutch woman insane. Ghetel tried to kill Mary, convinced her companion was the cause of her troubles.[27]

Escaping her grasp, Mary ran, then hid under the riverbank. In the moonlight, she found a canoe like one the Indians had used earlier, half buried in mud and leaves. She

This illustration shows flatboats and keelboats similar to those used on the Ohio.   Courtesy of Martha Daugherty

used a tree branch to clear the canoe and paddle it to the other side.

In the morning the woman discovered her, promised good behavior and begged to rejoin her, but a wary Mary kept the river between them.

Approaching her former Virginia home in cold and snowy weather, Mary's strength deteriorated rapidly. Her limbs were swollen from wading cold streams, frost and fatigue.[28]

After 40 days of traveling not less than 20 miles a day, she reached the Kanawha River. Following it upstream, she met a man she had known for years. Eventually he recognized her battered body. After she spent three days recovering at his house, he took her home.

Tormented with fears of recapture, Mary

---

[26] Collins, 53.

[27] Harrison & Klotter, 10.
[28] Collins, 53.

insisted the family move back east of the Blue Ridge Mountains. Help was sent to Ghetel and she too recovered.

Thirteen years later, one of Mary's sons was located and ransomed, the other had died in captivity not long after the forced separation, as had the young daughter. Mary died in 1813 at the age of 84.

A drama called "The Long Journey Home" is staged annually at Mary Ingles homestead in Radford, Va. James Alexander Thom describes her ordeal in a historical novel called *Follow the River*.[29]

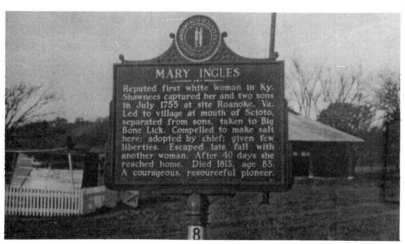

Sign commemorates Mary Ingles' escape. Photo by Bob Sharpe

Bone Collectors

Ten years after Mary Draper Ingle's ordeal, explorer and Indian agent Col. George Croghan (also spelled Groghan) of Pennsylvania visited Big Bone Lick to collect bones. He described his arrival in his journal.

"Early in the morning we went to the great lick, where those bones are only found about four miles from the river on the south-east side. On our way we passed through a fine timbered clear wood. We came to a large road, which the buffaloes have beaten, spacious enough for two wagons to go abreast, and leading straight to the Lick. It appears that there are vast quantities of these bones lying 5 or 6' under the ground, which we discovered in the bank at the edge of the Lick. We found here two tusks above 6' long. We carried one, with some other bones, to our boats and set off."[30]

Attacked by 80 Kickapoos and Mascoutins a week later, five of Croghan's men were killed and the others taken captive. The bones were lost. Croghan wrote to a friend, *"I got the stroke of a hatchet on the head, but my skull being pretty thick, the hatchet would not enter, so you may see a thick skull is of service on some occasions."*

Cresswell's Journal

Nicholas Cresswells journal from a decade after Croghan's visit, describes the site in 1775:

"Saturday, June 17th. This morning set out for the Elephant Bone Lick, which is only three miles southeast of the River. However, we lost our way and I suppose traveled 20 miles before we found it. Where the bones are found is a large muddy pond, a little more than knee deep with a Salt spring in it which I suppose preserves the bones sound.

"Found several bones of a Prodigious size, I take them to be Elephants, for we found a part of a tusk, about 2' long, Ivory to all appearance, but by length of time had grown yellow and soft. All of us stripped and went into the pond to grabble for teeth and found several.

"Joseph Passiers found a Jaw tooth which he gave me. It was judged by the company to weigh 10 pounds. I got a shell of a Tusk of hard and good ivory about 18" long. There is a great number of bones in a Bank on the side of this pond of an enormous size but decayed and rotten. Ribs 9" broad, Thigh bones 10" diameter. What sort of animals these were is

---

[29] William Conrad, An Educational and Historical Tour Through Northern Boone County, The Top of Kentucky, Community Education Program, Boone County Schools, 1986), 25.

[30] Jillson, 15-16.

not clearly known.

"All the traditional accounts by the Indians is that they were White Buffaloes that killed themselves by drinking salt water. It appears to me from the shape of their teeth that they were Grass-eaters.

"There neither is or ever were any Elephants in North or South America, that I can learn, or any quadruped one-tenth part as large as there was, if one may be allowed to judge from the appearance of these bones, which must have been considerably larger than they are now.

"Captain Hancock Lee told me he had found a tusk here that was 6' long, very sound but yellow. These tusks are like those brought from the Coast of Africa. Saw some Buffaloes but killed none. Several Indian paintings on the trees.

"Got plenty of Mulberries, very sweet and pleasant fruit, but bad for the teeth. One of the company shot a Deer. The loudest Thunder and heaviest rain I ever saw this afternoon. Got to the Camp well wet and most heartily tired. A D–d Irish rascal has broken a piece of my Elephant tooth, put me in a violent passion, can write no more."[31]

Croghan's Return

On his return to collect more bones in 1766 after an Indian peace treaty was signed, Croghan's party included army engineer Captain Harry Gordon and geographer Ensign Thomas Hutchins. Captain Gordon wrote:

"We encamped opposite the great lick, and next day I went with a Party of Indians and Batteau-Men to view this much-talked-of Place. The beaten Roads from all Quarters to it easily conducted Us: they resemble those to an Inland Village where cattle go to and from a large Common.

"The Pasturage near it seems of the finest kind, mixed with Grass and Herbage, and well watered; on our Arrival at the Lick which is about five miles distance South of the River, we discovered laying about many large Bones, some of which the exact Patterns of Elephants Tusks & others of different parts of a large Animal.

"The extent of the Muddy part of the Lick is 3/4 of an acre; this Mud being of a salt quality is greedily lick'd by Buffalo, Elk & Deer, who came from distant parts, in great Numbers for this purpose; we picked up several of the Bones, some out of ye Mud, others off the Ground; returned, proceeded next Day & arrived at the Falls 19th July."[32]

Franklin Shares Non-Carnivore Theory

Jan. 31, 1768
To Abbe Chappe:

I sent you sometime since, directed to the Care of M. Molini, a Bookseller near the Quay des Augustins, a Tooth.... It was found near the River Ohio in America, at what is called the Great Licking Place, where the Earth has a Saltish Taste that is agreeable to the Buffaloes and Deer, who come there at certain Seasons in great Numbers to lick the same.

At this Place have been found the Skeletons of near 30 large Animals suppos'd to be Elephants, several Tusks like those of Elephants being found with these Grinder Teeth.... Some our Naturalists here, however, content that these are not the Grinders of Elephants, but of some carnivorous Animal unknown, because such Knobs or Prominences on the Face of the Tooth are not to be found on those of Elephants, and only, as they say, on those of carnivorous Animals.

But it appears to me that Animals capable of carrying such large & heavy Tusks, must themselves be large Creatures, too bulky to have the Activity necessary to for pursuing and taking Prey; and therefore I am inclin'd to think those Knobs are only a small Variety. Animals of the same kind and Name often differing more materially, and that those Knobs might be as useful to grind the small branches of Trees as to chaw Flesh–However I should be glad to have your Opinion, and to know from you whether any of the kind have been found in Siberia.

Benjamin Franklin

---

[31] Jillson, 22-23.

[32] Jillson, 19.

Franklin's Mysterious Elephants

Some bones from this collection were sent to London's Lord Shelburne who was in charge of the American colonies. Others went to Benjamin Franklin, who was then in London. Franklin acknowledged receiving the bones saying:

"I return you many thanks for the box of elephants' tusks and grinders. They are extremely curious on many accounts; no living elephants having been seen in any part of America by any of the Europeans settled there, or remembered in any tradition of the Indians. It is also puzzling to conceive what should have brought so many of them to die on the same spot... the grinders differ from those of the African and Asiatic elephant, being full of knobs, like the grinders of a carnivorous animal; when those of the elephant, who eats only vegetables, are almost smooth. But then we know of no other animal with tusks like an elephant, to whom such grinders might belong.

"It is remarkable that elephants now inhabit naturally only hot countries where there is no winter and yet these remains are found in a winter country; and it is no uncommon thing to find elephants' tusks in Siberia, in great quantities, when their rivers overflow, and wash away the earth, though Siberia is still more a wintry country than that on the Ohio; which looks as if the earth had anciently been in another position, and the climates differently placed from what they are at present."[33]

Like his peers, Franklin believed that animals did not become extinct. Later, he accurately concluded that the mammoth's sharp teeth could have been used *"to grind the small branches of trees."*

Interspersed among the mammoth fossils (many, particularly the proboscidian skulls, were too large for men to move), early explorers found skeletal remains of other gigantic animals: the glacial horse, the ground sloth, the arctic ox, and the early and contemporary buffalo, caribou, moose, elk, reindeer and bear. *"It was all in all the greatest natural depository of the bones of the great Pleistocene mammals that man's eye had ever beheld in any part of the world."*[34]

Virginia sent Thomas Bullitt, Hancock Taylor, Robert McAfee, Simon Kenton and James Douglas to explore Big Bone Lick in 1773. Douglas recorded this impression:

"The lick constituted about 10 acres, bare of trees, no herbage of any kind, three flowing springs whose waters would produce one bushel of salt to every 550 gallons of water, also a large number of bones so large and long that we used the ribs for tent poles. The land being marshy, the animals (evidently) became mired in the mud and died of exhaustion, thus leaving many of their bones in an upright position."[35]

Filson's Extinction Theory

John Filson, a teacher and explorer from Chester County, Pa., theorized, quite accurately in some respects, about the origin of the bones *"which bespeak an animal of five or six times the cubic volume of the elephant."* In his book, *The Discovery, Settlement and Present State of Kentucke* (Wilmington, 1784), he speculated on the creature's origin.

"At a salt spring near the Ohio River, very large bones are found, far surpassing the size of any species of animal now in America. The head appears to have been about 3' long, the ribs 7', and the thigh bones about 4'; one of which is reposited in the library at Philadelphia, and said to weigh 78 pounds. The tusks are above a foot in length, the grinders about 5" x 8".

"These bones have equally attracted the amazement of the ignorant, and the attention of the philosopher. Specimens of them have been sent both to France and England, where

---

[33] Jillson, 28-29.

[34] Jillson, 31-32.
[35] Yealey, History of Boone County, Kentucky, 26.

they have been examined with the greatest diligence and found upon comparison to be the remains of the same species of animals that produced those other fossil bones which have been discovered in Tartary, Chili, and several other places, both of the old and new continent.

"What animal this is, and by what means its ruins are found in regions so widely different, and where none exists at present, is a question of more difficult decision.

"The ignorant and superstitious Tartars attribute them to a creature which they call Maimon, who, they say, usually resides at the bottom of the rivers, and of whom they relate many marvelous stories; but this is an assertion totally divested of proof and even of probability, it has justly been rejected by the learned; and on the other hand it is certain that no such amphibious animal exists in our American waters.

Mastodon illustration by Martha Daugherty

"The bones themselves bear a great resemblance to those of the elephant. There is no other terrestrial animal now known large enough to produce them. These external resemblances have generally made superficial observers conclude that they could belong to no other than that prince of quadrupeds; and when they first drew attention of the world, philosophers seem to have subscribed to the same opinion.

"But if so, whence is it that the whole species had disappeared from America? An animal so laborious and so docile, that the industry of the Peruvians, which reduced to servitude and subjected to education species so vastly inferior in those qualities, as the llama and the paca, could ever have overlooked the elephant, if he had been found in their country.

"Whence is it that these bones are found in climates where the elephant, a native of the torrid zone, cannot even subsist in his wild state, and in a state of servitude will not propagate?

"These are difficulties sufficient to stagger credulity itself; and at length produced the inquiries of Dr. Hunter. That celebrated anatomist, having procured specimens from the Ohio, examined them with that accuracy for which he is so much distinguished. He discovered a considerable difference between the shape and structure of the bones and those of an elephant.

"He observed from the form of the teeth that they must have belonged to a carnivorous animal; whereas the habits of the elephant are foreign to such sustenance, and his jaws totally unprovided with the teeth necessary for its use, and from the whole he concluded, to the satisfaction of the naturalists, that these bones belonged to a quadruped now unknown, and whose race is probably extinct unless it may be found in the extensive continent of New Holland, whose recesses have not yet been pervaded by the curiosity or avidity of civilized man.

"Can then so great a link have perished from the chain of nature? Happy we are that it has. How formidable an enemy to the human species, an animal as large as an elephant, the tyrant of the forest, perhaps the devourer of man.

"Nations, such as the Indians, must have been in perpetual alarm. The animosities among the various tribes must have been suspended till the common enemy who threatened the very existence of all should be extirpated. To this circumstance we are probably indebted for a fact, which is perhaps singular in its kind, the extinction of a whole race of animals from the system of nature."[36]

Delaware Legend

Delaware Indian legend gives another belief about the mammoths' extinction. In ancient times, the legend goes, a herd of these tremendous animals came to the Big Bone Licks and began a universal destruction of the bears, deer, elks, buffalo and other animals which had been created for the Indians' use.

Looking down and seeing this, the Great Man Above was so enraged that he seized a lightning bolt, sat down on a neighboring mountain (on a rock where the print of his seat and feet are still visible) and hurled lightning bolts until all the Mammoths except the bull were slaughtered.

The bull turned his forehead to deflect the bolts, shaking them off as they fell. As the onslaught continued, he missed one and was wounded in the side. In anger he sprung round, bounding over the Ohio, the Wabash, the Illinois and finally over the Great Lakes to where he lives to this day.

---

[36] Jillson, 32-34.

Chapter 2
1776-1809 The Pioneer Path

Mammoths and their origin, while intriguing scientists and explorers, held little interest for most early settlers. Settlers' motivations to bring their families to the dangerous and Indian-infested West seldom came out of a desire for adventure, but more often on the same searches that had sent their ancestors across the ocean.

Escaping the Church of England's rule motivated Baptist preacher William Hickman Sr. to explore Northern Kentucky in 1776. Despite the colonies' Declaration of Independence, the Old World Catholic Church's dictates were still followed and enforced in Virginia.

Other settlers came out of poverty. The script (paper money) used to pay soldiers for their Revolutionary War service rapidly declined in value, leaving former soldiers in poverty except for the Western lands granted to them. In the uncharted west they could still claim land and work it into whatever their industry dictated.

With Virginia's growing population making game scarce, farming supplemented diets. Preferring game and fish to grains and vegetables, some moved West, passing up the easily plowed Bluegrass prairies in favor of thick forests that sheltered multitudes of animals and birds. Kentucky's northern quadrant was described as so heavily forested that a squirrel could climb a tree in Georgetown and reach the Ohio River, never walking on the ground.

Flocks of wild turkeys, pheasants, quail and bald eagles filled the air. Many varieties of owls, hawks, buzzards, ravens, crows, wild geese, cranes and ducks populated the area too.

Finding plentiful game and rivers full of fish in what we now call Boone County, Rev. Hickman returned to Virginia sharing news of the bountiful wilderness where no government existed to challenge his religious practices.

Three years later, Baptist preachers John Taylor and Joseph Redding set out, walking and riding horses. They followed the Cumberland Gap path that Daniel Boone had "blazed" or marked by chipping bark from trees during his explorations in 1769. (While Boone thoroughly explored the entire Commonwealth, there are no formal records of him visiting Boone County.)

Like Boone and other long hunters who traveled without families or belongings, Redding and Taylor hiked winding well-trod trails. Herds of hoofed animals, following one another according to their rigid social structures, pounded solid paths throughout their Kentucky range. Smaller species also found the beaten trails easy to follow. The animals' constant movement kept brush and saplings from growing into the trails. While some bison paths were reportedly wide enough for two wagons to pass, others would have been so narrow that overhanging branches would strike a man on horseback.

Indian attack was a life-threatening risk until after the 1794 Treaty of Greenville. While some chiefs had "sold" Kentucky hunting ground, other tribes who also hunted here didn't respect those treaties. Seeing what European settlers had done in the east and encouraged and supplied with firearms by the French and British, they fiercely defended this ground.

Avoiding the Indians, the Baptist preachers took different paths after their first visit here. Redding continued his explorations while

Taylor returned to share the news of their discoveries.

Word of mouth was the most common communication, but even in this largely unsettled wilderness, *The Freemans Journal* and the *Cincinnati Sentinel* newspapers were sold from 1762 until 1799. The amount of paper available, rather than a publication schedule, determined the publishing dates. With the Ohio River as the primary transportation route, their news was as current as any available elsewhere.

Floating downstream required only one man on a moderately stable raft, but to row a keelboat upstream took a large crew of strong men. With oarsmen pulling on each side, the boats' pointed ends made them relatively easy to steer. The keel, a beam running the boats' length, helped with steering. A keelboat could carry goods cheaper than a wagon over the animal trails used as roads.[1]

Rogers' keelboats met Col. John Campbell (Campbell County's namesake) in Louisville where 30 reinforcements were guarding a cargo of flour for Fort Pitt in the summer of 1779. The now 65 men poled five boats up the Ohio, working about 10 hours each day to cover roughly 20 miles.

Upriver from Boone County, near what is now Dayton, Ky., Indians – led by Simon Girty and financed by the British in Detroit – killed Rogers and 39 of his men and took a dozen prisoners. Thirteen escaped, some barely alive.[2]

Girty was infamous for his survival skills and military strategies. Senecas had captured his Pennsylvania family when Girty was 15. Freed by a treaty years later, the short, swarthy man became an interpreter for the United States army. Appalled by atrocities perpetrated against the Indians, he switched sides. Girty's

This reconstructed flatboat sits outside Behringer-Crawford Museum in Covington.
Photo by Martha Daugherty

Revolutionary War

No doubt the papers carried stories about Revolutionary War battles in the East. During that War, the Ohio River began its long career as the region's major transportation link between the populous East and the wilds of the West.

While most water travelers relied primarily on the current to move unwieldy flatboats downstream, military contingents with their manpower could go upstream. In August 1779, Col. David Rogers (a cousin of George Rogers Clark) used keelboats to deliver a shipment of gunpowder and other military stores from the Spanish at St. Louis to Fort Pitt (Pittsburgh).

---

[1] Harrison & Klotter, 51.
[2] Thomas L Purvis, editor with Kenneth M. Clift, Betty Maddox Daniels, Elisabeth Purser Fennell and Michael E. Whitehead, *Newport, Kentucky, A Bicentennial History*, (Newport, 1996), 6.

understanding of both cultures and tactical and weapons skills made him a feared opponent.[3]

Lochry's Defeat[4]

Soldiers like Girty – financed by the British or French – continued leading and supplying Indian armies with European guns to repel settlers.

To stop those attacks, Gen. George Rogers Clark asked Scotsman Col. Archibald Lochry, county lieutenant of Westmoreland County, Pa., to raise a force and join the fight.

On July 25, 1781, Lochry headed down the Ohio River with 120 Pennsylvanians to meet Clark's force of 400 from Fort Pitt. Restless waiting for the others to arrive, 19 of Clark's men deserted. To quell growing dissent, Clark set out earlier than he'd planned.

Trying to catch up, Lochry sent Capt. Shannon and four men ahead in a small boat, hoping they could overtake the main army and obtain supplies for his hungry company that was low on ammunition. Instead, Indians captured the men and their letter to Clark detailing the situation. Reading the letter apprised them of Lochry's weaknesses. The Indians collected along the Ohio below the mouth of the Little Miami River (near Lawrenceburg, Ind.).

Using a common trick to stop river travelers, the Indians placed their five prisoners conspicuously on the Indiana shore near the head of what is now called Lochry's Island. There the men could implore river travelers to help them.

Promised release if they hailed their companies, the decoys planned to convince the troops to surrender. The Indians waited with 200 warriors on the Boone County side of the river and the other half of the war party on the other. Their plan didn't come together precisely as planned, but the results were the same.

Before reaching the island, Capt. William Campbell took a boat ashore to cook some buffalo. As his men sat around the fire or brought horses ashore to graze, Indians attacked with rifles. The troops defended themselves until their ammunition was gone, then attempted to escape by boat.

As soon as the boats began to move in the sluggish current, the Indians rushed out onto the Indiana sand bar and fired on Campbell's men. With rifle balls coming from both sides of the river, the Pennsylvanians surrendered.

Knowing military structure, the Indians murdered Col. Lochry before their chief arrived and stopped the massacre. More than 300 Indians killed 42 Pennsylvanians and took 64 prisoners. Two years later, most of the military men were ransomed for British soldiers taken prisoner in the Revolutionary War.[5]

A monument to Col. Lochry and his slain company was erected at an Aurora, Ind., cemetery in 1783. A veteran of that battle, Hugh Sears, is buried in Boone County behind Ryle High School on what is now the 18th green of Lassing Pointe Golf Course.[6]

Tanner's Station

In 1780, the year before the Lochry massacre, William Lynn, acting as agent for three men including William Holiday of Stafford County, Va., received title to 1,000 acres of unpatented land the trio had marked off during a 1777 visit to Northern Kentucky.

One parcel was described as "*on the Ohio River below a large pond about four miles above a large rock and ten miles below the mouth of the Big Miami River.*" Holiday had the land surveyed and registered legally in Virginia five years later.

He gave or sold it to James Garrard in 1787. Garrard, a politician and Baptist minister, lived near Paris, Ky. Fellow Baptist preacher John Tanner was a silent partner in a nearby parcel

---

[3] Allan W. Eckert, *The Frontiersmen*, Bantam Books, Boston, Mass., 1970.104.
[4] While the island, a creek and more on both sides of the Ohio are named after this man, the spellings of his name vary greatly: Laugherty, Loughrey, Locherty, Laughery, Lochery, Lockrey, etc.

[5] Collins, 54
[6] Bruce Ferguson

known as the Woolper tract because it had been granted to John David Woolpert (or Woolper) of Pennsylvania.

Tanner sold his interest in the Woolper tract to Thomas Mosby and settled on the Garrard tract along the river. His land became known as Tanner's Station (now Petersburg) and people traveling down the river began to settle there.[7]

In April 1785, a company from Pennsylvania including John Hindman, William West, John Simmons, John Seft, "old Mr. Carlin" and their families, cleared 30 or 40 acres 22 miles below Cincinnati on land claimed by Tanner. After a month or so, they went to Ohio to "make improvements" (claim unclaimed land by marking trees with a tomahawk or hatchet) but did not remain there.[8]

For access to water and fertile croplands, the Tanners and other early settlers often built their homes on the river or along creek bottoms just as the Indians and prehistoric people had.

Families generally moved the home place inland and to higher elevations after several years. In addition to reducing flood risks, it reduced their chances of contracting the mosquito-borne "fever" or the "ague." Even this far north, in the moist, warm, swampy bottoms, mosquitoes spread diseases.[9]

Early Boone County cabins were similar to this one built of hewn logs. Windows were added later and glass even later.   Photo by Jason Dunn

Tanner Boys Taken

Wherever homes were built, Indian attack and theft remained a risk. Around 1790, Rev. Tanner's sons were captured by Indians, but the details of the incident vary. One says in May 1790, while gathering walnuts in the woods, nine-year-old John Tanner was captured and adopted into an Indian family. The next year, his 15-year-old brother Edward was taken. The teen-ager escaped after two days and made his way home.

In a paper written as a high school graduation requirement in the 1930s, Petersburg native Mary Rector told the story a bit differently. Her research found that both boys were attacked under a walnut tree about a half-mile from their home when they were under 12 years old. The younger, wounded in the leg, was unable to walk, so he was carried and his brother forced to walk. Assuming one boy would not leave without the other, the Indians didn't secure them carefully. But in late night discussion, the boys decided that Edward would escape and bring help to rescue John.

After the Indians were asleep, Edward freed himself from his bonds, swam both the Miami and the Ohio (which was much narrower and shallower than it is today) and returned home

---

[7]William Conrad, editor, *The Loder Diary, Part 6, Jan. 1, 1893-Jan. 29, 1904,* (Boone County Schools, Florence, Ky., 1985), 1.
[8]Collins, 54.

[9]Clare, 35.

that same night. Despite his brother's heroics, the Tanners and their neighbors were unable to track the Indians and locate young John.[10]

John Tanner remained with the Indians. One story says at 27, he returned to Boone County in search of his Virginia family, although he was married to an Indian woman and raising a family in Michigan. Tanner's Station had grown, but he recognized Allen Morgan, an orphan his father had adopted.

After visiting with Morgan, John Tanner Jr. realized that he had forgotten much English and was disappointed that his family had moved on, so he headed north. Traveling through Indiana, he saw a man who looked like his father. Stopping the stranger, he met his brother Edward. Although their father had died, Edward took John to Missouri to meet the rest of the family. Later, John Jr. returned to Michigan and his Indian family.[11] In 1818, the United States government hired him as an Indian interpreter.[12]

In Rector's version of the story, Morgan traveled to Michigan searching for Tanner. Though *"his friends offered him every inducement to remain, he could not be persuaded to leave his wife and children and savage habits."*

First Ryle Baby

More settlers were arriving. During the autumn of 1789, James Ryle left North Carolina with his wife Sallie (some accounts call her Sarah) their children, and a slave. Nine-year-old James Jr. rode horseback behind the slave the entire trip up the Daniel Boone trail. One child rode behind pregnant Sallie and another in front.

Sallie Ryle delivered Mary "Polly" Ryle at Tanner's Station on Feb. 19, 1790. (Some sources say she was born in 1796.) Previous county histories have said she was the first white child born here.

In the spring, the family left the fort and moved to the mouth of Middle Creek. After two years of living in the swampy land, they contracted fevers. To get away from the mosquitoes, they purchased hill acreage from the government for 72½ cents per acre. The land was near Waterloo and Belleview.

Devout Baptists, the Ryle family walked 14 miles to Bullittsburg Baptist Church – carrying their dinner – each Sunday.[13]

The James Ryle family later moved near Rabbit Hash. Their primary farm crops were tobacco and corn raised with slave labor. (In his will, Ryle identified 23 slaves.)[14]

Cobbler Underhill Stays

Also in 1790, William Underhill and his family journeyed down river on a flatboat from Pennsylvania. Many flatboats contained a few cows and sheep, a horse or two and all the family's household goods. These rectangular rafts with 2' to 3' tall sides only went downstream. At their destination, boats were dismantled for their timber.

Most flatboats had a passenger cabin, often with a fireplace that allowed travelers to cook and warm up more safely than going ashore. A pen or stable sheltered livestock. A long rear oar and two or four shorter oars allowed some degree of steering. While costs varied, a 12'-wide boat might have sold for $1 per foot of length. Fifty to 100 miles (downstream only) was a good day's journey. Even small 12'x 20' flatboats could handle 8-10 tons. Larger 25'x 50' ones could carry 70-80 tons.[15]

The Underhills met the Craig family at the Taylorsport landing. Learning Underhill was a shoemaker, the Craigs implored him to remain and make shoes for their family and 20 slaves. As word traveled, other settlers came for shoes. With all the work he could do, Underhill built a cabin and settled in Boone County.

---

[10] Mary Rector.
[11] Conrad, *Loder 6*, 3.
[12] Collins, 55.
[13] Yealey, 18.
[14] Mrs. Mamie Williamson, History of the Ryle Family, Grant, Ky., 1955, 2, 22.
[15] Harrison & Klotter, 51.

The shoes Underhill made probably did not discriminate between left and right feet. Shoes lasted longer and wore more evenly when they were interchangeable. (Work shoes continued to be interchangeable until well after the Civil War.)[16]

Out of necessity, the cobbler became quite experienced in Indian warfare, arousing the settlers to arms and forcing marauding Indians to recross the Ohio in their canoes. On one occasion, thinking they were safely across the river, the Indians shouted epithets, only to watch a comrade drop from a bullet shot by Lewis Fitzgerald, a sharpshooting nephew of Mrs. Underhill.

Settlers chose Underhill as their leader for the "Squirrel Hunter's Brigade," organized to stop the raids. They marched to the Indian village in Chillicothe, Ohio. Finding no Indians, they set fire to wigwams and cut down the corn. They were not bothered again.

The Underhill family moved to the forks of the Gunpowder in 1804, but was ousted by another who claimed the land. The same thing happened at another location. Underhill gained clear title to property on the third move and the land eventually was passed to his son John.[17]

Although gaining clear title was often difficult, land was cheap. Many Revolutionary War soldiers who had received land grants weren't particularly interested in living in Kentucky and sold their property. While low, prices varied widely. John W. Conley of Beaverlick said his great grandfather was reportedly offered 100 acres adjoining his Walton farm for one horse.[18]

John Underhill, born Nov. 18, 1798, preached at Gunpowder Baptist Church for 50 years. Rev. Underhill was said to be the "Warwick" portrayed by John Uri Lloyd in his book, *Warwick of the Knobs*.[19]

Morrison Family Arrives

On Feb. 1, 1796, after Indian hostilities had cooled a bit, Samuel Jr. and Ephraim Morrison left Pennsylvania in a keelboat. Ephraim brought his pregnant wife, Agnes Nancy, and a young child.

Eight days later, they stopped at Tanner's Station because Nancy was ill. The settlement contained one frame building, four hewed log houses and three log cabins. They repaired an old 16' square cabin with no roof and a dirt floor and moved in on Valentine's Day. Ephraim Jr. was born March 1.

For several years, the Morrisons used a canoe as a ferry at Tanner's Station. People rode in the boat while their horses swam behind

Thomas Morrison said Shawnee Chief Blue Jacket borrowed a saddle from his father Ephraim to go to Detroit with Simon Girty. Blue Jacket, actually a Virginian who was wearing a blue jacket when he voluntarily joined the warrior tribe at age 17,[20] returned the saddle, then later attempted to steal it.

In another memorable incident, Morrison said he and his brother William treed two bear cubs while hunting with their dogs in southern Indiana. William climbed a tree and caught one. It let out a shrill scream, bringing its mother, who terrified the boys into releasing her cub. After a noisy fight between the dogs and bear, one cub was separated from its family and the boys caught it.

After a few years, the Morrisons moved to Indiana using a canoe made from a huge poplar tree cut near Rabbit Hash.[21]

Bullittsburg Baptists

A Virginian and veteran of the French and Indian Wars, Captain Thomas Bullitt and a company of surveyors contemplated plotting a town at the mouth of Sand Run Creek on property Bullitt received as a land grant. Although Bullitt never returned to Kentucky,

---

[16] Harrison & Klotter, 140.
[17] Yealey, 37
[18] *Boone County Recorder,* 1930 Historical Edition, (R.E. Berkshire publisher), Sept 4, 1930.
[19] "Early Historical Spots in Boone County," *Boone County Recorder,* Aug. 31, 1978, 10.

---

[20] Eckert, 19-21.
[21] Morrison family history documents provided by Rose M. Conner of Burlington.

Chapter 2 1776-1809 The Pioneer Path

Cave Johnson laid out the town of Bullittsburg 24 years later on 100 acres.

Lewis Deweese, a blacksmith, and Tanner, the pioneer who lost his son to the Indians, had preached on both sides of the river since 1792. Because settlements were so far apart and travel was primarily by foot or horseback, "preaching stations" were established throughout the region. After Gen. Anthony Wayne defeated the Indians and signed an August 1794 treaty, living and preaching outside fortified stations was safer.[22]

The oldest existing church in the county, Bullittsburg Baptist still has an active and energetic congregation. This photo, taken about 1952, shows the very edge of the old saddle house. Photo by Virginia Lainhart

A group of Baptists including Lewis Deweese, John and Elizabeth Hall, Chichester and Agnes Mathews, and Joseph and Leannah Smith had settled at Bullitt's Bottom (now called North Bend) in June 1794. Most came from the Culpepper, Orange and Madison counties of Virginia – a few came from New York and North or South Carolina.

Led by Joseph Redding and William Cave and accompanied by Elder John Taylor, they formed the Bullittsburg Baptist Church, the first church in what is now Boone County.

Taylor, who had explored the region in 1779, returned about 1783. This time he brought his family, animals and slaves slowly by boat on a low river, anticipating Indian ambushes the entire way. The family and four Negroes eventually arrived at Boone County's North Bend.

When the Taylors passed down the Ohio River, no settlements were visible. Within six years, log cabins formed a residential string along the Indiana side.

The church they had followed to their new homes was the pioneers' sole source of community and social interaction and ruled their activities. Despite the hardships they faced in daily life, "*church discipline was rigid and impartial and maintained with unshrinking firmness and vigilance. . .*"

Baptists who missed two successive meetings, spoke harshly to another, "*departed from the truth,*" became intoxicated, broke the Sabbath, or "*behaved immodestly*" were judged "*guilty of sin*" and could be suspended from church privileges until they proved their faithfulness or were excluded.[23]

John Conner clerked for the first house of worship, a log church built on two acres donated by George Gaines in 1797. By the century's close, Bullittsburg Baptist Church had four ordained ministers, one licentiate, two elders, two deacons and a membership of 72. Meetings were also held at Tanner's Station and Woolper's Bottoms.

Early Baptist churches allowed Negro members and slaves all the privileges of other members except voting. Voting privileges were withheld because it was believed slaves' votes would be influenced by their masters'.

The church continued to issue edicts about social activities. In 1797, the Baptist association issued an opinion that "*Funeral processions with*

---

[22]Collins, 55.

[23] Morith.

singing conform too much to the anti-Christian customs."[24]

Depew's Grist Mill

A few miles from Bullittsburg Baptist, a community initially known as Corneliusville and later Mitchellsville, would be renamed Bullittsville, also in honor of Capt. Thomas Bullitt. Eventually, six roads would crisscross there and the community would have a school, a steam saw mill, two churches, a post office, drugstore and a Masonic and Grange Hall.[25]

Near Bullittsburg, Captain Abraham Depew operated a water-powered grist mill. Grist mills used the power of moving water, caught in a water wheel, to turn large stones. Whole corn, wheat or rye kernels were placed between the stones. As the stones turned, the seeds were crushed into flour.

Water-powered grist mills couldn't function during droughts when the water got too low to turn the wheel. Some adapted to using steam so they could operate without relying on weather. Saw and grist mills used the same mechanics to saw logs, making the most of their investment and meeting more of their community's needs.

Gaines' Brick House

Another early settler, Revolutionary War Col. Abner Gaines brought his family and slaves from Orange County, Va., in 1785. Twenty miles from Cincinnati, along a fork in a bison trail atop a ridge, they built a log cabin.

With his wife, Elizabeth Matthews of Augusta County, Va., he had eight sons: James Matthews, John P., William H., Benjamin P., Augustus W., Archibald K, Richard M. and Abner L. Their three daughters were Elizabeth H. Hubbell, Mildred Pollard and Mary Wright Bush.

A few years later, as the slaves were hewing trees for a larger cabin, steamboat captain Walton, a well-to-do friend, stopped by and suggested the Colonel build with brick. When Gaines said he couldn't afford it, Walton offered him a free loan.

The Gaines house, completed in 1805.
Courtesy of Boone County Historic Preservation

Construction on a brick three-story house began in 1791 and was completed in 1805. Brick was made on the grounds. Slaves felled trees for joists and flooring and made the nails and roof shingles. Three stairways – including one of curly maple – connected the 20 rooms, a secret room and an underground tunnel. Ten carved mantles covered wood-burning fireplaces.[26]

Zebulon Pike

Near Depew's Mill, Captain John Brown owned a plantation called Sugar Grove. The

---

[24] Elizabeth McMullen Kirtley, *Burlington Baptist Church 150th Anniversary*, (1992, s.p.), 6.
[25] Jim Reis, *Pieces of the Past,* (Kentucky Post, 1988), 72.

[26] "The Haunted House – Walton, Ky.", *The Waltonian,* Sept. 19, 1984.

Chapter 2 1776-1809 The Pioneer Path

New Jersey man was a Revolutionary War veteran and one of the first Boone County justices of the peace. Suspicious when an unknown young man, Lieut. Zebulon Montgomery Pike, came to court his daughter Clara, Brown actually required Pike to give a bond that he would support his new wife. William Bates signed the bond that is recorded at the Burlington Courthouse.[27]

After Pike's marriage to Clara, he discovered Pike's Peak, then became a brigadier general. Shrapnel injured Pike in a powder magazine explosion in Toronto, Canada, while he was an officer in the War of 1812. With a captured British flag folded under his head for a pillow, Pike died on Lake Ontario and was buried at Sackets Harbor, New York.

Clara and their daughter Clarissa returned to Sugar Grove. Clara, who was known for her care of that British flag, is buried in a family graveyard at what is called the Harrison place below North Bend.[28] Clarissa married John Cleaves Symmes Harrison, the eldest son of southern Indiana's Gen. William Henry Harrison, who was elected president but died 30 days after his service began.

This illustration "Daniel Boone in the Wilderness" by William C. Allen in 1939 hangs in the Old State Capital in Frankfort.
Don Lainhart of Hebron is president of the Society of Boonesborough that is made up of Daniel Boone's descendants. Lainhart counts his heritage back eight generations to Boone's daughter Levinia. Several Boone Countians also can trace their heritage to Boone.
Courtesy of the Kentucky Historical Society.

Indian Battle

While Gaines now had an opulent home, most weren't living so comfortably. In 1789, Brig. Gen Josiah Harmar (also spelled Harmer or Harman) sent Captains Strong and Kearsey to find food for soldiers protecting Fort Washington (now downtown Cincinnati).[29]

Hungry troops were ready to abandon their posts. John S. Wallace, a trader who lived near the fort, sent hunters John Dement and John Drennon to Boone County. They reached Big Bone Creek, hid their canoe, and in a few days had killed enough deer, bear and buffalo to last the 70-man garrison until provisions arrived from Pittsburgh.[30]

One of Harmar's volunteers was Major John Bush, a member of the County Court Justices who lived in the North Bend bottoms when it was considered Campbell County. In 1790, Bush crossed the river and left with Harmar's army to chastise Indians who had been disturbing tri-state settlements.

Following the Big Miami River, the men reached Piqua and St. Mary before a two-day battle took place. Major Bush's 20-man advance guard had orders to fire on any Indians they encountered. Regardless of opponent's numbers, his orders were to charge through them and form at their back. With that plan,

---

[27] *Boone County Recorder*, 1930 Historical Edition.
[28] *Welcome to an Educational & Historical Tour Through Boone County*, (sponsored as a community education program by Boone County Schools, s.p., n. d.), 15.

[29] Eckert, 390.
[30] Yealey, 8.

Bush's *"detachment was drawn into ambuscade with a loss of one-third their number."*

After retreat orders were given, horsemen were to ride to the rear and retrieve the injured. Carrying two men, Bush's horse got mired in the mud. As they dismounted, two Indians appeared to take them captive. While Bush fled, a gun blast startled his horse into freeing itself. It ran past Bush – who leaped aboard and escaped.

In another battle, while retrieving the body of his superior officer, Bush's sword was shot from his hand and a ball pierced his cheek.

Bush's defeated army returned home, but word of his heroics spread. In 1793, in an effort to lure the war hero to Cincinnati, Bush was offered a city lot at the corner of Main and Front streets for a bargain price of $100. Bush refused the offer saying he would rather live in the North Bend Bottoms in Boone County.[31]

1799 Boone County Tavern Rates*

Breakfast, dinner or supper, each	1 shilling, 6 pence
Lodging per night	6 pence
Whiskey, half pint	9 pence
Peach brandy	1 shilling, 6 pence
French brandy or medary wine	3 shillings
All other wine or rum	2 shillings, 3 pence
Horse to hay per night	1 shilling
Pasturage per night	6 pence
Oats or corn per gallon	8 pence

English Coins
4 farthings = 1 penny or pence
2 pence = 1 shilling
20 shillings = 1 pound
21 shillings = 1 guinea

* Information supplied by Mrs. Ann Fitzgerald, Boone County Clerk's Office

Fur Trading

Six fur companies bought Ohio Valley pelts from 1780 to 1820. Most agents represented the Missouri Fur Company in St. Louis. Pelts were carried by horseback, then by boat to St. Louis. Boone County's Beaverlick may have received its name because trappers and pioneers brought their furs, including plentiful beaver pelts, to the junction of the roads leading to the salt springs or "lick."

Counties Organized

While soldiers and settlers were contending with Indians and wild animals, politicians and bureaucrats were drawing boundaries on maps and naming new territories. During 1776 a part of Fincastle County, Va., was divided off and called Kentucky County. In 1780, Kentucky County was divided into Jefferson, Lincoln and Fayette counties.

By 1784, residents of Kentucky County began calling conventions to discuss separating from Virginia. On Dec. 1, 1789, after eight conventions over five years, Virginia passed an act agreeing to separate its western annexation into a region called Kentucky. The act was accepted July 26, 1790. June 1, 1792, was set as the date Kentucky would be admitted as a state.

The new commonwealth included only nine counties. Because the smaller governmental units brought politics and services closer to the people, nearly every time the Kentucky legislature met from 1800 until 1870, more counties were delineated.

In 1785, Bourbon was organized out of Fayette. Three years later, Mason came out of Bourbon and Woodford from Fayette. During 1792, Scott was organized out of Woodford. Two years later, Campbell County was organized out of Harrison, Scott and Mason.

Boone County Formed

In December 1798, a state law was passed separating Boone – Kentucky's 30th county – from Campbell, but Boone County wasn't effectively established until 1799. The new government met in June 1799. The county was named in honor of Daniel Boone, although the area had no particular connection to him.

---

[31]Yealey, 5.

Chapter 2 1776-1809 The Pioneer Path

Bounded on the east by Kenton County, on the South by Grant and Gallatin and on the north and west by the Ohio River, Boone County has an average length of about 20 miles and an average width of 15 miles with roughly 40 miles of river frontage. The boundary at the Ohio River between Boone and Campbell (later defined as Kenton) counties was the mouth of a stream called Dry Creek.

No further changes were made in Northern Kentucky until 1840, when Kenton County was organized out of Campbell.[32]

County Seat

John H. Craig was one of Boone County's early merchants, carrying shelled corn, tobacco, flour and bacon in a 40'x 12' flatboat to New Orleans. *The Covington Journal* on Jan. 31, 1852, described Craig as the first white man *"to descend the Kentucky River, the Ohio River, and the Mississippi River to New Orleans."*[33]

Robert Johnson had met Craig while fighting off an Indian attack at Bryan Station in 1782. His brother, Cave Johnson, moved to Boone County to join him in 1798. Craig and Johnson donated 74 acres on which Boone County's seat of government was established in 1799.

County Government

Gov. James Garrard commissioned John Hall, John Conner, John Brown, Archibald Huston and Archibald Reid as Justices of the Peace of the Boone County Court.[34]

At their first meeting in June 1799, the group elected Cave Johnson the first county clerk. He was required to post a bond of $3,000 – as were several of the new officials. (The money these early Boone Countians used was British pounds, shillings, pence and farthings.)

Casting ballots, the majority of the new justices chose land on Woolper Creek offered by Johnson and Craig as the location for the public buildings.

Roads were the councilmen's second and abiding interest. They assigned various property owners to determine locations for and improve roads around the county, many to the new county seat location.

Moses Scott took several oaths required to be principal surveyor. Robert Stuffs qualified as deputy surveyor. John Cave was made sheriff and William Sebree his deputy. Thomas Allin was appointed coroner.[35] William Warren earned $30 a year as the first attorney.

In September 1799, John Conner was granted the first license to operate a tavern *"at his own dwelling."* He was required to pay *"security in the sum of 100 pounds."*[36]

In August 1800, when the court met at John Conner's home, the salary for Richard Southgate, the newly appointed attorney, was increased to $70 annually.

The first court record book listed the newly organized county's first recorded murder:

"Samuel, a Negro man, the property of John Brown, suspected to have committed the crime of murder by poisoning a Negro man named Lewis, the property of Jeremiah Kirtley, was produced in court by the aforesaid John Brown to whose custody he was committed by John Conner, Esquire Justice (a position similar to sheriff) for safe keeping until this court and thereupon no person appearing to prosecute said Samuel, nor any document appearing to justify any proceeding against him, order that he be discharged."[37]

In 1801, Boone County elected Squire Grant its first state senator. The first state representative was William Arnold.

---

[32] Yealey, 7.
[33] Jim Reis, *Pieces of the Past 3*, (Kentucky Post, Covington, Ky. 1994), 160.
[34] Boone County Court Order Book 1, 1799-1809, June 1799.
[35] Boone County Court Order Book 1, 1799-1809, June 1799
[36] Boone County Court Order Book 1, 1799-1809, Sept. 1799.
[37] Leland Sullivan, "History of Boone County Courts and Courthouse," *Boone County Recorder*, n.d.
* Boone County Court Order Book 1, 1799-1809, Sept. 1799.

Craig's Camp Courthouse

Also in 1801, a log courthouse was completed, adding to the few houses and log jail at "Craig's Camp." Fourteen years later, citizens constructed a fence around the courthouse. Just two years later, construction was underway on a "commodious stone courthouse."

The Craig's Camp name changed to Wilmington between 1798 and 1815, but that moniker didn't last long either. Likely because a Wilmington, Ky., already existed when the community applied for a post office, the name was changed to Burlington about 1815, but the town was not incorporated until 1824.

The name Burlington may have been chosen because local men fought in naval engagements near Burlington, Vt., during the War of 1812. Or, it may connect with Burlington County, N. J., which is across from Philadelphia.[38]

Piatts' Federal Hall

Jacob Piatt's family had left New Jersey in 1795 and traveled by wagon to Pittsburgh. He and his wife Hannah McCullough, of a wealthy and sophisticated East Coast family, had 15- and 16-year-old sons, Benjamin and John.

At Pittsburgh, the family boarded a boat, destined for property along the Ohio River south of Garrison Creek granted to Piatt for his military service. (This property is north of Petersburg, just south of where I-275 crosses the Ohio River.) There they built a log cabin, then gathered fieldstone to build a house. Constructed in 1804 on a hill overlooking the river, it was called Federal Hall (also Federal Hill).

The boys loaded flatboats with produce from theirs and surrounding farms, then drifted to New Orleans where they sold both the boat and its contents and returned overland, following little more than their instincts, since few roads or paths existed.

On Sept. 21, 1799, Benjamin married Elizabeth Barnett who was a year younger than he. Theirs was the first marriage recorded by the Boone County clerk. Benjamin was described as vigorous and handsome, and Elizabeth as tall and lovely.

She wrote of her wedding, "*Our marriage was not such a gay affair as my cousin Sally's but it was very nice, I assure you. I had a satin gown with a waist up under my arms. It came from my Mother and was the finest gown in Boone County. And will you believe it, children, your grandpa came dressed in his father's Revolutionary uniform as a Colonel and he looked so grand the neighbors scarcely knew him.*"

Benjamin and Elizabeth lived in the old log cabin near Federal Hall before moving to Lawrenceburg where calamities befell them – their home was burned and she contracted smallpox. After moving to Cincinnati, then to a smaller Ohio town, he studied law, eventually was granted a judgeship, then served in the Ohio legislature.[39]

Near the turn of the century, Jacob Piatt established a ferry to Lawrenceburg not far from his home overlooking the river north of Petersburg.[40]

Wilderness Trail Cleared

In 1793, Kentucky's first governor, Isaac Shelby, and the first legislature passed an act to clear the Wilderness Trail as a wagon road by 1799. That gave settlers who didn't have access to the rivers an overland option to bring their possessions west. Tree stumps were cut to a height of 12" by 1796, allowing wheeled vehicles to pass through the Gap.

As more people arrived and population centers began to appear, more roads were needed. On Dec. 14, 1793, the legislature authorized a road from Frankfort to Cincinnati.

---

[38] Reis, *Pieces of the Past 3*, 160.

[39] Blakely.
[40] Reis, *Pieces of the Past 3*, 22.

Now called Dixie Highway, it is also known as KY 25.[41]

On Oct. 15, 1796, the *Kentucky Gazette* announced that *"wagons loaded with a ton freight, may pass with ease with four good horses."* Wagons reduced costs and travails of bringing goods overland.[42]

In 1797, Kentucky's General Assembly gave county courts authority to oversee road development, construction and repair. Surveyors began evaluating routes where roads could be constructed. Costs were reduced by corvée (a Latin word meaning labor exacted in lieu of taxes by public authorities, especially for highway construction).

"All male laboring persons over 16 years of age" were required to *"work the roads, except those who were master of two or more slaves over said age"* and sent the slaves in their stead. Not working resulted in a significant $1.25 per day fine. Most local roads in Kentucky were built and maintained by corvée until 1849.[43]

Surveyors were ordered to *"make these roads out of stone, timber or earth and receive their pay from each county levy of taxes as the law provided."*[44]

Some roads were more difficult to construct and traverse than others. Between Hebron and Constance is "mile hill" where travelers still descend from 850 feet to 550 feet above sea level in one mile on what is now KY 20.

In 1799, "corduroy" – split logs laid crosswise in the road – was added to the Wilderness Trail. That reduced the possibility of getting stuck in the mud, but was far from a smooth surface. Wood also held the smells and leavings of animals that passed over it.

Kirtley's Arrive

In 1796, following the partially cleared overland trail, and buffalo, Indian and wagon trails, Jeremiah and Mary Kirtley emigrated to Boone County from the Rapidan River region of Virginia. Jeremiah's great grandfather, an Episcopalian, had settled there in 1710.

Jeremiah became a Baptist in 1788. Eight years later, he began moving his family west. On the way, they left their 10-year-old son Robert near Lexington to study with educated Englishman Parson Stubbs. Robert's only reading material was a Bible. The boy soon moved to Bullittsburg and continued his 18 months of education under Absalom Graves.

Robert Kirtley
Courtesy of Burlington Baptist Church

At 20, Robert married Polly Thompson, daughter of a Lexington-area family. The Kirtleys had nine sons and one daughter, some of whom died in childhood. Robert Kirtley was baptized during a revival in 1811. As a lieutenant in a Kentucky Militia company, he served under Gen. William Harrison in the War of 1812.

On June 8, 1817, Kirtley was ordained a deacon of Bullittsburg Baptist Church. Two years later, he was licensed to preach. At the age of 36, he was ordained as a minister. In November 1839, he baptized his sons Robert E. and James A. in the Ohio River. Both eventually became ministers.

---

[41] Paul Tanner, *Toll Roads in Kentucky 1817-1917 and Boone County*, (s.p. 1992) 1.
[42] Harrison & Klotter, 49.
[43] Harrison & Klotter, 125.
[44] Yealey, 10.

Polly, his wife of 45 years, passed away in 1851 when Robert was 65. He married Louisa Graves in June 1853, but she died five years later. Robert Kirtley Sr. died at 86 on April 8, 1872.[45]

Lick Ownership

A crude fort built at Big Bone Lick around 1780 protected settlers from Indian attacks as they boiled away the water in the tedious salt-making process. Within a decade the structure had deteriorated.

Since Indians didn't believe men could own land, ownership of the salt lick wasn't an issue until the close of the French and Indian Wars. Then England's King gave the Virginia governor the power to grant land to American soldiers who had fought against the French.

Virginia's governor from 1779 to 1780, Thomas Jefferson, granted land including the Big Bone area to Col. William Christian. In 1780, Christian sold a 1,000-acre tract including the salt lick for 1,350 pounds or approximately $4,455 – nearly six times the price of neighboring real estate.

David Ross, a friend of Jefferson's and a real estate operator who held title to about 100,000 acres of the Northwest Territories (what is now Ohio and Kentucky), bought the salt lick site from Christian. He obtained most of his land from disinterested soldiers who had received it as grants.

Early scientists had difficulty imagining these prehistoric creatures found at Big Bone Lick.
Photo by Bruce Wess,
Wild Walks Photography

Big Bones

Explorers kept returning to Big Bone Lick, intrigued by the giant bones sticking out of the ground. The best educated eventually surmised the bones came from elephants, oddly and inexplicably misplaced from their native reaches of Africa.

When Capt. Thomas Bullitt surveyed a Big Bone Creek tract on July 5, 1773, the old Indian who guided them said the big bones had been there *"ever since his remembrance (about 60 years) as well as that of the oldest of his people."* One of the men who arrived with Bullitt, Robert McAfee, wrote this description of the amazing site in his private journal:

"The bones were lying in the Lick and close to it, as if most of the animals were standing up side by side, sticking in the mud, and had died together. Some backbone joints lay on the solid ground and were used as seats by the men. The ribs were used as tent poles. One tusk stuck out of the bank 6' and was imbedded so firmly that they could not even shake it. The bones were much destroyed by the different companies who had visited them. The McAfee and Bullitt companies carried away many pieces as curiosities."[46]

---

[45] Kirtley, Burlington Baptist Church, 11.

[46] Collins, 55.

Bones Stolen

Bone collectors were not motivated purely by scientific curiosity; some paid cash for the odd skeleton fragments.

Aware of European interest in mammoth skeletons, Dr. William Goforth, a Big Bone Lick resident, dug fossils extensively between 1803-1807. While he didn't find a whole mammoth, he found many mastodon bones, teeth and three fluted projectile points.[47]

In 1803, Goforth sent bones from the Lick to the Royal College of Surgeons in London. From there, part went to Dublin, Ireland, and some to Edinburgh, Scotland.

In 1806, he entrusted his first collection of five tons of fossils – gathered at his own expense – to English traveler and writer Thomas Ashe. Ashe said he'd exhibit them in Europe for a percentage of the profits. The Englishman shipped the bones from Cincinnati to New Orleans, where he turned down $7,000 for them, saying it was not one-tenth their value.

From New Orleans, Ashe shipped them to London. There he exhibited the artifacts, sold the collection and pocketed the money. The purchaser later gave part of the collection to the Royal College of Surgeons in London and part was sold at auction. Goforth didn't receive a cent.

Goforth to Jefferson

President Thomas Jefferson was one of the people most intrigued about the findings at Big Bone Lick, discussing them with the best educated scientists of the time as well as developing his own theories of where the animal species originated.

Goforth was always looking for benefactors who would support his research and hoped for money from Jefferson or the new organization of which he was president, the American Philosophical Society in Philadelphia. When Jefferson requested information about Goforth's research, the Boone County man replied in part:

"The bones of one paw nearly filled a flour barrel; it had four claws and the bones regularly placed together measured from the os calcis to the end of either middle claw is 5' 2".

"The bones of this paw were similar to those of a bear's foot. Where I found these bones, I found large quantities of bears bones at the same time and had an opportunity of arranging and comparing the bones together, and the similarity was striking in everything particular except size.

"The vertebrae of the back and neck, when arranged in order with the os sacrum and coccyges, measured nearly 60', allowing for cartilage's. Though I am not confident the bones all belonged to one animal, and the number of vertebrae I cannot recollect.

"I had some thigh bone of incognita of a monstrous size when compared with my other bones, which I much regret I neither weighed or measured, and a number of large bones so much impaired by time it was fruitless to conjecture to what part of any animal they belonged. . . .

"From my long residence in this country I had long cherished a desire to make researches at Big Bone Lick, but my circumstances (having a large family, and my practice as a physician, though extensive, is not profitable owing to the poverty of the people) would not enable me to bear the necessary expenses. . . .

"About three years ago, some persons understanding the avidity with which skeletons of this kind were sought after in Europe, and believing a complete skeleton of the mammoth might be procured, said that it would sell well in Europe.

"After several exertions to obtain what might be necessary to carry my objection into execution, I accordingly proceeded to Big Bone Lick and with a few hands, such as my trifling resources would permit, and commenced my researches, when the agent of David Ross of

---

[47] David Pollack, *The Archaeology of Kentucky: Past Accomplishments and Future Directions*, Vol. 1, Kentucky Heritage Council, Frankfort, Ky. 1990, 74.

Virginia (who owns the tract of land), forbid my proceeding further.

"Since which time I have endeavored, by every means which my contracted situation enables me, to procure liberty to prosecute my search.

"Big Bone Lick was formerly a salt march – Salt is made there at present – we generally dug through several layers of small bones, in a stiff blue clay, such as deer; elk; buffalo and bear bone, in great numbers, many of them much broken, below which was a strata of gravel and salt water, in which we found the large bones, some nearly 11' deep in the ground though they were found upon the surface.

"The large bones were not found regularly connected together as those of a carcass, which has been consumed by time without disturbance, and I was led to form strong suspicions, that the carcasses of the large animals were preyed upon and the bones scattered here and there.

"I am so firmly persuaded that large – nay, almost any quantity of teeth, bones and tusks may be procured, – that I have long entertained a sanguine hope of bettering my circumstances by procuring skeletons, provided I could obtain permission to prosecute my search, perhaps it may be in the power of your learned body to procure me this permission, and if the society would wish collections of the bones of these nondescripts for their own use, I would undertake to superintend the collection and forward it to Philadelphia, or elsewhere, for such compensation as the Society should think proper to allow me for my trouble and quitting my business during the time of the work.

"I spent about four weeks in my former research, and with six, sometimes eight hands, and I think with ten or 12 hands (who must be found victuals and liquor), I could completely search the whole Lick.

The mastodon statue at Big Bone Lick State Park.
Photo by Bruce Wess, Wild Walks Photography

"The expense would be about $1.25 each man per day; we could take provisions from this town, or take a hunter to kill for us.

"I have now, respected sir, give all the information that suggests itself, and have mentioned the place where the collection is to be made, and the best method to pursue.

"With sincere wishes, that the Society may prosper, and that you may long continue your labors for the benefit of your country, I am, with sincere respect, your friend,

William Goforth"[48]

Megalonyx Jeffersoni

Jefferson asked William Clark, whose famous brother George Rogers Clark had just returned from an expedition to the far west, to go collect a large variety of bones at Big Bone Lick at Jefferson's expense. He also wrote Mr. Ross, asking for permission to search for particular bones on his property.

In 1796, Jefferson received a set of lion-like bones of the "great claw" Goforth had described. He then learned that a skeleton had been discovered of *"an enormous animal from Paraguay, of the clawed kind, but not of the lion class at all; indeed, it is classed with the sloth. . . The skeleton is 12' long and 6' high.*

---
[48] Jillson, 41-43.

There are several circumstances which lead to a supposition that our Megalonyx may have been the same animal as this."

The next year Jefferson read his first paper on paleontology before the American Philosophical Society. He included a description of the Megalonyx, now known to be a relative of the present-day tree sloth. The extinct giant was named Megalonyx Jeffersoni.

More than 300 bones traveled to Washington via the Mississippi. Jefferson wrote fellow Philosophical Society member Dr. Caspar Wistar when the bones arrived and Wistar soon became the society's fossil authority. They spread the bones on the floor of an empty White House room so they could study them leisurely. Jefferson's letter inviting Wistar to join him in studying the bones read in part:

"It is a precious collection, consisting of upward of 300 bones, few of them of the large kinds which are already possessed. There are four pieces of the head, one very clear, and distinctly presenting the whole face of the animal. The height of his forehead is most remarkable. In this figure, the indenture at the eye gives a prominence of 6" to the forehead.

"There are four jaw-bones tolerably entire, with several teeth in them, and some fragments; three tusks like elephants'; one ditto totally different, the largest probably ever seen, being now from 9-10' long, though broken off at both ends; some ribs; an abundance of teeth studded and also of those of the striated or ribbed kind; a fore leg complete; and then about 200 small bones, chiefly of the foot.

"This is probably the most valuable part of the collection, for General Clark, aware that we

Of the thousands of pounds of artifacts found in Boone County, little more than these tusk fragments remains at Big Bone Lick State Park.
Photo by Bruce Wess, Wild Walks Photography

had specimens of the larger bones, has gathered up everything of the small kind. There is one horn of a colossal animal."[49]

In a letter thanking Clark for collecting the bones, Jefferson shared his new identifications:

"The animal was neither a mammoth nor an elephant, but of a distinct kind, to which they have given the name of Mastodon, from the protuberance of its teeth. These, from their forms, and the immense mass of their jaws, satisfy me this animal must have been arboriverous.

"Nature seems not to have provided other food sufficient for him and the limb of a tree would be no more to him than a bough of a cotton tree to a horse."[50]

The finest specimen in Jefferson's collection was a skull of the great arctic musk ox Bootherium. The only one of its kind taken from Big Bone, the Academy of Natural Science in Philadelphia now owns it. Some bones were sent to Philadelphia, some to the National Institute of France to be studied by the

---
[49]Jillson, 54.
[50]Jillson, 55.

French naturalist M. Cuvier, and some stayed in Jefferson's private collection.

For decades after Jefferson's death, his private collection was thought to be lost. However, in 1987, a small, dusty collection of bones was discovered in the basement of the Virginia Museum of Natural History. No one on staff knew the package's origin although some knew Jefferson's grandson had donated a large bone collection in 1887. Scientists there have tested clay samples and found the soil to be the same as samples from Big Bone Lick. An unknowing Monticello tenant is said to have ground up the majority of the collection for fertilizer after Jefferson's death.

Clark's last collection marked a change in Big Bone's topography – the big bones laying about were gone. It had become very lucrative to sell them in the states and abroad and many had collected the profits.

Saltmaking

On July 30, 1806, debt forced Jefferson's friend Ross to sell the salt lick property to Wilson Allen, Edmund Rootes and Jacob Myers of Tidewater, Va., but Ross retained possession for two years, giving Jefferson permission to continue his investigation of the big bones.

The next year, the trio of new owners sold the property to a Scotsman, Mr. Colquohoun, who had visions of establishing a salt industry. This is a description of his process:

"The fuel is introduced into a grated furnace, whose mouth is closed by an iron door. The kettles rise gradually from the front to the chimney, so as to occasion a sufficient draught of air.

"The first kettle in the furnace is round and contains about 100 gallons, as this receives the greatest degree of heat, and evaporates the water much faster than the smaller ones, they are partly supplied from it after the water has boiled down considerable, and the small black kettles are supplied from those near the front.

"The kettles are filled with salt water in the first instance from a wooden pipe running over the middle of the furnace, having a spigot hole on each side; this is supplied by a pipe, from the general reservoir filled from the leading troughs."[51]

Water was drawn in buckets or pumped from wells using hoses or pipes. The saline solution poured into a trough then funneled into boiling kettles. Kettles of various sizes set parallel to each other on furnaces made of layers of stone that were cemented together with mud.

Furnaces were several feet deep and 12' to 15' long. Each boiler required a separate fire. And after each boiling, the furnaces had to be recemented. Salt distillers constantly cut and carried firewood, carried water and fixed the furnaces. Five hundred to 600 gallons of water were boiled down to make one bushel of salt. That process cost $4 a hundredweight, which made it too high to be exported.

Attempting to reduce the cost, Colquohoun built two furnaces and mounted kettles that would hold from 16 to 100 gallons of water. But he found that traveling a great distance over bad roads made the salt too expensive to deliver. He finally gave up. Ephriam Tanner's shop book shows Colquohoun bought salt on the Cincinnati market for $2.94 a barrel.

Because salt was so important to daily life, between 1798 and 1820, the Kentucky legislature passed a series of laws regulating and encouraging salt manufacture. Some set penalties for those who disrupted the manufacture or transport of brine or salt.

Indentured Servitude

While difficulties prompted most to relocate in Boone County – few travails were as lengthy and fraught with hardships as those of Boone County's first Lutherans. Originally destined for Pennsylvania, a dozen Protestant German families had set sail in 1717. When their ship stopped in England, the captain was imprisoned several weeks for debt. During the delay, passengers ate the ship's provisions, a foolish

---
[51] Jillson, 92-93.

Chapter 2 1776-1809 The Pioneer Path

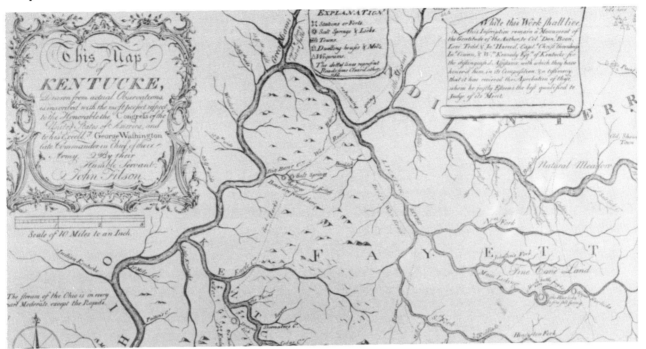

Internationally known cartographer John Filson's early maps of Kentucky showed Big Bone Creek, salt springs, and the note "Bones are found here." Note that the rivers are located differently than we now know.
Courtesy of Behringer-Crawford Museum

move that caused some to die of starvation during the crossing.

Storms pushed their ship south until it landed in Virginia. There the captain sold the Germans into indentured servitude to pay for their passage. Families named Aylor, Blankenbaker, Carpenter, Utz, Crigler, Crisler, Clore, Weaver and Yager worked in Gov. Spottswood's Orange County iron mines. They lived in a place called "Germanna" in what is now Madison County, Va. Seventeen more families, including the Tanners, Rouses, Beemons and others, totaling about 80, joined them later.

Unable to afford a church, the group asked Jacob Christopher Zollicoffer of Switzerland to visit European churches and solicit funds to help build a church and pay a minister. By the early 1730s, they had organized the Hebron Church in Germanna, Va., the oldest Lutheran Church in the south.[52]

Church members Michael Schmidt and Michael Holden went back to Europe to collect funds to endow the church and develop a library for the pastors. One-third of the money they collected paid their voyage expenses, another third built a frame chapel and bought farm lands and the remainder went to purchase slaves to cultivate the land.

The situation the early German Lutherans had found in the 13 colonies was not uncommon. "*The leading currency of Virginia was tobacco and the most valued property was the slave. The early servants were not Africans, but whites, who came from poverty or crime and had fallen into slavery.*" In 1671, there were three white servants to one black in Virginia.[53]

Frederick Tanner was one of the German Lutherans who had served in the Revolutionary War. Under Capt. Isaac Ruddell, he spent time in Kentucky from 1779-80. No doubt Tanner returned with stories of the fertile Kentucky soil and plentiful wildlife.

About 1800, fellow church-member Ludwig Rouse visited the area and returned enthused. In 1804, Hebron Lutheran's pastor William Carpenter,[54] investigated Boone County.

---

[52] William Conrad, *Yesterdays, An Enriching Adventure in Boone County's Past*, (s.p. 1987), 1.

[53] Rev. H. Max Lentz *A History of the Lutheran Churches in Boone County, Kentucky*, York, PA, 1902, 14,

[54] Some Zimmerman families adopted the English name Carpenter. William Carpenter's father was William Zimmerman who changed his name at the beginning of the Revolutionary War in which he served.

Hebron Lutheran Church
Courtesy of Barbara Dye

On Oct. 8, 1805, 11 families from Carpenter's church packed their belongings in covered wagons. They walked down Virginia's Shenandoah Valley to the Holston River, then followed it until they came to the road Daniel Boone made to Lexington.

Lutherans Found Hebron

The families of George and Elizabeth Rouse, John and Milly House, Frederick and Rose Zimmerman, Ephraim and Susanna Tanner, John and Nancy Rouse, and Elizabeth Hoffman took the ridge route too, arriving in a beech forest wilderness called Boone County on Nov. 25, 1805.[55]

Several days after their arrival, Susanna Tanner gave birth to a son, Simeon. (Susanna lived to be 86, bearing 14 children, several of whom – including Simeon – lived nearly to the turn of the century.)

"The greater part of the country was then a perfect wilderness. These families however were furnished with rough cabins" [likely ones the unaccompanied male explorers had built on earlier visits to convince the families to come].

To build a cabin, trees at least 18" in diameter were cut, then squared using an axe, saw, and footadze. Clay was mixed with lime to create "whiting" or "white chinking" to fill the space between the logs. (In 1969, when remodeling his 1808 log home, William Bruce Campbell Sr. found that 161-year-old chinking had remained hard and smooth.)[56]

The rafters and sheathing were of hard wood, fastened by mortise and black walnut pins 1" in diameter. A hand auger bored holes to join pieces with wooden pegs.

No cabin was available for George Rouse, a single man who pitched his tent in the dense forest, not far from where Hopeful Church now stands.

As soon as Rouse's cabin was completed late in 1805, Lutheran meetings began there. After a hymn and a prayer, Ephraim Tanner read a sermon in German by their Virginia pastor, Rev. Schubert. Services concluded with prayer and singing.

Father Carpenter, who had stayed in Virginia, responded to a letter from Tanner about how to organize a new church by sending a constitution.

In 1807, Rouse donated an acre for the church cabin of unhewn (not squared) logs. A clapboard roof and doors sheltered seats made of saplings that sat on a puncheon floor. Logs on both ends were sawed out for windows. Since no glass was available, the windows were open year-round. No stove or fireplace added comfort during the weekly winter services.

The settlers encouraged five new families to join them in 1806. Several of the men had

---

[55] Yealey, *History of Boone County, Kentucky*, 29.

[56] Campbell, 15.

fought in the Revolutionary War and witnessed Cornwallis' surrender at Yorktown.[57]

Trading Without Cash

Although more and more settlers were arriving, the region was still spacious and largely unpopulated. *"Where Covington is now, there was a farm and an orchard. Cincinnati consisted of two brick and two frame houses with a number of log cabins."*[58]

Even when pioneers found a place to purchase supplies they couldn't produce themselves, buying was complicated. Settlers' pockets weren't full of spare change. Just locating coins was a problem. Currency values weren't standard; the occasional coin used could have been minted in a number of different countries.

While some paid in English currency, others used United States' money. Leonard Crisler bought 224 acres for $560 in 1802, but William Wilhouit paid 75 pounds for 100 acres adjoining the Crisler tract on the southeastern side of Georgetown Road.

To deal with the currency problem, early legislative bodies enacted standards to substitute for coins. A pound of sugar was worth a shilling; the skin of a raccoon or a fox – a shilling three pence; a gallon of "good" rye whiskey – two shillings, six pence; a gallon of peach brandy or a yard of good linen – three shillings. A bear skin, otter skin or deer skin was to be worth six shillings.

The amusing standards brought jokes that at least this currency could not be counterfeited, but soon a bundle of "otter" skins were found to be less valuable racoon skins with otter tails sewn on them.[59]

Disappearing Frontier

The frontier was disappearing. In 1793, herds of bison still roamed Northern Kentucky. Seven years later, they were gone. Pioneers overtrapped any animal whose fur had commercial value, including panthers, otters, martens or mink. Then they either exterminated or greatly reduced small predators like foxes and wildcats. Wolves moved in to prey upon fearful settlers' domesticated sheep, pigs and calves. But bounties soon exterminated them too.

With no large flesh-eating animals to keep their numbers in check, rodents and rabbits devoured settlers' crops and sometimes invaded their homes.[60]

Clearing Land

Corn that had been planted in unplowed ground as soon as the new arrivals could get it in the ground attracted squirrels, mice and rats. Versatile and hardy, the golden grain was simple food for people and livestock. Ears made corn easier to gather and store than small grains and beans, pumpkins and melons could be grown among the hardy cornstalks.

While the first corn crop was growing, farmers cleared more land. A good hand with an ax might clear three acres during a winter. The easiest way to make a clearing was girdling a tree "Kentucky style" and leaving it to die. As soon as the dead leaves fell, sunlight came in to the crops planted below.

As the trees' branches fell, they were piled against the trunk and burned. Roots were cut and grubbed out. Eventually the tree stumps were dug, pulled or blasted out. Without trees to hold the topsoil, the ground's fertility was soon exhausted, so clearing new land became a lifelong job.

As more acreage became available, settlers cleared and tilled the ground, then planted wheat and oats to vary their diet. Women added vegetable gardens. A field of flax and several sheep, who could scavenge poor pasture, ensured raw materials for new clothing.

After food crops were growing, farmers began cultivating hemp or tobacco for cash. As

---
[57]Lentz, 13.
[58]Lentz, 20.
[59]Lentz, 13.

---
[60]Purvis, 28.

Blue-eyed Marys carpet Middle Creek Park in the springtime. Other wildflowers found in the area include trout lilies, bloodroot, trillium, Dutchman's breeches, squirrel corn, spring beauties, Jack-in-the-pulpit, May apples and more. Photo by Bruce Wess of Wild Walks Photography

it remains today, a small amount of tobacco brought many times more income than a similar-sized field of grain.

Horses multiplied a man's strength and provided transportation. The family milk cow offered butter, cream and cheese in addition to fresh milk. As game disappeared, hogs and chickens replaced them in settlers' diets. Apple and peach trees, transplanted with them or purchased from itinerant salesmen, added healthy variety to summer and fall meals. Both could be dried for winter snacks and pies.[61]

As soon as neighbors could get together to help, a barn went up to protect domesticated animals against both weather and wolves. Rail fences kept animals nearby and out of the crops. Hogs were often allowed to run wild in the forests, scavenging for nuts and plants. Salt kept the other animals close to home.

Few hired hands were available and fewer could afford to pay them. A landless man was likely to work as a tenant. Neighbors gathered from miles around for the labor-intensive tasks of log rolling, house and barn raising, and corn husking, making hard labor into social events.

Western Spy

While it seemed the land was still wild and empty, literate citizens could turn to the new weekly papers, the *Western Spy* and *Hamilton Gazette* for information and news. Articles in the Spy included:

- *"Andrew Jackson (Old Hickory) advertises his black slave (George) as having eloped from his plantation, $50 reward." April 26, 1802*

---

[61]Harrison & Klotter, 133.

- *"No Spy published for the last three weeks for want of paper. No mail for three weeks. There is great dissatisfaction and with good cause." May 27, 1803*
- *"The first sea vessel passed Petersburg April 27, 1801, called the Bright St. Clair could carry 100 tons. This vessel was so well constructed that it could cross the Atlantic Ocean.*
- *"To our county subscribers: The printers of the Spy want some turnips and potatoes for which a reasonable price will be paid."*[62]

Southern Slaves

The U.S. government's 1800 Boone County census showed a population of 1,104 whites, 325 slaves and 15 free blacks.

Kentucky was one of three states that allowed slaves to learn to read and write. Most prohibited it, believing educated slaves could lead insurrections. A few slaves living in the region were even allowed to earn cash for extra or independent labors.

State law allowed border counties to establish patrols to recapture runaway slaves. Men from 16 to 60 were paid $1 for patrolling for 10 hours. Patrol captains could order up to 10 lashes for recaptured slaves. Then a Justice of the Peace could order up to 39 more.

For catching a runaway from within the county, the patrol earned $25. If the runaway was from another county, the slave owner paid the patrol $50. Funds came from a $1 tax on each slave which was specifically set aside to pay the patrols.

Rev. Robert Kirtley, Lawrence Sanford, Thomas Tousey, and James Dickens patrolled Boone County between Woolper and Elijah creeks in 1808. Patrol reports said Kirtley's Negro Ben was caught without a pass and was given a severe "cowhiding." A patrol discovered some Boone County slaves trading merchandise stolen from their masters across the river. The slaves exposed the ring after being severely whipped.[63]

A 1798 act said if any Negro, mulatto or Indian was convicted of any offense, the offender was to be "*burnt in hand*" by the jailer in open court and "*suffer any other corporal punishment the court deemed necessary*." Burnt in hand meant branded – probably on the back of the hand so the palm would remain useful – likely with a T for thief or an R for runaway. The brand could be seen regardless of clothing and aided bounty-hunters who populated even free states.

Anyone believed to have ¼ or more Negro blood was deemed a "mulatto." The word Negro used in any statute included mulattos. By 1860, 13 percent of Kentucky Negroes were mulattos.[64]

Daily Boone County slave life isn't documented. Only information about the unusual is mentioned, like this story: On March 2, 1808, Lodick Campfield admitted to the Boone County Court that he beat his colored boy early one morning because the boy had "dirtied" himself. Later in the day, a passerby found the boy dead.

Salute Harrison

The man who recorded that information was likely Col. Cave Johnson, the first county clerk. Johnson had received a land grant of the rolling meadows at the intersection of Routes 237 and 8 along the North Bend of the Ohio.

Johnson began constructing his home in 1798. The Colonel is said to have rowed across the Ohio to visit his friend and fellow Revolutionary War veteran Gen. William Henry Harrison.

Elected the ninth president, Harrison only served 30 days. A cold caught during his inauguration turned to pneumonia which killed him. Four days later, his widow received a letter edged and sealed in black. His remains were

---

[62]Yealey, 31.

[63]Merrill S. Caldwell, "A Brief History of Slavery in Boone County, Kentucky," a paper presented to the Boone County Historical Society, June 21, 1957, 5.
[64]Caldwell, 2.

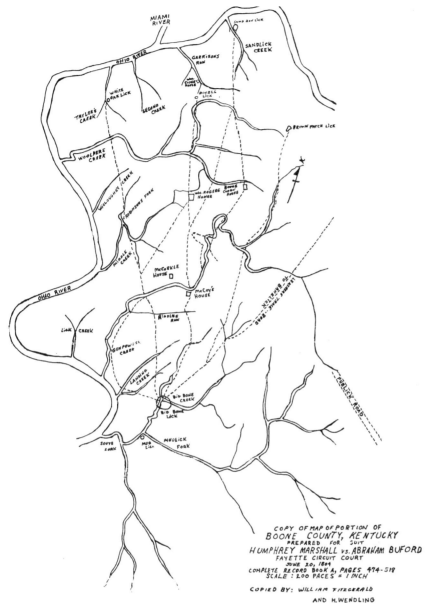

This Boone County map was drawn in 1804.
Courtesy of Boone County Historic Preservation

returned to his Indiana home by steamboat and his body was entombed at the base of the monument, visible across the river from his friend's property.

For many years, steamboats passing the landmark tolled their bells in respect for Harrison's war record as well as his short presidency.

When Gen. Andrew Jackson, a Democrat – the party opposite of Harrison's Whigs – was traveling down the Ohio, the riverboat captain explained the traditional salute to Gen. Harrison as they passed North Bend and asked if Jackson minded.

Jackson is said to have replied, "*Yes, give him two for his military service, but darn his politics.*"[65]

Johnson's interest in and support of the military continued. His Boone County land was used to train and drill troops before the war of 1812.[66]

Covington resident Thomas Kennedy, who had a stone residence at what is now Second and Garrard streets, also used his riverfront property to assist the military. Kennedy ferried soldiers across the Ohio to raid Indian villages.

People paid 12 cents to cross the river in a row boat. Kennedy used large flat boats with oars to ferry horses. In 1823, he began using the side wheel or treadle. Kennedy's crossing was reputedly the best in central Kentucky.

Fiddle in the Fire

Baptist preacher John Taylor had another use for rivers. And his goal was to get as many people in as possible. In 1801, Taylor returned from preaching at other churches to learn a series of dances had been held in Bullittsburg after a wedding. Angry and attempting to put a stop to this sinful activity, he held a service near the party place, but few attended.

A Sunday service at the meeting house however, had a different effect on the dancers. Taylor wrote, "*Soon after I began, a set of feelings overcame me, that exceeded any I had*

---

[65] Conrad, *Top of Kentucky*, 27.
[66] *Educational & Historical Tour*, 13.

ever felt in public speaking. They consisted of a profuse weeping that I could not suppress. The whole assembly seemed to reciprocate the same feelings, perhaps there was not a dry eye in the house. What the Lord did at this meeting entirely broke up all the dancing in the settlement."

This revival spread like wildfire, continuing for two years, adding 152 to the church's rolls.

By 1800, Boone County's population was 1,534. Although there was only one Baptist for every 20 Kentuckians at that time, in Boone County the ratio was one in ten.

One convert was Moses Scott, Boone County's first surveyor and a Pennsylvanian who came to Kentucky in the 1790s with his wife Mary Ryle, a sister of John and James Ryle from North Carolina. A fiddler, Scott played for community dances raising the ire of Baptist preachers.

Preacher Taylor described Scott as *"a small man in stature, but before his conversion, a very great captain for the Devil – and though some where in the east he was raised by a religious Presbyterian father – he came to Kentucky, and threw off even the form of godliness. Among other things he was a great fiddler, and fond of all the amusements connected with that practice. It may generally be taken for granted, that what is called a good fiddler is the Devil's right hand man. This Scott gloried in his native strength of intellect, connected with his wit, capacitated him to make wickedness acceptable to men. . . .*

"A number of Cincinnati gentry, male and female paying a visit to this near rich neighbor of mine, and desiring to have a dance, could not do it without Scott's agency with his fine fiddle – in this he accommodated them, and they had a long dance, and with this away went all Scott's religion apparently – he forsook meetings for several months, till a monthly meeting being at my house in dead of winter.

"Mr. Scott living almost in sight, came to the meeting – one of the finest young ladies that I knew in the country as to dress was also there. A companion of hers came forward and related her experience which so much affected this fine girl, which she strove to suppress for some time, at length broke forth in plaintive sorrow. . . .

"The young lady entreated me to pray for her, as a poor lost sinner – while she trembled from head to foot, while all her flouncery, jewelry, curls and feathers trembled as if an earthquake was under her feet. . . . After I had closed my prayer, with tremorous voice, before she left her knees, prayed herself at some length for the Lord to have mercy on her guilty soul. Perhaps no preaching could have affected the assembly more. This circumstance opened Mr. Scott's wound afresh."

Scott visited Taylor soon afterwards speaking *"of the weeping young lady and wishing he could be as she was, to which I replied – 'but Mr. Scott what will you do with your fiddle?' His reply was ... that he intended to make a present of it to me, to do with it as I thought proper. However, soon after his house got burnt with chief of his effects, fiddle and all."*[67]

Presumably Scott and the young lady were among the ten Taylor baptized the next month in the river among ice flecks. The Scott family continued to support the church and assist other regional churches.[68]

Letty's Conversion

Taylor also recounted this conversion: *"I had owned Letty as my property from a child and she was now the mother of children. She had ever manifested the greatest aversion to anything like religion, so that she could not be ruled except by harsh means to family worship, but otherways the most faithful servant I ever owned.*

"Her masculine strength made her equal to any black man on the plantation. Her high spirit and violent temper often brought her to bloody blows. As her body was strong, so was

---

[67] John Taylor, *A History of Ten Baptist Churches*, (Art Guild Reprints Inc., Cincinnati, Ohio, 1823), 98-101.
[68] Kirtley, *Burlington Baptist Church*, 12.

her mind. Nature had done more for her than common. ...

"The hour of sorrow being come with a woman in the neighborhood which has killed more of our mother Eve's poor daughters for her first sin, my wife sent Letty to give assistance in this distressing crisis. ... The husband, an Irishman and perhaps a Catholic as to religion, otherways he was a monstrous wicked man as to swearing and drunkenness.

"The situation prompted Letty to ponder conversion, but deciding she had no friend, she ran down to the river, perhaps to drown herself. Throwing her distraught self headfirst down the riverbank, she 'felt the anger of God turned away from her.'

"For more than 20 years this poor black woman has given good evidence that the work I have been stating was a reality. We may see in this instance that God is no respector of persons – and it is probable more slaves will go to Heaven than masters," Taylor said.[69]

Middle Creek Baptists

Baptist churches continued to multiply as Boone County's population doubled to 3,000 between 1800 and 1810. Settlers requested letters of dismissal from the churches they had walked miles to attend and started new ones closer to home.

By 1803, 23 Middle Creek Baptists – including two Negroes – had erected their own log church. *"Planks for the church floor were to be seasoned, jointed, and pinned down, the seats to be 1' wide and 2" thick, with a door and three windows. The house to be underpinned, chunked and crammed."*

Brother Moses Scott was allowed $2 to purchase a book and paper for his clerk duties. (This book still exists.) Deacons William Rogers and James Ryle were ordained on June 19, 1803. Christopher Wilson was selected preacher but soon left for the Bullittsburg church, so he and two other ministers from local congregations were asked to preach twice a month.

All free male church members were assessed $5. Fundraising "subscriptions" from members were not often paid in still-hard-to-find currency, but in tobacco, wheat, livestock, hemp and whiskey.

The church's first luxury was $5 spent to add backs to the benches in August 1803.

After little growth in its first eight years, an 1811 revival added 18 by baptism and eight by letter from another church. In 1814, the church moved to a new and larger 32' x 24' frame meeting house that cost $300 to build. In 1818, another revival added 103 members.[70] But by 1839, deaths and dismissals had reduced the church to 64 members.[71]

---

[69] Taylor, 111-112.

[70] *Belleview Baptist Church, 190th Anniversary booklet*, 1993 est., 1-2.
[71] Laura Rogers, *Boone County Recorder*, "Sketch of Belleview Baptist Church," Sept. 21, 1978.

Chapter 3
1810-1829 Settling In

Events of 1811 were even more remarkable than Rev. Taylor's amazing Baptist conversions: the Ohio flooded, a comet appeared, the sun was eclipsed, and earthquakes rattled homes hard enough to bring down stone chimneys. Settlers, who had just begun organizing their lives in the newly formed Boone County, were unsettled by the long series of unexplained anomalies.[1]

Adding to the turmoil, and coinciding with the comet's appearance, a new invention called a steamboat began navigating the Ohio. Huge paddlewheels churned the water, creating a bubbling wake. The superstitious said the comet plunged into the Ohio, because when it disappeared, the river "boiled" and the earth shook. Some thought the events portended the world coming to an end.

Even the squirrels acted oddly. Scientist and artist John James Audubon described a squirrel invasion of the Miami Valley – and watching the rodents jump into the Ohio and drown.

On Oct. 27, 1811, the steamboat New Orleans heading to New Orleans from Pittsburgh, sped past Boone County astounding river folk with its amazing 13 mph pace. (Rising Sun settler John Fulton was the uncle of steamboat developer Robert Fulton.)

Earthquakes centered at New Madrid, Mo., began Dec. 16, 1811, and lasted through the winter, creating gloomy moods among settlers.[2] Some families packed away their valuables anticipating a quick escape. Rumbling sounds and a peculiar atmosphere often preceded a quake – building fearful anticipation as neighbors gathered around fireplaces. Shocks recurred for a full two years.[3]

Indiana Connections

The river brought excitement – news, new technology, and visitors – somewhat unifying residents who lived along it. Proximity, rather than state boundaries, linked communities. Kentucky's growing string of river towns interacted more with their cross-the-river neighbors than their own county seat.

Although Boone County's population doubled by 1820 as it had the decade before, Indiana's riverfront communities of Lawrenceburg, Aurora, and Rising Sun offered goods and services not yet available on the southern side.

The Ohio was narrower then, less than half the width we now see. In winter and very dry seasons, people and animals could walk on ice or wade across the great waterway. (Since March 1784, the low water mark on the opposite shore has been Kentucky's boundary.)

Complicated Currency

Paying for goods and services on either side of the river wasn't as easy as reaching into a pocket for change. Spanish dollars were still more common in Kentucky than American coins. Some British money remained in circulation. Until the War of 1812, many

---

[1] Owen Findsen, "Disasters of 1811 left the city quaking," *The Cincinnati Enquirer,* March 30, 1997, F3.
[2] Harrison & Klotter, 156.

[3] Owen Findsen, "Disasters of 1811 left the city quaking," *The Cincinnati Enquirer,* March 30, 1997, F3.

Early Boone County roads may have looked similar to this path through Boone Cliffs. Photo by Bruce Wess, Wild Walks Photography

Kentuckians quoted prices in either pounds or dollars – often both.[4]

Traveling through Boone County, scientist David Thomas wrote, *"In this district, cut money is very common. If Change cannot be made, the chisel and mallet are introduced. But often there is speculation, even in the business, for one-fifth is often palmed on the traveler for a quarter. This invention is supposed to be of Kentucky origin and was probably caused by necessity."*

Ephriam Tanner's 1816 shop book says three silver dollars were laid on his anvil and cut into four equal parts, or quarters, worth 25 cents each. Dollars cut into eight parts were called "sharp skins" because of their wedge shape and sharp edges.

If the change amount was less than 12½ cents, the storekeeper generally gave pins, pencils or needles as change. Change was as inexact as the judgment of the person wielding the chisel. Some cut five "quarters" or 10 "eighths," saying they should be paid *"for the expense of coinage."*

When storekeeper John Bartle became exasperated at the wedge-shaped coins, he put them in barrels and shipped them up the river to Pittsburgh, then by wagon to Philadelphia. There, a mint recoined the sharp-edged pieces into easier-to-handle currency. Bartle also asked mint officials to send him several barrels of large pennies, dated 1824-1825, that some Boone County families still keep.[5]

Some banks and merchants issued paper "coins." Called "shin-plasters" because they "weren't good for any thing but a shin plaster," they were an effort to overcome the coin shortage problem.

First Banks

The state chartered 46 independent banks, including one in Burlington that received

---

[4] Harrison & Klotter, 144.

[5] Yealey, *History of Boone County, Kentucky*, 15.

Chapter 3 1810-1829 Settling In

$30,000. But the public distrusted paper money and all the banks' charters were repealed a year later. Because so many customers lost money, the banks gained notoriety as "The Forty Thieves."[6]

In 1821, Benjamin Leathers established a bank in connection with his Covington store to help with the currency problem. Leathers issued his own "promise to pay" or "shinplaster" in denominations of 6¼, 12½, 25 and 50 cents.

When Leathers collected the paper coins to redeem them, he threw them in his shop fireplace, not realizing that the wind carried them up the flue and deposited them in the street in front of his store. People picked them up and cashed them a second time. His assets nearly exhausted, Leathers discovered the problem and began depositing the paper in a trunk to burn at his farm.[7]

Road Travel

Cincinnati and Covington were growing and gaining reputations as major markets for farm produce and regional supply centers. Drovers with herds of cattle, sheep or pigs could arise early and be at the Covington markets' opening if they stopped in Boone County to spend the night. The tavern at the junction of Banklick and Ridge roads (U.S. 25) often housed 50 to 75 guests. Flocks of turkeys roosted on the fences and in trees under the care of a night watchman.

Buggies were becoming more common as surfaces appeared over which they could be driven. Ed Fowler brought a buggy to Boone County on his return from South Carolina in 1826. Henry Sayers drove a buggy on the Covington and Lexington Pike from Covington to his Kenton County home in 1827, reported S.S. Scott of Florence in the *Boone County Recorder*, Oct. 5, 1884.

When citizens like Fowler and Sayers wanted a better road, they petitioned the state legislature for a road charter. In 1819, the first Boone County state charter described a road from Georgetown to Cincinnati, through Walton. Called the Lexington Pike, it is now known as Dixie Highway or Route 25.[8]

If local landowners couldn't finance roads themselves, they sold stock or subscriptions. When a percentage of the road had been subscribed, the new corporation elected officers and began construction. Tolls could be collected after a few miles were completed to state specifications. Some roads didn't sell enough stock to start construction, others took years to build.

Boone County citizens and officials frequently relied on the General Assembly in Frankfort to enact special and local laws, especially those affecting roads. (The 1892 Constitution finally stopped the practice.) On Dec. 11, 1822, a state law allowed the county to levy taxes and require residents to work on the roads, rather than leaving the issue in private hands:

"It shall be the duty of the county courts of Boone, Campbell and Mason to levy as much on said counties as will be sufficient for the purchase of tools and instruments as said courts shall consider necessary to keep in good condition the roads in said counties."[9]

Representative Stephens

Leonard Stephens, who had moved to Northern Kentucky in 1807 as a 16-year-old, was eventually one of those legislators. Elected to the Kentucky General Assembly in 1823, Stephens also served in the Kentucky Senate, representing Boone and Campbell counties, from 1829 to 1833.

Stephens, his father and brother John made the bricks for a Colonial mansion on Richardson Pike (which was in Campbell

---

[6] Conrad, *The Top of Kentucky*, 15.
[7] Yealey, *History of Boone County, Kentucky*, 15.

[8] William Fitzgerald, "Walton Established in 1840." *Boone County Recorder*, Jan. 2, 1964.
[9] Tanner, BC-1.

County at the time). Northern Kentucky politicians gathered at that big house before heading to Big Bone Springs where they set election strategies.

When Kenton County was organized in 1840, Stephens became high sheriff (the elected sheriff in charge of the deputies). His political career continued as Justice of the Peace in Campbell County in 1839. He died at 82 in 1873 and was buried in a family cemetery near his home.[10]

Cincinnati Newspapers

Politics were gaining prominence. The weekly newspaper called the *Western Spy* had changed its name to the *Cincinnati Republican*. It and the *Hamilton Gazette* began taking sides in politics. The *Cincinnati Gazette, Cincinnati Chronicle* and *Cincinnati Republican* began advocating for Whig candidates to their combined circulation of 2,000. The *Cincinnati Advertiser and Journal* promoted Democrats to its 400 subscribers.

The *Daily Times*, read by 1,500, and the *Public Ledger*, with a circulation of 1,400, remained neutral. Boone County correspondents supplied the neutral papers with general news.[11]

These are news excerpts from 1813:

- "*Col. John J. Flournoy,* (Petersburg mill owner and town father) *who lives in the big house* (now called the Loder House) *in Petersburg, received a clock from Philadelphia, the first one in Boone County. People from far and near go to see the wonderful machine. . .*

- "*Our women are busy with spinning wheels and looms, making material to clothe the soldiers under Gen. Harrison and Dick Johnson.*

- "*Robert Mosby and Mary Spangler were married during the holidays. The bride was handsomely attired in a linsey dress of her own making from the spinning wheel up. The groom looked every inch a man in his regulation suit of brown jeans. Robert Kirtley, the youthful pastor of Bullittsburg Church, performed the ceremony.*"

Marshall and Emma Jump McCandles of Verona in their carriage. Emma was the aunt of Ruth Glenn Meadows of Walton.
Courtesy of Ruth Meadows

Taylorsport

On the far northeastern side of Boone County's horseshoe bend in the Ohio, below the mouth of Elijah Creek, Thomas D. Foulks built a warehouse and ferry crossing in 1827. James Taylor of Campbell County started a ferry above the creek in December 1836.

Five years later, he recorded a sketch of a town he named Taylorsville. Within five more years, postmaster John H. Crawford opened an office called Elijah's Creek. (The office closed in 1859.)

Caroline Hafer Sprague offered her home and orchard for meetings of the Taylorsport Methodist Episcopal Church. Rev. William Humpries crossed the river from Home City, Ohio, to become the first pastor. The church was built after land was purchased in 1863.

The 1870s census listed 120 Taylorsport residents including a doctor, retired doctor, two shoemakers, a printer, a plasterer, a tailor, a stonemason, a bricklayer, a grocer and several farmers. The Methodist church also sponsored a mission in Constance.

---

[10] Yealey, *History of Boone County, Kentucky*, 20.
[11] Yealey, *History of Boone County, Kentucky*, 31.

Chapter 3 1810-1829 Settling In

In 1909, the post office was re-established under the Taylorsport name with Louis H. Sprague as postmaster. Since that time, the river has claimed one original street, a row of houses and the first graveyard.

Piatt Ferries

The family of Jacob Piatt, who lived in Federal Hall north of Petersburg, operated three ferries. Moses Tousey, who had married into the family, ran one near the homestead at the mouth of Taylor Creek. Superstition surrounded the "Touseytown" ferry. Death, disaster, ruin and other calamities were said to have befallen the ferry's owners.

The fifth owner, John Kizex, died with a dagger in his heart. The weapon was owned by a man Kizex attempted to murder. Years later, Sen. S.W. Tolin of Burlington was indicted for unsafe facilities after a man using the ferry received near fatal injuries.[12]

Further down the river, the Piatt family operated ferries that were docked at Rabbit Hash and "Piatts Landing" in East Bend Bottoms.

Early ferries offered a rowboat for pedestrians and a barge for livestock, vehicles and freight. The ferryman pulled a rope attached to the barge upstream, then navigated the crossing using sweeps or oars.[13]

Low water, flooding, sharp rocks, sand bars and other obstructions hampered the Ohio's navigability. Discussion and plans to build a canal *"that would be of immense advantage to the Ohio trade"* around the Falls of the Ohio at Louisville began as early as 1804.

On May 24, 1824, Congress assigned supervision of the Ohio and Mississippi rivers to the Corps of Engineers of the United States Army. A $75,000 appropriation was to remove the *"planters, sawyers, and snags"* from the Ohio's channel. (The Army Corps still retains control of the river in the 1990s.)[14]

Landing Turns to Petersburg

Politician and Baptist minister James Garrard, who became Kentucky's governor, wasn't interested in living along the river north of Rabbit Hash. He sold his 1,000-acre tract to Philemon Thomas for $500. Thomas sold it to Col. John Grant, who then was making salt at Grant's Lick, for $1,000 in cash and $3,000 worth of horses.

By 1806, Grant had obtained permission from the Burlington court to open a ferry to the fledgling town of Lawrenceburg, Ind. He laid out a 100-acre town and named it Caledonia for his Scottish ancestry. With his salt businesses failing, Grant sold everything to John J. Flournoy and moved to Illinois.[15]

Boone County's justices granted Flournoy permission to establish a warehouse at Tanner's Station to inspect flour, tobacco, hemp and pork. The Frenchman took advantage of the burgeoning steamboat traffic to begin the Petersburg Milling Co. in 1816. Both his supplies and product could be delivered nearly to and from his door via the river.

Flournoy donated two acres for a town cemetery, about half a mile from downtown, but no one was buried there until 1880. A Scotsman named Macasilly opened a school in the old distillery building in 1816.[16]

Two years later the Kentucky State Assembly officially established the town of Petersburg. Also on Jan. 17, 1818, the legislature chartered a bank with Flournoy, Benjamin G. Willis and Absalom and Reuben Graves as stockholders. Willis was listed as president and John Grant as cashier.[17]

Flournoy represented Boone County in the Kentucky legislature for two years. In 1817,

---

[12] Margaret J. Blakely, paper "The Piatts of Kentucky," May 27, 1952.
[13] Conrad, *The Top of Kentucky*, 21.
[14] Clare, 48.
[15] Conrad, *Loder 6*, 2-3.
[16] Mary Rector
[17] Mary Recto.

he deeded 2½ acres to the Petersburg Steam Mill Company.

Later, Flournoy advertised in a Cincinnati newspaper that he would donate Petersburg city lots to tradesmen and mechanics who would settle there. Lots sold slowly. By 1823, only about 40 of the 172 measured lots were sold or reserved. Two large parcels, where the school and ball fields stand today, were designated "publik ground."

Uriah Hardesty, a cooper, received the first four lots on Grant Street, starting along the river from Water Street, in consideration of a fraction of a Cincinnati lot. He soon opened a tavern.

John H. Shepherd paid $340 for lots 32-33-34 on Market Street in May 1820. He operated a tavern in 1822 then sold to John and Catherine Schramm who continued the tavern into the Civil War years.[18]

Trustees of the Christian Church bought lot #66 on Tanner Street for $1 in 1842. It had been sold in 1818 for $75. Trustees included John Terrell, Charles L. Brasher, Charles O. Alden, Kirtley Youell, and William Snyder.

Burlington resident Lewis Riddell purchased Lot #46, where the Loder House now stands, for $200. That lofty amount probably meant a building was included. William Snyder sold the property to Julia Loder on Feb. 4, 1858, for $1,400.

A clause in the Loder's real estate contract excluded 16' 3" of that lot on the east, the Tanner Street side. Two years later, the Loders bought that odd parcel from William and Elizabeth Chapin for $275. L.A. Loder's brother George, a carpenter, built a barroom on the porch and added other improvements to the original building.

Meeks Founds Belleview
South of Lochry Island on the Kentucky side, Col. Edward Meeks laid out a new town in 1815. Originally called Mt. Vernon, it was re-named Belleview, (also spelled Bellevue) a word believed to be derived from French meaning beautiful to see.

Cincinnati's *Western Spy* newspaper advertised Belleview lots for sale in 1816: *"located in midst of a high fertile bottom and inhabitants wealthy and industrious with their surplus products such as wheat, flour, tobacco, cheese and butter sold."*[19]

Not far from Belleview was a path called Garnett's Mill or Big Bone Road, now known as Middle Creek Road. On it stood Middle Creek Baptist Church, a store, a shingle mill, a distillery, two water-powered grist mills, a saw mill and a carding mill where wool was untangled and combed.[20]

Big Bone's Curative Qualities
Still the best-known site west of the Alleghenies because of the big bones, by 1812 new sources made salt more easily available than the lengthy and tedious process of evaporating water from it at Big Bone.

The bones and saline springs had become one of the nation's earliest tourist and natural health spas. During the early 1800s, wealthy southern families came to Big Bone Lick to socialize and submerge themselves in the sulfur-saline springs' "curative qualities."

Big Bone was seen as a safe haven from summer yellow fever epidemics that swept Louisiana, Mississippi, Alabama, the Carolinas, Tennessee and Arkansas.

A hotel built in 1815 included a dance pavilion, bath houses adjacent to the springs, and stables for horses and carriages.

Famous Bluegrass residents including the Breckinridges, Todds, Crittendens, Clays, Marshalls and McDowells came to visit Big Bone over the Lexington-Covington toll pike, now known as the Dixie Highway. Traditional coachmen wearing linen or livery drove along

---
[18] Conrad, *Loder 6*, 5.

[19] Conrad, *Top of Kentucky*, 36.
[20] Conrad, *Top of Kentucky*, 36.

Chapter 3 1810-1829 Settling In

Benjamin Piatt Fowler built this limestone house on what is now U.S. 42 in 1817.   Photo by Jason Dunn

the ridge road through Union with their wealthy passengers.

Other visitors came by the new steamboats on the Ohio, then traveled to Big Bone on foot or by carriage piled high with luggage.

Fowler Builds Union Home

Shortly after Boone County was separated from Campbell, Jacob Fowler had purchased 5,000 acres. Half of his land was in Boone County where a fork of Gunpowder Creek is called Fowlers Branch.

His son Benjamin Piatt Fowler built a limestone house on what is now U.S. 42 in 1817. The walls were 22" thick. An endless chain laid in the mortar of each story acted as a band bracing the building. (In 1998, the Piatt Fowler house is owned by the Wayne B. McClellan family.)

East Bend Baptists

John Jones, John Neal, William Hodges, Washington Fuqua, John Hodges, Benjamin Hodges, William Smither, Agnes Neal, Nancy Neal, Rebecca Neal, Drucillah Fuqua, Elizabeth Hodges, David Fuqua, and William Neal built a new East Bend Baptist Church of bricks they fired themselves.

On Christmas 1819, settlers living near where the Ohio River bends and flows to the east, tired of their long walk to church, petitioned Middle Creek Baptist to start a church nearby.

In April 1824, Robert Piatt sold land to the trustees of East Bend Baptist Church "*in consideration of the love and goodwill, which Robert Piatt has and cherishes toward the cause of religion and for the consideration of one dollar, paid by the trustees, sells this parcel of land, including the ground where East Bend Meeting House now stands.*"[21]

Gunpowder Baptists

Baptists continued recruiting new members and building churches closer to their homes. Absalom Graves and 28 others were dismissed from Bullittsburg Baptist to start a church at the Forks of Gunpowder on April 29, 1812.

While the Bullittsburg Baptist congregation had been meeting in a log and frame building since 1794, in 1818 they built a brick auditorium with walls 16" thick. The building, which still stands, cost $1,850. All but $150

---

[21] Elizabeth McMullen Kirtley and Carlene Stephens, *East Bend Baptist Church 175 Years* (s.p., 1994), 4.

was on hand when construction began and the additional money was gathered quickly.

As was the current tradition, the pulpit was placed on the side, rather than the center of the sanctuary. The building was heated with a fireplace. George Gaines' servants supplied the fuel. The building was positioned so it faced the road leading to Burlington.

The Gunpowder Baptist Church's original building was a combination church and Indian fort made of massive stone walls without windows, only loopholes for rifle firing. The heavy oak door was reinforced with cross bars.[22]

Sand Run

A community called Francisville in the North Bend of the Ohio River was home to the Sand Run Baptist Church, a post office, general store, tobacco factory and later a hotel and school. A cemetery there includes the graves of County Clerk Cave Johnson and his three wives.[23]

Chichester Matthews, one of the county's original settlers, and 77 other members of the Bullittsburg Baptist Church, started the Sand Run congregation. Fifty-five members, including moderator Absolom Graves and clerk Moses Scott of Middle Creek, were of European descent and 23 were African.[24]

Sand Run Church met in members' homes until February 1820 when the church received a deed to three acres. Completed that year, the building cost $2,100. Part of the cost was paid in cash, the rest in tobacco – the county's primary crop.

Chichester Matthews preached at the church until he died in 1828. Many slaves regularly attended services, sitting in the gallery.[25]

The candle chandelier is all that remains of the original church. Homemade tallow candles lit the church for evening services. Each service, someone brought a lighted candle sheltered by a lantern to light the other candles. Candle holders, made of an L-shaped piece of wood, were placed around the meeting house walls.[26]

Benjamin Mitchell earned $7 annually for cleaning the church and the spring (which was used for drinking water) and furnishing candles. Two years later, his salary was increased to $10 a year. The church grew and acquired Brother Landon Robinson as an ordained minister. Free white males paid $12.50 a year to maintain the church.

Rev. James A. Kirtley
Courtesy of Burlington Baptist

In 1831, a saddle house was added to protect saddles during bad weather. Horses were tied to rings in a tree in front of the church.

The church's discipline remained strict. When a complaint was registered against someone, the accused could give his account to the church. If he didn't bother to, he was excluded.

Three men who had missed several consecutive weeks of services were called before the church. Two who came with satisfactory excuses were pardoned, the third – who didn't show up – was excluded.

Brother Andrew Brockman brought a complaint against himself for "*disorderly conduct and getting intoxicated with spirituous liquor.*" An investigation found him guilty of sin. He apologized to the church and said he would try not to do it anymore. The church forgave him and restored him to full fellowship.[27]

---

[22] Mrs. Lorie Morith, "History of the Old South," Jan. 12, 1960.
[23] Reis, *Pieces of the Past,* 73.
[24] Campbell, 42.

[25] *Boone County Recorder,* 1930 Historical Edition.
[26] Morith,.
[27] Vivian Blaker, *Sand Run Baptist Church 1819-1994.*

Chapter 3 1810-1829 Settling In

Burlington Baptist Church minutes document similar practices. The son of Boone County's first sheriff, Squire G. Scott, frequently confessed to the sin of overindulging in intoxicating drinks "*contrary to Christian character*."[28] Scott's son, Perryander Cadmus (P.C.), became Burlington Baptist's pastor and his daughter married Rev. James A. Kirtley, a later Burlington Baptist pastor.

Although the Baptist Church prohibited many things, it did not prohibit slave ownership. A bill of sale dated March 8, 1811, noted that Payliss Cloud sold a five-and-a-half-year-old Negro girl named Sharlot for $160 to Robert Kirtley.[29]

Members of the Mud Lick Church organized yet another congregation called Oak Woods Baptist Church on March 26, 1825, at the home of Brother James Finnells.

Frontier Baptist preachers feared educated Eastern missionary preachers would deride them and lure their parishioners away. Since frontier ministers didn't get paid for some years yet, Boone County's preachers didn't understand why missionaries should receive money.[30]

Lutherans Chastised

While church was a very serious matter, occasional events lightened the mood. As a toddler, Thomas Rouse and his contemporaries entertained themselves during spring services rolling colored Easter eggs up and down the aisle. When two eggs collided, the broken egg's owner howled until his mother supplied a new one.[31]

When William Carpenter became the first Hopeful Lutheran pastor in October 1813, he liberalized services by offering them in both English and German. Before his arrival, loyal parishioners had read in German sermons previously given in Virginia.

At a congregational meeting in 1823,

Leather flaps covered windows of the early stagecoaches to prevent rocks and debris injuring passengers.   Courtesy of Boone County Library

Carpenter shamed his congregation in German: "*You build fine homes for yourselves while leaving God in a tent!*" Within six months, parishioners had built a new 25' x 25' log church on the Rouse farm. The building featured an end gallery and a high pulpit. (The brick building existing in 1998 is the fourth church on that site.)

Carpenter, a Revolutionary War veteran who always wore knee britches and gold buckles, also preached in Episcopal pulpits. The dapper retired soldier had come through the Cumberland Gap with his wife Polly Aylor. They had nine children.

Carpenter was described as a man of means, but very kind to the poor. On discovering a neighbor stealing corn from his crib, he told the man to simply ask for it rather than

---

[28] Kirtley
[29] 175th Anniversary Historical Book, 52.
[30] Kirtley

[31] Emma Rouse Lloyd, *Clasping Hands with Generations Past*, (Wiesen-Hart Press, Cincinnati, August 1932), 64.

attempting to steal. He "sold" corn only to those who didn't have cash to pay for it. Shortly before his death in 1833 at the age of 71, he burned about $300 worth of due bills given for that corn.[32]

Carpenter's will, recorded on Sept. 27, 1831, granted freedom to his servant Ben and Ben's wife Caroline. They were to be allowed to live on Carpenter's son's farm as long as they did not "*entertain or harbor black people or suspicious characters*." The rest of Carpenter's slaves were to be sold among his own children – not among strangers. His nine slaves' value was estimated at $2,200.

Mulatto Runaway

With roads and steamboats now offering more mobility, the relative security of Northern Kentucky slaves' lives was gone.

After learning she was to be sold into the deep south, a young Boone County slave girl arranged to run away, first hiding in a straw pile near her master's barn. Crossing the Ohio in a skiff, she reached the home of an abolitionist family in Cincinnati. Disguised in a Quaker bonnet, she left with Mr. and Mrs. Levi Coffin, stopping overnight in Hamiliton, Ohio.

The next day, a Sunday, they continued to West Elkton, Ind. After seeing the beautiful young mulatto woman in a public exposition, the town soon became a major Underground Railroad depot.[33]

Forces were at work that would push the nation apart over slavery.

A large slave-owner named Norris had many difficulties with slaves escaping across the Ohio, through Richmond, Ft. Wayne and South Bend, Ind. He and his agents traveled frequently to retrieve slaves from Northern Indiana, always failing to get satisfaction from Hoosier courts. During his last trip with prisoners captured at South Bend, Norris was attacked by a band of sympathizers and his slaves were taken by force.

Norris brought suit in the U.S. Circuit Court at Indianapolis against Newlan Crocker and others, recovering a court judgment of about $2,800 plus $2,000 in costs, but many who assisted the runaways didn't pay the fines assigned to them.[34]

Gaines Begins Stage

Abner Gaines had become a Boone County justice in 1805 and served for 12 years until he was appointed sheriff. In 1813, he bought 200 acres from Thomas Kennedy for $810. A month later Gaines bought the 190 acres where he was living from Caleb Summers for $1,666.

A post office opened under the name Gaines Ford Road on July 14, 1815. The area had a tavern, two tobacco warehouses and about 50 residents.[35]

Abner began operating the first stage line from Cincinnati to Lexington on May 6, 1818. His four-in-hand coaches stopped at his tavern, halfway between Covington and Williamstown, where passengers disembarked to join him at a long dining table loaded with food and drink.[36]

The Lexington Turnpike, chartered in 1819, ran through Gaines Crossroads (Walton). The road became U.S. 25 and Dixie Highway.

Burlington

Incorporated in 1824, Burlington was as large as Cincinnati at the time. Expected to grow into a large city, the original houses were built without front yards. In 1830, the population was 276, but it declined slightly by 1850.[37]

"*In 1819 the town of Burlington contained 60 white males over 21 years of age.*"[38]

---

[32] 175th Anniversary Historical Book, 12.
[33] 175th Anniversary Historical Book, 52.
[34] Yealey, *History of Boone County, Kentucky*,. 42.
[35] Jim Reis, "200 and holding," Kentucky Post, Nov. 19, 1984, 10K.
[36] Conrad, 200th Anniversary, 19.
[37] "Early Historical Spots in Boone County," *Boone County Recorder*, Aug. 31, 1978, 10.
[38] *Boone County Recorder*, Vol. 1, No. 1, Sept. 23, 1875.

Chapter 3 1810-1829 Settling In

The son of the ferryman, Erastus Tousey built one of the first Burlington buildings on Jefferson Street. On land purchased in 1817 for $25, Tousey built a large, two-story brick house. The Federal Style building, completed in 1822, was equipped with a dumb waiter so that his two slaves who cooked in the basement on large stone fireplaces could send meals upstairs.

Burlington Seminary

As interest in education grew, in 1814 the Kentucky legislature granted 2¼ acres on Burlington's north side to create an academy. Burlington Seminary (also known as Boone Academy and later Morgan Academy) was at first a one-story, two-room building set in a beech grove on Bullittsville Road (also known as Jefferson Street or KY 338).

Thomas Campbell and his daughter June were hired to operate the school in 1819, but they soon left, disagreeing with some state laws.[39]

The academy offered a high school-like education. Optional primary schooling was available as convenient for winter months when farm work wasn't pressing.

---

[39] Conrad, *History of Boone County Schools*, 15.

Chapter 4
1830-1849 Steamboats and Stagecoaches

Farming was the primary way of life in Boone County. Long hours of hard work and 1,820 slaves made most farmsteads self-sufficient. In 1840, the population had increased to 7,214 whites, 2,000 more than in 1820. By 1840, the number of slaves in the county peaked at 2,183, while the number of "free colored" dropped to 27 from 41 in 1830. The number of slaves remained stable through 1850, but the number of whites increased to 9,044.[1]

Steamboats continued bringing visitors and new products to the river towns. Hamilton, down near Big Bone, claimed a population of 200 in 1830.

Petersburg had its own industry, making it the county's largest community with 500 residents. Petersburg founder William Flourney sold his flour mill to William Thornton Snyder in 1832. Impressed with the quality of water found in a well driven nearby, Snyder began a distillery in connection with the mill.[2]

In 1830, Burlington reached a population peak that wasn't matched for 130 years – anecdotal counts ranged from 276 to 350. Burlington Seminary was soon joined by a significant number of additional schools to meet a state requirement.

As roads improved, Florence more than tripled in size – from a population of 60 in 1830 to 200 in 1840. Drovers passed through, taking their animals to the Cincinnati markets. Stagecoaches – the newest transportation form – quickly began making regular mail and passenger runs between Cincinnati and Lexington, creating hotel businesses in the emerging villages of Florence and Walton.

Big Bone Lick continued to attract attention. Entrepreneurs marketed the Big Bone Lick's sulfur water for health and relaxation benefits. Alexander Wilson, called the father of American Ornithology, studied colorful Carolina parakeets there. Constantine Samuel Rafinesque, an early naturalist, searched for bones in 1841. Famous English geologist Sir Charles Lyell also pilgrimaged to Big Bone.[3]

> **Meteor Showers**
>
> Less frightening than the environmental irregularities of 22 years before, 1833 was called *"the year the stars fell."* Nightly meteor displays were brilliant and abundant, lighting the sky like a full moon. Seventeen-year-old Thomas Rouse remembered *"the stars seeming to fall before and all about him"* as he rode home from a party late on Nov. 12, 1833. He said the *"snowfall of stars"* frightened his horse so much it stopped and trembled.
>
> Like most Boone County youths of his time, Rouse preyed upon deer coming to the salt licks at Big Bone. Once, as the gunman for a group, Rouse stationed himself in a tree near a commonly used trail by the lick. His friends and their dogs hiked back to flush out the deer. Seeing a large wild cat, he couldn't resist shooting. He missed, leaving his gun empty and unable to kill a deer, much to his hunting companions' chagrin.*

---

[1] U.S. Census figures.
[2] *Boone County Recorder,* "History of Petersburg Community," Sept. 21, 1978.
[3] Edwin Way Teale, *Wandering Through Winter,* (Dodd, Mead & Co., New York, 1957) *248-249.*
*Emma Rouse Lloyd, *Clasping Hands with Generations Past,* Wiesen-Hart Press, Cincinnati, August 1932, 23-24.

Churches continued to play an integral role in Boone Countians' lives. Even those who weren't particularly devout came regularly to the "meeting house" to keep up with world and community news and attend social events. After-church invitations could bring a score of seldom-seen friends or neighbors home for Sunday dinner – a feast of impressive proportions.[4]

The population remained overwhelmingly Baptist, but religious options began diversifying – Lutheran, Methodist and other churches opened. While some religious orders continued bringing settlers here, others began evangelizing, converting new members.

The Farmstead

Thick beech forests that sheltered the game and attracted early settlers to Boone County were disappearing. Log cabins were being weather boarded, expanded or replaced with newer brick or frame houses.

While most Indians had been driven out and conflicts were fewer, more African slaves had been moved in. Conflicts were beginning between slave owners and abolitionists. Abolitionists were seldom farmers attempting to till and harvest large amounts of acreage.

Large farms resembled small villages with all their outbuildings. Slave cabins, ice houses, saddle houses, carriage houses, granaries, flax houses and other structures sprang up around the main house as farmers gained wealth and expanded their holdings.

On larger farms, each animal species was housed in a different barn – cattle in the main barn, sheep in another and hogs in a smaller one. Chickens lived near the main house in a small building of their own lined with nests from which eggs were collected daily.

Hay was stored in lofts above the animals. Oats logically were kept near the horses, in granaries built as solid as possible to deter rodents. Separate corncribs stored yellow cobs awaiting sale or use as food for pigs, cattle and horses.

While the men planted, tended and gathered field crops and kept track of the animals, women completed endless household chores. They often cared for large numbers of children and elderly family members who could no longer live alone. Women also cooked, cleaned, gardened, preserved food, milked cows, wove wool and flax, made clothes for themselves and the slaves, sewed carpet rags and wove them into floor coverings, and made butter, cheese, soap and candles.

Soapmaking

Like most tasks, making soap required planning and preparation. Four forked poles driven into the ground at right angles made a soap hopper. Poles laid in the forks formed a hollow square about 6' above the ground. A 3'-long log hollowed into a trough angled toward an iron kettle positioned to catch the lye.

Straw lined a slanting wooden box. Wood ashes saved throughout the winter were packed into the hopper, dampened and allowed to soak for several days. Each day water was added to run through the ashes and drip into the trough, carrying lye into the kettle. Poured through the ashes repeatedly, the lye solution was strong enough to use when an egg floated in it.

Cooking grease saved throughout the year was stirred into the lye. When the amber-colored mixture attained the consistency of jelly, it was soap.

Stronger "country" soap cleaned coarser clothes. Mixing salt with soft soap while it was cooking made two layers, a liquid and the top layer of "hard soap." Cream-colored hard soap was air dried, cut into cakes and used for dishwashing and heavy household cleaning.[5]

Candle-Making

Uncooked beef fat had another valuable

---

[4] Campbell, 16.

[5] Lloyd, 100-101.

use. With window glass difficult to obtain and electricity still many years away, any indoor activity after dusk required candles or lamps.

Beef tallow rendered (cooked) and heated to the exact temperature made candle wax. Since wood-burning stoves had no temperature-control knob, it was an exacting process. If the tallow was too cold, the wick could not be dipped. If it was too hot, the tallow wouldn't coat the wick.

Wicks long enough to make 10-inch candles were tied to a stick or rod then dipped in melted tallow and hung to cool and harden. Repeated dipping thickened the candles to the desired size. Dipped candles were generally about an inch in diameter at the base, tapering to the top.

Candle molds sold by peddlers simplified the time-consuming task. Sets of six, eight or a dozen molded candles were made at once by tying one end of a wick to a rod and drawing the other end through the tin molds. Filled with hot tallow, the molds were left to cool and harden overnight. Then the candles were ready to remove and use.

Before they were lit, candles were placed in tin candlesticks surrounded by trays. A pair of snuffers was nearby, if not on each candleholder. Snuffers opened and closed like scissors, their wide upright blade closing into a square receptacle. After the candle burned for an hour or so, the charred wick was snuffed off to increase the amount of light given off.[6]

The Ice House

While soap and candles were necessities, ice was somewhat of a luxury to chill tea, lemonade and other summer drinks and treats. Made like cellars, icehouses were about 10' deep with stone walls and floors. Only the roof extended above ground.

A layer of clean, new rye straw covered the dirt floor before the icehouse was filled. Ice was cut from a river or pond when it was frozen at least a foot deep. Sawed into blocks, it was thrown up on the bank with steel tongs and left to freeze dry. The rectangular blocks were layered in rows separated by straw, which insulated them. Layers were repeated until the house was filled. Then it was closed until summer. To reduce thawing as much as possible, the day's ice supply was removed early, before the summer sun rose.[7]

A drink cooled with this ice came with its own straws, of the wheat or rye variety.

Sassafras tea was a spring drink, made from the bark of red sassafras roots. Red sassafras

Hopeful Lutheran   Photo by Bob Sharpe
Print courtesy of Bruce Wess, Wild Walks Photography

is a deeper brown/red color and is more spicy and aromatic than white sassafras, although they look similar. Fresh roots were shaved into hot water. The potion was said to "thin the blood" and help ready the body for summer's heat.

'Poultry' Escape

Spring and summer brought more visitors to rural homesteads. Strangers stopped by

---

[6] Lloyd, 100-101.

[7] Lloyd, 100-101.

Chapter 4   1830-1849   Steamboats and Stagecoaches

farms offering goods for sale or just to visit on their way to market or a relative's house.

A white man named John Fairfield, who professed to be "*buying poultry for market*" one spring, helped 28 slaves escape. Sneaking away in the night, they climbed onto three skiffs tied to the Boone County riverbank in a wood-yard across from the mouth of the Great Miami River.

Fairfield's skiff sank before reaching shore, forcing the group to wade through waist-deep water. Heading toward Cincinnati, they were forced to hide in ravines when the sun came up. Fairfield requested passage on the Underground Railroad from a man named Coffin. Relying on his name for inspiration, Coffin suggested renting coaches and arranging a funeral procession for the group disguised in the heavy black face-covering garb of mourning.

The mock funeral became a real one when a tiny infant carried by its mother died. The runaways buried the baby on a hill overlooking Cincinnati and continued their flight north.

Altruistic goals met profit motives in individuals who assisted runaways. A poor white man who owned a boat and lived along the Kentucky shore ferried runaway slaves, met at appointed times and places, to Underground Railroad stops above Madison, Ind., for small fees.[8]

Lutheran Slave Owner

The contradictions of slave ownership were many. Native of a slave-free state, Pennsylvanian Rev. Jacob Crigler purchased a slave woman named Tina (or Tinie) for $180 from Joseph Kendrick and Jacob Clarkson on Dec. 30, 1839.[9]

While slaves attended Baptist churches, often sitting in specially designated balconies or rows, no records have been found that indicate they were included in Boone County's Lutheran church services.

Crigler became pastor of Hopeful Lutheran Church in 1833, after Rev. William Carpenter died. Like Carpenter, Crigler defied convention and preached in English and German.

Hopeful Lutheran "modernized" in 1836, adding a bucket of drinking water and employing someone to open the windows, start the fires and fetch water before services.

Despite those improvements, church members built a brick church the next year that they used until 1917. Members contributed labor to build the 35' x 50' structure. Materials cost $1,587.28½.

Milling Grains

Most churches were constructed along Boone County's creeks to be close to a drinking water source. The many Baptists who practiced immersion baptism also used them for cleansing the soul. Larger creeks and streams that held running water year-round were chosen as sites for gristmills that converted grain to flour.

One water-powered mill stood on Gunpowder Creek south of Hopeful Lutheran near the YMCA's Camp Ernst. Another sat on a different Gunpowder branch near Florence by the George Rouse Creek Bridge. Still another was on Salem Creek. Gabriel Crisler ran a gristmill above the forks on Long Branch.[10]

While some millers relied only on the stream for power, operating with steam allowed mills to run in dry weather when water levels were too low to turn the water wheel. Steam came from a boiler heated with burning wood. Saw and gristmills powered by steam or water both ground grain and sawed logs to make the most of their investments and serve their community's needs.

Buckets on a huge wooden wheel filled with water from a millrace, which was

---

[8] Merrill S. Caldwell, "A Brief History of Slavery in Boone County, Kentucky," a paper presented to the Boone County Historical Society, June 21, 1957, 8.
[9] Yealey, *History of Boone County, Kentucky*, 18.

[10] *175th Anniversary Historical Book*, 18.

sometimes narrowed and directed to ensure water would move faster. The water's weight in the buckets caused the wheel to turn until the water spilled out. Meanwhile, other buckets going through the same process kept the wheel rotating.

The rotating wheel turned an axle that extended into the mill house. There it transferred the energy to an intricate system of cogwheels, gears, shafts, belts and pulleys that powered the milling equipment. Huge stone wheels crushed the wheat, corn or oats. Only the top stone turned, crushing the grain against the stationary bottom stone.

Grain kernels fed into the top stone's center hole. As it turned, the grain was ground and pushed to the outside by grooves cut into the stone. Flour collected in a grain chest below the stones.

Boys often rode to the mill with wheat or corn divided evenly in the ends of a tied sack draped over their horse's back. The miller weighed the grain and accepted a fee or took a toll – a tenth to an eighth of the grain. Millers adjusted the flour's texture by raising or lowering the top stone, or burr. Boys who didn't want to watch the process brought a fishing pole and waited at the creek.

Stephenson Mill Road got its name from the mill on Salem Creek near Walton. (The site is now under I-71.) Across from the mill, which provided flour, corn meal and lumber, was a blacksmith shop run by the Hopper family.

Roy Elmer McCubbin, whose great grandfather Stephenson started the mill, said it was built from creek stone. The grinding burrs came from France. One was made into a gravestone for his cousin Raymond A. Stephenson who is buried in New Bethel Cemetery.

"The lumber mill had a bog saw that ran up and down and another called a whip saw that was later changed to a circular saw."[11] McCubbin was told the blacksmith across the creek cut the old whipsaw blade into hoes after it was replaced.

"The mill stood on the north side of McCoy's Fork Creek and the miller's home stood on the south side under a big sycamore close to the Verona branch." That was just above where Panther Creek Painter Branch emptied into McCoy's Fork. The mill owners had rights to all the waterpower in these creeks up to their headwaters.

Its' 20' to 25' tall overshot wheel had buckets holding about 50 gallons of water. A dam about ¼ mile upstream diverted water into the race or canal. About 100 yards further upstream was a *"low level dam"* of rocks 10' square by 1' thick that created an island and controlled the water flow.

Old Mill
Photo courtesy of Virginia Lainhart

Sometime in the 1880s the dam was washed out, damaging the race and mill. Homesteaders clearing a hillside upstream rolled logs and carried brush near the creek waiting for it to dry so they could burn it. But a summer storm blew up and washed the debris about 10 miles down the creek, tearing out road crossings and the mill race.

Mill owner Stephenson used burning brush to create lime for chinking and plaster. After building a huge brush pile, he and the neighborhood children collected a particular color of rock. They piled the rock on top the brush, then set the pile afire. After it burned for nearly a week, the lime was ready to use.[12]

Plaster was a mixture of lime, sand and animal hair, usually applied ¾ to 1" thick over 2" wide wooden lathe, split or "riven" from

---

[11] Roy Elmer McCubbin, *Boone County Recorder,* "I Remember," Sept. 21, 1978.
[12] McCubbin.

quartered logs. Floors were made of hardwood boards, often of white ash. Building styles varied with individual tastes. Most houses had wide porches or verandas, high ceilings and large rooms.[13]

Schoolhouses

During three winter months, some children took time away from tasks like making lime to attend school. However education wasn't a requirement nor particularly encouraged. In 1831, only 24 percent of young Kentuckians attended school.

Educated individuals offered subscription schools in their homes or churches for a fee. Some communities banded together to build schoolhouses.

In Virginia, "old field" schools had been located on poor, unproductive, or worn-out land. Since Kentucky didn't yet have worn out land, schools were located near population centers and close to water and wood supplies.

Buildings were simple. One description of an 1820s school said it was built of small, round logs, 14' x 16' square, then covered with clapboards held in place by heavy poles. Puncheon (10" to 12" diameter logs split lengthwise) benches sat on a puncheon floor. The seat's legs were round saplings driven into auger holes in the floor.

Wooden spikes driven into holes in the walls provided hooks for coats, hats and dinner baskets or pails. The ceiling was just high enough to allow the teacher and tall scholars to walk under. The one door faced south to allow the sun to enter for heat and light. No windows let the cold or the sun's rays in. (Later schools, particularly those built near the turn of the century that still exist, often had windows.)

With no public funding, each student paid the teacher – sometimes part in cash and part in 'coon skins or farm produce.

Many families couldn't afford to send all their children or didn't believe it was necessary. Some sent their brightest child, while others sent their dimmest, leaving the more resourceful to fend for themselves. Some large families sent children to school in turn, alternating terms. Some believed "book learning" was only for boys.

Often students chanted their lessons in voices a little above a whisper while the schoolmaster mended or made goose-quill

A school at Stringtown on the Pike.
Courtesy of Virginia Lainhart

pens. The pens used ink made from a mixture of pokeberry juice, oak galls and iron rust.[14]

In 1836, the state General Assembly passed an act establishing a common (public elementary) school system. Boone County magistrates appointed commissioners who surveyed the county and laid out 26 schools.[15]

The first Boone County public schools opened in 1838 with three-month terms. They used Eclectic schoolbooks, Ray's arithmetic and Mansfield's grammar, published by Truman and Smith, Cincinnati.[16]

School started in September and continued into December, coinciding with the slower

---

[13] Campbell, 15.

[14] William Conrad, *The History of Boone County Schools*, (Boone Co. Community Educational Council, Boone County, Ky. 1982), 7.
[15] Conrad, *The Top of Kentucky*, 39.
[16] Yealey, *History of Boone County, Kentucky*, 31.

farming seasons. Students ranged in age from four to early 20s.

Some schoolteachers held other jobs throughout the year, but most were itinerant teachers and boarded in the neighborhood where they taught. Boarding the teacher was one way to pay for schooling.[17]

In 1839, Walton's first school was located at the forks of Stephenson Mill Road and Beaverlick Pike. A brick building north of Walton replaced it in 1900.[18]

Squirrel Hollow School

Florence's first school was located at the foot of what is now Banklick Street. The building is described by various historians as measuring 14' x 20' or 16' x 24' with slab seats and a rock fireplace. Squirrel Hollow School (named for the plentiful gray squirrels) overflowed with pupils.

Town founder Thomas Madden and Dr. Menzies, who owned a drug and general merchandise store, set out to find a new location for a larger school. Menzies' store employed 15-year-old Thomas Rouse as a clerk. Rouse lived with his uncle, Joshua Zimmerman, who owned all of the land at the corner of Burlington and Price pikes.

Madden and Menzies talked Zimmerman – who had no children, but wanted a school nearby for his nephew – into donating land on Price Pike and construction began on a larger school.

A tax of 15 cents per $100 valuation paid for that building. Subscriptions paid the teacher. Squirrel Hollow School operated under the Florence trustees from 1831 until 1881 when the land was sold to S.S. Scott for $30. Scott now owned the surrounding land that Zimmerman previously occupied.

Schooling was becoming a statewide priority. In 1838, the Governor appointed a state Superintendent of Public Instruction who required public schools to offer three-month terms.

Before 1850, teachers created math books to include analytical arithmetic, algebra and geometry. Peter Parley's geography text was also used.[19]

Selling Big Bones

A school was offered at Big Bone Landing not far from the lick where George McGlasson was postmaster in 1834. In 1846, the post office was renamed Hamilton (after large landowner George Hamilton who may have been postmaster at the time[20]) and the community boasted a tavern, two doctors, three stores and 200 residents.[21]

Erosion continued to expose more bones at Big Bone Lick. The Western Museum Society had collected more bones in 1819. Collecting artifacts was becoming more lucrative.

In 1831, Captain Benjamin Finnell, who lived for a time near the licks, had sold bones for $2,000 to a Mr. Graves. Graves resold them to a New York company for $5,000.

Some speculated that the bones of at least 100 mastodons, 25 mammoths and other animals now had been collected by visitors from around the world who arrived on horseback or by boat. Because of these finds, Big Bone was better known in Europe at this time than New York City.[22]

Steamboats

In the 1830s and 40s, steamboats began traveling the Ohio River regularly, adding to transportation options that enhanced the county's economy and increasing goods distribution options for manufacturers and farmers.

Early river steamboats resembled small oceangoing vessels with deep hulls and masts

---

[17] Conrad, *The History of Boone County Schools*, 3.
[18] William Fitzgerald, "Walton Established in 1840." *Boone County Recorder*, Jan. 2, 1964.
[19] Yealey, *History of Boone County, Kentucky*.
[20] Barbara Dye, Dec. 9, 1997.
[21] Conrad 200th Anniversary, 20.
[22] "Early Historical Spots in Boone County," *Boone County Recorder*, Aug. 31, 1978, 10.

Chapter 4 1830-1849 Steamboats and Stagecoaches

for sails. Soon boat builders realized that flat-bottomed side-wheelers passed down the shallow rivers more easily.

Although the Ohio River's loop around Boone County is now deep and wide, before the dams were built it was less than half as wide in spots and sometimes only a foot deep in dry seasons.

Some boats drew less than a foot of water, opening localities that had been believed impassable. Sometimes a crew member from a nearly grounded boat waded ahead to find the best channel.

Sandbars still often stranded boats, leaving them to wait for a rain upstream. Newspapers sometimes listed departure times as "on the first rise of water." Between fires and accidents, steamboats generally lasted less than five years.[23]

Flatboats continued to offer cheap downstream travel when time wasn't a factor. Steamboat races became famous. Since it was now possible to travel upstream relatively cheaply and without a huge well-muscled crew, keelboat traffic ended.

As early as 1837, a packet boat ran regularly from Cincinnati to Rising Sun, Ind.

An advertisement in the Feb. 4, 1837, edition of *The Rising Sun Times* said, "*The Steamboat Dolphin will leave Rising Sun every Monday, Wednesday and Friday at sunrise, pass Aurora (Ind.), Petersburg, and Lawrenceburg from 8 o'clock to 1 o'clock, and return from Cincinnati on Tuesdays, Thursdays and Saturdays.*"

Store boats pulled off along the Ohio offering wares to local residents. This unattributed quote is taken from an Aug. 21, 1839, storekeeper's journal: "*Drew out at 3 o'clock – ran down to Mr. (Senior) Piatt's landing on the Ky. shore. Poor landing, water shallow and snaggy - river quite low. Fine brick house on the bank in which Mr. P. lives. M. as usual went to run down customers. Five families within a short distance – a number of blacks. Quite a number called, but none bought anything. Have a little store just above the landing kept by Moor, a boyish looking fellow. Sold only 75 cents worth. Sick this evening.*"

The next day: "*Some sick this morning – exposed myself too much yesterday. Was out all the time we were floating and steered the boat; being windy she was hard to steer, consequently fatigued too much. Some calls this morning but sell little. Pushed off about 8 o'clock, ran down to a little white cottage on the Indiana side...*"[24]

Northern Piatt's

Farmer Abram (Abraham) S. (Sanders or Sedam) Piatt patented a horse-drawn treadmill to operate his ferry to Lawrenceburg north of Petersburg. (Lawrenceburg Ferry Pike ran near where the I-275 bridge crosses the Ohio.)

Abram Piatt also installed a steam-driven boat that was destroyed in an ice floe the next year. So, he replaced it with another horse and treadmill-powered craft. In 1845, Abram sold the ferry to his brother, Jacob Wykoff Piatt.

Jacob Piatt moved to Cincinnati and became an attorney. As a city council member, the Boone County native advocated a paid city fire department. At the time, private volunteer fire departments made money by collecting from property owners. Angry fire fighters mobbed his Cincinnati home and burned Jacob in effigy. But he was safe, his loyal Irish Catholic supporters provided him with security.[25]

A mechanic named Lutta, encouraged by Piatt, invented and constructed a steam fire engine. Under Piatt's leadership, a new fire engine was purchased and a mechanic and crew were hired to operate it. A fight erupted at the first fire to which it was taken. "Volunteers" – seeing their lucrative business

---

[23] Harrison & Klotter, 129.

[24] James F. Shaffer *Piatt's Landing East Bend*, (Cincinnati Gas & Electric Co., Cincinnati, Ohio, 1978).
[25] Reis, *Pieces of the Past 3*, 23.

about to end – attempted to destroy both the new machine and the men running it. The melee ended in 20 minutes. The machine proved its worth, and the volunteers signed on as city employees. Soon other cities were following Cincinnati's example, hiring city employees to operate the more efficient new machines.[26]

After losing his young wife Caroline, then going into public service and bringing improved fire service to Cincinnati, Judge Jacob Wykoff Piatt married Martha Eugenie de Valcourt in 1855. She brought with her to Federal Hall, rare and valuable heirlooms from her prominent Baltimore family. Their nine children were the fourth generation of Piatts to grow up in Boone County.[27]

The large and growing Piatt family owned three of the six ferries that crossed between Indiana and Kentucky.

Macadam Roads

While the ferries were used regularly, inland, stagecoaches were becoming common as roads were improved. The buffalo and animal trails to or from Big Bone Lick were becoming roads and now led to Verona, Burlington and Walton. These paths allowed a horse or man to walk through the dense woods and underbrush, frequently following creeks. If the creek was too deep to wade, the path continued until it came to a ford or a spot shallow enough to cross. Soon county officials asked citizens to find and mark convenient crossroads and connecting roads.

Completing the Georgetown Road or Covington to Lexington turnpike (now U.S. 25 or Dixie Highway) in 1836 meant faster travel by stage or carriage.

Men used plows, picks, shovels and rock hammers to construct roads in the 1830s. A Scotsman named McAdam devised a road-building strategy followed here. Rocks broken into gravel (6 ounces or smaller) were laid on top of a base of larger rocks. The roads' higher-in-the-center, arched design, allowed water to drain off, reducing mud.

Roadways were graded 20' to 50' wide and stone was laid 16' to 20' wide. Broken stone was spread 9-10" deep. To maintain a dry surface to support the thousands of horse-, mule- and oxen-drawn vehicles that passed over it annually, rock was added continuously.

Broken rocks used for paving sank in the soft dirt, requiring years of additional layers to build a solid roadbed.

Gravel roads cost from $5,000 to $8,000 a mile to construct. The state contributed $1 every time a subscriber or stockholder contributed $30 toward a toll road.

Immigrants constructed the road near Florence. When German and Dutch laborers rebelled, complaining of coarse meat in their meals, Irishmen who didn't complain replaced them.

Macadamized roads allowed travel even in muddy weather, decreasing freighting costs. A horse, mule or ox team could pull a much heavier load over gravel than over dirt roads.

Tollgates

More roads were needed. In 1835, state money completed Dixie Highway's 15

Neighborhood Travel and Hauling with Common Tire or Tread

For each wagon or cart, loaded with grain, hay or other products of the farm, when drawn by two horses, mules or oxen, per trip for going and returning	37½ cents
Same, when drawn by three horses, per trip, as above	43¾ cents
Same, when drawn by four horses, per trip, as above	56½ cents
Same, when drawn by five horses, per trip, as above	75 cents
Same, when drawn by six horses, per trip, as above	$1

Broad Tread for Neighborhood Hauling

For each wagon or cart, loaded with grain, hay or other products of the farm, if drawn by four horses, mules or oxen, per trip as above	50 cents
Same, drawn by five horses,	62½ cents
Same, drawn by six horses,	87½ cents

---

[26]Blakely.
[27]Blakely.

southernmost and 10 northernmost miles, leaving 50 miles in-between. Twenty additional miles had been graded, but no stone or gravel was yet laid. The road was completed three years later with tollgates at crossroads to collect money for upkeep.[28]

Tollgate poles extended from the keeper's residence to a solidly set post on the opposite side of the road. An iron pin ran through the post and pole, allowing the weighted pole to rise vertically when the rope holding it was released. It was possible, but seldom heard of, for a keeper to drop the gate too soon, damaging the carriage or buggy top.[29]

While construction techniques likely varied, some used a stone-filled box as a weight to cause the pole to lift when it wasn't tied down. For convenience, it was often tied to the gatekeeper's porch.[30]

Dixie Highway had two gates between Florence and Walton. The Florence-Burlington Pike (KY 18) had two as well.

Tollkeeper's salaries were 10.6 percent of the road's receipts, plus housing. The fare varied according to the vehicle and number of passengers. Privileged travelers, like ministers, mourners, funeral goers and churchgoers were allowed to pass without paying tolls. They were usually identified by the Bibles they carried, the day and time of day.[31]

Avoiding tollgates was illegal – anyone passing "*through any private gate, bars or fence, or over any ground along or near a turnpike, or the gate erected thereon*" could be fined $10. Roads running within a mile of the turnpike to and from the same place were forbidden.

Farmers and others living along the routes could get on and off almost anywhere. Gates were required to be five miles apart and at least a mile from town.

State laws limited private road subscriptions to $7,000 per mile, which was considered the maximum cost. If profits exceeded ten percent annually, tolls were to be reduced to bring profits down to that rate. Tollgate keepers were authorized to require travelers to swear an oath regarding the distance they traveled. Keepers could be fined for failing to keep the road in good repair.[32]

Tandy Ellis told of "Uncle" Pat Lowry keeping a tollgate near Ghent. With Boone County's many tollgates, keepers' experiences here were probably similar. Late one night a

Tollgate Fares for General Traveling

For every horse or mule and rider, when the gates do not exceed five miles apart	6¼ cents
For each horse, jack or mule, led or driven	3 cents
For each head of cattle	2 cents
For each head of hogs	½ cent
For each head of sheep	¼ cent
For every cart, wagon, barouche, dearborn, gig or other vehicle drawn by one horse	12½ cents
Same as last above, when drawn by two horses or oxen	20 cents
For each family carriage or hackney coach, employed in the transportation of persons, drawn by two horses	25 cents
Same, having seats within for four passengers only, when drawn by four horses	31¼ cents
For each sleigh, drawn by one or two horses	12½ cents
For each wagon, drawn by three horses	31¼ cents
For each wagon, drawn by four horses	50 cents
For each wagon, drawn by five horses	62½ cents
For each wagon, drawn by six horses	75 cents
Empty wagons or wagons having no other loading than provender for the team, paid half.	

Broad Tread or Tire

For each wagon with four horses of four-inch tread and over	37½ cents
For each wagon with five horses of four-inch tread and over	50 cents
For each wagon with six horses of four-inch tread and over	62½ cents
For each coach or stage having seats within for six	37½ cents
Same, with seats for nine passengers only	56¼ cents
Same, with seats for 12 and drawn by four horses	75 cents
Upon all the above vehicles, drawn by four horses, two cents in addition for each passenger over four, to be paid by the owner of the coach, but which may be commuted for a definite sum.	

---

[28] Yealey, 9-10.
[29] Campbell, 18.
[30] Roter, 322.
[31] *175th Anniversary Historical Book*, 9.
[32] Tanner, 9.

stranger asked for lodging. Expecting his pay in the morning, Lowry let him sleep. By morning, the guest had disappeared without paying.

Furious, "Uncle Pat" started locking the gate down all the time– until someone sawed off the pole. A few months later, Lowry received a money order with a note saying the visitor had no money the night he stayed with him, but now was in the bootlegging business and had plenty of money.

The state now too had more money and was putting it into roads, reducing the need for private investors and tollgates. By 1837, the Commonwealth had spent $26,000 on 37 miles of ridge road from Covington to Williamstown. The completed 85 miles cost $170,000 – not including contributions by stockholders and subscriptions.

Tollgates helped repay private investors. Dixie Highway became the most traveled road in the state and paid the best dividend (4 percent) of any road in the state.[33]

The panic of 1837 and resulting depression curtailed road development. The General Assembly passed a law effective in 1840 allowing partially finished roads to charge half the allowed tolls.[34]

The seven toll houses between Georgetown and Covington increased to 14 in 1854. Yet their combined profit of $1,500 annually didn't offset public and private investments of at least $250,000. Annual receipts were a little over $1 a mile, while some Bluegrass turnpikes returned $300 a mile.

The turnpike above the bridge at Constance.
Courtesy of Boone County Historic Preservation

Stagecoaches
In 1818, stagecoaches left Cincinnati every Wednesday at 8 a.m. and arrived in Lexington at 6 p.m. the next day. The 34-hour trip was typical. Mail coaches switched horses at Florence and Williamstown, leaving for Lexington about 10 a.m. An 1825 account noted that stagecoaches took two days to travel from Maysville to Louisville. Their route was 140 miles long, through Lexington and Frankfort.

Teams of four or six horses were changed about every 10 miles. Allowing for stops during the day, coaches averaged three to four miles per hour. Despite the horses' fast trot, trips were not speedy for passengers.

By 1833, more than a dozen stages offered twice-a-week departures for the 86-mile trip from Cincinnati to Lexington. The 10-cent-a-mile fee allowed each passenger 14 pounds of baggage. One hundred pounds of baggage was considered equal to one passenger.

Stagecoaches sometimes literally plowed through ungraded ground, which resulted in two or three day delays. Roads were still poor, muddy mires when wet, and a rutted, bouncing trail when dry.

The standard Concord stage carried six

---
[33] Yealey, 11.
[34] Tanner, 4-5.

Chapter 4 1830-1849 Steamboats and Stagecoaches

passengers inside and one who sat outside with the driver. Mail and other baggage was lashed to the top, the back, and crammed inside with passengers.

Coach riders sat on wooden seats attached to springs made of heavy leather. Between jolts, they could peek out a window for a breath of fresh air. Leather hides draped over the windows kept mud and rocks from flying inside.

Along the Lexington Pike (U.S. 25) they saw green meadows, tidy gardens and bluegrass pastures separated by zigzagging split rail fences.[35]

Faster Roads

With the new "metalled" or graveled roads, stagecoaches doubled their average speeds to six to eight miles per hour. That included stops in Delphton, Georgetown, Big Eagle, Williamstown, Dry Ridge, Crittenden, New Lancaster, Florence, Dry Creek, Covington and southern Boone County's Gaines Crossroads.[36]

With the "artificial" road surface, the Lexington to Cincinnati stage journey that had taken two days now took less than one. By the early 1840s, the stagecoach pulled out at 5 a.m. and rolled into Lexington at 9 p.m. Stage service now ran three times a week between Georgetown and Cincinnati. By 1842, the one way fare from Cincinnati to Lexington was $5.

Point Pleasant

In the county's northeastern corner (near the airport exit off I-275), in 1834, Rev. Walter Scott held a two-week long meeting in the old Point Pleasant School. But he only converted two.

Five years later, Scott returned to hold another meeting, finding 61 souls to organize a new Point Pleasant Christian Church. Officers included James Ellis, Park Walton, and William McGlasson. James Cullom, Jedidiah Foster and Simpson Riggs became deacons and John Riggs Sr. was trustee.

The school and homes hosted services until 1841 when Mr. and Mrs. Joseph Brown donated land for a building. "Old Father Masters" preached for $12 a year.[37]

Rabbit Hash Store Opens

The first Rabbit Hash-Rising Sun ferry was a hand-operated flat hulled boat. A boat used in the 1830s was described as "a superior ferry flat – 50' long by 10' wide, well secured by substantial railings on the sides."[38]

George Anderson ran one from Rising Sun to Rabbit Hash between 1817 and 1840. Anderson built a stone house high above his ferry landing in 1830 for good reason. On Feb. 18, 1832, the Ohio River crested at 64' 3", flooding the area. But he remained and expanded his riverfront businesses. In September 1832, the Boone County court gave Anderson permission to operate a tavern.

Taverns or inns were nearly a necessity at river crossings to provide weary travelers with lodging and food, especially in inclement weather or at night when the boat was not operating. A nearby stable or pasture boarded their horses.

Folklore has it that hungry travelers waiting to cross the Ohio by ferry during the 1847 flood wistfully discussed the variety and availability of food on the Kentucky side. Despite their mouth-watering fantasies, the menu had one listing: "plenty of rabbit hash." Floodwaters had driven rabbits up the hills, making them easy to catch.[39] Barges and steamboats couldn't get in due to the flood or because the river froze.

Another story of how Rabbit Hash got its name is that on Christmas Day 1847 villagers gathered on the cold hillside in the snow watching things float down the flooded Ohio. A house with chickens on the roof, logs, stacks of hay, lumber, bridges and corn shocks passed

---

[35] Conrad, *Yesterdays*, 19.
[36] Tanner, CL-3-4.
[37] Morith, Mrs. Lorie, "History of the Old South," Jan. 12, 1960.
[38] Clare, 38.
[39] *175th Anniversary Historical Book*, 63.

down the river.

Discussion turned to Christmas dinners past. One wished for "*roast goose, another for a fat hen, and they continued from hog to hominy. At last, all but one, the village jester, had responded, so they turned to him. . . . He answered in just two words, 'Rabbit Hash.'*"[40]

The story was repeated until the name stuck.

A Madison County, Va., man named James Alexander Wilson had come to Boone County at the age of 10. Wilson moved to Rabbit Hash in 1826, married Jane K. Stephens and had 13 children. He opened the Rabbit Hash General Store in 1831.

Dinsmores Arrive

An adventurer who traveled far and wide, Silas Dinsmoor chose to move his family and spend the end of this life in Boone County. After graduating from Dartmouth College, teaching, studying law, celebrating Christmas 1798 with George Washington at Mount Vernon and serving in the navy in North Africa, Silas returned to the states and became Indian agent for the Cherokee and Choctaw tribes in the south for 20 years.[41]

He and his wife visited Cincinnati in the 1830s and encouraged his nephew to move here. Silas thought he had discovered a wonderful new place to grow grapes and make wine, so in 1839 the James Dinsmore (also spelled Dinsmoor) family bought 700 acres of southwestern Boone County. James built a homestead that was to house five generations of the family on $7 an acre ground in Belleview Bottoms.

A New Hampshire native, James was one of eight children born to John and Susanna Bell Dinsmore. His grandfather had been New Hampshire's governor.

A Dartmouth College graduate like his eccentric uncle, James continued studying law as he moved to Louisiana and Kentucky.

Dinsmore Homestead
Photo by Jason Dunn

Never in robust health, he married Martha Macomb in New Jersey and in 1829 moved to the southern climate of Natchez, La., where he tutored.

The Macombs were a prominent and wealthy family. Martha's father had rented a house to George Washington that became the presidential mansion during the short time New York City was the nation's capital. Martha was one of 19 children of a fur merchant and land speculator.

James Dinsmore later operated his own sugar plantation in Terrebonne Parrish along the Gulf of Mexico, about 50 miles southwest of New Orleans. Tired of the flat land, unstable sugar prices and the Deep South's yellow fever epidemics, he brought his family north.

Their Boone County home was apparently still under construction when Martha wrote to James on Dec. 14, 1841. She suggested he hold on to the southern plantation as security and give the family slaves the option of being sold to other plantations in Louisiana or being brought to Kentucky.

Martha was concerned about how the slaves would cope with Kentucky's cold winters. She also asked her husband to make sure that their slaves' new owners would treat them fairly. Despite his wife's doubts, James

---
[40] Conrad, *The Top of Kentucky*, 34.
[41] Conrad, 200th Anniversary, 35.

Dinsmore sold his Louisiana holdings and moved his family– including daughters Isabella born in 1830, Julia born in 1833, and Susan born in 1835 – to Boone County in 1842. Five slaves, including "Aunt Nancy" came with them.

Sour Vineyard

Silas purchased land nearby, as well as 30 acres on the river, including Lochry Island, which then was called Grape Island. But he was not to see prospering vineyards.

Silas Dinsmoor died in 1847 at 81. Four years later, his niece Susan (James and Martha's daughter) and her cousin Mary Ann Goodrich, a sister of B.F. Goodrich, drowned in Lake Erie. A storm blew up and capsized the girls' boat while they were vacationing at their uncle's home in Ripley, N.Y. Both Silas and the 15-year-old were buried on the farm.

Focusing on wine-making, James planted 1,000 catawba vines, but black rot and leaf rust wiped out most of the grapes. According to the Cincinnati Horticultural Society Report, James Dinsmore owned four of the 1,400 acres of vineyard within 20 miles of Cincinnati.

Not a man with a strong constitution, James soon found career paths other than farming. He became a county road surveyor in 1846 and a justice of the peace in 1848. In 1849, he assisted with an anti-slavery meeting at the Burlington Courthouse. Boone Countians elected 48 representatives to a state conference in Frankfort focused on proposing gradual emancipation for slaves.

Big Bone Resorts

Like the Dinsmores, other Southerners retreated to Kentucky's "northern" climate during the cholera epidemics of 1833 and 1849. In 1849, cholera killed 8,500 around the nation. Tourism boomed at Big Bone Lick's hotels. Since a microorganism that lives in water causes cholera, the saline springs probably were a healthier place than cities with their often polluted water supplies.

Social life at the resorts was as big an attraction as the purported medicinal water qualities. Cock fighting, bowling, poker, horse races and quoits, a game involving pitching flat iron rings at a stake, were also popular.

James Dinsmore
Courtesy of Dinsmore Homestead

Gaines Crossroads

While, the post office wasn't renamed Walton until July 8, 1840, one story says Abner Gaines named it after his benefactor as an act of gratitude. Another story is that it was named after a popular basket-maker named Walton. A third says it's an abbreviated pronunciation of Wall's town, after a well-liked businessman who owned a great deal of property.

Walton, whose charter the General Assembly passed on Jan 21, 1840, was a few miles east of Big Bone. Property owned by E. Brasher, William Pitcher, John Arnold, Reuben Noel, Michael Snyder, William Vanhorn, Margaret Leonard, Silas Bridges, Elizabeth Butts, Nathan Connely, Samuel McLean, Melville Rich and A.W. Gaines defined Walton's boundaries.

Overton P. Hogan, a Grant County politician and hog dealer, operated stage lines between Walton and Williamstown, Covington and Burlington, and Williamstown and Georgetown. All three connected at Walton.

L.N. Norman ran the general store there. By 1847, Walton included 50 inhabitants, one tavern, livery stables, two tobacco factories and carriage manufacturers.

Archibald Reid operated a tavern at the intersection with the newly completed stretch of the Covington to Lexington Turnpike. Col. Abner Legrand Gaines converted his three-story brick house into a tavern and stagecoach stop.[42]

Gen. Lafayette, a Frenchman who fought with the colonists as a Revolutionary War officer, may have stayed overnight at Gaines' Tavern on May 18, 1825. A.M. Yealey said he had an 1820-vintage silver half-dollar that Lafayette used to pay for his dinner there. (Some recall Yealey saying his half dollar was used to pay for Lafayette's dinner at the Southern Hotel in Florence.) Civil War Gen. Kirby Smith is said to have used the inn as his headquarters.

In the early 1840s, the home was known for hosting elaborate balls and lavish festivities. Abner's attractive granddaughters were often the guests of honor. Legends of the house's haunting began after two suitors of the same granddaughter attended a party.

The younger man threatened the older to stay away from the girl or he would pull his wig off. The older retorted he would kill if that happened. It did and he did, stabbing the younger man to death. The resulting blood stains remained visible until the floor planks were removed.

The home remained in the Gaines family until it was sold to Ira Cleek who stored hay and grain in the first floor and supposedly hid a horse inside to protect it from theft by Civil War soldiers.

Gaines' Sons

Abner and Elizabeth's eldest, storekeeper James, was named after his double-uncle (who had married Abner Gaines' sister). James was appointed Gaines Crossroads'* first postmaster in 1815. His brother A.W. succeeded him in 1832. Before that, A.W., sold subscriptions for the *North Kentuckian*, a Covington newspaper, at the Gaines Crossroads store.

From 1838-1842, Augustus W. Gaines held a contract that paid him $5,500 annually to carry mail between Lexington and Cincinnati. He made the 84 mile trip with four-horse post (U.S. mail) coaches. The mail coaches were the most timely of the stages.

> ### Legislative Resolution Honoring JP Gaines
> "*Resolved, that Major John P. Gaines has won the admiration of the people of Kentucky by honorably withdrawing his parole as a prisoner of war, when ordered by Gen. Lombardini to go to Toluca; by his escape through the lines of the enemy; by his successful junction with the American army and by his gallant bearing at Churubusco, Chapultepee, and all the battles fought before the walls and in the city of Mexico – he being the only volunteer from Kentucky who participated in the achievements of Gen. Scott and his army in those memorable victories.*"[1]

Gaines Goes to Oregon

Another son of Abner and Elizabeth, Major John Pollard (or Pendleton) Gaines, first represented Boone County in the legislature the year he turned 30 in 1825-27, and again in 1830 and 1832.

In May 1846, Gaines volunteered to lead the first Kentucky cavalry regiment in the Mexican War. In a military encounter that gained national recognition, his regiment was outflanked. Three thousand Mexicans took Major Gaines, Cassius Clay, George Davidson and 30 companions prisoner.

The Major escaped through enemy lines and rejoined the American army. After his long imprisonment, he located his favorite horse, named Black Sultan and rode him home to Kentucky.[43] On his return, he discovered he'd been elected to Congress.

In Washington, Gaines met Millard Fillmore who became president when Kentuckian Zachary Taylor died. President Fillmore asked Dr. B.F. Bedinger to become Oregon's first governor, but he declined the position and recommended Major Gaines.

---

[42] Jim Reis "Walton's Birthday," *The Kentucky Post,* Jan. 22, 1990.
* also spelled Gaines X Roads or Gaines Cross Roads.

[43] "The Haunted House – Walton, Ky.," *The Waltonian,* Sept. 19, 1984.

Bedinger threw a going away party for Gaines in December 1849. An invitation announcing *"the latch string is out"* brought hundreds to the last meal with the Major, despite snowy, cold inhospitable weather. Great heaps of logs were burning in the yard and barnyard, providing heat for guests to gather round. A huge dining room table was crowded with guests who retired upstairs for dessert – pies, cakes and jellies. As soon as one seating moved on, the table was cleared and reset for another to feast on turkeys, chickens, ducks, hams, fresh beef and pork.[44]

With no suspicions of the tragedies soon to befall him, Gaines sold his Boone County farm and personal property, taking a huge amount of silver to New York City, where his family boarded the store ship Supply. Both his daughters died from yellow fever near the coast of St. Catherines. Soon after the girls were buried on the island, his son died of consumption.

A short time after arriving in Oregon, Gaines' wife was thrown from her horse and killed. Gaines remained territorial governor until a conflict arose with the legislature over the location of the state capitol in 1853. He remarried, then died in Oregon in 1857.

Richwood Presbyterian

Just north of Walton, Rev. Joseph Cabell Harrison, a first cousin of President William Henry Harrison, founded Richwood Presbyterian Church in early May 1834. Joseph and his cousin, John Breckinridge, edited the first religious paper in Kentucky.[45]

Until Rev. Samuel Lynn began constructing a building in 1842, the original 13 members met in a school. The community that grew up around it, borrowed the Richwood name from the church.

> ### *The Western Christian Advocate*
> Sept. 19, 1834
> *I have the lamentable news that there are many stout hearted sinners that are too stubborn to submit to calls of mercy. Unpleasant as it is to me, I have had to leave them in their sins. Happy to have 240 souls to come into the gospel feast; 60 at Burlington where three years ago just one member (added), making 71 members, and are building a brick meeting house 34' x 44'. Unto him that hath loved and redeemed us be all the glory.*
> J.C. Crow, a Methodist preacher[49]

Florence Gets a Start

A day's 10-mile walk or a short horseback ride from Cincinnati, Florence was a useful stop for travelers coming from Lexington, Louisville or Maysville. By now, Florence nearly matched Verona in size with 63 residents. Both were considerably smaller than Burlington's 350 and Petersburg's 500 residents.

Legend has it that Florence was originally settled by Hessian soldiers who escaped down the Ohio and walked inland.

Benjamin Reiss, an old man who lived nearby, christened it Polecat because a den of 'cats (polecat was another name for skunk) gave it a distinctive smell.[46] Later, when Indians brought their furs to exchange, it was dubbed PowWow.

Since Union and Burlington roads intersected there with Ridge Road (now Dixie Highway), the community was called Crossroads. In 1821, anticipating growth generated by the new roads, young Covington lawyer Thomas Madden bought four acres on Georgetown Road (U.S. 25) from Leonard Crisler for $100. Madden planned to open a tavern. He also purchased a farm at the junction of Price Pike and Burlington Pike from Joshua Zimmerman.

A group of Methodists, the Wilhelm Wilhoit (Wilheut), Henry Crisler (Heinrich Kreusler) and Jacob Conner (Kohner) families were already living there and helped Madden lay out a village, calling it Maddentown. A year later Madden sold his land and moved to

---

[44] Paper written by Oliva Morgan Bedinger, July 5, 1922.
[45] *175th Anniversary Historical Book*, 13.

[46] Lentz, 108.

Illinois.

Since Madden was gone, the name was changed to Connersville, recognizing Jacob Conner, who was now the largest landholder. An 1829 post office application discovered a Connersville, Ky., already existed, so the community held an election for a new name.

Of the 25 votes cast, 16 were for the name Florence, possibly in honor of Jacob Conner's wife Florence. The town was incorporated in 1830 with a population of 63. Postmaster Pitman Clondas started daily mail service in Florence on April 27, 1830.

Mail came by stage. Florence was the first stop out of Covington where stagecoach horses were changed. Passengers often returned to the city by carriage for dinner or amusements, then came back to Florence to sleep so they'd be ready for the second leg of their journey. That built not only Florence's hotel business, but also the stagecoach, blacksmith, harness maker and carriage trades.

Growing Cincinnati markets prompted drovers to move hogs, cattle, sheep and turkeys down the new roads. Florence taverns and hotels provided fenced yards and pens where livestock rested and ate. (Steve Conrad remembers asking about the tall grass behind the hotel on Girard Street and Main in Florence when he was a child in the 1950s, and being told stock pens had been there.)

The largest pork-packing city in the world, Cincinnati earned the nickname Porkopolis. As hog demand grew, pedestrians were often forced off the road until the pigs passed. These passersby sometimes accumulated so much dust that they were mistaken for drovers.[47]

Little White Church by the Side of the Road preceded Florence Christian Church. (This photo was taken in 1925.) Photo courtesy of Florence Christian Church

Regular coach service and increasing traffic helped Florence grow to a population of 200. And more religious options were becoming available.

Little White Church

In 1831, the first Disciples of Christ Church was built of logs at the junction of today's Routes 25 and 42. The faithful sat on hand-hewn plank benches without backs for three-to-four-hour long sermons. Two disgruntled female members reportedly burned that church.

What became known as the Little White Church by the Side of the Road was built on the same site in 1835. Negro members of the new brick church were required to use the rear door. Musical instruments were not permitted. (It was torn down in 1964 to build a new Florence Christian Church, affiliated with the Disciples of Christ.)

Florence Baptist Founded

In 1840, militant Baptist abolitionists in the north organized a Baptist Anti-slavery Convention. To counter them, 293 delegates representing many diverse Baptist bodies organized the Southern Baptist Convention, saying, *"We will never interfere with what is Caesar's (slavery). We will not compromise what is God's."*[48]

A letter of dismissal from the Dry Creek Baptist Church in April 1845, allowed Benjamin Dulaney, Leonard Stephens, D.M. Scott, Henry F. Snyder, Sally Snyder, Paly Scott and Louisiana Finch to form the Florence Baptist Church. Melton and Harriet Wilhoit

---

[47] Conrad, *Yesterdays*, 18.

[48] Elizabeth McMullen Kirtley, *Burlington Baptist Church 150th Anniversary*, (s.p., 1992), 11.

sold a land tract 131' on the east side of the Covington and Lexington Pike for the church building in 1855.

Methodists Build Churches

Boone County Legislator Louis Riddle had arranged for Methodist preachers to visit the region in 1820. Repeated visits by J.C. Crow built a Methodist congregation in the Burlington circuit, which encompassed more than Boone County. By 1834, Crow claimed he had saved 240 souls from sin. Hanry N. Vandyke joined him in 1834. By 1837, he added 241.[49]

After meeting in homes and tents, Florence Methodists built a log church in 1832 (some say 1842). Trustees purchased land on Banklick Street for $80 from Samuel Craig. The Craigs owned the sawmill at Banklick and Main Street, so most lumber came from the mill. Seats were split logs. Parishioners sat on dirt floors strewn with straw – which was often infested with fleas, increasing squirming in faithful patrons.

Members left occasionally without snuffing out the candles placed between logs for light. Since the logs were green, the candles burned out without damage.

Other New Churches

Other churches appeared around the county. Chasten and Martha Scott gave a tract of their Union land to Samuel P. Cummins in 1844 to be used by the Methodist Church.[50]

Thomas Arnold was the first minister for Petersburg Christian Church in 1836. The first "Christian Meeting House" was built in 1840. *"The congregation took the inscription literally and records show that meetings were conducted there by ministers of the Baptist, Methodist, Universalist and Christian Scientist faiths,"* as well as women's societies, concerts, and other public events.[51]

For $1,150, Elias Coffman laid bricks for the Mount Pleasant Church of Predestinarian Baptist in less than a year. Completed Sept. 30, 1841, the church was on the Bullittsville-Burlington Road (now KY 20) about a quarter-mile from Bullittsville. (The visiting preacher quit in 1925 and the church no longer exists.)

Kirtley Family

Robert Kirtley became Middle Creek Baptist Church's third pastor in 1825 and served for nearly 40 years. Rev. Kirtley received the first recorded compensation issued by the Baptist church to a pastor when James Ryle paid him $9.12 for preaching at Middle Creek Baptist Church in October 1827.[52]

Robert Edward Kirtley, the fourth child of Robert and Polly Kirtley, was born Feb. 7, 1820. He attended a country academy, then spent a year at Hanover College in Indiana.

When his brother Jeremiah died in Illinois, leaving his widow Mary Lacy Kirtley with four children, Robert Edward married her and moved the family to St. Mary's, Ill. They then moved to Missouri where the Union Baptist Church ordained him in 1863.

After serving in the Confederate Army, Robert Edward returned to Kentucky in 1867 and preached at the Middle Creek, East Bend and Sand Run churches. He served as Sand Run pastor for 25 years, dying in 1898.

Brother Robert also preached at Big Bone Baptist when it was organized on May 25, 1843, until 1874. Deacons were Thomas Huey and John C. Riley.[53] Land purchased in 1843 cost $7 an acre. Two acres were donated.

Treasurer Thomas Huey recorded the first offering of $13.52½. Expenses came to $12.16½. In 1844, Henry Stanisfer of Florence was hired to build a brick meeting house at a cost not to exceed $1,200. He

---

[49] Ivalou H. Walton, *Historical Study Burlington Methodist Church*, May 1975, 6-7.
[50] Walton, 11.
[51] *175th Anniversary Historical Book*, 11.
[52] *Belleview Baptist Church, 190th Anniversary*, (s.p., 1993), 1-2.
[53] Morith

completed it two years later for $1,240. Stoves and fixtures cost $25.20. Churchwomen raised $32.36 for lamps, books, chairs and a table.[54]

Mentions of slavery creep into church records. *"It was reported that Samuel Huey has a boy George, who was unbecoming in conduct. He was sold and reported out of reach of the church and considered a member no more."*[55]

A charge was placed against Sister Sealey, another slave owned by Huey, who attempted to poison the family. She was found guilty and excluded from the church.

In 1842, the Kirtley family organized 16 people (including five African Americans) to form another church in Burlington, which first met at the home of Squire Scott, then in the courthouse. On a lot bought for $100, Mills Wilks laid bricks for a building costing $1,939.84. Twenty members dedicated it in May 1844.

The elder Kirtley led the congregation until 1845 when another son, Rev. James A. Kirtley succeeded him and preached for 27 years.

Touseys Arrive

While Erastus Tousey had paid only $25 for his lot on the west side of Burlington's Jefferson Street in 1817, he had built an impressive two-story red brick home there in 1822. Tousey married Catherine Piatt of the extensive Piatt family. She lived in the Burlington house until 1884, raising six daughters and a son.

The home featured carved pine fireplaces in every room, built-in floor-to-ceiling cabinets, cherry stair railings, and a stone-walled cellar with a kitchen and what may have been slave quarters.

The well-to-do family was served by four slaves – Lydia, Martha, Jefferson and Tommy – whom Erastus allowed his wife the option to free upon his death in 1863. Two of the slaves evidently chose not to be freed. Tousey left his wife an extensive estate including property in Kansas and Iowa.[56]

Catherine sold the property on March 12, 1884, to Rosie and H.P. Stephens for $2,050. Catherine lived another 11 years, likely with one of her children. The house was to change hands repeatedly – becoming a boys' dormitory, livery stable and tavern. Ownership stabilized in 1917 when it became the Gulley and Pettit general store, then remained in the Pettit family for 60 years.[57]

Burlington Grows

Mail ran on horseback to Lawrenceburg, Ind., through Burlington at 9 a.m. three times a week.

In 1836, Burlington's town trustees ordered the Touseys and other residents to install paved sidewalks.

By the 1840s, the county seat had 200 residents, four churches, schools, stores, taverns, seven lawyers, five doctors, and a wool factory.

By 1847, the trustees levied a poll tax.

New churches joined the new schools popping up along country and town roads. If only one building was available, it served both purposes, depending on the day of the week.

Five of the 16 who met at Squire Scott's home to begin a Burlington Baptist Church were "colored." In 1842, they paid $100 for a city lot and for $901 the brick church was built. Four ministers agreed each to preach one Sunday a month.

In 1846, charter member Perryander C. Scott was called as pastor. He graduated at the top of his class from Georgetown College and was ordained in 1847. On April 3, 1852, he was killed instantly in the explosion of the steamer Redstone near Carrollton.[58]

---

[54] *A Brief History of Big Bone Baptist Church 1843-1968*, (s.p., n.d.), 4-5.
[55] *Big Bone Baptist*, 6.

[56] Katie Presnell
[57] Katie Presnell
[58] Campbell, 43.

Chapter 4 1830-1849 Steamboats and Stagecoaches

Burlington's Tousey House was built in 1822.
Photo by Jason Dunn

Horseback Travels

Searching for Albert Stephens, the son of John Stephens, Thomas Rouse rode through Indiana, Illinois, Iowa and Missouri. He crossed the Mississippi in a skiff ferry with his horse swimming behind.

He spent the night about 10 miles inland at a settler's home. The next morning his horse was gone. He followed its hoofprints to the river then lost track of it. He procured another and continued his journey. Several months later, the horse showed up at its old Kentucky home.

Rouse's horseback travels continued when he was a delegate to the 1844 Presidential Convention in Baltimore.

Three years later, still searching for a better place to live, Rouse reached old Fort Dearborn (now Michigan). Looking for a place to spend the night, he followed directions six miles further to the banks of Lake Michigan. Soaked by the pouring rain, he rode through the swampy prairie. He then followed a walk of single-planks laid end to end to reach a wayside tavern. He put his horse in the shed and took a blanket to sleep on the floor. Today that desolate and inhospitable swamp is called Chicago.

While he could have bought Windy City property for $1 an acre, Rouse said he wouldn't give his Boone County farm for the whole Illinois prairie with the lake thrown in.

Returning to Kentucky, Rouse came across a band of 50 wagons filled with men, women and children on their way to Salt Lake City, Utah. The Mormons had been ordered to leave Nauvoo, Ill. Invited to join them, he declined and headed home.[59]

During the winter, Rouse indulged his penchant for travel by running flatboats from Cincinnati to Vicksburg or New Orleans. Like others of his time, he bought a boat in Cincinnati and loaded it with staples like flour, prepared tobacco, hams, bacon slabs (entire halves of hogs) and whiskey.

Rouse's whiskey could have come from distilleries at Petersburg, Hamilton's Landing or Aurora. He bought tobacco packed in casks at the landing near the mouth of Big Bone Creek.

Rouse made no effort to sell his products until he reached the Mississippi, then he hawked them at every landing. News of his arrival would precede him, drawing planters to make their purchases. When his supplies were gone, he sold the boat and returned by steamboat or bought a horse and rode back, carrying his money. Thieves were never a threat.[60]

On Jan. 20, 1849, Rouse arrived home to read an announcement of his death from cholera in that day's *Burlington Advertiser*. He had indeed contracted the dread disease in Vicksburg and been left to die. However he lived to a ripe old age, until April 9, 1906.

---

[59]Lloyd, 25.
[60]Lloyd, 29.

Chapter 5
1850-1861 The River Rules

Boone Countians were settling in. The county's 1850 population of 11,185 would remain in that range for 100 years. Twenty percent of the 1850 population had African roots.

Between isolated farmsteads the communities we know today were growing. New post offices delineated settlements around the county. Burlington and Florence each had about 250 residents. Walton and Union each had a population of 50.

With larger settlements came more politics and crime, but also diverse entertainment, medical assistance and labor-saving inventions. The Florence Fair began. More locals began traveling for pleasure. Some had already begun campaigning for temperance.

The first Catholic Church brought variety in the previously all Protestant religious options.

Property owners continued contributing labor to improve roads. Stagecoaches ran regularly. State mandates expanded school terms to five months, rather than three.

The ever-increasing steamboat traffic kept Petersburg supplied with visitors, news, entertainment and products. Still the county's largest city, it had roughly 400 residents, but 100 fewer than two decades before.

Petersburg's innkeeping diarist, L.A. Loder, documented many elements of what we now see as "modern life" emerging then, including details like insurance. In 1861, *"Henry Faris from Lawrenceburg was over and insured J.C. Jenkin's new home on the hill. J.C. took a policy on the house of $6,000 at ¾ percent on the hundred dollars."*[1] Appraisers evaluated property.

Three men's clubs soon appeared – the Masons, Odd Fellows and Sons of Temperance. Eventually Petersburg hosted chapters of the Knights of Pythiasis, Modern Woodsmen and Royal Neighbors.[2]

The county had built a "poor house" on 20 acres deeded by John Cave and others on Sept. 14, 1847. In 1849 and 1854, Court Order Books noted that James Perkins, "overseer of the poor," was paid $16. In October 1858, Dr. B.W. Chamblin was paid $60 a year to be the *"physician for the paupers in the Poor House and Jail."*[3]

Weather's Role

Across the Ohio Valley, weather and the river's rise and fall significantly controlled citizens' lives and activities. In journals he kept for 47 years, Loder documented the weather daily.

Crops were planted and harvested according to the weather. Hogs were butchered when freezing temperatures aided in meat preservation. Ice was cut after ponds, creeks and rivers froze a foot thick. The river's height and the amount of ice in it controlled travel for business and pleasure and products' arrival and departure.

Between 1818 and 1870, records show highs of 102 degrees on Sept. 3, 1854, and Aug. 14, 1870. On Jan. 19, 1857, the temperature fell to 24½ degrees below zero.

The most dramatic weather anomaly Loder

---

[1] William Conrad, editor, *The Loder Diary, Part 1, The Ante-bellum Years, Jan. 1, 1857-April 21, 1861*, Boone County Schools, Florence, Ky., 1985, 63.
[2] Mary Rector
[3] Elizabeth Kirtley and Beverly Roland, "History of Maplewood," 1998.

Chapter 5 1850-1861 The River Rules

recorded in the mid 19th century occurred on May 21, 1860, when a tornado cut a path 40 miles wide and 245 miles long from Louisville to Portsmouth, Ohio.

Loder wrote: *"The Forest Queen was rounding out from the warfboat when it commenced blowing. The wind blew her back to the shore at the road at Tanner Street and kept her there until it ceased blowing.* Several days later he wrote: *A lot of coal men here who reported they were in the river in the storm. . . and all their boats sunk and several drowned."*

Felix Moses

Highly regarded peddler Felix Moses was a French-speaking Jew whose parents were murdered in Europe before he arrived in the United States as a refugee. Born in 1827, he pledged allegiance to the United States at the Burlington court in April 1858. He began his career carrying his wares on his back. Later he made his rounds on horseback, but speed wasn't his interest. The only Jew in Boone County at the time, but befriended by Baptist minister James Kirtley, he boarded at a Florence hotel.

Eventually the itinerant peddler drove a spring wagon loaded with goods he sold or traded for produce or furs, earning the nickname "the beloved Jew."[4]

Peddlers and hucksters opened their stores of needles, pins, thread, buttons, muslin, table linen, silk dress patterns and even spectacles at each home, allowing the homemaker to reduce the weight of the pack on his back. When roads became passable on horseback and wagon, they carried more, often swapping for country produce like butter, eggs, and rags that he sold in the city on his return.

"He made regular trips, usually punctual to the hour as well as the day. Such was Felix Moses, the Jew. Always pleasant, he was a welcome visitor to the children in the country. He always had a kindly word and many times a little gift for each one," said Emma Rouse Lloyd who grew up in southern Boone County.[5]

(In 1930, John Uri Lloyd paid a Cincinnati publisher to print his book called *Felix Moses*, about the peddler. The book is on reserve at

The only known photograph of peddler Felix Moses, astride a mule in Florence's Stringtown. Photo courtesy of the Lloyd Library, Cincinnati

Boone County and regional libraries.)

Other itinerant workers soon followed the regular peddler. City clock repairers often walked through the country repairing farmhouse clocks and watches. Menders of tinware and umbrellas also tramped around the country, saving farmers a trip to the city.

Self Sufficiency

Peddlers offered unusual, specialty goods that settlers couldn't easily make for themselves. Out of necessity, individual farmsteads had become completely self-sufficient. Women and girls put up enough food to last the winter.

---

[4] Conrad, *Yesterdays*, 26.

[5] Lloyd, 102.

In the fall, home pantries looked like grocery stores. Apples and peaches, peeled, quartered and dried in the sun, were added to pies and stewed in the winter. Green corn was cut from the cob and dried in the sun. Dried fruits and vegetables were soaked overnight before cooking. White and brown beans were dried in the hulls then threshed on the barn floor and stored in barrels. Walnut chests held brown loaf sugar and spices.

Apples, potatoes, turnips and cabbages were stored underground for winter. Gardens were converted to large cold storage mounds. Foundation boards were laid on the ground and covered with straw. A layer of apples or vegetables was added, then covered with more straw, and topped with boards. When the final earth covering was added, the mound was 8' to 10' tall. A small door at the base of the mound was just large enough for someone to creep through.

Another food preservation technique was used to make hominy. Corn, placed in a hollowed out section of a tree, was pounded with a maul – a round block of hickory with a handle inserted in the center – to make hominy. The corn was soaked overnight in clear water to soften it, then it was cooked.

Soaking selected white corn overnight in lye made lye hominy. In the morning, the skin or husk of the kernels had softened, the edges loosened, curled up and could be washed away. After soaking in clear water for another day, the corn was rinsed many times to remove the lye taste, then it was ready for the table.

Emma Rouse Lloyd told childhood memories of another major household task. A new back log was added to the fire twice a week in the winter:

"A big green hickory log was brought from the wood pile to the porch, either on a sled drawn by a horse or rolled there by several Negro men who then carried and placed it in the big fireplace in the living room. The fire built in front of it was kept going for another three or four days.

"Putting on a new back log was always a nerve-racking experience, the fire allowed to die out, the doors all open, the house cold, Mrs. Henderson standing on the porch, hands on hips, giving orders, the grandchildren huddled in a corner and everybody else keeping out of sight.[6]

"The cooking was done in two kitchens. Peggy, the head cook in the brick kitchen, prepare the meals for the "big house." For this purpose there was a great fireplace where logs of wood were burned. A crane fastened on the inside of the chimney about four feet from the hearth, swung out to receive kettles of water, soup or any liquid to be boiled when swung back over the fire.

A Lloyd family portrait begins with grandmother Sophia Webster Lloyd, John Uri Lloyd, his children John Thomas and Dorothy Lloyd and wife Emma Rouse Lloyd
Photo courtesy of the Lloyd Library, Cincinnati

---
[6] Lloyd, 104-105.

Chapter 5 1850-1861 The River Rules

"The oven, a large, flat-bottomed kettle about 10" deep, stood on three legs. It had a tight-fitting cover with an upturned rim. When baking was to be done in this oven, coals of fire were placed under it, hot ashes being piled on the lid. Frying was done over the coals in long-handled skillets and frying pans. Cooking for the slaves was done in the same way by Letty in one of the cabins."

Petersburg deed books only record property transfers after 1820, so the date this home was built is uncertain. John Schram used it as an inn for many years. This sketch by Caroline Williams ran in the 1957 Cincinnati Enquirer. Courtesy of Christine Godsey

Constance and Hebron

Up in the far northeastern tip of the county, Postmaster William Turner opened the Constance Post Office in December 1853. The community was named after Konstanz, Germany, a town on the Rhine River adjoining the Switzerland border that had been settled in 780 A.D. Many inhabitants of Kentucky's Constance came from those provinces in the early 1800s.

Southwest of Constance, the community locally called Briar Patch or Briar Thicket requested a post office. They took their new name from the Hebron Lutheran Church. Established in 1854, the church was named to recognize a Madison County, Va., church that donated to its construction. Francis Lafayette Gordon, a local merchant, opened the Hebron Post Office in 1858.

Petersburg

Straight west of Hebron was the bustling community of Petersburg. With steamboats stopping daily, it had grown into a typical river town of the time. Animals escaped their confines and whoever discovered the problem returned them. Babies were born every week while children and the elderly died just as frequently. Unidentified bodies discovered in the river were brought ashore and buried in the local cemetery.

A new mowing machine helped Petersburg farmer Joseph Jenkins cut clover on June 13, 1858, rather than using the tedious hand scythe. Several curious neighbors came by to watch the machine work.[7] Another river bottom farmer, J.H. Walton, bought a thrashing machine.

The thrasher separated grain from the chaff and straw in the field. No longer was Walton

---

[7] Conrad, 6.

required to cut the stalks by hand, tie them in bundles and build sheaves, let it dry, then load it all on wagons, unload it in the barn, and run it through a grain mill.

But the modern horse-drawn thrashing machine with its moving knives and whirling gears brought unaccustomed dangers. Some of its many moving and cutting parts took a piece of Dr. Ed Grant's foot.

No Lincoln Votes

Petersburg residents took an active interest in state and national political issues. Politicians lectured and campaigned from whatever stage was available, sometimes attracting thousands. A lieutenant governor candidate "*spoke for two hours and half and not half* (of what) *he said was true,*" Loder recorded on July 5, 1859. Three weeks later, Democrats rallied in Lawrenceburg.

On Nov. 6, 1860, the Democratic party was split between John C. Breckinridge and Stephen A Douglas (who had stopped during a train trip to speak for 10 minutes in Lawrenceburg). John Bell was on the Whig ticket.

A new party, the Republicans, backed an Illinois man named Abraham Lincoln. Of the 224 votes called aloud in Petersburg – as was the custom of the day – not one was for Lincoln. Nonetheless, on Feb. 12 (his birthday) Lincoln made a public appearance across the river in Lawrenceburg on his way to the White House.[8]

Racial turmoil was underway. Word traveled down the river from Virginia to Petersburg about abolitionist and insurrectionist John Brown being hung at Charleston and the Negro executions that followed.

Temperance

More so than slavery, the divisive issue in Boone County was temperance, particularly among the Methodists and Lutherans, who were a minority in the largely Baptist county, but the majority in Petersburg.

On Dec. 5, 1859, Mrs. E.A. Monroe spoke on avoiding alcohol at Petersburg's Methodist Church. (In 1850, Allen Stott "burned" bricks for the church. Alfred E. Chambers Sr. had

John S. Taylor and his horse Prince.   Photo courtesy of Linda Green

preached the first sermon. The Bullittsburg Baptist Church rented the Methodist Church, holding Baptist services on dates that didn't conflict with Methodist activities.)

Objecting to Hopeful Lutheran Church Minister Rev. Harbough's views favoring temperance, on April 8, 1854, a dozen brethren met at Tanner School to discuss organizing another church.

The discontented Lutherans decided to collect funds and erect a church on a corner of Enos Tanner's land. The Ebenezer Lutheran

---

[8] Conrad, Loder 1, 9.

Church began Jan. 22, 1856, with 11 members.[9]

Commerce

With better roads and a variety of ferry services, Boone Countians crossed the river to buy the newest products Cincinnati had to offer. In February of 1861, J.N. Green opened a Petersburg grocery in the same downtown room where John Loder already sold beef.

Itinerant sellers of nearly anything one could imagine stopped by Petersburg. Many products arrived nearly or literally at residents' doorsteps.

- A Cincinnati boat brought candy.
- A man named Singleton spent six days selling patent rights to make soap.
- Samuel Martin returned to Petersburg with a patented piston churn.
- Glass arrived by boat.
- A man sold book subscriptions.
- Many offered patent medicines.
- One sold bells.
- A man and a boy sold dulcimers.
- An Indianapolis couple named Norrith came by selling embroidery.
- A man from New Albany, Ind., delivered fruit trees.[10]

Currency minted by the U.S. government paid for those goods. The jumble of odd coins, gold, silver, and paper produced in various European countries or by local entrepreneurs was finally gone.

Prices had also stabilized somewhat for hard goods. In May 1855, a double-barreled shotgun cost $20. Three plates cost $1, lamp wicks were $.30, and 1½ gallons of coal oil cost $1.50.[11]

J.C. Jenkins invested in a fine gold watch and chain for $275.[12] A bolt of cloth was worth $45. Loder bought a coal oil lamp in Aurora for $1.25 in 1859.[13]

A new roof for the Sand Run Baptist Church cost $75.50.[14] John Loder bought lumber in Aurora to build a slaughterhouse. A

A showboat on the Ohio.   Photo contributed by Virginia Bennett

man from Cincinnati brought his wagon through to buy blackberries in Petersburg. In 1860, Boone County produced 34,405 bushels of Irish potatoes (2,064,500 pounds).

Taverns filled their patrons with a variety of brews to accompany those potatoes. Wine was only for connoisseurs at 37½ cents a half pint. Half pints of peach brandy, French brandy and other spirits sold for 12½ cents. Tavern goers could sleep for the same amount. Meals were a quarter. A gallon of corn or oats or a half-day of pasture for the drinker's horse cost 12½ cents in 1852.[15]

Livestock was big business in Boone County. Farmers drove their stock to the sale

---

[9] Mrs. Lorie Morith, paper titled History of the Old South, n.p. Jan. 12, 1960.
[10] Conrad, Loder 1, various dates.

[11] A Brief History of Big Bone Baptist Church, 9.
[12] Conrad, Loder 1, 23.
[13] Conrad, Loder 1, 31.
[14] Vivian Blaker.
[15] Conrad, *The Top of Kentucky*, 15.

An unidentified woman with a surrey with a fringe on top and a Guernsey cow.
Courtesy of Virginia Lainhart

pens in the cool of early mornings. Animals stayed in pens on the river's shore until the boats that carried freight upriver from Louisville to Cincinnati, arrived.[16]

William Snyder had moved with his family from Albermarle County, Va., to Petersburg in 1833 when he was three. He married Permulia (handwritten source) Chambers, the daughter of Alfred and Amanda Chambers. Later, he married Susan Frances Whitaker, whose parents were William and Judith Lacy Whitaker.

Snyder helped his father in the distillery, then was appointed to the Revenue Service by President Cleveland until his health forced him to resign.[17] He returned to run Petersburg's distillery and mill as well as a large farm.

Snyder paid an impressive $450 for an imported bull. He sold a large steer for $200 to a butcher. Loder paid 5 cents a pound for 42-pound feeder pigs. William Jenkins, a Petersburg livestock broker, and Snyder shipped 500 hogs to Buffalo, N.Y., on April 30, 1861, and another 500 three days later.[18]

Horse Traders

Horses of all colors, breeds and qualities were bought, sold, traded and raced. Evidently, the animals brought whatever the market would bear. L.P. Scott showed off his new two-horse spring wagon with yellow running gears in Petersburg. He'd paid $125 for it in Cincinnati.

Loder paid $65 for an open-topped buggy at Aurora and $45 for a bay filly. He recorded one horse selling for $135 and another going for $250 in the same year. Jack Carson sold Col. Appleton's horse in Cincinnati for $70. William Lyon sold a bay horse to Edwin Gaines for $16.

A horse bought in Cincinnati for Mr. Snyder cost $152. James Alexander bought a brown horse for $175 from William Wingait – their agreement was payment in patent rights on washing machines.

A mule-buyer spent $190 on a kicking mule, then bought two for $300 from S. McWhethy, and another for $190 from J.N. Early.[19]

Entertainment

While some may have considered a kicking mule good entertainment, Loder tells of many amusements regularly arriving in Petersburg.

The Showboat Banjo played steam music and brought performing dogs, monkeys and goats on Oct. 29, 1857. A week later was a presentation of sleight of hand and magic tricks. A man swallowed a 20" sword, sang and performed other tricks. An Indian show filled the schoolhouse on the 20th and Kawshawgance, an

---

[16] "Belleview As Remembered," *Boone County Recorder,* Sept. 21, 1978.
[17] Mary Rector
[18] Conrad, Loder 1, dates as indicated.

[19] Conrad, Loder 1, various dates

A U.S. Mail Packet Courier unloading.   Photo courtesy of Virginia Bennett

Indian chief, lectured in the Christian church the next day.

On April 20, 1858, a cloudy and rainy day, the John Robinson animal and circus show entertained in Burlington – with steam music. Their performance didn't have a chance to bring the house down – their tent fell on top of them just as the show began.

On Aug. 28, "*Dan Rice's Great Circus Show*" arrived in Lawrenceburg. Organ players came to Petersburg another day. The Spalding & Rogers European Circus performance on June 7, 1859, lasted from 7 p.m. until well after midnight. Toward the end of the year, a man "*played some very good tunes*" on a "*harp of a thousand strings.*"

On Jan. 31, 1857, Loder reported a number of men from Aurora and Lawrenceburg brought 19 chickens to Petersburg to fight. Two of the Aurora chickens were killed.[20]

Prize fighting was popular sport: "*The news come to Petersburg today of the great prize fight between Heenan and Sayers. The news is that Heenan got the best of the fight and the English rushed into the ring and carried Sayers off the ground. They fought two hours and eight minutes and for 40 rounds. Heenan got all the rounds but one. Sayers drawed the first blood and Heenan the first round.*"[21]

While unloading corn barges, the steamer J.P. Tweed presented Mr. Snyder with a live bear. Several months later, the bear injured the arm of "*the small Johnson boy.*" A month later, "*Mr. Snyder's bear got loose and bit his Negro girl and run half over the town. But he jumped over into Mrs. Snelling's yard and Perry McNeely caught him and tied a long cable to the piece of a chain that was to him and took him back to his box.*"[22]

That Christmas Eve, Snyder killed the bear "*because he was so mean he could not be trusted.*"[23]

Entertainment was often free. A very large flatboat passed Petersburg on Oct. 12, 1859. The band it transported played tunes as it

---

[20] Conrad, Loder 1, various dates

[21] Conrad, *Loder 1*, 53.
[22] Conrad, *Loder I,* 10.
[23] Mary Rector

passed the town. A steamboat, the Gray Eagle, played its calliope as it passed on July 6, 1860.

Crime

Despite technology's emergence, some age-old practices prevailed. Men still fought in Petersburg streets or in taverns. More unusual crimes occasionally occurred. A Petersburg woman poisoned herself. A Cincinnati man, Patrick McHugh, was hung for cutting his wife's throat.

Infrequently, money and possessions were stolen, but the culprits were usually apprehended quickly and taken to the Burlington jail. Edward Fowler was appointed superintendent and keeper of the poor from 1856 to 1859. He was deputy sheriff under W.H. Baker from 1861 to 1865.

Charles, the eldest son of Benjamin Piatt Fowler, one of the county's first settlers, married his stepsister, Susan Scott Brown. They were not related by blood, but met during their parents' second marriages.

In 1866, Fowler was elected assessor. He served 12 years before spending a year as constable.[24]

On Sunday, Sept. 15, 1860, two men attacked Jackson Rice about 9 p.m. on a Petersburg street between John Chapin's and J.C. Jenkin's homes. *"But they were unsuccessful and got nothing."*[25] Five broke out of the Burlington jail on Nov. 23, 1859. Two had stolen P.W. McNeeley's boat. Another, named King, had stolen J.H. Moore's horse. The fifth had stabbed a man near Belleview.

Accidents with animals were common. A Petersburg child got a leg broken by a sow (a mother pig that could have weighed up to 800 pounds). Accidents also happened while shooting or hunting.[26]

Privately Maintained Turnpikes 1850

Union and Florence	5.5 miles
Union and Beaverlick	5.0 miles
White Haven and Richwood	2.5 miles
Burlington and Florence	6.0 miles
Beaverlick and Richwood	5.0 miles
Cincinnati and Lexington	11.0 miles

Road Construction

1854
Gunpowder to Buffalo Hill
Florence to Union
Union to Richwood
Union to Beaver,
Buffalo to Hamilton
Union to Big Bone

1856
Union and Burlington Road to Big Bone Church and Hamilton

1858
North Bend Road (KY 237)
Sand Hill to Mitchellsville and Dry Creek
North Bend and Woolper
Francisville to Taylorsport to Constance

Tourists and Picnics

Travel for business and pleasure was more comfortable and common now. A group of local tourists including the Crisler family left on the Jacob Strader steamer from Covington March 28, 1859, intending to visit Pike's Peak.

Visitors arrived from as far away as California. Some returned with strange and exotic gifts: While in Memphis, Sarah June Sebree's father sent her two guinea pigs.

Churches remained the strong cohesive force in the community, holding "basket dinners" during pleasant weather. Everyone ate together under the trees surrounding the church. On Aug. 4, 1860, a barbecue on Elijah Creek attracted a Monters band.[27]

In the southern part of the county, farmers in the Buffalo Hill area near Big Bone traditionally celebrated the completion of corn planting with a fish fry at the "hole," a pond in Gunpowder Creek. Participants brought corn bread and other dinner "fixins."

---

[24] *Boone County Recorder*, 1930 Historical Edition.
[25] Conrad, Loder 1, 60.
[26] Conrad, Loder 1, various dates
[27] Conrad, Loder 1, various dates

Two men waded waist-deep into the creek with a seine to catch the main course. The crowd cleaned and fried the fish as soon as they came out of the water. Emma Rouse Lloyd remembered as a child riding to these picnics on horseback on a pillow in front of her father.[28]

Rabbit Hash Doctor

Medical help was now available. A dentist practiced in Lawrenceburg, frequently pulling problem teeth.

Dr. Adolphus Sayre, who was born along Gunpowder Creek in 1821, earned his degree from the University of Louisville's Medical College in 1851.

Setting up housekeeping in Rabbit Hash with his bride Nannie Lodge, Sayre practiced both in his log cabin and from the back of his mule. Their son Frank became a doctor and returned to Hebron to practice – but used the more sophisticated transportation of a horse and buggy. The younger Sayre soon began to rely on a new gadget called a thermometer, rather than his father's reliable hand on the forehead.[29]

Buffalo Hill

When Thomas Rouse married Nancy Ann Henderson, they moved to Buffalo Hill, three miles west of Union on the Big Bone Lick and Riddell's Run roads. The Rouses bought 163 acres for $4,912 according to a deed dated May 31, 1853.

The Rouse family multiplied on Buffalo Hill. *"An old mammy named Patience went with the young bride to teach her housekeeping and how to manage her household affairs. She remained* (to help the family) *until three children came into the home, then a sister of Nancy's married and needed her guiding hand in starting another new home."*[30]

One story says Buffalo Hill was named for a trapper who built his cabin on the main route to the salt lick with the vision of meat coming to his door. But it didn't make his life easier. As a buffalo herd passed, he shot and wounded a cow. The bull charged and killed him.

In the 1850s, old buffalo paths were still visible, worn several feet deep into the ground and creating trees with a peculiar stunted growth and exposed roots. Bordering the trail were several circular ponds, thought to have been buffalo dust wallows in dry weather and mud-baths in wet. Farmers deepened many of these depressions to make drinking ponds for cattle.

Thomas and Nancy Ann Henderson Rouse, 1930 Recorder Historical Edition, Courtesy of Ruth Glenn

In 1847 Union was the largest community in the area, with one store, two churches, one doctor and 50 residents. Union Masonic lodge was founded in 1854.

Morris Lassing had been Union postmaster and storekeeper since 1827. He also was ordained as an Old School Baptist preacher at Old Sardis in April 1854. Converts were baptized at Elm Hole, in the creek by an old elm.

His son, Henry Clay Lassing became a doctor. Henry's son, John M. Lassing, born in 1864, became a Burlington attorney, then county attorney, then circuit court judge for many years.[31] (Lassing Pointe golf course, which is located on part of the old Lassing farm, was named after the family.)

Big Bone Baptist Church Established

In 1857, the first Big Bone Baptist Church

---

[28] Emma Rouse Lloyd, *Clasping Hands with Generations Past*, Wiesen-Hart Press, Cincinnati, August 1932, 34.
[29] Chester Geaslen, "Strolling Along Memory Lane #3," *Chronicles of Heritage*, (Otto Printing Co. Newport, Ky. est. 1975), 23.
[30] Lloyd, 32.
[31] Conrad, *Yesterdays*, 55.

members heard Rev. Robert Kirtley preach. James Kirtley assisted with the service.

In 1843, 42 members created a congregation for the new church, led by deacons Thomas Huey and John C. Riley. They spent $1,240 on the building. James Kirtley served as pastor for 49 years, resigning on Nov. 17, 1900.[32]

Road Improvements

Bridges were being added to improve the new roads constantly under construction. Henry Mallory, a Zanesville, Ohio, carpenter built two 40' covered bridges crossing Woolper Creek between Burlington and Petersburg in 1851. The bridges lasted until the 1917 floods.[33]

A man named Rogers framed a covered bridge over the Taylor Creek crossing at the foot of Market Street in Petersburg (now KY 20) during a mild January in 1859. It was painted red.

Tolls and conscripted labor weren't enough to finance roads. An 1859 poll tax helped, charging $1.50 on each white man over 16 and $.50 for black men. Road work was generally done from April to July each year.

Labor for state-financed roads was paid at a rate of $.75 a day. A team, plow and plowman earned $1.75. A team, wagon and driver earned $2.25. An overseer received $1 a day, but not more than $8 a year.

In 1860, work began to replace the mud road (KY 18) between Florence and Burlington. Construction began on more covered bridges.

Highway Accidents

Despite a horse's relatively slow speed (four miles per hour at a walk or six to eight miles per hour at a trot), travel over those new roads included some dangerous incidents.

Loder recorded on Sept. 11, 1857, that: (Petersburg mill and distillery owner) "*Mr. Snyder and Mr. Jenkins* (livestock dealer) *started to Covington with a two-horse buggy. On the pike between Botts' and Gaines' the horses got skeared and run some 50 yards and*

Covered bridge — Photo contributed by Virginia Lainhart

struck a log and broke the buggy considerable. They gathered up the pieces and went on to Gaines. There they procured another buggy and resumed their journey." In July of the following year, the pair drove to Covington in a two-horse carriage. While there, Mr. Snyder's young horse called Morgan died.[34]

Jack Winston's horse ran off down Walton's hill with its buggy, injuring Winston and his wife.

"*Thomas A. Stevens' black boy got thrown from a horse in the lane below Petersburg and was dead for some time but came to again,*" Loder noted on Jan. 30, 1859.

River Travel

Horses powered the Rabbit Hash-Rising Sun ferry in the 1850s. Horse teams walked treadmills that connected to paddle wheels. Some said blind horses were used to power the boats because they were less easily spooked by

---

[32] Mrs. Ora B. Presser, *Boone County Recorder*, 1930 Historical Edition.
[33] Conrad, *The Top of Kentucky*, 16.

[34] Conrad, *Loder 1*, 3.

the river's motion. Others say the horses originally had normal sight but eventually were blinded by the sunlight's glare on the water. These ferries were used until steam and gasoline engines arrived.[35]

When the river froze, ferries weren't needed, the ice created a convenient and well-used bridge. On Jan. 12, 1857, Loder noted: *"Snyder sent two four-horse teams over the ice to haul whiskey from the mouth of Tanner's Creek to Lawrenceburg. His teams and loads weighed six tons each. He was hauling whiskey this morning with two one-horse sleds across the ice. The ice was between 8" and 10" thick and clear."*

Several weeks later, Snyder was continuing his work despite rain, sleet and rising temperatures that left *"considerable water running over the ice."* After four or five trips, he was obliged to quit because *"Tanner's Creek commenced to running out so much (from the Indiana side). The temperature dropped a few days later and Snyder was back at it using a mule and a sled."*

On Feb. 9, Loder said that there had been no mail since Jan. 1 due to the winter weather. As soon as the ice broke up, steamers and other boats began running the river. The mill and distillery received coal and corn by barge.[36]

River Tragedies

River tragedies were common. On April 13, 1852, an explosion of the steamer Redstone near Carrollton killed popular Burlington Baptist Pastor P.C. Scott.

The sternwheel steamer Fanny Fern blew up at Medocks bar, killing a number of people on Jan. 28, 1858. A woman's body was found in the river near Cyrus Clark's. Several weeks later her father arrived and paid her burying expenses: coroner's fee $6, burying expenses $16.95. Captain Woodward's body was caught in the river near Rising Sun. His stepson J.S. Crawford came for it two days later.

On Dec. 26, 1858, the steamer Motropolis (cq) stoved and sank at the mouth of Kentucky's Sugar Creek. The next week on Jan. 3, the steamboat Madison – coming from New Orleans to Cincinnati – collided with the steamboat Iowa at Aurora. The Madison sank to its lower boiler deck.[37] The steamer was repaired within a few weeks and continued its service.

When Perry McNeeley's boat was stolen, he pursued the thieves, overtaking them near Maysville, then brought them back to Burlington to stand trial and be committed to jail. He also recovered the boat's stolen contents.[38]

New steamboats passed Petersburg every few days. The Steamer Jacob Strader took 7 hours and 15 minutes to go from Cincinnati to

Steamboats like this one lasted an average of five years with constant risk of fire, explosion and wrecks. Courtesy of Rabbit Hash Museum

---

[35] Clare, 38.

[36] Conrad, *Loder I*, various dates.
[37] Conrad, *Loder I*, 27.
[38] Conrad, *Loder I*, 43.

Louisville.[1] Loder also saw *"two locomotives drawing 11 passenger cars and one drawing seven passenger cars going to St. Louis to have a celebration on June 4, 1857."*[2]

Holmes-Gibson Disaster

In one of the worst steamboat disasters of the time, the Nathaniel Holmes and David Gibson steamers collided on March 28, 1859, across from Snyder's saw mill in Petersburg.

Coming up from New Orleans, the Gibson was bound for Cincinnati, loaded with sugar and molasses. The Holmes, with Captain Kennedy and pilot John L. Conway, was headed for St. Louis with full load of passengers and cargo. Gibson pilot William Irwin lost his license for *"negligence and unskillfulness"* in causing the collision.[3]

Both boats sank quickly; the Holmes' cabin went down and the Gibson's cabin went up. Thirty to 35 from the Holmes and three to five Gibson crew members drowned. Aurora citizens rescued and cared for survivors.

A submarine went out to the hull of the Holmes, but couldn't do anything because the water was 30' deep.[4] On Aug. 25, the Deputy U.S. Marshal sold the Holmes wreck to a Covington man named McDonald for $1,400.

On March 10, 1860, with a very cold wind blowing all day, a loaded coal barge ran into the David Gibson wreck and sank a short distance below Swings ferry.[5]

Slave Defined

River travelers had many motives and purposes. Emma Rouse Lloyd recalled going to Louisiana with her father when she was about five *"to buy a flatboat load of little Negroes. These were brought on the boat in droves – always fat and sleek and greasy – about my own age. And strangely, they were always nude."* They were her playmates when she returned home.[6]

The Kentucky legislature had prohibited importing slaves into Kentucky in 1833, but 15 years later that law was repealed. On Feb. 3, 1849, the Kentucky House of Representatives unanimously passed a resolution *"that the people of Kentucky were opposed to the emancipation or abolition of slavery in any form except as currently provided in the state constitution..."*

Two years later, the word slave was defined. *"No persons shall be deemed a slave in this state except such as are now slaves by the laws of this Commonwealth of some other state or territory of the United States or such free Negroes as may be sold into slavery under the laws of this state and future descendants of such female slaves."*

In 1855, Boone County had 1,745 slaves and 48 free colored – about average in Kentucky slave population. In 1860, Petersburg had 26 slaves. On Jan. 8, 1855, seven slaves owned by Boone Countians who had died were sold at prices ranging from $1,015 to $1,505 each.

Occasionally slaves had opportunities to earn money, raising chickens, eggs or garden produce. A few managed to secrete that money away, or with the help of a sympathetic banker, have it forwarded to them after an escape. Most weren't so fortunate.

While some were looked down upon, others were an accepted part of the community. *"Old free black Milly fell dead in the street of Petersburg supposed to be the breaking of a blood vessel,"* Loder noted on Nov. 15, 1857.

He also noted that a wedding took place at 9 p.m. on May 4, 1860, for *"Owen Kirtley's black boy Andy and William Snyder's girl Eliza."*[7]

Many rules, most of them unwritten, dictated behavior in blacks' lives. These conventions carried to all with dark skin, free or slave. Mrs. Lloyd described women's hair

---

[1] Conrad, *Loder I*, 4.
[2] Conrad, *Loder I*, 7.
[3] "History of Petersburg Community," *Boone County Recorder*, Sept. 21, 1978.
[4] Conrad, *Loder I*, 32.
[5] Conrad, *Loder I*, 50.
[6] Lloyd, 35.
[7] Conrad, *Loder 1*, various dates.

style in her book.

"Slave women and children always wore their hair 'wrapped.' This was done about every week by parting the hair into sections and wrapping each section with cord, very tight and close to the scalp, and the cord was drawn from one roll to another in such a way as to make them all lie flat on the head.

A Boone County family.   Photo courtesy of Virginia Lainhart

"A Negro was never seen with bushy hair. The women also wore a headcloth, a large, three-cornered muslin kerchief, bound neatly and closely around the head. A woman was never permitted to go into the kitchen or out of her cabin without this cloth unless she was 'dressed up' to go visiting Saturday afternoon or Sunday."[46]

African-American Crime

Right or wrong, need or logic aside, slaves or "free coloreds" often were assumed to be guilty when crimes occurred.

On June 27, F.M. Bess brought a Negro man from the Lochry Ferry to Petersburg, saying there was a $400 reward for returning him to Henry County. Perry McNeely of Petersburg caught a Negro with a bag of corn, a basket of eggs and an empty half-gallon jug around midnight near Petersburg. *"Perry tussled with the Negro some time but did not succeed in keeping him as it was quite dark."*[47]

In his capacity as a Justice of the Peace, Loder heard a case in circuit court of a black boy (no indication of age) owned by Miles Marquiss accused of killing Eliza Bryant, the nearly six-year-old daughter of J.C. Bryant.

Judge Nutall ordered that the boy, who was valued at $900, to be hung on March 19, 1858. With James Calvert as the hangman in Burlington, *"he swung off 25 minutes past 1 o'clock p.m. and hung 26 minutes, then cut down."*[48]

Slave Families

Mrs. Lloyd wrote of her family owning only two slaves, *"Jack, a finely built, ebony black young fellow whom my father heired from his family, and Mary, a middle-aged woman, half Indian, who did the cooking, cleaning, milking, etc.*

"My grandmother Henderson owned three families: a white minister married John Robinson and Peggy Smith before my grandfather owned them. Their children were Lewis, George, Aaron, Andrew, Julius and Liza. Lewis, after the Negroes were freed, went to St. Louis and was coachman for one family for 29 years. George and Aaron died in infancy.

"Andrew married Kate, daughter of 'Moss' Sechrist, owned by Charles Sechrist. They had 18 children. Andrew died in the summer of 1931, aged 92 years. Kate died several years previous. Grandmother did not

---

[46] Lloyd, 105-106.
[47] Conrad, *Loder I*, 9.

[48] Conrad, *Loder I*, 16.

own Kate.

"Julius was a stupid young fellow, of not much account. After the war, he lived on the Whitney Wilson place on the Independence Pike. Liza married and was living in Williamstown when we last heard of her. She had two children. She lived with the Rouse family for a few years as a nurse for Henderson and John T. The Robinson family lived in a log cabin in the lot north of the "big house.

"After they were freed, John and Peggy lived on the Nath Thompson place and later went near Richwood. After John died, Peggy lived with Andrew's family. She and John are buried in the family burying ground on Andrew's farm near Richwood. Andrew was a good citizen and a prosperous farmer. He owned his own home and farm where one of his sons now lives. Grandfather bought this family of six from Robert Daniels.

"Patience had six children: "White" whose father was an Indian, Harve, Parthene, Ruth, Milly (Pig) and Jim.

"Parthene was maid in "Miss Lizzie's" family. Ruth was 'Miss Hannah's' maid and Milly, known as 'Pig' lived with 'Miss Nan' and was nurse for the first baby in the family. Pig became a hairdresser in Lexington. Whit lived with her and assisted in her business.

"Dan's wife belonged to the Collins family and lived with them. Dan and Whit got into some trouble and Grandma sent them to Tennessee. Whit returned after the war, but Dan never came back though he often wrote to Grandma."

Old Ame

"Amos Harrison was not one of my grandmother Henderson's slaves. He came to Crittenden from Harrison County, Ky. shortly after the Negroes were freed and hired to grandmother to split rails.

"He was a young fellow, just entering manhood, strong, broad-shouldered, husky, with face as black as jet and always with the appearance of having been greased. He was an expert rail-splitter as well as a good workman at all kinds of farm work. After my grandmother's death, Ame (Amos) remained with my father and mother on the old place.

"During the last years of my mother's life, Ame, then an old man, became careless and negligent about the work on the farm. After having been reprimanded a number of times without improvement, my mother called to him one evening and said: 'Ame, I can not be

Unidentified boy.   Courtesy of Virginia Lainhart

bothered with you any longer. You do not attend to your work and I must have someone on whom I can depend. Now I am through with you. You may pack up your things and leave.'

"In silence, with bowed head, hat in hand, the old man turned and went home to his little cabin. Next morning, Ame was at his work as *usual though he kept out of Mother's way. That evening, when my brother who managed the farm arrived, Ame's conduct was reported to him. He called the old Negro and asked if he had been dismissed.*

"'Yes, Mr. John.'

"'Well, why don't you go?'

"'Mr. John, the las' words old Mas' said to me was 'Ame take good care of old Miss as long as she lives.' How kin I take care of her if I leaves the place?'

"Ame remained in his little cabin on the farm as long as he lived, many years after 'old Miss' was gone." The family laid Ame to rest as he requested, in a couch coffin delivered to the grave in a real hearse.[49]

Garner Family Escape Attempt

On Jan. 28, 1856, five members of the Simon Garner slave family escaped from Richwood Station farms owned by James Marshall and Archibald Gaines. The group included Simon's parents, Simon and Mary, and from the Gaines' farm, his wife Margaret, 23, and her four children, Silla, a 9-month-old boy, Mary, 3; Samuel, 5; and Thomas, 6.

Following the path that had successfully taken eight Boone County friends to freedom, they left the two horses and sleigh they'd used at a Covington hotel. Across the river, they searched for Elijah Kite, who had been a slave with them until his father, Joe, purchased his freedom.

At the Kite home on Sixth Street, Mary Kite fed them while Elijah ran to Levi Coffin's store. The Quaker was "president" of the Underground Railroad. Coffin warned the successful escapees had gone further west, beyond the jurisdiction of the U.S. Marshall.

Early in the morning, Gaines with neighbor Major Murphy, William Marshall – the son of the Garners' owner, and other Kentuckians came looking for the Garner family. At the Kite house, Cincinnati marshals smashed in the door. The younger Simon shot an officer's finger off before the gun was taken from him.

Realizing escape was futile and rather than see her children return to slavery, Margaret Garner grabbed a butcher knife and nearly decapitated her daughter, then slashed at the other three, begging her mother to help as the older boys struggled for their lives.[50]

During the trial, crowds lined the streets as the Garners were taken to the courtroom. *"Free African-Americans waved handkerchiefs, cheered, sang songs of freedom and taunted the marshals, who were pro-slavery Kentuckians deputized to prevent rescue efforts."*

Gaines demanded the Garners be returned to him. The defense asked that Margaret Garner be tried for murder in a Cincinnati court. Although she would have been hung, it would have struck a blow against the Fugitive Slave Law that could have saved others.

Cincinnati anti-slavery attorney John J. Jolliffe said, *"These people would go singing to the gallows rather than go back into slavery. The mother of these children, rather than permit them to be returned into bondage, would murder them with her own hands. Yes, she would imbue her hands in the blood of her own children and go to the gallows joyfully, rather than permit them to be taken back to Kentucky."*

Jolliffe argued that by freely allowing the slaves to come to Ohio (to attend church and do errands), the owners had given them their freedom. John W. Finnell, who represented the slave owners, said state lines were immaterial, the laws of the Union overrode them.

The 14-day-long trial was reported in newspapers across the nation. William Marshall, 19, who grew up with the younger Simon on his father's farm, said he considered him *"more of a companion than a slave. If money can save him from the effect of any rash act he has committed, I am willing to give it in any amount."*[51]

---

[49] Lloyd, 175-178.

[50] Owen Findsen, "Posse follows escaped slaves across the Ohio," *Cincinnati Enquirer*, Feb. 1, 1998, F7.

[51] Owen Findsen, "Fugitive preferred death over slavery," *Cincinnati Enquirer*, Feb. 8, 1998, F14.

The Utz family ran a tollgate near Florence. Courtesy of Linda Green

Legal maneuvering continued after Col. Gaines took the Garner family back to Kentucky. They stayed in the Covington jail for one week, following legal orders, then he put them on the steamer Henry Lewis, bound for the Gaines family plantation in Arkansas. A riverboat collision sank the ship and 15 died, including Margaret's baby but she was pulled from the water. Margaret was put on another steamer and sent back to slavery.[52]

Florence Agricultural Fair

In April 1855, the Northern Kentucky Agricultural Society leased 40 acres of Florence woods and pasture for 10 years for $1. A dozen Boone and Kenton county men planned to hold Boone County's first agricultural fair there in September.

John Barton's leased land was west of the Covington-Lexington Turnpike. Organizers were President John C. Walton, Joseph C. Hughes, John W. Leathers, George M. Bedinger, Thomas C. Graves, W. B. Watts, H. M. Buckner, Volney Dickerson, Dr. Braxton Chamblin, John C. Swetnam, Sam K. Hays, and Washington Watts.

The first display included a Pippins apple weighing 1 pound, 6 ounces and a Queens variety measuring 18" in circumference and weighing 2 pounds, 4 ounces.

The fair was held annually for the next six years, gathering participants and spectators from throughout the region.

The Covington Journal listed fair premiums in June. Awards were given for categories including fruits, vegetables, farm products, poultry and livestock. Some Indiana and Ohio residents participated in the annual fair in late September, but most were from Boone and neighboring Kentucky counties. Women displayed the handiwork of their looms and

---

[52] Owen Findsen, "Slaves case ended in tragedy," *Cincinnati Enquirer*, Feb. 22, 1998, G11.

Chapter 5 1850-1861 The River Rules

spinning wheels while men brought hand-smoothed ax handles, wooden rakes, butter churns and more.

Lemonade, root beer, cider and ice cream were favorite refreshments, chilled with ice cut in late winter and stored underground in thick layers of straw or sawdust. Ice cream was cream set in a metal bowl surrounded with crushed and salted ice and stirred with a wooden spoon. Big iron kettles of burgoo were suspended over hot beds of smoky embers. A variety of meats roasted on turning spits nearby.[53]

L.A. Loder said that in 1858 nine lady equestrians rode for the coveted silver pitcher. Eliza Riddell received the $25 keepsake. Miss Woodford got the $15 cup and Rebecca Clutterbuck won the $10 cup.[54] The next year Julia Aylor won the top prize, Miss Clarkson was second and Miss Murphy third.

John Hornberger's horse took the premium for the fastest pacing horse with a time of 1 minute 44 seconds. A brown mare of Gaff's (probably John Gaff, the Scotsman who owned the Aurora mill and distillery. His spectacular home, called Hillforest is now available for tours.) took the premium for the fastest trotter at 2 minutes 1 second for three times around the track. Jack Carson got one premium on his horse for light harness and won $10.[55]

At the Lawrenceburg fair, John Carson got two premiums for best light harness stallion $10, one for sweepstakes and one $20 award for best all purpose horse.

During a colt show at Petersburg, "*John H. Walton's horse colt took the $10 prize. First premium for a mare colt,*" and another coveted $10 bill, went to William Allen. Second went to Nate Allen.

On Oct. 3, 1859, Loder wrote about a horse that impressed him while he was attending a fair in St. Louis: "*Lexington is a light bay stallion, long tail and all of his feet are white and some white on the end of his neck. Lexington made the fastest race that had ever been made either in Europe or America. He ran against time when he was four years old for $35,000 and won it having made the four miles in the unprecedented time of 7 minutes 19¾ seconds.*"[56]

Catholics Build Churches

Irish immigrant Cornelius Ahern arrived in Florence to find only three other Catholics, Mrs. Scott, wife of the town doctor, and innkeepers Mr. and Mrs. Joseph Ferneding. The Rev. Thomas R. Butler from Covington came to say Mass every three months.

In June, Ezra Fish, who was not Catholic, donated two lots at Shelby and Center streets for a church. Built for $600 in 1855, the 75' x 40' frame building featured a 30' tall steeple. Pine benches accommodated 400. It became St. Paul Catholic Church.

During construction, a group called the "Know Nothings" vowed to burn the church before it was finished. As members prepared to defend the building, Col. H. Buckner, a non-Catholic, attended a "Know Nothings" meeting. Laying his revolver on the table and calling God as his witness, Buckner promised to shoot the man who lit the first match. Since he was known to be a man of his word, the threat was not carried out.[57]

The first pastor, Father John J. Brent, lived in a brick house on the south side of Shelby Street. One original church member was Irishman Andrew Collins who had arrived in New Orleans, then made his way upriver to Taylorsport by horseback.

(A new brick church was erected in 1910 and the old building became a hall with a stage. After electricity arrived in 1918, motion pictures were shown there. The old building was razed in 1926.)

Another group of Irish immigrants, including Thomas Dwyer, founded St. Patrick's Catholic mission at Verona in 1850. Father Lambert Willey came from Covington for monthly services. Verona resident John

---

[53] Conrad, *Yesterdays*, 11.
[54] Conrad, *Loder 1*, 5.
[55] Conrad, *Loder 1*, 40.

[56] Conrad, *Loder 1*, various dates.
[57] Conrad, *Top of Kentucky*, 14.

Dempsey donated a lot for the church in 1865. Within two decades, 40 families were attending the mission and Verona became a parish center with a resident priest.

About 1895, Walton property was purchased for a Catholic Church. After 1950, with the founding of All Saints, Walton became the parish center.[58]

Five-Month Schools Begin

With no parish schools, the few Catholic children were among the estimated 1,619 pupils taught by 21 teachers in Boone County in 1850. Schools, particularly grammar and writing schools, were flourishing and the school year was extended to five months. Each community established its own schools.

Florence's census counted 46 children between five and 16 and reported that 75 percent attended the local school taught by Robert Varner.[59]

In 1849, the state had levied a tax of 2 cents per $100 property valuation for education. Funds were distributed to counties based on the number of children from five to 16 who lived there.

The Squirrel Hollow and Zimmerman schools had served Florence until 1856. From 1856 to 1865 John Uri Lloyd and his father Nelson opened a private school in Florence's Old Town Hall on Main Street.

Nelson Lloyd, a civil engineer, had come to Kentucky to work for a proposed railroad from Covington to Louisville. It was to run along Gunpowder Creek past the Weaver and Christler Mills.[60]

When the railroad's plan fell through in the panic of 1854, he was stranded without a job. So Nelson and his wife Sophia, well-educated New Yorkers, became teachers. Sophia conducted a girls' school across the road. Women were just beginning to be allowed to teach. The Lloyds moved between Petersburg and Florence as better teaching positions were

The parlor of a house on Middle Creek Road.
Courtesy of Kathryn Rudicill

offered.

School trustees had suggested a tax to repair the schoolhouse on Price Pike, but taxpayers rebelled, so the Florence Town Hall was the only building available for the public school. The Good Faith Lodge #95 had constructed the building. The first floor was to be used as a school and community building and the second floor for the lodge's private use.

An inventive man, Professor Lloyd devised a means of ringing the school bell, which was outside the building, from inside. He ran a rope through a window to the bell. Lodge members, who built and shared his building, objected to his ingenuity, so Lloyd was forced

---
[58] Conrad, *Top of Kentucky*, 14.
[59] Conrad, *The History of Boone County Schools*, 19.
[60] "Early Historical Spots in Boone County," *Boone County Recorder*, Aug. 31, 1978, 10.

to continue ringing the bell traditionally.[61]

About 1860, Florence Baptist Church was used for school exercises that didn't include music, which the church forbade. Will Conner offered a public school in Florence, a Mr. Fullmaker had a German school, Irene Bradford offered a private juvenile school and D.Y. Bagby taught high school.

A "common" school opened in 1859 at the intersection of Union-Frogtown and Richwood roads. School #39 opened in Union in 1869 on the Union-Visalia Road, now Mt. Zion Road. The Clarkson School, a subscription school, existed west of Union as early at 1840.

Morgan's Academy

In 1841, a Boone County man named Allen Morgan who lived on Woolper Road near Petersburg died, leaving no known relatives. According to laws of the time, proceeds from the sale of his estate were given to the Boone (or Burlington) Academy which had opened in 1814.

Located in the north end of Burlington off Temperate Street (next to what is now Urb's Garage), Boone Academy was originally financed through the sale of seminary lands that the state had set aside years before. Boone's share of seminary lands was 4,500 acres.[62]

In August 1856, the trustees decided against repairing the old Boone Academy and planned a new 27' 5" tall building. Morgan's money paid for a 60'x 30' two-story school with two first floor rooms and one large room on the second. The school's name was changed to recognize Morgan.

Two years later, after the building was completed, principal Sackett Mead taught for an annual salary of $800. Mary Greenwood taught primary grades for the tuition fees. About 50 students attended for five months.

An ad in *The Burlington Advertiser* promoted Morgan's Academy, offering advanced classes like Latin for $13; chemistry and surveying for $10; English grammar for $8; and primary classes for $5. Fuel to heat the school cost extra.[63]

The Limaburg sawmill and lumberyard.
Courtesy of Boone County Historic Preservation

During the next few years, the school attracted up to 80 students from prominent Boone County families and others in Indiana and Ohio. However, tuition fees couldn't maintain the building. Some of the Cumberland Lake land granted by the original plan was sold, netting $1,500 for 3,000 acres, but it was used to repair the fences, buy new desks and benches and partition the second floor to create another classroom.[64]

Limaburg Appears

Between Burlington and Florence along what is now KY 18, Jeremiah Beemon built a grist mill in about 1849 using the water from

---

[61] Conrad, *The History of Boone County Schools*, 8.
[62] Conrad, *The Top of Kentucky*, 39.
[63] Conrad, *The History of Boone County Schools*, 16.
[64] Conrad, *The History of Boone County Schools*, 17.

Gunpowder Creek to turn the grinding wheel. A few years later, Israel and Robert Rouse added a sawmill in partnership with Beemon.

Beemon was to receive two loads of sawdust a year from the Rouse brothers and the grist mill was required to operate on Tuesdays. (Much later, the community that grew up around this enterprise was named Limaburg.)[65]

Burlington Grows

In the 1830s, Willis Graves, who had been the Boone County clerk in earlier decades, built a brick two-story house a few lots down in the next bend in the street from his log cabin. (Nancy and Bob Swartzel now operate the house, with a modern addition, as a bed and breakfast run by Nancy's parents, Bob and Jean Brames.)

The Presbyterian Church was built on Jefferson Street on an alley not far from the courthouse at the same time Graves was building his house.

The Baptist Church, on an alley west of northern Jefferson Street, was organized in 1842.

The Methodist Church, a block away at Jefferson and Gallatin streets, was built in 1837. (After the church moved to a new building, Betty and Charlie Sallee renovated it into Burlington Antiques in the 1980s.)

The building next door was constructed in 1856. (It now houses "The Herb Works" operated by Brenda Mullins and Jodena Kelly, "Don's Antiques" owned by Don and Jackie Johnson, and "Healing Touch of Northern Kentucky" operated by Deborah K. Griffith, R.N., and Lyle E. Allen.)

The two-story red brick "Foster-Sanford House" in the next block was built in 1831.

After completing his renowned stone house near Union, Benjamin Piatt Fowler built Burlington's Boone House just up Jefferson Street from Boone Academy. He operated the hotel there for a time.

---

[65] William Fitzgerald, "History of Florence," written in 1958, republished in the *Boone County Recorder*, Aug. 3, 1978.

Chapter 6
1861-1869 Civil War – Balancing on the Line

In 1860, Boone County, with its long stretch of riverfront, was quite literally on the border of the North South conflict. Just as residents' lives were beginning to have some predictability, the Civil War's divisive forces began drafting the men, conscripting their newly accumulated goods and farm animals, and destroying their well-built mills and farmsteads.

The conflict pushed out of mind much of what had begun in the last decades – schools, post offices, the Florence Fair, travel and agricultural improvements.

Citizens were constantly pulled from one side to the other for emotional, political and financial reasons. Aurora residents like wealthy mill and distillery owner John Gaff did their best to encourage their southern neighbors to stay out of the conflict.

Kentucky tried to remain neutral during the Civil War, "*but finally abandoned this position and, being a border state, soon became a recruiting station and battleground for both the North and the South,*" said teacher and historian A.M. Yealey. Boone County men enlisted in both the Union and the Confederate armies. Sometimes brothers in the same family faced each other in battle.

Boone County native Henry DeCoursey Adams speculated that Kentucky was the only state to have met its full quota of every Civil War draft by both the North and the South.

Locals ran the gamut in their beliefs about slavery. Boone County included slave owners, slave hunters, abolitionists, those who had freed their slaves, and those who secretly helped slaves escape.

Boone County's 1860 population included 9,403 whites, 48 "free colored" and 1,745 slaves. Nearly 16 percent of the residents were slaves, four percent less than 20 years before.[1]

On Nov. 30, 1860, a Burlington public meeting focused on slavery. Dr. Samuel S. Scott said if the U.S. Constitution could not be enforced – including slave owners' rights – perhaps another government should be formed to guarantee those rights. Union supporter J.C. Wilson said no constitution should be so weak as to allow its own destruction.

After the war began, marauding soldiers – seeking food for themselves, their platoons and horses – took it wherever they could find it. Many homeowners lost the fruits, vegetables, meat and crops they'd grown or preserved for their own use in the coming winter.

Hundreds, perhaps thousands, of hungry men moved through Boone County, anticipating a major battle in Cincinnati. After that was defused, they came back through to defend or attack Lexington.

Word Travels

On Saturday, March 13, 1861, Boone Countians learned that shots had been fired at Fort Sumter, S.C. The next day, news arrived that Major Anderson had surrendered and Fort Sumter was on fire. Petersburg resident G.H. Frazee took his Negro woman on the mail boat and left. A week later, two men brought a Negro in from the mailboat and put him in the Burlington jail. He'd escaped from Union County, Ark.[2]

On a cool and cloudy March 20, 1861,

---
[1] U.S. Census figures
[2] Conrad, *Loder 1*.

Soldiers dressed like these moved through Boone County constantly during the Civil War. Photo by Virginia Lainhart

influential Aurora men John W. Gaff and O.P. Cobb held a meeting in Petersburg to discuss what to do about the violence, mobs and potential consequences of seceding from the Union.[3]

Lee M. Fulton's Petersburg census showed a population of 577 and 26 Negro slaves in 1860. It remained, by far, the county's largest town.[4]

Through the confusion and turmoil, Adisson Gaines' Negro woman and her five children ran off on April 3, 1861. Two days later, a Lawrenceburg man named Ferguson was in Boone County hunting for a "*boy who ran off*" several weeks before.

Meanwhile, Aurora's Dr. Sutton and Petersburg's Dr. Graves discovered a Petersburg child with a bad case of smallpox, an often-fatal disease that left its few survivors badly scarred and disfigured. Although some refused Edward Jenner's vaccine because they thought it might give them the contagious disease, the local doctors vaccinated nearly 100 that day. So fearful was General Rice that he moved his family across the river.

Public meetings about the war continued. A constable and delegates to a Border State conference were elected in Petersburg on May 4, 1861. A state legislative session was called the next day.

But the conflict was still distant and many local events continued as usual. A few weeks later Petersburg held a squirrel barbecue with the 32 squirrels shot that day.

Several cannonballs struck the river on May 22, startling Petersburg residents. Aurora men were testing a new cannon positioned to aim upriver.

On June 18, 1861, Watt York and an Aurora man caught a Negro across the river and brought him through Petersburg on the way to the Burlington jail. Jasper Halloway and J.G. Hamcrick came from Louisiana to claim the man a few days later.

On July 16, 1861, Widow Piatt's horse ran off dragging a spring wagon. He cantered up Petersburg's Front Street from Snyder's mill, turned down Tanner Street, then ran into some locust trees, badly breaking the wagon. He ran on to Jack Walton's and was caught.

The next week, Dr. Grubb's Burlington house caught fire, destroying its contents. A few days later a group gathered for a picnic at Captain Collin's woods. Linn Boyd McNeely fell into the river from a boat and nearly drowned.[5]

Nearly 40 years after the county enacted a tax levy to purchase tools to build public roads, resurfacing began on Dixie Highway, the first road chartered to be built in Boone County.

---

[3] Conrad, *Loder 1*.
[4] Mary Rector

[5] Conrad, *Loder 1*.

Petersburg distillery workers. Courtesy of Boone County Historic Preservation

Enlistment Begins

The Civil War came closer to home in the late summer and fall.

Florence residents were surprised one day to see 40 Union ambulances carrying yellow flags accompanied by 50 female nurses and a dozen Sisters of Charity heading down the partially completed Dixie Highway to Richmond (Ky.) to bring home sick and wounded soldiers. Confederate Gen. Kirby Smith who was monitoring Dixie Highway gave them permission to pass.[6]

On Sunday Aug. 18, 1861, soldiers arrived at Lawrenceburg. They got off the steamboat to take the train to St. Louis. Ten carloads departed the next day. The next Sunday, four steamboats from Madison, Ind., passed Petersburg going the other direction, each loaded with 100 horses and 100 soldiers on their way to Pittsburgh.

At a "peace meeting" at the Burlington courthouse on Sept. 2, 1861, Boone Countians adopted a series of resolutions calling for compromise to end the fighting. If that could not be arranged, the group said, Southern states should be allowed to secede because that was preferable to war. The gathering demanded strict neutrality for the Commonwealth, saying the federal government should not use state tax money in the war effort.[7]

Later that month, four slaves ran off: John

---

[6] Conrad, *Yesterdays*, 27.

[7] Reis, *Pieces of the Past 3*, 161.

and Frank, owned by Mrs. Joseph Norris, a "boy" of John Terrill's and Ed, owned by John H. Walton. They crossed the river at North Bend.[8]

Covington (Union) recruiters came to Petersburg on Oct. 9, 1861, but no one enlisted. On Oct. 28, a company of Capt. Foy's soldiers camped on the Petersburg commons.[9]

Farmer and Petersburg drug store owner John William Berkshire joined the Orphans Brigade under John Hunt Morgan. (He returned to marry Petersburg girl Melicent McNeeley on Oct. 30, 1866.)

Distillery owner Jenkins build his retirement home on the highest hill above Petersburg with a great view of the Ohio River. Caroline Williams sketched this scene in November 1957. Courtesy of Christine Godsey

Military men moved constantly. Petersburg residents saw six stern-wheel steamboats loaded with soldiers go down the Ohio on Monday, Oct. 21, 1861. The City of Madison boat came to Lawrenceburg to pick up soldiers. Three more steamers went by that day, each filled with soldiers headed to Louisville. That process continued – varying only by the numbers of horses, men and wagons transported on each ship or barge.

As the year edged toward a close, Confederate officers secretly began enlisting men from the river counties – although Kentucky was, at least theoretically, still a Union state. Well-known French peddler Felix Moses joined the rebels, riding south on a mule carrying a Confederate flag made by some Florence women. (This is the man immortalized in John Uri Lloyd's book.)[10]

Two days before Christmas, five men came to Petersburg with four black men and a woman they caught at Dillsboro, Ind. The slaves had escaped from Warsaw, Ky., and were returned there.[11]

Slave Enlistments

Many slaves escaped or were stolen and transported across the Ohio to enlist in the U.S. Army. The bounty offered for each enlistment was seldom collected. Each county's provost marshal could order captured slaves to enlist in Kentucky regiments.

While some were forced into military

---

[8] William Conrad, editor, *The Loder Diary, Part 2, The Civil War Years, April 21, 1861-Sept. 30, 1868;* (Boone County Schools, Florence, Ky., 1985), 80.
[9] Mary Rector.

[10] Conrad, *Yesterdays*, 26.
[11] Conrad, *Loder 2, 97.*

service, others eagerly anticipated it. In January 1862, Florence citizens began organizing a cavalry company.

William Snyder sold his Petersburg Distillery to J.C. Jenkins and William Appleton in 1862. (The flour mill had been forced to close by law.) Many of Snyder's slaves were among the property sold at a Feb. 3, 1862, auction at the Burlington courthouse.[12] A month later, the sheriff sold more of Snyder's cattle, wagons, buggies, carriage, plows and equipment.

Jenkins had built his retirement home in 1860. Called Prospect Hill, it was a mansion on a hill overlooking Petersburg, the Ohio River and much of Indiana. There Jenkins bred trotting horses and Shorthorn cattle.[13] (Mary Jo and Steve Amann are rehabilitating and living in the house in 1998.)

Jenkin's brother-in-law George Terrill attempted to outdo him in constructing an equally posh home on the hillside just below Prospect Hill. (The John and Sharon Smarr family now lives in the white mansion on Petersburg Road.)[14]

On Aug. 1, 1862, a Federal soldier from Lawrenceburg tried to persuade Old John Norris' Negroes to leave (and likely enlist). Norris threatened to shoot the soldier.[15]

Divided Loyalties

Since sympathies were divided, information was constantly conveyed across Boone County's 40 miles of Ohio riverfront to military authorities on both sides. The federal headquarters at Fort Mitchell received much information concerning Boone County's Southern sympathizers.

Gen. Stephen Burbridge ordered citizens arrested for having sympathies with the South. Those arrested included Dr. John Dulaney who practiced medicine throughout Boone County during the war and Spencer Fish who owned extensive acreage, including a subdivision west of Florence's Shelby Street.

Throughout the war, the Union army controlled the Ohio River. Many Boone Countians who came from Virginia and other Southern states interacted daily with Indiana residents whose leanings were decidedly Union.

Southern soldiers tended to join neighborhood companies, but changed companies frequently, making it difficult to track them. *"Perhaps they didn't get along with their officers – or their cousin was in another company and they wanted to be together,"* theorizes Jack Rouse of Walton who wrote *The Civil War in Boone County, Kentucky*.

"Many men were transferred to other companies and their records lost or destroyed. Many men marked deserted on one company's roll are listed on another." [16]

Conscript or Theft?

Federal forces usually gave paper redeemable for money when they moved through the region taking food for men and animals. Self-righteous Yankee soldiers reportedly angered local families by the rude manner in which they removed conscripted goods. The other side, like Lexingtonian John Hunt Morgan, employed their Southern manners to make homesteaders' losses more palatable and win supporters for their effort.

To assure their own survival, many families hid food, clothing and valuables. Invading men took hams, side meat, canned goods, eggs, and garden produce to feed the troops. Corn, hay and fodder were conscripted to feed their animals. Hungry soldiers stripped ripening fruit trees and young cornfields as they walked past.

Homeowners' laboriously created split rail fences made convenient, dry cook fires when hundreds of men camped in one location.

The 18th Michigan Regiment, under Captain Hardeman, camped in the pond field

---

[12] Conrad, *Loder 2*. 86.
[13] *Boone County Recorder*, "History of Petersburg Community," Sept. 21, 1978.
[14] Alice Jarrell, April 2, 1998.
[15] Conrad, *Loder 2*, 92.

[16] Rouse, 60.

across the pike from the Thomas Henderson House. *"The family suffered much from their depredations. When they broke camp to leave, they destroyed all provisions they had not used, threw the windlass into the well, destroyed crops and did many other things to annoy the family."*[17]

Hog market traffic increased and hundreds of horses and mules were driven north through Florence for the Union army. Late in the war, hog or pig orders prevented free trade in hogs, making life even more difficult for farmers.

Troops also raided Boone County farms for horses. Farmers hid badly needed and favorite horses in the woods, paw-paw thickets, old buildings and anyplace else.

On Aug. 8, 1862, James Calvert and eight cavalrymen took two horses from Richard Parker's, one from Henry Terrill and another from W.C. Berkshire. They brought them into Petersburg, but let them go again.[18]

Hannah Weaver's Horse

During the Civil War, Hannah Weaver, Betty Weaver Roter's great grandmother, had lived on what became the Charlie Delph farm on Longbranch Road near Union. When Yankee conscriptionists visited the farm to take horses, she tried to intervene, asking that her favorite riding horse be left.

"The men refused, beating her severely. Our father led us to a huge upright hand-hewn post – a part of the old barn's frame. On the aged post still remained the stains of blood from Hannah's hands, wounded as she tried to hold onto her horse.[19]

"Ephraim Weaver, coming to his mother's defense, was beaten and threatened by a soldier named Silas Merchant. After that, Ephraim always carried a pistol when he left home. Years later, during a court day in Burlington, word came to him that Merchant was in town boasting of his threat.

Civil War soldiers' camp scenes looked like this reinactment photo.
Photo by Virginia Lainhart

"When an opportunity came that he (Ephraim) could be first to fire without endangering others, he stooped down at an upward angle, to further prevent injury to others. Grandpa shot and killed the Union soldier Silas Merchant. Later, in a trial by jury, Ephraim Weaver was acquitted. It was considered shooting in his own defense – justifiable homicide."

Charlie Fowler, a friend of Ephraim's who was 12 years old at the time, wrote an account of the incident he had witnessed. For more than 80 years, the gun was locked away. When it was opened, only one bullet was missing, the others remained in the chamber.[20]

Tobacco and Tom Thumb

On Sept. 2, 1862, Cincinnati, Covington and Newport were placed under martial law. A war meeting had been held the week before in Burlington, attracting men from Aurora as well.[21]

Despite the changes, some aspects of day-to-day life continued as if the war didn't exist. Celebrated dwarf Tom Thumb appeared in

---

[17] Lloyd, 105-106.
[18] Conrad, *Loder 2.*
[19] Roter, 140.
[20] Roter, 142.
[21] Conrad, *Loder 2.*

Lawrenceburg and Cincinnati. Mrs. Carey's boy (Loder did not note whether this was her son or her slave) got scalded falling in a slop tub and died the next day.

The Petersburg tobacco auction was held as usual on Nov. 21. The large harvest brought $10 to $14 per hundredweight.

Oyster suppers celebrated Christmas. A popular delicacy often served on special occasions, oysters were shipped from the East Coast in gallon cans, similar to paint cans of the 1990s. Those who brought cedar trees inside the house would have chosen three- to five-foot-tall trees to set atop tables in their drawing or living rooms.

John Loder hosted a New Year's Eve party. Taylor Lyons had a dance. The next day, two gunboats went down the river to help capture Vicksburg, Miss. A few days later, Fletcher Clore brought Mr. Brown's Negro boy from Florence and put him on the mail boat.

Dr. Graves left for the Frankfort legislative session. Miss Mary Fischer opened the Petersburg school.[22]

Troops with bayonets affixed to their guns guarded some voting booths. Some polling places required voters to swear allegiance to the United States before voting. Southern sympathizers and those who had sons in the Rebel army weren't the only ones offended by this order. Some ministers refused to swear the oath, saying their only allegiance was to God. Those who refused to swear weren't allowed to vote.[23]

Snows Pond Encampment

Boone County's largest role in the Civil War came when Gen. Kirby Smith was moving his army to Lexington. Brig. Gen. Henry Heath was camped at Corinth with 5,000 seasoned Confederate troops and several companies who had reached Snow's Pond[24] near Walton. Their plan was to threaten Cincinnati, Covington and Newport. They first began searching for mills, used for grinding corn, to procure supplies.

Will Aydelotte remembered as a 10-year-old stopping his wood cutting to watch wagons drawn by four mules, loaded with ground corn and slabs of bacon, heading for Snow's Pond.

For three weeks the Union army camped there, drinking the stagnant water covered with three inches of scum called frog spittle. (After the men and horses drank from it for so long, it became apparent that they had been drinking the decaying carcasses of 13 mules, thrown in by retreating Rebels.)[25]

Florence Fight

John Uri Lloyd recalled a battle fought around the Florence Christian and Baptist churches around Lexington Pike.

Union Gen. Lew Wallace who was defending Cincinnati sent men on a reconnoitering expedition. About 150 of Morgan's veterans met them on the road. Despite being "*outnumbered 10 to 1, the Confederates attacked fiercely, creating the impression that their strength was on a parity with the Federals.*"[26]

Taken by surprise, Union troops were thrown into confusion. "*There was much shooting and sabering. The attack resulted in a complete rout of the boys in blue.*" When things quieted down, the 19 dead and wounded were carried into the shade of the trees surrounding the Baptist Church.

Later, the dead were laid out on the grass in the Christian Church yard before being sent back to Cincinnati. The battle is not mentioned in any Civil War account. Frank Grayson mentioned it in an Aug. 28, 1933, article about historic spots in greater Cincinnati published in the *Times Star*.

---

[22] Conrad, *Loder 2,* 98.
[23] Rouse, 36.
[24] Rouse, 26-27. The field is on the east side of old Lexington Pike, about 1/10 mile north of what is now Kensington. Rouse recovered 50 Civil War era minie and pistol balls from this field in 1992 and 1993. The pond is now a barely visible depression. U.S. 25 and the Southern Railroad bisected the site. Rouse notes that the railroads constructed many ponds rumored to contain Civil War guns and cannons well after the Civil War.
[25] Rouse, 19.
[26] William Fitzgerald, "History of Florence," written in 1958, republished in the *Boone County Recorder*, Aug. 3, 1978.

Rouses Arrested

Smith's army advance companies procured many loads of ground corn and wheat from Julius Rouse's mill on Burlington Pike and Gunpowder Creek, 2½ miles from Florence. On Sept. 15, 1862, mill owners were arrested on the charge of aiding the Confederates and taken to a prison camp in Lawrenceburg, Ind. Gen. Wallace's troops blew up the mill while the Rouse family watched, under armed guard, from their front porch.

While living in tents at the prison camp, the Rouses had Sunday visitors. Yankees pulled back the tent flaps and *"stared at us as if we were wild animals."* After two weeks, the men were sent to Cincinnati, where they asked an influential Hebron resident to assist them. They swore allegiance to the U.S. Government and came home.

After their return, an organization was established to pool money, so when men were drafted who didn't want to serve, they could purchase substitutes. *"Yet by skillful manipulation, substitutes seldom received what was allotted for them,"* said A.M. Yealey. The treasurer of the organization claimed to have $5,000 to purchase substitutes.[27]

Romantic Image

Confederate Gen. John Hunt Morgan epitomized the romantic image of a dashing Southern gentleman who charged headlong into battle, then emerged unscathed to kiss a young woman's hand in thanks for a drink. Although his raids had little lasting military accomplishment, they prevented Union troops from moving to battles in the South. Morgan's raids also bolstered local sympathizers' morale.

Those with less altruism than Morgan often simply took advantage of the wartime chaos to collect cash, boots, clothes, food or whatever struck their fancy as they raided homesteads at gunpoint. Some of these men were regular soldiers cut off from their units, locals too young or undisciplined to handle regular military duty, deserters and occasionally just criminals.[28]

While the romantic image no doubt attracted some, many were forced into military service. All male citizens, including ministers and the elderly, were drafted. Anticipating a major Cincinnati battle, earthworks were thrown up at Ft. Mitchell and Ft. Perry.

Gen. Lew Wallace's Cincinnati forces encountered a Confederate advance guard at Florence on Sept. 15, 1862. One man was killed in the skirmish and the Confederates fell back to Walton. In another conflict, a company of Union soldiers was captured and the regiment retreated south of Covington.

Sightseer Killed

On Sept. 17, 53 Union soldiers engaged a company of 101 Confederates near Florence. The Rebels were defeated. Five Southern soldiers were killed and seven wounded. The Union army suffered one fatality and one injury. Curiosity killed a Florence resident, Larkin Vaughn, who was struck by a stray bullet as he watched from a nearby barn.

Meanwhile, Rebel scouts stationed on the Boone County hills above the Ohio discovered boats of Union soldiers steaming toward Louisville. Having learned that Cincinnati was no longer a target, Union forces pushed Confederates south, past Walton, to conceal a build up of Union forces in Louisville. Scouts also saw infantry and cavalry units camped north of Walton to carry out the ruse.

Under a flag of truce, Confederate Capt. Samuel Morgan delivered dispatches to the Union commander – betting the commander that he would drive in his pickets within 48 hours. Morgan left for Falmouth, giving Confederate Col. Basil Duke an update on the strength of the Walton encampments. Duke marched his troops all night toward Lexington Pike (U.S. 25).

---

[27] Yealey, "History of Boone County, Kentucky," 24.

[28] Reis, *Pieces of the Past 3*, 58.

Duke's Account

Basil Duke's account of the battle is reported in *History of Morgan's Cavalry*:

"Just before General Heath came down into that country, 15 young men of Boone County who had long wished to join Morgan banded together and attacked a train guarded by 51 Federal soldiers, dispersed the guard and burned the wagons. This party, with some 25 of their friends, then equipped themselves and set out to join us. They were assigned to a new company – 'I.'

"On the road, however and before I reached Falmouth, scouts brought the information that the enemy had fallen back to Walton and also informed me of what his strength was. It was plain that no force of that size would attempt to march on Lexington. Shortly afterward, other scouts, who had been sent to Warsaw to watch the Ohio River, reported that a number of boats laden with troops had gone down river toward Louisville.

"This information explained everything. Finding that Heath has withdrawn and Cincinnati was no longer threatened, this force, which had to drive us away from Walton had been sent to clear the country of troublesome detachments, and also to attract attention in that direction and conceal the concentration of troops at Louisville. Walton is 25 miles from Falmouth.

"On the day after reaching the latter, I sent a flag of truce to Walton, with dispatches, which Gen. Smith has instructed me to forward to Cincinnati. The flag was borne by Capt. S.D. Morgan who betted with the aide of the Commanding General that he (Morgan) would drive in his pickets within 48 hours – He won the wager. The entire strength of the six companies, which Col. Hutchinson had taken to this country was not quite 500 men – the additional A and I, did not swell the total effective to 600. All of these were large ones, but many men (from 4 or 5 of them) were on furlough."[29]

Robert's Coup

At daybreak 10 guards were spotted ahead of an infantry regiment near Walton. Ten men

A Civil War encampment may have looked like this reenactment photo. Photo by Virginia Lainhart

were dispatched to attack the pickets and the entire column galloped forward. Covington native Sgt. Will Hayes and six Confederate cavalrymen compelled 60 Federal infantrymen to surrender. Lt. Roberts captured one company and caused nine others to flee.[30]

This account of that event also was taken from Duke's book:

"...When I reached the little squad of Lieutenant Roberts with the company which I took to assist it, I found it, or rather a fragment of it, in a situation which perhaps was never paralleled during the war.

"Lt. Roberts was still further down the road and toward the encampment, with a portion of the detachment, picking up stragglers. Sgt. Will Hayes stood with six men in the midst of a company of 69 Federal infantry. The infantry seemed sullen and bewildered, and stood with their rifles cocked and at the ready.

---

[29] *175th Anniversary Historical Book*, 50-51.
[30] Conrad, *Yesterdays*, 111-112.

"Hayes had his rifle at the head of the commanding Lieutenant, demanding he order his men to surrender, and threatening to blow his brains out if he encouraged them to resist. Hayes' six men stood around him, ready to shoot down any man who should raise a gun. 'I thought it was the finest sight I had ever seen.'

"The arrival of the company decided the infantry to surrender. Caps and bayonets having been taken off of their guns, they were sent off guarded by the men who had completed their capture. Lt. Roberts had gone with his mere corporal's guard into the infantry regiment, had captured one company and run the balance back to camp. The men of this company were very green and raw. Hayes had persuaded them for some time that he was an officer of their own cavalry, and it was only when he peremptorily ordered them to follow him to Walton that they suspected him.

"After sending off the prisoners, four or five of us rode on down the road to join Lt. Roberts whom we found to be bringing back more prisoners.... A staff officer came galloping toward us, evidently not knowing who we were, and taking us for some of his pickets not yet driven in. He came right up to us, thinking his capture certain.

"Capt. Morgan, who thought that he recognized him as the officer whom he had made the bet two days previously, rode forward, saluted him and told him he was a prisoner. He, however, did not seem to be of that opinion, for he wheeled his horse, coming so close to us in doing so as to almost brush the foremost man, and dashed back at full speed, despite the shots that were fired at him.

"The skirmishers, who were not more than 200 yards off, soon induced us to leave and we galloped off after the column. Eighty or 90 prisoners were taken and sent off to Lexington as soon as we got back to Falmouth. The enemy did not know for several hours that we had entirely gone, and indeed rather expected during that time to be attacked in force...."[31]

Confederate Prisoner

A Telegraph operator from Boyd, Ky., and a kinsman of Thomas Schiffer of Gunpowder Road, George B. Durant wrote this account of being taken prisoner by the Confederate advance toward Covington in September 1862. (The punctuation and wording taken from the diary has not been changed.)

"Tuesday Sept. 9 - Yesterday morning the camp horn blowed at 3 o'clock and at 4 we were ready to march. I, with Mr. Ravenscraft who was to be my fellow prisoner, and the only prisoners they had, were placed under the provost guard. We went ahead of the main army.... We marched six miles below Williamstown and encamped for the day and night reaching there about noon, a distance of about 18 miles. This morning at four we started again and are now camped near Walton coming about the same distance we did today at Crittenden.

"Before Covington – Wednesday, Sept. 10. Beautiful weather. This morning at an early hour we left our camp and are now within range of the Federal guns on the fortifications. Our camp being in front of the Five Mile House. Every moment we expect the battle to commence. I have been well so far, have slept in the open air every night. The men have treated me with unusual kindness, allowing me many privileges sharing their blankets with me and faring the same as they do in the mess. I cannot but admire the conduct of these men toward me – no one has yet treated me only in the most kind and gentlemanly manner. About a dozen prisoners have been added to us today whom the pickets have brought in.

"Thursday -11th; Rained this afternoon and evening considerably. This morning we were moved ¾ mile nearer town and encamped in a narrow piece of woods on the other side of which are plainly to be seen, the fortifications of Covington hills. Pickets have been skirmishing all day and two Federal (soldiers) are said to be killed. A severe

---

[31] Basil W. Duke, *History of Morgan's Calvary*, (Miami Printing and Publishing Co., 1867), 240.

shower coming up this afternoon – permission was given to move into and occupy a barn nearby. I have had no supper nor anything to eat but a biscuit this morning. I have to lay down to sleep on the straw supperless and thirsty, but am thankful of a barn to shelter me from the cold rain this evening.

"Friday – 12th; Pleasant day. Last night at 11 o'clock we were ordered to be ready to march at a moment's notice and forthwith we were all in readiness not knowing which way we were to go. A heavy rainstorm was coming up at the time and lightning flashing fearfully. As we fell into line, I thought my time about come. I thought of my nice little room at Mr. Boyd's and how happy I might be were I there. But NO, I was a prisoner in the Rebel Army and God only knows where I might be released – the order was given and came our backward trip. The rain soon began to pour and the mud over shoes, we marched to Walton 17 miles where we are to remain a few days.

"Rebel Camp near Walton. – Saturday, Sept. 13; Beautiful fine day. I apprehended . . . the rebels thought best to change the base of their operations, leave Covington to be taken another day and at the same time look out for their own safety. So here we are at Walton the whole Rebel Army. We have now in our mess 35 prisoners. Mr. Woodson from Falmouth, a Provost Marshall is one. The Rebels are mortified at not being able to march on Covington. They bragged so much on our march down – about the Damned Yankees not being able to fight them – they did not care for numbers but with one big yell and a scare they intended to turn them like a flock of sheep and run pell mell into Covington, but the scare didn't take.

"Sunday, 14th, Walton, warm delightful day. Have spent the day reading the Bible and <u>Life in Oregon</u>, and talking upon the scriptures with several of the guards. One in particular who is very staunch Methodist and zealous member of the Church. The men are very social in their manner and are not so uncivilized and barbarous as many think them. They treat all prisoners with the kindest disposition. Mr. Ellsworth, the notorious Morgan Operator and another operator named Capt. Burke called on me and spent half an hour. Our conversation was amusing. Three operators – two Sesech and one Union. They asked me if I was Union – I says 'Yes, Sir, always – and always will be.' Very good fellows.

"Monday – 15th; Walton. Same day – beautiful weather. Several of the prisoners have been released... I addressed a note to Gen. McCrey today something as follows: Dr. Gen. I write you a line to ask at your hand a favor which if improper you will please pardon me. It is to ask you to give my case a hearing as soon as practible feeling confident that when thoroughly investigated it will not appear a very aggravated one. I wish to remain within your lines. I would return to Mr. Boyd, who together with his family and the most of my friends are your strongest sympathizers. And I pledge you my life that if again found aiding directly or indirectly your enemy my blood may pay the forfeit of my indiscretion. Hope Dr. Gen. I am G.B. D. (George B. Durant)"

"Rebel Camp near Williamstown. Tuesday, Sept. 16. Happy day. Tonight I am once more a free man. The note I addressed to Gen. McCrey yesterday had the desired effect. He sent me word that as he was going to march to Williamstown today he would like me to come along as far as that with him as it was right on my way. This morning he sent his liet. with a horse for me to ride. Quite a favor when all the rest were obliged to walk. We reached here about noon and camped (on the) side of the road. At 1 o'clock I was overjoyed to see Mr. Boyd and John Berry. They had been to see Gen. Churchill and Gen. Heath and they had ordered my release but Gen. McCrey countermanded them just to be contrary. About dark McCrey sent for me – made out my papers I took the oath and was released.

"Wednesday, 17th. Boyd Station, Ky. Ravenscraft (who was also released last night) and myself started this morning at 4 o'clock *for home reaching there about 9 coming 14 miles on foot. Mr. Boyd's people were glad to see me and had left nothing undone towards bringing my case before the proper authorities for my release. They had worried themselves not a little in my behalf and the old lady received me with both hands. Mr. Boyd offered Heath to be security to a number of thousands he might name that I should be forthcoming at anytime he might name if he would let me go home. But he did not want a Bond, they made me a unconditional release.*

"Thursday, 18th. Seems good to be a free man once more. I am quite sure hereafter I will appreciate it more. Here is my oath taken before Gen. McCrey (T.H. Mcray). 'I do solemnly swear that I will not take up arms or fight against any of the army or citizens of the Confederate States of America nor give any information nor disturb or destroy any of the public property of the said Confederate Government or of the citizens of the Confederate States.' I could not object very much to taking a pill of that calibre for it is an oath which heretofore I had scarcely transcended. McCrey told me I had better effect an exchange for someone at Camp Chase when this would cease to effect.

"Friday, Sept. 19. McCrey gave me a pass as follows: 'Headquarters 1rst Brigade, 3rd Division, Army of Kentucky, Sept. 16, 1862. Mr. George B. Durant having taken the oath and been regularly paroled as a citizen has permission to pass the lines of the Army of the Confederate States and is heretofore exempt from molestation in any business he may enjoy in so long as it does not conflict with the oath taken. By order of T.H. McCrey Col. Com. 1rst Brg., 3rd Div. Army of Kentucky, C.G. Kilgore Capt. Adj. General.' Lee Boyd left this morning for Fosters Landing with a letter from me to father. I feel he will be intercepted. . . . Rebel scouts everywhere."[32]

Boone Countians Serving

Jack Rouse documented numerous Boone Countians who served in the conflict. The type and amount of information about each varies.

- Dr. Daniel M. Bagby, who moved to Walton in 1864, was a Confederate soldier in Co. K-2nd KY Mounted Infantry. He was wounded at Camp Morton in Indianapolis

A row of cannons along Dixie Highway, that may have looked similar to this, protected Union troops from an attack coming from Lexington.
Photo by Virginia Lainhart

while he was under the command of Col. Roger Hanson's Co. K. Juvenile Volunteers. Born in 1841, he married Julia F. O'Neal in 1868 and was buried in Walton Cemetery in 1916.

- Florence native John C. Crisler joined a company of Confederate sharp shooters commanded by B.A. Bulaney. He was transferred to the Tennessee cavalry for three years and fought in the south until paroled at the surrender in Gainesville, Ala., on May 11, 1865. A beekeeper, he fathered nine children before his wife died. He died Jan. 5, 1918.

- After being wounded in the leg and contracting pneumonia, Dr. Robert Andrew Edwards Jr. asked to recover at home under his father's care. A graduate of the Edinborough, Scotland, medical school, he enlisted in the Ohio regular infantry in Cincinnati on May 29, 1862. In 1864 commissioned a 2nd Lt. of company L, 4th Kentucky Volunteer Cavalry regiment, he was given a pension of $24 a

---
[32] Rouse, 29-34.

month in 1901. He died in 1914 and was buried in Wilmington, Del.

- R.A.'s brother, Samuel Lycurgus Edwards (called "Kurg") enlisted in Company G of the 84th Ohio Infantry and served as a nurse in the regimental hospital. Born in 1843, he married Ella Nora Pettit and had five children. He and his wife are both buried in Walton Cemetery.

- Joseph Glenn, who moved to Walton from Kenton County in 1858, enlisted in the Confederate army at Beaverlick on July 22, 1862. Captured a week later while serving in Company B of Jesse's Battalion Mounted Rifles, Glenn was sent to Vicksburg in November and exchanged as a prisoner of war. He married Annie Arnold and had a son named Herbert.[33]

- On Oct. 31, 1862, Bill Bennett and his brother-in-law got off the mailboat at Petersburg. They had been taken prisoner near Cumberland Gap and were paroled.

- Robert Terrill delighted his family by arriving home on Christmas day, after having been taken prisoner at Hartsville, Tenn.

- Some returns weren't so happy. B.W. Sherrill returned on the mailboat with the body of his son Ben who died on the steamboat as he was returning from Nashville. He was wounded in Murfreesboro, Tenn.[34]

War Increase Toll Revenues

The Civil War had increased traffic and road wear substantially, especially around camps. The federal government had committed to pay tolls at half the regular rate for transferring troops and army supplies, but that was rescinded in 1862. The Secretary of War reinstated the agreement the next year.

The Kentucky Board of Internal Improvement published a six-month *Report of Turnpike Roads* in July 1864. It said the 50 miles of road between Covington and Lexington cost an estimated $6,000 per mile and brought in $26,207 in tolls, averaging $524 per mile.

That was the second highest revenue in the state, exceeded only by the Danville, Lancaster, Nicholasville and Lexington road which averaged $1,409. The lowest revenue road was a 12-mile stretch from Versailles to Anderson County, which averaged $54.

The Civil War dramatically increased the dividends the state received. The years 1864, 1865, and 1863 were the three most productive years in more than 150 years of state ownership. Yet in 1864, the $67,111 investment returned only 2.6 percent.[35]

Tolls Collected on ***Dixie Highway*** *Covington to Georgetown*	
1859-62	$22,162
1863-66	$33,897
1867-70	$27,377

Back in Petersburg

While many of its sons were hiking down roads far away, Boone Countians went on with occasional reminders of the ongoing conflict. The two Tennessee Negroes that Botts and Riddell had put in the Burlington jail last fall were captured again on Feb. 27, 1863, near Petersburg.

The steam propeller Robin struck a snag a half-mile below Taylorsport, then crossed to the Ohio side and sunk on April 14, 1863. The steamboat Prioress burnt at the mouth of Mill Creek, just below Cincinnati two days later. A month later, the mailboat ran into the Robin, knocking a hole that caused the ship to sink. Three days later, the Robin was repaired and running again.

During Court Days, John W. Menzie (a Union candidate) made a speech and declared himself a candidate for re-election to Congress from the 6th District.

Horses not conscripted by the war effort were swapped and sold. Col. Appleton sold nine mules to John Stuard for $135 each. Jack Carson sold his bay horse for $180 to the same man. Stuard loaded the animals on the mailboat and took them to Louisville.[36] John

---

[33] *150th Anniversary, City of Walton*, (Jan. 21, 1990, n.p., n.d.), 19-20
[34] Conrad, *Loder 2*.

[35] Tanner, 13.
[36] Conrad, *Loder 2*. 104.

Loder bought a horse for $125.

Three men were charged with stealing a horse from Filman. One was also named McMurry, another one Hall. Nothing was proven against them so they were released, then arrested as deserters and taken to the Burlington jail.

Two days later on June 17, 1863, two Dutchmen stayed all night in Petersburg buying grease for soap.

On the 24th, Col. Appleton, Jack Carson and J.G. Gaines went to Louisville on the mailboat to buy some horses condemned by the government.[37]

On July 10, Lawrenceburg and Aurora were abuzz with news of John Hunt Morgan's Rebel raid in Indiana. Smoke hung in the 94-degree air for days and the mailboat didn't run. Morgan was reportedly within 25 miles of Aurora. No steamboats moved. The New Madison Packet Brilliant went down the river at 4 a.m. as far as Bellevue, then returned to Cincinnati.

Fifteen transport boats and four gunboats loaded with soldiers ran the river. On the 16th, an exceptionally cool July day, the Brilliant took its first trip to Madison, Ind. The next day, the Roberson Brothers Circus and Menagerie performed in Lawrenceburg.

Word came on the 27th that Morgan and his forces had been captured. On Sept. 1, 1863, Morgan's horses captured at Aurora were sold. When he passed through southern Indiana, Morgan had exchanged his exhausted horses for fresh ones. Col. Appleton bought seven the first day and three the second. William Wingait bought four. J.C. Jenkins bought one.

D.R. Peck opened his school. Miss Sebree's started two weeks later.[38]

A Negro boy of Rich Parker's, another of John Norris' and a girl of Fanny Parker's ran away on Sept. 27.

On Oct. 21, two men attempted baling hay using a portable press in Berkshire's field. Mrs. Martin, who peddled china parlor toys, came to Petersburg and Burlington.[39]

Morgan's Escape

On the night of Nov. 26, 1863, Gen. John Hunt Morgan and eight other Confederate soldiers confined in the Columbus, Ohio, penitentiary, tunneled out. Beyond the prison walls, the men divided in pairs. Morgan and an aide, Captain Thomas Hines, bought railroad tickets to Cincinnati where they arrived before daylight. At the lower part of the city, they pulled the bell rope, signaling the train to stop. Just as the train slowed and a conductor appeared on the rear platform to ask why they wanted to get off there, they jumped.

Opposite Ludlow, they gave a boy with a skiff $2 to row them across the river. On the Kentucky shore, they found the home of widow Ludlow where they had breakfast. Dr. John Dulaney's son, J.J. Dulaney, piloted them to Daniel Piatt's home near Union. They walked three miles then were given horses. Piatt's two sons, Asael (cq) Daniel Piatt and William Cain Piatt, had been in their command.

From there, R.G. Adams escorted them to Henry Corbin's on the Burlington-Big Bone Road for Saturday night. (Corbin's sons were also in Morgan's command.) Word of their escape traveled quickly. Friends appeared, supplying fresh horses, money and firearms.

At 9 p.m. Sunday they resumed their journey south, W.P. Corbin said. (Corbin was in his early 30s at the time but was missing his left arm near the shoulder – likely the reason he was not drafted and was available to assist in the notorious escape.)

Charles B. Smith of Big Bone gave Capt. Hines a good horse. Gen. Morgan rode off on a bay mare Corbin had just purchased from Jacob Piatt at East Bend. Seeing Gen. Morgan wearing a black cloth suit entirely too light for the weather, Corbin pulled off his new blue jeans and gave them to Morgan who put them on over the others. Corbin also gave Morgan his saddle, bridle and spurs. The men

---

[37] Conrad, *Loder 2*. 105.
[38] Conrad, *Loder 2*. 108.

[39] Conrad, *Loder 2*.

continued south past Big Bone Church.

Near the South Fork, the party stopped to warm themselves at old Mr. Richardson's home about midnight. Despite the hour, the elderly couple received the group warmly, encouraging them to build up the fire and warm themselves. The Richardsons were curious to know why the men were traveling so late and so quickly. Gen. Morgan invented a story on the spot, saying they were selling hogs in Cincinnati and a sudden rise in the market had sent them rushing back to Owen County to stock up before people there got word of the rise. A half hour later they left, to arrive at Clay Castleman's Gallatin County farm about 4 a.m.[40]

Hines and Morgan successfully escaped. While southern Boone Countians aided the subterfuge, word came to Petersburg that Morgan escaped from Camp Chase and went to Canada.[41] After the war, Hines earned a law degree and eventually became a Kentucky chief justice.

No Hard Feelings

The warm helpfulness Hines and Morgan found escaping through a supposedly Union Commonwealth was common.

"In 25 years of study, I have not found any instance of hatred between neighbors due to which side the neighbors fought on," Jack Rouse says. *"Men came back from the War who fought for the South and ran for public office and were elected by voters from both the North and South. They joined lodges, went to church, served on juries, were election officials, traded work with neighbors whom a few years before would have shot them in battle."*

"My investigations have led me to believe that the men of Boone County laid down their arms and got on with their lives working together in pursuit of raising and educating their families. Personal vendettas were rare for such an emotional division as a Civil War which not only pitted neighbor against neighbor, but brother against brother and father against son...

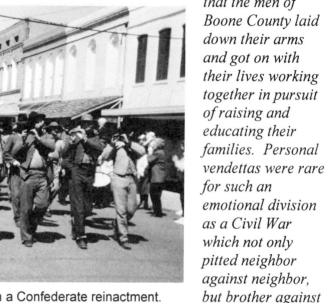
Fife and drum corps in a Confederate reinactment.
Photo by Virginia Lainhart

"When it was over, it was over. They went back to their largely agricultural life on the farms, some to the merchandizing trade or other forms of tradesmen, some to politics or law, and pursued quiet lives as compared to their former wartime adventures."[42]

Cold Snap and Fires

Back on those farms, the challenges continued. An early January cold snap in 1864 killed nearly all the peach trees along Boone County's river bottoms. Ice in the river stopped the mailboat and others, but provided an early opportunity to fill icehouses. A good many empty flatboats and one barge went down, frozen in the ice, Loder noted.

The sun came out on the 12th and 42-degree temperatures began melting some of the snow. The ice in the Licking River broke on the 19th and the steamboat Tempest sunk. Sallee Sebree headed back to Memphis from

---

[40] Conrad, *Yesterdays*, 9, 59.
[41] Conrad, *Loder 2*.

[42] Rouse, 60.

A Southern officer rides astride while his lady rides sidesaddle.
Photo by Virginia Lainhart

Petersburg on the St. Cloud.

On the 6th, Petersburg young people met at the Christian church and established a Sunday school. Gilbert Fisher's house roof caught on fire, but it was extinguished before much was damaged. On the 12th, renowned circus headliner Tom Thumb returned to perform in Cincinnati with his wife.

The last car of an O&M freight train burned in Lawrenceburg on Feb. 18. After several days of snow flurries, the weather improved on March 4.

"*Feeling his oats*" in the spring-like weather, Col. Appleton's horse ran off with Hute Appleton, threw him and skinned up his face. The same day Jack Carson's mare threw Omer Porter, injuring him. Two weeks later, Pete Snelling was driving W.C. Berkshire's team. They ran off and into a locust tree near Shan McGuffin's house.

Petersburg gave a big dinner for the 23rd Kentucky Regiment in the schoolhouse on Easter Sunday. On April 3, someone broke into Henry Tou's house and stole a lot of clothing. On April 10, Jenkins and Gaff, the mill and distillery owners, bought the steam distillery – formerly known as Snyder's Mill – from Col. Appleton.[43]

Slaves Freed to Fight

In July 1862, when the war was going badly for the North, Congressional order freed all Confederate slaves crossing Union lines.

Arguing that slaves doing the farm and factory work aided the Confederacy while Southern white men served in the military, Union military leaders had pushed Lincoln to abolish slavery. On Sept. 22, 1862, five days after the Union rallied to win the Battle of Antietam, President Abraham Lincoln issued an ultimatum saying if the South did not return to the Union by Jan. 1, 1863, he would declare their slaves forever free. On Jan. 1, 1863, he issued the Emancipation Proclamation.

Since the Proclamation governed only areas under Confederate control and excluded border states, it didn't free most slaves.

By April 1864, the Federal Government began offering male Kentucky slaves the same opportunity others had been offered the year before – freedom for enlisting in the Union army. At first only slaves who had their owners' permission were allowed to join, but the Army quickly overturned that policy and began taking all able-bodied men. By August 14,000 Kentucky slaves had enlisted.

Fearing for their families' safety if they were left behind, African-American men often brought wives, children and even parents with them to the recruitment camp. The Army camps soon became refugee centers. In March 1865, the offer of freedom for military service was extended to include families of slaves who enlisted – increasing the number freed to nearly 100,000.

Yet a month later, Boone County court records show John Cooper accused of aiding

---

[43] Conrad, *Loder 2*. 114-117.

the escape of a slave named Hiriam belonging to the heirs of A. Souther. *"On or about March 28, 1865, the aforesaid was accused of setting the slave Hiriam across the Ohio River with the intent and for the purpose of assisting said slave to escape..."*

The April 15, 1865 records show a slave named Sandy owned by Clarrise Blaksly accused of attempting to aid and entice five slaves owned by W.W. Hedges to escape across the Ohio.

By July, an estimated 28,000 slaves were living in Union military camps. By April 1866, 29,000 Kentucky slaves had enlisted.

President Andrew Johnson estimated that of Kentucky's 230,000 slaves counted in 1860, the majority had been freed by the fall of 1865 through enlistment or the automatic freeing of Confederate soldiers' slaves.

The remaining 65,000 were freed in December 1865 when the 13th amendment was ratified without Kentucky's support. (In 1976, the Kentucky legislature ratified the 13th, 14th, and 15th amendments to *"erase the shadow on Kentucky's history."*)[44]

The Freedmen's Bureau tried to force slaveowners to pay back wages to the wives and children of ex-slaves who had enlisted in the Union Army, but their effort primarily created hostility. Despite labor shortages, farm wages were low for former slaves. Most migrated to the cities. Many Kentucky cities passed vagrant laws or "slave codes" to regulate their growing populations. Covington's African American population increased 304 percent while the European-American population increased only 44 percent.

Slaves Released

Boone County's Henderson family was one of few who released their slaves after Lincoln's proclamation.

"After the Proclamation of Emancipation was declared, Mrs. Thomas Henderson called all her Negroes into the back yard and standing on the porch, she explained to them that they were free–their own masters. She had no more authority over them.

"Dick, a boy about 12 years old, jumped up and down, slapping his sides, exclaiming: 'Free niggah, free niggah!' There were no other demonstrations among them. Andrew, Peggy's son, bought a farm near Richwood, where he went to live, taking his father and mother with him. He reared a family of respectable citizens. The others scattered, all returning now and then to see 'old Miss' and the old home." [45]

Black Harassment Continues

Negro marriages were not recorded in Kentucky until after the Civil War. Boone County's first Negro Marriage Bond Book is dated Dec. 1, 1866. The first marriage recorded was Lucy Duncan and Philip Coleman on Dec. 8, 1866. Coleman signed his name legibly, but the white minister who performed the ceremony could only sign with an X.[46]

The Klu Klux Klan grew out of the Civil War. It was a secret organization with membership open only to native-born, white, Protestant males, 16 and older. Negroes, Catholics and Jews were excluded and were often targets of animosity and persecution.

Some disguised Klan members, in long white robes and pointed hats, entered local churches during services. No special disturbance was reported, as *"they just wanted to make the people aware of their existence."*[47]

By 1870, only 11 percent of the African Americans in Kentucky had $100 worth of personal property. Although 45 percent of Kentucky's population, they owned only 6 percent of Kentucky's wealth.[48]

War Winds Down

No doubt releasing tension left from the

---

[44] Harrison & Klotter, 180.
[45] Lloyd, 105-106.
[46] Caldwell, 10.
[47] Elizabeth McMullen Kirtley and Carlene Stephens, East Bend Baptist Church 175 Years, (n.p., n.d), 8.
[48] Pollack, 610-611, 618.

war, a good many men got drunk and fought during a barbecue on Ashby Fork Road on a cool rainy May Day, L.A. Loder noted in his diary. John N. Colsher arrived in Petersburg on June 21, 1864, with his final discharge papers after three years of service.

A week later, Dillon Bradley returned home from Mt. Sterling where his son William had been wounded. The boy died before his father arrived. Two days later, George Comer and Henry Bradley left in a spring wagon to bring the body home, but they returned on the first without it.

A man came to Petersburg selling small sewing machines. A picnic at Wash Watts' woods included music by the Reeves band. And pranksters were hard at work: "*Some low-flung scamps smeared Giesler's Shoe sign all over with cow manure.*"[49]

On Aug. 18, 1864, George Fulcher stabbed John C. Kissick at the Piatt Ferry. Kissick died three minutes later. Two days later Fulcher was tried, found guilty and sent to jail.

On Aug. 26, five days after school began at Petersburg Academy, General Burbridge issued an order that Kentuckians had to have a special permit to sell produce in Indiana or Ohio.

On the 30th, soldiers came to Petersburg from Burlington. Gilbert Fisher got home from his 100 days of service.

On Sept. 5, 1864, an order was issued to draft 50,000 men. Sunday, Sept. 18, Slater's Cavalry Company went through Petersburg returning to join their regiment. On Sept. 19, 854 Boone County men were drafted. Notices were served on the 22nd.

Efe Anderson and Webster Robinson came to Petersburg buying horses for the government. They bought three.

The Nov. 11, 1864, election brought 114 votes for Gen. McClellan and George Pendleton and 21 for Abe Lincoln in Petersburg.

On Dec. 6, 1864, Richard Hardesty was attacked by two men at the water's edge at the foot of Petersburg's Tanner Street. He was robbed of $500 – $150 in gold, $20 in silver and the balance in greenbacks. Old Mrs. Alloway fell on the steps of J.C. Jenkin's house and broke her leg just above the ankle.[50]

Gunpowder Creek from Limaburg.
Courtesy of Boone County Historical Preservation

Horses Returned

On Jan. 11, 1865, commanding a squad of 55 Kentucky Cavalry, Doc. Butts took a little bay mare named Kit from L.A. Loder, giving him a government voucher.

On Feb. 3, they returned looking for horses in Burlington and took Charles Norris' sorrel mare Tasso. The next week, Collector Nixon was in Petersburg collecting government taxes. On the 13th, Loder's mare was returned.

On April 10, 1865, news came to Petersburg that Gen. Robert E. Lee had surrendered to Gen. Grant. The next day, two men came by selling patent rights to wind mills for cleaning grain.

On the 13th, guns were fired celebrating the war's end. On the 15th President Abe Lincoln died after being shot in a Washington theater. On the 17th, Col. Appleton's Negro woman

---

[49] Conrad, *Loder 2*, 120.

[50] Conrad, *Loder 2*, 124.

and children ran off in the night.

The 27th brought news that John Wilkes Booth, Lincoln's assassin, died in a fire when the barn he was hiding in was burned.

Elijah Parker returned home from serving in the Rebel Army on May 1. He had been with Giltner when he surrendered at Mt. Sterling. Richard Parker's and John Terrill's Negroes left on May 12. Two mares stolen from J.C. Jenkins were returned in March – three weeks apart – by the same man.[51]

Canby Accepts Surrender

Boone County native Gen. E.R.S. Canby accepted the final surrender of Confederate forces from Generals Kirby Smith and Richard Taylor in May 1865, at Citronella, Ala. Edward Richard Spriggs Canby was born Nov. 9, 1817, to Dr. Israel Canby of Maryland and Elizabeth Piatt Canby, at Piatt's Landing in a house called Winfield Cottage.

After attending local schools, Canby moved with his family to Indiana where he attended Wabash College then gained acceptance to West Point military academy.

After graduation, he was sent to Florida where his troops fought the Seminoles. During the Mexican War he was promoted to chief of staff and participated in several battles.

When Texas Confederates attempted to invade California, Canby's Union force was defeated, but he avoided direct attack and began a series of harassing guerrilla-like raids until the Texans retreated. Rewarded with a promotion to brigadier general, Canby was sent east. After reorganizing retreating troops, he planned to capture the vital Mobile, Ala., Confederate supply port. President Lincoln personally commended his success.

After the war, the Boone Countian served in various capacities, then was placed in charge of Army activities on the Pacific Coast. On April 11, 1873, he took 800 regular troops and hundreds of local militia to Northern California's lava beds to return a group of 50 Modoc warriors to a reservation in Oregon.

Modoc leader "Captain Jack" or Kintpuash smoked cigars with Canby, passing them symbolically as in a peacepipe ceremony. Since they had nothing to lose, Captain Jack signaled his men to attack. Hearing the shots and knowing the officers were unarmed, Canby's men advanced to find him stabbed and shot in the head. Canby's body was returned to Indiana and buried in Crown Hill Cemetery in Indianapolis.

Typical dress of the 1860s.
Photo by Virginia Lainhart

Despite their superiority in numbers and firepower, it took the Army three months to round up Captain Jack and his men. The chief and three others were hanged for the murders. Indians who refused to move to Oregon were marched to Oklahoma reservations. Five Indian warriors had been lost and 65 soldiers killed in a skirmish that cost the U.S. government an estimated $500,000.[52]

Finnell's Narrow Escape

Living in Missouri during the war, Boone County native Weden Finnell was a Southern sympathizer. His neighbor was a Union man, but the Kentuckian thought nothing of it until a squad of Federal soldiers arrested him on charges of being a rebel. Under arrest, Finnell was taken some distance from his home and ordered to take a position on a stump where he was to be shot.

He jumped over the stump and ran to a

---

[51] Conrad, *Loder 2*.

[52] Jim Reis, *Pieces of the Past 2*, (Kentucky Post, Covington, Ky. 1991), 45-47.

creek, under fire from the soldiers. Hiding in a secluded pool, he allowed only his nostrils to protrude. Dense undergrowth obscured small pools on both sides of the creek. Soldiers diligently searched the creek, firing their muskets into the larger holes, but Finnell survived.

After the search was abandoned, Finnell joined the Quantrill band and remained with them until the war's end. When Finnell died, his remains were returned to Kentucky and buried in the family cemetery in 1901.[53]

Unusual Petersburg Happenings

Now that the war had ended, Boone Countians found other hardships and frustrations.

In the spring of 1866, photographer C.A. Johnson tied his boat at Petersburg's Tanners Street landing. Ten days later he left, taking citizen's money and photos with him.

A fire broke out on First Street in Petersburg on Sunday, May 20, burning five buildings, including the J.G. Gaines' corner store. Thieves broke into the store on Aug.14, blew open the safe with powder, and took $2,000.

Nelson Greene's old sorrel horse fell dead in the two-horse hitch while pulling a wagon in the street across from the mill office. It died before John Snelling could get the harness off.[54] The next day, two spans of the O&M railroad bridge passed Petersburg on boats.

Steamboats loaded with soldiers passed by on Sunday, June 11, 1866. The end of the month, the mill stopped after spending the month grinding corn and wheat flour.

William Bradley's remains were finally returned to Petersburg by mailboat and buried in the graveyard below Petersburg. George R. Moore lived 24 hours after falling into a tub of hot slop at the Mill Creek distillery. On Dec. 12, a flaming coal barge with no crew passed Petersburg.

As bookkeeper for the distillery, J.A. Loder went to Cincinnati to pay $16,004 in taxes on 8,002 gallons of whiskey. The lower whiskey house in Petersburg caught fire on Dec. 1, but was quickly extinguished with little damage.

After a cold and snowy week, four or five men spent Sunday, Dec. 17, 1866, trying to cut a corn-laden barge out of ice at the mouth of Tanner's Creek. The rain, hail and snow continued the next day.

Thieves broke into the J.C. Jenkins office on March 29, 1867, blew open the safe, and stole $292.48 and some valuable papers.

Three boys – sons of Sam Panborn, Calvin Wingait and Mrs. Kirkoff, were struck by lightning on Aug. 8 as they walked along the road near John Loder's. Speechless for a while, they recovered. In another freak incident, a woman named Anne Eliza Leak held an exhibition in the schoolhouse on the 25th. She had no arms.

The Petersburg Methodist church began holding a fund-raising strawberry festival in 1869. That April the town planted maple trees on the riverbank.

L.A. Loder's chestnut mare named Lucy, which he had sold to R.S. Strader and Strader had sold to W.S. Briggsen, sold again. This time, Briggsen sold her to a Boston man named W.P. Balch for $10,000. She *"trotted string to string in 2:26 minutes. She will be entered in the Buffalo race to come next month."*[55] A few weeks later, Balch sent Loder $1,000 for Puritan, Lucy's three-year-old bay colt which had been gelded. The next week, a Boston man came to get him.

On Aug. 27, horse trainer J. Foster drove his horse and buggy through Petersburg without using a bridle or driving lines, much to the locals' amazement.[56]

Crossing the River

Charles Kottmyer opened a ferry in 1865 using a cypress boat called Boone #1. Kottmyer switched to steam rather than horsepower and operated the ferry for 64

---

[53] Rouse, 155.
[54] Conrad, *Loder 2*, 145.

[55] Conrad, *Loder 2*. 22.
[56] Conrad, *Loder 2*, 23.

years.

Cork filled cracks between the boards so that when the wood was submerged, it would swell and seal the joints. There were times that the water was so low that horses pulling wagons or carriages could ford the stream at Anderson's ferry.

Florence Fairgrounds as depicted in John Uri Lloyd's book "Our Willy" set in the 1860s. Courtesy of the Lloyd Library, Cincinnati

The German immigrants had four sons. Henry Kottmyer took over after his father's death at age 84. Henry's three sons George, Ollie and Henry remained in Constance. George Kottmyer bought the General Store in 1920 and Ollie and Henry Kottmyer became the third generation to operate the ferry.[57]

After 11 years of construction, the Cincinnati-Covington Suspension Bridge opened Dec. 1, 1866. John Augustus Roebling designed it before building the Brooklyn Bridge. It opened to vehicular traffic in 1867.

Parlor Grove Amusement Park

Parlor Grove Amusement Park, located along the Ohio in Boone County's northern quadrant, offered wrestling, dog and cock fights, boxing, picnics, dances, band music and a "Flying Dutchman" (now called a merry-go-round). Picnickers came by steamboat from Cincinnati, Petersburg, Lawrenceburg and Aurora to spend the day in the shade of huge beech trees. Parlor Grove sponsored a baseball team in 1869. [58]

The Petersburg Artics baseball team played the Parlor Grove Club of Taylorsport on May 28, 1869. Although the Artics led, a disagreement ended in a draw game.[59]

Soon competition came from amusement parks like Parker's Grove across the river. The Parlor Grove land was eventually sold to Charles Hempfling who cleared it and planted vegetables and orchards. The property remains in the Hempfling family as fruit orchards.

Florence Fair Resumes

The Northern Kentucky Agricultural Society Fair restarted in 1863 after being suspended during the first war years.

Horse-drawn buses brought Covington patrons to Florence for $1.25 round-trip.

Premiums for items exhibited in 1868 were: *"best 10 yards of white and best 10 yards of colored flannel, $4 each; Rag carpet, $5 (a gentleman won this); Best pair homemade blankets, $6; Silk embroidery by a lady, $4, by a girl under 12, $4; Woolen hose, $3; Woolen gloves, $2; Best 5 yards of cotton diaper, $3;*

---

[57] "Kottmeyer Family History," *Boone County Recorder,* 1930 Historical Edition.
[58] Welcome to an Educational & Historical Tour Through Boone County, 10.
[59] Conrad, *Loder 2.* 20.

White counterpane, $10; and Hair work and shell work, $3 each." Maple sugar and syrup, sorghum molasses, pies, cakes, pickles, preserves, candies and other goodies appeared as did new varieties of fruits and vegetables introduced to supplant the old types.

Horse shows offered ladies' and gentlemen's hitching contests, side-saddle riding, trotting races and costume contests.[60] On Sept. 17, 1863, five ladies rode for the premium. Miss Murphy took first. Mrs. John Barton was second and Miss Senior was third in the week of contests at the Florence Fairgrounds.

Cave Clore's daughter won best horsemanship for a lady on Oct. 11, 1866. The next year, John Riddell's "prettiest" horse won $25. Ned Forest won $100 in the President's Ring. Miss Hogan took first in the ladies' riding category. Mrs. Kate Lail (or Lale) was second. The great prize fight between Aaron Jones and Mike McCool went 25 rounds in 34 minutes. McCool was knocked down once.[61]

Kate Lail won $30 in 1868. Ad Nixon was second and Mrs. Waterman took the $10 prize. In 1869, only two women competed although the top prize was now $40. Maria McGryar (also spelled McGryore) was first, Miss Dickerson, second.

White Haven Academy

Rev. W.G. White, pastor of Richwood Presbyterian Church from 1866 to 1869, founded White Haven Academy on the road between Beaverlick and Union. White's son, the Rev. William White, became a missionary to China.

Offering education in social refinement, algebra, Latin and other subjects, the co-educational academy prepared students who had completed public school an opportunity to prepare for college.

When the school flourished, dormitories housed both boys and girls.

The boys' dormitory caught fire and burned, despite efforts by a bucket brigade. They saved the girls' dorm.

John Uri Lloyd, 1930 Recorder Historical Edition, Courtesy of Ruth Glenn

New owner Lynn Frazier discovered it was built of 4x4s and 2x14s when he remodeled it in 1934. A railing with pegs held bridles and saddles for riding lessons. Some girls had scratched their names and dates into the glass.

Prof. John D. Brown and his wife left their academy in Petersburg to teach at White Haven in 1865. One White Haven alumnus was Emma Rouse who eventually married John Uri Lloyd and moved to Cincinnati. Another alumnus, James Lynn Frazier, was the first cashier for the Union Deposit Bank in 1903. He later purchased the White Haven property. Patronage eventually waned and the land and buildings were sold.[62]

Surveying Rail Lines

Surveyors began charting a railroad route between Louisville and Covington in March 1866. The Louisville to Lexington route included a stop at LaGrange, where the Covington route connected.

In July, two years later, workers began laying track from LaGrange to Worthville, from Worthville toward Walton and from South Covington toward Walton. With tunneling and bridge-building, the South Covington section progressed slowly. By April 1869, two construction trains ran daily from the city to two miles past Walton. The last four miles were completed April 18, 1869.

Under director John LeBosquet, the Walton

---

[60] William Conrad, "Conrad Chronicles Boone County Fair," Recorder Newspapers, 1995 County Fair Guide, 20, 22, 24.
[61] Conrad, *Loder 2*. 154.

[62] Conrad, *Yesterdays*, 55, 64.

Chapter 6 1861-1869 Civil War – Balancing on the Line

train began running the 18-mile route July 10, leaving the city at 4 p.m. and arriving at 9:30 p.m. Walton's hotel business increased and new businesses began. On Aug. 9, a coal-burning locomotive began pulling the night express' elegant sleeping cars. The Aug. 10 run from Louisville to Covington set a record for transferring 27 passengers in four hours and 10 minutes.

At the end of the Civil War, the south desperately needed goods from Cincinnati and the north to help repair damages. Commercial trade was stopping at Louisville or held up by steamboats laboring upstream. Cincinnati too needed railroads, but couldn't bear the expense. Lawyers devised a plan for the city to issue bonds to pay for the tracks and $10 million worth of bonds were sold.

Construction began in 1873 and finished in 1880, $8 million over budget. Interest alone was $1.25 million annually. Cincinnatians even turned off street lights on moonlit nights to save money for the railroad. Cincinnati Southern followed Dixie Highway so closely that people couldn't tell which was the muddy, dusty road and which was the railroad during construction.[63]

Cincinnati was the only municipality in the United States that owned a railroad. The Cincinnati, New Orleans & Texas Pacific line started here and went to New Orleans. (The CNO&TP abbreviation was painted on all the box cars.) It was the original and major component of what was known as the Southern Railroad.[64]

---

[63] Conrad, *Yesterdays*, 113-114.
[64] Martha Daugherty

Chapter 7
1870-1889 Boone Communities Grow

After the Civil War ended, men returned to their farms and communities and Boone County grew in the classic after-the-war boom economy. It took years to replace the 60,000 horses and innumerable cattle that had been killed and stolen from the Commonwealth.

General stores became the heart of each community. Most sold dry goods (bolts of fabric), groceries, hats, caps, boots, shoes, queensware (ceramic dishes), tinware (pie pans, cookie sheets, etc.), hardware, lumber, shingles, salt and coal.

In addition to meeting residents' basic needs, the general store's proprietor was often the postmaster. Mail came regularly by steamboat, horseback or rail. Transportation options were increasing with the new rail lines through Walton. Steamboats still stopped at Petersburg and other Boone County riverfront communities.

While a few African-Americans remained on Boone County farms, most newly freed slaves had moved to the cities. Boone's African-American population went from nearly 1,800 in 1860 to just over 1,000 in 1870. Covington's population jumped to 29,720 and Newport's to 20,433.

Boone was still the smallest of the three northern counties with an 1883 population of 11,900. Kenton County's population was nearly 44,000 and 37,440 resided in Campbell. By 1890, Boone would reach a record 12,246.[1]

Tollroads

A more efficient network of better-surfaced roads was making getting from one community to the next easier. Buggies and carriages were now common. Although people had once accepted the practice of paying for road use by the trip rather than paying taxes for roads, that attitude was changing. Travelers were tired of waiting for the gates to be lifted.[2]

Turnpike construction was frequently delayed, adding to the frustration. The Burlington and Belleview Turnpike (now KY 18 East) was chartered on Feb. 3, 1851, but construction didn't begin for 26 years. Work began in March 1877 and by October a tollgate had been constructed – even though the road was not completed.

Most tollroads were not profitable. It's likely that owners lived out of whatever amount of receipts exceeded expenses. Not everyone paid state assessments exactly or appropriately. From

The front porch of this general store advertised Oliver Plows and hosted the usual crowd.
Courtesy of Boone County Historical Preservation

---
[1] U.S. Census figures
[2] Tanner, 22.

1883 to 1885, the Burlington-Belleview turnpike paid the state only $16.50.

Avoiding tolls became common. Joining funeral processions to escape paying became so common that a state law was passed on Feb. 1, 1872, to exempt only the hearse and five carriages from paying tolls on Dixie Highway.

Others exempted in an 1820 state act regarding the Covington and Lexington Turnpike included *"public express, post riders, children under 10, persons on foot, persons going to and from divine services, to and from muster, and witnesses and jurors going to and from court."*

In 1860 this act had been added, *"All persons passing over the turnpike roads in this state to or from church or public worship on Sunday and in attending funerals are hereby exempted from the payment of tolls."*

A special act pertaining to the Petersburg and Burlington Turnpike read: *"That hereafter all persons going to or returning from funerals, school, mill or church and persons passing to and from different portions of the farm occupied by them, shall be exempt from the payment of tolls at any and all said gates; Provided, however, that the said exemption shall apply only to persons attending church on the Sabbath day, to persons going to and returning from mill on horseback, and to school children and their necessary escort or driver."*[3]

The exemption for traveling to or from the mill on horseback assumed that a rider on a single horse would only be carrying enough

An early Boone County tollgate.
Courtesy of Boone County Historic Preservation.

grain for his family's use. Those transporting wagonloads of grain to market were charged.

Exemptions for schoolchildren were so abused that on April 22, 1880, an act required full toll payment if anyone other than a student and a driver were in the vehicle.

Because much traffic had been avoiding one of their tollgates, the company owning the northwestern Boone County road between Burlington and Petersburg (part of KY 338) appealed to the state and was allowed to erect another gate. Their proclamation allowing the additional pole read:

"Whereas, nearly the whole of the Petersburg and Burlington Turnpike Road lies between the two gates now on said road, one of which is nearly adjoining the town of Petersburg, and the other about one quarter of a mile from the town of Burlington, leaving about ten miles of said road between said gates;

"and whereas, a large trade and business is done by the people of the northern portion of Boone County over said road and between said gates, with the City of Lawrenceburg, Ind.,

"and whereas there is a very large intermediate travel upon said road between said gates, and upon portions thereof most

---

[3] Tanner, 16.

expensive to keep in repair, from which travel no tolls are received;

"and whereas, said road runs over a hilly and rough country, and crosses large ridges through nearly its whole route, making repairs very heavy and burdensome, by reason whereof the tolls now received at said gates are insufficient to keep said road in good repair."[4]

The gate was added.

Constance

Tollgates were everywhere. To get from Florence to Ohio through Constance on the Anderson Ferry meant two tollgate stops.[5]

The busy ferry brought some notoriety to Constance. On May 23, 1876, a mob took Smith Williams from the jail and hung him. The Negro was accused of killing a Dutchman near the Anderson Ferry the previous July.[6]

Not a large town, Constance's population was 135 in 1880. Its northern riverfront neighbor, Stringtown, had 42 residents. The Taylorsport magisterial district, which also encompassed North Bend riverbottom farmland and the Hebron community several miles inland, included 1,635.

Constance resident James H. Walton represented Boone County in the Kentucky legislature from 1881 to 1888.

W.B. and W.S. Walton, who lived just south of Constance and four miles north of Florence imported the Norman horses "Albatross" and "Nimrod" from France. The large saddle horses had been used as war and cavalry horses and were also raced. They may have demonstrated their abilities on the trotting track northeast of Elijah Creek and the Constance-Burlington Road.

The 1880 Constance population included three retail grocers, one retail merchant, one stonemason, one wagon maker, one gardener, one painter, three shoemakers, one stock trader, one roller mill worker, four steam engineers, nine seamstresses and one washerwoman.

In 1880, homes lined the Mitchellsville-Dry Creek Turnpike from Hebron to Constance. A solid string of houses began at the Boone-Kenton County line on what is now KY 8 nearly to Parlor Grove Park and the schoolhouse east of Taylorsport.

In a weather oddity for Constance, L.A. Loder noted in his diary that on June 21, 1875, two white men and one Negro were struck by lightning at North Bend. Adams, one of the white men, was quite badly hurt, but all survived.[7]

Orchards

Several other families joined the McGlassons in starting orchards along the North Bend riverbottoms, but fickle weather made locals skeptical of fruit growers' profit potential.

As happened with some frequency, on March 6, 1879, the *Recorder* reported frost damage to the local fruit crop: *"Several orchards checked, nearly all peaches, cherries*

Boone County Recorder
Vol. 1, No. 1, Sept. 23, 1875

Public Sales

On the 15th inst. the personal estate of Jeremiah Smith, deceased, was sold by the administrators at public sale. The crowd was very large, the bidding rapid, articles bringing near their full value. Old red wheat brought from $1.80 to $1.40 per bushel, and old white wheat from $1.51 to $1.55 per bushel. Hogs sold for about seven cents per pound, horses from $130 to $160 per head, sheep $5.25 per head and corn in the field brought $20 per acre. The sale was made on a six month credit.

The crowd, on the 16th inst., at the sale of the personal estate of Geo. Goodridge, deceased, was small, but the spirited bidding showed that a majority of those present desired being purchasers, instead of spectators. The buyers were given till the first of next January to pay for the articles they purchased. Lard sold for 14 cents per pound; side meat, 10 ¼ cents; shoulders, 9 cents; hams, 15 cents; new hay $12.50 to $15 per ton; old hay $12 per ton, hogs 7 cents (per pound); calves $15 per head; milch (milk) cows from $22 to 37; horses from $57 to $65; road wagon $91.

---

[4] Tanner, 12.
[5] Tanner, BC-5.
[6] Conrad, *Loder 3*, 94.

[7] Conrad, *Loder 3*, 83.

Chapter 7 1870-1889 Boone Communities Grow

German immigrant G. Henry Stevens built this house in 1870 between Bullittsburg and Petersburg. He had three sons and two daughters. One son was responsible for each animal species – cattle, sheep and hogs. Those animal barns were visible from the upstairs bedroom they shared. Their grandsons, James and Gaines Stevens, still reside in the area. The house is now First Farm Inn, a bed and breakfast operated by Jennifer Warner and Dana Kisor. Courtesy of Jennifer Warner.

killed and tenderer and small fruits. Farmers preparing to plant unusual amount of tobacco and potatoes."

Short-season crops like potatoes offered their challenges as well. L.A. Loder wrote in his diary on May 17, 1871, *"This summer the potato bug made its appearance."*

Farmers were also disappointed on May 29, 1859. Loder recorded: *"Peach trees all in bloom – frost."* But some years, fruits excelled in Boone County.

On April 3, 1879, the *Recorder* said: *"Taylor Red apples make superior cider, fine flavor and good keeper. It was brought to this county by John Taylor, an early Baptist minister, from Pennsylvania."*

On Feb. 3, 1886, the paper said, *"The Ben Davis apple is a native of Owen Co., Ky., and was developed by Ben K. Davis who lives on the Sparta Road in Owen Co."*

Baptist Churches Expand

South of the North Bend orchards, the 49-year-old Bullittsburg Baptist Church had been remodeled in 1858. The $1,594 renovation nearly matched the original construction cost. In 1873, Bullittsburg parishioners added a unique key-hole shaped baptismal font beside the church. The rock-lined pool is fed by a spring. (It was last used in the mid-1990s.)

In 1878, on the other side of the church, a burial vault was built into a hillside. The cave-like stone structure stored bodies awaiting burial.

Fifty-five Bullittsburg Church members had begun Sand Run Baptist in 1819 to reduce the distance parishioners must travel to attend services. After the Civil War, Sand Run Baptists paid $1,200 to expand and remodel the church. Prompted by a need for more burial ground, the church bought an additional six acres for $200.[8]

Owen Kirtley organized the first Sunday School in April 1873 under the direction of

---

[8] Vivian Blaker, Sand Run Baptist Church 1819-1994.

superintendent Jonathan Graves.[9]

About that time, Brother Robert E. Kirtley (the younger) was first paid for his services as pastor. He earned $100 a year.

In 1877, Sara Scothorn became the first woman on the church finance committee. In October 1887, the first carry-in basket dinner was recorded. Later that year, the church adopted the envelope system to submit monthly donations.

Bullittsville Christians

Lexington Elder W.S. Keene organized Bullittsville Christian Church in 1879 after a "protracted meeting" at the Baptist Church in Francesville. After the first week, the meeting moved to Grange Hall at Bullittsville, a few miles south of Bullittsburg.

Forty-three converts joined the 19 original members. They contributed $1,205 to start a new building, which was completed the next year. (Lightning destroyed the building in 1910, but it was rebuilt on the same site.)[10]

Hebron Grows

The Hebron Lutheran Church remained the undisputed center of the community that had taken its name. With 96 residents in 1880, Hebron was the second largest community in the Taylorsport magisterial district.

Magistrate A.B. Whitlock was a farmer, as was B.B. Rouse who bred poultry. G.M. Riley campaigned on the Democratic ticket for county assessor. The election was held the first Monday in August 1883.

Hebron's strong community framework supplied the basics and more to those who lived in the area. John Kahn made boots and shoes. Along what is now KY 20, between 237 and Limaburg Road, the Hebron saw and grist mill provided flour and lumber.

Robert Bradford guaranteed satisfaction with the harnesses and saddles he made at the intersection next door to A. Clore's general store.

Across the road (where the Flick's grocery is today), stood M. Clore's drug store. J.A. Davis' stable was on the southeast corner, up from the Lutheran Church and cemetery.

Many new products were becoming available, taking people away from their traditional agricultural livelihoods. W.H. Clayton had a new kind of career, in sales. He traveled Boone County selling sewing machines.

"Have you examined the new No. 7 American Sewing Machine with self-threading shuttle and self-threading needle? The many valuable improvements embodied in this machine are so positive that it cannot fail to please you," Clayton claimed. *"Repairing promptly done,"* he added.[11]

John Beall (or Brall), an agent for George Huresehart & Co. in Lawrenceburg, sold tombstones and monuments.

James A. Davis likely bought a tombstone on Feb. 16, 1880, after his wife, Atheleen Davis, shot herself through the heart with a pistol. She joined a primarily male group of those who chose suicide using guns, knives, poison or jumping in the river.

Hebron's resident doctor, L.B. Terrill, of the Petersburg family of physicians and surgeons, had many unusual cases to attend.

In 1874, in an attempt to save the life of a Hebron man who had a cancer on his hand, a trio of father and sons, Doctors W.H., L.B. and J.E. Terrill, came to a farm near Hebron and cut off one of Bill Henthorn's arms.[12]

Petersburg's Terrill family was among the first to use the telephone. But L.B. was forced to wait. Ten years after the telephone was invented, a line was planned from Covington to Constance, then along what is now U.S. 20 through Hebron to Petersburg. Another line was to run from Hebron to Burlington. But the route was moved to the Ohio side, so neither Hebron nor Constance had telephone service until after 1900.[13]

---

[9] *Boone County Recorder*, 1930 Historical Edition.
[10] *175th Anniversary Historical Book*, 12.
[11] Griffing, 13.
[12] Conrad, *Loder 3*, 82.
[13] Conrad, *Historical Tour*, 12-13.

Chapter 7 1870-1889 Boone Communities Grow

Charcoal Sales

The Hebron column of the March 6, 1879, *Boone County Recorder* explained that the dense hardwood forests, which covered the county just a few decades before, had been turned into charcoal.

It was a wood and labor intensive process. Two to two-and-a-half cords of wood were burned to make 100 bushels of charcoal. Woodcutters earned $10 per 100 bushels. Boone Countians sold between 800 and 1,000 bushels of charcoal in Cincinnati each month.[14]

Passing many fields now denuded of their forests, a stage from Covington delivered mail three times a week to Hebron and Bullittsville.

Downtown Petersburg. Courtesy of Boone County Historic Preservation

Gainesville

Midway between Hebron and Petersburg on what is now KY 20 is Gainesville or Idlewild. In the 1880s, in partnership with Charles Schramm, Petersburg grocer Frank Grant sold dry goods and groceries there.

A.S. Gaines, one of many Gaines family members who lived in the Bullittsville/ Gainesville area, traveled the county dealing in all kinds and grades of livestock.

Petersburg Reaches 400

Just west of Gainesville and Bullittsville, Petersburg bustled with 400 residents in 1870 and 441[15] a decade later. (In 1874, another census estimated 600 living in Petersburg.) Average land value was $24.68 an acre, an increase of $10.29 in the last 23 years.

Steamboats brought mail twice a day. Just south of town along the river, Boone County Distilling Company made whiskey. (Longtime mill owner William Snyder had sold out to Freiberg & Workum.)

Kentucky's whiskey production nearly tripled between 1871 and 1880. By 1882, the 1880 number had doubled again, to more than 30 million gallons.

A tannery operated on Petersburg's outskirts. (The stone building has been converted into a home.) Its tanning pit is now a slight dip in the road leading out of Petersburg.[16]

Near Petersburg, G.W. Terrill built the Lawrenceburg Ferry, a horse-operated boat. On May 23, 1872, S.S. McWethy badly mashed his hand trying to start it.

A new bell was delivered from Cincinnati for Petersburg's Christian Church on Feb. 23, 1880. The old bell weighed 130 pounds.[17]

> **Boone County Recorder**
> Vol. 1, No. 1, Sept. 23, 1875
> **Petersburg**
>
> One night last week some miscreant entered the culinary departments of our friend Frank Grant's house, and supplied themselves with a quantity of the good things with which his cupboard abounds. Mr. Grant knew nothing of the marauder's intrusion until he rose in the morning, by which time the thief had made a successful exit.
>
> George W. Terrill was badly hurt last week by being thrown from his horse. He had just returned from meeting, when his horse took fright and ran under the clothesline, dragging him off and throwing him on his head and shoulder. He was badly injured by the fall, but is now improving.

---

[14] Conrad, An Educational and Historical Tour, 30.
[15] Griffing, 4.
[16] *Boone County Recorder*, "History of Petersburg Community," Sept. 21, 1978.
[17] Conrad, *Loder 4*, 15.

Thirteen preachers came to Petersburg for a Methodist District Conference on April 24, 1876. In 1880, the Methodist Church's Burlington circuit (which include a huge region encompassing more than Boone County) asked its members to refrain from using tobacco.[18] The church history doesn't mention how the congregation responded. Methodist circuit rider D.E. Bedinger was a Princeton graduate and a Boone County native.

On May 8, 1874, farmer and livestock dealer J.C. Jenkins moved the graves of his entire family from his private graveyard to the public one below Petersburg.[19] Jenkins bred Shorthorn and Jersey cattle, trotting horses, Cotswold sheep and Chester White hogs at his Prospect Farm on the hill overlooking Petersburg.

The Loder House, a large frame building with a veranda overlooking the Ohio River, had opened as a rooming house in the mid 1800s and offered lodging for nearly a century. (Under renovation in 1998, owners Dale and Alice Book aspire to renovate it into a modern bed and breakfast.)

Chapin's Memories

Petersburg native Edward Young Chapin nostalgically remembered the town of his youth. (He owned the Loder House for a time, making it into apartments.) He wrote his reminiscences of the 1870s and '80s for the 1930 *Boone County Recorder* Historical Edition.

"*The Boone County I knew in the late '70s and the early '80s was a land of bucolic plenty*

People explore ice on the Ohio River.
Photo courtesy of Dorothy Richie

of stalwart men reaping the harvest from fat acres, of charming women creating homes redolent of domestic joy.

"*We villagers looked at this little enviously. We ground the grain and set it for fermenting; and gathered a vapor from it that Bishop Cannon would not praise; but had its attraction for the outer world. And we carried on the modest commerce that exchanged the products of the farm for the output of the loom, the factory and the foundry.*

"*This latter occupation was carried on in stores where trade never pressed, where there was abundant leisure for the exchange of gossip along with the exchange of commodities; where issues, local or national, found time for debate. These stores were the gathering places for our philosophers; and of audiences who hung upon their words.*

"*We had keen appetites for news. A favored few would read the* Enquirer *after the 'Water Witch' had brought it down on her first trip from Lawrenceburg. True, there were other papers published in Cincinnati in those days – the* Commercial *and the* Gazette*, but those were radical sheets, and found no readers in Petersburg – barring perhaps a government officer or two. But they were foreigners and did not count. We would not believe the news in the* **Commercial** *or* **Gazette** *even if we had read it.*

"*The two churches were our principal gathering places. Each had its preaching once – sometimes twice – a month, with services conducted without a minister between. But if there was a secular gathering in the meantime, it was held at a church. Itinerant lecturers were heard there.*

---

[18] Ivalou H. Walton, Historical Study Burlington Methodist Church, May 1975, 11.
[19] Conrad, *Loder 3*, 70.

Chapter 7   1870-1889   Boone Communities Grow

"I remember one, with picturesque locks and fervid rhetoric, who spoke on the Battle of Gettysburg one night, temperance the next and was never able to speak after that, although he remained in town a day or two longer, because our local sons of Belial got him drunk and kept him so.

"Don't imagine from this that we were a 'wet' community or that drunkenness was not frowned upon. Petersburg was among the first towns in the state to take advantage of the "local option" law, despite our distillery, and our local lodge of Sons of Temperance was a virile body whose memory I revere.

"Communication with the outside world was by boat – largely by our own little steamer that ran to Lawrenceburg and Aurora. There was no telephone and radio then, but we were alert to what was going on. And we reacted to it as sensitively as you would react today.

"We had our concerts and our amateur theatricals. I remember when 'The Lady of Lyons' was given at the Methodist Church on a stage supported by whiskey barrels. And we had our singing schools when a teacher from the outside world would enliven the winter, closing, in a blaze of glory, with a concert in the spring.

"Our farmer friends – they were our aristocracy – produced blooded stock as well as grain. They were formidable contenders at the fall fairs in Northern Kentucky and southern Indiana. These were among the notable occasions of the year. My heart quickens now as I think of our own John Moody taking a 15 minute recess from his duties as ringmaster at the Aurora fair to appear in the Gentleman's riding contest with a stern rigidity of deportment that overshadowed competition.

"It was a wonderful life, lived in an environment where rugged hills and a graceful curving river inspired delight that was enhanced by a soil so generous in its yield that our fields and gardens had to smile in spite of themselves. And the people who lived on it were worthy of their inheritance."

Water and Ice

Chapin's rosy memories omitted the rigors of life in those days, including coping with the Ohio River's fluctuations. Loder, in his continuing documentary, remained focused on the weather and its implications for the community and commerce.

On a rainy Feb. 26, 1870, when the Ohio was busy with towboats, pieces of newly-sawn lumber floated down the river. Enterprising Petersburg residents caught more than 100.

A few months later – like several residents did each year, old Jack Howard jumped into the river and drowned. This poetic suicide note was found in his hat: *"Gentle River, where art thou flowing or going. I will take a ride upon thy gentle bosom and baptize myself, and leave this world of pain and theft and self; and bid farewell to all I leave behind."*[20]

Low water the spring of '71 left the sand bar in the river opposite Petersburg out of the water, *"a circumstance that never has been for 100 years,"* Loder recorded.

On Christmas morning 1872, although the river had risen 3-4' during the night, the Petersburg Methodist Church had its first Christmas tree. The next year both churches had Christmas trees.

Dams Proposed

The river also brought useful, if unusual, items. A floating saw mill landed at Petersburg on May 23, 1873. A week later, it was towed to Aurora.[21]

An 1875 survey resulted in a proposal to maintain a year-round 6' depth along the entire 981-mile Ohio River. Although construction began on a series of moveable dams, rock blasting and dredging, many river people believed "the Ohio would come back for what she left behind" in previous floods – regardless of man's efforts.[22]

On Sept. 22, 1876, the river set a record – *"higher than it was ever known this time of year"* – for the fall season.

---

[20] Conrad, *Loder 3*, 30.
[21] Conrad, *Loder 3*.
[22] Don Clare, *Ancestry-Our Ohio River Heritage*, 1996, 48-49.

The Steamer Golden Rule on the Ohio River.   Photo contributed by Virginia Bennett

Icy River 1876-1877

On Dec. 18, 1876, breaking ice that had closed the river several times during the week, the steamer Minnie made two trips from Petersburg ferrying whiskey over and bringing malt and rye back from Lawrenceburg. The next day, it took the boat two hours to get through the ice, which extended above the cat hole. Minnie didn't get back that night. But with temperatures climbing to 32 on the 20th, the Minnie continued. Four or five horse teams hauled whiskey to fill the boat.

Temperatures rose to 40 on the 22nd. *"Minnie come down through the gorge to the Mill landing but had a pritty hard time of it."* On Dec. 23, *"Minnie made one trip to L'burg with a lot of cattle and come back as far as the mouth of Tanner Creek. They commenced running and filled up where she went along. She had to return back and get to shore above the gorge on the Kentucky shore."*

Despite dropping temperatures, nearly constantly breaking ice and spitting snow, the Minnie continued ferrying whiskey, supplies and cattle across the river. On the 28th, mill teams hauled whiskey halfway to Lawrenceburg on the ice, then the Minnie took it across. On the 31st, the Minnie received three loads of coal to help it get out of the gorge, but the effort was to no avail. Workers hauled whiskey on hand sleds over the ice from Hartman's place to the other side.

The Huddleston family with four children crossed the ice in a spring wagon. Several Petersburg men went with them.

Two more inches of snow had fallen. Four more mill teams now were pulling sleds, hauling rye from Lawrenceburg on the ice. Four mules with sleds hauled whiskey to Lawrenceburg. Each sled held six barrels. One mule fell through the ice and drowned. By Jan. 9, the mules were dragging hay from Aurora to their barn despite temperatures of 22 degrees below zero and several inches of new snow.

On the 13th, the *"gorge (a rush of water created by a dam of breaking ice) ran 45 minutes then stopped."* Sunday it started three times then stopped until noon the next day. *"It then let loose again and the ice was (thrown) from shore to shore. Over 100 barges (that had been stuck in the ice) passed down in the ice. Eight or ten of them were loaded. Some had an end stoved in, some had sides mashed in."*

On Jan. 15, the steamer Minnie got back to Petersburg after spending 23 days at the Hartman Landing. The oldest rivermen said this winter's ice on the Ohio from Pittsburgh to Louisville had destroyed more boats than they had ever seen. A few days later, the Minnie left to get new rudders. On Jan. 18, the steamer Golden Rule was the first boat to go upriver since the ice was broken.[23]

The next several winters were milder. Steamer traffic was still busy. William H. Kirby & Co. bought the steamer Virgie Lee for $17,000 on Oct. 25, 1877, planning to run it from Cincinnati to Madison, Ind.

In January 1879, while hauling whiskey, coal and rye over the ice the second week of the year, horses fell through frequently, but were usually hauled back to safety and survived.

Through rain, snow and sleet, the Minnie continued to force its way through the ice back and forth from Petersburg to Lawrenceburg.

The traditional river route continued to be a major conduit to commerce, even after rail lines were laid. On March 16, 1879, Irwin Balsley shipped walnut logs from the Petersburg landing. Others sold more walnut trees. On March 26, 1880, the river peaked at 59' 2". It was a milder flood than other years.[24]

River Gives and Takes

River levels and ice thickness controlled whether or not the mailboat made its scheduled twice daily stops.

Steamboat stops determined if and when freight arrived to keep the Petersburg distillery working, farm animals could be shipped to Cincinnati sales, and travelers started on or returned from their journeys.

Drowning accidents were common. Evidently the ability to swim wasn't particularly valued. When skiffs sank, even near the shore, most passengers drowned.

Accidents and suicides upriver often brought unknown bodies to the surface, caught in tangles along Boone County's riverbanks. Bodies were searched for identification and the

Anderson's ferry boat embedded in the ice.   Photo courtesy of Virginia Bennett

justice of the peace held an inquest. If no information was discovered, money and valuables were turned over to the county government.

Two men drowned trying to cross at the Lawrenceburg ferry in a skiff on a snowy March 20, 1881.

A week later Henry Parker's body washed up on the Petersburg landing. In his capacity as Justice of the Peace, Loder held an inquest about the drowning. Parker was wearing a silver double-case watch with a gold chain, two finger rings, one "shall" pin and in his pockets had $125 in gold, $8 in greenbacks and $1.22 in silver as well as a pen knife with a white handle and a silver-mounted cartridge pistol.[25]

Nearly a month later Wash Parker's body was found near Col. William Applegate's landing. He was carrying $100 in gold, one $2 bill, and $3.52 cents in silver.

---

[23] Conrad, *Loder 3*, 99.
[24] Conrad, *Loder 3*.

[25] Conrad, *Loder 5*, 30.

Loder only noted one instance of anyone swimming: On May 16, 1881, when the air temperature was 58, he wrote: "*Capt. Paul Boyton past down swimming with his armory on at half-past 11 o'clock a.m. Several boys went out in a skiff and talked to him. He told them he was going to Evansville.*" Temperatures reached 60 that week, but it frosted two days later.[26]

The next month brought another curiosity. Sky watchers marveled at a comet visible in the northwestern sky for more than a week.

Ice in the river on Feb. 7, 1883, broke the Freiberg & Workum coal barge loose from its moorings. The new Petersburg distillery owners' barge floated down to Lochry Island and sank. The next day the river rose 3" an hour as the ice melted. The next several days the steamers ran, but the trains stopped.

On the 11th, the Cincinnati water level was 59' 6". "*The people of Petersburg took up a lot of provisions for the sufferers of Lawrenceburg yesterday and a lot today,*" Loder recorded. On Feb. 15, 1883, the Ohio River crested at 66' 4".[27]

Telephone Service

The river, through the newspapers and people it brought, carried the news until 1876 when Alexander Graham Bell invented the telephone. But the odd gadgets were often viewed as an amusement or plaything rather than something useful.

Early telephone service was one line connecting two places. A year later the switchboard was invented so lines could be interconnected. The man operating the exchange worked a treadle, similar to an old-fashioned sewing machine, to produce the electrical energy to ring the call bells.

Operators memorized subscribers' names. Phone users had to hold down a button throughout their conversation to maintain the connection. If a finger slipped, the line disconnected.[28]

Lines crossed the suspension bridge from Ohio in 1879. Merchant J. Frank Grant ran a line from his store to his Petersburg home on Jan. 24, 1880. The next week he added a line to the doctor's house. The next day, Dr. Ed Terrill put a line in from his office to his home.[29]

A contract signed May 1, 1882, with Bell Telephone Company of Boston authorized the Cincinnati City and Suburban Telegraph Association and Telephonic Exchange to offer "communication devices" in a circle 25 miles from Cincinnati. (Parts of that contract are still in effect – allowing toll-free calling across state lines in the region.)

Ed Chapin and Charley Grant installed a telegraph wire between their Petersburg area houses on April 14, 1883. In September 1885, men ran a line from the Petersburg Distilling Company Office to the Lawrenceburg Ferry and from there across the river to Lawrenceburg.

The next September, Robert Hazelton ran a wire from the mill office to the government office at Boone County Distilling.[30]

Distillery workers took down telephone poles for the Petersburg to Lawrenceburg line on the Kentucky side in April 1889. On Jan. 17, 1891, two men put up new telephone lines from Gaines & Berkshire's store to William L. Gaines' residence.

Riverboat News

On Valentine's Day 1884, a parade of houses and lumber floated down the river.[31] After cresting at 71' ¾", the river began falling. Ten days later, the hull of the steamer Wave was found opposite Petersburg. "*Today they took out her engine and some other parts of her and hauled the machinery and put them in a wood shed in Petersburg,*" Loder wrote on Feb. 25, 1884.

Riverboat news was Petersburg news: On

---

[26] William Conrad, editor, *The Loder Diary, Part 5, Jan. 1, 1885-Dec. 31, 1892,* Boone County Schools, Florence, Ky., 1988, 106.
[27] Conrad, *Loder 5,* 51.
[28] 90th Anniversary, The Cincinnati and Suburban Bell Telephone Company 1873-1963, 9-11.
[29] Conrad, *Loder 4,* 14.
[30] Conrad, *Loder 5,* 92.
[31] William Conrad, editor, *The Loder Diary, Part 4, Jan. 1, 1879-Dec. 31, 1884,* Boone County Schools, Florence, Ky., 1988, 63.

Chapter 7 1870-1889 Boone Communities Grow

May 12, 1869, six steamboats burned in Cincinnati. Elihu Alden bought a half interest in the steamer Western Wave for $250. Captain Ray Blaum was discharged from the steamer Minnie and Bass Fenton took his place. In July 1884, the steamer Ben Franklin left for Madison, Ind., where it was to become a wharfboat.[32]

With the river rising in August, Captain B.B. Bradley's Charles L. Grant partially capsized at Lochry Island. The steamer Minnie went down to bail water and help get it ready to run.[33] When the boat was up and running, the Captain installed a mocking bird whistle which uniquely announced his arrival.

All kinds of news surrounded the river. On a 30 degree Jan. 5, 1886, Loder recorded, "*A man by the name of John A. Gibson tied his hands together with a lady's hands and jumped off the suspension bridge and was drowned.*" (The couple was probably from Cincinnati rather than Boone County.)

On Sept. 1, 1886, the river took a backseat to an earthquake that shook the region between 9 and 10 p.m.

General Stores

People no longer had to rely on their own skills and ingenuity or itinerant peddlers to supply their wants and needs. It was easier to get to town and most communities now hosted their own general stores.

Petersburg had two. J.H. Snyder dealt in "*staple and fancy groceries, canned goods, fancy flour,*" and drugs from his store on the northeast corner of Farmer and First streets.

J. Frank Grant offered dry goods, groceries, notions, caps, hats, boots, shoes, coal, and lumber.

Frank had lived on his father's farm until 1870, when he bought the Petersburg store in partnership with his brother W. Ed Grant. Their father, Dr. E.L. Grant was also a physician. W. Ed later left for Louisville where he studied medicine and returned to practice.

J. Frank remained in Petersburg and was the leading layman at the Methodist Church. He loaned his large collection of books – including those written by the popular author Charles Dickens – to community residents. Active in politics, he once ran for Congress.

On May 12, 1881, Grant had "*80,000 or 90,000' of hemlock lumber drawed out of the river.*"[34]

In partnership with Charles Schramm, Grant sold dry goods and groceries up the road in Gainesville (also called the Idlewild area in northwestern Boone County).

Bank of Petersburg

A man named Lassing (likely Dr. Henry Clay Lassing of Union or his son John M. Lassing who later became circuit court judge) helped J. Frank Grant start the Bank of Petersburg in 1888. In March, the building got a new tin roof. On April 4, 1888, its safe arrived from Cincinnati aboard the steamer Minnie. By the next day the safe was in the vault and the bank was open.

Grant ran the bank until 1897, when he went to Baltimore to become the grand secretary and adjutant general of the Independent Order of Odd Fellows. (He died in Baltimore in 1904 and his remains were interred in the Petersburg Cemetery.)

The Petersburg bank closed on March 19, 1898. The building was used as a doctor's office, then reopened as a bank in 1903.

Out-of-Town Shopping

Exotic and new-fangled inventions could be purchased in Cincinnati or Covington, a short steamer ride from Petersburg or a train ride from Walton.

Bricks sold for $7 per 1,000 and coal was 14 cents a bushel. A daisy stove cost $11. Morocco-top boots cost $6 in 1884.[35] Loder paid $8 for "*fine sewed boots made by Jacob Goenawein of Aurora*" in 1885. While shoes

---

[32] Conrad, *Loder 4*, 69.
[33] Conrad, *Loder 4*, 69.
[34] Conrad, *Loder 4*, 30.
[35] Conrad, *Loder 4*, 73.

were available from the local stores, the next year he bought some "low shoes" for 90 cents from O.N. Cobb & Co.

Loder bought a new gadget called a thermometer in Cincinnati in May 1873. The next year, he bought a hotel license for a $50 fee plus $1.50 for the clerk. Two years later, he got a license to sell the tobacco and cigars displayed in the case he paid $2.50 for in Dillsboro, Ind.

Traveling merchants or "drummers" still stopped by Petersburg selling tombstones, window shades, patent medicines, Singer Sewing Machines, jeans, Smith's liniment, wafers to kill rats, toilet (perfumed) soap, lamps, hedge fences and more. The Loder family acquired a coal cook stove. In August 1889, Angelo J. Worth sent a box of dried apricots from California.

A boatload of coffins from Lawrenceburg was unloaded at Petersburg and hauled to Florence on May 25, 1876. In September, three men bought walnut logs from near the William Wingait farm.

A Dutchman named Bronson opened a barbershop on Petersburg's Front Street on Easter Sunday, 1879. Two men came through Petersburg in 1879 making bed springs. A glove cleaner came through town and disappeared without paying for his lodging.

J. Frank Grant started a store at Voshalls, near the Ashby Fork of Woolper Creek on Feb. 14, 1880. He didn't stock anything as fancy as the barrel of oranges Mrs. P. McNeely's sons sent her, via the mail boat, from Memphis in November.

In May 1882, J.J. Daughters sold encyclopedias in Petersburg.[36] A man named Simpson began doing tailor work for Grant's store in October 1882, but left within a month.

Modern Refinements
In May 1883, B.B. Bradley brought his boat from Rising Sun to have it fitted with carpets and furniture so he could sleep in it.

Peter Keim installed the first tin roof in Petersburg over his kitchen in March 1883.

James J. Loder sold his barber chair and stool to S. Bricken for $3.50 on Feb. 5, 1886, and went into the house-painting business. In June 1887, John M. Botts began removing the drug store's roof to add a second story.

A June 1887 strawberry festival at the distillery gathered money to build a sidewalk to the graveyard. The Petersburg community came together to repair the schoolhouse too. And, when the Christian Church wanted an organ for its Sunday School in 1889, it held a community supper to raise money.

Industrial Accidents
Mill accidents happened several times a year. Aboil Dean was hurt trying to start the flywheel at Petersburg.

> **Boone County Recorder**
> Vol. 1, No. 1, Sept. 23, 1875
>
> The country seems infested with tramps, and nearly every day they pass through our town. It would be well for people to take warning and look well to the fastenings on their doors.
>
> From the tone of the tax notice in this issue, we are almost persuaded to believe that our Sheriff's stock of indulgence is about exhausted and that he intends to replenish with a determination to make "fellers" shell out.
>
> The Zoological Garden, in Cincinnati, was opened on the 19th inst. This garden has an area of sixty-five acres and is located in the northern part of the city and adjoins Burnet Woods Park. It is destined to be one of the greatest resorts in the city, and while visits to this garden will be largely entertaining, they will be equally instructive.
>
> We learn that Mr. Ben Deering, the late newspaper emigrant from Boone, has met with the wall of typographical desistance at Cynthiana, Ky. Mr. Deering, as we are aware, took his exit from this county about three months ago. He located shortly afterward at Cynthiana, a flourishing town in Bourbon County. There he commenced publishing a tri-weekly paper, entitled the Sun; and *note* The Sun is defunct, and Mr. Deering is embarked in seeking "wider success."

---

[36] Conrad, *Loder 4*, 42.

Chapter 7 1870-1889 Boone Communities Grow 141

A few days after Christmas 1880, Jake Nipher lost two fingers when his hand was caught in a straw cutter at the distillery. A week later Dr. Terrill and Dr. Green from Lawrenceburg amputated his arm just above the elbow. He died the next day.

On March 27, 1882, Denis Holden got his left arm caught in wire with the mill stone. It tore his hand and arm nearly off. Doctors Will Terrill and Green came from Lawrenceburg to consult with Dr. Ed Terrill. They took Holden's arm off between the hand and elbow.[37]

The next week both of Andy Lenard's hands were badly mashed while he was fixing a pump at the mill.

A miller named Siementel caught his right hand in a mill on Oct. 7, 1884. It was so badly damaged it had to be taken off between the wrist and elbow.

Medical Report

Local doctors kept busy tending to illnesses and accidents away from the mill as well.

Doc Mussy took a tumor out of Mrs. Sally Parker at Mrs. Walton's house on Nov. 9, 1874.

Mark Gordon broke his arm "rasseling" with Harry Lyon. A young Fuller boy, eight or ten years old, was run over by a log wagon and killed on Aug. 26, 1875. Evan's oldest boy fell out of a mulberry tree and broke his arm in June 1883.

Although many, like the three-week-old Dill Snelling baby, died young, some, like wealthy Aurora industrialist James W. Gaff, lived to be as old as 91. Mark Whitaker died at 83. Also in 1879, Richard Parker died at 76. Mrs. Susan Foster died at 95. Paschal Rucker died in April 1888 at the age of 97.

Blind James Bradley went to Cincinnati to have his eyes operated on and stayed for four weeks.[38] On May 25, 1880, an optician named Smith spent three days in Petersburg.

A pistol Frank Cox was looking at in an Aurora gun shop went off, shooting him in the hand.

Doc Tanner went on a 40 day fast in the summer of 1880. His weight started at 157½ pounds and dropped to 122. He ate a peach first, then a watermelon, then drank some $24 a gallon Hungarian wine.[39]

Petersburg residents crossed the river for dental care "*to have teeth plugged.*"

Dr Ed Terrill took Sam Hensley's son to Anchorage to the asylum on July 21, 1882.

Petersburg paid Doctors J.E. and W.H. Terrill $50 "*to do the pauper practice*" in 1882. The senior Terrill, W.H., later moved to Louisiana. In 1884, the Ed Terrill family began moving to Florida for the winter.

In August 1885, Doctors J.D. Terrill, J.E. Duncan and W.H. Dunn operated on Mrs. McWethy's leg, cutting it open and removing a piece of the bone. A few days later all three Dr. Terrills – J.E., W.M. and J.D. – removed a hen's-egg-sized tumor from Mrs. D.C. Alcorn's breast.

That night Dr. J.E. Terrill moved into a new house. He died between 6 and 7 p.m. His funeral, held two days later, was well attended.[40]

Evidently without the doctors' assistance, Ed Walden's wife had triplets on Aug. 11, 1886. All were girls.

In March 1888, Ralph C. Tilley left Petersburg for Louisville to attend Medical College.[41]

Veterinary Medicine

Animals were now getting more sophisticated medical attention as well. While Boone Countians were aware of an "epizootic" disease that was killing Cincinnati horses, they were mystified to find more than a dozen dead cows around Petersburg on July 23, 1873 (possibly caused by a mid-summer lightning strike or grazing on a poisonous weed.)

The Cincinnati horse disease increased the demand for oxen teams, which sold for $300 a pair. A few weeks later, a Covington man

---

[37] Conrad, *Loder 4*, 41.
[38] Conrad, *Loder 4*, 12.
[39] Conrad, *Loder 4*, 21.
[40] Conrad, *Loder 5*, 80.
[41] Conrad, *Loder 3*.

came by with cholera medicine to cure hogs, cattle and chickens.

Lock-jaw killed young, healthy horses owned by Solon Early and Ed Terrill in mid-August 1884.

While veterinary insights were making some inroads, the old cures passed down for generations still found their uses. On May 26, 1884, Loder chronicled: *"Our cow got into a clover lot and eat a good deal of green clover. We give about as much shot as would load a shot gun which relieved her in a few moments."*

Whiskey Voted Down

Elections were major news in Petersburg. And with Petersburg's mix of Christians and Methodists, minus the large Baptist population in the rest of the county, some elections turned out differently there.

A Sept. 2, 1880, Petersburg election counted 47 votes against the sale of whiskey licenses and 42 for. Voters also elected a Court of Appeals Judge, Circuit Judge, Commonwealth Attorney, Circuit Clerk, Sheriff, Constable, Police Judge and Town Marshall.

Election results in Petersburg on Feb. 5, 1886, were:

- Circuit judge: Geo. C. Drane 307, P.U. Major 459, Warren Monfort 866
- Commonwealth Attorney: John S. Gaunt 873, Thos R. Gorden 677
- Circuit Clerk: J.W. Duncan 114, W.L. Riddell 894
- County Judge: E.H. Baker 938, M.C. Norman 786
- School Superintendent: H.J. Foster 732, Ryle 788.

In the Aug. 1, 1887, Petersburg election, Solon Early was named sheriff and J.W. Duncan was selected clerk. John Carson and S.G. Botts were the new judges.

S.B. Buckner received 150 votes for governor while W.O. Bradley got 50. John S. Hoggins received 150 votes for representative and George W. Baker got 51.

The new sheriff had knocked Charles L. Grant down in a fight and Grant brought charges against him. When the case came before L.A. Loder, he found the sheriff guilty, but fined him one cent and costs.

Assaults and Theft

A sheriff was needed occasionally. And, as they are today, protection and prosecution weren't always fair. On May 22, 1873, Jim Jerral chased a Negro man and woman out of Petersburg. The next week an assault and battery case was brought before Judge J.N. Early on their behalf. Jerral was found guilty, but fined one cent and costs.[42]

Thieves cut a hole through the back door of Petersburg's Grant & Graves store on July 19, 1873, but were scared off, leaving their burgling tools behind.

Throughout the summer, vandals placed logs and debris on Burlington Pike causing travel hazards.

Bill Jenkins had pulled a pistol on Billy Stott in the drug store on a Saturday night, but didn't shoot. Sunday a week later he *"got into a mess at George Brindel's. Brindel hit him a lick with a piece of iron or something hard which killed him. He was struck about 8 o'clock and died the next morning about 3."* The next day, Brindel was brought before J.N. Early and L.A. Loder on murder charges. His bail was set at $1,000 to ensure he appeared in Burlington's Circuit Court.[43]

Frank Simpson was taken to court on May 25 for beating his stepchild. He was found guilty, fined $30 and imprisoned for 30 days by constable J.H. McWethy.

Two men broke into James Thomason's house and stole Mrs. Thomason's gold watch and chain and $9 or $10 in cash on June 19, 1879. In early August, some Aurora boys crossed the river and got caught stealing Aboil Dean's watermelons.

Bar fights involving two, three or sometimes more men occasionally ended in

---

[42] Conrad, *Loder 3*, 60.
[43] Conrad, *Loder 3*, 65

trips to the jail and court appearances. Just as often, participants walked away.

Burglars broke into the Loder House on Feb. 9, 1882, stealing four silver tablespoons, six teaspoons, a silver mug and a pair of gold spectacles. Total value of the goods was $40. Vandals also broke into Morgan Academy.

On Sept. 4, 1884, Loder noted, *"Some Negro stole 20 or 25 of William R. Green's chickens and took them to Lawrenceburg and sold them to Ebbs Brothers."*

In a description of what may have been a duel, Loder wrote on March 5, 1885: *"John W. Gaines killed William Corbin with a pistol. Gaines was hurt bad."*[44]

On May 19, 1885, S.G. Botts and Dr. Ed Terrill went to Aurora to buy marble posts for D. Rigg's wife's grave. Vandals removed that stone as well as a marble urn off G.R. Loder's grave, and a marble headstone off a Smith child's grave.

Several Petersburg residents were among the nine graduated from Lawrenceburg's high school on May 22, 1885. Petersburg did not yet have a high school so those who wanted more education crossed the river to get it.[45]

Moses Murdered

Itinerant peddler Felix Moses met an untimely end in March 1886, apparently victim of a robbery and murder on the steamer Fleetwood.

His body washed up on the riverbank in North's Landing, Ind., and was taken to Florence for burial. The newspaper reported, *"The deceased, being a trader in furs, etc., was extremely acquainted in this and adjoining counties and will be greatly missed. Mose (as he was called) was a Jew and was a member of Good Faith Lodge No. 95, F&AM."*

Some speculated that Moses may have been killed for a diamond he reportedly carried. He was buried in Cincinnati after a great deal of dissention between his Boone County friends and the Cincinnati Jewish community. A memorial service was held at Florence Christian Church. In 1901, the Cincinnati chapter of the Daughters of the Confederacy erected a monument at Cincinnati Walnut Hills Cemetery in his honor.[46]

The grave of Felix Moses in Cincinnati.
Photo by Virginia Lainhart

More Violence

In another violent scene, on Aug. 8, 1885, one of Peter Zimmerman's sons hit his father with a crowbar and nearly killed him.

On Jan. 1, 1886, Henry Reif got reprieved from the Indianapolis Penitentiary where he had been confined some 10 years.

Two men fought in Aurora in August 1886, one killing the other. "Justice" was nearly instantaneous: A mob formed and lynched the survivor.

The same day, *"Ralph Tilly followed a Negro woman, who had stolen some clothing from Mrs. Lemon, out the pike and got the clothing back."*[47]

The next week, L.A. Loder held an inquest over the body of a white female baby pulled from the river.

Pranksters became the focus of Petersburg conversation in July 1888 when they cut off the mane and tail of Mr. Passon's old brown mare. On May 11, 1889, the "horse barbers" visited both of Henry North's horses.

On Nov. 21, 1889, William Early was

---

[44] Conrad, *Loder 5*, 76.
[45] Conrad, *Loder 5*, 78.

[46] Reis, 14.
[47] Conrad, *Loder 5*, 91.

Members of the Witham, Christy and Hensley families gathered for a fall dinner outdoors. The woman labeled 1 is Mary Witham, 2 is Sally Ann Christy, and 3 is Clay Hensley's wife. Courtesy of Mary Rector

brought before the court for carrying a pistol. He was convicted, fined $25 and let out on bail until he could appear before the next term of the Circuit Court.

Fire Fighting

Fire was a bigger fear than crime, and more common. Lightning struck L.F. Jackson's stable on the river just below Petersburg on June 3, 1872. It burned to the ground. Several Petersburg residents installed lightning rods the next week.

The steamer Pat Rogers caught fire halfway between Aurora and Lochry Creek between 3 and 4 a.m. Aug. 4, 1874. Sixty-six lives were lost.

The winter of 1875 brought fires in the Piatt's stable on March 12, and five days later at Mrs. Martha C. Riddell's house. The roof nearly burned off the house before the fire was put out, but the stable was discovered early and not damaged much. In August 1876, Bradley & Wilder's planing mill burned.

In early May 1879, Alfred Rucker's house caught fire. A fire on the General Lytle burned three or four staterooms.

A faulty flue caused L.F. Jackson's house on the riverbank below Petersburg to burn down in late March 1880. That November, Willie and B.R. Gaines lost a fine horse when their barn burned down despite a hard rain that night.

The Boone County Distilling Co. caught fire on April 4, 1881. The end of May, J.C. Jenkin's hen house burned to the ground.

In April 1882, Petersburg residents watched a Lawrenceburg fire consume several houses, the dry goods store and McGranahan's grocery. In early September, an Aurora fire burned eight or 10 houses along the river.

On June 20, 1883, Petersburg man John Bolen received a $250 check for helping put out a ship's fire in New Orleans during the previous winter.

Another fire at the Petersburg distillery broke out in the early hours of April 5, 1884,

Chapter 7 1870-1889 Boone Communities Grow

and burned W.T. Snyder's house. The next day, Sunday, sightseers came to see the damage done to the former distillery owner's home.

While cooking breakfast on Aug. 4, 1885, Mrs. Chapin's cooking stove exploded, burning her and Lizzie Olds.

Boilers blew up frequently on steamboats. The boiler at Merit E. Leming's saw mill blew up on June 22, 1887, burning the mill and badly injuring Harry Graves.

An April 7, 1889, fire at Joseph J. Ferrise's stable killed 13 horses, three mules, five cows, one bull, three fine sheep, three buggies, a two-horse carriage, a sulky, a road cart, 600-800 bushels of corn and a lot of oats.

Fun and Games

Many forms of entertainment and diversions were available in the evenings after chores were done. Petersburg youth put on a play in the Methodist Church on Dec. 28, 1876. Children played marbles or ice-skated in the streets.

Organized baseball maintained its popularity, attracting good crowds. Town teams traveled up, down or across the Ohio on steamers to games.

If the church allowed, individuals hosted dancing parties in their homes. Three Negroes who worked for John D. Norris played for a dance in Polus McNeeley's home on Jan. 13, 1870. Norris dealt in and bred thoroughbred trotters at his Petersburg farm.

And performers arrived by riverboat. The great P.T. Barnum Show came to Aurora, attracting many from the region.

Several Petersburg residents had purchased pianos in the 1860s. Anora Loder took lessons from Laura Willis.[48] Three more pianos arrived in Petersburg on Feb. 22, 1880. They were delivered to J. Frank Grant, Graham, and Thomas Collier.

The Merriman Sisters, one of whom was blind, drew a large crowd playing piano at Petersburg's Methodist Church in May 1879.

Soon piano tuners were among the itinerant merchants stopping in Petersburg.

Community Festivities

Petersburg ladies' Grand Lodge of Temperance continued to regularly hold schoolhouse meetings, lawn parties and picnics. The Masons met and had picnics. They organized a new lodge in Petersburg on July 16, 1875, hosting a big supper. On July 30, the steamer Minnie took people to Parlor Grove for a Masonic picnic.

Sportsmen shot birds and animals for the dinner table and often sold the pelts. Elder Keen and Jimmy Lloyd killed 6½ dozen quail, nine rabbits and one fox squirrel on a January 1876 hunting trip. Canadian geese, which had been hunted almost to extinction in the east, were rare then. *"When B. B. Bradley shot a wild goose in the river it was quite a curiosity in Petersburg."*[49]

Prizefighters attracted the men. On March 19, the steamer Levi J. Workum anchored in the river between Petersburg and Tanners Creek to host two prize fights, one between whites, the other Negroes.

On June 20, 1877, the steamer Minnie took 120-140 people from the Petersburg Sunday School on a picnic to the Cincinnati Zoological Garden. The tugboat Antelope took another group to the Cincinnati theaters on Jan. 3, 1878.

The end of February 1889, a group of young men from Petersburg left for Georgetown to attend a regional gathering of the Young Mens Christian Association (Y.M.C.A.).

Stage Shows

In 1874, a chubby and aging Gen. Tom Thumb returned to Lawrenceburg where his appearances had been popular the previous decade. Professor Tucker brought his rabbit and bird show to Petersburg and other river communities in 1879.

Petersburg residents were still big travelers,

---

[48] Conrad, *Loder 3*, 48.

[49] Conrad, *Loder 4*, 16.

visiting places from Montana and California, to the ever-popular St. Louis by steamer. On one St. Louis trip, William Hayden sent James J. Loder a jack rabbit's ears.[50]

On a much bigger adventure, two men spent March 17, 1879, in Petersburg preparing to head to South America in their 42-foot boat.

Volintine Vox brought his caravan to the Petersburg schoolhouse on Dec. 30, 1874. A spotted pony pulled a buggy. Two matched sorrels were hitched to a covered spring wagon. Two men, a little boy and a spotted dog rounded out the show.[51]

Two Dutchmen performed in Petersburg on New Year's Eve 1882. One played an accordion with his hands while a bass drum with a triangle attached was on his back and slap jacks were fastened to his boot heel with a strap.[52]

Professor Tucker brought his rabbit and dove show to the Petersburg schoolhouse "*but the boys cut up so he did not have much of a crowd*," Loder reported on June 15, 1884. A month later a "Mexican Gymnasium" show brought its own tent.

A company built a portable dancing platform and held its first dance in the Petersburg schoolyard on Saturday night Aug. 14, 1886. A few weeks later, Loder recorded, "*Tom Smith got on a high horse on account of Miss CarSmith* (cq) *dancing and ripped around a good deal.*"

Race Horses

Horses remained a perpetual form of entertainment. Buying, selling or racing only required two men and two horses. Horse racing was making the national news: Robert Bonner purchased the trotting horse Grafton from Richard Penniston of Lexington. He paid $35,000. Grafton trotted a trial mile in 2:15½ minutes in 1875.[53]

In a Louisville race, Mollie McCarley led for two miles before being overtaken by Ten Broeck in a time of 8:19¾.

Loder, a big horse-racing fan, noted that the famous trotter Dexter died on May 22, 1888, in Robert Bonner's New York City stable. The 30-year-old horse was the first to trot a mile in 2:17¼. Bonner, who paid $35,000 for Dexter in 1867, had the horse buried on his farm in Tarrytown.

Col. John W. Conley's purchase of the three-year-old trotting stallion Axtell for $105,000 caught Loder's attention as well. He said it was "*the highest price paid for horse flesh in the world.*" His 2:22 record was set at Terre Haute, Ind. Conley also owned Johnston, who held the 2:06¼ minute pacing

---

> **Boone County Recorder**
> Vol. 1,   No. 1,   Sept. 23, 1875
> **Bellevue**
>
> Some predacious miscreant recently entered the dwelling of William Moody and overturned his furniture, scattered it promiscuously about the room, and made it difficult to tell what he would have done if he had not been stopped. Mr. Moody and his family, as it happened, were away from home that day: but as luck would have it, something led his wife home; and when she opened the door she discovered the rogue scrutinizing articles in the clock. She being frightened at the sight, gave a scream and ran for some of the neighbors; and as neighbors were readily aroused, Mr. Rogue was compelled to take his departure without giving things a farewell shake. On his path were found several articles which he dropped. The loss sustained by Mr. Moody we have not yet learned.
>
> ◆
>
> The farmers in this vicinity are cutting up corn and sowing rye. The uncertainty of the wheat crop of late years has rendered it unpopular, as well as unprofitable. Very little wheat will be sown in this neighborhood, although at one time it was noted for that crop.
>
> ◆
>
> The Grand Hall at this place is not completed, but will be soon. It will add considerably to the looks of our little villa, and be of great value to the Patrons of Husbandry and the Brothers of the Mystic Tie, who assisted in its building and will hold forth therein.
>
> ◆
>
> Albert Corbin is building a new storehouse. It is to be 20 x30 and located on the lot opposite the blacksmith shop.

---

[50] Conrad, *Loder 3*, 70.
[51] Conrad, *Loder 3*, 77.
[52] Conrad, *Loder 4*, 38.
[53] Conrad, *Loder 3*, 85.

Chapter 7 1870-1889 Boone Communities Grow

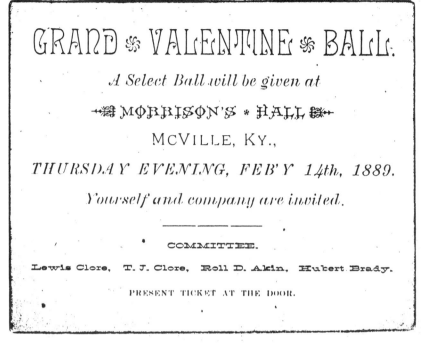

Courtesy of David and Jeanette Clore

world record.[54]

In the spring of '90, Morgan S. Davis, (Loder's son-in-law) was training trotters at Chester Park.

Piatt Wedding

Mary Catherine Nolan and Charles D. Piatt, son of Martha and Jacob Wycoff Piatt, were married at Covington's old Cathedral in June 1878. Piatt's friend, Dr. Ed Grant of Petersburg and his sister Adele Piatt, joined the couple on their honeymoon to Louisville where they stayed for three days and returned by boat. The steamer landed at Lawrenceburg where they took the ferry across to the family landing. They, along with friends and relatives there to greet them, went by carriage to Federal Hall.

The entire entourage, including the Berkshires, Waltons, Graves, Gaines, Willis, Kirtley and others stayed until the morning's early hours, dancing, singing and celebrating.[55]

Belleview Flourishes

Belleview included two tobacco warehouses, a hotel, several stores, a basket factory and a grade school. A post office established there in 1869 was named Grant to recognize prominent local landowners.[56]

Horse shoeing was W.W. Grant's specialty in Belleview (spelled Bellevue in 1883 and also called Grant for a time), less than eight miles down the river. He also promptly repaired machinery and promised his customers *"blacksmithing and wagon-making in all its branches done with neatness, accuracy and dispatch."*

Belleview's magisterial district counted a population of 713 in 1880. The village itself included 124 and a hotel for visitors.

"The public will do well to call me before purchasing elsewhere," said A. Corbin who had a *"first class country store"* on Fourth Street in Belleview.

H.C. Botts offered to pay the highest market price for first-class tobacco in Belleview.

Joseph Maurer and John Deck each owned basket-making shops. Willows cultivated in the surrounding creek bottoms were woven by hand after they were cut, bundled and the bark was stripped from each switch. Wild willows weren't used.

When baskets were shipped out by boat, one size nested into the next larger. Baskets rather than trunks carried luggage and goods shipped by boat.[57]

McVille Founded

South of Belleview a few miles, Green

---

[54] Conrad, *Loder 5*, 118.
[55] Blakely.
[56] Reis, *Pieces of the Past*, 72.
[57] *Boone County Recorder*, "Belleview as Remembered," Sept. 21, 1978.

(Isaac) McMullen laid out McVille in 1881. His home was on Main and Scott streets.

According to an inscription on a closet door, a man named McIntrye built Jonas Clore's McVille home in 1878. The home on Front Street overlooking the Ohio used an unusual mixture of styles and building techniques.

Paint dealer, contractor and builder, G.B. McMullen offered *"house and sign painting of every description."* The Constance wharfmaster dealt in tobacco and sold *"mixed and liquid paints, leads, oils, brushes and varnishes."*[58]

Saving the Dinsmore Place

James Dinsmore's daughter Isabella had married her first cousin, Charles Flandrau in 1859, one week before her mother died. Born in 1828, Flandrau, a Minnesota judge, earned renown in August 1862. With the young men away fighting the Civil War, Flandrau commanded 115 civilians who turned away a Sioux Indian attack on New Ulm, Minn.

Isabella died at 37. Flandrau sent six-month-old asthmatic Sally (named Sarah 1866-1947) and six-year-old Patty (named Martha 1861-1923) to be raised by their grandfather and Aunt Julia on the Boone County farm. Their father eventually remarried and had two sons and a stepson from that marriage.

Julia Stockton Dinsmore (1833-1926) had been named for her mother's friend, Julia Stockton, whose uncle Richard signed the Declaration of Independence.

Julia Dinsmore waits at the horse mounting block. Courtesy of Dinsmore Homestead

Reportedly a popular girl, Julia never married, possibly heartbroken over the death of a Confederate colonel who was killed early in the Civil War. (Two brass buttons from a Confederate uniform were found tied together with a red ribbon in a tiny buckskin bag after her death.)

At her Uncle Silas' encouragement, Julia was well educated in private schools in Cincinnati and Lexington. (Theodore Roosevelt is said to have called Julia one of the best educated women in the nation.)

James Dinsmore's orchards and his Bakewell or Southdown sheep were multiplying by the 1870s. He experimented with silkworms, raised honeybees, and used osage orange trees as hedges and for dyes. He planted osage orange in creek bottoms from seeds shipped from Louisiana. Dinsmore also planted madder, a plant with small yellow flowers and a red, fleshy root. Madder roots also were used for dying fabrics.

He searched for a breed of large dogs with light-colored long shaggy hair, called Spanish Shepherd's dogs to assist with his sheep business.

Dinsmore had been harvesting osier or basket willows along Middle Creek. By 1870, seven of the county's 14 basket makers worked in Belleview for Dinsmore's basket factory. He shipped out as many as 30,000 pounds of surplus willow switches each time a steamboat stopped. Willow brought about $50 per ton in the 1860s.

When her father died in 1872, Julia Dinsmore inherited a farm laden with debt. She invited her cousin Belle Raymond and her

---
[58] Griffing, 15.

Chapter 7 1870-1889 Boone Communities Grow

husband to live just outside of Burlington with her for a year. Their $10,000 gift enabled Julia to pay bills and keep the farm in the family. For 54 years, Julia continued to manage it with the help of family, tenants and laborers.

Even with hired hands doing or overseeing the physical work, managing the farm was a stress for Julia. Robert Miller described her as *"a woman with the strength and fiery determination of Scarlett O'Hara, and yet at other times, the fragility and vulnerability of Blanche DuBois."* She joined the men in fox hunting, enjoyed killing snakes and visited the sick.[60]

Julia earned a little money teaching piano lessons on the massive Steinway piano in the parlor. Trinkets and photographs arranged atop the piano illustrate the family's impressive connections to the wealthy and well-known. One photo shows a sculpture by Gutzon Borglum, a friend of Isabella Greenway's who created Mt. Rushmore. Teddy Roosevelt sent a huge mounted elk that hangs in the main hall.

Other photos show Dinsmore cousins, known across the country for their achievements in architecture, photography, business, languages and flight.

All 54 years that she ran the farm, Julia maintained a diary. At 55, she began writing poetry. Doubleday published some of it when she was in her 70s. Many diary entries reflect her loneliness and exhaustion in keeping up the family farm.

In the 1870s, she paid day laborers 75 cents to grub fields, shuck corn, strip tobacco or shear sheep. The Dinsmores hauled their farm produce, corn and wheat to Belleview where it was loaded on boats.

1872 Lodging Rates[59]
(fixed by the county court)

Breakfast, dinner or supper	$.50
Lodging, or horse fed on grain	$.50
Horse fed on hay	$.25
Steam whiskey, beer or ale	$.10
Distilled whiskey or wine	$.15
Brandy	$.20

Providence Moves Church

Middle Creek Baptist Church also had its difficulties. During the 1870s, the congregation worried over securing enough subscriptions to pay the pastor's salary, but that was resolved quickly when the treasurer was instructed to report the names of those *"delinquent in their giving."*

On top of a hill overlooking Middle Creek toward Belleview, the church could only be reached on foot or by horseback. The brethren were unmoved by Brother Kirtley's efforts to convince them that the saddle was giving way to the buggy. Pastor Kirtley resigned in frustration.

Providence intervened in the form of a windstorm or "baby cyclone" which destroyed the church in 1876. Congregation members said it was *"the hand of God's providence, for not even a branch was torn from any of the trees around the church."*

Members met in the Locust Grove School for two years. Still disagreeing on the location to rebuild, they sold subscriptions for both the old and new sites. Planning to build on the site that gathered the most funds, they collected $541.40 for the old site. A total of $1,240 plus an acre of bottomland donated by Michael Clore determined the new. The church was completed in 1878. A parsonage was added for Brother A.M. Vardiman. Crediting its new location, Middle Creek was renamed Belleview Baptist Church in 1885.[61]

Brother E.N. Dicken was a strict disciplinarian there, excluding many members for various offenses.

In 1885, after Brother J.H. Fullilove became pastor, the church's authority was *"severely tested by an outbreak of dancing among its members."*

The situation was resolved by the discipline

---

[59] Conrad, *Top of Kentucky*, 21.
[60] Chastang, Gail, "The Dinsmore Homestead," Northern Kentucky Heritage, Vol. V, No. 1, Autumn/Winter 1997-98, 20.

[61] *Belleview Baptist Church, 190th Anniversary, "A Look at the Past – A Vision for the Future,"* 1993 est., 3-4.

committee, but was controversial for several years. In 1897, the church purchased 5½ additional acres from Clore to lay out a new cemetery.[62]

Rabbit Hash

A 3½ mile hop down the river from Belleview is Rabbit Hash. The river community was granted a post office under the name Carlton on Jan. 3, 1879, with Mrs. Elizabeth C. Kennon as postmaster.

Carlton was confused with Carrollton, just a few miles down the river, so the Rabbit Hash name was restored three months later. In 1912, with the advent of rural routes, the post office was closed.

James Alexander Wilson operated the Rabbit Hash ferry for eight years and was twice elected to the Kentucky legislature, in 1866-67 and 1873-74. He was also school commissioner and deputy county clerk.

Hamilton

On the other side of the Ohio River's East Bend was a landing called Hamilton where boats stopped every day. In 1883, Hamilton had a post office, likely named for Hamilton Mills where W. Saunders dealt in grain and custom milling. John Hamilton lived in the Indian Hill area, just off Big Bone Creek.

The riverfront community was off Ryle Road, (south of what is now the East Bend Power Plant,) a few miles north of the county line and where Big Bone Creek flows into the Ohio.

Normansville

North of Hamilton, where Big Bone Church Road intersects 338, was the community of Normansville (also called the Landing or Norman's Landing). J.W. Kennedy traded in tobacco and ran the general store there. J.L. Johnson's store offered tinware and patent medicines. Local physician and surgeon Dr. John A. Wood specialized in chronic cases.

Beaverlick's Adams Family

Directly east of Big Bone, Beaverlick included a post office, several schools, the Mud Lick Baptist Church, and a dozen houses at the intersection of what is now 338 and 1292. Beaverlick's mail came three times a week from Walton.

Between Beaver and Big Bone, on Gum Branch Creek was a farm owned by John Preston Hampton "Hamp" Adams. A Confederate veteran and former prisoner of war, Hamp married Sallie Ann Kennedy and began raising a family and foxhounds. Beef cattle, flocks of sheep, pens of hogs, and acres of corn, wheat and rye fed his large family and built his prosperity.

Three families – the Adams, Greens and Hances – went together to build and maintain a school for their children there. Teacher Miss Ellen Porter boarded at least part time with the Adams family.

Hamp was gathering materials to build a new house when Maggie, his second oldest daughter, came down with tuberculosis. Then called consumption, it "consumed" her body rapidly and went on to take her sister Lizzie. Soon eldest daughter Rose Ann, who had just gotten engaged, returned home. After overhearing her bereaved father say he couldn't imagine getting along without her, she called off her engagement. New baby Fannie died soon after birth. Then Annie, one

---

> **Boone County Recorder**
> Vol. 1,   No. 1,   Sept. 23, 1875
> **Big Bone**
> There was a Centennial Association held at this place last week. Efficient ministers, "plenty of victuals." And a large number of people were in attendance. Things passed off very quietly until the last evening, when the carriage of Mr. Harry Baker collided with the buggy of Mr. Addison Huey. No injury was sustained, with the exception of a wheel demolished for Mr. Huey.
>
> We feel sorry to pen that the attempt made by the County Attorney to stop the sale of whiskey at Hamilton was futile. He will have to come down and make another effort.

---

[62] *Belleview Baptist Church*, 3-4.

of the twins, came down with diphtheria. Although it is now preventable and curable, she died. Soon, May contracted the same disease.

In 1982, Hamp went ahead with his house building plans. Lifting a heavy beam, he ruptured a muscle. All Dr. Sam, Hamp's brother who was also the minister at Big Bone Baptist, could do was administer medication to reduce the tremendous pain. To get to a hospital would have meant riding in a wagon or buggy to Hamilton Landing, then going by steamboat to Cincinnati. Gangrene developed. Hamp died just 15 days after his daughter May, at the age of 54, leaving nine-year-old Ella (one of the twins) and seven-year-old Wayne. Eldest son Harry had been away at college in Lebanon, Ohio, with his sister Rose.

Rose and her mother kept the farm, relying on tenant farmers to care for the livestock and tend the crops. Wayne served on a Navy mine sweeper in WWI, then married Etta Keyhoe Carpenter, and eventually moved back to the family farm. Harry married Katie Hance and named his son, who was born in 1897, Hampton.[63]

Big Bone Spa

Interest in Big Bone Lick as a resort revived for a time. Squire Lucas and Thomas Coombs operated a bath house at the springs. A huge U-shaped white frame hotel was built

Storytellers at the Beaverlick store around 1900.
Photo courtesy of Linda Green

on the hill opposite the Big Bone Methodist Church. An old spring behind the church offered drinking water.[64]

In 1870 another hotel was built north of the salt springs at Big Bone Lick. However the Civil War had destroyed Southern fortunes and ended mineral springs' prominence as Kentucky vacation retreats.

Dr. J.E. Stevenson varied the marketing approach, offering the "*healing waters of Big Bone Springs*" at a hotel for invalids. In 1883 he advertised, "*physician of 38 years experience. Special attention shown to all who visit these springs for cures. Also a pleasant resort for those desiring sport.*"[65]

Others were digging and installing pipes and wells to make it easier to put the springs "medicinal" mineral water in barrels to be sold.

As they dug, they found a wagon load of mammoth bones including a tusk 12' long and 10" thick, and a tooth 15" long, 6" thick and

---

[63] Roter, 297-306

[64] Conrad, *Top of Kentucky*, 20.
[65] Griffing, 22.

The last Big Bone Hotel was razed in the 1940s when it was about a century old. Courtesy of *A Peek Into the Past*.

weighing about 20 pounds. These artifacts likely were allowed to deteriorate.[66]

Bones to Harvard

While the medicinal water salesmen didn't value the bones, scientists were still interested in Big Bone Lick. Nathaniel Southgate Shaler spent the summer of 1868 extensively excavating. The Newport native became Kentucky State Geologist in 1873 and eventually Dean of the Lawrence Scientific School at Harvard.

He discovered Elephas Primigenius, the glacial or hairy mammoth, 8' below the surface with Bootherium, the arctic musk ox. Above the Pleistocene level, he found Mastodon Ohioticus. Above that was a horse, probably Equus-Complicatus. Above them were modern caribou and elk, now driven to the far west.

Nearer the surface he found buffalo, bear, and deer with enough evidence to show they did not encounter the glacial age beasts.

Shaler met his goal of stocking the Harvard museum with big bones, but as had many before him, he had difficulty financing his studies. While the largest collection from Big Bone Lick still resides in London, Harvard maintains the largest U.S. collection, thanks to Shaler.

The Academy of Science in Philadelphia has a diverse collection showing seven species.[67] New York City's American Museum of Natural History also maintains a large collection of bones from the Boone lick. At Monticello, Jefferson's home near Charlottesville, Va., a mammoth tooth is displayed on a table. That tooth is all that remains of Jefferson's extensive collection. After his death, an unknowing tenant ground up the rest of the bones and used them as fertilizer.[68]

Orphan Becomes Landowner

In 1868, John L. Jones was 10 years old when his mother died. He was living in Missouri where his great-grandfather had traveled with Daniel Boone. His father died soon after. In his words, "*I wasn't raised, just growed up.*"

Because his generous father

> ## Big Bone Springs Hotel
> "This popular resort which has been entirely refitted will be
> open for the reception of guests
> **May 10, 1881.**
> Every arrangement has been made to insure the comfort and pleasure of visitors.
> The sulphur baths can be taken hot or cold.
> Terms $7 and $8 per week.
> Big Bone can be reached by taking the 3 o'clock p.m. Madison Packet at Mail Boat Landing, Cincinnati which lands at Hamilton where an omnibus will meet the boat every day."
>
> Cincinnati advertisement placed by C.A. McLaughlin Jr.[1]

---

[66] Willard Rouse Jillson, *Big Bone Lick*, The Standard Printing Co., Louisville, Ky. 1936, 63.

[67] Jillson, 65.
[68] Asa Rouse.

had endorsed many notes for friends, the 160-acre farm was sold to pay them, leaving the boy a pauper.

Remembering his uncle's story of the 30-day trip in a covered wagon from Kentucky to Adair County, Mo., John undertook the reverse trip himself at the age of 20. After arriving, he earned $12 a month working on a farm near Big Bone.

On Feb. 24, 1881, Jones married Sofie C. Reib and had six children. Their three boys all farmed. By 1930, he was one of the largest land-owners in the county.

Jones raised brown Duroc hogs on his River View Farm that his son John L. Jr. eventually took over. An active member of the Methodist Church, Jones delivered the first load of stone used in its construction. A director of the Boone County Insurance Company, he was known for his charitable works.[69]

Berkshire Mail Delivery

On the farthest southwest edge of Boone County near the Gallatin County line, a post office called Berkshire opened in 1881.

The South Fork Christian Church was the neighborhood's center. The settlement included a steam saw mill, a general store, public scales and a blacksmith shop.

The original Old Louisville Road, part of the escape path chosen by Gen. Morgan and Capt. Hines, ran by the community formerly known as South Fork, due to its proximity to the South Fork of Big Bone Creek. Springs peppered the region.

Railroad Comes to Verona

Completed in 1875, the Louisville, Cincinnati and Lexington Railroad – the first rail line between Covington and Louisville – ran through Verona, along what is now routes 14 and 16. However in 1872, before the line was completed, a train fell through an iron bridge near Verona, killing two and injuring 53.

Mail arrived daily at the Verona Depot.

Train crossing bridge Photo courtesy of Virginia Lainhart

Postmaster J.N. Dickerson ran a grocery that included dry goods, notions, boots, shoes, hardware, tinware, schoolbooks, cutlery and an assortment of ready-made clothing.

Lizzie Roberts taught school in Verona in 1883. Miss Nannie E. Hamilton taught at the League Institute of Verona in the 1880s.

The Vest House offered lodging. Kennedy & Whitson bought tobacco. L.J. Hume sold livestock. Magistrate J.J. Bromback was a farmer. C.D. Lewis and his son did carpentry and construction work.[70]

The Verona magisterial district nearly matched Walton's size with 836 residents, including the 153 who populated the village.

Walton Train Depot

Walton is five miles northeast of Verona, following the 1868 L&N rail line. Including the town, the magisterial district totaled 1,072 in 1880. By 1883, the Louisville, Cincinnati

---

[69] *Boone County Recorder*, 1930 Historical Edition.

[70] Griffing, 12.

and Lexington railroad ran one line through Walton while less than 20 rods away ran a line for Cincinnati Southern. (A rod is a distance measurement, 5.5 yards, 16.5 feet, or 5.029 meters.)

Trains were reducing road and river travel, offering three fast trips a day between Cincinnati and Lexington. One left Lexington at 7:05 a.m. and arrived in Cincinnati at 10:20 a.m., then returned at 4 or 7 p.m., arriving at 7:15 or 9:57 p.m. The later one, the night express, didn't make as many local stops. The comfortable train trip took less than a third of the time required by stage.

Cincinnati Southern Railway bought 30 miles of road between Boone and Scott counties in 1875 because the tracks crossed the road so often it became unfit for driving.[71]

Trains brought a construction boom, adding hotels, depot buildings and new businesses. The next year, A.J. Whipps of Covington built a new tobacco warehouse.[72] Two hotels offered accommodations for those using the Walton depot.

The Covington and Lexington Turnpike (Dixie Highway or 25) bisected Walton, running for a distance in the narrow strip of land between the tracks.

Jerry Glenn renamed his old brick house at Gaines X Roads Drovers Inn and opened as a hotel. Drovers herding cattle, hogs and sheep to Cincinnati rested there. Prices charged for food, drink and lodging were set by the court and strictly enforced. Sheriff's reports show landlords were fined for overcharging guests.

John Murphy, John Arnold and W.I. Norman owned large tracts of town. Most of Murphy's was northeast. It included the Cincinnati Southern train depot and bordered the public school and the Baptist Church.

Arnold's land was southeast. His home was on the turnpike, between A. Arnold's and J.W. McBee's. The Rouse Brothers Saw and Grist Mill lay between the tracks, along the highway near a pond that was created when the Southern Railway dug a pit to use the fill dirt. A.M. and W.R. Rouse's mill was steam driven. They lived near the Mill Pond on South Main Street.[73]

W.L. Norman's property laid west. His home was across the tracks from his grocery. A.J. Whipper's tobacco warehouse stood between them as did T. Rice's property. George Ransler's property and tobacco warehouse bordered Norman's on the north. D. Bedinger also dealt in tobacco and farmed.

Just across Dixie Highway from Norman's Store, T.F. Curley promised "*a full and complete assortment of choice goods at lowest prices.*"[74]

Dr. W.M. Lowry lived north of town. Dr. D.M. Bagby lived toward the south. W.E. Vest offered surveying and civil engineering work. H.C. Dahling made boots and shoes. J.J. Kipp promised "*boots and shoes of best quality. Satisfaction guaranteed and a neat fit. Repairing promptly done.*"

Frank Smith painted houses and signs, whitewashed ceilings, hung wallpaper, and did graining and glazing from his location at Richwood Station.[75]

Walton Deposit Bank opened in 1879, the only bank on Lexington Pike between Covington and Williamstown. (It merged with Equitable Bank and Trust Company in Walton in 1927.)

Zion Baptist Church was built in 1872. Solomon Watkins, the first pastor, is buried in an unmarked grave at the foot of the steps. The building has remained the hub of the African-American community in Walton, serving as a school until minority students were consolidated at Burlington.

The progressive community published its first telephone book listing 500 subscribers in 1880. Boone was the sixth Kentucky county to be added to the telephone system.[76]

---

[71] Tanner, CL-13.
[72] Jim Reis, "200 and Holding," The Kentucky Post, Nov. 19, 1984, 10K.
[73] A.M. Rouse was the great grandfather of Asa and Jack Rouse of Walton.
[74] Griffing, 20.
[75] Griffing, 20.
[76] *150th Anniversary, City of Walton*, 38.

Chapter 7 1870-1889 Boone Communities Grow

Walton's Bucket Brigade

In 1880, Walton's "Bucket Brigade," men on foot or horseback, answered fire calls for the community of nearly 300. Their equipment included three ladders, two poles, hooks, spikes, ropes, 25 buckets and two tubs.

They dug and filled 12 fire cisterns along Walton roadsides. Reserved only for fire fighting, the cisterns were maintained until 1936 when the city installed a water system. Eventually a hand-powered piston pump, designed to be pulled by men rather than horses, was purchased.[77]

Fire was a particular threat in towns where flammable buildings stood side by side. In big cities it could become a disaster. On a beautiful 80 degree Oct. 8, 1871, word came that a huge fire in Chicago had burned much of downtown, including the important banks and telegraph offices.

Road Laws

Boone County firefighters traveled over macadamized roads, made from creek rock hauled by horse and wagon to the road site.

Chipping rocks into gravel was a labor-intensive process. Rocks were stood on end in slightly slanting rows along the road. Men sat on a rock, breaking off small pieces with a little round hammer and moving back as the rock chipped off between their legs.[78]

John Taggart, who lived for a time in the tollhouse at the corner of Fowler Creek Road and Florence-Union Pike was an expert napper. Using a napping hammer with a 12-15" handle and a circular head 2" across, he broke 1 to 1½" rocks to resurface the pikes.

"The smaller the rock pieces, the more stable and smooth the road when the spread rocks were covered with a layer of dirt and packed down. The dirt for this top layer was usually obtained by scraping a drainage ditch on each side of the road.

"John Taggart was a man of honor, a man never known to deceive, to 'cut corners' as some did, by napping the large stones into sizes bigger than the desirable kind, or by covering a mound of the less desirable size with a shallow layer of the acceptable small ones."[79]

The 1882 General Assembly enacted several laws pertaining only to Boone County roads. At the time many local decisions were made at the statehouse. Chapter 664 was *"An act to amend and reduce into one all the laws relating to opening repairing, keeping in repair, and levying and collecting taxes, for the benefit of public roads in Boone County."*

Another General Assembly provision passed that year authorized Boone County to hold an election on *"taking stock to the amount of $750 per mile"* to construct and complete roads.[80]

1882 Boone County Road Laws Enacted by the Kentucky Legislature

1. Annual tax of 5 cents per $100.
2. Assessor to keep books by magisterial districts.
3. Tax receipts to be distributed by districts.
4. Each magisterial district divided into four road districts of approximate equal size.
5. County judge to appoint surveyor for each road district.
6. Surveyor to notify each person required to work on road when and where he was to work two days between April 1 and September 1. Person to report with proper tools and implements. Person may be exempted by paying $2.
7. Failure to work could result in fine of $2 per day.
8. Work in district should take into account the condition and amount of travel on various roads.
9. Public roads include streets in towns which are a continuation of same, and not part of turnpike charter.
10. Surveyors were allowed $1.50 per day, not to exceed $20 a year.
11. Surveyors to make financial report to county court at end of term.
12- 14 Provisions for fining and removing surveyors for failure to perform duties.

---

[77] *150th Anniversary, City of Walton*, 44-45.
[78] Tanner, UF-4.
[79] Roter, 325-326.
[80] Tanner, BC-6.

Richwood

The county's major road, the Covington and Lexington Turnpike or Dixie Highway, ran north through Richwood Station. The railroad tracks followed the road, crossing it frequently.

Residents of Richwood, which took its name from the Richwood Presbyterian Church, could board the train at the local depot. Wesley Hoggins had a horse barn, a cattle barn and a scales next to the tracks. Next to him, James Lampton offered a school across the tracks from his house.

Halfway between Richwood and Union on the White Haven-Richwood Pike, stood White Haven Academy. Tollhouses at both ends of that road exacted payments from travelers.

Union

About five miles southwest of Florence on U.S. 42, the town of Union was incorporated in 1871.[81] Union's mail came three times a week from Florence.[82]

Misses Nannie D. Bristow and Eliza Lampson (or Lampfon) taught at the school just east of the intersection, next to Jennie Fall's land and across from J.H. Corbin's.

The Eagle House provided lodging. In 1883, Magistrate H. Bannister offered blacksmith services and H.P. Stephens practiced law.

Conner & Utz sold general merchandise on R.I. Conner's city lot. Their store stood on the southwest corner of the intersection of what is now 127 and 536.[83]

William H. Stamper bartered produce for the groceries and dry goods he sold from his store 2½ miles northwest of Union.[84] Four miles southwest, Mrs. Emily I. Conley accepted produce in exchange for the dry goods, groceries, boots, shoes, hats, caps and other items she sold.

H.A. Hicks bred trotters and dealt in horses, sheep and cattle. A.J. Utz also dealt in livestock.

Pleasant Ridge/ Gunpowder

The 5½ miles from Union to Florence were a one-hour buggy ride in 1883, stopping to pay several tolls and traveling through a heavily populated area called Pleasant Ridge. A saw and grist mill on the South Fork of Gunpowder Creek sat across the road from Tanner's store. Pleasant Ridge School #9 was just down the road. The Crigler, Tanner and Rouse families owned much of the land in 1880.

Gunpowder was the next community. It included a restaurant, two stores, a blacksmith shop and a saw and gristmill. Before that the crossroads was called Pinhook, later Sugartit – names that came from the shape of the hill there.

Florence Fair Closes

Farmers, craftsmen and women came from around the county to the annual Florence Fair to exhibit their products, produce, fruit and livestock. The fairgrounds sat on the southwestern corner of the U.S. 25 and U.S. 42 intersection.

Like many things, the fair had stopped during the Civil War. By 1874, the second 10-year lease on the fairgrounds had expired. John Barton now received $200 rent annually for the land.

A wood-fence bordered the grounds and a racetrack was built. The track was used exclusively for trotting races from May 15 to Nov. 15. Taverns and hotels did a brisk business thanks to fairgoers. During evenings of the fair, Florence's Southern Hotel offered "social hops" or dances. On July 4 and other days, Florence lodges held picnics at the fair grounds.

Attempts to rally interest for the 1881 fair included prizes for:
- the greatest number of hawk scalps obtained from April 1 to Sept. 1, and
- *"the lady getting up the best meal in the shortest time with the least fuel."*[85]

---

[81] *175th Anniversary Historical Book*, 8.
[82] Tanner, BC-5.
[83] Griffing, 19.
[84] Griffing, 10.

[85] Conrad, *Yesterdays*, 12-13.

But enthusiasm dimmed and the Florence Fair closed on Sept. 3, 1881.

Over the next years, the Harvest Home Association – which had sponsored fairs at an amusement park on the Ohio years before – held one-day fairs with events including horse shows and pretty baby contests just off Limaburg-Hebron Road (where the golf course is now).

The Presbyterian Church looking toward uptown Florence on Main Street from the corner of Dortha Ave.   Photo courtesy of Virginia Lainhart

Florence's Limitations

The fair wasn't the only thing losing interest in Florence. Much was changing. Rails for new steam locomotives followed Lexington Pike and ran along the Boone County line, bypassing Florence. Farm animals, once herded to Cincinnati or Lexington through Florence, were driven to stock pens in the new town of Erlanger and loaded onto rail cars.

Travel by road was slow and annoying. Going to Erlanger's railroad depot meant paying a toll, as did going to Covington. Heading to Lexington meant stopping two miles south of the city and again north of Walton. Between Covington and Lexington were 13 tollgates.[86]

Boone County had as many as 30 tollhouses by this time. Five toll gates ringed Florence. One could only maneuver in an area about two miles in diameter without paying a toll.

The Covington stage brought mail daily to Florence and Burlington. In the 1870s, Florence's population was 374, but by 1880 it had dropped to 309.

Florence's Business District

Still the largest town in the county, in Florence's business district, Girard Street ended on Main, face to face with Mrs. R.V. Grant's Southern Hotel. The Florence Hotel also offered lodging and meals.

T.L. Swetnam dealt in dry goods, groceries, notions and general merchandise. F.J. Burke made and repaired harnesses and saddles and sold whips, lap robes and dusters.

C.C. Bradford built carriages, promising special attention to painting, finishing, trimming and repairing. Carpenter W.H. Tanner put together wagons and other wooden items, committing to attend to all kinds of repairs personally.

Blacksmith Fred Reich made wagons and did repairs. Civil engineer W.R. Terrill did surveying and ran a bus line from Erlanger to Florence.

Dr. A. Sayers lived on a sizeable tract on the north side of Covington Pike (Dixie Highway), next to Dr. John Delaney. Physicians and surgeons J.A. Corey and Charles R. Slater also practiced in Florence in the 1880s.

S.S. Scott, who was a doctor and an attorney, sold "*drugs, medicines, chemicals, paints, oils, varnishes, glass, putty, dye stuffs,*

---

[86] Tanner, BC-5.

dye woods, and pure wines and liquors for medicinal use."[87]

On Nov. 27, 1870, Glassford's stable and house burned at the south corner of Main and Shelby streets. A carriage shop and Osborn's store burned on the north corner. No fire department existed yet to stem the blaze.

Florence Presbyterian became the community's fifth church. Bells in several Florence churches were cast in the early 1870s, possibly to celebrate the 100th anniversary of the Declaration of Independence. The Christian Church stood on the southwest corner of Union and Lexington (Dixie Highway) pikes, across from the Baptist Church.

Lloyd Douglas

A pastor named Douglas took over at Hopeful Lutheran Church in 1881 bringing his five-year-old son Lloyd and daughter Lou.

Lloyd C. Douglas went on to become one of the most widely read novelists of his time, publishing bestsellers including *The Magnificent Obsession* (1929) and *The Robe* (1942) between 1929 and 1951. His books were translated into 54 languages and several were made into movies.

In *Time to Remember*, his final novel, Douglas includes several pages of reflections on his childhood in Boone County. This is his description of the Lutheran parsonage in 1881.

"If a man had a mind to, he could almost make his living from the four fertile acres belonging to the place. One acre was in blue grass. There was a good barn, a high-wired chicken run, and a pigpen at the far end of the pasture field.

"The latest parson to live in the rambling old house, with the huge brick chimney and wide verandahs, had amused himself by tapping the sugar maples in a grove just across the road."[88]

Douglas mentioned James Blodgett, a Florence blacksmith his father once described in a sermon, who handled horses in a friendly and compassionate way.

White Hall shows in the background of this photo of Walter Ferguson and his son Walter playing with some kittens. Courtesy of Bruce Ferguson

Buying Teaching Rights

Rev. Joseph J. Bent established a parish school in an extension added to St. Paul's Church on the northeast corner of Florence's Shelby and Center streets. Mary Powers is believed to have taught at St. Paul's.

The right to teach at Florence's Town Hall was still being auctioned to the highest bidder. Bids ranged from $1.50 per month to $3. From 1865 to 1880, Professor D.J. Daughters generally had the top $3 bid.[89] Irene Bradford was the last teacher who purchased the right to teach. Florence had no public school from 1881 to 1887.

Dissatisfied with that situation, voters

---

[87] Griffing, 18.
[88] Lloyd C. Douglas, *Time to Remember*, (Houghton Mifflin Co., Boston, 1951), 42.
[89] A.M. Yealey, "History Concerning Florence Schools," *Boone County Recorder*.

elected a new board of school directors in 1887. They purchased a plot of land and built a public schoolhouse (behind today's Florence Elementary).

William A. Clutterbuck and L. Conner Yeager Jr. taught school in Florence. A.M. Yealey, a later teacher, principal and historian, said, *"After considerable argument, an acre of land was purchased from Ned Galway with an outlet 30' wide on a continued lengthening of Montgomery Street. Here a building was erected which had two rooms. This was the first public school house at Florence which aimed to separate the primary and advanced grades."*[90].

The first public high school opened in Florence in 1887. Mabel and Harry Tanner, Ruby Corbin and Robert Robbins were the first to receive diplomas in 1915. Graduation didn't come after 12 years in the classroom as it does now, but after students demonstrated they could read, write and do arithmetic – regardless of the number of years they attended school.

Forty Schools

While Zach F. Smith, state School Superintendent had mandated five-month terms in 1867, Boone County schools took some time to comply. Some school terms were expanded from three months to five or six months in 1869, starting in September and ending in February.

In 1875, about 3,247 children attended schools in 46 Boone County districts.[91] A third of the county's population was of school age, a percentage that remains consistent in the 1990s.

By 1881, 40-some one-room Boone County schools taught five-month terms and five schools taught three-month terms. Buildings were brick, log or frame. Fourteen private schools and three academies supplemented the county's educational offerings. Boone County school funding was $1.90 per student in 1875.[92]

M. Riddell's store in Burlington. Courtesy of Virginia Lainhart

Morgan Academy Closes

By the 1870s, Burlington's Morgan Academy had closed. The *Boone County Recorder* began publishing anonymous letters chiding the trustees for not opening the school and questioning the whereabouts of the academy's treasury.

Soon trustees began responding they had tried to get an instructor without success and the funds were being used for building maintenance. Advertisements often appeared in August saying the school would open if there were enough subscriptions.

By the 1880s, the school was operating again. In 1887, Professors James Maurice Lassing and William Gaines announced the five-month term would cost between $12.50

---

[90] Yealey, *Florence Boone County, Kentucky*, 12-13.
[91] Conrad, *Boone County Schools*, 19.

[92] Boone County Recorder, Vol. 1, No. 1, Sept. 23, 1875

and $15 per pupil.[93] In 1888, Prof. Henry Newton and a Miss Arnold taught the last classes there. The land reverted back to the heirs of the original donors when the first school was built.[94]

Teachers' Institutes

Teachers' Institutes were held in Burlington beginning in 1872. County teachers gathered to certify new teachers, examine current teachers, discuss new approaches and learn teaching methods.

In 1878, Thomas Zane Roberts was one of the newly certified teachers. He began working for $28 per month at Locust Grove School for five months. Recognized for his mathematical expertise, in 1886 Roberts earned the title of professor and was consistently elected to the four-person executive committee at the annual Teachers' Institute.

The Aug. 24, 1892, *Boone County Recorder* said: "*T.Z. Roberts is another Boone County bachelor who takes pleasure in developing the youthful mind, and since 1878 he has spent much of his time in the school-room, surrounded by his neighbors' children. He is well posted and defends with vigor, every method he pursues in the school-room.*"

Wealthy Burlington District

Maude Kirkpatrick taught at the Burlington school on Orient Street, just north of Washington Street or Florence Pike (KY 18). Burlington encompassed 277 residents and several churches.

In 1870, a 50 cent per $100 real estate tax was passed in Burlington. In 1889, Burlington was listed on county tax roles as the third wealthiest of 11 districts in the county. Florence and Taylorsport had higher property values.

In 1883, four physicians and surgeons practiced from Burlington – J.F. Smith, R.H. Crisler, J.G. Furnish, and J.M. Grant. Dr. Grant lived on the corner of Jefferson and Union streets, just south of the courthouse.

Burlington's Boone County Deposit Bank was founded in 1885. (The bank moved into a new building across from the courthouse in 1925, then merged with the Peoples Deposit Bank two years later.)

W.E. Piper sold dry goods, groceries, notions, hats, caps, boots, shoes, flour, salt, hardware, tinware, and queensware.

Fine teas were the specialty at Dudley Rouse's grocery, which stocked the same things as Piper. Rouse's store was on the corner opposite the courthouse.

Owned by C.L. Crisler, then W.L. Gedge, Boone House was west of the store on Washington. Gedge promised a "*table furnished with all the luxuries of the season. Good bar attached. Give him a call.*"

Boone House caught fire on New Year's Day 1882. "*It burned a good deal of the kitchen and dining room before it was put out.*"

Attorney R.C. Green owned the Central House across the street from the store on one side and the courthouse on the other.

Other Burlington hotels included The St. James Hotel, The Burlington Hotel, and The Sanford House.

"*J.M. Riddell is now having his new shop weather-boarded. Perhaps if he should have it ceiled and then plastered it would render it still more comfortable.*"[95]

The Methodist Episcopal Church sponsored 25-cent oyster suppers at the Palmer House Hotel to raise money for charity.

Above Rouse's store, Albert M. Acra sold and repaired leather goods – harnesses, saddles, bridles, whips, fly nets, dusters, lap rugs, trotting boots, etc.[96]

J.F. Weaver ran a saw and grist mill southeast of Burlington on Gunpowder Creek, promising to fill orders for all kinds of hard wood promptly at the lowest prices.

---

[93] Conrad, *Boone County Schools*, 17.
[94] Conrad, *Top of Kentucky*, 40.
[95] *Boone County Recorder*, Vol. 1, No. 1, Sept. 23, 1875.
[96] Griffing, 10.

George Gilpin Perkins

George Gilpin Perkins, who was born in Burlington in 1839 then moved to Covington, had passed the bar in 1863. Election to the General Assembly in 1867 started his 30-year career in public office – a record almost unparalleled in the history of Kentucky jurisprudence."

Smith's *History of Kentucky* said, "*It is doubtful if any man of his age has continued in such a position so long, and the public confidence has been won by marked capacity and fidelity to everything belonging to the high trust. But few men are more popular or live in more the affections of their constituents.*"

Judge Perkin's political success came from his character, dignity, honorable dealing, simplicity and directness. "*The docket of his court is kept free from accumulated cases, and his opinions are well considered, clear, terse and strong and rarely reversed. He is able, fearless and just, an no political prejudice or zeal could deflect his mind from its honest and intelligent convictions.*"[97]

Burlington courthouse   Courtesy of Virginia Lainhart

New Courthouse

Burlington's stone courthouse built in 1817 burned on Jan. 4, 1875. The court met on Feb. 1 to decide what to do about not having a jail anymore. In 1883, Sheriff T.W. Finch took prisoners to the Frankfort penitentiary.[98]

In July 1888, contractors began tearing down the old courthouse so it could be rebuilt. The next summer the brick building that still stands was completed. The new courthouse, with many fire safeguards, was completed for $20,000.

Deputy Clerk J.W. Duncan owned several lots on Jefferson Street in the block north of Gallatin Street. County Clerk L.H. Dills was elected county judge in 1883. W.L. Riddell was circuit court clerk.

Little has changed about politics. An old fashioned Burlington barbecue on Aug. 14, 1872, just a week after the election, attracted lots of politicians and a big crowd.

Hogan House

Property transfers on a log cabin and the quarter-acre lot next to Morgan Academy kept the clerk's office busy in the 1870s. On Dec. 3, 1855, John Cave had received the property from Willis Graves' estate. The next day, Cave transferred it to Joseph Chambers. The next spring, Chambers sold it to James Boyd for $190.

Quite an entrepreneur, Dr. J.R. McKensie (or McKenzie) bought it in 1873. Dr. McKensie sold drugs, medicines, stationary, sponges, brushes, tobacco, fine cigars, perfumery, and fancy and toilet articles at his Burlington drugstore according to an 1875 advertisement in the *Recorder*.

In 1874, the druggist then sold the tract to

---

[97] H. Levin, *Lawyers & Lawmakers of Kentucky*, (Lewis Publishing Co., Chicago, reprinted by the Filson Club of Louisville, 1982), 735-737.
[98] Conrad, *Loder 3*, 81.

Linda and Dan Whittenburg have restored Hogan House in Burlington to house Cabin Arts, a shop offering quilting supplies, classes and unique local handicrafts. Courtesy of Linda Whittenburg

Aaron Slaughter Zeller for $500. Four years later, Zeller sold it back to McKensie for $200. In 1881, McKensie sold it to J. Hogan for $325.[99]

In 1912, Hogan resold the property for $1,800 to Elmer Kirkpatrick who resold it three years later to Hubert Rouse. Hubert and his wife Stella owned the house for most of the century.

(Dan and Linda Whittenburg bought the Hogan house in 1992, and began restoring it, exposing the original logs and the fireplace. Linda operates "Cabin Arts" there. Dan's business, Superior Imports, repairs imported cars on the lot behind it.)[100]

Boone County Recorder

Ben Deering edited the *Boone County Journal* in the 1870s. Its slogan was: "*Independent in all things, neutral in nothing. Hew to the line; let the chips fall where they may.*"

Bob Berkshire began printing the *Boone County Recorder*, one of the first ten papers in Kentucky, in 1875.[101]

Some excerpts from the news of the day:

- "*We are indebted to Capt. Finch of this place for a late Kansas paper from which we learn that the West is threatened with devastation by the grasshoppers again this year.*"
- "*A vast quantity of wool has passed through Florence this week going to the Cincinnati market.*"
- "*As Albert Price attempted to mount his horse with a loaded shotgun in his hand at Cain's tollgate on the Lexington Pike, his saddle turned, throwing him to the ground, when both barrels of the gun exploded, some of shot striking Mr. Cain, John Wilson and John Conley who were standing near, wounding them severely, but not seriously. Price was greatly frightened.*"
- "*At a meeting of the North Kentucky Trotting Association, R.S. Strader was re-elected president; Volney Dickerson, vice president; Jacob Strader, secretary and treasurer; H.A. Hicks, L.H. Dills, Owen Gaines, John Horshall, Columbus Carlisle, William N. Smith, and Benjamin H. Stansifer, directors.*"[102]

Attorney H.J. Foster became the *Boone County Recorder's* editor in February 1882 assisted by his son.[103]

The Lloyd Scientists

Boone County native John Uri Lloyd had shown an early aptitude for chemistry. Born

---

[99] Boone County Recorder, Vol. 1, No. 1, Sept. 23, 1875.
[100] Whittenberg, Linda, current owner
[101] Conrad, *Loder 4*, 3.
[102] Yealey, *History of Boone County*, 44.
[103] Griffing, 10.

in 1849 to well-known schoolteachers Nelson and Sophia Webster Lloyd, at 14 he apprenticed to a Cincinnati apothecary. He earned $2 a week working from 7 a.m. until 9 or 10 p.m.

To earn his certificate of proficiency, Lloyd studied a different drug's dispensary record each night. Employed at Egger's Pharmacy, he apprenticed himself a second time to learn the German prescription business. Meanwhile, he attended lectures at the Ohio Medical College and took an anatomy course at Miami Medical College.

In 1878, Dr. Lloyd was named a professor at the Eclectic Medical College. President from 1896 to 1904, he edited the Pharmaceutical Review and the Eclectic Medical Journal.

John Uri and his brother Nelson Ashley joined a third man to form the Thorpe and Lloyd Brothers drug manufacturing company. The prosperous company soon became just the Lloyd Brothers Company.

After their younger brother, Curtis Gates, became a pharmacist, then dabbled in bookkeeping and printing, he joined them in 1886. Unlike his brothers, Curtis channeled his interest into mycology, the branch of botany dealing with fungi. He identified new and exotic plants, which he sent to John to analyze for their medical benefit. Nelson ran the business end.

Curtis traveled to Europe and set up offices in London, Paris and Berlin to collect information and plants. He traveled to Egypt, South America and to the Samoan Islands on a trip that lasted several years.

Curtis erected a monument to himself in Crittenden, because, he said, no one else would.[104]

The *New York Times* quoted the country's largest ginger ale manufacturer about one of John Uri Lloyd's inventions for the industry: *"We submitted the problem to Prof. John Uri Lloyd, a leading authority on botanical chemistry. He spent months in painstaking research – experimenting, testing, rejecting – until at last he discovered a process so revolutionary and far-reaching that it necessarily takes its place among the important business secrets of the nation."*

Sheet music cover Courtesy of Katie Presnell

John Uri also wrote books on Northern Kentucky's folklore and legends: *Etidorpha, Stringtown on the Pike, Red Head, The Right Side of the Car, Felix Moses: The Beloved Jew* and *Warwick of the Knobs*. Among his many awards, the American Pharmaceutical Association presented John Uri with four medals, including the Remington Honor Medal in 1920 for research in colloidal chemistry.[105]

---

[104] Jim Reis, *Pieces of the Past 2,* (Kentucky Post, Covington, Ky. 1991), 43.
[105] Boone County 175, 59.

Chapter 8
1890-1899 Commuting Begins, Population Declines

With more communities around the county and faster transportation, lifestyles were changing. Boone County's population hit a high point of 12,246 in 1890. Trains and steamboats, as well as the reliable horse and buggy, made goods and services easier to locate, encouraged leisure travel, and made it feasible to commute to work off the farm.

A huge monument to President George Washington, which opened in 1888, encouraged travel to Washington D.C.

Increased mobility brought *"small crowds at first, then the last two days 1,000 to 1,200 people came"* to hear Methodist circuit rider, Rev. W.A. Penn during a 10-day camp meeting at Parlor Grover in August 1892.[1]

Subtle change arrived in other ways. On Oct. 1, 1892, voters began using secret ballots. No longer did they name the candidates they supported aloud and watch the information being recorded.

Florence's population dropped by 124 to 258 between 1870 and 1890. Even Masonic Lodge #95 dwindled to 10 members. After 58 years of meeting at the town hall in Florence, the lodge moved to Erlanger where membership soon jumped to 17.[2]

Railroad towns like Walton and Erlanger were growing, offering more services and bringing more diversified career opportunities for those eager to leave the relentless and intensive labor of the family farm.

No longer did families need to raise their own food, milk their own cow and make their own clothes.

General stores, even in the smallest communities, made essential "store-bought" goods accessible.

Covington stores like A.L. Brown's advertised their hats: *"Soft and Stiff hats and straw hats – in all the latest colors, styles and qualities. Also Boy's and Children's hats. I have just received a large shipment of Hats from the celebrated J.B. Stetson & Co. manufactory. Being agent for Covington, I will sell them lower than elsewhere. Give me a call and be convinced."*[3]

At Loebecker's Cheap Shoe Store, ladies slippers sold for $.75 while men's custom-made boots topped out the price list at $4. Loebecker used the headline: *"Money Saved is Money*

Boone County Recorder
Jan. 6, 1892

INSURE AT HOME The Farmers' Mutual Fire Insurance Co. of Boone County is now completely organized and receiving applications for insurance. Its rates are lower than those of any other Company and it gives the farmers of Boone County hitherto unknown advantage in keeping their property insured. Every farmer in the county should take a policy at once.

◆

The Baptist church built a chimney of candy in boxes, each one representing a brick. The children were delighted of course.

◆

UTSINGER
Henry Stephens has thirty young lambs.

Sam Wilhoit eat (cq) 16 bananas in seventeen minutes on a wager.

Hunters shot at some quails the other day and shot one of Tom Riddell's children.

Some of our shootist attended the clay pigeon match at Anderson's ferry the other day.

About one mile west of town is a sink hole from which issues boiling water all the time.

---

[1] Ivalou H. Walton, *Historical Study Burlington Methodist Church*, May 1975; 11.

[2] Conrad, *Yesterdays*, 30.
[3] Boone County Recorder, June 12, 1879.

Made" on his advertisement in the *Boone County Recorder*.[4]

A Lawrenceburg tailor also promoted his services. The newspaper included a fashion column that mentioned mauve was the color for spring of 1888 and black and white sashes were stylish with black evening dresses. Johnson & Clark of New York advertised for representatives to sell their "New Home Sewing Machine" around the nation.

Farming Continues

Agriculture, in all its variations, remained the primary livelihood. Land was valued at an average of $27 an acre.[5] The value of Kentucky's farm products surpassed every southern state except Texas.[6] In 1890, Kentucky was third nationally in apple production. Wheat production doubled between 1870 and 1900, then declined. Between 1889 and 1907, hay acreage increased 40 percent.[7]

Grains, tobacco and livestock were the most common crops, but some also marketed vegetables and fruits in Covington.

In August 1879, William McWethy and James Loder took a load of watermelons to the Grange picnic then to Constance to sell the rest.

Boone County Recorder
Feb. 13, 1889
Boone's Wealth
The following shows the taxable property in the county and its value as set out by the Assessor's book:
Land, 159,216 acres $4,319,051
Town lots, 608 250,440
Thoroughbred stallions, 2 900
" geldings, 1 200
" mares & colts, 5 ...250
Common stallions, 84 8,850
Horses and mares 103,050
Mules 39,890
Jacks, 11 2,440
Jennets, 9 400
Thoroughbred bulls, 5 275
" cows, 68 1,675
Cattle 76,574
Sheep 40,086
Hogs 37,040
Stores 74,875
Gold watches, clocks, &c.........6,935
Gold and silver plate 1,605
Jewelry 125
Diamonds 500
Household furniture 1,450
Paintings 15
Pianos 12,695
Professional library, 1 200
Safes 205
Buggies &c......................51,810
Agricultural implements 150
Steam boats 4,660
Wines, whiskeys &c..............81,690
Money at interest 664,850

Voters 2,440
Males over 21 years 2,441
School children 2,713

Wealth by districts:
Taylorsport ....$...802,395
Florence 1,048,645
Verona 357,375
Walton 520,455
Petersburg 710,785
Bellevue 246,902
Hamilton 286,634
Carlton 341,785
Union 521,120
Beaver 247,025
Burlington 787,040

A number of farmers shipped loads of melons out on steamboats.

Fewer were raising their own chickens. Egg prices went from 20 cents in 1870 to as high as 70 cents a dozen in 1899. On March 2, 1899, L.A. Loder wrote: "*Eggs have been higher all over the county the last four or five weeks than they have ever been known* [to be]."[8]

Tobacco Prices Drop

Boone County farms' diversity still included hogs, cattle, grains, fruit, vegetables, chickens and horses, but tobacco had begun to emerge as the primary cash crop. Traffic in horses and mules for riding, driving, working and racing had increased as well. William Bruce Campbell Sr. recalled his grandfather, with several other men, driving horses and mules to Selma, Ala. in the fall.

Despite Boone County farmers' access to Cincinnati, Louisville, Lexington, southern Indiana and other Kentucky markets, tobacco prices were dropping to unbelievable levels. Nationally, tobacco companies were banding together, creating monopolies to keep prices low.

In January 1892, the *Recorder* reported, "*The farmers have their crops all gathered and most of the tobacco is stripped, and is*

---

[4] *Boone County Recorder*, June 12, 1879.
[5] *Boone County Recorder*, Feb. 13, 1889.
[6] Harrison & Klotter, 298.
[7] Harrison & Klotter, 296.

[8] William Conrad, editor, *The Loder Diary, Part 6, Jan. 1, 1893-Jan. 29, 1904*, (Boone County Schools, Florence, Ky., 1988).

now being prized (bundled) and sold. Most of the crop here is shipped to the Louisville market, where shippers say they receive better prices."

Elsewhere the paper noted, *"Cum and Jule Bristow have sold their new crop of tobacco for 8 cents all round to Mr. Kennedy. These gents know when to turn loose."*[9]

The next year, *"J.W. Berkshire and M.F. Wingate tried the Louisville tobacco market last week. They report prices no better than at Cincinnati."*[10]

In 1894, C.L. Crisler *"sold and delivered his tobacco last week to Prague and Malson, in Covington, at $10.50 for first, and $5 for the second grade."*[11] (These prices were per 100 lb. bundle.)

The next year, B.W. Adams was in Hathaway (half-way between Rabbit Hash and Union on Hathaway Road), paying 1 to 4 cents a pound for tobacco.[12]

Verona tobacco dealer George W. Roberts paid 1 to 6 cents a pound for the tobacco he bought in February 1897.[13]

It now was costing farmers more to grow, harvest and transport their tobacco to market than they were getting paid for it.

Horse Trading

For the next decade, horse trading – with all its risks – was likely to be more profitable than raising tobacco, despite the increasing number of horse-less carriages motoring about.

During an auction at R. Strader's farm, 36 horses of all ages sold for a total of $1,500 – an average of nearly $42. In the 1880s, a "yellow horse" sold for $6 in Petersburg. Evidently not a prize winner, L.A. Loder noted that the same horse was on the market again a few months later, but didn't sell. A few years later, a horse sold to a butcher for $45. In 1887, a little black mare sold for $300 to a Cincinnati man.

In 1894, a horse sold for $112.50. The next year, Loder recorded horses selling for $58 and $50. In 1899, horses sold in Cincinnati for $75 each. In 1901, Chester T. Davis sold his bay horse Skinner to a Cincinnati man for $200.[14]

Many advertised their stallions' services in the daily paper. On July 8, 1896, H.H. Hays offered Declamont, *"a solid bay with black points, level headed, good bone and muscle"* at his Bullittsville farm.[15]

"Red Hornet," a chestnut stallion who had a record of (running a mile in) 2:23¼ minutes, stood at W. Ackemyer's stable *"one mile below Bullittsville."* For $10 he ensured a mare in foal.[16]

At his Petersburg farm, J.T. McWethy showed an imported French coach stallion called Lantier. For a $15 stud fee, McWethy guaranteed a *"colt to stand up and suck." "Every farmer should see this horse before breeding elsewhere,"* he advertised.[17]

L.H. Crisler of Bullittsville practiced veterinary surgery and equine dentistry. He came to Burlington the first Monday of each month.[18]

Boone County Recorder
May 30, 1888
FARM FOR SALE
Farm of 90 acres, situated on the Ohio river, 2 miles below Anderson's Ferry, well watered; house of 7 rooms and cellar, tenant house, barn and all other outbuildings, orchard of 4 acres of well selected fruit. Part bottom and part hill land well adapted to gardening and dairying purposes. Terms $70 per acre, ½ cash, balance in 1 and 2 years, equal payments, notes bearing legal interest from date of sale. Title shall be good. For further particulars inquire or address O.C. Lutz of Ludlow and W.L. Riddell of Burlington, Ky.

---

[9] *Boone County Recorder*, Jan. 6, 1892.
[10] *Boone County Recorder*, March 9, 1893.
[11] *Boone County Recorder*, March 9, 1893.
[12] *Boone County Recorder*, April 17, 1895.
[13] *Boone County Recorder*, Feb. 17, 1897.
[14] Conrad, *Loder 6*.
[15] *Boone County Recorder*, July 8, 1896.
[16] *Boone County Recorder*, June 27, 1894.
[17] *Boone County Recorder*, June 27, 1894.
[18] *Boone County Recorder*, June 27, 1894.

Chapter 8 1890-1899 Commuting Begins, Population Declines

Leaving the Farm

Horse teams still did the heavy farm work, plowing, disking, planting, mowing, and hauling manure, hay, corn and other crops.

"Matchless grain-saving, labor-saving and time saving" threshing machines were now using steam power to separate wheat, oats, barley, rye, and other small grains from their grass stems. Ads for the huge machines promised they would reduce grain waste so much, they would pay for themselves.[19]

Despite such new technology, there was no end to the hard physical work involved in farming. Many still relied on familiar, safer, but more labor-intensive harvesting alternatives.

In May 1888, well after the threshing machine was available, a man came through Petersburg selling grain cradles. Also used to harvest small grains like oats, wheat or rye, the grain cradle was a simple implement. The farmer walked through the field using the cradle to pull the seed heads off the tops of the dry stalks.

Although most knew only farming as a livelihood, some saw opportunities elsewhere and gave it up – likely with few regrets. After years of milking his cows by hand every morning and evening, Elijah Holton quit the dairy business in May 1889.

In 1892, Susie Saxton left for Kansas City, where she *"has a good position . . . as a stenographer and type-writer and likes the city very much."*[20]

William Brittenhelm of Walton devised a moveable corn crusher for dairymen. He could crush 3,600 pounds of corn and cob. He set it up at Ben Stephens' on the Lexington Pike two miles south of Florence and ran it on Tuesdays and Fridays.[21]

Some, like Benjamin H. Berkshire, remained on the farm, working large tracts to make it profitable. Berkshire farmed 500 acres, 225 of them river bottom land. Cattle and sheep grazed on his hillsides. Hogs cleaned up the grain and fodder the other animals left behind.

Berkshire married Ethel Norris of Petersburg and they had four children. Their home sat on a high bluff along the river in Petersburg *"affording a wondrous view of his own fertile acres as well as many miles of the Indiana shore line and undulating hills."*[22]

Petersburg women began commuting to work, crossing the river in rowboats or on the ferry to work in Aurora's match factory. A tomato canning factory began in Walton, offering more non-farm employment.

> **Boone County Recorder**
> Jan. 6, 1892
>
> The Lawrenceburg granite and marble works are turning out some very fine work at the most reasonable prices. Boone county people who desire to purchase tombstones or monuments will find it to their advantage to call there. John Beall, of Hebron, is the agent.
>
> ●
>
> Geo. G. Hughes sent south and got some very fine pecans, which he has planted for the purpose of propagating that nut. Although naturally a southern production, it is claimed that they will grow and do well as far north as the great lakes. The result of his pecan venture will be watched with much interest – especially by the small boy of the future.
>
> ●
>
> Prof. J.H. Craven and brother, of Walton, were in town Saturday. The Professor says his school gave an entertainment from the proceeds of which he purchased the latest edition of Webster's Dictionary for the use of the school.
>
> ●
>
> A.F. Lerch (of Bellevue) bought several crops of tobacco here last week at prices ranging from 10 to 12 cents per pound.

Ohio Floods

The primary economy still depended on agriculture. With many living along waterways, floods and droughts continued to make news.

While too little water troubled those moving goods and services on the river, too much was a bigger problem for Boone Countians. River

---

[19] *Boone County Recorder*, June 12, 1879.
[20] *Boone County Recorder*, Jan. 6, 1892.
[21] *Boone County Recorder*, Feb. 17, 1897.
[22] *Boone County Recorder*, 1930 Historical Edition.

Main Street looking west in Hebron.
Photo courtesy of Boone County Historic Preservation

levels kept folks on edge, watching their gauges, evaluating past records and speculating on the future.

"There has been more water in the Ohio River at this point during the months of January, February and March of this year than ever before since a record has been kept. The great floods of 1883 and 1884 filled the channel for about a month, but at no time since the new year began has the river been lower than 30' except perhaps for a single day," Petersburg's diarist L.A. Loder wrote in early April 1891.[23] When the Ohio reached 60', flood damage was extensive. Between 1900 and the 42 years since the Weather Bureau began keeping records in 1859, the Ohio overflowed the 52' flood mark 24 times. A minor flood now could be expected, on average, every other year.

High and low water were only two of the hazards facing steamboats. Temperatures were below freezing on Jan. 16, 1892, and ice was running in a quickly rising river. The steamer New Mary Houston broke loose in Cincinnati and began floating away. The Levi Workum caught it near Petersburg.

More people were using reliable overland transportation than the unpredictable river, but the steamer's passenger rates were reasonable. The Louisville and Cincinnati Packet Co. operated two boats, named after the cities. In 1899, a daylight round trip between Cincinnati and Louisville on the Cincinnati cost 25 cents. (On Jan. 30, 1918, ice damaged both and they were taken out of service.) The steamer Pittsburgh charged 50 cents for the same trip.

During droughts, even these low-water steamboats couldn't move up or down the narrow and shallow Ohio.

A record low pool of 1', 11" was recorded on Aug. 1, 1883. Riverfront residents waded across the Ohio to Indiana.

The Army Corps of Engineers began making plans to dam the river to maintain a minimum 9' year-round depth that would enable river traffic year-round.

Winter also hindered the steamboats.

"January and February 1895 plunged into a deep freeze, solidifying the Ohio, stopping steamboat travel and building a free bridge that eased commerce – at least in Petersburg where mules pulled sleds of whiskey to Indiana and returned with corn, the raw material to make more."

Temperatures listed in the Recorder for Jan. 18, 1895 included: Burlington -16; J.J. Tanners -18; W.H. Pope's -19; Petersburg -14; and Limaburg -20. (Residents always claimed that Limaburg had the lowest temperature in the county, summer or winter.) Chickens reportedly froze to death. At Gunpowder, a well 26' deep reportedly froze over.[24]

Weather anomalies continued. On April 2, 1894, a cyclone blew down the two-story East Bend Methodist Church. It was rebuilt as a one-story building.

---

[23] Conrad, *Loder 5*, 129.

[24] Conrad, *Yesterdays*, 60.

Chapter 8 1890-1899 Commuting Begins, Population Declines

On Oct. 8, 1895, Loder wrote: *"Ohio River lower than it has been for 50 or 100 years. The dry weather extends over a large scope of the country. People have to haul water a great many miles. There are no steamboats running between Cincinnati and Louisville."*[25]

An earthquake came with rain on the 31st. The odd weather continued, with another cyclone striking Cincinnati and other places on Nov. 26, *"blowing down chimneys and tearing up things generally."*[26]

Doctors News

Waterways other than the Ohio became hazards as well. On a cold and rainy Feb. 1, 1891, when rivers were up and rising, Dr. Tilley lost his surgical instruments and medicine packets while crossing Woolper Creek.

Local doctors were doing more and more surgery. A few days later, doctors Jonas C. Terrill, Luther B. Terrill, James M. Grant and W.H. Dunn took a tumor out of Miss Vie Snyder's breast. The group, minus Luther, removed a tumor from Sue Smith's breast the next month.

New transportation modes brought dangers with them. Dr. R.P. Gordon, while visiting Chicago, fell off an electric car on June 21, 1893, and was so badly hurt that he died the next day. Two years later, Frank Laws was fatally injured on the electric cars in Indianapolis.

Julia A. Loder, wife of the diarist, died on Dec. 26, 1893, at the age of 74. Her remains were placed in the Petersburg Cemetery vault two days later, then buried two weeks later, possibly due to frozen ground.[27]

The hanging tree on Burlington Pike (now KY 18) Courtesy of Boone County Historic Preservation

Making News

While Loder only recorded the bare facts about his wife's death, he extrapolated on rare, unusual and major disasters.

Sallie McAllister, a Petersburg woman who weighed 700 pounds, died at 82 on Nov. 30, 1893. Her coffin measured 4x5'. It took 17 men to lower the coffin into the grave. She had not been able to sleep in a bed for years and died in the chair she sat in. However, Loder noted that John Hanson Craig, who was known as the "Kentucky Giant" for his 900-pound bulk, outweighed her.[28]

That same week, a Louisville bridge under construction fell, killing 25 to 50.

J.J. Ferris went to Chicago on Oct. 9, 1893, to locate his grandfather's gold watch. The $300 watch had been pawned for $25. It was marked J.C.J. for Joseph Carter Jenkins who died on Sept. 21, 1889.[29]

On June 1, 1894, John M. Botts went to Cleves, Ohio, to have the "mad stone" put on a dog bite. The "mad stone" was a common treatment for animal bites, mentioned in later issues of the *Recorder* as well.

On Dec. 11, 1895, Dr. Kile of Aurora came to Petersburg to open a cancer on Philip Hoffman's face, but said it was neglected for so long that he could not cure it.

Boone County Distillery's still called "the column" blew up on Jan. 8, 1898, badly scalding Frank Collier and Adam Hoffman Jr., both of whom survived.

Crime

Accidents and sickness weren't the only tolls on human life, despite the rosy retrospect many hold for these days. Numerous other

---

[25] Conrad, *Loder 6*, 160.
[26] Conrad, *Loder 6*, 161.
[27] Conrad, Loder 6.

[28] Conrad, *Loder 6*, 146.
[29] Conrad, *Loder 6*, 143.

unfortunate events took place, some precipitated by Boone County residents. Their mention in Loder's diary shows they were the unusual and not expected events of the day.

Someone broke both windows and sashes from Mrs. Green's house on the corner of Peterburg's Mill and Second streets on March 7, 1893. On May 19, Jule Hoffman "had a fuss" at the distillery with John Grisley. Hoffman shot twice at Grisley then was arrested and held on $100 bail to appear before the Circuit Court in Burlington.

A woman was badly cut in a fight at Solon Early's farm. Dr. R.C. Tilley used 12 to 15 stitches to close her wounds. On Dec. 15, 1897, thieves stole $40 and a lot of dry goods from the Gainesville Store.

On March 22, 1901, burglars broke into Petersburg's bank and stole $250 in money and stamps.

Bloodhounds were put on Wood Huff's trail after he stoned T.B. Mathews at the Ben and James Jarrell house on Oct. 9, 1904.

Lafferdette Lynching

With eight lynchings in 20 years, Boone County was gaining "a national reputation as the abode of the lawless and the lynchers." In May 1884, Charles Dickson was taken from the jail and lynched.

Boone County Recorder
Jan. 6, 1892
Petersburg

On New Years night Mr. & Mrs. T.B. Matthews entertained a party of their friends with a peanut hunt. Everyone always has a good time at their home, and it is useless to say more than that the enjoyment on this occasion was fully up to the average. J.J. Ferris and Mrs. Hattie Gaines won the prizes. On the same evening Philly Hoffman and wife gave the young people a party and they tripped the light fantastic until the wee small hours.

Petersburg society has enjoyed several very pleasant gatherings lately. On New Year's Eve the White Bow Club gave an excellent oyster supper at Mrs. Maria Terrill's. The evening was spent with games of all kinds and about ten o'clock about 30 guests sat down to the elegant repast. The organization of W.B.C. is of quite recent date, but it is hoped it will be long-lived and often repeat the entertainment last Thursday evening.

On Thursday evening Mr. & Mrs. J.J. Ferris entertained the ladies who constitute the T. and G. club, and their guests at their elegant home on the hill. An excellent supper was served, which, in point of elegance and grandeur, was surpassed only by the beauty of the ladies and their toilets. Mr. and Mrs. Ferris are the best entertainers, and everyone enjoyed one of the pleasantest evenings of the year.

FARM FOR SALE

I want to sell my farm about one mile from Hebron on the North Bend road. It is the best farm in the neighborhood, containing some 250 acres with good fences, plenty of timber and good water, a new barn (unfinished) and 40 acres of the best wheat in Boone county – balance mostly in grass.

I want to sell because there is not snap enough in that country to build a turnpike, and I don't want to move my family on a dirt road. Anyone willing to live on a dirt road can get a bargain – I will sell at a loss.

GEO. M. BEDINGER

A drunken mob removed William Scales from the jail and did the same in September 1885.

Louie Lafferdette, a man who had started a fight with A.B. Whitlock near the Anderson ferry, was lodged in the Burlington jail. Angry citizens threatened to lynch him on a Saturday night, but then their ardor had seemed to dim.

However at 1 a.m. Monday, July 16, 1894, Jailer Crisler woke surrounded by four or five men with drawn pistols. While Crisler resisted their demands to unlock the jail, the gunmen prevailed. Lafferdette was roused and dressed, asking for mercy, but told he had shown none to their friend.

With a handkerchief over his mouth and hands tied behind him, Lafferdette was rushed into a wagon. The mob had come through Hebron, then Bullittsville, taking a hay wagon from a barn and pulling it to Burlington.

They left town quietly without waking citizens. He was hung from an oak tree about ¾ mile out Bullittsville Road. Sheriff Roberts and Dudley Finnell removed the body about 7 a.m.

The hangman's knot had failed to work and Lafferdette died of strangulation by a seagrass rope. The mob had remained until its victim was dead.

Chapter 8 1890-1899 Commuting Begins, Population Declines

While the lynchmen had thrown the jail keys on the cell floor, a boy named Green who was also imprisoned was found sitting in his cell, too terrified to escape.

The coroner's jury determined that Cincinnati newspaper reporters Kirby Snow and William J. Keefe incited the mob. They were the only members of the 30-man mob who were identified – despite the fact that none wore hoods or masks. Snow and Keefe were charged with murder. Snow claimed he simply attended in his capacity as a reporter.[30]

Elections

Elections were another news-making event, but Loder didn't mention any campaigning, much less contentious races. The Recorder announced candidacies and vote tallies.

On May 26, 1890, grocer J. Frank Grant was sworn in as Chairman of Petersburg's Board of Trustees. A few days later, Surveyor Vest completed the town survey that was turned into the federal census bureau. A week later, more than a dozen citizens rode the mailboat to Carrollton to nominate

---

Boone County Recorder
Jan. 6, 1892

In the departure of the old year, Burlington was given a pretty general shakeup, and rather a demoralized state of affairs met the optics of the citizens when they came forth on the morning of the first day of the new year.

It was about 11:45 o'clock when the discharge of a shotgun on the street signaled the beginning of the general hurrah which lasted for some time.

When the signal was given the hotel bells, the church bells and the court house bell commenced ringing simultaneously, and kept up their chorus for about half an hour in which time the old year had given way to its young successor.

While the old year was retiring, things moveable about the town cut some queer antics.

Several large stones blockaded the gates opening into the yards in front of Dr. Furnish's and John Lassing's offices, and seemed to dispute the right of anyone to enter.

At the corner of Washington and Jefferson streets a bucket had a commanding view from its elevated position in a maple tree. While Everett Hall's barber sign had left its position at that corner and ascended the court house portico, and exchanged the morning's salutations with a sleigh that had secured a position astride the roof of the bank building.

A couple of buggies and a spring wagon were stationed about the bank as though they wanted the job of transferring the wealth of that institution to some other point.

A superannuated buggy and 2 or 3 sets of harness were trying to obtrude themselves into the presence of the jeweler, as though he was the proper person to administer unto their wants.

A two-horse carriage, recently used by an attorney of this place, made its way into the courthouse hall, from which place it took several able-bodied men to eject it Friday Morning.

The proprietors of the livery stable expecting that inanimate objects might get a move on them Thursday night, attempted to forbid such action on part of their rolling stock, by locking it up that night at the close of business hours, but all to no avail, as their buggies were among the most frisky of any in town.

No property was destroyed, all the mischief being done only as a new year's frolic and an adieu to '91.

---

a congressional candidate to fill John G. Carlisle's seat. After Senator J.B. Beck's death, Carlisle had moved into that position.[31]

The Oct. 1, 1892, primary election was done "under the Australian plan" – by secret ballot – rather than calling one's preferences aloud as had been the previous custom.

In November, the Democrats rallied in Petersburg. N.S. Walton, Dr. Furnish, Enos Nixon, and Ben Huatt "*made short speeches to a powerful crowd,*" Loder noted.

L.A. Loder assessed the town of Petersburg as well as took the census in December 1896. The population was 268 males and 291 females. Just after he finished the census, Loder became a grandfather. On Dec. 31, 1896, the A. Leon Loder family had twins, Julia Barbara and Milton Bryan.[32]

Petersburg Free Schools

Loder's grandchildren could now

---

[30] Louie Lafferdette Take From Jail and Hanged, *Boone County Recorder*, July 18, 1894.

[31] Conrad, *Loder 5*, 123.
[32] Conrad, Loder 6.

MUSICAL AND DRAMATICAL
ENTERTAINMENT
At Burlington, Kentucky
MARCH 10, 11 & 12, '92
PROGRAMME:
"THE TOODLES,"
Or the Brothers' Revenge

A Drama in Two Acts, in which, with Dr. FURNISH as "Toodles," Miss FANNIE FINCH as Mary or the Farmers' Daughter, and the following cast, no one can fail to be entertained:

Mrs. Toodles .... Miss Ora Conner
George Acorn .... Joe Reed
Farmer Acorn .... Ed McKim
Charles Fenton .... Elmer Beall
Lawyer Gibbs .... Stanley Clutterbuck
Farmer Fenton .... Arthur Rouse
1rst & 2d Farmers .... J.W. Palmer and G.W. Sandford

"HANDY ANDY,"
Or the "IRISH DUKE."

A Drama in Two Acts, in which, JOE REED, will play the Irish man in his inimitable style, and "Mad Nance," presented with great force by Miss ORA CONNER, supported by the exceptionally strong cast:

Squire Edgar .... J.M. Lassing
" O'Grady .... D. Beall
Dick Dawson .... Elmer Beall
Mr. Furlong .... Ed McKim
Edward O' Conner .... Stanley Clutterbuck
Simon .... G.W. Sandford
McQuade .... J.W. Palmer
Oonah Roney .... Miss Pinkie Cowen
Fannie Dawson .... Miss Olga Kirkpatrick

A Side Splitter,
The HEROIC DUTCHMAN of '76.

A Comedy in Five Acts, is full of Fun and startling incidents and with the following cast will not fail to entertain:

SAM, a gentleman of color .... J.M. Lassing
The Heroic Dutchman .... Elmer Beall
Reble Captain .... N.E. Riddell
A Tory .... Ed McKim
Ex Col. Brown .... Arthur Rouse
Captain Lile .... G.W. Sandford
A British Corporal .... J.W. Palmer
May Brown .... Miss Ora Conner
Kate Brown .... Miss Pinkie Cowen

The Farce,
30 Minutes for Refreshments.

Will give the audience Thirty Minutes of as Hearty Laughter as it will desire. In which will appear in his Happy Style D. BEALL, the Blastering Bachelor supported, in a style not to be excelled, by the following cast:

John Foxton .... Elmer Beall
Major Pepper .... Eddie McKim
Clarence Fitts (servant to Bachelor) .... N.E. Riddell
Mrs. John Foxton .... Miss Ella Duncan
Miss Polly Patton .... Miss Olga Kirkpatrick
Miss Arabella Pepper .... Miss Pinkie Cowen

ADMISSION 25c. Children under 12, 15 c.
Doors open at 7 o'clock.   Performance begins at 7½ o'clock.

Boone County Recorder
March 9, 1892
LOCAL NEWS

All those wanting painting, papering &c., can have it done in first-class style by calling on CHAS. E. CLORE, Hebron, Ky.

Hear that James L. Clore has been awarded the contract for carrying the mail on the Erlanger and Burlington route for the next four years.

A flock of 53 wild geese passed over the town last Thursday evening going from east to west. Wild geese are seldom seen passing over here in these latter days.

NOTICE – All those indebted to me will please come forward and settle at once, as I need money badly.

A valuable Jersey cow belonging to J.R. Clutterbuck fell into a sink hole one afternoon last week, where she remained til morning. The injuries the animal sustained will likely render her useless forever.

Mr. Bolton requested me to state to the reading public that he considers himself one of the handsomest and most graceful and accomplished gentlemen in Boone County.

Mr. Ran Rouse with our minister, Rev. Duvall, was riding on a box in a wagon with the children as drivers, when the horse gave a sudden start throwing the minister and Mr. Rouse out breaking one of Mr. R's arms.

Some of the farmers have their lambs sold at $4 and their wood at 25 cents per pound.

Our friend James W. Barlow, of the Limaburg neighborhood, was in town one day last week and by some means it was reported on the streets that he intended, that day, to make application for his marriage license; but we were satisfied that it was a reckless statement of a thoughtless person and so it proved.

Dr. L.R. Terrill, of Delhi, O., has many friends in this country who have been particularly solicitous about his condition since he contracted blood poisoning by assisting in a post mortem and they are glad to learn that he is improving. He had a very severe attack from which to recover.

Wood sawings are all the go at present, with an oyster supper or fish fry at night.

The Boone Co. Distilling Co. shipped a lot of whiskey to Germany one day last week.

It takes 5000 gallons of slop and two tons of hay daily to feed the cattle at the Petersburg Distillery.

Petersburg had a dancing school where the waltz and the glide, the skirt dance and the Ward McAllister are taught.

Chapter 8 1890-1899 Commuting Begins, Population Declines

attend a two-room school. Petersburg's elementary "free school" had begun on Sept. 22, 1890, under Principal William Terrell's direction with Mrs. Mary . Walton and Miss Lizzie Gordon assisting. The teachers continued with Frank Laws as principal when school began on Sept. 18, 1893.

On Sept. 17, 1895, Beverly Nelson was principal and Orlando Snyder and Miss Lawring assisted. Lula Souther directed the free school in 1899.[33]

Petersburg began offering more than one grade about 1896. Some other county schools had a third room, allowing not only separation of the primary and elementary classes, but also advanced subjects. A typical teacher taught 35-40 pupils 11 subjects in an eight-hour day.[34]

On Sunday, Oct. 7, 1894, Mr. and Mrs. McKinley lectured at the schoolhouse on a short method of doing arithmetic.[35]

Boone County's superintendent of schools from 1886 to 1890 was John P. Ryle who grew up a few miles down the river in

---

[33] Conrad, Loder 6.
[34] Conrad, *The History of Boone County Schools*, 20.
[35] Conrad, Loder 6.

JIM CROW

The combined harness and Saddle Horse and renowned breeder of Ky., will be found at George E. Rouse's farm, half way between Burlington and Florence, every day in the week, and will be allowed to serve mares at $10 to insure a living colt.

JIM CROW is too well known to require a description. He has proven himself an excellent breeder. At the Harvest Home last year, his colts were awarded first premiums in the following rings: Best general purpose colt; best draft colt; best harness colt. In this last ring there were 31 other handsome colts.

His colts have fine style, good size and excellent disposition.

J.E. ROUSE Limaburg, Ky.

PIGS! PIGS! PIGS!
FROM MATURE STOCK
PURE BRED
Chester White Hogs

LA BELLE HERD is made up of a very select lot of breeding animals from five different States. Several prize winners – one that captured a ribbon at the World's Fair.

World's Fair stock for sale at all times. Can furnish pairs or trios no akin. All either recorded or eligible to record, and pedigrees furnished whenever wanted.

Every one invited to visit herd.
T.J. HUGHES, Beaver Lick, Ky.

Prospect Simmons 14221,
(2 year old record 2:37.)

Sired by Simmons 2744 (2:28); 1rst dam by Almont Boy 4308 (2:33 ¼); 2d dam C.M. Clay, Jr., 22 (2:30 ½); 3d dam Leviathan, thoroughbred.

Will make the season at Prospect Stock Farm, Petersburg, Ky. At the following rates:

$10 Single Service – spot cash.
$15 By the season, money due at time of service, with privilege of returning in 1895, or money refunded at my option.
$20 To insure a mare with foal, money due when fact is ascertained or mare parted with.
$25 to insure living colt.

For further information address
J.J. FERRIS, Petersburg, Ky.

Boone County Recorder
June 27, 1894
NEIGHBORHOOD NEWS.

PETERSBURG – Mrs. A.B. Parker lost her pocket-book which contained about $20. It was found by a boy who refused to surrender it after she had described it, and an officer had to take it from him.

The day was dreadfully hot, and several came near receiving sunstrokes as they were returning from the grounds.

G.W. Taylor furnished two 'buses. The horses attached to one of them gave out on the way home and the passengers had to walk to town.

The program included singing, praying, preaching and blackboard lectures. The band had to walk home.

The band played at the residence of W.T. Crisler, Wednesday night, the occasion being the first anniversary of the marriage. Billie and his wife have the best wishes of the boys, who hope they will live to celebrate their diamond wedding. The ice cream, lemonade, and other delicacies served, were delightful.

U should see Buchanan's show window. In it he has a fountain and a tank filled with fish. The fountain is small and quite a curiosity.

Petersburg would be the best city in the United States if her people would wake up, and shake off the lethargy that has overtaken them. If it were not for her churches and Sunday schools, the town would have the blues.

TAYLORSPORT – One depredation after another is committed at Parlor Grove by the bad elements of Cincinnati and Covington participating in dog fights, prize fights, gambling, selling liquor, etc. The people of this community think it ought to be stopped.

The social and festival was a grand success in every respect. Joyful notes rang out from old Taylorsport, and the bountiful supply of ice cream, cake and lemonade cooled and refreshed the inner man. The old members were so delighted that they did not know when to stop eating.

Harvest is at hand, and the wheat in this neighborhood has been put in the shock sooner than ususal. Some say the heads are not well filled.

Our lamb buyers have a forlorn look since the bottom fell out of the market. Cheer up boys, the future may be some brighter.

MOUNT AIRY – Two young men of this neighborhood, I wont say who, inform me that peach pie, mustard, Aurora beer and gin combined, make a good dish for a restaurant, but you must partake of the last two very freely.

H.P. Crisler was the first man in this neighborhood to commence cutting wheat. He began last Thursday.

LIMABURG – Kirb Tanner has bought a new buggy.

Adam Heist's little son fell into the cellar, one day last week, receiving a very ugly scalp wound, which was sewn up by Otha Rouse.

Eddie Helm, Chad and Otha Rouse have organized a string band.

Cutting wheat is the order of the day here.

CONSTANCE – K. Zimmer's horse ran away with a plow and crippled itself quite badly. Henry Havely cut his foot very badly with an adz.

Grant (now called Belleview). Two of Ryle's seven children remained in Boone County. In 1915 Solon Ryle became known for raising registered Jersey cattle and Chester White hogs.[36]

"Scent"sation

In what was probably the most shocking science lesson for any local resident, an Eastern entrepreneur brought a 65' whale weighing an estimated 80,000 pounds down the Ohio by barge. He stopped at Cincinnati, Petersburg and Belleview, attracting the curious.

L.A. and Leon Loder and Mr. Stephens were among the Petersburg residents impressed with the 20' jaw spread and 45' girth.[37]

Isabella Selmes, who had been raised on the Dinsmore farm, recalled seeing the whale at Belleview when she was about 10 years old. The whale's mouth was propped open and carpeted in red with two benches sitting inside. She was told people along the way had gotten married inside the whale's mouth.

She said she could still smell the whale after she got home – a mile away![38]

New Flour Mill

Petersburg's businesses were growing as well as its educational offerings.

James Barnet began delivering milk in Petersburg using a horse-drawn wagon on March 17, 1886.

Grant and Graves bought Ira & M.F. Wingate's (or Wingait) Petersburg butchering business on Jan. 14, 1888.

Stonemasons began building the foundation for a new flour mill at the upper end of Petersburg in April 1889. By mid-May the boiler had arrived on the steamer Minnie. The mill began grinding flour on Sept. 3. On Nov. 16, 1890, Loder noted, *"Last week there was quite a lot of excitement in Petersburg of the running away of Day, one of the proprietors of the flour mill."*

On Sept. 24, 1890, *"The Boone County Distilling Co. got up steam today to pump water to swell the tubs before commencing to still."*

R.A. McWethy and Thomas Cowan left Petersburg the end of February 1891 to start a

Looking east from Hebron.
Courtesy of Boone County Historic Preservation

store selling groceries and queensware in Ada, Ohio.

A distillery fire on Sept. 13, 1891, burned a barn full of straw. *"Made a big fire for a little while,"* Loder said. By the end of the month, the distillery was *"starting its first mash of 1,250 bushels."* [39]

In September 1892, Reese and Mark Gordon came to Petersburg to refill their storeroom with groceries. The distillery finished another brick government warehouse seven stories tall on Sept. 25, 1892.[40]

---

[36] Solon B. Ryle, *Boone County Recorder*, 1930 Historical Edition.
[37] Conrad, *Loder 4*, 28.
[38] Hannah Baird, from the Dinsmore Diaries.

[39] Conrad, *Loder 5*.
[40] Conrad, *Loder 5*.

Mrs. Lightfoot took over the Loder house on March 9, 1893, when its namesake was 74 years old. In June, Levi Spencer opened an ice cream and lemonade stand in part of Mrs. James Bradley's house. Petersburg citizens began taking up money to drill a town well. They found plenty of water at 107'.

Government men began fixing the river shore in mid-October 1895, in preparation for installing a dike at Lawrenceburg. The end of November 1896, Joe Morrison began building a new ferry at the foot of Petersburg's Tanner Street for S.W. Tolen at the Lawrenceburg Ferry.

In March 1897, an Aurora man came to Petersburg looking for girls to work in a match factory. The next week, 21 women began crossing the river to work for him.[41]

Sunday Visiting

The new factories, of course, observed the unwritten rules of no work on Sunday. With primarily the young, unmarried women and men working away from the family farm, lifestyles changed little.

Throughout the region, isolated farmers gathered at country stores to see friends and neighbors, discuss politics, and exchange news and advice.

Winter, after machinery was cleaned and repaired for spring plowing and tobacco was sold, was slow time in the agricultural economy. Many whittled away the dreary hours telling stories around the general store's ever-present wood stoves.

Sundays were the natural day for family travel or hosting guests. The decree reserving the seventh day for rest was impinged on only by the necessities of feeding livestock and tending to emergencies.[42]

Theater and Baseball

There was plenty of entertainment to be found. On Aug. 7, 1900, men stopped by Petersburg and took photos – several of A. Leon Loder's family, Anora and her daughter Fannie Davis, and L.A. Loder and his dog Davey. Two men brought two grizzly bears to Petersburg, which *"created quite an excitement in the town"* on Nov. 8, 1890.

The next May, a four-horse rig from Lawrenceburg that included three Indians, four white men and one Negro, came to Petersburg. They gave a lecture, sold medicine, *"and had some good music and singing."*

The Knights of Pythias entertained at the Petersburg Methodist Church on Feb. 10, 1891. In April, the group planned to go to Burlington to organize a lodge but the *"conveyance that they had employed failed to come and they had to postpone their trip."*[43] The group sponsored a celebration on Sept. 23, 1894, that attracted 500-700 and included Chinese (Loder said "China") lanterns hung all over Petersburg, a big supper, speeches, three bands and fireworks.

The Empire Theater performed for six nights in Petersburg one November, then traveled the winding road to Hebron and did it again. The next month, the *"Home Talent Entertainment of Theatrics Performance"* from Hebron played in Gordon's Hall in Petersburg. On a return engagement, the group gathered $70-$80.

The Petersburg Base Ball Club held a festival in the distillery's malt house raising $176 on Aug. 12, 1891.[44]

Courtesy of David and Jeanette Clore

---

[41] Conrad, *Loder 6*.
[42] Campbell, 21.
[43] Conrad, *Loder 5*, 128.
[44] Conrad, *Loder 5*.

The Rogers family place on Route 20 between Belleview and Petersburg. Courtesy of Mary Sue Rudicill.

Petersburg's Podge

Two years later, local boy Arthur "Podge" Alloway who had grown up playing baseball in Petersburg, was pitching for Memphis in the Southern League. His mother, Caroline Clark, had died in 1874 when Arthur was five, so he grew up in his father's busy blacksmith shop.

Orville Alloway's son Podge played with independent teams around Cincinnati, then tried out for Louisville. Bill Rourke, a man who later scouted for the Cincinnati Reds, is credited with keeping Alloway out of the big leagues. While Rourke was managing the Omaha team, he hit Podge at practice. "*'Podge' retaliated by giving Rourke a thorough trimming.*"

In 1895, Alloway played for Petersburg, Va. Two years later, he pitched every other day, winning the pennant for Evansville. Sold to Cleveland, he was farmed out to Ft. Wayne, Ind., where he played for two years. In 1901, he went to Indianapolis, then on to Omaha where he was traded to Peoria, Ill., in 1903.

Alloway recalled playing in Cripple Creek, Colo., where the altitude was so high the Midwesterners had difficulty running bases. After hitting a ball he was sure would be a homer, he fell down four times getting to second base and had to stop there. Later that day, a cloudburst literally washed away the diamond, halting the game and sending spectators fleeing.

Alloway jumped to the Association League in Kansas City. In 1904, he was sold to Birmingham,

Arthur "Podge" Alloway
1930 Recorder Historical Edition
Courtesy of Ruth Glenn

Chapter 8 1890-1899 Commuting Begins, Population Declines

The Rabbit Hash Ferry ran to Rising Sun, Ind., was powered by horses. Ben Wilson stands on the front of the boat, Willie Stephens is at the back. Hubert Ryle is on the wagon delivering a load of tomatoes to the Rising Sun cannery.   Photo courtesy of Wanetta Clause

Ala., then to Grand Rapids, Mich., in the Central League.

In 1907, he umpired for the Western Association for two years, then for the Blue Grass League for another two. He umpired in West Virginia's Mountain League in 1911, then in Pennsylvania's Tri-State League.[45]

Riddell's Store

James A. Riddell also moved away to take a non-farm job. Born at Petersburg in 1846, he attended Sackett Mead's private school in Covington, then worked in William Berkshire's dry goods store in Petersburg.

At 18, he moved across the river to clerk at John Ferris' Lawrenceburg drug store. He worked for several pharmacists and in 1874, moved to Aurora to open a drug store in partnership with John B. Morrison.

The J.A. Riddell Co. became his own when they dissolved the partnership in 1883. After 56 years of working in the same room, he sold his store to an Indianapolis man. Unmarried, Riddell lived with his sister in Aurora, enjoying the flowers and birds.[46]

Winston, Harvard Attorney

Bullittsburg native Charles A. Winston left the region too, making a name for himself as an attorney. Born on Dec. 6, 1865, he graduated from Harvard University in 1893. After practicing law in Chicago, he studied in Europe, the Near East, India, Australia and Tasmania.

After attending some additional Harvard courses to specialize in constitutional, corporate and civil law, he taught in the University of Minnesota's law department for a time. Finding the university job financially limiting, he returned to Chicago and practiced law.

During a visit to Rome, he met a Michigan woman who was staying in his hotel. In June 1890, Winston married Nina Wright. (They returned to Rome to celebrate their 25th anniversary.)

Mrs. Winston, who spoke five languages fluently, had studied in France, Italy and Greece. She too was a member of the Illinois and Chicago Bars, having attended Chicago University Law School.[47]

---

[45] "Arthur Alloway," *Boone County Recorder,* 1930 Historical Edition.
[46] *Boone County Recorder,* 1930 Historical Edition.

[47] C.A. Winston, *Boone County Recorder,* 1930 Historical Edition.

Dinsmore Sausage Business

Mrs. Winston was as much an anomaly in her time as the forward-thinking and well-educated Dinsmore women. In 1886, Patty Dinsmore Selmes had returned to the family home to give birth to a daughter, named Isabella in honor of her grandmother. Ten years later, after her husband Tilden Selmes' death, Patty and Isabella moved in with Julia at the Boone County homestead.

In the late 1890s, Patty began a ham and sausage business in partnership with another woman. Meanwhile, Julia raised her grandniece, accompanying Isabella on European trips.

Described as beautiful and gifted, Isabella took her first trip to Europe at 16. One account says a crowd of men gathered around Isabella as she sketched the Tuileries Gardens in Paris. The crowd became so large that the Paris police escorted her to her hotel and advised Julia to select a more secluded place for Isabella's painting.[48]

Additional Tolls

While the Dinsmores were traveling around the nation, simple overland travel was still an issue here.

On July 6, 1893, state laws regarding tollroads added a provision charging $1 for "each traction or other engine" using the road. Twenty cents a mile became the automobile toll, amid concerns that the weight of horseless carriages would damage the roads, not to mention frighten horses and disrupt buggy and wagon traffic.

Some improvements were being made. The Petersburg Turnpike Co. built an iron bridge one mile from Petersburg in July 1894.[49]

Agitation against tollroads increased in the 1890s, resulting in violence in Anderson and Washington counties in 1896. Tollgates were destroyed, occasionally the house with them. Some gate operators just took down the barrier and walked away, leaving the counties to repair the roads.

Statewide, individuals who had put up roughly $30 million received only irregular dividends and ultimately lost most of their investment. However, their money had stimulated growth and development in their hometowns.

Kirtley Sr. Resigns

After more than 40 years of leading the Baptist churches at Bullittsburg and Big Bone, Rev. James A. Kirtley offered his resignation. He had pastored the Bullittsburg church with his father Robert from 1853 until 1871, until the older man retired, when he was on his own. Then, James rode a horse from his Bullittsburg farm to preach at Big Bone on alternate Sundays. The congregations declined to release him in 1894, but he resigned for good in 1898.

Improvements had been made at both churches during his tenure and he had baptized, married and consoled many in neighborhoods in-between.[50]

In 1886, Big Bone Baptist extended to Union, organizing a new church on property it had bought and built on a decade before. Bro. LaFayette "Lafe" Johnson led the congregation that included Mr. & Mrs. J.A. Huey and Annie A. Bristow.[51]

In 1887 Big Bone Church paid $4 to insure its meeting house. Coal cost 10 cents a bushel and the minister's salary was $550 that year.[52]

In 1901, Bullittsburg paid the Excelsior Company of Cincinnati $379 for new pews. The steamer Workman carried them to the

---

> **Boone County Recorder**
> Feb. 17, 1897
> **Verona's Free-silver Debating Club**
> The Free-silver Debating Club's topic was 'Resolved that a man can be of more benefit to his country religiously than politically.
> T.E. Roberts, J.H. Craven and George McPherson argued for the resolution.
> E.E. Fry, John L. Vest and George W. Johnson argued the negative.
> Judges James Hind, J.H. Marshall and William McPherson found in favor of the resolution.

---

[48] Reis, 45.
[49] Conrad, *Loder 6*, 150.

[50] Campbell, 20.
[51] Campbell, 45.
[52] A Brief History of Big Bone Baptist Church 1843-1968, 13.

landing at the mouth of Garrison Creek, about a mile from the church. Church members delivered them to the church with horse-drawn wagons. Sixty years later, the pews were returned to Cincinnati for another refinishing – at three times the original cost.[53]

In 1903, James A. Kirtley Jr. was ordained to the ministry at Bullittsburg. His father died the next year. James Jr. served the Big Bone Church.[54]

Two years later, the Bullittsburg Church spent $160 to install an iron fence around the cemetery.[55]

Norman's Landing Store

Parishioners could purchase most of their supplies from John C. Miller, who began operating one of the general stores at Norman's Landing, a bit west of Big Bone. After his son Lurrel R. married Bertha D. Miller (no relation) in 1899, Lurrel took over the store. While the younger Millers had no children by birth, they reared a niece, Bertha Newberry.

The Millers' store stocked hardware, farm implements, notions, groceries and produce.[56] A wool mill operated at the Landing for a time, and then it was converted into a flour mill. The structure was dismantled in 1921.

---

[53] Campbell, 22.
[54] Campbell, 21.
[55] Campbell, 22.
[56] Lurrel R. Miller, *Boone County Recorder*, Historical Edition, R.E. Berkshire publisher, Sept. 4, 1930.

Just upriver, the East Bend Baptist Church was growing. It reported, *"two baptisms, three by letter, eight excluded, for a total of 39 members."* The 1894 regional meeting also reported that the pastor's salary and church expenses totaled $130.

Boone County Recorder
Feb. 17, 1897
Verona Fox Hunt

The greatest event of the season in the Mudlick neighborhood was the pulling off of that fox chase near Hume's Store. The Houston boys and James Hume caught a fox the day before and sent out word of the time and place where the reynard would be turned loose.

When the time came, there were 45 men and 26 dogs at the appointed place. David Houston was made master of ceremonies.

At 9 a.m. the fox was liberated and was allowed four minutes before the start of the hounds. The dogs were sent off on good order. During the first hour, they gained little on the fox.

At the end of two hours of the hardest running that has been witnessed in this country for many years, the fox was caught on the ground.

Of the 26 dogs that started the race only these five were at the catching: Arthur Stephenson's Brady, Ben O'Neal's Bob, Rube Houston's Kate, David Houston's Dinah, and Jim Hume's Flora.

It seemed that every man within a radius of several miles of here was a fox hunter that day.

William Conrad said, *"Quite often the fox would enter a den, and picks and shovels were brought into the action. It has been related that hunters once dug from the same burrow six skunks, three groundhogs, and not one, but two foxes."*

Verona School Grows

Records also were well documented at Verona's school which, like the Baptist Church, had grown considerably.

In 1897, Verona principal John Henry Craven and teacher Mrs. Lillie Rouse reported the term closed Feb. 1 with 161 pupils in the district, 116 of whom were enrolled. High attendance was 101, low was 55, average was 84. The average grade for scholarship, deportment and neatness was 96. Five students received corporal punishment.

Verona had its own column in the *Recorder*. This was published on Nov. 21, 1894:

"While driving home from Crittenden one day last week, Miss Bettie Kennedy met with quite an accident. Her horse while hitched to the buggy running away with her, upsetting the buggy and dragging Miss Kennedy quite a distance. She was bruised and severely hurt, but not fatal. The buggy was completely wrecked while the horse escaped without injury.

"C.C. Roberts and family were the guests of friends and relatives here, last week. Charley

was after the taxes that are unpaid in this part of the county.

"Scott Myers, one of our hustling machinists, will soon have in running order a fine new saw and grist mill. Scott talks as though he will soon start a roller flour mill in town.

"The Houston boys killed a monster eagle down on Mudlick while enroute to the (new church) dedication at Beaver. The eagle was devouring a goose when captured.

"There are too many loafers around town since the recent election.

"Farmers are busy gathering corn and hauling coal."

A series of accidents injured the sons of Dr. S.M. Adams of Beaver in 1897. While little Presley was attempting to carve letters on the barn door, the knife slipped and struck his eye. The next day, his older brother Johnnie was handling a shotgun that went off accidentally, tearing off his heel and badly injuring his ankle.[57]

Walton Street Lights

That same newspaper announced a "masque ball" at Walton's Opera House on Thanksgiving evening, local Catholics' plans to build a church, and that Christian Church ladies were seeking the hungry in need of a Thanksgiving dinner.

George Youell was acclaimed for killing 15 birds with one lucky blast from his shotgun.

Minutes of the 1890 Walton city council show a preoccupation with getting sidewalks installed throughout the town. Ditching streets, collecting delinquent taxes, dealing with the jail and other issues were assigned to committees.[58]

While the trains had arrived, expediting commerce and making commuting easier than by stagecoach, nothing had alleviated Walton's ever-present dust and mud. Main Street was either a dry, dusty, manure-laden road or a fragrant mud churned by rain and animal hooves. Steam engines belched black soot to the consternation of Walton housekeepers who hung their Monday washing out to dry.

Still a frontier town in appearance with its false-front buildings, Walton installed the county's first streetlights. Mr. Hedges, the first lamp lighter, carried an oilcan and a ladder to reach the Dietz lanterns, which were mounted on posts about 8' high. He filled each lamp with just enough oil to burn out after daybreak.

Fred Calendar took over and held the lamp lighting job until the first electric plant was built across from city hall in about 1913.[59]

Walton attorney C.Y. Dyas practiced law in Boone, Kenton and Grant counties, promising *"prompt attention given to all cases entrusted to my care."*[60]

The county's major manufacturing enterprise was Walton's cannery that opened in 1894 to process locally grown tomatoes. It operated sporadically until WWII. At one point, when prices fell to about a dime a bushel, local tomato growers banded together and withheld their produce until the plant paid a reasonable price.[61]

In 1897, there was talk that a Cincinnati firm was buying the Phoenix Hotel with plans to turn it into a summer boarding house with a grocery attached.

Union Attorney Elected

Union boy John Maurice Lassing, born at Elm Tree in 1864, was the first son of Dr. H.C. and Anna Lassing.

In 1886, after graduating from Central University (now Eastern Kentucky University) in Richmond, he taught school and studied law under Burlington attorney Fountain Riddell. Lassing completed the two year program at Cincinnati Law School in one year, ranking 7th of 90.

---

[57] *Boone County Recorder*, Feb. 17, 1897.
[58] 1890 Walton City Council Record Book.
[59] William Fitzgerald, "Walton Established in 1840." *Boone County Recorder*, Jan. 2, 1964.
[60] *Boone County Recorder*, June 27, 1894.
[61] Bruce Ferguson, Jan. 13, 1998.

The next year, he was elected County Attorney, then re-elected in 1894. When Circuit Judge John W. Green died in office, Lassing was appointed to fill the term. He was elected and re-elected until a vacancy appeared in the Appellate Court. In a repeat of his experience with the lower court, he was appointed, then elected and re-elected. He served until ill health caused him to resign.

During his 21 years of public service, Judge Lassing assisted in managing several hotly contested gubernatorial, senatorial and judicial campaigns. He was known for his focus on improving Boone County roads.[62]

Horse Shows at the Fair

During Lassing's term as county attorney, the Florence Fair revived. Construction began in 1896 on leased ground in Carpenter's Woods at the southwest corner of the U.S. 25 and KY 42 intersection. Workmen moved a sawmill in to construct an amphitheater with 10 rows of seats. A roof covered the seats and promenade to shade viewers.

Promoters thought complimentary tickets and easy access were the reasons the original fair failed, so these grounds were secured with a solid wooden fence surrounding even the stalls and stables.

Women showed off their baking, canning, and preserve-making skills. Awards were offered for nine varieties of pies and 18 kinds of cakes at the first fair.

Main Street looking south from the hotel in Union
Photo courtesy of Boone County Historic Preservation

Six tobacco stalks from each crop were selected for judging. The finest pecks of corn, rye or oats won ribbons. The poultry department listed awards for 22 chicken breeds and two each of ducks and geese.

Hampshires, Chester Whites, Durocs and Poland China hogs competed. Sheep included Oxfords, Southdowns, Hampshires and Shropshires. Beef cattle were rare then, but Holsteins and Jerseys were driven to the grounds in herds of 10 to 20 cows with a bull.

The Queen and Crescent railroad ran special trains to Erlanger where horse-drawn buses carried fairgoers from the depot to the fairgrounds.

Trick dogs or ponies performed in the center ring. A gaily-uniformed brass band from the city occupied the second floor.[63]

Although Boone County's population was only 11,170 in 1899, on Friday evening of the fair, attendance was estimated at nearly 15,000. Wagons, buggies, carriages and carts brought crowds to Florence. The last day included beautiful baby contests, sales of winning cakes and horse shows.

"Horses from the north crossed the river at Aurora, Ind., and were walked through Petersburg," said William Conrad in a

---

[62] Boone County, a brief history of the much honored land located just 12 miles from Cincinnati, (1940, n.p.), 6-7.

[63] Conrad, *Yesterdays*, 31.

Recorder article. "Some came secretly, carefully covered except for their eyes. A blue ribbon at the Florence Fair added value to a stallion or mare. Horsemen roamed the stalls and stables looking to trade or deal.

"With every grandstand seat occupied and the aisle and promenade deck crowded with spectators, the band played loudly. Just before the horses were to enter, the music stopped. When the heavy, double gates at the south end of the ring swung open, the band began again as cheers greeted horses and riders entered the ring.

"Gaits changed in response to the ringmaster's shouts until he commanded 'Bring them in' and the class lined up facing the spectators. Judges inspected the individuals, then dismissed the group, the blue ribbon winner leaving the ring first amid cheers and applause. Then a water wagon, driven by Lewis Thompson in the 1920s, came in to spray water to settle the dust. When it finished, ringmaster Hank Tanner in that era, rang the bell for the next class to enter.

"Stands sold balloons, whips, canes and kewpie dolls. Games of chance included throwing balls at targets or driving a nail into a wooden board with so many blows from a hammer. Smells from wieners, bratwurst and frying fish tempted fairgoers. Church ladies sponsored dining halls that offered sit-down meals. Barrels of drinking water with floating ice offered a tin cup or dipper hanging on the side, but some preferred to bring their own individual folding cup."[64]

Highland Stock Farm's Thoroughbred stallion "Hildur." 1930 Recorder Historical Edition, Courtesy of Ruth Glenn

Prominent Boone County farmer, John J. Aylor, frequently judged at livestock shows and fairs around the region. He also organized the county's first purebred registered hog association.

Aylor raised a variety of purebred animals on his Springwater Stock Farm along Gunpowder Creek. Hogs, sheep, Shetland ponies and three-and five-gaited saddle horses thrived on his farm.[65]

Respess Breeds Thoroughbreds

Jerome "Rome" Bristow Respess, who grew up on a farm near Union, brought a different kind of horse to Boone County – the Thoroughbred.

Born on his grandfather Bristow's farm between Florence and Independence, his mother Katherine Bristow was a Boone County native and Union resident. Rome's maternal great grandfather was Leonard Stephens, one of the wealthiest men of his day. Stephens, who owned 5,000 acres between Florence and Independence, and another man paid the entire cost of constructing Florence Baptist Church.

Jerome Respess, Jr. was born in 1913, 1930 Recorder Historical Edition, Courtesy of Ruth Glenn

When Rome was 16, his father bought a new farm near Florence.

In 1883, Respess began showing Saddlebreds. In 1898, he began breeding Thoroughbreds at Woodlawn, Ohio. His stallion Dick Welles, foaled in 1900, was

---

[64] William Conrad, "Conrad Chronicles Boone County Fair," *Recorder Newspapers*, 1995 Boone County Fair Guide, 22, 24.
[65] *Boone County Recorder*, 1930 Historical Edition

Chapter 8 1890-1899 Commuting Begins, Population Declines

John Aylor, Irvin Baker, Hube Beemon, Willie Utz, Jerry Quigley, and Jim Pettit on the porch of Prock Brothers Store, under a sign for Sharples Tubular Cream Separators. Barrels and chicken crates sit behind the hitching rack to the right.   Photo courtesy of Katie Presnell

called the greatest Thoroughbred until Man O' War. In 1903, Dick won $7,200. He started 15 times, winning 14. His overall winnings totaled $42,000.

In 1903, Wintergreen, Dick Welles' son, won the Kentucky Derby, paying Respess a handsome $9,000. Another Respess horse, Billy Kelly, sold for $1,500 as a yearling. Named best two-year-old of 1917, Billy later sold for $40,000.

Respess moved his Thoroughbred operation to 555 acres near Florence. Called Highland Stock Farm, his nine horse barns had 140 box stalls. In 1930, he had 44 mares, five stallions, 17 yearlings, 25 suckling colts, and 28 runners in training.[66]

The farm was on the west side of Dixie Highway, south of Florence, where the Northern Kentucky Industrial Park is now.

Florence Ordinances

When Florence's first Board of Trustees met in March 1897, their primary concern was getting the cattle off the street. And they defined the word cattle to mean *"horse, mule, ass, sheep, hog or goat of any age or sex, bull, cow, calf and ox."*[67]

Those driving animals through town were excepted, but anyone who let their animals roam was subjected to a $1 per day fine and risked the animals being auctioned off to pay the fine.

Ordinance #2 prohibited baseball playing in the streets or alleys, enforced by a $1 per incident fine. Clerk J.W. Nead also penned the third restriction, prohibiting throwing trash in the streets.

"It shall be unlawful for any person to throw out, empty or deposit any ashes, feathers, fruit

---

[66] *Boone County Recorder*, 1930 Historical Edition.

[67] Florence Ordinance Book #1.

Limaburg School
Photo courtesy of Boone County Historic Preservation

Looking west from Gunpowder Creek Bridge in Limaburg
Photo courtesy of Boone County Historic Preservation

profane swearing or drunkenness, shooting, and fast riding through town. Chairman D.H. Brown also signed penalties for assault with a deadly weapon and contempt of court.

The next year, city fathers bought land for a cemetery, Clerk J.F. Murray recorded. In 1889, Chairman J.C. Buckner required landowners to install sidewalks. A tax on the sale of *"spirituous, vinous and malt liquors"* and contracts to improve the streets came in 1900.[68]

Limaburg

At a crossroads midway between Florence and Burlington (on KY 18), a community had sprung up with no particular name. Surrounding a pre-Civil War saw and grist mill on Gunpowder Creek, it was sometimes called Florence Crossroads or Needmore and eventually Limaburg.

Irishman John Welsh lived on the creek near the mill in a house that stood until 1916. His neighbors described him as *"the kindest man who ever lived."*

The Morgan C. Crigler family occupied the tollhouse there. The J.W. Rouse family ran the general store across the creek from the blacksmith shop.

A tiny schoolhouse stood on land adjoining the store atop a hill along Hebron road overlooking the settlement. It was the gathering place for religious, educational and any other community gathering. Parties, plays, debates and other forms of entertainment filled the schoolhouse.

One popular debate topic was *"which is the most destructive – fire or water?"* Residents had first-hand experience with both, a flood had washed out the mill and the bridge and filled the store's cellar with water. Mrs. Mary Crigler's blacksmith shop washed out and was never rebuilt. George Baker built a new shop

or vegetables, green or spoiled melons, decayed or spoiled meats, vegetables, grains or fruits, peelings, old boots, shoes or harness worn out; spoiled or broken dishes, glass, tin or wooden or crockery ware or any garbage, offal or refuse of whatever kind. Any person violating this ordinance shall be fined $1."

Ordinance #4 established a chain gang for men over 18 imprisoned in the Florence jail. They would receive $1 credit toward their debit or fine for each eight-hour day worked.

Punishment for breaching the peace was defined in Ordinance #5 as a fine of not less than 1 cent nor more than $100 or imprisonment for five to 50 days.

Others, passed in August 1897, prohibited carrying concealed weapons, disturbing religious worship, provoking an assault,

---
[68] Florence Ordinance Book #1, 1-23

on his own land. Water covered the floor of the Welsh house in which James Utz was living.

Another time, deep snow made the road impassable.

Near the school, in the local cemetery, were buried those lost in the 1849-cholera epidemic that nearly decimated the village.

While the war had divided residents, the community survived, needing a larger general store by 1870. Farmers J.W. and S.J. Rouse moved their general store into a new two-story building.

Factory-made, rather than traditional homemade, articles were becoming popular. The Rouse store operated from sun-up to after dark using only family members, not hired clerks, to sell those factory-made items to their customers. They also stocked yard goods, boots, flour, spices, dried fruits, green coffee, sugar, crackers by the barrel, candy, oil, turpentine and more.

Like most general stores of the time, Limaburg's was the center of discussion and dissent. *"Many weighty problems were aired and decided around the stove"* in the store. A later storeowner, J.P. (Prock) Brothers became a Democratic political leader, aided by his knowledge gained in those conversations.

Miss Ada Aylor introduced homemade ice cream to Limaburg.

In 1884, the community applied for a post office. The name Needmore had been used, but most called the place Florence Crossroads. Residents weren't happy with either. Someone suggested Lima, but was concerned about confusion with Lima, Ohio. The postal representative suggested Limaburg and filled out the form, ending the discussion.

Burlington Baptist Church was built in 1892.
1930 Recorder Historical Edition, Courtesy of Ruth Glenn

Silas J. Rouse was the first Limaburg postmaster. The first cancellation stamp was issued on Feb.17, 1885.[69]

Harvey S. Tanner left for Cincinnati to learn the barber trade in 1897.

A half-dozen years later, W.O. Rouse entered medical school. He opened an office in the old store after he graduated in 1895. But he soon moved to Burlington, convinced it was a better location.

After Silas Rouse passed away in 1901, his partner J.W. Rouse sold the general store to J.W. Quigley and Clark Beemon. Quigley soon married Beemon's daughter Eva. Rouse returned to his farm.

Quigley and Beemon added delivery services and bartered "store-bought goods" for poultry and fresh produce. They expanded the inventory to include farm implements, wire fencing, fertilizer, paint and feed.

At Christmas time, the store filled with fresh fruits, fancy candies, toys, bright handkerchiefs, new bolts of yard goods, nuts and other festive items.

The advent of rural free delivery service in 1907 eliminated the post office and the town began to fade away. James P. Tanner was the first rural mail carrier to use the new boxes appearing along roadsides.[70]

Newton Not Assassin

Just west of Limaburg, Dr. O.S. Crisler attended Morgan Academy in Burlington. His teacher was Professor Henry Newton. A rumor had gotten around that Newton, who was a slender man with a crippled foot, was actually John Wilkes Booth, who broke his ankle and

---

[69] William Fitzgerald, "History of Florence," written in 1958, republished in the *Boone County Recorder*, Aug. 3, 1978.
[70] Mrs. J.P. Brothers, "Limaburg Community Flourishes in Early Days," *Boone County Recorder*, Aug. 10, 1978.

escaped after shooting President Abraham Lincoln. Here's what Crisler said in a letter:

"...The rumor got around. The Trustees investigated and found there was nothing to it. He was a good man and one of the best teachers I ever had. He had a wonderful education, could teach and did higher mathematics, English, Latin and all other subjects. He even taught a class in surveying. His students were admitted to colleges of higher learning such as law, medicine, etc. He was a brilliant man. We referred to him as 'Sir Classic.'

"He never got after me but once. I was sitting at my desk leisurely looking out the window. He said to me, 'You're wasting your time, which can never be regained. It is not like money, which can.' He pulled a silver dollar from his pocket and held it up. I never forgot...

"Professor Newton brought his dinner with him. Often times during the noon hour the boys would have target practice. One day they asked him to join them. They handed him a .32 caliber revolver. He picked a knot in a board fence next to the cemetery and when he had fired until the gun was empty, the knot was neatly surrounded with six holes. Some shot.

"He used tobacco but never chewed. He would take the plug out of his pocket, take out his knife, cut off a sliver and put it in his mouth. He would never chew or spit. Quite a man."[71]

Morgan Academy closed soon after the investigation and the land reverted back to its original owners. The old school building was torn down and replaced with a barn.

A New Courthouse?

A proposal to tear down and replace Burlington's courthouse brought rallies around the county protesting the outrageous cost of a new building. At a meeting in Union protesting the new courthouse, G.W. Baker of Hamilton said the people in his district wanted to move the county seat to Florence.

"Why not go ahead and build a $20,000 court-house now rather than wait two years and then may have to pay taxes to erect public buildings to cost anywhere from $30,000 to $75,000?" asked the *Recorder* on May 30, 1888.

L.W. Lassing stated that he wanted to repair the old historic landmark built by the county's founders. Dr. Scott called for a vote on where the county seat should be, saying he was perfectly willing even for it to go to Rabbit Hash if that was what the majority wanted.

Dr. Blanton said a Union lot was already approved for a new courthouse. John Whitson said he was too busy quarrying stone for the courthouse to be built at Union to attend the meeting.

The people of Burlington were said to be *"as calm as a May morning"* about the issue.

A few blocks down Jefferson Street, a new courthouse was built in 1894 with red bricks made in the county for the outrageous cost of $18,400.[72]

Boone County Deposit Bank of Burlington was founded in 1885. A new bank was erected across the street from the courthouse in 1925.

Burlington Baptist Church dedicated a new building, on Route 18 on the east side of the courthouse on Dec. 21, 1892. Ten years earlier, Brother Owen Kirtley had organized the first Sunday School at Burlington Baptist Church.

---

[71] *175th Anniversary Historical Book*, 41.

[72] Leland Sullivan, "History of Boone County Courts and Courthouses," *Boone County Recorder*.
[72] Purvis, 142.

Chapter 9
1900-1909 Telephones, Cars & Baseball

The decade began with newly elected Kentucky Gov. William Goebel becoming the only governor in American history to die in office from an assassination attempt. His Democratic cronies had counted the votes in the narrow election, and with no Republicans present, had declared Goebel the victor. Indignant Republicans armed more than 1,000 of their own men and faced an equal Democratic force in Frankfort. Previous Gov. William S. Taylor fled the state under indictment as an accessory to the murder. Thirty-year-old John Crepps Wickliffe Beckham, grandson of a former governor, took office.[1]

Boone County's population began to decline from its 1890 peak of 12,246 to 11,170 in 1900, then to 9,420 in 1910.

Railroads were hauling growth to Walton. With a population of 538, Walton was nearly as large as Petersburg.

The horseless carriage rolled into Florence – careful not to exceed the 6 mph speed limit, designed to help prevent frightening the horses. A motorcar assembled in Charlie Bradford's buggy shop *"was not too successful, but it ran some."*[2]

Medical advances were arriving as was news from around the world. Under a headline *"Revival of the Dead,"* the *Recorder* told of a New York physician, Dr. Robert Kemp, resuscitating chloroformed dogs by cutting a hole between their ribs and pressing on

---

> ### Boone County Recorder
> **Aug. 10, 1903**
>
> *"The farmers with exceptions of few are in excellent financial shape in the percent of indebtedness being quite small and it is doubtful if there is another county in the State that can show as few mortgages recorded. This with the fact the Boone is one of the largest counties in the State, speaks volumes for the prudence, sagacity and high standing of our husbandry.*
>
> *"Cereal raising and tobacco raising are the chief agricultural products. The fine grade of white burley tobacco grown her is always sought for a fancy price.*
>
> *"The splendid macadamized highways of Boone County is ever the source of advantage. Principal roads are maintained by corporations who charge a light toll for travel, yet with this revenue it is said the receipts are inadequate to cope with the expenditures for increased improvements. A great many who favor free pikes generally change their minds when they compare our fine roads to the free roads of Kenton, Carroll, Grant and Owen counties.*
>
> *"The picturesque scenery of Boone County is beautiful to the extreme. The pleasing story of John Uri Lloyd, The Warwick of the Knobs," was inspired by the rich landscape views in the south part of the county, and the silvery brooks and creeks that sing sweet notes in their ripple to the lover of nature. Big Bone Spring with its old style hotel and waters known far and wide through their great curative power is a place of great interest to the traveler.*
>
> *"A few miles from Burlington along the clefts, again one comes in contact with ornate creation of diversified scenery. Here too is found sparkling springs, with waters pure and remarkably cold. The most admired of these springs is the great "Split Rock," set out seemingly without support and from which gushes fresh, cold water clear as crystal.*

---

[1] Harrison & Klotter, 272.

[2] Conrad, *Yesterdays*, 32.

their heart while blowing into their lungs with a special kind of pump.[3]

When rural free delivery came to Boone County some Florence businessmen thought that if mail was delivered to homes and farms, fewer customers would stop in their shops on their way to the post office. That delayed home delivery's arrival in Florence. The Erlanger office began a route covering parts of Boone County around Florence.[4]

Catalog companies like Sears and Roebuck and Montgomery Ward delighted rural residents with merchandise delivered to home mail boxes. If roads were impassable carriers did not make deliveries, so homeowners quickly cleared them.

Covington, Newport and Cincinnati stores advertised furniture, appliances and other goods in the *Boone County Recorder*. A three-piece oak bedroom set cost $25. A special on "*roll arm reed rockers*" promised $4 rockers for $2.49. "Estate gas ranges" sold for $10. The "*Miller all-steel*" gas range sold for $20.[5]

The Aug. 10, 1903, *Recorder* offered "*sketches of the leading institutions and business men who vie with each other in making Boone County one of the greatest in the state.*"

Writers effusively complimented everything and everyone here. "*Big courts in Boone County seem a thing of the past. The legal business is light inasmuch as litigation is concerned. Like all county seats, a jail is in evidence, but as six months has elapsed since a prisoner has entered its doors, so little is this place of county property used that weeds have grown up high around the main entrance.*"

> **Boone County Recorder**
> Aug. 19, 1903
> A young man who had filled up on bad whiskey at Lawrenceburg, last Saturday, came to this side of the river full of fight, and seeing nothing to go up against, he attacked, with his knife, a rick (stack) of sacked wheat lying on the wharf, and belonging to Geo. W. Terrill, and slashed them in a terrible manner, wasting a large quantity of wheat.

Judges and Attorneys

Despite the *Recorder*'s rosy sketches, politicians were elected to keep the peace and set policies for residents to follow.

Boone County's John M. Lassing was the youngest circuit judge in Kentucky. The oldest son of Dr. H. C. Lassing of Union, he attended White Haven Academy, Central University in Richmond, then Cincinnati Law School.

Twice elected county attorney without opposition, in 1901 he was appointed circuit court judge to fill the term of Judge Greene, who died in office. He was nominated without opposition, elected, then re-elected to the post.

"*His mature judgment and fair rulings have lent conspicuous lustre to the exalted dignity of Bar and Bench,*" the *Recorder* article said.[6]

A staunch Democrat, Lassing was a friend of Sen. William Gobel, the Governor killed in office, and the famous orator and presidential candidate William Jennings Bryan.

Lassing married Mary Lillard Brady, daughter of Boone County farmer R. A. Brady, and lived in Burlington with their two sons.

Another very young man, P.E. Cason, was elected judge of the fiscal court at 24. The youngest man ever elected in the county, he graduated from the University of Louisville College of Law and returned to practice in Burlington. Named Inspector of Chinese Immigration in 1894, Cason moved to Tacoma, Wash., for 15 months, but resigned and returned to Burlington to practice law.

S.W. Tolon, another University of Louisville law school graduate who practiced

---

[3] *Boone County Recorder*, Aug. 10, 1903.
[4] Conrad, "A Story about Florence," 9.
[5] *Boone County Recorder*, Aug. 19, 1903.

[6] *Boone County Recorder*, Aug. 10, 1903.

in Burlington, was the state senator.[7]

County Officials

Manlius Thompson Garnett clerked for the county court for eight years and served as deputy of the county and circuit courts for 17 years. When Fountain Riddell resigned as president of Boone County Deposit Bank, Garnett was elected to replace him.

Petersburg farmer and livestock dealer, J.A. Duncan was elected circuit court clerk, succeeding his father, J.W. Duncan who had served for 18 years. (Another article in the same *Recorder* says 30 years.)

County surveyor W.E. Vest, a former student of Prof. Henry Newton, dealt in city and farm real estate.

O.S. Watts was elected assessor in 1902. A livestock dealer in partnership with J. L. Riley, Watts lived on a farm 5½ miles east of Burlington.

Mud Lick native B.B. Allphin was elected high sheriff in 1899 after serving as a deputy in 1898. As many did, he named his son, J.C. Allphin, a deputy. Benjamin B. Hume, who was born on Mud Lick Creek, was also a deputy sheriff. Mrs. Allphin, the former Pink Edwards, was the office clerk. The senior Allphin was known as the best mule buyer in the region and also dealt in horses.

Longtime teacher and "examiner" D.M. Snyder farmed and was superintendent of schools. L.H. Voshell of Union, another longtime teacher, had been elected superintendent in 1894.

Dr. J.G. Furnish, an ex-legislator, was superintendent of the Central Kentucky Lunatic Asylum. In addition to attending the Ohio Medical College, the Owen County native took a post-graduate course at Belleview in New York City.[8]

Petersburg man G.C. Grady was deputy revenue collector for the Sixth Congressional District, appointed in 1902. Known for his taste in well-bred horses, he dealt in livestock. He "*discharges his manifold duties in such an obliging way as to make him a popular personage in all circles, both business and socially speaking.*"[9]

Preacher Jones

While nearly all the men noted as community leaders were natives of Boone or bordering counties, a few newcomers settled here.

A Texan who was orphaned as a child, Edgar DeWitt Jones came to Boone County in 1902 to preach at the old Point Pleasant Church, but his popularity took him to Petersburg, Bullittsville, and other churches. "*In fact, there are few Christian pulpits in Boone that he has not filled at some time or other.*"

He married Boone County girl Frances C. Willis and they had five children. Jones gathered funds to build the Erlanger Christian Church, moved to Illinois, then to Detroit. His book "*Fairhope, the Annals of a Country Church,*" published by New York's McMillan Co. in 1917 took place in Boone County and included characters drawn as composites of local people.

1904 Ferry Rates

Kottmeyer's new ferry crossed the river at Constance on Aug. 10, 1900.

Foot passenger	5 cents
One horse team and driver	15 cents
Two-horse team and driver	25 cents
Additional horses	10 cents
Additional wagons	15 cents
Cattle, per head	10 cents
Sheep, per head	2 cents
- under 25 head	3 cents
Hogs, per head	5 cents
Calf	5 cents
One cow and drover	15 cents

---

[7] *Boone County Recorder*, Aug. 10, 1903.
[8] *Boone County Recorder*, Aug. 10, 1903.
[9] *Boone County Recorder*, Aug. 10, 1903.

Corn planting time. Photo by Mrs. Bessie Kirtley. Courtesy of Barbara Fallis.

Jones quite accurately predicted Boone County's future when he said, "*Twenty-five years from now there will be hundreds of city dwellers who will have their homes in the country, with plenty of fresh air, an abundance of small fruit, surrounded by a few acres, intensively cultivated, close enough to the city for all practical purposes, yet able to live amid the high hills on the Kentucky side with perfect highways and a heap of happiness thrown in for good measure.*"[10]

Road Improvements

Jones' predictions were not to come to pass for a half-century. Natives still relied primarily on horses to navigate 1,120 miles of mud roads and 83 miles of gravel roads – hardly an efficient road system to attract outsiders.[11] When mechanical rock crushers were introduced about 1905, road conditions began to improve.

Problems were exacerbated by landowners who would not allow roads more than 16' wide through their property. A few roads had been topped with cement roads by 1910.

Tobacco Wars

Highly profitable on small acreage, tobacco was the most valuable crop for most Kentucky farmers, Boone Countians included. But around the turn of the century, The American Tobacco Company and two overseas groups dominated the market and agreed not to compete with each other when buying tobacco.

This created a monopoly that forced farmers to accept well below what it cost them to produce their crops. Overall, the farm economy was declining, but the drop in tobacco prices made farmers desperate.

In an attempt to survive, farmers formed the Planters' Protective Association, a two-state cooperative that would hold tobacco off the market until prices rallied.

An offshoot, the Burley Tobacco Society, organized to decrease production and increase demand. But if farmers defected and sold their crops, the pool wouldn't be effective. Farmers on the edge of bankruptcy felt forced to take what they could get. Called "hillbillies" by the cooperative, they were the focus of retribution

---
[10] *Boone County Recorder*, Sept. 4, 1930.
[11] *175th Anniversary Historical Book*, 9.

Chapter 9 1900-1909 Telephones, Cars & Baseball

in Western Kentucky, more so than this area.[12]

Despite farmers' financial pain, they didn't focus their frustration on local men who worked as tobacco dealers. In a profile of native son, O.P. Conner, the Aug. 10, 1903, *Recorder* says, *"Tobacco growers have long since learned that he is their friend and for their product pays as high price as can be obtained in any nearby market."*

In addition to buying 200,000 pounds of tobacco annually to process at the Burlington Tobacco Warehouse, Conner operated a 233-acre farm four miles south of Burlington. A son managed his farm and owned "Max Ledger," a stallion who had won 47 blue ribbons and passed his winning traits on to the foals he sired.[13]

Another local man, L.H. Voshell, organized interest in a Boone County division of the Burley Tobacco Growers' Association, and distributed a meeting notice that ran in the Aug. 19, 1903, *Recorder*.[14]

Like their contemporaries around the state, Boone County farmers literally sold their crops for pennies.

Mrs. Elizabeth Kirtley recalled her father traveling south to Cynthiana in search of a tobacco market that would make his work worthwhile. But at 2 cents a pound, it cost him more to haul his crop than he earned.[15]

From 1905 to 1909, an estimated 10,000 Night Riders, or "The Silent Brigade" vigilantes organized across the Commonwealth to "persuade" farmers who remained outside the pool. A bundle of tobacco sticks thrown on a porch was a warning. If that was unheeded, young plants could be destroyed or a more mature crop burned in the field.

If the grower still didn't join the fold, vicious violence erupted. Some were beaten with thorn bushes. Others were killed. One noted, *"To join the Night Riders was both fire and life insurance."*

"Political leaders either openly or tacitly supported the PPA and usually the Night Riders as well. Those who were fighting saw the conflict as a people's war against a monopoly that strangled them, and all means were justified. Others saw property being destroyed and individuals being hurt, and they cried out against the use of illegitimate violence to achieve legitimate goals."

Some began to use this opportunity to harass, beat or kill black families. Soon the movement took a racist turn and became more out of control.

After winning the 1907 gubernatorial election with a promise to end the Night Riders' violence, Louisville Republican Augustus E. Wilson activated state military units to stop the Silent Brigade.[16]

In 1908, Night Riders covered with sheets rode into Walton on horseback and burned a large tobacco barn. The barn was used to "prize" or pack tobacco into hogsheads to ship to Louisville. Tobacco was selling for about 2 cents a pound.

In 1909, Congress removed an oppressive tobacco tax. Two years later the American Tobacco Company was convicted of violating antitrust acts. Prices rose. The PPA and Burley Tobacco Society dissolved in internal problems.[17]

Petersburg's Loder Dies

Petersburg diarist L.A. Loder died at his son Leon's home in Constance in March 1904. He was 84 and had lost his wife nearly a decade before.

The *Boone County Recorder* said on March 22, 1904: *"He was a man of learning, and for many years was the trusted bookkeeper of Gaff & Jenkins when they operated the big flour mill, now the Boone County Distillery. He lived an honorable and useful life, and has now gone the way of the world."*

Loder's son added occasional bits to the diary for a few years.

---

[12] Harrison & Klotter, *A New History of Kentucky*, 280
[13] *Boone County Recorder*, Aug. 10, 1903.
[14] *Boone County Recorder*, Aug. 19, 1903.
[15] Elizabeth Kirtley

[16] Harrison & Klotter, *A New History of Kentucky*, .280.
[17] Harrison & Klotter, *A New History of Kentucky*, .280.

"Night Owl," the ferry run by the Kottmyers in 1910, carried "you pick" customers from Cincinnati to the riverfront orchards on Boone County's northern edge.
An LC Packet Line Steamer passes in the background.   Photo courtesy of Virginia Bennett

Riverfront Orchards

Until the turn of the century, at least one milk cow and a small orchard were part of every Boone County farm. Bottom lands along the Ohio were ideal for growing fruits. The Dolwick, McGlasson and Hempfling families planted apple, peach and other fruit trees in the area below Stringtown. Fog and moisture-laden air from the river gave some protection from frosts, but severe winters often damaged trees, reducing especially the peach yield.

Kenton County native H.F. McGlasson owned 400 acres near Anderson's Ferry. He served as president of the North Kentucky Agricultural Fair Association and was president of the Boone County Harvest Home Association for 13 years.[18]

Charles O. Hempfling bought the 84-acre Parlor Grove property near Taylorsport from McGlasson in 1903. Cincinnatians had come by the boatload to picnic at Parlor Grove. The Hempfling family cleared the giant beech trees the area was known for to plant orchards. Specializing in the "Big Red" apple variety, Hempfling sold "*thousands of bushels through brokers handling fancy eating fruit.*"[19]

Hempfling also purchased the 272-acre Webb Hall estate from the family who had owned it for a century. He converted it from general crop production to Big Red apples and peaches.

His German-immigrant parents, John and Elizabeth Dolwick Hempfling, had arrived in Cincinnati in 1836, moved to Constance in 1847 and began farming. After attending Cincinnati schools, Charles traveled the Midwest selling structural steel. In 1890, he married Lillie Kottmeyer of Constance, worked for Jones Fertilizer Company, then Fleishman & Co. of Cincinnati before purchasing the farms.[20]

Hood's Store

The fruit growers could have obtained their

---

[18] *Boone County Recorder*, Aug. 10, 1903.

[19] *Boone County Recorder*, 1930 Historical Edition.
[20] *Boone County Recorder*, 1930 Historical Edition.

necessities including coal at J.L. Hood's store in Constance. Hood purchased the business from C. Davis & Co. in 1900. In addition to drawing customers from the riverfront community, many crossed the river to shop the store's low prices. R.S. Hood, a brother of the owner, managed the enterprise.

Hood's coal yard offered the celebrated Kanawha River coals including Raymond City, Plymouth, Raymond, and Belmont. *"Their trade for coal extends far back into the country for miles and miles, the people knowing that to get coal at this yard they not only get quality but a fair deal at fair prices for goods."*[21]

Coal fallen from barges or carried on barges that wrecked or sank often washed up on the small islands in the Ohio. Mrs. Elizabeth Kirtley recalled her father frequently taking a small boat to Lochry and the other islands to glean coal for her mother's cook stove.

Basley's Bullittsville Store

Just a bit inland, North Bend native C.S. Basley owned a 225-acre farm. In 1878, he established a Bullittsville general store offering "*quite everything needed by an agricultural community*." He was named postmaster by the Garfield administration.

"*Bullittsville, one of the principal points of trade in Boone County, is justly proud of the distinction of having within her confines one of the most extensive general stores in this section of the state.*"

Basley married Ada Clore and had a son Kenneth who graduated from the Rugby College of Covington. Basley's grandfather, George L. Basley, was the first Democrat elected to the state legislature from Boone County.[22]

B.F. Zimmer & Sons Grocers at Constance
Courtesy of Boone County Historic Preservation

Burial Prohibited

In 1902, Brother W.S. Taylor was hired for $100 to be pastor of Sand Run Baptist Church in Francesville. His salary was doubled the next year. Membership growth prompted purchasing 42 new hymnals for 25 cents each plus 77 cents for postage.

In May 1906, Holland Goodridge initiated a move to prohibit Negro burials on the church premises and in the cemetery. In 1910, for $66.16, defrayed by a $5 credit for the old organ and 75 cents for the organ box., the Sand Run Church bought a new organ.[23]

Hebron Farms

Below the river-edged North Bend horseshoe, Hebron was the center of a

---

[21] *Boone County Recorder*, Aug. 10, 1903.

[22] *Boone County Recorder*, 1930 Historical Edition.
[23] Blaker.

productive farming community.

T.S. Aylor and W.A. Hafer owned and operated Hebron's general store. Limaburg native Aylor had been an attaché for the Kentucky Central Railroad in Covington, then became a salesman for C.E. Clore.

Attorney A.G. Winston lived on a 255-acre farm near Hebron. Winston, who fathered five daughters and a son, served a term as clerk and Master Commissioner of the Boone Circuit Court.

"During his career as a lawyer, he was engaged on one side or the other of every important case tried in Boone Circuit Court. . .

A creamery in Hebron.
Photo courtesy of Boone County Historic Preservation

For years he has been regarded as the best financier in the County and has made many remunerative deals in real estate which in less proficient hands would have proven heavy losses."

His farm was located *"on a good turnpike and within a few minutes ride of the street cars."*[24] Winston *"being considerable beyond the meridian of life"* and desiring to retire, offered 255 acres for sale – for $17,500 if purchased within 30 days of his Aug. 13, 1903, advertisement. *"It is all meadow and fine grass except about 10 acres. . . It is the greatest bargain in farm lands ever offered in this end of the State. It cost nearly double that sum."*[25]

East of Hebron, the farm owned by Hubert Conner and his wife Lillie Goodridge included the general assortment of animals and crops common to the day.[26] But their black and white spotted dairy cattle were registered Holsteins – a larger, higher producing dairy cow than the brown and white spotted Alderneys (an antiquated name for Guernsey) and delicate fawn-colored Jerseys popular for their milk's high butterfat content. In efforts to improve the animals' conformation and milk-producing abilities, progressive farmers were beginning to buy better quality, purebred animals.

Not every farmer switched from the high milk-fat producing cows to higher quantity-producing Holsteins. One common retort by those who preferred the traditional breeds was *"the only reason to keep a Holstein was in case you needed to put out a fire."*

Hebron dairy farmer Malchus Souther, who married Alice Gordon, milked Jerseys.

Further west toward Petersburg, C.S. Chambers and his wife, the former Alta Terrill of Petersburg, raised "high class horses" on 269 acres. Oak Knoll Stock Farm, with its Colonial house surrounded by oak trees, was seven miles from Burlington on the Burlington and Petersburg Pike. Chambers had a reputation as one of the best horse judges in the county.[27]

Petersburg Parties and Plays

Traveling entertainers still rode the river and stopped at Petersburg.

---

[24] *Boone County Recorder*, 1930 Historical Edition.
[25] *Boone County Recorder*, Aug. 10, 1903.
[26] *Boone County Recorder*, 1930 Historical Edition.
[27] *Boone County Recorder*, Aug. 10, 1903.

"*Showboats often tied up at or near the ferry landing. The calliope would play and could be heard as far as Florence. Crowds would come to hiss the villain and applaud the hero and heroine.*"[28]

Another form of entertainment was invitational parties held after supper time. "*You would receive a letter inviting you to attend a party given by a boy or girl at their home. Of course, the main attraction was the kissing game provided by the host.*

"*Candy pulling and fudge making was also popular. After a while molasses candy turned white with a few streaks of soil from the bare hands which only added to the flavor. Games included spin-the-plate, post-office and musical chairs.*"[29]

Tradition dictated April 1 was garden planting time and after May 1 children could go barefoot.[30]

Petersburg Merchandising

While Petersburg was no longer growing, its merchants still served a significant number of residents and area farmers who had arrived the previous century.

J.W. Berkshire and R.A. McWethy bought leaf tobacco in Petersburg and Grant/Belleview. Berkshire, a Petersburg native, was a candidate for sheriff in 1898. McWethy, also a Boone Countian, married Mattie Lyons. After she died, leaving a daughter, he married Katie Weindel of Petersburg in 1890.[31]

Farmers Bank of Petersburg opened July 1, 1903, under the direction of Solon Early, former Petersburg sheriff, area farmer and fiscal court magistrate. J. Henry Stevens, who farmed several hundred acres near Idlewild on what is now called Stevens Road, was vice president and succeeded Early as president.[32]

"*Occupying a very pretentious business house in Petersburg with a salesroom 45' x 60' in area, the W.L. Gordon General Store*" was established in 1890. Gordon, a Boone County carpenter, had a construction business before opening the store. A town trustee, he also served on the school board.[33]

Indiana man, S.C. Buchanan, quit teaching to open a Petersburg drug store. He married Irene Alloway and had one son and four daughters.[34]

William J. Weindel returned to Petersburg to practice medicine, leaving a practice across the river where he had attended high school due to the "*earnest solicitation of friends in his hometown to come and serve them.*"[35]

Belleview (Grant)

Down the river, Belleview Baptist celebrated the church's centennial in 1903 by building a new, larger church at the cost of $2,900 and $160 worth of new fixtures. When

---

> **Boone County Recorder**
> Nov. 14, 1900
> **Bellevue Wedding**
>
> The marriage of Mr. Weeden Williamson and Miss Mamie Rogers at the Baptist Church here at 7 p.m., Nov. 7, was a most beautiful wedding. The friends of the bride and groom had the church handsomely decorated with natural flowers for the occasion, and before the hour for the ceremony arrived the house was crowded to its utmost capacity.
>
> Promptly at 7 o'clock the bride leaning on the arm of her brother, Clayton, entered the church and approached the altar by one aisle, while the groom, accompanied by Johnnie Moody, came in by the other aisle. They met over the altar, and there in a most impressive manner Rev. Atwood pronounced the ceremony that united the hearts of the loving couple. The bride and groom were each handsomely attired.
>
> Immediately after the ceremony the bride and groom, accompanied by numerous friends, repaired to the home of the bride, where a sumptuous and elegant supper was served. The bride's cake was a handsome production of culinary art. It contained a gold ring, which the groom was so fortunate as to draw.

---

[28] Welcome to an Educational & Historical Tour, 7.
[29] Adams
[30] Adams
[31] *Boone County Recorder*, Aug. 10, 1903.
[32] James and Gaines Stevens are his grandsons
[33] *Boone County Recorder*, Aug. 10, 1903.
[34] *Boone County Recorder*, Aug. 10, 1903.
[35] *Boone County Recorder*, Aug. 10, 1903.

Pastor T.L. Utz died, his widow was given $100.

A. Corbin & Son general store at Belleview opened in 1864 and dealt in coal, lumber and shingles. Son M.J. Corbin, who wore a handlebar mustache like many of his time, managed the business after his father's death. Mrs. A. Corbin owned the majority of the stock. The store was handling $25,000 worth of transactions annually.

Cyrus Kelly ran a nursery *"that met with fair success"* at his Belleview farm until 1882, then became a merchant, running a store affiliated with the Granger Order. The Grange or Granger Order was a national men's club made up of farmers. They pooled their resources to start co-operative stores that could buy and sell agricultural goods in quantity.[36]

J.W. Kite operated a country store at Waterloo. He sold dry goods, then was superintendent of the Farmers' Cooperative Store at Belleview. After nearly a decade, he returned to farming the Ohio River bottomland, then got back into merchandising in 1891.

Kite had enlisted in the Union Army during the Civil War, serving in the 55th Kentucky Regiment. He married Josie Clore, was a *"Republican and cast his first vote for President to U.S. Grant."*[37]

Riverboat Pilot

Edward Maurer left Belleview in 1899 at the age of 22 to begin his apprenticeship as an Ohio River pilot. He worked on several steamers running the river between Cincinnati and New Orleans, learning the winding channels of the Ohio and Mississippi rivers.

Maurer became a first class pilot on Sept. 5, 1900, and earned his master's license two years later. He began piloting the Henry M. Stanley. For 17 years he served as master or pilot primarily on the City of Cincinnati or City of Louisville steamers. He traveled an estimated 1 million miles without a serious accident – an unusual record.

Edward Maurer
1930 Recorder Historical Edition

Edward's three brothers also became licensed masters and pilots. With his brother William, Edward served on the Cincinnati for four years. William died in 1908.

Edward was the last pilot on the steamer Louisville before it was lost in ice in January 1918. He held a record for making the run from Cincinnati to Louisville in five hours and 50 minutes downstream and upstream in nine hours and 42 minutes.

Edward married and had two children, then decided to give up steamboating to spend more time with his family. He passed an examination and became U.S. local inspector of hulls and steam vessels first in Pittsburgh, then in Louisville where he remained.[38]

Macksville Merchant

Owen County native W.H. Stamper stayed closer to home, running the Macksville (McVille) general store and two farms. He moved to Boone County in 1849 and married Nancy Henderson four years later. They had nine children, four boys and five girls, before she died in 1867. In 1883, he married Amanda Louden, who died in 1892.[39]

---

[36] Bruce Ferguson, Jan. 28, 1998.
[37] *Boone County Recorder*, Aug. 10, 1903.
[38] *Boone County Recorder*, 1930 Historical Edition.
[39] *Boone County Recorder*, Aug. 10, 1903.

Two unidentified men stand beside riverboat pilot John Maurer (third from left), next is his wife Lou, then his mother Rebecca and father Joseph Maurer. Courtesy of Sandra Rudicill Cupps.

Rabbit Hash Store Changes Hands

Rabbit Hash's General Store also began as a Granger Store. Cal G. Riddell began clerking there in 1877. He, with J.A. Wilson, (spelled Willson here) bought the store in 1883. In the spring of 1900, Wilson sold his half interest to E.L. Stephens. Stephens was a farmer who had started a huckster wagon, selling farm produce door to door.

Four years later, Stephens was running the store on his own and operating a fleet of four huckster wagons "*that make regular trips through the rurals, distributing goods and money and caring for such produce as the farmers may have to sell.*" B.W. Nelson was one of his clerks.

Even with all the huckster wagons and the produce they brought in, the store couldn't always keep up with the demand. In August 1907, the City of Louisville steamer could not get through the Rabbit Hash channel and remained docked at the landing all day. Rabbit Hash and Rising Sun were "*denuded of all eatables*" by 700 hungry passengers.[40]

Coal barges docked at Rabbit Hash to sell coal. Buyers drove horse-drawn wagons to pick up their supplies. They parked the wagon on the huge scales, weighed it empty, then reweighed it full of coal.

Bustling Businesses

Practicing in Rabbit Hash was lucrative for Dr. Y. Frank Hopkins, who had graduated from the Kentucky School of Medicine in 1901. The Grant County native earned $3,000 the first year after friends convinced him to

---

[40] Conrad, *Top of Kentucky*, 34.

move across the river to join them. After Dr. Hopkins moved away, his house became a hat shop.

Pleasure craft buyers came to Rabbit Hash to order a boat built to their specifications by expert craftsman George Hillis. "*He is never without orders for fancy skiffs and boats. There are few outing resorts along the Ohio that do not look to him for their supply of pleasure craft. . . . Not only does he model his skiffs and boats to please the eye, but they are built strong, capable for to undergo great endurance. Yet they are light and glide through the water as if propelled by magic.*"

The Rising Sun native was also an expert painter.[41]

S.N. Riggs of Gunpowder Creek was a wheelwright and blacksmith who ran planing and grist mills and a blacksmith and wood working shop in Rabbit Hash. (Planing mills planed or smoothed rough-sawn boards.) Mrs. Smith Riggs ran a hat shop.

In his wood finishing mill, Riggs used a scroll saw to make ornamental trim, including brackets, ornamental gables and columns. Riggs built two houses with gingerbread trim, one just below, the other just above Rabbit Hash.[42]

On certain days, Riggs ground feed and meal for the neighborhood.

In his blacksmith and woodworking shop, Riggs made plows, harrows, wagon boxes, hay beds, shoveling boards, farm gates, ladders and more. The multi-talented man was also president of the Rabbit Hash and Normansville Telephone Co.[43]

Rules for Phone Use
1. Have patience.
2. Business messages have the right of way.
3. Don't meddle with the phone.
4. Raise receiver from hook and listen before ringing bell to avoid interrupting someone. If line is in use hang up and wait until parties ring off.
5. Eavesdropping is strictly forbidden, also improper, obscene or profane language and if indulged in your telephone will be removed and you forfeit your box.
6. Never place receiver over phone or do anything else to annoy those who may be talking. This subjects to same penalty and forfeit as improper language.
7. Phones are free to subscribers and their families. If others are allowed the use, it will be charged at exchanges against subscribers at whose phone it originated.
8. Phone to be free to all in case of sickness or for calls for a physician. [44]

Rabbit Hash Telephone Rings

On April 25, 1903, a group met at Rabbit Hash to decide how to build a phone line from Normansville at the intersection of Ryle Road and KY 338, roughly five miles down river.

Surveys determined 205 poles were needed for the main line, so the 12 stockholders were assigned poles to erect. Each stockholder was to make his own connection with the main line.

Outsiders were charged 10 cents each time for using the line. Their calls were limited to five minutes. Anyone paying or donating $20 or more toward line construction was allowed free phone use indefinitely. Those donating less than $20 were allowed to use the line for 10 cents per message until the amount of the donation was spent.

In December, minutes recorded by Solon Stephens reported the board agreed to pay B.W. Nelson $1 per year for each box on the phone lines from Normansville to Rabbit Hash and Belleview to Rabbit Hash. The switch

---

[41] *Boone County Recorder*, Aug. 10, 1903.
[42] Lib Stephens, Feb. 4, 1998.
[43] *Boone County Recorder*, Aug. 10, 1903.
[44] Rabbit Hash Telephone Co. board minutes, 1903-1914, 11-12.

was to be open from 6 a.m. until 8 p.m. and until midnight on Sundays.

Burlington Telephone Service

Henry DeCoursey Adams recalled his role in using the new phones in Burlington. *"My family had moved to a two-story frame house. The telephone switchboard had been installed with Emma as operator. Sam and I acted as relief operators without pay. It was a small switchboard with just a few lines and six to 15 subscribers on a line.*

"Little more than a 'party' line, this was a 'congregation.' Particularly in the evenings, everyone listened in on all conversations. A lot of pleading was needed to get them to hang up so we would have enough power to get a call to faraway Hebron or Idlewild. After every ring – click, click, click – all the receivers went down again.

"Even in Burlington the number of telephones was very limited. I got the messenger fees, delivering messages or calling someone to the phone: the main part of town 10 cents, the suburbs, like the Charley Hughes place, 15 cents. An electrical storm usually burned out everything. I could make most of the repairs, either inside the switchboard or climb the pole out front to the platform and metal box containing most of the main connections. If it was too complicated, I sent for Edison Riddell."[45]

Big Bone/Beaverlick

New technology was appearing everywhere. The first photos of Big Bone Baptist Church were taken in 1900. One was given to Pastor James A. Kirtley Jr., the other to the church.

J.S. Taylor was general manager of

Harry Roseberry and other farm hands with Julia Dinsmore outside the cookhouse around the turn of the century.
Courtesy of the Dinsmore Homestead

Beaverlick Mercantile Co. J.W. Cleek was president; W.C. Johnson, secretary; and J.O. Griffith, treasurer. The post office was in the store and Taylor was deputy postmaster.

Just a few miles away, James W. Kennedy ran a general store at Normansville. He operated a flourmill there for a few years before returning to farming. He dealt in tobacco, then moved to a home overlooking Union where he built a large warehouse. A loyal Democrat, Kennedy was elected to the legislature and was nominated for re-election without opposition.

Roosevelt Connection

Much changed for the well-known Dinsmore family this decade. The niece named Martha but called Patty ran a ham and sausage business at the farm until about 1901. Then Patty took Isabella to New York City to attend school. While there, Isabella met Eleanor Roosevelt who remained a life-long friend. Isabella Selmes was a bridesmaid for Eleanor in her 1905 marriage to her cousin Franklin Roosevelt.

In July of that year, Isabella married Robert Munro Ferguson, a Scotsman who had ridden with Teddy Roosevelt's Rough Riders. Three years later, he developed tuberculosis, so they moved to New York, then to New Mexico.

---

[45] Adams, 17-18.

The Fergusons had two children, Martha Ferguson Breasted (1906-1994) and Robert "Bobby" Munro Ferguson (1908-1984).

Now a grandmother, Patty moved between the Boone County farm, her sister Sally's in New York and her daughter's home in New Mexico.

Dinsmore farm caretaker Harry Roseberry was trained as a carpenter and furniture craftsman. Born in 1881, he married Susan Reily who joined him on the Dinsmore farm.

Several generations of the Roseberry family grew up on the Dinsmore farm, living in a house built from a structure that originally was a slaughterhouse.[46]

Verona Grows

While Patty's second grandchild was toddling about, Boone County's southernmost village was incorporating and gaining its own general store.

Arthur and Lulu Powers Roberts opened Verona's General Store in December 1908. Arthur, a carpenter, also "*engaged in wall paper decoration and painting*" and wrote a community column for the *Recorder*.[47]

A few months later, on April 13, 1909, Verona incorporated.

Verona native John L. Vest was an attorney who avoided criminal cases and participated in a variety of business ventures around the Commonwealth. He was a large stockholder and director of the Income Life Insurance Co. of Louisville, Anglin Ave. Tobacco Warehouse in Lexington, Formica Insulation of Cincinnati and the Bank of Independence.

In 1926, Vest took over the Chevrolet dealership for Boone and Gallatin counties. Denver Bassett managed the Boone County dealership that sold about 500 new and used cars a year. "*They keep a complete line of Chevrolets on display at all times, including roadsters, phaetons, coupes, coaches, sedans and trucks.*"[48]

Walton Development

In 1906, a crew that had failed to strike oil at Big Bone Lick moved to Walton. At 250', they hit gas, just as they did at Big Bone.

Attorney J.G. Tomlin, a former schoolteacher, served as Deputy Revenue Collector, then moved to Walton to practice law. One of the few Republicans in the county, Tomlin had been a nominee for Commonwealth's Attorney, county attorney, state senator and county representative.

Sons of a miller, A.M. and Rand Rouse built Walton Roller Mills in 1879. The old burr process was upgraded to a roller system that produced high-grade flour using steam power. The flour was sold as "*bolted and unbolted meal.*" Finer flours were bolted, or strained through a cloth to remove coarser pieces.

W.R. "Rand" Rouse was superintendent of the Methodist Sunday School and a member of Walton's town council. He also owned Limaburg's saw and gristmill. For several years, Rand served as president and owned a "*very large block of Burlington and Florence Turnpike stock.*" He married Ada Wilhoit.

Boone County Recorder
Aug. 22, 1900

THE LEAGUE INSTITUTE,
VERONA, KY.
The Sixth Term Opens Sept. 24, 1900
N.E. Hamilton, Prin.

Tuition and Board $130 per school year.
Instrumental Music $16 per school year, for one lesson per week;
$30 for two lessons per week.
The entire course is divided into four departments – Classical, Scientific, Teachers' and Musical.
A pupil may choose and complete either and receive diplomas for same.
A competent and experienced teacher furnished for every 12 to 15 pupils.
For full information address,
N.E. HAMILTON, Verona, Ky.

---

[46] Bettie Thomas Siffel, December 11, 1997
[47] Arthur C. Roberts, *Boone County Recorder*, 1930 Historical Edition.
[48] *Boone County Recorder*, 1930 Historical Edition.

Walton Schools

A.M. Rouse (great grandfather of Walton residents Asa and Jack Rouse) married Mary Coffman who died in 1882, leaving two children, William O. and Pearl Rouse Johnson. Rouse, who then married Ella Rogers, was a trustee of the grade school and school board treasurer.

The Walton school district became independent in 1900. Two years later, new elementary and high schools were built on Main Street.[49]

"*After considerable legal trouble, the present building of the Walton Graded School was completed in 1902 at a cost of about $11,000.*" Principal William Pinkney Dickey was a Mississippi native, educated in Georgetown, Ky. Teachers were Harriett Bedinger, Alice Coffman, Jean Chambers and Mary Rouse. The school was expected to attract many pupils from outside the district.[50]

Chambers Move to Walton

Some new pupils for Walton's red brick school arrived in 1906 when Cleveland Scott Chambers moved from Idlewild to Walton.

He brought a brand-new funeral car built in Lawrenceburg, Ind. In partnership with Ben B. Allphin, he opened a funeral home that has become Chambers and Grubbs. As was the custom, they also had a livery stable.

Born on a farm, Chambers attended the Cincinnati College of Embalming and passed state accreditation tests in Indiana, Kentucky and Ohio. He married Alta Terrill of Petersburg on Nov. 7, 1900, and had two daughters, Aleen (born in 1902) and Mary Scott (born in 1904).

Mary Scott Chambers shadowed her father, conducting her first graveside service at the Richwood Presbyterian Church at 13. She graduated from high school three years later and rode the train daily from Walton to the Cincinnati College of Embalming.

She had to wait until she was 21 to receive her license and become the first female embalmer in Kentucky. She married Wallace K. Grubbs, who also had funeral director and embalmer's licenses. Their youngest son Jimmy later became the third generation to own and operate the same funeral home.[51]

In 1928, "*a dear little girl four years of age from the Orphans Home in Louisville came to*

Jeanette Grubbs (Mrs. David Clore) stands beside the new Chambers and Grubbs' hearse that doubled as an ambulance. Courtesy of Boone County Historical Preservation

the Chambers home on a visit." Mr. Chambers became so attached to Ella Mae that "*out of sympathy and the pure kindness of his heart he has kept this little girl and given her parental care, which she seems to realize, for she says, 'I have the best daddy in the world.*'"[52]

About that time, Chambers purchased a new hearse that served as an invalid coach and ambulance. (Funeral homes ran local ambulance services before fire departments were established.)

A *Recorder* article said, "*The very latest

---

[49] Conrad, *History of Boone County Schools*, 20.
[50] *Boone County Recorder*, Aug. 10, 1903.
[51] 150th Anniversary, City of Walton, 76.
[52] *Boone County Recorder*, 1930 Historical Edition.

The Walton Canning Co. on Nicholson Ave., owned by John Metcalfe, father of Faye Conner and Lucille Brakefield. Courtesy of *150th Anniversary, City of Walton*.

type tents, awnings, and lowering devices make this service one of beauty and Mr. Chambers himself a genius in the arranging of flowers."[53]

Walton's Trains

A switch in front of what is now the Chambers and Grubbs Funeral Home allowed one train to be manually switched to a section of track off the main, while another passed. As many as three trains ran north daily carrying passengers, freight and deliveries from Sears and Roebuck on the L&N Railroad while two ran south on the Southern Railroad. Walton was the local passenger stop.

[53] *Boone County Recorder*, Sept. 4, 1930.

Just south of Walton was a pump station on a large lake where steam-powered trains stopped to refill with water.

Southern firemen were advised to "*watch the engineer to see how he was working and fire accordingly, to make sure the engine was properly drafted, to stop leaks around the smoke box and never to place more coal than necessary in the firebox.*"

Boone County residents rode to Covington and Cincinnati to shop. Henry DeCoursey Adams recalled a gentleman from the Grubbs family who carried large baskets to shop for those who could not make the trip themselves.

Many rode the commuter train to Cincinnati to work or attend business schools. It passed through Walton at 5:45 a.m. then left

Chapter 9   1900-1909 Telephones, Cars & Baseball

Steam engine near Walton. Photo courtesy of the Dan Finfrock Collection

Cincinnati at 5:30 p.m. and returned to Walton about 7 p.m. Fare for 54 one-way trips was $4.50 a month.

The Southern Railroad made an extra trip on Saturdays, turning the engine around on a turntable before heading back to Cincinnati. The trains were so full some passengers stood. Smoking was permitted only in the front car.

Popular excursion trains went from Cincinnati to High Bridge, a few miles south of Lexington, then returned late in the evening stopping at all stations. Tourists took their own lunches. The L&N Railroad ran excursions to Louisville for baseball games and zoo visits.[54]

Traveling circuses like Barnum & Bailey, Ringling Bros. or Hallenbeck & Wallace filled a whole train. Kids offered to carry water for the animals, pound stakes or do just about anything to get money for a ticket, Wilford M. Rice recalled. *"Going to the depot to see the animals and equipment unload from the train was a sight to see."*

Intimidated by a headlight *"like a giant eye above the cow catcher,"* Betty Weaver Roter recounted boarding the train the first time as a child: *"The wheels squealed on the tracks, and the great blacksnake of a train screeched to a halt. . . The conductor called, 'All Aboard!' A belch of smoke, a rattling of cars as each one bumped into motion and its wheels rolled into action on the rails. Clickety-clack! Clickety-clickety-clack! Clickety-clack! The wheels underneath muttered as we crossed the ties, speeding along the tracks."*[55]

Aunt Bettie

Mrs. Bettie Steele, known as "Aunt Bettie" around Walton, was born into slavery in Missouri around 1833. She, her husband Nat and son Layton were sold to a Kentucky landowner and made the pilgrimage from Hannibal, Mo., to Kentucky in a covered wagon.

In about 1854, they settled in Steel Creek Bottoms near the Ohio. Several years later

---

[54] *175th Anniversary Historical Book*, 56.

[55] Roter, 41-42.

they were freed and migrated to Walton where they had two sons, Frisby and Willie, and five daughters, Louisa, Fannie, Sallie, Elvira and Darkas.

Mrs. Steele, grandmother of Gladys Ingram of Walton, purchased a log cabin on Church Street from Walton attorney J.G. Tomlin for $50 which she earned from scrubbing clothes on a wash board and ironing for 25 cents (perhaps by a bushel basket or some other measure) in the early 1900s. She recalled Civil War soldiers coming through the area. Local residents were required to feed them and their horses. Five generations of her family were born on Church Street. Mrs. Steele died in 1923 at the age of 90.[56]

James "Stoney" Ingram, great grandson of Mrs. Steele, lives on Church Street and is the janitor for Star Bank in Walton.

View of Union.   Courtesy of Boone County Historic Preservation

Union Gains Bank

The new Union Deposit Bank that opened in 1903 planned to avoid any problems like robbery. The new brick building had a fireproof vault and an "*improved Mosler Screw-Door Time-Lock Safe.*" It also offered trust boxes. Former legislator Dr. M.J. Crouch was president.

Although he owned a drug store and bluegrass farm in addition to his medical practice, Crouch conceived the bank concept. With the help of farmer and businessman J.W. Conner, Crouch organized the bank. Union area farmer J.L. Frazier was selected cashier.

L.W. Lassing

L.W. Lassing, the judge's brother, also chose a farming career. He clerked in their father's store in Union from the time he could see over the counter until he reached 18. Then Lassing turned to agriculture and soon owned his own farm. He became known for raising Shorthorn cattle and Shropshire sheep.

A member of the state legislature in 1882 and 1883, Lassing also participated in the constitutional convention in 1887. A Democrat, he was known for bringing the party together.

The Aug. 10, 1903 *Recorder* wrote this glowing description of L.W. Lassing: "*a disposition hospitable in the extreme, blessed with a heart full of sunshine. . . . staunch as a friend, pure as a citizen, unsullied in character, courteous with an apology for being courteous, he stands a man among men, one of the true emblems of a typical Kentucky gentleman.*"

Lassing's wife, Jennie M. Kennedy, died in 1896 after 38 years of marriage. They had a daughter, Theresa who died when her dress ignited as she was standing in front of a fireplace.

Hathaway Love Story

Joseph Ephraim Weaver ran the grocery store and post office at Hathaway, midway between Union and Rabbit Hash. A narrow dirt road wound over the hills to Big Bone Baptist Church. Weaver, a tall man with black hair, mustache and cowboy hat, rode his

---
[56] *175th Anniversary Historical Book*, 53.

pacing saddle horse named Brad to church on Sunday.

Ella Porter Adams sat on the opposite side of the church with the other women. After the service concluded, when Deacon Lee Huey came to greet her, she asked about the man. Huey introduced them, beginning a courtship that ended in a Sept. 6, 1906 marriage.

Ella and Joseph were married at the Adams family home on a high hill above Big Bone Lick. Ella wore a tailored dress of brown fabric, popular at the time. They moved into the new house Weaver had built on another hill above Fowler Creek Road, about 1¼ miles north of Union and lived there for 40 years.[57]

A show horse   Photo courtesy of Virginia Lainhart

Gunpowder Blacksmith

Just north of Union, near Gunpowder, L.H. Busby was the blacksmith at Busby Heights. The protégé of W.A. Tanner, he lived with the Tanners, became a business partner and later learned he had been named an heir.

"Oct. 21, 1899, Mr. Busby moved his shop from Gunpowder proper to its present site, built a new and very commodious shop, and has since had all the business that he could look after, and oftentimes he had two or three helpers. He makes horseshoeing one of his specialties, gives special attention to deformed or irregular shaped feet and cracked heels, etc."[58]

W.N. Surface bought E.O. Rouse's store at Gunpowder in 1893. The next year Surface married Susie Carpenter. In 1895, a fire destroyed their home, business and supplies. He rebuilt.

E.E. and J.S. Rouse owned the primary industry in Gunpowder, a lumber manufacturing plant. They rough-sawed walnut, oak and other woods and shipped lumber out. *"Their resource for desirable timber is sufficient to keep the mill running steadily for several years yet to come. The owners are also interested in farming and own some very desirable lands."*[59]

Showing Horses

Horses hauled wagons loaded with the Rouse Brothers' lumber to the river or the train. Buying, selling and training equines of all sizes and abilities remained a business, diversion and pleasure. Most newspapers contained a half-dozen advertisements for stallions offering stud services on Boone County farms, usually at prices of $10 to $15.

The best stallions were exhibited at April Court Days when people pilgrimaged to the county seat. Horses like Old Dexter, owned by Jim Aylor, were trotted from the Cowan

---

[57] Roter, 413-414.
[58] *Boone County Recorder*, Aug. 10, 1903.
[59] *Boone County Recorder*, Aug. 10, 1903.

Fairs Start Again

The Harvest Home Fair and the Florence Fair offered more opportunities to show off horses, farm produce, dairy and poultry products, and needlework.

The Harvest Home Association added dancing for young people to help attract spectators to its grounds near Limaburg. To attract exhibitors, the Association paid premiums as large as those paid by county fairs.

The county fair brought people, their crafts, and animals from all over the region to Boone County's northeastern town.

Florence farmer and livestock dealer, F.A. Utz was a director of the North Kentucky Agricultural Association that sponsored the Florence Fair. Utz also was a director of the Erlanger Deposit Bank, the Florence-Burlington and Florence-Union pikes and treasurer of Farmers' Mutual Insurance Co. of Boone County.[60]

Henry DeCoursey Adams remembered Dick Utz not allowing anyone to pass his passenger-filled buggy on the way to the fair. Meeting another vehicle head-on on the narrow county roads tested buggy-racers' equitation abilities. During dry weather, informal races produced huge dust clouds, no doubt flavoring the baskets packed with food for families and friends to enjoy at the fair.

Horses without buggies showed off in a special ring. Pens held livestock and poultry. Ribbons were awarded for the best vegetables and canned items. Boys met girls on an elevated walkway called a promenade that circled the show ring.

Adams said one year, Otto Crisler sold rubber "come-back" balls about the size of a golf ball attached to a three-foot long rubber line. The boys hit girls with theirs, and the girls hit boys. *"When the promenade became congested, girls in under-sized shoes and over-tight corsets fainted and were carried to the shade of a tree. Sometime helpful friends poured water over their heads, soiling their dresses."*[61]

Adams' sister Elizabeth, who was known for her horsemanship, rode a yellow horse during presidential campaign parades for William Jennings Bryan. Bryan's promise of 16 silver coins for one gold dollar was illustrated with 16 white horses and a Palomino in the center.

Bryan was well-supported in the county. As the sixth Congressional District's representative to the National Convention in 1896, N.S. Walton voted for Bryan. Walton, a veteran who fought for the Confederacy under Co. B "Jessie's Batallion," farmed 540 acres near Idlewild on Burlington-Petersburg Pike. He was a legislator in 1883-84 and 1891-93.[62]

> **Boone County Recorder**
> April 26, 1905
> *"Please say to the old Confederates of Boone County, you must each get a suit of gray and get ready to go to..."* Louisville in June to Postmaster T. H. Baker's.
> *"You know Tom is a Boone County boy and he will be glad to have us. ... If I can't do any better, I am going to try to borrow a suit of gray that my old friend Billy Stott of Petersburg has. We will not take any excuse from a any rebel soldier of Boone County for not going to the reunion of Confederate states as they never will in our life meet again in Kentucky."*
> William Grimsley
> Confederate veteran

First City Ordinances

Florence city fathers hired a town marshal, whose salary was $42 annually, paid quarterly, plus an extra $2 a day during the Florence Fair. Ben Osborn, Virginia Lainhart's grandfather, was the first Florence marshal. The council began emphasizing the need to install curbs and improve roads.

---

[60] *Boone County Recorder*, Aug. 10, 1903.

[61] Adams.
[62] *Boone County Recorder*, Aug. 10, 1903.

Chapter 9 1900-1909 Telephones, Cars & Baseball

In 1905, with T.L. Utz as the chairman and J.C. Buckner as clerk, the trustees set a 6-mile per hour speed limit for automobiles. Autos were required to have brakes, bell, horn or other signal and a white light in front and red light in the rear for night driving. Other requirements for automobile drivers included:

"On meeting or approaching persons who are walking with horse or team must give signal with horn or bell, and must stop if necessary and do everything in reason to avoid frightening animals.

"If they meet a person with restive horse must come to a stop when signaled by hand or at request."[63]

Florence Businesses

Florence prohibited gambling and breaking street lamps in 1905.[64] Perhaps patrons at the town's several saloons got out of hand too often. J.M. Finch ran a saloon in Florence. A.S. Cates ran one near Erlanger on the Florence-Erlanger Turnpike, offering Owen County whiskey and Bavarian bottled and keg beer. John Veerkamp ran a "Last Chance" bar midway on the Erlanger-Florence Turnpike. He offered "Forget Maryland Rye" and "Dan Barton Bourbon" whiskies.

Florence's business district was growing. In a commodious and handsome brick building, C.W. Myers offered general merchandise, dry goods, groceries, hardware and more in 1897. He employed several salesmen to serve *"the surging crowds that daily may be seen entering the portals of the establishment."*

T.B. Castleman, who married Grace Raymond Yeager, operated an Erlanger drugstore before opening one in Florence. During the Cleveland Administration, Castleman was Florence's postmaster. After graduating from Cincinnati Dental College, Castleman opened a practice with a main office in Florence and auxiliary offices in Burlington, Latonia and Big Bone Springs.

"As a dentist, he employs all the latest ideas suggested by modern practice and in the execution is said to be one of the most skillful representatives of the profession. Artificial work, bridge and crown building, treating diseased teeth, extracting without the usual attending pain are but a few of the special incites to his practice."[65]

Florence Deposit Bank opened on July 25, 1904, with capital stock of $15,000.

German immigrant Fred Reich built wagons and did blacksmithing in Florence. Arriving in 1856, he apprenticed to a Covington smith. In 1865, he bought the Florence business from John Olsner. Jan. 27, 1901, he married local girl Georgia B. Snyder.[66]

Florence High School

With business development came more students for city schools. In 1890, Florence school expanded into a two-room building on Shelby Street on an acre purchased from Mr. Galway. Enrollment increased rapidly.

In 1900, Almer Michael Yealey contracted to become principal of the Florence school. Lizzy Vest was the primary teacher. School board members were Ezra Rouse, Henry Tanner and Lewis Thompson. Thompson had taught in the county system.

School consolidation began in 1907 with a high school in Burlington, after a state law required at least one high school in each county seat. All county taxpayers were required to support the high school. High school students completed two years at Burlington or paid tuition to go to Erlanger.[67]

Parents began protesting the distance and cost of transporting pupils – especially the large number from Florence – to Burlington.

To address the problem, two more rooms were added to the Florence elementary school.

---

[63] Florence Ordinance Book #1
[64] Florence Ordinance Book #1, 27-29.
[65] *Boone County Recorder*, Aug. 10, 1903.
[66] *Boone County Recorder*, Aug. 10, 1903.
[67] Conrad, *History of Boone County Schools*, 10.

Boone County High School in Burlington
Courtesy of Boone County Historical Preservation

The first Boone County graded high school began in Florence in 1908.[68] Mabel Tanner, Ruby Corbin, Harry Tanner and Robert Robbins were the first Florence High School graduates in 1915. (Walton's high school was already established.)

The county judge outlined another school district in Pleasant Ridge. A schoolhouse was built in the northwest corner of Hopeful Road and U.S. 42.

John Uri Lloyd returned to Florence after his folklore novel, *Stringtown on the Pike*, was published. Then he asked permission to restore the Old Town Hall as it was when his father taught school there 40-50 years before. The old building was "*straightened amid a great groaning and whinny of ancient hewn rafters and joists until it was enabled to again look straight.*"[69] Mr. Lloyd established a fund to maintain the building, which was demolished over protests in the 1970s.

Adam's Knee Infection

A small Burlington boy was struggling with health problems. In 1893, when he was about five, scarlet fever destroyed the drum of Henry DeCoursey Adams' right ear. In 1899, his left knee was infected, putting him in bed for nine months. Adams colorfully recounted the experiences of his youth in an undated manuscript.

"*In the beginning, Dr. Furnish recommended a Cincinnati hospital, but Father would have none of that. There was a widespread belief that if one went into a hospital, he never came out alive. It never occurred to anybody that the patients were 9/10 dead before they entered. The leg was swollen to more than double normal size, with all the accompanying debilitating conditions.*

"*Dr. Furnish operated. He did not believe I could survive a general chloroform anesthetic. So, he resorted to 'freezing' with ethyl-chloride, so superficial it is not even effective on soft tissues. Swollen and infected as the knee was, he cut to the bone without an anesthetic. No success, nothing gained.*

"*A week or so later, he decided to try again. I had just enough strength to say that he wouldn't. They would have to tie me down. I won. If I could not live through chloroform, it was alright with me. Dr. Smith, a Civil War surgeon was called. He administered chloroform. Again the operation was not a success. In time, nature did better, opening up*

---

[68] A.M. Yealey, "History Concerning Florence Schools," *Boone County Recorder*.
[69] Jones, 8.

drainage.

"*If a horse trotted down the dirt road or alley to the livery stable, the vibrations awoke me screaming. At one time the muscles contracted so much the foot would be drawn halfway up, the pain close to unendurable. A six-pound flat iron was tied to the foot to keep the leg straight. The contraction increased and pulled up the iron.*

"*They had tied on a huge nine-pound tailor's iron, but it was too heavy. I couldn't stand it. My much older sister Elizabeth fought many of my battles and won most of them. She agreed, took the iron off, carried it to the kitchen and returned with the smaller one plainly visible. When hidden by the foot board, she tied on the nine-pounder, which she had hidden in her apron. It was so comfortable, it was perfect. I didn't learn of this delusion until a year or two later.*

"*As usual, it was not all bad. The grownups and boys and girls dropped in for visits. When so many of the good folks had a special dinner, they shared it with me. When shopping in Cincinnati, Mrs. Revill often brought me a storybook or toy.*

"*To while away the hours, I learned something of simple crocheting and pieced a four-patch quilt of one-inch pieces in four patch squares. That news spread and just about all of the women brought scraps of cloth to go in that quilt. When finally finished, the Ladies' Aid came and quilted it.*

"*Months and months of recuperation were helped by Jo Revill Furnish's little wagon upon which was placed a platform and sort of a mattress to make a substitute wheelchair so I*

Dr. Furnish and his buggy. Courtesy of Virginia Lainhart

could get around the house and eventually out in the yard.[70]

"*In September 1902, Dr. Furnish got me into a children's hospital in Louisville. Brother Sam took me by buggy to Gunpowder Creek, through Sugar Tit to Verona then Walton where he left me with Scott Underwood, a former neighbor, who now was running a little hotel in Walton.*

"*I lost the battle to the bedbugs, millions of them. Early the next morning Scott put me on a train to Louisville. During that lonely 39-mile ride, remembering the frequent hearsay that only the dead came out of a hospital, I thought of escaping but decided it couldn't get worse. The hospital's reception was informal and friendly but when they unpacked my little box they were greeted by some of the victorious bedbugs. I convinced them they were from the hotel, not from my home. They put me to bed. But my appetite left when dinner was served on the same white granite plates we used for the prisoners* (at the Boone County jail where his brother served as jailer).

"*Saturday morning, the surgeon Dr. Ap Vance said he'd try to save my leg but gave no promises. After the chloroform-ether wore off I still had my toes. With water limited, I*

---

[70] Adams, 12-13.

dreamed of all the springs and streams within a mile of Burlington.

"Monday night there was a new undergraduate nurse on duty whom I talked into bringing me a pitcher of ice water. I drank all of it. When she returned she was scared. It was just what I needed. I got a good night's sleep.

"On visiting day some of the society girls came driving beautiful horses in tandem with a footman in the rear seat. They brought expensive toys, books, and good stories. I was in the hospital four months with a heavy cast almost from hip to ankle."[71]

Clore Joins Circus

Adams tells of another Burlington boy who had a different kind of exciting trip. *Bruce Clore (whose father ran the bus and mail line and lived in the Tousey house) was so impressed with the sideshow and animal acts when a circus came to town that he decided that was the life for him. About 14, he departed with the circus. He quickly learned that the animals didn't help taking down the tent and seats nor live on a few hours of sleep in a rolling wagon before setting up for another show in the next town. He was soon back in Burlington."*[72]

Burlington Blacksmith

Other Burlington residents left an impression on young Henry as well. Col. Crisler, who ran the Burlington blacksmith shop, *"was a mighty man, about 6'5" who wore the heaviest boots and shoes I had ever seen. They had the usual heavy soles, but the first thing he did with a new pair was to half-sole them, which he could do either by sewing or nailing. He taught me how to do both, and that saved me considerable money.*

"In his shop I made a turtle hook, like a large fishhook but without the barb, strong and sharp with a rather long stem that fit into the end of a light pole, with a welded band to keep the stem tight...I got a right big one, dressed and fried him. Delicious, with seemingly many different kinds of meat, but dressing one was enough for me."

Henry also made iron or steel sled runners from an old buggy wheel to speed his winter fun. And, he made a garden hoe from one of the Colonel's discarded rasps.

Just down the road was another interesting bit of news. *"The Kirkpatrick family of Jesse, Roy and Katie kept a skeleton in their carpenter shop, all bones wired in place in a long narrow box. Their turning lathe was the closest thing to a modern tool in town."*[73]

> **Burlington's Bucket Brigade**
> In Burlington, the efficient fire brigade made flames a lesser threat than in many places. There was no bell or gong, but people seemed to materialize with buckets and ladders when the need arose.
> Some manned the cistern or well pump, others lined up passing a full bucket in front and an empty bucket behind on its way to be refilled. If the cistern ran dry, they moved to a pond.[1]
> Henry DeCoursey Adams

County Jail

Henry DeCoursey Adams learned intimately about the jail's workings. *"Following Father's death (in about 1902), brother Sam was appointed jailer, then elected and served about 10 years. As a contribution to my board and keep, I took over the chores of janitor of the court house, jail and Baptist Church."* He also did those chores at the school, but for an enterprising $2.50 a month.

"At the courthouse, it was my job to 'wash the windows and scrub the floor and polish up the knocker on the big front door,' but I did not polish it so bu-tif-lee that they made me ruler of the Queen's Na-vee. And instead of the knocker, there were the big brass spittoons. The chewers did not often hit the hole.

"Those big windows got their turn in spring

---

[71] Adams
[72] Adams

[73] Adams

Dr. Furnish, who treated Henry DeCoursey Adams, and later became a state senator, is seated in the back row with this group posing on the Burlington courthouse.   Photo courtesy of Virginia Lainhart

housecleaning, washed with a lot of kerosene in the water. Kerosene and hands were never compatible.

"It required a lot of those snout-shaped buckets of coal to fill the box. I carried coal from the bin in the jail yard across the pike, up two flights of steps and emptied it into the big box by the stove. It was easier to ring the bell about 15 minutes before court assembly. That bell had a lousy tone.

"Another chore was to wait upon the court and see that the judge had a pitcher of ice water if any ice was in town. Usually there wasn't. Judge Lassing had the only icehouse and the supply did not last throughout the year. I also rounded up the jurors in case one had met an old friend and forgot he was supposed to be on duty. In special cases, I'd scout the town and try to find 'six men good and true.' The women did not then qualify.

"Once I could find only five. Judge Perry Cason was presiding. My good friend Mrs. Bailey was to be committed to what was then known as the Kentucky Asylum for the Insane, since given a more humane name. She had spent the previous night in our home under constant guard. There was no doubt as to her condition.

"I reported to the judge that I could not find the sixth man. He told me to sit. So at age 14 I served on a jury, but the judge's reputation was saved. At the moment the jury was to be polled, a man came in and was asked to take my place."

"The jail was not so much care. The prisoners, if any, could sweep the cells. The surrounding floor was easy to mop. The second floor was never used -- it was reserved for the ladies, and they must have been (ladies), for we never had a female prisoner.

The stove was small and no problem in winter. Fresh water came from the cistern in front of the court house.

"Once when Sam was in the hospital, I was acting as jailer, illegally of course because I wasn't of age. A young teenager is never where he is expected to be. I got home late in the afternoon and found a note that a prisoner had arrived, so I grabbed the keys and went to the court house.

"All the offices were vacant, every man had gone home. As I entered the building, I noticed a stranger standing on the front steps. Being the only one inside and having nothing else to do, I went out and stood beside him. The stranger told me he was the prisoner and handed me his papers. With that, we crossed the street and I locked him up. It was for some minor offense, he served about 10 days. The judge knew he would not run away."

Attempted Lynching

"Another time Sam was hospitalized and (brother) Lute was acting jailer. Early one evening, somebody in Walton called to alert us that a mob was forming with the intention of lynching a prisoner.

"We made our plans. Lute, with the real keys, was to hightail it across the garden to the nearest safe hiding place. I was to meet the mob, argue and delay them as long as possible, but if they got too persistent, give them the keys to the upstairs part of the jail, which was empty.

"Except for shoes, we went to bed with our clothes on. It was bitter cold weather. The ground, even the old pike, was deeply frozen. Sounds traveled and magnified. About midnight we heard horse hooves pounding the pike, first faintly, then unmistakably. In almost nothing flat, Lute was in his shoes and gone. On they came, closer and closer. They stopped in front of the house. The horses were pawing the frozen pike, two dozen of them at the least. I went to the window just in time to see and hear one man say to another, 'goodnight,' and they rode away in opposite directions on Washington Street. In time, Lute came sneaking in." [74]

Schools

Some of Adams' experiences were more common for youth of his day. *"We had the little room and the big room, both exactly the same size. The distinction was that the beginners started in the little room. Eventually with luck, endurance, plenty of time, the good will of the teacher, sometimes an ill will that wanted to get rid of you, maybe a little bit of studying, they got promoted to the big room.*

"There were no grades (grade levels). Classes were called to the long front benches for individual recitation. In ability, most of the teachers were limited to the textbooks, wholly unable to enlarge upon any subject or stimulate inquisition.

"Professor Hughes introduced the classics. I think it was during his term that finally

---

Adams Reflects On Youthful Behaviors

"It is easy, if not popular, to criticize the youth of today. Could they be any worse than we were and stay out of jail? Why did we behave as we did on that picnic?

"Why did some boys take a rooster out of a coop in the Clutterbuck barn, pour gasoline and set him on fire? Fortunately, he ran for a hole in the barn door instead of the hay. And that act stirred the town. Some memories engender remorse.[1]

"My last teacher, Miss Lizzie Rogers of Walton was the best. Able, alert, classes on time, moved about the room to aid any who needed help, interested in everybody, always smiling. There was no disorder. How could there be in such a situation?

"After regular school hours she had classes in Latin and Benn Pitman Shorthand. The charge was $2.50 a month each, the exact pay for my janitorial services. It was worth it. Latin laid the foundation for my limited vocabulary and it is of inestimable value in medicine. The shorthand saved me the time and money in a business course."

---

[74] Adams, 22.

Chapter 9 1900-1909 Telephones, Cars & Baseball

McGuffey Readers were supplanted and new readers and a geography were adopted. Professor Hughes and I had a mutual hatred. He enjoyed disciplining me and I delighted in annoying him. He collected my bean shooters as fast as I could afford to buy them -- those metal cylinders with a rubber eraser in one end and pencil in the other, both removable, left the cylinder for the shooter.[75]

School Picnic

"In the last week of one term of Professor Hughes' school, he took the big room on a picnic to the cliffs by hayride. We loaded up in front of the Post Office.

"After departure, sharp-eyed Carrie Riddell got to wondering why dry hay would leak, but there was the evidence where the wagon had stood. Curiosity grew into suspicion. She hitched dobbin to the buggy and took off for the cliffs. And what a sight!

"Boys sprawled all over the hill drunk. Do not know how it got started, but the idea spread to take some liquor along, everyone to bring whatever he had. In addition, two boys the previous day or night sneaked a horse and buggy, drove to Florence and got a quart of whiskey.

"My donation was a half pint of what was presumed to be wine, long hidden beneath a rock under a walnut tree at the edge of the garden, origin unknown. No wine was permitted in our house. The conglomeration was poured into a kettle with a chunk of ice alongside. There were very few boys who did not partake. I did not go down, but felt very wobbly.

"Few incidents stirred Burlington more than this disastrous picnic. Of course, alcohol was verboten in dry Burlington. It was expected that when the grand jury next met it would investigate. When they met sister Emma was out of town. I was operating the switchboard and all the other boys were visiting their grandmas. That left me to tell everything I knew.

"One morning I looked out the window only to see Sheriff Allphin approaching. I knew the old 'possum trick, but falling off the stool did not seem like such a good idea. The sheriff came to make a direct call to Cincinnati so that everybody would not be listening in. That call went through fast. My feeling was that if I got out of that mess I would never get into another one like it. For many, many years, I would not taste even eggnog.[76]

Grandma and Dinah

Two more memorable characters Adams remembered were his grandmother and Dinah. Grandma Riddell, widow of Cy Riddell, lived in one of three white brick houses in

---

Boone County Recorder
Aug. 15, 1900
Midway

W.C. Johnson is engaged sawing lumber for the building of a large barn on the farm of John Hartman.

T. Jake Hughes pulled his threshing machine into Beaver, last Saturday evening having threshed 8,000 bushels of fine grain for the farmers.

Work on the pike leading from Big Bone to Beaver is progressing nicely at present. The grading is almost completed and quite a portion of the road is macadamized.

Miss Annie Wolfe, of Verona, has the contract for teaching the Beaver public school. She taught the school there last term and gave good satisfaction, hence, the selection of her services by the trustees for the present term.

Sleet Yarnell, the popular young barber at Walton, is visiting at Hamilton, sojourning at the hospitable home of our clever mail carrier, Will Hume, where he is devouring fish, watermelons, and other dainty edibles of the season.

T. Jake Hughes, the Beaver telephone magnate, has the poles set from the central office in Beaver to Crittenden and will string the wire this week. Mr. Hughes keeps a good man constantly employed attending to the line, consequently, it is never out of repair for any length of time. Mr. Hughes left here Tuesday for Chicago to visit a wholesale dry goods firm and the company from which he gets his up-to-date phones.

---

[75] Adams

[76] Adams

Burlington. *"In any distress, she was apt to be the first helper to arrive with her big basket that was always filled and ready. She was a tall, heavy, but active person.*

"Always with her was Dinah, an ex-slave and a typical one -- honest, dependable, the wants of others first, not her own. Dressed in tradition, always the big, white apron and a red bandanna perfectly adjusted. She walked about three feet behind Grandma and carried the basket.

"Dinah was the only black with the liberty of approaching by the front door and sitting in the parlor. She made regular visits to everybody and carried a basket the same size as Grandma's. Once I asked her why. 'Somebody might put something in it,' she said. And they always did.

McKim's Store

"Once I was in the right spot, talking to Frank McKim who ran the store, when the first bakery wagon to visit the burg showed up. He bought for me a baker's loaf of bread and a dozen doughnuts, the first of either I had seen and were they good. Father called the bread 'light bread.' Being accustomed to big, hot biscuits and cornbread twice a day, he scoffed at the light bread. Said you might as well let the moon shine in your mouth.

"Frank once pushed his teasing too far, I thought. Remember those little round, usually pottery vessels that were so essential before the days of inside plumbing? Ours got broken. I was sent for a new one. Frank refused to wrap it. My protests and the biggest threats I could make got me nowhere.

"Wrap it he would not. 'Just put your finger through that little round handle and you won't drop it.' As he had hoped, all of Burlington was on the street that morning, smiling as I toted the chamber pot home."[77]

Star Routes

Burlington's post office adjoined the general store on the corner of Jefferson and KY 18. The narrow rectangular room had one door, one window and the usual pot-bellied stove for heating.

In the winter, people crowded inside waiting for the mail to come from Erlanger. The post office *"had the combined smells of everything bad for miles around,"* Adams recalled. A Star Route was a route between two post offices.

"The Star Route system was operated by contract to the lowest bidder. That is if politicians or somebody else did not interfere, when it was always easy to find a flaw in the lowest bid.

"Rural delivery was one of the congressman's favored tools for political maneuvering. The Civil Service Commission supplied the Congressmen with a list of those eligible for appointment as rural delivery carriers.

"If he was a Democrat, and only Republicans were eligible, there were ways to rearrange routes. One patron may have to move his box a mile or more to another road and a few might be left without service.

"The answer to the yowls and protests was, 'This change is believed to be in the best interest of the service.'

*"Meanwhile, an examination was held and the desired person was added to the eligibility list. After his appointment, the statement was issued, 'It now appears that this change has not worked out to the advantage of the patrons and the original routes will be re-established.' In the meantime, a well-liked man, with no

---

> **Horse Tricks**
> Henry DeCoursey Adams' cousin Bluf (Bluford W.) Adams was county clerk and an excellent horseman.
> *"On a Court Day he pulled the stunt of standing a handkerchief on its edges a high as possible and, short and fat as he was, (bent down and) picked it up from the saddle at full gallop."*

---

[77] Adams

Florence's 1921 baseball team included Frank Sayre, Charlie Carpenter, Russell House and L.T. Utz, shown in the front row.   Photo courtesy of Tom Utz

"Jim Clore underbid somebody and got the contract for carrying the mail between Burlington and Erlanger. He was the first to have a special bus, with seats on either side for passengers with his name and U.S. Mail impressively painted on the outside.

"When the mail was all sorted, maybe one sack, I can still hear Miss Olga Kirkpatrick's voice, 'All Out,' which meant that those with boxes could open them up and the others could take their turn at the general delivery window.

"Olga worked behind a little counter and the rack of private boxes. Sometimes when the mail was more massive, Edison Riddell, never an introvert, would step in and help sort. He was the only one who dared violate the sanctity of the little swinging door, the entrance to behind the scene."[79]

Baseball

"Olga's brother Herbert had close to a fanatical devotion to baseball. When not trapping that was his only thought and subject. He laid out a diamond in the park across the road from the old cemetery with a ruler, fine-tooth comb and level. Burlington had some good players."

Son of sheriff James R. Clutterbuck, *"Roy Clutterbuck the first batter, nearly always got on base. His brother Homer was about as good but had arthritis in his feet and didn't play much.*

"Mont Slaback and Ed Hawes were catchers. Jack Sanford of East Bend Road played first base using a right handed glove, probably for economic reasons, even though he was left-handed. He could catch the ball, jerk off the glove and throw apparently without the loss of time."[80]

Women played too. Bloomer Girls baseball teams from Chicago came to compete with the

---

[79] Adams

[80] Adams

local baseball team.

"*The girls wore bloomers and middies, used regular baseball gloves and bats, and for sure, they were good. First their management would erect a canvas fence all around the field so outsiders couldn't peek in. Softball hadn't been heard of then,*" Wilford M. Rice said.

Clutterbuck Brothers' Store in Burlington   Courtesy of Virginia Lainhart

Reds Game

"*Hubert Brady, a farmer on Woolper or Middle Creek, was a pitcher with marvelous control and the ambition to get a game with the Cincinnati Reds. After years of pleading and sort of a lark since Burlington was much too small for them, with a guaranteed sum of money and a good fried chicken dinner, they agreed.*

"*The entire Reds team came. Except for a hired semi-pro catcher, it was Burlington's regular team. Billy Hughes pitched the first three innings, but the catcher would not let him use his out-drop. A Conner followed, then Brady.*

"*In the 9th, the score was 12-0 Cincinnati. Brady managed to reach third base. When the Reds pitcher started his windup, Hubert took off for home. He had huge feet, about a 14 shoe. I can still see those feet rising and falling like ocean waves.*

"*About 10' from the plate, he went into a mighty slide and made it! Edison Riddell was umpiring. The game was delayed. The Reds argued for 15 minutes that the runner was out. They didn't want to see in the papers that a farmer stole home on them. That pitcher well knew the ribbing he would get from his teammates. Edison stood his ground, and as he was right, that run saved the shutout. Even the Reds praised that Burlington diamond as one of the best.*[81]

Clutterbuck Brothers Store

"*Homer and Roy at the Clutterbuck Brothers Store were equally good at baseball and merchandizing.*" At the corner of Union and Jefferson streets, "*this was sort of a men's club without dues, a social gathering place with a few chairs, boxes, even a cracker barrel where they could meet around the big fat stove and prop their feet up. There was a frame box-like thing around the stove filled with sawdust for those who missed the spittoons.*

"*This was the most active and best stocked store. Of course there were no fresh vegetables, everyone had his own. I am not too certain, but they may have carried a limited supply of canned goods -- tomatoes, peas and corn. I do remember the small cans of cove oysters. The women were just learning how to can tomatoes, etc. so they would not blow up, and even then only the brave*

---
[81] Adams, 4.

attempted it.

"There were boxes of salted fish and a barrel of blackstrap molasses. The center isle was sometimes crowded to the point where it was as much for storage as a passageway. You might have to push the cat off the prunes to get down to the barrel of Navy beans. On the shelves were Levis, calicos, muslins and bolts and bolts of cloth. Mary and Catherine Furlong could take a customer who wanted a dress to the store to select the fabric and they'd make it.

"In the back room were plows, harness, saws, axes and heavy farm equipment. They may have had wagons, but no buggies. On the second floor was the town, or maybe at one time the Grange, hall. It was never used that I know of." [82]

Roy married Anna Garrison in October 1899. That December, his brother married Anna's sister, Charlotte Garrison.[83]

After 1903, Roy moved to Beverly Hills, Calif., in an effort to improve his son's health. But the boy, Lawrence, passed away in 1907. Roy was a wholesale grocery salesman and remained there.[84]

Mrs. John Roberts should have traded at Clutterbuck Brothers. *"Story is she read an ad in some magazine for an unbelievable number of yards of silk of any selected color at an amazingly low price. She sent her money and received the specified number of yards in the right color -- but it was thread, not fabric. That was before the Truth in Advertising Act.*[85]

Livery Stable

"Watt Browns owned and operated Burlington's livery stable. He was tall and thin and usually lightly dressed. Even in right cold weather he sat on the stile block in front of the Clutterbuck store. (A stile is a wooden step used to climb over a wire fence.) Its four to five-foot square top was the best whetstone in town. That stone had been used so much that little, middle size and big notches had been worn on all four edges, just right to fit any knife.

"Watt kept a few horses on hand for hire. Dr. Furnish and Dr. Duncan kept their horses there. It was one of Willie Duncan's chores to saddle or hitch up the horse for his father. The stable was well cared for, but it was still a stable and made its contribution to the inestimable fly population." [86]

Burlington Farmers

A few blocks away was another livery stable owned by James L. Clore and managed by his son Bruce (who had run away with the circus as a teen). The Tousey House on Jefferson Street became the Burlington Hotel managed by Mrs. Clore.

James Clore had traded his farm to Judge John Lassing for the Tousey house in 1902 and operated the Burlington and Erlanger bus and mail route twice a day from there. His *"elegant, roller bearing bus"* ran on schedule with the punctuality of a train, offering accommodating and courteous service.[87]

The newspaper said the senior Clore's *"early life was spent making money and in making it fast with an insatiable desire to spend it just as rapidly, thus in experience 'Jim' as we should judge, is in the neighborhood of a centenarian in age, but in reality would class down to about 35 or 40 years."*[88]

Outside of town, near Limaburg, W.H. Rouse bred Shorthorn cattle, fine sheep and Poland China hogs on 200 acres.

A mile and a half west of Burlington, Rabbit Hash native Daniel E. Lawell and his wife, the former Frances A. Craig, began raising sheep on a 161-acre farm. Lawell received a medal and diploma at the 1893 World's Fair in Chicago for his wool exhibit.

---

[82] Adams, 6-7, 9-11.
[83] *Boone County Recorder*, Aug. 10, 1903.
[84] *Boone County Recorder*, Sept. 4, 1930.
[85] Adams
[86] Adams, 22.
[87] Katie Presnell research.
[88] *Boone County Recorder*, Aug. 10, 1903.

B.C. Kirtley sold this 32-month-old Poland China barrow at the Cincinnati market for the highest price ever received for a Boone County hog. The 800-pound "Big Ted" brought $106. The newspaper held the bill of sale to prove the price to disbelievers. Photo by Mrs. Bessie Kirtley. Courtesy of Barbara Fallis

Deacons of the Burlington Baptist Church, the Lawells advertised their farm for sale in 1903, planning to move to Central Kentucky.[89]

Four miles west of Burlington, J.J. Lillard raised Thoroughbred horses and Shorthorn cattle. He had served in the Confederate Army. Captured at Mt. Sterling, Ky., he was imprisoned at Johnson's Island for six months.

W.C. Goodrich farmed land his forefathers had claimed early in the county's history. He was born in a log cabin surrounded by dense forest, now included in the acreage he owned. His sons, Elmer and Raymond *"have been a valuable aid in the farm work. Mr. G. is one of the neatest and most successful farmers in this county and makes money rapidly."*[90]

Locust Grove native W.J. Rice worked in the carpentry and building business as well as living on a 139-acre farm just south of Burlington. He married Fannie A. Crisler and had two sons, then two daughters who died in infancy. On Rice's farm, which Charles Chambers had owned, was a two-story brick house built in 1835 with bricks made by Jessie Kelly and woodwork by Thomas Roberts.[91]

Holiday Pranks

Life in and near Burlington wasn't all business or farming. Then and now pranksters created amusements and holidays were celebrated in individual ways. Adams recalled a particular Halloween:

"The Burlington boys collected all the carts, buggies, surreys and wheelbarrows they could find and dragged them into the courthouse corridor, turning them different directions so the wheels locked together. In another stunt, the boys took a farm wagon apart, carried the parts up ladders and reassembled them on the bank roof. Residents began taking precautions, removing gates, porch chairs and stray implements and locking them in the parlor for the night."[92]

Holiday merchandizing began long ago. W.M. Rachal offered a Christmas special at his Union store – 20 pounds of sugar for $1, plus promoting oysters, candies, nuts, fruits, toys, glassware, fancy goods and fancy neckwear. Christmas shoppers received a free calendar.

Hog Up?

Another memorable event in Burlington was the contentious "hog up?" election. The

---

[89] *Boone County Recorder*, Aug. 10, 1903.
[90] *Boone County Recorder*, Aug. 10, 1903.
[91] *Boone County Recorder*, Aug. 10, 1903.

[92] Adams, 37.

previous decade, Florence City Council men had passed a strongly worded ordinance prohibiting all species of free-roaming animals.

A vote was called on the question *"Should hogs be allowed to roam free or should they be penned? The ayes position was: My hogs have the same privileges to the streets that the loafers have to the bank fence. Why should six to eight gentle, friendly 400-pound sows be deprived of their siesta on the Cowan porch? The nays countered: 'I don't pay my taxes to fatten your hogs. I'm tired of repairing fences and I love my potato patch.' The hogs lost their freedom."*[93]

Peoples Deposit Opens

Another step toward adding sophistication to the county seat was Owen Watts' effort to begin the Peoples Deposit Bank in Burlington in 1904. Planning to sell $20,000 in stock, *"his success was not immediate, and so not to delay longer, W.P. Beemon was asked."* Soon the stock was oversubscribed.

In May 1905, Watts chaired the first stockholders meeting and D.E. Castleman served as secretary. The stockholders voted to offer a $600 annual salary for a cashier *"if a competent man could be obtained for that figure."*

The directors elected B.W. Adams president and O.P. Conner vice president. A committee was appointed to select a building site, which was bought within the month.

No cashier was appointed, so D.E. Castleman became temporary treasurer. *"A call for 10 percent of the stock was ordered payable to him at once"* to cover the lot and begin construction.

The vault was made of 2½' thick concrete, reinforced with steel. The 10" steel door weighed more than 20,000 pounds and was claimed to be "burglar proof." Community groups could meet on the second floor.

In mid-August, A.B. Renaker was unanimously elected cashier. Forty percent more stock was called to enable construction to be completed. At the end of its first year, the bank paid a 3 percent semi-annual dividend – eventually increasing to 10 percent in 1920.

On Nov. 6, 1905, the Peoples Deposit Bank opened with deposits of $10,297.98. By Nov. 6, 1918, deposits passed the quarter-million mark. On June 30, 1925, deposits had doubled. By 1927, they totaled nearly a million.[94]

Burlington Professionals

M. Riddell and L.H. Crisler increased their offerings at Dudley Rouse's Burlington store when they took it over Feb. 1, 1903. Known for its low prices, the store also featured a soda fountain in the back. Riddell had operated a soda fountain at another Burlington location before joining the partnership.

Crisler, a graduate of the Ohio Veterinary School, practiced veterinary surgery. *"The percentage of his losing cases being but a minimum compared to the amount of business he is called upon to do."*[95]

Limaburg native Dr. W.O. Rouse opened a medical practice in his Burlington home after graduating from the Lutheran College of Springfield, Ohio, then the Ohio Medical College of Cincinnati.

Son of Dudley and Eliza Rouse, A.B. Rouse graduated from Louisville Law School then set up practice in Burlington. He was made secretary to Congressman Gooch and assisted in setting up Boone County's telephone system. Treasurer of the North Kentucky Agricultural Association, he was also chairman of the county Democratic Committee.[96]

Campbell's International Role

Leaving Burlington when he turned 18,

---

[93] Adams, 41-42.

[94] *Boone County Recorder*, Sept. 4, 1930.
[95] *Boone County Recorder*, Aug. 10, 1903.
[96] *Boone County Recorder*, Aug. 10, 1903.

Historic Dinsmore Homestead

Burlington, Kentucky

A horse-drawn hay rake sits on the Dinsmore Homestead. Photo by Bruce Wess, Wild Walks Photography.

B.W. Campbell moved to Cincinnati and became an international businessman. His first job was selling candy wholesale. Five years later, he moved to a wholesale harness house. Then, on Jan. 1, 1879, with H.A. and W.S. Perkins, also Boone County natives, they formed the Perkins-Campbell Co. Their business was said to be the largest saddlery manufacturing concern in the world.

In addition to being vice president of the saddle company, Campbell was president of Decatur Traction & Electric Co, and a director of the United States Trading Co. of Manilla, Philippine Islands; and Brown & Patterson Grain Co. of Cincinnati. He was a Nova Scotia coal company officer, director of a Washington D.C. gun company and had financial interests in many other enterprises.

The National Association of Manufacturing appointed him European Commissioner to evaluate trade opportunities. He visited Norway, Sweden, Germany, France, England and Denmark. In Copenhagen, he met the King of Denmark. He also helped establish a warehouse to distribute American products in Hamburg, Germany.

Rouse's Life in Burlington

Like most Boone Countians, Frank H. Rouse never traveled internationally. He spent his life in or near the town where he was born. He began keeping a diary in 1906 when he was running a Burlington butcher shop and kept writing daily entries for more than half a century.

During this decade, Rouse found that keeping the storefront open, butchering, rounding up animals and doing all the chores himself at the store and on his farm became impossible, so he planned to hire a helper.

He offered Irvin Rue 50 cents a day for three months with an increase to 80 cents a day, working only when he was needed. Rue refused, demanding 75 cents per day and $1 when he was driving a wagon. Rue was working by March 1, so evidently they came to an agreement.

On March 5, 1906, Rouse *"butchered hog, worked and rendered it all up in morning. Staid in shop in morning. Sent buggy to Florence to Bradford Bros. for repairs on and to have new axles, axle caps, wheels, all new side curtains, painting and general repair."*

A month later, on April 12, Rouse spent the morning in his shop. Then, *"Ira Sanders and I cleaned off garden. Planted lettuce, radishes. Fixed fence, brought cow to Burlington. Got Mr. Rivell's marketing and to Mr. Sullivans after chickens at night. Rented house, barn and lot from T.G. Willis in Burlington, paying him $80 from 2/1/06 to 3/1/07. Rent to be paid*

Burlington's Main Street looking north. Photo courtesy of Virginia Lainhart

one half in Aug., other in winter."

Rouse ran a huckster route for a while, delivering meat and groceries. In July, he traded corn and $10 for a colt from Elmer Kelley. During the summer, he sold hides in Cincinnati from the animals he'd butchered and returned with a load of ice. Nearly every summer evening he watched a live baseball game or played croquet.[97]

On Aug. 28, 1906, he bought three old sows from W.J. Rice for $28.50, then made a hog trough, fixed fences, and hauled water to Thos. Rouse's, before butchering in the evening. B.W. Kelley had dinner with him and his wife Lena. A few days later, Rouse worked until 12:30 a.m. cleaning and repairing the wagon he'd just taken to Cincinnati and back.

The next month, he and Dudley Blythe went to Thornton's farm after calves. They rode in the rain *"until 3 p.m. and couldn't find sight of one."* So, he bought a calf from C.C. Alore (possibly Aylor or Clore, the diary is handwritten)and drove it home. He spent the evening working in his shop. A week later he returned to Thornton's to get a heifer (young female cow), but again returned cow-less.

In January 1907, Rouse participated in a shooting match, picked up loads of coal for the sheriff's office, ran his meat route, helped neighbors fill all their ice houses, attended Hopeful Lutheran Church, and sold rabbit hides.

A member of the local telephone board, in 1908, Rouse helped Wilbur Wilson put in a telephone.

Democratic Barbecue

Getting ready for the annual Democratic barbecue at Florence Fair Grounds was a huge undertaking. Quarter-page banner advertisements across the front of the *Boone County Recorder* invited one and all to the big

---

[97] Diary of F.H. Rouse, July 1909-12/31, 1912.

event.

On Oct. 15, 1908, Rouse cooked, cleaned, and dug a trench from his rented slaughterhouse to wash the animal blood away. Then he, Irvin Rue and another helper "*butchered three beeves*" weighing a total of 3,930 lb. and killed 11 lambs. "*Net meat we dressed, 2,600 lbs. Elmer Kelley in shop most of day.*"

"*William Kirkpatrick furnished the cattle and sheep. Effie Kelley and Bonnie Rouse cooked dinner for us.*"

The next day, Rouse ran his meat route through Limaburg, Hebron and Bullittsville, and was home by 11 a.m. He changed horses, had dinner at the James Clore Hotel, took his tools and went to the Florence Fair Grounds....

There he "*peeled potatoes, onions, turnips and cabbage all night. Swept dining hall, opened tomatoes and corn, etc. Carved meat from 8 a.m. until 7 p.m. Lena met me at barbecue coming from institute* (likely teachers' institute at Morgan Academy). *Got aprons and tools together, came home, went to Hebron Lodge.*"

In January 1909, the nine telephone company directors, including Rouse, went to the moving picture shows. In June, Rouse wrote a non-compete agreement for butchering, agreeing to work five days a week for grocers W.E. & Elmer Kirkpatrick, to be paid $360 whether they provided daily work or not, minus $1 per day if he was sick.[98]

Charivari

Henry DeCoursey Adams and Zellah Barker were married on Sept. 1, 1909, in Covington. They came home to Burlington in a topless buggy drawn by a pair of Palominos owned by Horne's Medicine Show. Their first night was a charivari.

"*All the pots, pans, shotguns and other noisemakers were there. After marching around the house several times, we greeted them at the front door. And of course, had a supply of cigars to hand out. This expression of friendship and continuance of an almost obsolete custom was appreciated.*"[1]

---

[98] F.H. Rouse diaries, 1906-1909.

Chapter 10
1910-1919 World War Changes Women's Roles

After the 19th century turned, changing transportation modes were beginning a dramatic evolution for Boone County.

With trains replacing steamboats and its distillery closing on the eve of prohibition, Petersburg was shrinking. North, across from Valley Orchards, Fernbank Dam opened in July 1911 with a lock chamber that measured 600' x 110' with a lift of 7.8'. The new dam maintained a 16' deep pool for 20 miles upstream.[1]

In the southern part of the county, trains running on new steel rails hauled growth to the progressive town of Walton. Northern Boone Countians stepped over the county line to board the train at Erlanger. Some businesses continued to slip from Florence's grasp to that growing community's rail access and the crowds it brought.

In 1911, the last Kentucky stagecoach ran over the rough macadamized roads peppered with tollgates. Road travelers had demanded that costly and time-consuming tollgates be discontinued. Expensive fees designed to keep noisy new automobiles off the roads backfired. More and more left their horse and buggy in the barn while cranking up horseless carriages in their new garages. Automobiles were the trendy new hobby for successful businessmen and farmers.

With more vehicles, improving road conditions became a primary political campaign promise. Statewide, a plan was designed to connect the county seats. In 1915, Gov. A.O. Stanley said, *"To say that you are in favor of good roads is like saying you are in favor of good health or good morals."*[2]

By 1913, the county's first school bus was delivering pupils from the Berkshire and Terrill school districts to Petersburg consolidated school. No longer did students have to cross the river to advance their education. By 1914, there were high schools in Walton, Verona, Union, Belleview, Florence and Hamilton.[3]

> **Boone County Recorder**
> April 11, 1918
> HEADLINES
>
> **BOONE CO. THE FIRST**
> *County in the United States*
> *To take Her Quota in the*
> *Sale of Liberty Bonds*
>
> **HAS EVIDENCE**
> To Show German Agents Have Been Sent Into Ky. To Injure Horse Industry
>
> **150,000 MORE MEN**
> To Replace Those Over There:
> Movement to Begin April 26
> Ky. To Furnish 3,398
>
> **Women to Register**
> Miss Margaret Anderson, the newly appointed chairman of Boone county, announces the personnel of the working organization of the Women's Committee, Council of National Defense of this county.
> . . .No service is asked or expected of a woman except what she may freely offer, but she is requested by the Government to register. . . . Headquarters for registration will be the Walton Bank and Trust Company Building. . . .

---

[1] Conrad, *Top of Kentucky*, 24.
[2] Harrison & Klotter, 315.
[3] Conrad, *History of Boone County Schools*, 20.

World War I had broken out in Europe, but the United States remained neutral. Overseas demand increased farm prices significantly between 1915 and 1917. Congress finally declared war on Germany in April 1917.[4]

The Nov. 14, 1918 *Recorder* announced that Private Joseph Hammons of Petersburg was declared missing, a week after the paper published a letter from him. (However, he is not included in the list of soldiers who gave their lives in that conflict.)

Banks were growing in size and number. Charles Ernest McNeely reported deposits increasing 600 percent since his election as cashier of the Citizens Deposit Bank on May 2, 1913.

Snowy Winter

The winter of 1913-14 brought a remarkably heavy snow, preventing mail delivery even by horseback. Flurries came and went, piling up three or four feet of snow. Sleet topped it with a hard frozen layer.

On Jan. 12, 1918, Burlington teacher Eunie Pettit wrote in her diary: *"The wind blew hard and it snowed all night. This morning the thermometer was 14 below zero and the wind has blown hard all day and it has been the coldest day for years. We set by the fire and then almost froze."* For several days there was so much snow on the roads that people drove through the fields.

That same month, the *Kentucky Post* reported that an ice gorge sank Boone #5, the ferry at Constance.

Boone County Recorder
April 11, 1918

PRIVATE HOMES

Must Cut Wheat Consumption One-Half of Normal – Pound And a Half of Wheat Per Person a Week

The Allies need wheat – they must have it. Only America can furnish it.

"If we fail," says Mr. Hoover, "the people behind the armies will be in want and suffering. Should that happen, the war could last only a few weeks.

…A German victory, if the Allies are Forced to further curtailment of their food supplies, is not only possible, it is probable. We are far from victory as things stand today. We will be close to defeat in another month unless we get food across the sea….

(Joining total abstainers clubs, planning wheatless Mondays and Wednesdays or cutting back to three slices of bread a day were recommended ways to meet the quota until after the next harvest.)

Dug from snow-covered piles, firewood was hauled to houses on sleds. Rural residents didn't worry about running to a grocery. Smoke houses held meat, cellars contained fruits and vegetables and cows gave fresh milk daily. The snow was such an oddity that after cows were milked and other animals fed, parents gave up their usual chores and joined children playing on homemade wooden sleds, sliding on scoop shovels, building snowmen and throwing snow balls.[5]

Proper dress for children was frequently a function of the calendar date rather than the actual weather or temperature. Long underwear season began with the first hard frost and lasted until May, regardless of temperature. Clothing styles covered more rather than less year-round.

"When I was a sprout, there couldn't be a square inch of hide showing," recalled Betty Weaver Roter who grew up in the Union area. *"Only your face was exposed so you could eat, breathe and see. We wore long, black stockings with garters just above the knees to hold them up. That was all right until the elastic began to lose its grip –then the stockings slipped down and it was a day-long battle."*

Dressing was much more complicated for children in the winter. Long underwear called union suits was required attire. *"One garment covered your whole body – except head, hands and feet. The union suit buttoned down the front – from the neck to, well, you know where.*

---

[4] Harrison & Klotter, 289.

[5] Roter, 48.

On the back there was a barn-door (that's what my daddy called it) . . . held shut by three big white porcelain buttons – unless the buttonhole stretched out too big, or a button fell off.

"To get those long, black stockings over the underwear legs, you had to work out a real strategy. The ankle part of the long underwear had to be folded over just right – and then the tricky work began: Holding that underwear leg with one hand and pulling the black stocking up with the other.
Lots of times it didn't work – you couldn't hold the folded ankle tight enough, and that sucker would creep half-way up to your knee and you had to start over again. Sometimes it took three or four tries.[6]

"At school, the barn door was far from convenient! But the worst thing that could happen: Just as you'd get up to read, or write a times table on the blackboard, one of the barn door buttons could pop off, hit the floor spinning, and land right up in front of the teacher. All the kids would giggle, and you'd feel the barn door hanging part-way down, and just know everybody could look right through your dress and petticoat and see a little patch of your naked body!"[7]

Child's Play

Summer brought more comfortable clothes and more time for children's games. Boys wore britches and girls wore calico dresses their mothers made.[8]

A board stuck through a wooden fence in the yard became a seesaw. If only two children were available, jumping rope required tying one end to a tree. Swings hung from trees.

Pictures in the Sears and Roebuck catalog or McCalls magazine became paper dolls. Mrs. Roter's favorite toys included a metal Log Cabin Syrup house (her father cut around the door so it would open to allow her homemade paper dolls to enter), a set of wooden blocks, and paper cows she drew and cut out herself.

Marbles was a spring game that resulted in winning or losing a beautiful collection of small glass balls when *"played for keeps."*

Summer evenings often included working in the garden or sitting together stringing and

Child and chicks Courtesy of Linda Green

snapping beans or hulling peas to cook the next day. Identifying birds by their calls, locating bullfrogs by the croaking, catching fireflies and listening to the music of crickets filled the tranquil evenings.

Boys played tin can, batting a can with a stout stick, running for a base before the can was caught or the catcher got to the base. Beaverlick area men enjoyed the electrically lighted horseshoe grounds below Jack's Grocery that even included benches for spectators. Before State Road 1292 came through, men loafed on homemade stools at the road's edge in front of Roter's Garage. In

---
[6] Roter, 62-63.
[7] Roter, 64.
[8] Roter, 50.

Beaverlick Families

Roy Kenney of Beaverlick had to take a test to see if he could get into Burlington High School in 1914. Printed on 3"x 5" cards, 100 questions checked spelling, grammar and general math and asked students to measure land in rods and figure amounts of linoleum, paint and wallpaper needed for rooms.

Roy passed the test and rode his horse to Mattie Hudson's stable, where he left it while he attended Walton High School. Boys planning to attend UK engineering school took extra math classes after school from the principal.

Roy was a member of Walton High School's first basketball team that played on an outdoor court.[10]

Aunt Jennie Ossman's millinery shop stood across the Florence-Louisville Pike from the Beaverlick Baptist Church, a white building with green shutters.

"Ladies brought last year's hats in for new trim – flowers, feathers, ribbon bands and bows. Or they would bring in new hats of plain straw or felt, ready for a complete Ossman fashion production. Aunt Jennie also sold hats already trimmed."

Mrs. Lee Afterkirk, who married Joe Besterman, and her sister Fannie Underhill Howard operated Beaver's telephone exchange. They taught a niece, Bertha Brown, who married Jack Ossman, to operate the board as well.[11]

Beaver laundress Pearl Murry's baby daughter. Courtesy of Linda Green

Minority Community

Herbert and Russell Baker farmed on U.S. 42 south of Beaver. Their sons James and Charles helped with the farm work and sold cars. Herbert eventually became a minister. Herbert's wife Henrietta was renowned for her excellent blackberry cakes.

Mrs. Roter remembered a tiny house between Union and Florence where two African-American men she knew only as John and Coon lived. *"John was brown, stout and sturdy-looking. Coon, a blacker, much smaller man"* sat on the porch playing his fiddle. John played banjo.

Invited to her family home, *"they entertained us with music played with the feeling only black people seem to possess. Some tunes were sprightly – some were sad – but all performed in beautiful harmony and with utmost, impressive humility. Afterward my mother served them cake and grape juice. Then John and Coon returned to their little shack."*[12]

The Big Bone Baptist Church's few African-American members sat in the church gallery on Sunday. Susie Riley was the janitor. Frances and John Brown lived just behind Jack's Grocery. Frances was a Beaverlick laundress.

Women's Work

After baking cakes, fixing meals, cleaning house, caring for children and all the other

---

[9] Roter, 417.
[10] Melinda Fillmore, "Kathleen Kenney Wiley," *A Peek Into the Past*, 104.
[11] Roter, 415-416.
[12] Roter, 68.

traditional women's work, farm women often joined their husbands and sons in the fields. While a few conveniences had improved their lot since pioneer days, women's work was literally never done. Mrs. Roter wrote this description of her mother's life.

"Four a.m. with crowing roosters was getting-up time. My mother was out of bed along with my dad, who built the fires then went to the barn. Mother ground coffee beans to brewing size grains, then coaxed the fire in the kitchen range to baking heat. She cut slices from a side of bacon, a ham or sack of sausage and fried them with eggs, while Father milked the cows and fed the cattle, horses and hogs.

"Two more meals each day required even more preparation and cleaning up afterward. When Dad had hired hands, I remember Mother baking three large loaves of yeast bread every day.

"The kitchen range. . . not only cooked all Mother's delicious meals, it kept us cozy warm as well. But in summer that blessing turned into a nuisance – the heat drove us out of the kitchen. (No electric, no paddle fans.)"

Modern Kerosene Appliances

The two-burner kerosene stove was an improvement – especially in the summer, but didn't allow for baking biscuits fresh each morning. *"So what did Mother do? She fried the biscuits and they turned out to be a special treat,"* Mrs. Roter said. An oven for the kerosene stove was a step forward, allowing for baked biscuits, cakes, pies and cobblers.

"Kerosene played an important part in early country life. Besides the stoves, all glass lamps that lighted our house had wicks that carried the 'coal-oil' from the fount portion when the small key on the side was turned up clockwise." Turn the key counter-clockwise and the light was out.

"A metal kerosene lantern furnished light at the barn. All of these had glass chimneys covering the flames. The lamps were entirely made of glass. Mother had to clean the glass things daily, and see that each lamp and lantern was filled with kerosene. When the Aladdin lamp came along with its mesh-like burner inside the chimney, it was almost as important to folks without electricity as Edison's light bulb was to folks with it. Its light was brighter and covered a wide circle."

Nannie Berkshire Gaines at her gate at 80 years old.
Courtesy of Mary Sue Rudicill

Kitchen Cleaning

"When breakfast was over, the cooking area, the stove, the cooking utensils, the dishes – all these had to be cleaned. But no garbage disposal awaited the leftover scraps – her disposal was the hungry, begging shepherd dog. (There was no such thing as bought dog food, nor money to waste buying it, if there had been.)" Liquids and vegetable scraps went to the "slop bucket" for fattening hogs. Using scalding hot water heated in a teakettle, Mrs. Weaver filled one dishpan for washing, another for rinsing dishes.

"There was no special soap powder to assure scum-free, spot-free china and glass. Her cleaning was done with a bar of yellow Fels Naptha soap and a little scouring with Dutch Cleanser or Bon Ami.

"Several years later, a brand-new white speckled gray enamel Home Comfort Range

was bought for Mother's kitchen. It had a water tank on the firebox side that furnished lots of hot water for all uses, besides having a huge oven with a thermometer. Baking temperatures no longer needed to be guesswork. But every day there was still a big bucket of ashes to carry out.[13]

Laundry and House Cleaning

"Using that same yellow cake soap she used for dishwashing, Mother tackled clothes on wash day. . . . In winter, water was heated in a copper boiler on the kitchen range. After clothes were vigorously scrubbed on a ribbed washboard in a galvanized tub, the white items were put into the copper boiler to boil until they were snowy white.

"Some pieces – dresses and aprons – were dipped in boiled starch so they would later iron smoothly and stay fluffy instead of being limp. I remember best Dad's dress shirts, with separate collars held onto the shirts by a little collar button, stiffened with cold starch and later ironed to glass-like perfection.

"All ironing was done with flat irons that could be heated sizzling hot on the cooking top of the kitchen range. The same procedure was followed in summer, except the water heating and boiling afterward were done in the large iron lard kettle used at hog-killing time. After a rinse in cold water, clothes and other items were wrung out by hand. Then, in summer, things were pinned with wooden clothespins on an outdoor line to dry in the fresh air. In winter, drying was done around the stoves.

"Mother's rag carpets were swept with a simple straw broom. Wood or linoleum-covered floors were scrubbed in soapy water with a mop, or sometimes on hands and knees with rags. At spring house-cleaning time, the rag carpets were hung on the outdoor clothesline, shaken, slapped with a broom and left to blow in the wind to remove accumulated dust.

Ella Flege Coleman cared for chickens. Filling the mound cellar behind her was also women's work. Courtesy of Martha Daugherty

"Lace curtains were washed, starched and stretched on special frames to dry. Despite lack of modern aids, Mother's house was well kept. At the end of spring cleaning, our house always looked so clean and smelled so fresh.

"In her spare time, (How would she ever have had any spare time?) my mother sewed dresses and other garments for Sister and me." Her feet worked the treadle back and forth on the Singer sewing machine while her hands guided fabric under the needle. She also made cotton-filled comforts (or comforters), pieced quilt-tops, and cut, sewed together and rolled into balls rag strips that would be woven into carpets.

"Added to all the rest of her accomplishments, Mother found time to sew covers onto baseballs – a home-job done by a lot of women in that era." Church activities,

---

[13] Roter, 388-392.

Raising Chickens

"After kitchen cleaning was finished, Mother's next chore was caring for her flock of chickens. In winter, it consisted mostly of opening the small doors close to the floor of the chicken-house, and feeding the chickens whole-kernel or cracked corn – inside on snowy or rainy days. The chicken house needed to be swept out regularly."

A row of nest boxes stood along the back wall in another room of the chicken house. Chickens shaped wheat straw nests before laying their brown or white eggs. Egg color depended on the hen's breed – Rhode Island Red, Barred Rock, Buff Orpington, Leghorn or tiny Bantam. Eggs were gathered in late afternoon.

Spring increased the chicken chores. Brooding hens were moved to another building with fresh straw nests. *"Mother placed as many eggs in each nest as the hen could cover"* with her feathers. Three weeks later, tiny fluffy baby chicks pecked open their shells and toddled out.

"As soon as all the eggs under a hen were hatched, Mother placed her and her brood in daytime in a small coop built with tobacco sticks. It was laid up in a square, rail-fence fashion, covered with boards and weighted down with a heavy rock. This penned the mother hen, but with a slight wedge under one corner, the chicks could creep out and back in. At night they had a warm dog-house type coop.

"Occasionally a hen would slip away, hide her nest in the tall grass of a surrounding field, lay her eggs, sit on them, and hatch a brood of chicks that were wild as a covey of quail.

"In later years, it became a better plan for Mother to purchase baby chicks from a hatchery instead of hatching them at home. An

[14] Roter, 395-398.

FOND DU LAC
$255 King of Tractors 255

It will do what five horses will do – do it better – do it faster – will work continuously – needs no rest – feeds only when it works – requires one half the value of feed – it will pull plows, listers, graders, etc.

REASONS WHY

Every farmer and every one who needs a tractor should have a FOND DU LAC TRACTOR combined with a Ford.
It combines a pleasure car with a tractor.
It costs 50 percent less than a good complete traction engine.
It is more easily handled than any complete tractor.
It can be operated where neither tractors nor horses can be used.
It costs less for gasoline than a complete tractor.
It is more convenient than a complete traction engine or horses.
It does not require the care of a horse.
It does not have to be fed, watered nor bedded.
It does not get sick and die.
It requires attention only when in use.
It is always ready.
It always works at full capacity.
It does more than is expected of it.
It will work 24 hours daily.
It is so simple a child can operate it.
It costs less to keep and operate than two horses.
It does its work from 50 to 100 percent faster than horses.
It makes farm life easy.
It solves the labor problem.
It is the only farm implement that carried a top, protecting from the sun and rain – the only one which permits the farmer to dress as well as the businessman while engaged in his business.
It lengthens life.
There is nothing that turns work into pleasure and profit as does the FOND DU LAC.

What the "Fond Du Lac" Will Accomplish

⇒ Will pull two 12 or 14 inch moldboard plows, 2 to 2 ½ miles per hour, plowing 5-7 acres per day of ten hours, where 5 horses can pull the same plows.
⇒ Will disc 20 to 25 acres per day.
⇒ Will harrow 40 to 50 acres per day.
⇒ Will harvest 15 to 20 acres of grain per day.
⇒ Will pull a wagon loaded up to 6,000 pounds on an ordinary road.
⇒ Will seed 30 to 35 acres per day.
⇒ Will roll 40 acres per day.
⇒ Will pull more than one of many machines and implements.
⇒ Will pull several wagons, mowers and other implements in train.
⇒ Will pay for itself and a new Ford in two years.
⇒ Will pull any implement or machinery with all the speed the implement can stand, regulating the speed by the use of the varying sized gears, which can always be furnished when desired.

BETHELL AUTO SALES CO.
COVINGTON, KY. PHONE S. 4289
Boone County Recorder, Nov. 7, 1918

Agriculture and Extension Service

In 1910, Boone County had 1,540 farms, averaging 95 acres. Tractors had arrived.

In 1913, corn sold for 70 cents a bushel, cattle for 6 cents a pound, hogs for 7 cents a pound, tobacco for 10 cents a pound. A new car cost about $1,000. Farm labor paid less than a dollar a day.

Boone County's first extension agent Robert D. Brockway, a New York state native, began work in 1914, the year Congress passed the Smith-Lever Act to distribute *"practical and useful information on farming, homemaking and related subjects."*

The Walton Advertiser noted in 1916 that W. L. Johnson of Walton had four sows who had 52 pigs. That was an average of 13 pigs to a sow, but one had 18.[16] Two years later the *Kentucky Post* reported that 3,000 Burlington hogs had cholera. The *Recorder* corrected the story, saying not more than 50 hogs had died, that large numbers of hogs had been vaccinated and that there weren't 3,000 hogs in the Burlington vicinity.[17]

Tobacco prices still hadn't stabilized. In November 1918, Belleview tobacco dealer Pepper Smith wasn't willing to hazard a guess as to what the markets would do.[18]

In an effort to cultivate as much acreage as possible, many fields that once held family burial plots were plowed or pastured, disregarding old gravesites.[19]

In 1918, W.D. Sutton took over the agricultural extension service, started 4-H Club work, conducted demonstrations and increased interest in purebred cattle, hogs, poultry and sheep.

Shunpikes

While farmers were learning new information about animal husbandry and crop management, they stuck vehemently to the old road system. Boone County was the last in Kentucky to remove its tollgates.

Boone County's road system included 84¾ miles of macadam road maintained by tolls while 350 miles of dirt roads were maintained by a 10-cent tax. The question of freeing the roads had been defeated in a November 1905 election 438 to 1,255. Apparently voters didn't want to pay extra taxes to maintain free roads or they thought users should pay for the roads' upkeep.[20]

Road Rules
(From the April 5, 1910, Fiscal Court Order Book.)

- All roads to be graded by July 1.
- Metal (gravel) to be placed on road and spread by November 1, except that knapped stone may be spread at any time.
- Eight hours constitutes a day's work.
- Overseers to report to fiscal court at term first Tuesday after first Monday in January, April, July and October on expenditures for labor and material.
- Overseers allowed $1.50 a day when overseeing four or more.
- May pay for one man and team of two horses up to $3 per day, 50 cents for each additional horse; and pay $1 per man day except stone masons and carpenters who may be paid the prevailing wage.
- Overseers may work at $1 per day, but will receive pay in but one capacity at the same time and will not be paid as an overseer when in charge of a team.
- Overseers may do as much of the work themselves as they see fit.

---

[15] Roter, 392-394.
[16] *The Walton Advertiser*, R. D. Stamler, April 1, 1916.
[17] *Boone County Recorder*, Nov. 14, 1918, 1.
[18] *Boone County Recorder*, Nov. 14, 1918, 1.
[19] Roter, 113.
[20] Tanner, BC-9.

"Boone County is the only county in the State that still retains the old system of tollgate turnpikes. There are several miles of turnpikes in the county owned and controlled by private companies and kept up by the old tollgate system. There are also about 100 miles of turnpikes in the county owned by the county and kept up by same," the 1910-11 report of the Bureau of Agriculture said.[21]

In 1912, the county road fund contained $7,500. The year before, the county had agreed to invest $500 per mile in a road from Union to Hathaway. The first tolls were collected on that road in 1913.

Travelers used Tanner's dirt lane to bypass Bailey's tollgate on Burlington Pike. "Shunpikes" permitted travelers to avoid, or shun, tollgates. When road owners realized what was happening, the gate was moved farther out Burlington Pike, past Tanner's Lane so travelers had to pay tolls for whichever road they used. The lane connected Ephraim Tanner's Union Pike farmland with his son's farm on Burlington Pike. Populated largely by the Tanner family, the area was once called Tannertown.

Paul Tanner of Huey's Corner, said a visit in a buggy to see his grandparents cost 13 cents each way in tolls at three gates. When his father went to Covington to purchase supplies in his two-horse wagon, he paid 32 cents at five stops. When his wagon was full, the return trip cost 64 cents. A Covington-Union round trip by car cost 80 cents.

In 1914, the Kentucky General Assembly restructured turnpike fees. Lower rates discouraged construction of new tollroads.

In September 1914, Dr. M.T. Crouch and 534 others filed a petition asking for a vote on eliminating tolls from Boone County roads. The Nov. 4 vote tallied 914 yes and 655 no ballots. While it carried, Florence citizens again voted against it, 136 to 36.

More motor vehicles increased road wear, but fearing imminent takeover, road owners made only minimal repairs. Tollgates and operators' homes had been violently destroyed in other places.

Driving horseless carriages was the new entertainment.
Courtesy of Virginia Lainhart

For $7,000, the Burlington and Florence Turnpike Company offered to sell to the county. They accepted $6,000 and the gates were lifted Sept. 7, 1915, opening the first major road in Boone County to free travel. The county soon spent several times the purchase price on reconstruction and repairs.

On Aug. 19, 1916, the tollhouse near Florence sold for $125 to E. H. Blankenbaker who owned the adjoining farmland. This property is now part of the I-75/U.S. 42 interchange.

Some owners wanted cash for their road. Some gave away a road with a provision the county fix it. Others just gave up the toll business. For $30,000 the county acquired roads that had cost as much as $200,000 to construct. The last toll paid in this era was on a small rural road in Boone County in early

---

[21] Tanner, BC-9.

Posing for a photo on a Sunday afternoon drive.
Courtesy of Virginia Lainhart

1917. By 1920, a state gasoline tax was financing roads.

Sunday Drives

Gasoline power was taking over the roads. Speed limits had increased with the automobile's popularity. In 1904, the limit was 15 mph, 6 mph for curves and bridges. By 1915, Henry Ford had produced one million cars. By 1920, limits increased to 20 mph, 8 mph on curves, 10 mph in the business portions of cities.

Sunday automobile rides became popular. Garages were designed for those who had no barn or stable. Blacksmith shops began to double as auto repair shops and to offer free air for tires. General stores added pumps that sold gas for 10 cents a gallon as well as motor oil and tires. License plates cost $2.

A Petersburg trio of Gaines Wingate, John Norris and Hubert (or Herbert) Walton banded together to buy that community's first motorcar.[22]

Rabbit Hash's auto dealer provided free driving lessons before new car owners left in their vehicles.

There were no "options" like tires that could be removed from rims, heaters, windshield wipers or electric lights. Side curtains protected the driver and passengers from bad weather.

Those startling a horse-drawn vehicle, were expected to stop their motors. Restarting meant getting out and cranking it up again by hand.[23]

Hitching racks and posts, once in front of every tavern and store, vanished from main streets to make more parking places. Soon parking areas for cars even began replacing hitching posts at country churches.

More and more laws were passed as increasing numbers of automobiles traveled Dixie Highway, the old Lexington Pike.

Bullittsville

"*With the advent of the automobile, some found attractions away from the church,*" recalled Bullittsburg Baptist deacon William Campbell whose father, J.W. Campbell, became pastor of the Bullittsburg Baptist Church in 1912. "*Some had always hated to leave their faithful driving horses tied out in bad weather, but now they could turn their switch keys and hurry into church*" so attendance was aided a bit, too.[24]

In 1916, Bullittsburg deacon E. A. Martin built three large mission designed pulpit chairs using golden oak the Women's Missionary Society furnished.

---

[22] Mary Rector

[23] Rice and Fitzgerald.
[24] Campbell, 27.

Students at Woolper School with teacher Agnes Carver in 1918-1919.   Courtesy of Mary Rector

Bullittsville native Carleton C. Crisler followed his father's footsteps to become a doctor. He earned a fellowship in the American College of Surgeons in June 1914.

William Winston Gaines, who was born on the George W. and Elizabeth Winston Gaines farm near Bullittsville, provided news for the *Recorder* before earning a law degree and moving to Atlanta.[25]

Despite having newspapers and telephones, Campbell said the best source of news was Templeton Graves.

Called "Cousin Temp" by most, he was a very sociable bachelor who visited his many friends and acquaintances frequently. After driving hay to Cincinnati or attending to his other enterprises, he tired of his own cooking.

"So, dressing in his Sunday best, he would no later than Friday get into his buggy and go to any of a dozen homes where he was warmly received, and spend a most enjoyable weekend... He always had the latest news or rumors at the country stores, the courthouse or the city. He knew all the courtships, law suits and so on – a veritable storehouse of knowledge."[26]

Hebron Pediatrician

Dr. Lewis C. Hafer, who grew up on his father's farm in Hebron, returned to Florence to open a practice specializing in treating children's diseases. He earned his medical degree in 1902 from Miami Medical College (now a part of the University of Cincinnati), then worked at the St. Louis Children's Hospital and Children's Memorial Hospital of Rochester, Minn. (owned by the Mayo Brothers).

Dr. Hafer moved to Covington in 1914. He devoted his energies *"toward the correction of*

---

[25] *Boone County Recorder*, 1930 Historical Edition.

[26] Campbell, 24.

diseases among children of the poorer classes. Many of these are brought to him mere 'walking skeletons' who are soon turned into chubby youngsters full of the natural vigor in normal children."[27]

For a time, Dr. Hafer maintained a small farm near Hebron where he raised registered Jersey dairy cattle. His wife, Katherine Crigler was the daughter of Hebron farmers John W. and Agnes Walton Crigler. They were descendants of George Walton, who signed the Declaration of Independence.

Dr. Hafer's brother, Owen Clyde, worked at the post office for a short time before attending a college agriculture course. In 1920, Owen purchased his father-in-law's 125-acre farm and raised registered Jersey cattle. His son, Robert, raised a heifer whose milk production record ranked highest of any Calf Club member in the county.

The Hafers' father, George Owen Hafer came from a line of German immigrants. George's grandfather, Philip Todd Richardson, had served as an ensign in the 19th infantry during the War of 1812.

Commissioned a second lieutenant, Richardson was captured by Indians while fighting in Ohio. More or less adopted into the tribe, he was allowed to go on hunting parties and eventually began to hunt alone. He remained away for longer and longer periods until it was acceptable for him to be gone nearly a week.

On one of these trips, he ran away, reaching civilization after a hazardous trip through the wilderness.[28]

Petersburg Distillery Dismantled

As of June 30, 1919, selling intoxicating liquors in the United States was prohibited, although liquors could still be produced for export. Whiskey manufacturing had been stopped soon after WWI began. Wine and beer production was phased out over two years.

The Petersburg Distillery had closed in 1910, but its owners continued bottling the aging whiskey stored in their warehouses.

The Dec. 25, 1919 *Recorder* carried a front-page article saying, *"A $24 million stream of whiskey began to flow thru Cincinnati yesterday from Kentucky to the Eastern Seaboard for export."*

As warehouses were emptied, the buildings were dismantled and their bricks reused in Petersburg and surrounding towns. The Petersburg General Store, the community center that was remodeled from a school building, the Baptist Church, the jail and several homes were constructed of distillery brick.

In 1919, Kentucky voters adopted prohibition by a 10,000 vote majority – a year before the nation.[29]

W.A.M. Wood

Petersburg's Baptist Church was dedicated in 1917. W.A.M. Wood – who referred to

Edna Lee Hubbard and Beal Martin Richie on their wedding day Dec. 22, 1917.
Photo courtesy of Dorothy Richie

---

[27] *Boone County Recorder,* 1930 Historical Edition.

[28] *Boone County Recorder,* 1930 Historical Edition.
[29] Harrison & Klotter, 286.

himself as Walnut, Ash, Maple Wood – helped start the church.

"Although having had the misfortune of losing a leg earlier in life, he would not allow this to handicap his work for the Lord. Using only one crutch, he would move about rapidly indeed. In walking with him, one had to hurry as he took a three-foot 'step' with his crutch and a corresponding one with his remaining limb.

"At that early period of no automatic drive on automobiles, he had a device rigged for him whereby he could operate clutch and brake pedals with his one foot," recalled William Campbell.[30]

Belleview Baptists

Baptists were active south of Petersburg as well. With its agrarian congregation facing tough times, deacons decided in 1910 that any Belleview (formerly Middle Creek) Baptist Church member asking for a letter of dismissal must first pay off all financial obligations to the treasurer. The church used $45 of the money collected to buy a Delco lighting plant in 1911. (Several churches bought these battery-operated systems to provide their first electric lights.)

H.B. Hensley came back to Belleview to serve as pastor at a salary of $45 per month. That salary was reduced to $30 because he needed to spend more time working on his farm. The church was continually modernizing, adding a cistern in 1913 and a furnace three years later.[31]

Roberts' Life

Born on a farm near Burlington, Thomas Zane Roberts was the ninth child and fifth son of Thomas and Rozanna Odell Roberts. The New England family had come to Boone County in 1842 when the senior Roberts bought 250 acres bordering Middle Creek.

Belleview Baptist Church in 1903.
Courtesy of Sandra Rudicill Cupps

Boarding with his sister's family in Burlington, Roberts attended Morgan Academy. After he returned to the family farm, he became a popular speaker for the Farmers Grange or Patrons of Husbandry. He spoke during the annual gathering of local chapters, usually held on the Harvest Home grounds.

Using his middle name, Roberts wrote poems – most satirizing love and marriage – and submitted them to the *Recorder*. After a broken love affair in his youth, Roberts never married.

When his father died suddenly in 1876, Roberts was the only child left on the farm to support his mother, so he focused on farming and milling.

In 1877, he organized a literary society at the Locust Grove schoolhouse. Literary societies, common at this time, organized

---

[30] Campbell, 46.
[31] *Belleview Baptist Church, 190th Anniversary*, 5-6.

intellectuals for debates, sharing essays, reading poems and singing.

Roberts taught school off and on from 1878 to 1899. His varied activities included teaching vocal music on Saturdays in Belleview and leading a singing school at Big Bone. In 1891, he was president of the Beech Grove Debate Society.[32]

Roberts' Giant Clock

During the summer of 1911, Roberts lost track of the days of the week and missed a Sunday service. That upset him. *"Whenever he was unsatisfied, he set out to do something about it. If it took an invention to solve his problem, then an invention he undertook."*[33] The musician, master clockmaker, wheelwright and amateur astronomer had built a tall lookout tower in back of his house. Even though he'd lost an eye in a woodcutting accident on Feb. 13, 1884, Roberts watched the stars through his telescope for hours every night, stroking his distinctive, waist-length beard.

He began building an 8' tall cabinet clock from native woods and walnut salvaged from old furniture. His huge creation showed positions of the moon and the relative positions of the Earth to Jupiter, Mars and Venus as well as the time and date.

The clock's workings came from a large Seth Thomas mechanism with a pendulum, an eight-day spring motor and a weight that required raising twice a year. Should the clock run down, all of its calculations would be upset, so Roberts designed an alarm buzzer that sounds if the spring is not wound.

In addition to keeping Eastern Standard Time, the clock has a 14-segment dial with one hand that tells the day of the week and indicates the diurnal and nocturnal hours.

The third face shows a model of the Earth's moon, larger than a grapefruit, which rotates on an invisible axis in a recess of the cabinet, showing the moon's phases.

The largest display is a yard-wide model of planets Venus, Earth, Mars and Jupiter, each somewhat larger than a golf ball. Roberts' choice of the second, third, fourth and fifth plants in our solar system was made almost 20 years before Pluto was discovered. Although viewers don't understand how, the clock even compensates for leap years.

Visitors from around the world, including Swiss clockmakers, traveled to the modest

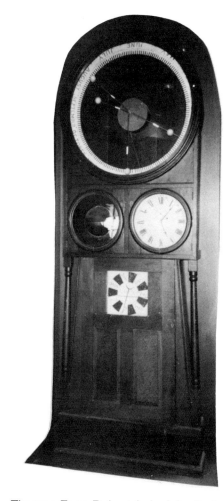

Thomas Zane Roberts' clock is displayed at Heritage Bank on KY 18 just outside of Burlington. Photo by Martha Daugherty

---

[32] Anthony W. Frohlich, "Thomas Zane Roberts and the Clock of Middle Creek," *Boone County Recorder*, Aug. 3, 1978.
[33] Bill Thomas, "His Solar Clock's a Puzzler," *Cincinnati Enquirer*, no date listed.

Chapter 10 1910-1919 War Changes Women's Roles

home in southwestern Boone County to see the unique timepiece that was completed in 1913.

After Roberts' death in January 1925, his nephew Ralph Cason moved into his home and the clock remained where it had always been. Then, for about 15 years it was displayed at Northern Kentucky University's science building.

Now, a copy of the diary Roberts kept for nearly half a century and the "clock of Middle Creek" are displayed at Heritage Bank on KY 18 between Burlington and Florence. Several of Roberts' heirs serve on the bank's board.

Electricity for Walton

Construction also was underway at Walton. The Mayfield Electric Co. was built across from city hall in 1913 to serve a population now numbering 538 – the largest in the county. Warren Stephenson operated the plant for Harry Mayfield. Stephenson, whose nickname was "Goat," was a mechanical genius, despite an education that had ended before high school.[34]

Stephenson, William Breeden and Bruce Wallace wired the Baptist Church first, then moved on to other buildings and homes around town. A lighting ceremony in August included a brass band from Cincinnati and attracted more than 1,500 to witness the first electric street lights being switched on by young Sybil Hart.

After the original plant burned on Feb. 17, 1917, Mayfield rebuilt it. Ten years later, a Texas corporation moved in and installed streetlights.

> **WALTON ADVERTISER**
> **APRIL 1, 1916**
> **Lost Boy**
> A small boy who was in charge of the conductor on train No. 27 of the Q & C railroad Monday afternoon, slipped the notice of the conductor at this place and got off. He could neither speak nor write English and was a puzzle for quite a while, but after numerous telephone calls it was found he was a Servian and on his way to his people in Lexington. . . .
>
> **Runaway – Leg Broken**
> Last Thursday a team of horses attached to a wagon ran away near Big Bone Springs near the farm of Mrs. F. M. Howlett, and one of the occupants, a Mr. Land, was thrown out and had his right leg broken below the knee. Dr. R. E. Ryle was called.

Technology Comes to Walton

Dr. B.K. Menefee had installed a Delco lighting plant in the back of his office in 1907 to use for medical treatments. Drop cords connected one light in each of his three rooms and a "goose neck" light outside.[35]

In 1913, First Baptist Church members built a new building on the west side of Walton's South Main Street. It replaced the 1866 brick church that stood where Walton Cemetery is on Church Street. Rev. D.C. Wayman was its first pastor. The 1913 building was torn down and a new church built on the same property in 1967.[36]

Founded in 1867 by Pastor J.W. Beasley, the original Walton Christian Church building was frame. African-American stonemason Eugene Watson laid a sturdy rock foundation for the new brick church in 1917. Watson carved his name and the date into a rock that was found in the foundation. That foundation was reused when the church was rebuilt after a Thanksgiving eve fire in 1947.[37]

The Walton school district became independent in 1900 in an effort to provide better schools than the county was offering. With two railroads running through town, Walton had a much larger tax base on which to draw than the rest of the rural county did. Two years later, new elementary and high schools were built on North Main Street.[38] Schools sometimes

---

[34] Asa Rouse, Feb. 24, 1998.

[35] Wilford Rice and William Fitzgerald, "Walton Established in 1840." *Boone County Recorder,* Jan. 2, 1964.
[36] Rice and Fitzgerald.
[37] Conrad, Yesterdays, 121.
[38] Conrad, *History of Boone County Schools*, 20.

showed movies to make money for the Parent-Teacher Association.

Previously, Walton students attended the Myers Academy, just north of the Walton Christian Church. Walton-Verona High School was built in 1954 on Alta Vista Drive. Walton and Verona high schools consolidated in 1935 to form the independent school district.[39]

"Loafers" Garage

Main Street was ankle-deep in dust. About six Walton residents drove cars. The first car, an E.M.F., belonged to Walton druggist Robert W. Jones. Manufactured in Indiana from 1908-1912, the vehicle was named after three men. Everett, Metzger and Flanders vehicles were later known as Studebakers. Jesters said the initials stood for "Every Morning Fixit."

Each fall Jones removed the tires, wrapped them in tissue and stored them inside his house for the winter. The next spring he replaced them on the wheels.[40] His drug store building became the Rouse Law office in 1976.

Stanley Vanlandingham had run a blacksmith shop across Main Street from the old IGA. Recognizing that cars were the coming thing, he built the Walton Garage, the first automotive repair station between Lexington and Covington.

Male commercial and social life revolved around Walton Garage and its' across-the-street neighbor, Powers Conrad's well-stocked Conrad Hardware for as long as the two existed. Every evening, weather permitting, dozens of men gathered on benches and window ledges to loaf.

Throughout the next three decades, *"loafing was refined to an art form. It included conversations laced with wonderful rural and small town humor, included a little gossip, of course, but more often related to business and world affairs, the weather, politics, the weather, the prowess of the high school basketball team, the weather, the Cincinnati Reds, the weather, the quality of the season's tobacco crop, and the weather,"* Asa Rouse recalls.

The numbers lessened in the winter. *"The hardcore loafers would sit around the big stove in the hardware store or hang out in the garage office, which also later served as the Greyhound Bus Company office."*[41]

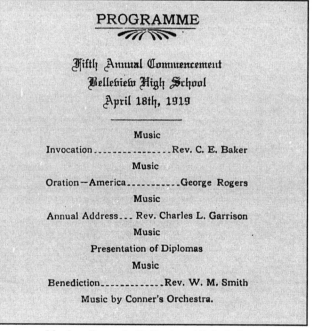

Marion Roger's Belleview High School commencement program. She was David Clore's aunt. Courtesy of David and Jeanette Clore.

Walton Advertiser

G.B. Powers and Roy D. Stamler, who ran a pool hall, founded the *Walton Advertiser* on Aug. 14, 1914. *"Published as often as necessary,"* the original *Walton Advertiser* was four 6" x 9" pages. In February 1915, Powers produced a news edition called *"Walton Outlook,"* carrying editorials and small local advertisements. James R. "Jim" Wallace joined the partnership in 1916.

---

[39] Asa Rouse, Feb. 24, 1998.
[40] Rice and Fitzgerald.

[41] Asa Rouse, March 1, 1998.

Stacking wheat on the Kirtley farm in 1918. Photo by Mrs. Bessie Kirtley. Courtesy of Barbara Fallis

Chautauquas and Silent Pictures

About 1912, annual visits of the chautauqua (an educational entertainment in the form of lectures, concerts or plays, usually presented outdoors) began in a tent behind Walton's high school. The company brought a brass band, singers, musical combinations, speakers, comedians and more. "*It was like having a vaudeville show right in our little community*," Rice said.

"Uncle Joe" Reed used local talent to put on operas, then went to dramatic plays at the Walton Opera House at Depot and Main streets. Later the opera house converted to offer silent picture shows.

Walton Advertiser owner Roy D. Stamler opened the Royal Airdrome Moving Picture Show in February 1917, about where Jack's Barber Shop is on Walton's Main Street. He promised his pictures would be as good as those in the big city. Bright electric lights decorated the front. Patrons sat on benches to watch movies on the big screen. If it rained, the movie ended.

People traveled from all over the county to see moving pictures like *Uncle Tom's Cabin*, *Kentucky Squire* or *The Moonshiner, A Kentucky Feud*, in 1904. *The Kentuckian* appeared in 1906. *In Old Kentucky* was released in 1909, 1920, 1927 and as a talkie with Will Rogers in 1935.[42]

"*Admission was a dime. After you entered and went around to the front, it appeared to be a grandstand. If a rain came up, we retired to the Opera House to complete the show*," Rice recalled.

"*Either Miss Bess Houston or Miss Syble Hurt played the piano. They used sheet music and didn't watch the picture. Sometimes a murder scene would be on the picture and they would be playing Ragtime. Of course, we didn't notice that because we were so interested in the picture – or our girlfriends.*

"*Harry Dixon, nicknamed Unique, converted A.M. Edwards' livery stable into a moving picture house. Mrs. Burdetta Feagan Powers played the piano there for about five*

---

[42] Klotter, *Portrait in Paradox*, 90.

Minister R.C. McNeely baptises Mrs. John Louden in the river at Rabbit Hash. Photo by Mrs. Bessie Kirtley
Courtesy of Rabbit Hash Museum

years. Shortly after James Falls took over the showhouse, he built the brick James Theater at Alta-Vista and Main streets from a former garage. After Jim's death, his wife Alva took over."[43]

Union Memories

Movies attracted some children, but nearly all were now attending school. Most – including the six and seven-year-olds – walked to school, often a mile or more. Older, wealthier or more distant students drove buggies or rode horses.

At Union Independent, primary teacher Miss Jessie Cleek was *"pretty and very nice"* while principal Mrs. McKee was *"a little stout, stern and authoritative,"* in Mrs. Roter's memory.[44] Mrs. McKee offered an extra-curricular elocution class that required memorizing lengthy poems.

Four years after graduating in the first class of Union High School in 1918, Miss Lillian Bristow became the assistant cashier at Union Deposit Bank. A Union native, she was the daughter of Napoleon and Annie Anderson Bristow.[45]

Susie Garrison taught piano lessons, whacking students' knuckles with a pencil or ruler if they missed a note. A large, stately woman, Mrs. Garrison directed singing and played the piano at the Union Baptist Church. Her husband John, a short man, had a farm on Big Bone Road.

Roseann Borders and two grown daughters, Artie and Eunie, lived near where Fowler Creek emptied into Gunpowder Creek. They supported themselves by weaving rag carpets and raising geese. They dressed geese they sold at Christmas so they could keep the feathers to stuff featherbeds, bolsters and pillows.

John and Bessie Taggert and their daughter Hymer lived in the old tollhouse at the intersection of Union and Florence Pike with Fowler Creek Road.

---

[43] *175th Anniversary Historical Book*, 58.
[44] Roter 122.
[45] *Boone County Recorder*, 1930 Historical Edition.

Lon and Lou Voshell ran a hotel in downtown Union. John Platt ran a blacksmith shop near the Presbyterian Church. Marietta, Eugenia and Harry Riley lived far back from the pike. The red-brick Union Deposit Bank and Frank Smith's grocery were across Hathaway Road.

The Rachals had a concrete sidewalk in front of their house across from the Voshell Hotel. Dr. O.E. Senour's office stood beside Sam Hicks' brick garage that had replaced Ben Norman's frame grocery. The small white frame building at the concrete sidewalk's end was the telephone company office. Pretty, blonde Fannie Utz worked and lived there with her mother Alice.

Matson Rachal operated a grocery in a frame building at the corner of Mt. Zion Road until he and Ben Norman built a new brick building that became a store and post office. On the way to or from school, children often spent their money on bananas, cookies and candy at Rachal & Norman's.

The Union community looked out for its own. Betty remembered a man named Sim House who *"seemed to be homeless and wandered from home to home – always arriving just in time for a meal."* House helped with chores and stayed with the Weaver family when Betty's father was away at night.

Leslie Sullivan, who lived in the last home in town with his wife Susie and son LaVerne, was the mail carrier.[46]

A postcard sent to Master William Rogers penciled from Laura and Manan on Aug. 19, 1915. Courtesy of David and Jeanette Clore

Spanish Flu Epidemic

Richard and Annie Smith lived in the fieldstone Fowler house across Fowler Creek from Clarkson Lane with their daughter Eva. Their son Frank, who had run a Union grocery, was one of the first to die from the great flu epidemic. His widow Hattie and their three children then went to live with his parents in the old Fowler House.[47]

In October 1918, the influenza outbreak canceled meetings at churches including Big Bone. Many 1918 community columns in the *Recorder* listed individuals recovering or dying from influenza. Several Boone County boys were sent home from the State College in Lexington (now the University of Kentucky) during the outbreak. The "Spanish influenza" took more than 14,000 Kentuckians before it ended in 1919.[48]

Huckster Wagon Delivery

Huckster wagons delivered produce and groceries from Boone County farms to Covington stores and families. Mrs. Roter recalled packing a spring wagon and delivering the goods with her father. Early in the week, they made butter, formed it in pound or two-pound blocks and pressed it with decorative patterns. Eggs were candled (held in front of a candle flame which allowed one to see if the egg was fresh or if a baby chick was growing inside) and sorted to meet individual orders.

On Thursday, chickens caught and caged in slatted coops were loaded into a covered

---

[46] Roter, 131-132.

[47] Roter, 129.
[48] Harrison & Klotter, 290.

Florence uptown looking from Girard Street. Courtesy of the Lloyd Library, Cincinnati

spring wagon. It was packed with everything it could hold – even the spring seat was removed and replaced with a box full of butter and eggs. After rising at 3 a.m. Friday, the farm chores were done, the mules were hitched, and the trip to Covington began.

Sometimes the wagon stopped along the way to pick up or deliver produce, chickens, eggs or butter. Some drove buggies or wagons filled with their goods to crossroads to meet the huckster wagon on its way to the city.

Creeks and railroad tracks could be hazardous to cross with the wagon, but drivers dreaded the Willow Run hill near what is now called "Death Hill" or the "Cut in the Hill" on I-75/I-71. Holding the wheel brake with one hand while reining the mules back with the other, the driver hoped and prayed the wagon wouldn't gather momentum and roll out of control.

Customers were friendly and grateful to receive fresh-from-the-farm goods. Mrs. Roter fondly remembered the brightly colored comic pages Mrs. VanPelt saved from her Sunday paper. They featured Hans and Fritz, the Katzenjammer Kids, Maggie and Jiggs and Snuffy Smith with his ever-popular adage "Time's a-wastin'."

Back to Union in the dark meant crossing the same creeks and waiting for the toll bars to lift. The mules knew the way home and were as grateful as their passengers for their meal, regardless of the hour.[49]

Florence Sidewalks Laid

Florence was modernizing. During A.M. Yealey's first term as Florence mayor, cement sidewalks were laid on Main, Shelby and Girard streets. As soon as sidewalks were completed, the trustees made it illegal to ride bicycles or roller skates on them and required homeowners to keep them clean.[50]

In April 1916 the first city property tax was passed with W.E. Osborn as Council chairman and L.E. Aylor as clerk. It required a payment

---

[49] Roter, 43.
[50] Florence Ordinance Book #1, 55-57.

Mr. Riddell, Pearl and Lester Gulley, and Newton Sullivan inside the Gulley & Pettit Store in 1926.
Courtesy of Katie Presnell

of 50 cents on each $100 worth of taxable property and a 50-cent poll tax.[51] The next year, the clerk was paid $1.50 per meeting.

"Electric lights began replacing coal oil lamps in Florence homes and the village lamplighter faded away. No longer was there a need to trim wicks, clean and polish chimneys, fill oil tanks, light lamps in the evening and put them out in the morning." [52]

Florence High School

In 1911, after a two-day inspection by state officials, Boone County was ready to offer a four-year high school curriculum at the Florence school. First year students studied rhetoric, composition, algebra, Latin, general science, and ancient history.

Second year courses were English grammar, plane geometry, Latin, biology, physics, and modern history. English literature, algebra, physics, English history and Latin were third year classes.

Seniors studied American literature, advanced arithmetic, American history, Latin and civics. In addition, girls attended "domestic science" one period a week while boys went to "manual training."

The first Florence High School graduates, in 1915, were Mabel and Harry Tanner, Ruby Corbin and Robert Robbins. After the graduation ceremony, Florence residents united in a vote for additional funds to add a fifth room to the school and employ another teacher.[53]

The Gulleys and Pettits

The Gulley and Pettit grocery opened in Burlington in 1917. The shop was in two of the first-floor rooms of what is called the Tousey House on Jefferson Street. The two families, L.W. and Pearl Gulley and Albert and Fannie Pettit, operated the store, swapping eggs

---

[51] Florence Ordinance Book #1, 61, 65.
[52] Conrad, *Yesterdays*, 33.

[53] Conrad, *History of Boone County Schools*, 11.

for flour, canning supplies, kerosene and other necessities when customers were short on cash.

They sold Coca Cola, silverware, cigarettes, shoes, coffee, stove parts, nails, milk strainers, home remedies, clothing, meat, oysters, paint, penny candy, seed, feed, hats, caps, cigars, and more. Proctor & Gamble delivered Ivory, Lava and Naptha soaps as well as Oxydol, Dreft and Chipso detergents.

Making use of their wagon going both ways, Gulley and Pettit carried produce, eggs and milk from Boone County to Covington, Louisville or Indiana to sell for their customers and returned with products from those locales.

Their business grew quickly, so they soon purchased a building a few blocks south on Jefferson and expanded.

The two families were closely entwined. Pearl Pettit Gulley was a sister of partner William Albert Pettit. Three of the Gulley brothers had married three of the Pettit sisters.

Fannie Pettit

Fannie Elizabeth Horton Pettit was the eldest of seven children who grew up where the Boy Scout camp is located off Grange Hall Road (now Camp Ernst Road).

As the oldest child in a family whose father had died of typhoid, Fannie had begun earning money when she was old enough to stand on a box and rub laundry on a washboard. The money she earned bought shoes and socks for her brothers and sisters.

A local man hoped the bank would foreclose on the farm so he could buy it, but Fannie's mother carefully documented every mortgage payment until the farm was debt free.

When Albert was courting Fannie, he rode a black horse from his family's East Bend Road farm past one of Fannie's friend's houses. Since the telephone's party lines invited gossip, the friend called, speaking in their own code, to say a *"black crow was going to fly over her house"* – giving Fannie time to "spruce up" before Albert arrived.

Fannie continued working after she and Albert were married and living in Francesville. Driving her horse and buggy, she ran a route selling products, like Rosebud Salve and flavorings, to other women.

After moving into the Tousey house, she raised four daughters and a garden, preserving food and storing it in the old dirt-floor cellar in the stone-walled basement. Their two eldest daughters, Alberta Pettit Robinson and Laura Pettit Ogden were married in the front room on the right and had their first babies in the same room at the top of the stairs on the left where they had been born.

James Pettit
Courtesy of Katie Presnell

Lester Gulley's wife Pearl, who was childless, kept the books and dealt with the business part of the store. Pearl used large aluminum kettles and strainers to bottle milk from the cows kept in the barn out back. The Gulleys too lived in the house.

After Mr. Pettit retired in 1956, Mr. Gulley continued the store. He and Pearl moved to the single-story house a few doors down (now a child-care center). In 1970, Gulley died of a heart attack while leaning over the store's counter. The Pettits lived in the Tousey house until Mrs. Pettit died in 1976.

Eunie Adams, Teacher

The Pettit family included another career woman. Burlington schoolteacher Eunie B. Adams eventually married James B. Pettit, which made her a sister-in-law to both store owners.

Eunie kept a diary for most of her lifetime, chronicling her day-to-day experiences. Like most women of 1909, she picked butter beans, made preserves, picked blackberries, washed, ironed, sewed, mended, cleaned and canned beans, tomatoes, peaches and apples.

Attending the Baptist Church at Gunpowder or Big Bone, "*going to Uncle Owen's to eat ice cream*," attending the Florence Fair, going to a fish fry on Gunpowder Creek, visiting a new baby or taking a drive were special events.

Eunie graduated from what is now Eastern Kentucky University and began teaching school in Burlington in 1918. That year she dated James B. Pettit, who took her out to dinner and to the theater on a Thursday night, then came to see her again on Friday. Their extended courtship included visits to the Florence Fair as well as attending church.

In 1919, Eunie had 31 pupils in her class. She attended chatauquas and ball games, mowed the lawn and helped cook supper for 23 on threshing day – likely when her family lived on the old Grange Hall Road.

The Pettits married on Aug. 21, 1926 when Eunie was 34 and James was 30. They never had their own children, but doted on their nieces, nephews and Eunie's students. She died in December 1977 and Jimmy, who had been in poor health, died a month later.[54]

Dancing Jailer

Born to Edward and Susan Scott Fowler of Burlington in 1857, Charles A. Fowler was the youngest of 11. He had attended Burlington schools, then learned to mix paints and took up painting as a trade. Fowler was appointed county jailer in 1917, then was elected and served 12 years. He traced his heritage through Benjamin Piatt Fowler, one of the county's earliest settlers.

Fowler moved to Athens, Ohio, in 1885, painting in the summer and teaching dance in the winter. Fowler married Ellen Logan and had two children. The Fowlers later returned to Burlington and ran the old Boone Hotel for two years.[55]

Miss Artie Ryle, great-aunt of Mary Sue Rudicill   Courtesy of Mary Sue Rudicill

Burley-Buying Sheriff

A loyal Democrat, Lewis Albert Conner was high sheriff from 1917 to 1921 with a well-known "Get Your Man" philosophy. He made his son Harold a deputy, possibly the youngest deputy sheriff in the state. Young as he was, Harold captured one of the first stills found in Boone County.

L.A. Conner had become a loose leaf tobacco dealer in 1906. The next year he handled tobacco for the Pool organization. From 1914 to 1921, he was a stockholder, director and active in the work of the warehouse in Walton. Burley prices soared during WWI and Kentucky led the nation in the amount of tobacco grown. One hundred pounds of tobacco sold for $9.09 in 1915, $17.41 in 1917, and $28.47 in 1919. More pounds of tobacco were produced that year than any time before or since in Kentucky.[56]

In 1925, Conner sold his Burlington home and moved to Florida for the winter. He

---

[54] Katie Presnell research.
[55] *Boone County Recorder, 1930* Historical Edition.
[56] Klotter, *Portrait in Paradox*, 128-129.

returned to Florence the next summer, and moved back to Burlington in 1927 with his wife of 31 years, Fannie Mae Latham of Florence.

Burlington High School

Conner was elected to the school board and drove the stakes for the new Burlington (Boone County) High School building (now Burlington Elementary). In the face of considerable opposition from board members Charles Kelly and S.L. Craven, Conner believed he had selected the right location.

The county infirmary. Courtesy of Maplewood

They hired an architect who inspected the ground from all angles, then announced Conner had picked the best site.

Conner's team drew the plow to break the ground to excavate the school's foundation. It opened in September 1910. Conner's son Harold was among the 1915 graduates. Harold became a bookkeeper in Florida then returned to Burlington and bred, raised and raced greyhounds.

County Infirmary

In June 1883, a committee had investigated moving the old frame Poor House (located on the edge of Burlington where the Animal Shelter and Highway Department are now) to a new location.[57]

In 1911, Frank H. Rouse ran the county infirmary for $1,752.31, caring for 18 indigent residents who assisted by raising the food they ate. Rouse reported to county officials that he had $193.93 left on hand from the budget he was allotted. Annual expenses per inmate totaled $76.69 including his salary. The fiscal court renewed his contract for 1912 giving him a $350 salary, a $50 increase.[58]

Rouse kept busy maintaining both his own farm and the infirmary grounds and residents. He and his wife Lena bought and prepared any food needed that wasn't grown on the grounds. He pitched in to help neighbors press hay, fill silos, and complete other major farm or building chores. He hauled coal from Erlanger to heat the huge building.

A very conscientious bookkeeper, Rouse recorded these prices in his 1911 journal: peaches $1.50 to $2 bushel, beans 25 cents a bushel, and apples 33.5 cents a bushel.

On a warm and muddy Christmas Eve 1911, he was busy preparing *"for Xmas for inmates and helping with dinner for 25. Marce Rouse & Effie Kelly came in afternoon. Marce & I decorated dining hall with evergreens, bells & balls. Gave each inmate plate of candy, nuts, orange, banana, dates, peanuts and handkerchief. Also some little gifts such as knife, coin holder, etc."*[59]

A few weeks later, a cold snap brought very low temperatures to the area: Aurora –24,

---

[57] Elizabeth Kirtley, "History of Maplewood," 1998.
[58] Diary of F.H. Rouse, 1911
[59] Rouse, Dec. 24, 1911.

Boone County Recorder

BURLINGTON, KENTUCKY   THURSDAY, NOVEMBER 7, 1918

R.C. Hammond Write to Home That Peace is Near and Will Come by Christmas

(Written Oct. 10, 1918 to his cousin Helen Ryle)

. . . It is a fresh air ward and about half the patients sleep out on the porch. I had to sit out on the porch all night with one because he wanted to put on his clothes and go home. He had the fever and pneumonia both and was delirious most of the time. . . .

I am not allowed to write much about my work and I don't care to for it is far from pleasant. There is only one thing that I like about the work and that is that I can do many little things that help to comfort and cheer my boys who are not able to help themselves.

There is a steadily growing rumor that peace is near and that it will come by Christmas. I only hope to God it's true.

I think I could stand to suffer myself without flinching, but to see the other boys, many of whom were my comrades and pals back in the States, suffer and die is much worse Some of the boys who were in camp with me and came over on the same boat are buried in the cemetery near here....

FROM HAMPTON ROADS

Writes Jameson Aylor to Home Folks is Feeling Good and Likes It Fine

Prices for Turkies will Soar

Turkey prices will soar sky high this year. . . .In Cincinnati they are now quoted at 25 cents on foot. Substitution of chickens, ducks and geese for the Thanksgiving Day turkeys in order to supply the men of the army and navy with turkey dinners is urged on the public by market experts. The government has contracted for the entire supply of cold storage turkeys, it is said, and has also arranged to purchase most of the fresh killed fowls. . .

Gussie Rich Dies In France

Gussie Rich, who was born Aug. 24, 1894, grew up to manhood at his home on Gum Branch, nearly in sight of Big Bone Baptist Church . . . was the son of the last W.O. B. Rich.. . .

He went to France and proved to be a Hero by killing eight of the Huns on a sniping expedition and getting back to his company; and on Sept. 13th, 1918, he was severely wounded and was taken to Base Hospital No. 116 in a very critical condition. . .

GASSED

Dr. E. W. Duncan received a letter from Frank Milner, son of A.F. Milner, of Constance. . . .

Young Milner was in a hospital in England recovering from the effects of a gas, a dose of which he got at the front in France. He was repairing a telephone line at the front and used his gas mask over his mouth and nose, leaving his eyes exposed, and they were blinded by the gas. He was badly burned on the body and lower limbs and the burns giving him considerable pain. . . .

ARRIVED IN FRANCE

Had Fine Voyage Over and the Weather was Fine – Attacked by U-Boat

(C.E. Witham wrote his sister:) . . . We were attacked by a submarine going over, about 11 o'clock at night. The destroyer dropped ten depth bombs about three miles from us and they shook our ship. It was reported the submarine sank. Several ships that have been torpedoed made it into port all right.

We carry nearly one million dollars worth of oil, mostly aviation. I will get to see some of New York as long as we are in port. . . . I have traveled nearly 20,000 miles this year.

The largest ship carries 15,000 soldiers besides 1,500 sailors to run it, and crosses in seven days. . . . I am well and weigh 168 pounds.

DROPPED 1500 FEET

Without a Scratch Writes J.R. Hammond, Who Has Been In Two Big Drives

. . .Just this a.m. I saw dead German boys of 16 and women chained to machine guns. The Germans are inhuman.

We are whipping them on every front. I was shot down the other day, made a 1,500 feet drop without a scratch. . . .

(Sent to Miss Kittie Kelley from her cousin James R. Hammond.)

Harvey Herbert Rusche Dead.

Private Harvey Herbert Rusche died of Influenza-pneumonia at Camp Zachary Taylor.

A member of the Petersburg Christian Church, he was quiet and reserved. To the sound of "Taps," he was buried at the Petersburg cemetery with salutes fired by veterans of the Civil War.

CALLS FOR 290,773 MEN

To Be Made Up of Older Men Selects to Leave Next Week

. . . It was announced 253,335 white men, physically qualified for general military service, will entrain, making the largest single call issued under the selective service act.

The remainder. . . will be made up of negroes for entertainment Nov. 19 to 21.. . . Total number of men inducted into military service under the draft will have passed the 3,000,000 mark, and the number of men in the U.S. Army in the field or training will total more than 4,000,000.

BADLY GASSED

Being in Hospital Better than Lying in No Man's Land Got Started on the Big Drive

Mrs. A. F. Milner of Constance received the following letter from her son Frank who is in a base hospital at Dartford, England. . . . A little mustard gas made me blind as a bat for a few days and some burns on my body which are as raw as raw can be. My throat and lungs feel the same way. I will be confined to the hospital at least six weeks longer.

I got started on one of the biggest drives of the year and I certainly am sorry I could not finish it. Oh! Its great mother and I am so anxious to get back and be able to go to Berlin and hang the telephone in the Kaiser's castle or Reichstage which will inform the world that autocracy has gone down in favor of Democracy.

What an experience to dodge lead. For five days I worked as I never worked before. I never slept and I ate very little. It is remarkable how you learn to judge a shell – that is how close it will hit. Had a nice bit of shrapnel to knock off my helmet very nearly but I was glad I had a helmet on. Another time I hugged the ground so close on a perfectly level place that I made a hole. It was necessary because a wily German had spied me and was proceeding to get some practice with his machine gun. A shell hit under a pair of horses standing outside my dugout and the fragments were never found. It piled the dirt so high in the door of the dugout we had to be dug out.

It is quite true that men in action know very little about the gigantic struggle in which they are participating. . . .

---

[60] This page, like other articles taken from media of the era, was reproduced as exactly as possible, with original spellings and punctuation.

Petersburg -26, Burlington -14. One of the elderly residents was gravely ill. *"Lonnie Acra came to see his father Lark Acra. I went to Burlington in afternoon, built fires and waited on Acra. Give the inmates apples to eat every evening. At the infirmary one year today. Snow on ground, good sleighing. Lark Acra died at 7 p.m. Washed and dressed Acra. Made bed and put Hunt* (presumably, another patient sharing his room) *upstairs. Telephoned to Lonnie Acra. Worked until 10 p.m. Infirmary 6 below zero. Burlington 13 below. George Rouse's on Burlington & Florence Pike 20 below."*[61]

The next day, he worked around the house aired out Acra's clothes and rode to Dr. Peddicord's office in Burlington to get a death certificate. H.C. Blanton, Lonnie Acra, and Otis Acra came out for dinner. Then he and the Acra brothers went to the Burlington IOOF (International Order of Odd Fellows) Cemetery, bought a lot, and staked off a gravesite.

Rouse went to Burlington to get Blanton's wagon to take back to the infirmary to get the corpse, then put the body in the vault. He returned, did the evening chores, then disinfected the room with formaldehyde. *"Acra was 68 years, 6 months and 16 days"* old, he recorded.

On the 18th, he returned to the IOOF Cemetery to dig the grave, then *"went to William Kirk's after boards for grave"* and finished digging with the help of Ward Coleman. *"Blanton brought casket and put corpse in."* Seven attended the burial. Rouse went home to dinner, then butchered a beef.[62]

Bill Horton
Courtesy of Katie Presnell

World War I

In April 1917, three years after WWI began, the United States declared war and joined France and England in fighting Kaiser Wilhelm's German army. Almost immediately, farm prices, wages and material costs skyrocketed, jumping 10 to 70 percent. The president was given control of all telephone systems throughout the war effort.

The well-organized draft conscripted all able-bodied young men. Many were shipped out on trains that ran through Walton and Erlanger to Fort Knox where men received artillery training.

Citizens' Deposit Bank oversold its quota of Liberty Bonds and War Savings Stamps, taking in $75,000. Zeal for buying war bonds was so extreme that those who didn't purchase them were called enemies of their country.

Until 1918, German had been the second language of Northern Kentucky. In a wave of anti-German sentiment, the state legislature prohibited teaching German in schools. School officials dropped German classes in mid-term. Some switched to Spanish. Boone County high schools didn't begin offering German classes again until the mid-'70s.[63]

George B. Pierce sent a German helmet to his new wife, the former Edna Beall of Francesville who had taught in Burlington. Postal employees were intrigued by the 3½-pound package wrapped in burlap. *"Those at the post office when it arrived would have*

Boone Countians Lost in World War I

Frank J. Bell	Alfred Stanley Cason
Benjamin C. Cook	Thomas E. Coyle
Charles E. Farrell	Thomas J. Garrison
Samuel Holt	William Jackson
Pearl Kite	Jacob B. Morris
Gussie Rich	Harvey Herbert Rusche
Joseph Smith	William Snow
Allen Slayback	Charles Walters

---

[61] Rouse, Jan. 16, 1912.

[62] Rouse, Jan. 1-18, 1912.
[63] Reis, *Pieces of the Past*, 177-178.

Boone County Recorder
Nov. 14, 1918
Written on Oct. 13, 1918

Hello Mr. Riddell!

I am feeling fine. I am now in France trying to talk French and change French money. I am getting plenty to eat in my company between meals – grapes and grape wine at night 30 cents a quart without any sugar in it. Some sour wine I say.

This part of France is sure nice – good roads and no mud, but prices for stuff we buy are sky high. Grapes are 20 cents a pound and other things the same way. The U.S. issues us boys all the tobacco we want to smoke and chew and soap, and all we want to eat and wear.

They use two wheel carts over here and two oxen to a cart. You see lots of burros but mighty few horses, just now and then you see one.

For a bunch of boys who left on Feb. 27th, two of us are not very far apart. The other boy is Edward Gross of Constance.

Please send me your paper as first-class mail and father will pay for it.

Your friend, Wagoner Otto Souther

Boone County Recorder
November 14, 1918

THE WAR OVER

Germany Surrenders – The Armistice Has Been Signed and The Boys at the Front Are Taking a Rest.

Germany as a Nation Wiped off the Map

The greatest war in the history of the world closed when Germany surrendered . . .

A revolution was sweeping many parts of Germany, the people having determined to have peace at any cost. During last week many men were shot in Germany for ignoring the notices calling them to army service which enraged the populace and they resented this action on the part of the government by an uprising.

The Kaiser and the entire Hohenzollern outfit will have to leave Germany and there will be a thorough house cleaning as regards rulers in Germany. To the American soldiers will fall a large portion of the job of policing Germany and other countries fighting the allies, and some predict it will be at least two years before they will get back home.

(*The newspaper listed all the terms of the surrender on the front page.*)

Boone County Recorder
Nov. 28, 1918

FIRST BOONE COUNTY SELECT TO REACH HOME AFTER BEING DISCHARGED AT CLOSE OF THE WAR

William Presser, of Waterloo, one of the 28 selects of this county who entrained for Camp Taylor on the 27th day of last June, arrived at home last Monday carrying an honorable discharge from Uncle Sam's service. He was sent from Camp Taylor to Camp Funston, Kansas, at which camp he was discharged a few days since and lost no time in reaching home to give his folks the pleasantest surprise of their lives.

He and Miss Clara Ryle, daughter of Mr. and Mrs. J. Mat Ryle, of Waterloo neighborhood, were married on the third day of June last and in about three weeks thereafter he was in the service. Mr. Presser says the boys are being discharged at the rate of 300 a day at Camp Funston.

Up to the time of his arriving in Burlington his people did not know he had been discharged and he was anxious to reach home before they received the information. He like the rest of the selects was anxious to go over seas so long as the war was in progress, but as soon as hostilities suspended, he was anxious to get back home.

So far as is known Mr. Presser was the first Boone county soldier to be discharged under the demobilizing orders.

given a great deal to get a look at it. The shape of the package showed plainly its contents."[64]

Belleview native John Samuel Clore had enlisted in the army at 17. On Feb. 23, 1918, he left Hoboken, N.J., on the French liner Maui. After 13 days, the ship landed at St. Nazaire, France. Clore inhaled poisonous gases on the front lines, but did not leave his company until after they were sent back to rest camp. After a few days at a hospital in Longuyon, France, he left and returned to his company. He became a mounted dispatch messenger for military operations in Luxembourg until the company moved to Treves, Germany.

Clore ended up in Luxembourg hospital with "the flu" and double pneumonia (possibly effects of the gas). The hospital was the Grand Duchess of Luxembourg's palace turned over to the Americans. *"He entered the hospital on Feb. 20 and on March 13 was operated on after several attempts had been made to draw the pus off his lungs."*

Clore was repeatedly transferred between hospitals, ending up at Brest, France, where he was shipped to New York on the liner Agamemnon. After 15 months in Europe, he returned to the states in nine days. He spent time in several New York hospitals, then was sent to Camp Zachary Taylor in Louisville where he was discharged two years after he'd enlisted.[65]

In 1918 came the news that World War I had ended. All the church bells were rung and five boys kept the bell in the Presbyterian church ringing all day."[66]

Local editorials showed no sympathies whatsoever for the Germans: *"It is better for this country that Germany surrendered before the armies reached her territory for had she been invaded, the destruction of property in retaliation would have been awful, entailing a larger burden on the United States."*

---

[64] Boone County Recorder, Nov. 14, 1918, 1.
[65] *Boone County Recorder*. 1930 Historical Edition.
[66] Conrad, *Yesterdays*, 33

Chapter 11
1920-1939 A Flood of Change

The next several decades were difficult ones, full of economic trials and social change. About 20 percent of those living in Boone County in 1900 had left by 1920. By 1930, a few would move in, beginning a population increase that now shows no signs of stopping.

Union's C.W. Lassing sold his farm and moved to Florida in 1920 – another trend that continues today. W.L. Satchwill bought 135 acres in Aurora, but ice on the river kept ferries from operating, preventing his move from Locust Grove for a time.[1] Telephone operator Bess Kirkpatrick accepted a position with Cincinnati Bell and moved.[2]

Strong European markets during the war years had encouraged farmers to produce more crops. After war's end, those crops glutted the market and prices plummeted. Impoverished farm markets brought the depression to Boone County in the 1920s.

By 1928, Kentucky ranked 47th of the 48 states in farm income. In 1930, its average per capita farm income was $148, well behind the Southeast's mean of $183, which was behind the national norm.

Then 1930 brought an unprecedented drought. Precipitation averaged less than half the normal levels. By August, statewide crop losses exceeded $1 million.[3] Seven years later, a record-breaking flood took another massive toll.

The one advantage of farming was that it fed the family, and often the extended family and friends who intentionally visited at mealtime to eat their fill – something they could seldom do at home.

"Everything we ate year-round was off the farm except the salt and pepper," recalls Bruce Ferguson, whose family of four shared a single bedroom in 1932 so the other two bedrooms could be rented to boarders who ate breakfast and supper with the family.

City dwellers did everything they could to put food on their tables, raising gardens in tiny yards and even keeping chickens on the terrace.

> **Boone County Recorder**
> December 25, 1919
>
> **Dollar ToDay, Cheap Dollar**
>
> The wastage of war excess of demand over production and extravagance following the strain of war, have forced down the market value of the dollar until it is worth only about half as much as it was in 1914. These are words of a Government expert and are true as to the purchasing power of the dollar. As has been the case after every great war, prices are up now, causing the purchasing power of the dollar to be low, but that situation has reversed itself in the past and will probably do so again within the next few years as production assumes a normal output.
>
> While we believe prices for farm products will never reach the low levels of five years ago, nor of clothing or machinery, yet values of all kinds that are controlled by supply and demand will gradually settle down to actual worth and our cheap dollars will have an enhanced value.
>
> **FARM BUREAU**
> **Organized by Farmers of Boone County – Expect to Enroll 1000 members.**
>
> ...It having been decided to organize a County Farm Bureau temporary officers were elected as follows: F.H. Rouse, Burlington, President; Eli Surface, Florence, Vice-President; Hubert Conner, Hebron, Secretary; B.C. Gaines, Burlington, Treasurer. . . .
>
> Influential farmers in each voting precinct in the county have volunteered their services to boost the drive for members and it will be about the liveliest drive ever conducted in the county. . . . Annual dues were fixed at $6.00. . . .
>
> **Hate to See Him Go.**
>
> The farmers of Boone County will be sorry to learn that the probability is that they will lose the services of County Farm Agent W.D. Sutton. . . having decided to take charge of his father's farm.

---

[1] *Boone County Recorder*, Jan. 8, 1920, 1.
[2] *Boone County Recorder*, Nov. 11, 1920, 1.
[3] Harrison & Klotter, 359-360.

Jobs were scarce and many were temporary – or ended abruptly without notice. Farmers did carpentry work and whatever else their skills allowed on the side.

A salary of $125 a month was an impressive income in 1932, providing enough money to meet expenses and buy a car.[4]

For most, social life continued to revolve around church activities and visits to the general store. Every store had a pickle barrel and bulk supplies of peanuts, cookies and candies that encouraged lingering and catching up on the news.

New Products

Classic after-war inflation had sent prices skyrocketing. A dozen items that cost $53.20 in 1913, cost $138.20 in 1920 – an increase of almost 160 percent.

While general stores carried an increasing variety of goods, catalog shopping was the rage in rural communities. In 1926, an entire house could be purchased through the Sears and Roebuck catalog. For $2,232, one received lumber, shingles, millwork, flooring, plaster, windows, doors, hardware, nails, siding and enough paint for three coats. It came with blueprints and a construction manual. A shipping schedule outlined when building parts would arrive by rail. A guarantee promised sufficient quality materials would be received to complete the house.

An article described the new look in home design as furniture made of bleached blonde woods and dressers with rounded, unframed mirrors. Three-piece *"come apart sofas should sit atop floor coverings with small patterns in plain colors – not the large, gay patterns of the past."* Chrome-plated electric appliances allowed the modern homemaker to cook at the table. Irons with heat gradations and wringer washing machines were advertised.[5]

In 1936, Sears and Roebuck offered demonstrations showing how the Kook Kwick Pressure Cooker, endorsed by the Good Housekeeping Institute, could *"cook an entire meal in one-third the usual time, over one burner, without the blending or intermingling of any flavors. Foods prepared in the Pressure Cooker way are more palatable than when cooked in an open kettle, fried or oven roasted. Meats are more tender, vegetables more healthful, with their natural juices and mineral salts retained to furnish the vitamins which science has found so necessary to health."*[6]

Change

Technology also brought entertainment including radios, Victrolas and moving pictures. Like anything new, some looked askance at them. One Kentucky judge declared that *"the majority of delinquent boys are movie fiends."* A legislator tried to set up a censorship board to control movie viewing.[7]

Some blamed comic books on corrupting the young – especially ones like the sexy "Sheena of the Jungle."

Many condemned women for taking on non-traditional roles, cutting their hair, wearing pants and riding astride, rather than sidesaddle. Some attributed these "declining values" to evils brought by automobiles and movies with their "scantily attired" women. Vehicles, for the first time, gave young people a private, unchaperoned place to gather and

---

> **WALTON ADVERTISER**
> MARCH 25, 1926
> ### WET OR DRY?
> A question that is agitating the minds of the people of the United States is the prohibition problem. . . .
> **THE WALTON ADVERTISER** is submitting the question to its readers . . . to ascertain if possible the consensus of opinion . . . Without bias or any ulterior motive whatsoever, but solely for the purpose of attempting to acquire information on the attitude of our subscribers, this paper is placing in the hands of adult men and women this ballot for the expression of their views on the subject. The editors will keep an accurate account of the vote and after being registered, the ballot will be destroyed.
>
> *(A headline above this box read NOT MUCH INTEREST SHOWN and indicated the vote was 15 against and 7 for)*

---

[4] Bruce Ferguson and Martha Daugherty

[5] *Walton Advertiser*, Jan. 16, 1936.
[6] *Boone County Recorder*, Jan. 30, 1936, 1.
[7] Harrison & Klotter, 345.

Lodge supper at Petersburg. Courtesy of Mary Rector

the dark of movie theaters was just as suspicious.

Motorcars

Improving roads for rapidly growing numbers of motorcars was a top political priority. Roads had three ruts, one from the horses' hooves and two on either side of that from wagon, cart or carriage wheels. In 1930, 47.6 percent of state funds were spent on constructing rural roads and replacing old macadamized road surfaces with asphalt.

The number of vehicles on the roads was multiplying dramatically. Nationally, 1.5 million passenger cars and 305,142 trucks were produced in 1919. Burlington's W.L. Kirkpatrick advertised Maxwells for $985 in 1920.[8]

Otho "Coonie" Hubbard of Union recalled his father buying a used Model T in 1920, paying a little over $300. By 1924, starters and batteries were optional equipment on new cars – selling for $12. Hand-operated windshield wipers were standard.[9]

In 1938, Al Jeager of Independence sold used cars: '29 Ford Coach $95, '31 Chevrolet Coupe $125, '34 Ford Sedan Deluxe $225, '37 Dodge Coach $495, or '37 Plymouth Deluxe Coach $525.[10] The county clerk collected a $25 registration fee.[11]

Automobiles were showing their limitations. This item appeared on the front page of the Jan. 8, 1920, *Recorder*: "*Joseph Hogan, mother and sister, Miss Loretta, of the Hebron neighborhood, got stranded on the Walton hill on the Burlington and Belleview Pike, last Friday night. Their machine had refused to pull the hill and they had to send for relief. Newton York of Burlington responded to their call. It was a very uncomfortable situation as a stiff wind was blowing and the mercury was traveling towards the zero mark pretty rapidly.*"

A front page *Recorder* story on Oct. 28, 1920, told of G.S. Marksbery of Florence and Mr. Adams who had been checking on some trucks and machinery Marksbery owned and stored east of Florence. About 1 a.m. they

---

[8] *Boone County Recorder*, Jan. 8, 1920, 1.
[9] Ann Fillmore, editor, *A Peek Into the Past*, (Ryle High School, Gray Middle School and New Haven Elementary, Windmill, Mt. Vernon, Ind., 1998) 77.

[10] *Walton Advertiser*, Dec. 22, 1938, 6.
[11] *Boone County Recorder*, Nov. 25, 1920, 1.

B.C. Kirtley crossing a creek in 1918. Photo by Mrs. Bessie Kirtley. Courtesy of Barbara Fallis

heard someone trying to crank up a Ford. They went out to help Floyd Read and William Brassle get a car back on the road and running. The next morning, they discovered the vehicle – belonging to Carl Anderson – had come from Hugh Carey's barn.

Sheriff Conner and Deputy Hume caught the thieves who admitted to also stealing another vehicle in Grant County and several additional attempts in Boone. The car, which had been sold to a Cincinnati saloonkeeper, was returned and the car-theft ring dismantled.

Another *Recorder* article on Nov. 11, 1920 said that around the nation an auto accident took a life every 31 minutes. *"Why should there be so much of haste, and so little of care? Drivers of cars in congested districts and pedestrians both are to blame. . . ."*

General stores had barrels of 15-cent-a-gallon gas, which was run into a bucket, then poured into the vehicle. Opening the gas tank required removing the front seat, filling the tank under it, then reinstalling the seat.[12]

Eight-Passenger Bus

While school buses had operated for some time, passenger buses arrived in Boone County in 1921. The first held six passengers, three on each side facing each other. Next came seven-passenger Studebakers, then a 13-passenger bus with three doors on the side.

Two buses ran north each day and two ran south. Grant Countian Mr. McMillan drove an eight-passenger bus through Walton on a daily trip to Pike and Madison in Covington, returning late in the afternoon carrying people who worked in town, said Wilford Rice. The vehicle didn't have a reputation for comfort.

"Going over the pike, which was not paved, the passengers were like rocks in a box, falling all over the bus and each other, resembling some of the rides at Coney Island. After a few months, Jewett and Prather from Williamstown started a bus line using seven passenger cars which were not so bad, except when it was overloaded and you had to let someone sit in your lap.

"One nice feature was if they arrived in front of your house in the morning and you were not quite ready, they would wait for you. Nobody minded, for they might be late the next morning. The same passengers were regular riders." If a tire blew, all the men on the bus got out to help.

---

[12] Fillmore, 78.

Chapter 11   1920-1939   A Flood Change

"What a time we had! If there were only a few aboard we would stop at one of the barbecue stands for a sandwich, sing and have fun."[13]

Boone County native and local congressman Arthur B. Rouse purchased the Dixie Traction Co. of Erlanger and bought more modern buses. Greyhound took over about 1930 and doubled the price of a ride to the bus depot in Cincinnati to $1.

Beacon Light

Technology was flying over Boone County as well. By 1937, 88 Kentuckians held pilots' licenses. In 1932, the U.S. Commerce Department constructed a 100-acre landing field west of Warsaw in Gallatin County as an emergency field between Cincinnati and Louisville. A 23" rotating beacon light was erected on a steel tower south of the field.

To aid night flying, another beacon light was placed in Boone County on a high point between Union and Beaver Lick on US 42. The huge searchlight became a landmark, and later "The Beacon Light Motel" kept the name alive.

Barnstormers landed planes, often WWI "Jennies," and gave rides to those willing to invest $5 or $10 for a bird's eye view of their homeland.

In the 1920s, small aircraft flew a line between Cincinnati and Louisville. A small airplane landed near Union. A crowd quickly gathered at the landing site. The pilot offered to take Mrs. Bessie Baker, an older woman, on a free flight. She took him up amidst cheers from the crowd! He offered to take anyone interested in a ride up for $5.[14]

Women Get the Vote

Another change was in the air. On Jan. 6, 1920, Kentucky had become one of only four Southern states to ratify the 19th Amendment, allowing women to vote that November.[15]

On Oct. 28, 1920, a front page note in the *Recorder* said some women weren't going to vote because they didn't want to be placed on the list of potential jurors. *"Do not think you can avoid jury service by not exercising the right of suffrage that has been conferred upon you. Do not shirk this responsibility. Exercise your right and vote."*

Speaking to a crowd of 600 at a Democratic rally at Florence Fairgrounds, Sen. John Beckham (governor 1900-1907, senator 1914-1921) admitted voting against suffrage twice. He had believed *"the good and noble women of Kentucky did not want this added responsibility and would not exercise the rights of suffrage."* He was now of the opinion that *"the good women of Kentucky would be at the polls protecting their state and country by their votes."* [16]

Robert Mosby Wilson, a Rabbit Hash farmer who traded livestock and served two

---

> **Boone County Recorder**
> November 25, 1920
> ## New Equality Bill is Feared.
> Columbus, Ohio – Announcement from Cleveland of the election to a lawmakers seat of Harry E. Davis, Cleveland negro lawyer, came as a shock today to Republican leaders. They had hope that all six black candidates had been buried by the voters and that they would have a 100 percent white General Assembly.
>
> Ostensibly, the organization in the various counties supported the negro candidates, but secret orders to knife them went out and in a number of places tickets were issued in which the negroes specially were marked as "black." In the heaviest Republican districts the negroes generally ran worst. In Cleveland, Davis's election is attributed to the similarity of his name to that of the Governor elect, Harry L. Davis. The same mistake in identity was held to be responsible for his nomination, voters not discriminating carefully.
>
> The reason for lack of joy in political circles is the threatened revival of the negro issue, which was made acute last year by the Beaty bill to compel all keepers of public places, under heavy penalties, to grant full equality to members of the negro race. This measure was stifled in the Senate after it had passed the House.
>
> For social reasons the Republican leaders, profiting by the negro solidarity, have not desired this issue to appear again. The negroes themselves are divided into two factions, one favoring the bill as being necessary for "the rights of our people," while another faction thinks that the true position of the negro race is in a state of dependency on the whites as a sort of subject race, with minor political, but no social rights accorded to it.

---

[13] Wilford M. Rice and William Fitzgerald, "Walton Established in 1840." *Boone County Recorder*, Jan. 2, 1964.

[14] Roter, 183.
[15] Harrison & Klotter, 289.
[16] *Boone County Recorder*, Oct. 28, 1920.

terms as a state representative, was another staunch Democrat who opposed women's suffrage. He found another reason: *"Women are not taxed for poll tax and they should help pay the expense of running county affairs to help build roads and schools."*[17]

The new female voters were already having an influence. Women largely supported a League of Nations, believing it was the only possible road to world peace. *"Men fully appreciate that 93 percent of all Federal appropriations are made for war. . . . But to women of America, disarmament does not mean so much a saving in money. It means that by every gun, every battleship, every piece of fighting machinery we scrap, by just so much have we reduced the chances of war, and that is what American women, and women all over the world, want."*[18]

Changes for Women

While men had always attended lodge and club meetings, not until 1926 did eight women form the Boone County Women's Club "for fellowship and education." By 1930, the club included 25 women who were musicians, dramatic readers, writers and amateur poets. An organization for women was new – as was any step out of traditional boundaries.

A gathering of women
Courtesy of Virginia Lainhart

In 1936, Walton had a Woman's Literary Club. During the February meeting at Mrs. Sidney Gaines' home on South Main Street, Mrs. J.C. Bedinger reviewed a story of a foreigner becoming a U.S. citizen.

Statewide, working women received $.87 per day while men averaged $1.63. By 1930, almost nine of every 10 women remained outside the organized work force.

The only accepted career for women remained school teaching. Often that job ended with marriage, either because the woman followed tradition and quit working outside the home, or because she was fired outright as soon as the schoolboard discovered her marriage.

Betty Weaver Roter of Union wrote of a Southern Boone County school classmate in the '20s who may have been one of the more radical women seen here:

"Della Mae Booth was a very rebellious member of the student body, flaunting her rebellion with a man's haircut, by dressing mannishly, smoking, and racing around horseback in jodhpurs – considered unthinkable in that day and time."

Despite her scandalous and talk-provoking teen-age behavior, she later "succeeded" in a conventional way, marrying Ivan Clements, son of a Big Bone Baptist deacon, 'Nase' Clements. *"Della Mae and Ivan were parents of Nathan Clements, who achieved love and admiration from wide areas as a Baptist minister, for a brief period at the old Beaver Lick Baptist Church."*[19]

Dinsmore Heir Excells

Granddaughter of James Dinsmore, Isabella Selmes Ferguson, like the Dinsmore women before her, had broken out of many molds restricting her gender. In 1918, she had been appointed chairwoman of the New Mexico Chapter of the Women's Land Army, an organization founded to encourage women to take the places of drafted farmers during WWI. Her husband died in 1922, leaving Isabella with two children, Martha and Robert Ferguson.

The next year Isabella married John Campbell Greenway, vice president of the Calumet and Arizona Mining Company in Santa Barbara, Calif. Their son, John Selmes Greenway, was born in 1924. Two years later

---

[17] *Boone County Recorder*, 1930 Historical Edition.
[18] *Boone County Recorder*, Oct. 20, 1920.

[19] Roter, 372.

the senior Greenway died of gall bladder surgery complications. Also in 1926, Julia Dinsmore died on the Boone County farm. The property passed to her niece, Sally Cutcheon.

In 1928, Isabella Greenway was elected Democratic National Committeewoman for Arizona. She was re-elected in 1932. In 1933, she was elected to fill an unexpired congressional term – becoming the first woman from Arizona to serve in Congress. She was re-elected in 1934, but chose not to seek re-election in 1936.

In 1939, Isabella married Harry O. King, president of the Institute of Applied Econometrics, with whom she had worked in Congress to write the Copper Code. During WWII, Isabella was National Chairwoman of the American Women's Voluntary Service and the American Arbitration Association. Although she remained a friend of President Franklin D. Roosevelt, she strongly opposed his re-election to a third term in 1944.

Social Changes

Contentious issues just kept arising. In March 1922, an anti-evolution bill was defeated by one vote in the Kentucky legislature. University of Kentucky educator John T. Scopes was the center of attention in the 1926 "Monkey Trial" in Dayton, Tenn. Anti-evolution bills reappeared in 1926 and 1928 General Assembly.[20]

The Roaring 20s encouraged bootlegging businesses that always had prospered in Boone County, but the gambling and prostitution that followed seemed to stay in Kenton County.[21]

In 1936, Kentucky took a first step toward providing social services. The legislature passed an old age pension law providing a $15 per month stipend for the needy over 65 years old. The state's estimated annual cost was $3 million.[22]

Gov. Happy Chandler – a charismatic politician well known to many Boone Countians – made the old age pension law in 1936. His race up the political ladder began with election to state senator. He moved to lieutenant governor then governor – all before he turned 37. Chandler later served as U.S. Senator, again as governor, then baseball commissioner.

Osborn's store in Florence readies for Christmas 1934. Owner Ed Osborn is behind the counter with Ardelle Fox and Mary Roberts and an unknown shopper. Courtesy of Virginia Osborn Lainhart

On the *Recorder*'s Oct. 28, 1920 front page, a few inches from comments about suffrage was this article: *"The colored candidate for member of the school board in Louisville refuses to quit the race, giving as his reason that his people represent about one-fourth of the Republican vote in Louisville and they were entitled to representation on the school board and proposed to have it."*[23]

In 1936, President Roosevelt won re-election, carrying 46 states. Boone County's

---

[20] Harrison & Klotter, 346-347.
[21] Bruce Ferguson

[22] *Walton Advertiser*, Feb. 20, 1936, 1.
[23] *Boone County Recorder*, Oct. 28, 1920.

vote was: Roosevelt 2,761; Landon 1,036; Lemke, 79.[24]

First Park

The county's first park appeared in this era. Emily Hughes Cleek and her husband Jacob, a dentist, donated a strip of land between the new U.S. 42 and the old turnpike for a park (the corner of Richwood Road and 42). The Works Progress Administration and the Civilian Conservation Corps planted pine trees there.

The wealthy and well-respected Cleeks lived on Richwood Farm. Active in the parent teacher organizations although she had no children, Mrs. Cleek hosted community meetings at her home and ran what was nearly a private social service agency. "Miss Emily," a big imposing woman, had helped bring the first home demonstration agent to Boone County. After homemaker clubs were established in the late '30s, they added shrubs, trees and flowers to the little park. The state contributed picnic tables, grills and comfort stations and it became the first state park in Northern Kentucky.

Victrola Arrives

More entertainment forms were appearing. Winter evening entertainment for many families, like the Joe Weavers in Union, had meant reading aloud. Then an aunt from Cincinnati brought a Victrola, just like the ones popularized in advertisements showing a little white dog listening intently to a large horn.

"Records were small tubes about the size and shape of a biscuit can in today's grocery cool section," recalled Betty Weaver Roter. *"That Victrola was a huge monstrosity sitting on top of Mother's sewing machine. But it was a novelty. And we kids wound it up by the crank on the side and played it a lot till something better came along, even though the outdated, poorly recorded songs weren't too enjoyable to hear."*[25]

Crystal Radio

An extraordinary craftsman and mechanic, Betty's husband Raymond built his family's first radio. His Beaver Lick neighbors came to enjoy the new invention.

The son of the aunt and uncle who brought the Victrola soon presented Betty's father with a crystal set – an early radio. *"It was tedious to tune something in and required a lot of time and patience. I liked to tinker with it, and with the earphones clamped tightly, and by maneuvering that cat-whisker just so on the crystal, I was able to hear a man singing in Pittsburgh! It was* (clear channel) *radio station KDKA.*

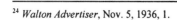
Betty Roter
Courtesy of Betty Roter

"Next we had a real radio. It wasn't pretty, just a long, black, box-looking object – not near as attractive as those shaped like a cathedral window. But it proved to be very entertaining and truly demonstrated how useful radio would become.

"To operate, it required a storage battery like the ones used in cars. Every so often, we had to take the battery to a filling station for a recharge. A table with shelves to hold the battery was brought from Grandma Adams' house.

"This radio provided our entertainment when Lum 'n Abner, Fibber McGee and

---

[24] *Walton Advertiser*, Nov. 5, 1936, 1.

[25] Roter, 161.

Florence High School students in about 1928 Back row: George Miller, Lawrence L. Aylor, Virgil L. Kelly, Bill Scott, Mason Schlader, John G. Laulusch, Lewis Higgins, Robert Tanner, Robert L. Aylor. Middle row: Lorraine Osborn Dahli, Mrs. Flossie Campbell Martin (teacher), Evelyn Tanner, Lucille Taylor Stephens, Dorothy McHenry, Dorothy Zimmerman Byland, Hazel Satchwell Tanner, Zellna Lee Odgen, Cora Wessler, Principal A.M. Yealey. Front row: Mary Higgins White, Jessie Lucas, Marjorie McKebben, Evelyn Aylor, Catherine Bethel Aylor, Lula Easton Tanner, Dorothy Sullivan Fichlie, Helen Ellrott Collins. Courtesy of Helen Collins.

Molly, George Burns and Gracie Allen, The Fred Allen Show, and the Jack Benny Show were such fun. My dad arranged his barn chores so he could get to the house in time for our favorite programs.

"In the morning, everyone got off to a better start after listening to Mrs. Cadle sing, 'Ere you left your room this morning, did you think to pray?' Afterwards, her husband, E. Howard Cadle, preached a brief (Methodist) *sermon. They did the broadcast from The Cadle Tabernacle in Indianapolis, Indiana. Years later, after my father died, Raymond and I took my mother to visit the tabernacle, because the program had always meant so much to her.*

"That radio was a valued piece of equipment at our house in January 1937. When the Great Flood took away all electric power, battery radios and kerosene lamps were premium property.... Mother and I sat glued in front of our radio to hear news about the flood, calls for help, and rescue efforts. In the midst, our battery was growing weak, but we hated to part with it for the time necessary to recharge. So we just sat closer and strained our ears for news."

Since electricity hadn't come to Fowler Creek Road, the radio remained a source of entertainment. *"Life would never be the same as it had been before the advent of radio. On its heels, television was born and became the focal avenue of entertainment."*

Mrs. Lee Besterman owned the first television in Beaver. Raymond and Betty

Roter, as well as other neighbors, gathered at Besterman's to watch wrestling matches.[26]

Schools

While Betty and Sarah Weaver taught school as teen-agers, they attended summer classes at Richmond working on their college degrees. Kentucky high school teachers were not required to hold college degrees until 1935, and it was another 25 years before elementary teachers met that requirement. The Kentucky Education Association had organized in 1907, so teaching jobs were no longer always the result of political patronage.

Donated books, magazines, shelves and a "neatly varnished reading table" began a library at the Florence high school in late 1920.[27]

The lack of standards and meager teacher salaries gave Boone County schools such poor reputations that during the war students often lived with relatives so they could attend school elsewhere. School enrollment began declining in 1936, but a decade later, the postwar boom started an upswing in student population that is still climbing.[28]

In the late 1920s, citizens donated beef and other foods to prepare hot lunches for Boone County schoolchildren. Parents operated the lunchrooms.

Public Health

In November 1925, Eunie B. Willis began inspecting school children, "*notifying parents of defects found and personally urging medical advice and care. 'Sometimes I met with resentment on the part of the parents saying I was interfering with their private affairs,'*" Willis said in an article in the *Recorder*.

Boone County's first one-woman health department focused on educating citizens about the need for health care. Using $3,000 left over from Red Cross war drives and working out of her home, Willis spoke at churches, parent-teacher associations and mothers' meetings, and gave demonstrations in schools.

After nearly five years, parents began seeking her out for advice. In that time, 856 "physical defects" thought "*to be disease-producing*" were addressed. Willis estimated "*the county folks have been saved $80,484, not speaking of the cost of heartaches, anguish and disrupted homes which illness exacts.*"

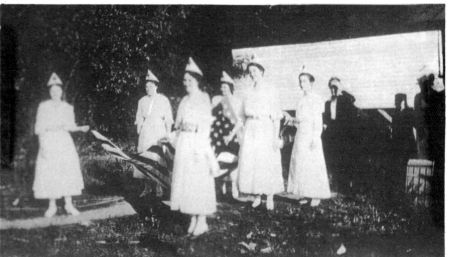

Mrs. Bessie Kirtley labeled this 1917 photo she took "Red Cross girls at Rabbit Hash." Courtesy of Barbara Fallis

Willis offered baby and pre-school clinics in her second year, recruiting physicians and child specialists from Covington and Cincinnati who donated their services. She placed four crippled children "*in the hospitals provided by the State Crippled Children's Commission and the Shriners.*"

In 1928, Willis attended a Colorado course to teach home hygiene for the sick. After returning, she attempted to have the course included as a requirement for high school girls who would, of course, become mothers and homemakers.

When war funds ran out, Willis met with

---
[26] Roter, 164.
[27] *Boone County Recorder*, Nov. 11, 1920.
[28] *175th Anniversary Historical Book*, 38.

Chapter 11 1920-1939 A Flood Change

the fiscal court requesting funding annually. *"Each request has been met with a unanimous vote from the court for the appropriation necessary. . . They know the worth of the Red Cross Nursing Service.* The national Red Cross recognized Willis' work in rural health care by sending a Filipino nurse to learn from her in 1929.[29]

Santa Claus Fund

A mysterious "Santa Claus Fund" paid the Red Cross to distribute baskets of necessities and small luxuries to the less fortunate. The *Recorder* disclosed that its benefactors were Alvin Boyers Renaker (Renneckar in German), his wife the former Henrietta E. Riddell and their daughter Mary Louise Renaker.

Son of the Dry Ridge Deposit Bank president, Renaker was cashier of Boone County's largest bank, Peoples Deposit of Burlington, at the age of 22. In November 1905, his salary was $70 a month, a higher wage than usually paid. He had worked without pay at the Dry Ridge bank for six months before that, a common apprenticeship practice.

As a sideline, Renaker ran a real estate business and managed a 127-acre farm. During the War, he was treasurer of the Boone County Red Cross, treasurer of the State Bankers Association and oversold the bank's quota of Liberty Bonds and War Savings Stamps.

He donated land for the Missionary Baptist Church and substantially contributed to the building fund. An automobile hobbyist, his first car, bought in 1911, was the second in Burlington. Described as one who loved country life, Renaker had been courted by big city banks but declined their offers.[30]

Farming

Even though agricultural extension agents were active in most places by the 1920s, farming of all kinds still remained almost unchanged from decades earlier.[31]

Kentuckians spent only 1 percent of their farm income on fertilizer in 1929 (versus 2.3 percent in Indiana) and only 2.8 percent of the farms had a tractor a year later (versus the national average of 13.5 percent).

Using machinery, farmers could produce 50 bushels of oats with one day (10 hours) of labor, versus the six bushels, one-ninth as much, in 1830.[32]

Mary Louise Renaker
Recorder, 1930 Historical Edition
Courtesy of Ruth Green

Nationwide, with no war machine to feed, farm products were glutting the market. By 1933, farmers were killing pigs and dumping milk rather than lose money selling their products at extremely low prices. Pork, beef, and corn prices fell and stayed low until President Roosevelt established the Farmer's Home Administration, Civilian Conservation Corps, Agricultural Stabilization and Conservation Service and the Federal Department of Agriculture.[33]

Modern improvements arrived slowly on Boone County farms. While the number of Kentucky farms lighted by electricity doubled in the twenties – from 2.2 percent to 4.3 percent – that figure lagged behind the U.S. percent of 13.4.[34]

By 1920, silos were catching on. *"A few years ago, you could count the silos in this county on one hand. Today there are real numbers of them as it has been proven that silage affords not alone the most economical*

---

[29] *Boone County Recorder*, 1930 Historical Edition.
[30] *Boone County Recorder*, 1930 Historical Edition.

[31] Klotter, 245.
[32] *Boone County Recorder,* Nov. 25, 1920, 1.
[33] Bruce Ferguson
[34] Klotter, 245.

feeding for the winter, but also gives the stock more real benefit with little of the feed wasted."[35]

By 1938, the Rural Electrification Association was signing up more outlying residents. Rev. Will Smith of Burlington said lines would be extended throughout Boone County as soon as an average of three customers a mile could be secured. Local volunteers signed up new members and secured right-of-way easements.[36]

The Kentucky Agricultural Experiment Station in Lexington warned farmers to vaccinate their pigs to prevent hog cholera from killing their entire herd. Low hog prices and the depressing economic state prompted many not to invest in vaccines, creating conditions in which the disease could spread rapidly.[37]

Sixty percent of treated hogs recovered from the disease. Ninety percent of hogs lost from all ailments died of cholera. In 1916, Kentucky losses totaled $1.5 million, by 1918 that had been cut by two-thirds.

The state veterinarian also noted that tuberculosis affecting 8 percent of Kentucky's children originally came from cows.[38]

Boone's dairy herds received considerable recognition. The Kite and Purdy Beech Grove Dairy Farm set a record for producing 54 pounds of butterfat from the 12-cow herd, but only nine were lactating. Assistant County Agent David Colville attributed the record to carefully culling cows and feeding balanced rations.[39]

O.R. Russ' nine-cow Jersey herd produced an average of 590 pounds (74¾ gallons) of milk per cow with 30.1 pounds of butterfat. P.B. Gaines' 57 cows averaged 727 pounds of milk per cow and 39.4 pounds of butterfat, leading the state for the month.

Walter Robinson and Sons poultry flock of Rabbit Hash produced 8,385 eggs from 573 hens in January 1936, an average of 14.5 eggs per hen. Grant Maddox's 996 hens produced 11,608 eggs, an average of 11.65 each at his farm near Florence.[40]

Putting up a silo. Courtesy of Mary Sue Rudicill

4-H and Extension Service

The federal government created a subtle way to reach farmers and homemakers who weren't aware or focused on using new and improved methods – 4-H Clubs. Kentucky was one of the first states to offer them. Boone County's were organized in about 1925. At the time, 4-H – which stands for Head, Heart, Hands and Health – was the largest youth organization in the world, committed to its members' educational, economic, social and recreational advancement.

Sponsored by the Cooperative Extension Service under the federal Department of Agriculture, 4-H Clubs taught kids a new agricultural or home economic technique. They then went home and practiced it,

---

[35] *Boone County Recorder*, Oct. 28, 1920.
[36] *Walton Advertiser*, Dec. 22, 1938, 1.
[37] *Boone County Recorder*, March 30, 1922, 1.
[38] *Boone County Recorder*, Jan. 8, 1920, 1.

[39] *Boone County Recorder*, Feb. 4, 1937, 1.
[40] *Boone County Recorder*, Jan. 18, 1936.

piquing the curiosity of their parents.

In Union, 4-H leader Mrs. Mills, who lived in the Ada Sanders' house near the Union Baptist Church with her daughter Louise (called Cindy), helped each 4-H member sew an unbleached muslin apron with the 4-H emblem on its bib.

In 1930, Boone County had 1,563 farms and 93.2 percent of the county was still farmland. Nevertheless, 1932 was the last year for the Florence Fair. The grounds were turned into an amusement park with Tom Thumb golf courses, carnivals, picnics, boxing and other events. A dance hall there known as Dixie Park offered square and round dancing, a juke box and big band sound.

One-day fairs continued from 1933-35. Success moved them to the Harvest Home

Bobby McClelland and John M. Baker started farming in 1932. John's father, Hubert Baker was principal at Walton and New Haven schools.
Courtesy of Linda B. Green

grounds off Limaburg Road in 1936. Activities, awards and contests were listed in a 26-page catalog. Popular bands, like the Old Kentucky Fiddlers and the Papaw Knockers, performed without charge. Then the Harvest Home location was sold and one-day fairs were held on the Burlington School grounds.[41]

But the weeklong fair soon would be revived in Burlington by the 4-H and Utopia Clubs. In 1933, about 500 young men and women between 15 and 21 belonged to a dozen 4-H and Utopia Clubs. Utopia Clubs were organized in about 1930 to include youth 19 or older who were interested in agriculture and home economics. Although 4-H membership ended at 19, there was no age limit for Utopia members.

Tobacco Inflation

European demand during war years had encouraged American farmers to plow every inch of tillable soil. Tobacco went from 12.5 cents a pound in 1914[42] to 34 cents in 1919 for the state's largest-ever crop.[43]

Delighted with their profits, burley farmers plowed ahead into 1920. A poor harvest, a glutted market and a decline in overseas demand brought average Kentucky tobacco prices to 13.4 cents. In 1921, tobacco prices fell to one-seventh the previous level. Politicians and agricultural leaders feared a recurrence of the Black Patch Wars little more than a decade before. A new Burley Tobacco Growers Cooperative was formed.

Pooling brought 1922 prices up to 28.4 cents a pound. But independent farmers, often impatient and strapped for money, could not remain united. The next year, with only 71 percent of the crop in the pool, prices fell to 21 cents. By 1926, with the majority of farmers outside the association, prices tumbled again, to 12.5 cents.[44]

The Tobacco Control Act of 1934 recognized the overproduction problem and

---

[41] Conrad, William, "Conrad chronicles Boone County fair," *Recorder Newspapers*, 1995 Boone County Fair Guide, 22, 24.

[42] Klotter, 239.
[43] Harrison & Klotter, 295.
[44] Klotter, Portrait in Paradox, 128-129.

allowed growers to vote for mandatory quotas in exchange for federal minimum price guarantees. In 1936, Kentucky farmers reduced tobacco production by 28 percent, increasing their income by several million dollars.[45] Radio and magazine advertising and the romantic image of smoking in talking pictures likely contributed to a 75 percent national consumption increase between 1939 and 1945.[46]

In 1938, while 82 percent of Boone County's farmers voted for burley quotas, nationally the referendum lost by less than four percent of the two-thirds majority required in votes taken in the 15 tobacco producing states.[47]

Hog killing in Boone County. Courtesy of Ruth Glenn Meadows

Farm Communities

While living on a farm could be isolating, traditions born before mechanization brought rural residents together. A group of neighbors could do in one day what might take one family a week or more working independently.

As well as lightening the workload, the gatherings lightened the mood, offering time to joke, gossip, talk politics and catch up on others' news and views.

Even more so than they do today, these activities always included a big meal. Menus were often traditional, like fresh meat on butchering day or chicken soup after corn cutting.

Former Union/Beaver resident Betty Roter describes the infinite details of these events of her youth in her book *White Kittens and Four-Leaf Clovers*.

Hog Killing

The day before hog killing was as busy as the day itself, she said. The outdoor firepit was cleaned, then filled with firewood and more was stacked nearby to add, along with kindling wood. *"Then the long, deep hog-box that had lain upside down in the grass for a year was turned right side up and placed over the fire pit."* Water was hauled in barrels to fill the box.

"Two fork-topped poles were set in the ground to support a long pole." There the hogs would be hung after scalding. Long, thick boards set on sawhorses made the cutting-up table. Another table was set up for rubbing the hams and shoulders with salt, pepper, brown sugar and saltpeter before they were hung in the meat house. Butcher knives were sharpened.

"Inside the house, my mother had cooked green beans and potatoes with ham, soaked prunes for cooking, roasted a large cut of beef, baked pies, cakes, light bread and made all her cooking plans for the day ahead. In addition, she had scrubbed the lard press and sausage mill that had been stored away for a year."

She made sure the large iron lard kettle, used for heating wash water in summer, was clean. All the five-, two- and one-gallon lard crockery jars and galvanized tubs were washed. She also sewed slender cotton sacks for stuffing with sausage.

"By two or three a.m. on that crisp, chilling morning, my father and mother were up and going. The first thing in order was

---

[45] Harrison & Klotter, 297.
[46] Harrison & Klotter, 298.
[47] *Walton Advertiser*, Dec. 22, 1938, 1.
*Zella Hale Weyant, *ABC of Canning*, n.p., n.d.

lighting the fire under the hog box. While my mother cooked breakfast, Dad did the barn chores." Then he separated the hogs to be slaughtered.

"One of the first men to arrive was the sharp shooter with his rifle. One by one the neighbor men arrived, some with wives accompanying." Those who helped the Joe Weaver family were Emerson Smith (the rifleman), Arch Rouse, Lute Bradford, Joe Wilson, Harry Wilson, Robert Wilson, Ab Robbins, Lloyd Gulley, Henry Beil, George Smith, Will Smith, Cooney Schwybold and Lewis Weaver.

Roter remembered Carrie Bradford in particular because she taught *"me how to scrape the small intestines to make casings for sausage. Fannie Wilson always mixed the sausage and seasonings by hand in a galvanized tub."*

The 200- to 300-pound hog was killed by a shot in the middle of the forehead. Then four men carried it by its legs to the scalding box. *"The hog was sloshed in the scalding water and (removed, then) most of the hair scraped off. A short, stout stick, pointed at each end, was thrust between the cartilages of one hind foot, placed over the readied pole, . . . then thrust through the other hind foot. This kept the body hanging just right for deft, quick hands to continue scraping till the skin was (completely) free of hair and ready for the next step. Meanwhile, other men were scalding another hog."*

The organs were removed quickly and precisely before the hog cooled. Then the carcass was taken to the cutting-up table. There the head, feet, hams, shoulders, ribs, backbone and slabs of fat meat for bacon were cut off. Sometimes the backbone was split in half to make pork chops. Some men shaped and trimmed hams and shoulders, cutting fat and lean strips for lard or sausage. After trimming, the hams were taken to the meat house and rubbed. *"My father always liked to do this himself for he knew just how much and where to apply it to achieve the taste the family preferred."*

Dinner was somewhat timed by the separation of the edible organs. *"Mother always made a delicious stew for the meal, cooking together small chunks of heart, melt (kidneys) and liver and making fluffy dumplings to float in the thick, luscious gravy. The men liked it. Work never stopped, dinner was sandwiched in-between."*

After everyone ate, lean scraps were ground into sausage. In a galvanized mixing tub *"salt, pepper and sage were added until patties fried and tasted were pronounced just right."* Then the sausage was stuffed into the cotton sacks or transparent casings that had been prepared from small intestines.

Men emptied and washed the intestines before bringing them to the women in the house to finish cleaning. *"In pans of cool water they were scraped of all outside coating, then slipped over a dull silver knife blade to turn them inside out for scraping the inner portion. When finished, the casing was thin and transparent, yet strong enough to withstand the pressure while being stuffed. The stuffing was done using an attachment to the lard press.*

"By this time, the men at the cutting table had chopped all the surplus fat scraps into small bits ready for the lard kettle. A fire underneath the large black iron kettle soon had the fat pieces cooking and steaming. One particular neighbor always tended the lard kettle because of his earned reputation: knowing just when the liquid fat was

---

Directions for Making Head Cheese

Clean hog's head by removing snout, eyes, ears, brains and all skin. Trim off all fat. Cut head in four pieces and soak in salt water for 3 to 5 hours to draw out all blood. Drain from salt solution and wash well in clear water.

Hearts, tongues and other meat trimmings may be cooked with the head meat. Cover meat with hot water and boil until meat can be removed from bones. Remove all meat from bones. Strain broth and measure. Chop meat fine.

Add salt, pepper and spices to the meat and mix thoroughly with broth. Cook mixture 15 minutes. Pack into clean jars to within 1 inch of top. Put on cap, screwing band firmly tight. Process in pressure cooker 60 minutes at 15 pounds or 180 minutes in water bath.*

sufficiently cooked to produce snow-white lard. This man kept stirring with a long wooden paddle to prevent scorching. While he stirred the hot fat, the rest of the men sat around the woodpile on unsplit blocks of firewood, smoking, chewing tobacco, keeping warm by the fire under the lard kettle, helping replenish the fire now and then.

"When the expert lard cooker said it was just right, the hot liquid fat was dipped out and strained through white cotton cloth into black and white crockery jars." When cooled, it would be solid, but soft – ready for making biscuits, pie crusts, cakes and frying chicken, rabbit and squirrel.

The children's excitement was making "cracklings." *"Using the lard press to extract the last drop of liquid fat for lard, the cooked fat pieces were pressed down till all that remained were tasty, brittle morsels. Some of the crispy bits that we sorted out of the galvanized tub had streaks of lean meat. We hunted for them, they were the tastiest of the 'cracklings.'"*

Helpers were usually invited to take some of the pork with them. *"Most wanted a package of sausage. Someone might want a slab of ribs, a backbone, or maybe a liver. After the neighbors had taken their treats of fresh pork and scattered to their homes, then clean-up time began for Mom."*

Cleaning the kitchen, scrubbing the lard press, the sausage mill, tubs, and lard kettle took lots of hot, soapy water. *"Outside, Dad dismantled all of the things he'd built for the occasion and emptied the huge hog-box and turned it upside down. . . . All the portions of meat that couldn't be processed that day were put into tubs of cold water – the heads, ears, feet, livers, heart. That meant work for Mother for many days to come."*

In 1930, this sycamore tree on the Harmon Jones farm measured 37' 7" in circumference. *Boone County Recorder*, 1930 Historical Edition Courtesy of Ruth Glenn

Brains for Breakfast

"Our favorite meal from the entire hog-killing was breakfast the following morning. The brains, cleaned of blood and membranes till snowy white, were mixed with eggs and scrambled to make a gourmet feast. Fried 'sweetbreads' ran a close second.

"For long days after that, Mother worked diligently to prepare every remaining edible portion of the slaughtered hogs to be consumed later in the year. The feet, toes removed and remainder packed in jars and covered with vinegar, became 'pickled pigs feet' which I like even today – although those bought from a store cannot match the ones my mother made.

"Ears and part of the head meat (after some jowls were cut away for 'jowl bacon.') were cooked and made into 'souse' – head meat pressed into a crock to be sliced and eaten cold or fried. Head meat mixed with meal and fried was what we called 'pon haus.'

"Mother cooked heart chunks and made stews with dumplings. Fried liver and onions made many good meals. Some of the leanest head meat was mixed with raisins, currants, apples and spices to make mincemeat for pies. Delicious!

"The lean tenderloin strips were cut into serving-size pieces and put into glass jars and 'cold packed' – which meant immersing the sealed jars in water and boiling for several hours. This was done in an immense kettle or copper boiler. This canned meat was kept for use the following summer.

"The tongue made a delicious and unusual meat dish. Then there were meals of backbone, pig tails with sauerkraut, spare ribs, and porkchops. All through the year,

Mrs. Bessie Kirtley took these two photos of threshing wheat on the Kirtley farm in 1917.
Courtesy of Barbara Fallis

after Dad smoked them with hickory wood smoke, we ate delightful sugar-cured ham and shoulder slices, usually with eggs, and, of course, red eye gravy!

"It has been said many times, but it can well be repeated about my parents at hog killing time: Everything was used but the squeal!"[48]

The Weaver's custom was repeated with little variation around the county. In the Bullittsburg area, William Campbell said the tradition was that no one left the butchering place until all the supplies were cleaned and ready to move to the next farm. Five or six farmers whose land adjoined pooled their resources to acquire a scalding box, lard kettles, sausage mill, lard press, sausage stuffer, etc.

Campbell recalled that being allowed to go "*as a hand*" to help with a neighborhood hog killing was a maturity milestone for a young boy. Working together, in one day a crew could process enough pork to last a family for a year.

Threshing Time

The gatherings were repeated in the summertime when the wheat thresher arrived. Campbell recalled the unforgettable whistle attached to the huge, black, coal burning steam-engine that pulled the massive machine from farm to farm and powered the separator.

Threshing required teams with hay wagons and drivers from several farms. The roving machine operator took a percentage of grain or pay by the bushel for his machine's labors, but no other cash was required.

During these hot summer days, helpers drank liberally from ten-gallon milk cans filled with ice chunks and long-handled dippers. Some indulged so heavily in the expansive noon feasts that they didn't feel well afterwards.[49]

Corn Cutting

Corn cutting was a communal task of the autumn season. When the ears were full and dry, men gathered on moonlit nights bringing their sword-like corn knives. "*Several men working quickly could cut what would take my father many days to do. It worked fine if all the men were mature and careful. Younger ones sometimes came just for fun and cut the stalks too far from the ground, leaving much longer stubs than most farmers liked. But it was a neighborly, friendly gesture,*" Roter said.

Wives each brought cut up chicken or vegetables that were tossed into the huge cast iron lard kettle to make a steaming supply of chicken soup – ready for what turned into a neighborhood party.

Eventually, chicken soup parties were held without the corn cutting. Each family brought their own cups or bowls to eat from. With the

---

[48] Roter

[49] Campbell, 29.

Mrs. Bessie Kirtley took these photos of making sorghum molasses on the Kirtley farm in 1918.
Courtesy of Rabbit Hash Museum

November elections nearing, politics was the common discussion topic.[50]

Sorghum Making

Betty's father, Joe Weaver, grew sorghum cane to produce molasses in the early 1920s. *"When the tall stalks in the cane patch became mature in the fall, it was time to harvest them and prepare for making molasses. Sorghum stalks grow very much as corn, except no ears develop. Up and down the stalks are long, narrow blades – the leaves of such plants – and a bushy seedhead develops on top."*

After school, daughters Betty and Sarah helped strip the leaves. *"Father wouldn't allow us to cut down the stalks, which had to be done a few inches from the ground with a very sharp corn knife. The seed tops too were cut off, these and the blades became cow-feed. The stripped stalks were loaded on the wagon; everything was ready for molasses-making day.*

"Dad's cousin, Charlie Delph, had a sorghum-mill at his farm on Longbranch Road. Early the next morning, Dad hitched his mule-team, Jack and Judy, to the wagonload of cane and headed for the Delph farm."

After walking 1¼ miles home from school, the sisters changed clothes and rushed 1½ miles to Cousin Charlie's farm – afraid they'd miss molasses-making.

"When we got there, Old Judy, the patient one of the mule team, was walking – leaning out a bit dizzily – round and round in a circle" turning the sorghum mill. *"From the grinding, squeezing mill drained a dark, syrupy juice which was transferred to a large shallow pan with a fire underneath. The juice was stirred constantly as it boiled down to a dark, thick, slow-pouring molasses that we knew would taste delicious on top of Mother's light, fluffy, butter-spread biscuits."*[51]

Harmon Hayes Jones Family

Unlike the majority of Boone County farmers who farmed the land on which they were born – or bought farms adjoining their family property, the Harmon Hayes Jones family moved several times. After the Bullittsville man married Jennie Pearl Aylor, Jones moved from Constance to operate a farm near Union. Later, they moved to Gunpowder, where they lived for 10 years.

---

[50] Roter, 410-411.

[51] Roter, 142.

Mrs. Jones, who grew up on a farm, learned to ride early. The *Recorder* said, "*She was never defeated in any Fair in a contest for the quickest harnessing and hitching up of a horse. She also won many prizes in Kentucky, Indiana and Ohio as a champion lady rider. No lady in the county can surpass her record for prize-winning on cakes, rolls, bread, jellies, preserves, pickles and canned fruits. She also was the blue ribbon winner for being the best lady driver. She is one of the greatest Buff Rock chicken breeders in the country today.*"[52]

Virginia Jones with rooster
1930 Recorder Special Edition,
Courtesy of Ruth Glenn

Four children arrived between 1911 and 1920. The eldest, Ira Huey, won many county and state fair prizes for his registered Holstein heifer. Her milk-producing records surpassed all in the region and won Ira a free trip to the St. Louis Dairy Show.

Joseph H., the second son, earned a reputation at the fairs for showing Hampshire and Chester White hogs. As a freshman, he was also a gold medal winner in algebra in the county scholastic tournament.

Daughter Virginia Pearl was captain and star player for the Walton High School girls' basketball team. Also active in 4-H, she marketed certified golden buff Plymouth Rock chicks around the world.

Youngest son, Earl C. was just 10 years old when this account was written in 1930.[53]

Hot Lunches at Constance

While more were moving out of the county than around it like the Jones family, Boone County's northernmost riverfront community was growing. In the '20s, Constance's one-room schoolhouse that had been built on Henry Kottmyer Sr.'s property in 1868 gained another room and another teacher.

Ralph (R.V.) Lents came to teach at the newly enlarged school in 1920. The Western Kentucky native had married Mollie Newman from Union. She attended Union High School and Eastern State Teachers College at Richmond, then graduated from Murray State Teachers College.

Two rooms allowed Mollie to teach grades one through four and Ralph to teach grades five through eight. The frame building with a narrow hall housed a large bell that could be heard all over town. Two pot bellied coal stoves heated the school.[54]

Joseph Jones with prize pig
1930 Recorder Special Edition,
Courtesy of Ruth Glenn

The Lents' students won county scholastic tournaments for three consecutive years, gaining Constance recognition as one of the best schools in the county.

Students walked as much as two miles to school, bringing their own lunches. After a PTA was organized in the mid-1920s, annual oyster suppers helped raise money for a lunchroom, a new teacher and a brick three-room building by 1930. Oyster suppers were a common fund raiser. The delicacy was shipped from the coast to country stores in one-gallon tin buckets.

The Kottmyer family supplied most of the

---

[52] *Boone County Recorder*, 1930 Historical Edition.
[53] *Boone County Recorder*, 1930 Historical Edition.
[54] Conrad, Tour Through Northern Boone County, 8.

towns' needs. George W. Kottmyer bought the Constance General Store in 1922. It carried feed, hardware, notions, groceries and more. A machinist by trade, Kottmeyer was also the Constance postmaster and a member of the Masonic Lodge. George's brothers Ollie and Henry continued operating the Anderson Ferry, started by their great-grandfather in 1864, after their father Charles had retired. Charles died in 1921 at the age of 84.

Francesville Electric

West at Francesville, the Sand Run Baptist Church added a Delco electric system operated by an engine in the buggy house. Hanging light fixtures had mantles that were pumped up with air, then lit by turning a knob. *"When electricity came to town, we signed up and from then on, we had lights that we didn't have to take care of,"* said Vivian Blaker in the church history book.

The church also dug a cistern when members tired of carrying water. Some materials were donated, as was part of the labor. The pump cost $4. John Utzinger, Franklin Ryle and R.S. Wilson oversaw the work.[55]

Parlor Grove Orchard

Up toward the river, Charles O. Hempfling's apple variety called Big Red won many cups and ribbons at fairs and fruit shows. The family also brought the first extra-sweet "Delicious" apple varieties to Kentucky.

Eldest son C. Liston operated the Parlor Grove Farm while middle son Charlie managed Webb Hall. Daughter Anita Florence taught school in Boone County before marrying H.W. Bentham and moving to Baltimore where her husband was in the wholesale seafood business.

Hempfling designed an apparatus to spray insecticide on his trees. Since little was known of effective pesticides, they mixed lime, sulfur and salt creating a toxic substance that sometimes removed skin and fingernails as it was applied. Hempfling worked with the university experimental stations to refine the mixture.

Liston married Elizabeth Mae McGlasson, the daughter of William T. and Alice Quiggley McGlasson of Hebron, on June 9, 1915. A former schoolteacher, Elizabeth was the first woman juror to serve on a criminal case in Boone County circuit court.

In addition to managing an extensive dairy of 20 purebred Holsteins, Liston was interested in organizing farmers for mutual benefit.[56] In 1920, the senior Hempfling helped organize and was named chairman of the Burley Pool. As president of the Warehousing Corporation, he controlled 22 loose leaf houses in 11 counties in Northern Kentucky as well as a redrying plant at Carrollton. He also helped form the Boone County Farm Bureau.[57]

Liston Hempfling

Charles O. Hempfling, *1930 Recorder Special Edition*, Courtesy of Ruth Glenn

---

[55] Vivian Blaker, *Sand Run Baptist Church.*

[56] *Boone County Recorder,* 1930 Historical Edition.
[57] *Boone County Recorder,* 1930 Historical Edition.

Hebron

Hebron Deposit Bank opened in 1920 in a small shot-gun style building on Main Street. Capital stock was $20,000 and had increased to $30,000 within ten years. Joel C. Clore was elected president and John B. Cloud vice president.

Charles W. Riley, of the C.W. Riley family in Hebron, left his family farm to become the bank's cashier in December 1922. He replaced his father-in-law who was in ill health. Riley was elected the next year. After attending local schools, Riley went to Covington High School and Transylvania College in Lexington, then began studying law. Riley married Oma Hankins in 1910.[58]

Hebron native Chester Goodridge graduated from Burlington High School in 1920 and began teaching at Hebron Elementary. After the schools consolidated in 1925, he was principal of Hebron Consolidated from 1935 to 1954. Then he became principal of the first consolidated Boone County High School. In 1972, Goodridge, who died recently, completed 52 years of teaching at Conner Junior and Senior High Schools.

Fire protection arrived while Goodridge was elementary principal. Hebron's first fire chief, Earl Aylor, relied on a fire truck made from a Model T Ford bought for $25. With 21 volunteers, he began serving Hebron, Bullittsville, Idlewild, Petersburg, Constance and Taylorsport in 1937. James E. Hart donated land for a firehouse in 1945. Ambulance service began in March 1951.

The Conner family including Paul in the car and Marie and William.
Courtesy of Elizabeth Craig Stephens

Petersburg

Clinton Gibbs, an African American born in Petersburg on Aug. 8, 1891, the son of Francis and James Gibbs, grew up in Cincinnati and studied piano with teachers from the Cincinnati Conservatory of Music. He later taught music at several schools.[59]

Petersburg farmer Francis M. Voshell won recognition for the hogs he raised. In 1929, he raised a litter that at market time was second in the county in total weight and was recognized around the state. He also bred registered and grade Jersey cattle, milking 14 cows and raising their replacements.[60]

Belleview

Alpha Rogers was born near Belleview, attended high school across the river in Rising Sun and studied at Burlington's Morgan Academy under Henry Newton. After marrying Viola Huey who also grew up in Belleview, he began farming. In 1903, he purchased Belleview's General Store. He operated it for 13 years, then retired, selling to Robert Hensley.

Interested in politics and solicited to run

---

[58] *Boone County Recorder,* 1930 Historical Edition.

[59] Reis, Pieces of the Past, 13.
[60] *Boone County Recorder,* 1930 Historical Edition.

Leveling the bottom of the Dam #38 lock chamber on Oct. 8, 1921.

Pouring the upper arm of the foundation abutment for the dam on Aug. 1, 1921.

Driving piles for the upper guide wall and completed land wall forms on Aug. 15, 1922.
Photos courtesy of Sandra Rudicill Cupps

Chapter 11   1920-1939   A Flood Change

In the 1930s, the general store at Belleview/Grant sold regular gasoline and "ethyl" or high test from these pumps in front of the store.
Courtesy of Boone County Historic Preservation

several times, Rogers always declined. Active in the Belleview Baptist Church, he was a director of the Peoples Deposit Bank for several decades.

The Rogers' only child, James Edward, operated one of his father's three farms in the mid 1920s. James married Laura Whitenack of Harrodsburg and they had two boys. They raised hogs, corn, cattle and general farm produce on 135 acres.[61]

J.D. McNeely, a director of the Belleview bank, settled on a 50-acre tract along Gunpowder Creek given to him by his father-in-law. He and his wife, Fannie Ryle, turned the land into a profitable farm. Their five boys helped with livestock and tobacco. After the youngest moved away, McNeely purchased an 80-acre farm near Waterloo.[62]

In 1931, Belleview Baptist Church Sunday School began a baseball club that met on Sunday evenings, starting the Baptist Young Peoples Union. In 1932, one offering a month was set aside for poor relief. The church was insured for the first time that year. In '37, the church raised $17.17 for flood relief. The next year the church built a new "sanitary closet" or outhouse at a cost of $64.65. On May 1, an all-day service raised money for a new cemetery fence.[63]

McVille Lock & Dam # 38

The Ohio River's lock and dam #38 was built near McVille in 1924. Boone Countians welcomed the local construction jobs, although the dam flooded some farmland and a small island that many used for picnics and camping. (Markland Dam would replace it in 1962.)[64]

Pleasure boaters enjoyed "locking through" the dam on Sunday picnics or weekend camping trips. Teenagers spent hours watching boats go through the locks.

Mrs. Elizabeth Kirtley recalled President Hoover traveling down the Ohio in '28 or '29. Schoolchildren were bused over to see him pass through the locks. Because the day was rainy and dreary, the children were allowed to wait inside the powerhouse – a rare treat. The interior was seldom seen.[65]

Rabbit Hash

Down river, Rabbit Hash residents crossed the Ohio regularly. Whitlock Grocery in Rising Sun brought groceries across the river. Many Kentuckians worked in the Hoosier tomato cannery. James Wilson rowed women across the river to work and went back to pick them up.

Raymond Bedgood operated the ferry to Rising Sun from 1937-1945 when ferry service stopped for nearly 40 years.

Auctioneer Bluford C. Kirtley, the son of William and Missouri Kirtley of Rabbit Hash,

---

[61] *Boone County Recorder*, 1930 Historical Edition.
[62] *Boone County Recorder*, 1930 Historical Edition.
[63] *Belleview Baptist Church, 190th Anniversary*
[64] Lib Stephens, interview, Jan. 8, 1998.
[65] Elizabeth Kirtley interview.

had crossed to attend Rising Sun school. He married Christina Stephens of Grant (Belleview) and had three children Howard, Reuben and Marie. A 32nd degree Mason and a member of the Knights of Pythias Lodge, he was a member of the Boone County fiscal court from 1922 to 1930.[66]

A Ford Motor dealership sold new cars in Rabbit Hash in the 1920s – teaching new owners how to drive before they could leave the lot.

In the next decade, a creamery was located in the log building where the Kentucky Huckster gift shop is now. Lib Stephens' family collected cream, tested it, added lactic acid (to help preserve it without refrigeration), then took it to the Cincinnati Merchants Creamery to sell.

A huge scale located left of the store weighed wagon loads of coal as it was taken off barges and sold. Drivers drove the empty wagon on it, then filled it, reweighed and paid. Like much of Rabbit Hash, the creamery and the scales were eliminated in the '37 flood.[67]

Near Big Bone

In 1938, University of Kentucky scientists began excavating two prehistoric mounds found seven miles southwest of Union. One was in a cornfield, the other was covered with trees. Fort Ancient excavation of the Fort Ancient village began in the 1930s.

In 1929, a 34' x 50' brick church was built at Middle Creek. It was described as "quite substantial but poorly arranged." Brother Kirtley preached at Middle Creek the second and fourth Sundays and at Bullittsburg, Burlington and Big Bone.

Big Bone Baptist Pastor J.A. Miller was granted permission to raise tobacco on church grounds in 1921. That same year the church passed a resolution unanimously against Sunday baseball. Two years later, J.H. Broom took over as pastor for a salary of $1,200, but he resigned a month later without explanation.[68]

Two doors and two aisles at Big Bone Baptist separated the sexes. The men entered on the left, the women on the right, sitting on their respective sides.

Baptising day was an exciting event. Betty Roter remembered her mother packing basket lunches to eat in the grove behind the church.

Immersion took place in the Ohio River at Hamilton's Landing. "*Girls and women to be baptized dressed in white. The men and boys wore white shirts and dark trousers. The gathered crowd sang, 'Shall We Gather at the River?' There was a solemn, reverent prayer. The pastor walked into the river. The line of candidates followed, halting a few steps behind him. A few deacons waded in at each side of the line, to assist the baptized ones as they took slippery steps out of the water. As they emerged, women and girls were welcomed into Mrs. Bertha Huff's home to change into dry clothes. Men and boys went to Tom Huff's store to change. After singing*

Clayton Ryle, Wilford Aylor, Ivan Ryle, Lewis Stephens, Sheenie Craig and Russell Stephens. Courtesy of Elizabeth Craig Stephens

---

[66] *Boone County Recorder*, 1930 Historical Edition.
[67] Lib Stephens

[68] Big Bone Baptist Church, 27.

Chapter 11 1920-1939 A Flood Change

'Blest Be the Tie That Binds' and a benediction, the witnessing crowd turned homeward."[69]

Richwood Presbyterian Church

Roberta Kenney Schneider and Kathleen Keeney Wiley attended Richwood Presbyterian with Mrs. Agnes Roberts and her family. Aunt Kittie Taylor promised fourth and fifth graders Roberta and Ruth Wade Cox a surprise if they memorized Bible verses. They zealously committed to memory the 23rd and 100th Psalms, the Beatitudes, the Apostles Creed, the Apostles names, the books of the Bible, John 3:16, the Lord's Prayer and other Psalms. Impressed, Aunt Kittie made a special trip to Cincinnati and bought a New Testament for each of them.

Throughout the 1930s, Margie Arrasmith walked from her Hicks Pike home to Richwood Presbyterian Church for services every other Sunday. There she played, "Nearer the Cross" on the pump organ while Mrs. Agnes Roberts sang. They were often the only two who arrived in time for Sunday School.[70]

Sisters Elizabeth Flage and Dolly Flage Martin taught school. Here they pose on the woodpile. Courtesy of Martha Daugherty

Union School Life

Basketball was popular at Union. On Friday afternoons when the school team traveled to play at other schools, a cattle truck and driver were hired to haul all the kids to the game and bring them back.

O.E. Purdy taught at Union, a school with three large rooms, and a hall that served as a room, for 12 grades. Mr. Purdy directed the band, which had about a dozen members. Being financed well enough to buy an instrument was the primary criteria. Bill Townsend played trombone. Harold Weaver saxophone; LaVerne Sullivan, clarinet; Virginia Jones, piccolo; Hubert Townsend, banjo; Roy Bachelor, drums. Sarah Weaver accompanied them on the piano during practice and at school functions. They didn't play in parades, athletic events or band competitions – simply played for their own fulfillment and the entertainment of others.[71]

Countywide school tournaments brought students from all the schools together to compete in scholastic and athletic events. Students entered races, high jump, broad jump, history, English, math, science, art and music categories – some without classes or coaches. Sarah Weaver sang "My Wild Irish Rose." Betty Weaver (Roter) recited "Out to Old Aunt Mary's," a James Whitcomb Riley poem. Mary Setters recited the "*entire poem 'Hiawatha,' which put most of the audience to sleep. It was a remarkable display of her ability to memorize.*" Winners received a small square pin. Many lifelong friendships were made at the county tournaments.[72]

1926 Union Graduation

Students carefully selected an usher to

---

[69] Roter, 153-154.
[70] Kathleen Kenney Wiley, "Richwood Presbyterian Church on the First Sabbath in May," *A Peek Into the Past*, 105-107.
[71] Roter, 184-185.
[72] Roter, 188-191.

walk with them into the graduation ceremonies. Girls and their mothers selected fabrics and sewed fancy dresses for the day, selecting matching accessories on shopping trips to Covington. Floral corsages completed the outfits.

Four students graduated from Union in 1926, Bill Townsend, Sara Wilson, Sarah Weaver and Betty Weaver. Lyle Williams dropped out his senior year. His cousin, Carrie Williams and James Feldhaus moved away.

They selected a modest class ring, *"indicative of the era, but probably more so, of the financial status of the families represented."* Invitations were also simple and inexpensive, but included sophisticated name cards they exchanged with classmates. *"We build the ladder by which we rise,"* a line from the poem "Gradatim" by Josiah Gilbert Holland was the class motto.

The baccalaureate service was held on the Sunday evening prior to school's end at the Union Baptist Church – because its sanctuary was larger than the Presbyterian Church's. The Weaver girls' cousin, Hampton Adams, pastor at the Christian Church in Stanford, Ky., gave the sermon. Graduates sat on the front pew taking in the service and music by the Baptist choir.

The day before graduation, students gathered dogwood and snowball blooms to decorate the church. Crepe paper streamers in the class colors of "old rose" and silver marked pews reserved for special guests.

A string trio from Cincinnati's Conservatory of Music entertained during the ceremony. Sarah and Betty wore white crepe dresses sewn by their mother with white silk stockings and shoes – there were no caps and gowns. (Door-to-door salesmen sold tiny mending kits for silk stockings.) They carried rose bouquets, the class flower. Their photographs were taken in Cincinnati the next day.[73]

After graduation, Betty and Sarah studied old teachers' exams, then traveled to Burlington to take the teacher's examination. No college experience was required, only being 18. Though Betty was still 16, both passed the exam in 1926.

Sarah applied for a Boone County teaching position and was assigned to the one-room Stephenson Mill School, in a hilly area off the

Excursions on the Island Queen were popular from the '20s through the '40s when the boat burned during repairs in Pittsburgh.
Courtesy of Virginia Bennett

Walton-Beaver Road. With several large boys, the school had a reputation of being a discipline problem. Sarah boarded with three generations of the Luther and Sarah Sturgeon family on their farm on Mudlick Creek. Clarence and Hattie Straub Sturgeon's son, Chester Lee, was one of Sarah's students.

Professional Painter

Since she wasn't old enough to teach, Betty explored her artistic talents. Alma Head provided some of the printed cards she

---

[73] Roter, 199-204.

was painting for Gibson Art in Cincinnati. Betty loved doing it.

So, Betty and Sarah went to Cincinnati for an interview. They drove a horse and buggy to Florence, caught a jitney bus to the Greenline trolley in Ft. Mitchell, rode to the Dixie Terminal, then walked down Fourth Street to Gibson Art.

After demonstrating her painting skills, Betty was given a box of cards to take home and paint. She was paid by the hundred, based upon the amount of painting, its intricacy and quality.

Betty painted during the day and read in the evenings. Zane Grey was one of her favorite authors. *"I would read so late into the night that the kerosene lamp would run dry and I'd have to get to bed in the dark."*[74]

Teaching at Pleasant Valley

The next summer (1927), with a certificate from Supt. J.C. Gordon that allowed her to begin teaching even though she wouldn't turn 18 until December, Betty attended teacher's institute in Burlington. Given a broom and chalk box, she was assigned to Pleasant Valley, near the Fork of Fowler Creek with Big Gunpowder.

The first school day, she stopped her horse and buggy to pick up little Lucian Bradford who had only agreed to go to school if he could go with her. The Ed Borders family had already cleaned the school and blackboard, so she didn't need her broom.

Eight students showed up that day. One, Helen Borders, had completed the eighth grade the year before but wanted to repeat it just to be in school. *"We had morning exercises, Bible reading, Lord's prayer, salute to the flag and stories. We had classes, recess, lunch hour – when we ate in the sunshine, sitting on the cistern top in front – then the kids played till I rang the bell. The days flew by."*

Young people in the community had formed "The Owls' Club" that met at the schoolhouse. At a box supper shortly after school began, they played games similar to square dancing, singing and clapping to "Skip to My Lou" and "Turkey in the Straw." *"Helen Border's oldest brother, William, bought my box, so I ate supper with him. In recent years, William became a favorite subject for many of the paintings of Union artist Gary Akers."*

A month into the school year, Supt.

Aunt Lou Craig holding Sydney and Uncle Lewis with Sadie. Walter Ryle stands in the background. Courtesy of Elizabeth Craig Stephens.

Gordon announced the school was being closed because there were too few students. Betty would be transferred to the two-room Beaver Lick school, teaching grades one through four for the same $50 a month. Mrs. Ida Conner, a widow supporting four children, also taught there.

The route to Beaver Lick School – the Florence to Louisville road – was being replaced with concrete to become U.S. 42. With mule teams pulling hand-guided scrapers it wasn't going to be completed

---
[74] Roter, 208-210.

Third and fourth grades at New Haven Elementary School in 1939. Teacher Ora Belle Rouse Presser stands at the far right. Her husband Cecil "Pie" Presser was the county jailer for many years. Students included: Avery "Tick" Clinton Shields, Allie Mae Shields, Bill Weaver, Gene Weaver, George Howard, Betty Lou Sturgeon, Chester Ryan, Bruce Ferguson, Wilferd Gurelle, Mary Katherine Setters, Ed Knox, Charles "Jim" Black, Ray Craddock, Jimmy Rivard, and Hattie Jean Black. Courtesy of Bruce Ferguson

quickly. So, Betty arranged to board with her mother's cousin, Daisy Jack, who lived in Beaver, for $20 a month.

Off to College

The next summer, the still teen-aged Weaver sisters prepared to go to Eastern Kentucky State Teachers College. After spending Saturday night with relatives in Covington, they boarded the train to Richmond for their first trip away from Northern Kentucky. Getting off the train in a downpour, they hailed a cab to take them to a boarding house since all the dorms were full.

College student Corey Slater Acra, who they knew from home, and his friend, Charlie Plummer, who drove a huge touring car, took them to Boonesboro on picnics and home for an occasional weekend. The trips sometimes included flat tires or breakdowns.

That fall both taught at their Boone County schools. Betty boarded with the Sleet family whose daughter Anna Mae was only three years younger than Betty. The Sleet family owned the grocery at the corner of Beaver Road and Mudlick. When Sarah came to visit for a weekend, Henry Sleet offered to drive her home on Sunday afternoon, beginning a courtship that led to marriage.

Mudlick Box Supper

To raise money for supplies, Sarah held a box supper at her school. To reach the school meant walking a footbridge over Mudlick Creek. In the midst of a cold snap, the wind was so biter men entered the cozy schoolhouse with white-frosted mustaches and women's eyelashes were frozen white.

"All the patrons and friends came hungry and with money to spend. Boxes were always decorated with fancy paper and ribbons to make them attractive to buyers." After the

Chapter 11 1920-1939 A Flood Change

auction, women and girls who prepared the boxes traditionally ate with the high bidder on their box. That night it was so cold, Betty said, she got in bed with her parents to get warmed up after the ride home.[75]

In the summer of 1929, Union High School Principal Ira L. Harrison submitted his resignation to Joe Weaver, who chaired the school board. He announced he was becoming the Verona principal and asked if Sarah and Betty would like to teach grades one and two or three and four there. Both resigned from Boone County and began teaching at Verona for $75 a month.

Verona Dissolved

While life in Verona continued as usual, this note appeared on the front page of the *Boone County Recorder* on Dec. 25, 1919:

"The town of Verona, this county, was wiped off of the map by an order of the court. There seemed to be no one who desired that the corporation be kept intact and the court entered an order dissolving the corporation."

During the late 1920s, 12 passenger trains went through Verona each day, six east and six west. One each way was the all-Pullman, state-of-the-art Pan-American running between Cincinnati and New Orleans in 23 hours.[76]

In January 1934, Sarah Weaver and Henry Sleet had secretly been married. In May, Sarah was dismissed: Verona did not allow married teachers. She began working for Boone County Schools.[77]

In the fall of 1935, Walton-Verona Schools were consolidated into one district with first through sixth grade in Verona and grades seven through 12 at Walton.

Verona's Female Basketball Coach

In the '20s, Frances Stevens Wilson began coaching the Verona High School boys basketball team that included George Powers and Joe Leary. Doubtless one of the few female coaches of a boys' high school team, Mrs. Wilson's 1932 team included Fred Hamilton, Harold Speagle, Clyde Chapman, Ernest Bingham and Francis Ransom.

Verona's court, like most, was outside. Fred Hamilton, who later built the Hamilton Funeral Home on the Walton-Verona Road in the '60s, recalled rain turning to ice during a game at Petersburg. The boys slipped and slid so much, the referees stopped calling them for traveling.

Each player paid $3.50 for a uniform that didn't always match his teammates' outfits. They rode to and from games in the back of a cattle truck, often walking miles to get home after they were returned to the school. Equipment was equally Spartan – they had one basketball.

"One night we played in Dry Ridge and when we got back to Verona we didn't have a basketball. Everybody thought somebody else had brought it.

"So, the next morning, we got Raymond Hahn to drive us in his Model-T Ford to Dry Ridge. The car didn't have any body, just a board across the frame in back and the driver sat on the gas tank. When we got to Dry Ridge, we got someone to open the gym and we found the basketball. I rode all the way back to Verona sitting on that board in the back and holding on to that basketball," Hamilton said.

Unlike most schools, Walton had an indoor court – a tobacco warehouse. At Sparta, players dodged two buckled boards, at Mason a huge hot air register nearly took their breath away, at Corinth was a hot water radiator that constantly threatened burns.[78]

Walton Improvements

A new gymnasium for the high school was one of many improvements that came to Walton in the '20s. George Nicholson and Sons built the new gym facing High School Court, directly behind the Walton High

---

[75] Roter, 233-235.
[76] Conrad, Yesterdays, 86.
[77] Roter, 250-260.

[78] Omer W. Johnson, "Were they really good old days?" *Kentucky Post*, March 19, 1985.

School that fronted on North Main. In 1935, Walton consolidated with Verona to form Walton-Verona High School. The school was moved to Alta Vista Drive in 1955.[79]

A new municipal water system and concrete paving for Main Street came with new electric service. Citizens voted overwhelmingly, 268 to 58, for a bond issue to provide electric lights in Walton. Rather than the 20-hour service they'd had, city trustees were asked to provide 24-hour service, either by operating a local plant or contracting for service.[80]

When the L&N Railroad dug what is now called Boone Lake in 1926, they offered the town the opportunity to use it as a city water reservoir. In an effort to eliminate some curves, a bridge was removed and rebuilt. Since a great deal of fill dirt was needed, they simply dug a lake and poured a concrete retaining wall. Plans called for a lake 1,200' long, 600' wide and 30' deep.[81]

The structure collapsed twice during construction. After it was stable, the wooded valley was allowed to flood. Eventually protruding treetops were cut off, but huge tree trunks are still preserved under water.

When steam engines stopped there to refill with water, enterprising locals climbed on top the coal cars and threw as much off as they could before the train left. They returned in the dark to load the free fuel. Otis Readnour, local coal dealer, said the coal snatchers ensured that he never got an honest weight on a Blue Diamond Coal car.[82]

Walton's telephone switchboard was in the Dixie State Bank building on the second floor from the 1920s to early 1967. The first "hello girls" – including Mary Worthington and Katherine Robinson Jamison of Walton – began working. Consolidated Telephone Company operated in Boone County until Bell acquired it in 1967. Other operators were Shirley Jack, Melva White, Bertha Jack, Faye Stephenson and Mrs. Brannum.

Walton Bank, Laundry, Theater

About 1921, Theodore Burdsall erected the county's first do-it-yourself laundry. Located across from the old IGA grocery (later Western Auto store), a large cistern below it collected water from the roof of the J.D. Mayhugh Lumber Co. next door. Clothes washed in Bendix washing machines were dried in a metal housing heated with an oil heater.[83]

Walton Bank and Trust merged with the Equitable Bank and Trust Company to form Walton Equitable Bank in February 1927. Their combined resources were $750,000. A new two-story limestone building was erected on Main Street at a cost of $52,000.

A marble facade and two columns decorated the front. Interior woodwork was natural quartered oak finish. A ten-inch door guarded the public's money as well as a McClintock Burglar Alarm. R.C. Greene was the first president, followed by J.D. Mayhugh, then Wilford M. Rice who held the office in 1930.

The Walls family founded Walton's Methodist Church,[84] a frame structure at the north end of town next to the old Walton school. In 1930, under Pastor Lewis, a new church was built on the opposite end of town.

Residents from around the region traveled to Walton to attend the theater. On Jan. 16, 1936, two selections at the Unique Theater in Walton were: Rochelle Hudson and Henry Fonda in "Way Down East," and Buck Jones and the Wonder Horse Silver in "Ivory Handled Guns."

By the '20s, the Walton Opera House housed the neon plant of Rouse Sign Service on the second floor. After the Kroger fire, Charles Rouse ran the Model Food Store on the first floor. In 1994, the site became the Boone County Library.

Prize Drawing

The Crash of '29 devastated Walton, like

---

[79] Asa Rouse, March 1, 1998.
[80] *Boone County Recorder,* Nov. 11, 1920.
[81] *Walton Advertiser,* March 25, 1926.
[82] Jack Rouse, Feb. 18, 1998.

[83] William Fitzgerald, "Walton Established in 1840." *Boone County Recorder,* Jan. 2, 1964.
[84] Rice and Fitzgerald.

Chapter 11   1920-1939   A Flood Change

the rest of the country. To attract potential customers, Walton merchants held a weekly drawing at 1 p.m. Saturday in front of Tom Percival's Dry Goods Store, just south of Walton Garage. Customers received a ticket with each $1 purchase from any Walton merchant that week. The big prize was $10 and you had to be present to win. The crowds exceeded anyone's expectations – until a state Attorney General ruled that it was too close to a gambling lottery to be legal.[85]

Three town blacksmiths, R.M. Callender, Waite Cross and Burgess Ford, shod horses and made horse-drawn wagons. Funeral director Scott Chambers and A.M. Edwards ran livery stables that rented horses and buggies by the day.

Walter Whitson and J.F. Hawkins of Walton advertised purebred White Rock eggs, 15 for $1 or 100 for $5. Mrs. M. Cleek of Verona sold eggs for the same prices, but they came from "*dark red Rose Comb Rhode Island Red hens mated to cockerels from Longfields.*"[86]

"Drummers" (salesmen) came from the city by train, living at one of the two hotels for the week while they drove to a different town each day to sell their wares. Henry Dears managed the Atlas Hotel at the corner of High and Main Street. Floyd Underhill managed the Phoenix Hotel (now a parking lot).

The hotels both served three meals a day and rang the bells in their towers to call guests to dinner before each meal.

Youngest Bank President

Walton Equitable Bank elected Wilford Monroe Rice, who then became the youngest bank president in the state. A Newport native, Rice's grandparents were born in Walton of English parents. Wilford's father, William Felix Rice, grew up there then moved to Latonia and Covington where he worked for the L&N Railroad.

Wilford started out as Walton's postmaster, then became a bookkeeper at Fifth-Third National Bank in Cincinnati. He resigned to become cashier of the Hebron bank. When the WWI broke out, he was 17, but sold $90,000 worth of war savings stamps on one day and $70,000 on another day. In 1930, he married Grace Mattie McCormick Dudgeon whose father was then the Walton postmaster.

Ku Klux Klan

Despite Gov. Augustus Wilson's actions to eliminate vigilantism that grew from the Black Patch Tobacco Wars, the Ku Klux Klan appeared in Walton about 1920. Hooded Night Riders, both men and women, burned crosses in yards and harassed Jews, Catholics and Negroes. An initiation ceremony in Walton's south end across from Holder Pond attracted 4,000 to 5,000.[87]

Walton Basketball

Loafers still hung out at the Walton Garage and Conrad's Hardware. The 20s brought much to discuss – the Charleston, Coolidge, Hoover and, before the stock market crashed of 1929, the greatest Walton High School basketball team ever. John DeMoisey, Jimmy Vest, Ward Rice, John Hartman, John Feagan, Red Robinson, Pete Johnson and George Sharp were coached by the much-loved Raymond Beverly who remains a local legend. Beverly's untimely death in 1937, saddened the town.[88]

Adolph Rupp took over coaching University of Kentucky men's basketball in 1930. Walton High School graduate John "Frenchy" DeMoisey was Adolph Rupp's first University of Kentucky recruit. He joined the Wildcats in 1931 and led the team with his left-handed hook shot. Captain of the 1933-34 team, he was named All-American that year.

Costume Party

In 1936, the Parent-Teacher Association masquerade brought many characters and

---

[85] Asa Rouse, March 1, 1998.
[86] *Walton Advertiser*, March 25, 1926.
[87] Wilford M. Rice and William Fitzgerald, "Walton Established in 1840." *Boone County Recorder,* Jan. 2, 1964.
[88] Asa Rouse, March 1, 1998.

costumes to the high school auditorium. Mrs. R.P. Hughes, disguised as an old Negro fisherman carrying some live catfish and a live turtle on a string, won for the most unique and original costume. No one knew her identity until she was unmasked.

Miss Sue Evelyn Mann won the finest costume prize. Perry Hughes and Mrs. Ronald Bossong of Cincinnati dressed as coal miners with lamps on their cap visors, taking the best representative character prizes.

Miss Evelyn Coffman took the children's prize as a fancy costumed Spanish lady. Nordine Mills had the prettiest children's costume. Jack Hughes had the tackiest and Marvin Hudson Jr. had the best competitive costume. "*Jack Roberts as a young and vivacious girl occasioned considerable amusement.*" The ladies collected $45 for their fund.[89]

Oddities

Growing up in his father "Ali" Roter's blacksmith shop, Raymond's mechanical talents were soon apparent. Seeing the popularity of "horseless carriages," the family built an automotive garage. Soon, word of Raymond's extraordinary skills traveled. A shy, quiet man, he worked diligently in the garage while his storefront became the gathering place for local loafers. An independent man, he didn't rush, nor did he do work for people he didn't like.

One day a Cincinnati man pulled up "in a car a mile long," demanding to see Roter. His curiosity piqued by overhearing the man's comments to the group gathered out front, Roter crawled out from under the vehicle he'd been repairing.

"*Everybody's worked on this damn thing and it still doesn't run right,*" he sputtered. Roter quietly asked him to push on the accelerator. He did. Roter began fiddling with the windshield wiper. The impatient man growled that there was nothing wrong with the wipers, but Roter continued.

Suddenly the sound changed and the car ran smoothly. Roter quietly explained that an incomplete vacuum connected to the wipers was preventing the engine from running correctly. The driver demanded to know how much he owed. Roter replied, "*Nothing.*" The man threw a wad of bills out his window and roared off.[90]

In the early '30s a croquet ground was built just off old Beaver Road behind Mayor D.L. Lusby's home on South Main. Lighted for night play, the court attracted many men who played or sat on the plank benches solving the world's weightiest problems.

Another gathering place was Stephens Restaurant, where Dewey Mulford's barber shop now stands, across Main from where Depot Street intersects. Mary Stephens prepared home cooked food with help from Jess Hopperton and Helen Gillespie.[91]

James Falls operated the picture show in an old barn-like building next door to the Phoenix Hotel until 1937 when he remodeled

Emma Frances Barlow and John M. Baker play in the Hopeful Cemetery on Sept. 27, 1927.   Courtesy of Linda Baker Green

---

[89] *Walton Advertiser*, Nov. 5, 1936, 1.

[90] Asa Rouse, March 9, 1998.
[91] Asa Rouse, March 1, 1998.

Chapter 11 1920-1939 A Flood Change

the Ford garage on North Main into the James Theater. Any kid with a dime or adult with a quarter went to the show during the Depression.

In February 1936, the Walton Fire Department sponsored the area's first Amateur Night, offering cash prizes totaling $25.

A dramatic fire burned the Kroger grocery in the center of town, across from Dixie State Bank in 1936. Harold "Connie" Conrad suffered severe burns rescuing the cash register. Charles Rouse, father of County Clerk Jerry Rouse, had managed the store.

In 1937, John and Madeline Gault bought Walton's oldest house, the 20-room brick with curved stairways at the north end of town. Stories about the house, built in 1791 by Col. Abner Gaines included secret rooms, murders, hauntings and tales of its history as an inn used by the wealthy and famous. Perhaps to enhance his marketing effort, John Gault reported seeing a fair-haired ghost child skipping through the house as well as several headless men. Local lore says an electrician wiring the house became so frightened that he ran two miles home, leaving his car behind.[92]

In another eerily odd situation, longtime *Walton Advertiser* partners Jim Wallace and Roy Stamler died in November 1937 one week apart. James H. Jump bought the paper and published it until 1940, when Mark Meadows became the owner and publisher. *The Walton Advertiser* came out every Thursday and was a Walton staple until about a decade ago.

Walton's CCC

In 1935, the federal government began the Civilian Conservation Corps to offer jobs for men, ages 18 to 25, from needy families. Men enlisted for six months and were paid $30, $25 of which was sent directly to their families. The age range was soon expanded to 17-28 and some World War I veterans were allowed to enlist.

Kentucky hosted 44 CCC camps, including the one in Walton. Run by the Army, the Soil Conservation Service also taught the men to prevent soil erosion and deal with crop problems. Located where Walton-Verona High School now stands, the camp had been a ballpark.

That changed quickly after July 17, 1935, when 23 men commanded by Army Capt. Robert Adams arrived with four truckloads of camping equipment and other supplies. They pitched five tents, converted the ballpark grandstand into a kitchen, and began arranging housing for 200. They dug ditches for water lines, brought electric and telephone lines in and used the Walton school's showers.

On Aug. 8, 152 men arrived by train and 17 local men joined the crew. They were soon unloading 17 railcars filled with wood and equipment shipped from Albany, Ga. Volunteers used the supplies to build barracks, mess hall, educational center and other buildings. The men had no control over their assignments. Some claimed they were

Wholesale Prices 1930*	
Reinhart & Newton Manufacturing Confectioners, Cincinnati	
24 O'Henry bars	$ 1.60
24 Tootsie Rolls	$ .80
Cracker Jacks (case)	$ 1.95
#25 pail Hershey Kisses	$ .35
Boss Brand Ovens, Stoves, Ranges Firestone Tire & Rubber Co.	
30" x 3" gray tubes each	$ 1.25
Roosa & Ratliff Chemical Co. Phamacists & Chemists, Cinci.	
1 doz. bottles iodine	$ 1.35
1 doz. bottles carbolic acid	$ 2.25
2 doz. bottles Rise Up	$ 3.50
Bourbon Remedy Co., Lexington	
2 doz. Bourbon Poultry remedy	$16.00
2 doz. Shipp's Linement	$ 9.60
W.D. Creasey's Sons Wholesale Grocers, Cinci.	
#1 Maxwell House Coffee	$ .51
Strawberry Jello, doz.	$ 1.15
Kelloggs Bran Flakes	$ .102
8c Bull Durham Tobacco	$ .032
J.M. McCullough's Sons Co. Seedsmen, Cincinnati	
Price per 100 lbs. of seed	
Kentucky Wonder	$12.50
Sugar Corn	$ 9.50
Musk Melon, Acme	$25.00
Peas, Alaska	$11.50
Procter & Gamble Distributing Co.	
Ivory, 100 lg.	$ 8.85
Camay	$ 3.65
Lava, 50 med.	$ 2.55
Oxydol 24	$ 4.60

---
[92] *175th Anniversary Historical Book*, 62.

The Florence High School basketball teams in 1932-33. The Nightingales were: Alta Fogel, guard; Helen Elliott, forward; Virginia Miller, forward; Mary Laubisch, guard; Mary Higgins, center and captain; D'Everette McCauley, mascot; Catherine Bethel, guard; Mary Marksbery, guard; Dorothy Sullivan, forward. The "Knights" were Lawrence and Winifred Aylor, forwards; Stanley Kern, guard; Charles Higgins, guard and captain; Forest Fergeson, center; John Powell, guard; Cornelius Reagan, guard; Robert Groger, forward. W.R. Davis and C. G. Lamb professors and coaches.
Rules were very specific, forwards were the ones who shot the ball, Mrs. Collins said. School colors were orange and black as they are today. In 1932-33 the girls' county high school basketball championship went into overtime twice. Then Hebron missed a shot and Florence missed a shot, maintaining the tie. Officials flipped a coin and declared Hebron the winner, despite a near riot in the middle of the gym – led by Arch Rouse and Roy Lutes who didn't have children but were huge fans,. They demanded the Florence Nightengales get an identical trophy, but it never came about.
Courtesy of Helen Collins

misled into believing they'd travel to more exotic locales like California if they signed up.

William "Mickey" McKinley of Covington who lived at the camp recalled some clashes between city boys and those from the mountains that resulted in the combatants being assigned to clean the latrine.

Life began with a 6 a.m. breakfast and flag raising. Men left in groups of 30 or 40 at 8 a.m. to work on Northern Kentucky farms. They dug erosion ditches, planted trees, erected fences and taught farmers to rotate crops to preserve the soil. A lunch arrived at 1 p.m., then work continued until they returned to camp for dinner at 5. Basketball, football, softball and the camp's library filled the evenings. Some rode buses to Simon Kenton High School in Independence to earn high school equivalency degrees. Others watched movies at Walton's James Theatre.

The camp of 200 young single men had a considerable impact on Walton's population of 1,000 – which included fights and marriages. On April 1, 1938, *The Kentucky Post* carried a feature about the camp's annual open house commemorating the CCC's fifth anniversary and the camp's third.

A story said 71 Northern Kentucky farms and 10,600 acres of farmland were assisted by the CCC. An editorial the next day said the agency had offered many city men their first chance to eat three good meals a day and do hard physical work. The typical recruit gained 4 to 10 pounds in his first two months in camp. One grew five inches and gained 40 pounds in six months.[93]

Concrete Paving

A few miles west of Walton, U.S. 42 ran north through Union and Florence. Southwest it led to Louisville. In the early 1930s, its two lanes were paved with concrete, making it a very fast route.

School superintendent J.C. Gordon, concerned about dangers to students walking along U.S. 25 and the new U.S. 42, planned to erect a school in the center of the Richwood, Stephenson Mill, Beaver Lick, Mud Lick, Hathaway, Union and Midway districts. Gordon died suddenly, so the new Boone County superintendent, Dallas H. Norris saw New Haven High School constructed in 1931 near the site of the old White Haven Academy.

The Union boys' basketball team beat Verona on outdoor courts during the first Boone County School tournament in Florence on April 28, 1925. The Union girls team was evenly matched with Petersburg, winning by only two points.[94]

Florence High School

Florence High School grew by a sixth room and a seventh teacher in 1925. Florence and New Haven consolidated schools opened in 1929.

By the time Helen Collins started there, it had eight rooms for first grade through high school. A dozen teachers assisted Mr. Yealey. *"When Mr. Yealey taught a lesson, you remembered it. He was so broadminded. He wanted you to learn something besides what was in the book."* Collins recalled Yealey taking students to a murder trial at the Boone County Courthouse during class hours. Students knew to be quiet if he shook his finger at them and said, *"Tut, tut, in this finger runs the blood of Pokey Hauntis."*

The new school meant an outdoor dirt basketball court. Mr. Yealey organized a girls' team, the Florence Nightingales. The boys, the Florence Knights, wore the school colors of black and orange. Helen was a forward and wore black bloomers and white middies. Her teammates were Captain Mary Higgins White, Mabel Davis Hoffman, Alta Fogel Miller, Dorothy Sullivan Fichlie, Virginia Adkins and Mary Frances Markesbery Henman.

Florence tied Hebron in a tournament. Girls games were only allowed to have three overtimes, since the game was still tied, a coin was tossed and Hebron took the trophy.

The class of '32 was the first senior class to graduate from the new building, which is now Florence Elementary.[95]

Principal A.M. Yealey took a break from schoolwork to build the first motel in Florence, the Wildwood Tourist Court on Route 42. His son-in-law Russell House helped design it.

Favorite son and now author, John Uri Lloyd presented the 1929 graduation address to a packed and wildly cheering audience at the RKO Theater on Main Street.

A new school opened on Center Street in 1931 under the direction of Principal W.R. Davis.

Gypsies at Fairgrounds

In the autumn, gypsies came from Cincinnati to the Florence Fairgrounds. They camped in the center of the two-story amphitheater and roasted lambs, pigs and chickens that some people thought they stole.

One year when a gypsy queen died, Prof. Yealey offered to take children to the funeral, if they brought notes from their parents allowing them to attend. Helen Collins did, observing auto licenses from many states and a pretty casket. Piled on top the corpse was with fruit and silver and gold money. Around 300 attended with decorated cars and singing happy, peppy music without instruments. A

---

[93] Reis, *Pieces of the Past 2*, 227-229.
[94] Conrad, *History of Boone County Schools*, 11.
[95] Betsy Conrad's interview with Helen Collins, Feb. 3, 1998.

A group posed in front of the John Delahunty house in Florence on May 18, 1930. Delahunty was president of the Florence Bank. In 1998, the Florence YMCA is located on this lot.
Courtesy of Linda Green

hearse took her to be buried at Spring Grove Cemetary. In the late 20s, they "left and never came back."[96]

Florence Incorporated

Florence's Main Street was being paved with concrete, prompting the sale of the Presbyterian Church (which had been disbanded) to its four surviving members for $1,200.

The money from the sale of the church and its organ was sent to mission schools in the Kentucky mountains. (The old building was remodeled into a motion picture theater where silent movies turned to piano music. When talking pictures arrived, the building was remodeled into offices.)

Throughout the 1920s, town trustees occupied themselves with street and sidewalk maintenance, and regulating parking, vehicle noise, smoke, dogs and licenses. One of the last handwritten ordinances, entered between 1927 and 1929, set forth guidelines for installing natural gas mains and lines throughout the town.[97]

Many of Florence's streets were named for the famous men in her past: Shelby, Girard, Montgomery and Youell. Center was named because it divided the west end of town into equal parts. Locust trees along the street gave Locust Street its name.[98]

Utilities to Florence

Incorporated in 1930, Florence's fledgling government began flexing its muscles. The first step before approving city ordinances was public posting, which included putting one copy in the bank, one at the post office and another on a light pole.[99]

Gas lines came to Florence in 1926, a water system in 1933, and the Consolidated Telephone System soon after.

Boone County Well Drilling Company provided natural gas from its 28 wells to Florence residents after the '37 flood when Cincinnati's main lines were turned off. A Feb. 11, 1937, *Recorder* article said being able to supply the city "*proves that Boone County gas wells are sure to be a success.*" The two wells being drilled made a total of 30 – all connected to a main line in Florence.

"*It is believed that enough gas could be furnished to supply the demand of Cincinnati and outlying suburbs. Many farmers are anxiously awaiting the pipeline which is to be laid from Burlington to Florence, which will mean many dollars to the farmers. . .*"[100]

Many had originally drilled for oil around Boone County, looking for quick riches in petroleum, but found only natural gas. Discovering gas on his farm (which is now the I-75-U.S. 42 interchange) Clint Blankenbaker eagerly ran lines into Florence to serve city residents, but the supply gave out

---

[96] Betsy Conrad's interview with Helen Collins, Feb. 3, 1998.
[97] Florence Ordinance Book #1, 100-116.

[98] William Fitzgerald, "History of Florence," written in 1958, republished in the *Boone County Recorder*, Aug. 3, 1978.
* information supplied by Katie Presnell from Gulley and Pettit store records.
[99] Florence Ordinance Book #1, 162-163.
[100] *Boone County Recorder*, Feb. 11, 1937, 1.

Chapter 11 1920-1939 A Flood Change

quickly.[101]

In August 1931, Florence hired a water engineer to supervise construction of water mains. A water system was installed, although it didn't work reliably for several decades.

Eldora Cole's subdivision was the first annexed by the town trustees in 1930. That same year, in-town speed limits were increased to 25 mph.[102]

Klan Visit

While 12 or 14 year-old Helen Collins was singing in the girls' choir during a Sunday evening service at Florence Christian Church, eight men wearing Ku Klux Klan hoods and robes burst through the doors. Rev. Harlan Runion said, *"Stop and give your cause for interrupting our service."*

When the robed men reached the front of the church, the leader asked the congregation to help burn the Catholic Church. Brother Union responded, *"Gentlemen, that's our choice"* and directed them out the church door. Rather than finishing his sermon, Rev. Union asked his male parishioners to go with him to guard the Catholic Church. Members followed him out the door.

The Klan burned a huge cross that night, but didn't burn the church because it was surrounded by Protestant men.[103]

Myers Ford

Born in Alexandria to German immigrant parents, Charles Winfield Myers Sr. attended Florence schools when his father was in the meat business there. At 15, after assisting his father, Myers began clerking for the F.L. Swetman store. Four years later, he opened a dry goods store in Florence. He ran it for 34 years before opening the car dealership.

In 1921, Myers began selling Ford vehicles in Florence, promising the lowest possible prices for his services. He sold about 175 new cars annually and about an equal number of used vehicles. His line included Standard Oil products and Goodrich, Goodyear and Firestone tires. Myers sold a 1937 Ford to Wendell Rouse, father of Jack and Asa, for $700.

Myers married Georgia B. Snyder, the daughter of Boone Countians James P. and Sallie Springer Snyder. Mrs. Myers' cousin, Reuben Springer of Cincinnati, donated Music Hall to the city.[104]

Charles Jr. "Winnie" Myers worked with his father's business after attending Woodward High School and Littleford Business College, both in Cincinnati. A father of two and member of the Baptist Church, he was a golfer, tennis player and fisherman.

Kentoboo

What seemed to be a relatively inconsequential construction project began in this decade on the northeastern edge of Boone County bordering Kenton County. Little did anyone realize that Kentoboo, the county's first subdivision was the precursor of housing developments to come.

The frame two-bedroom houses were built on lots with 25' of road frontage. Modern new asbestos shingles covered the exteriors of some. During the depression, many of the standard, four-square houses were begun but never completed.[105]

Volunteers Fight Fires

On Memorial Day 1929, Markesbery's Hardware and Huey's Express office in Florence opposite the Shelby street intersection caught fire. The outcome was the same as the fire at the same intersection 59 years earlier –with no water supply other than cisterns, there was little the bucket brigade could do. In 1870, McNeal's carriage shop and James Osborn's General Store had burned.[106]

Those two devastating fires prompted Albert Hue to organize a Florence fire

---

[101] Bruce Ferguson
[102] Florence Ordinance Book #1, 126-127.
[103] Betsy Conrad's interview with Helen Collins, Feb. 3, 1998.
[104] *Boone County Recorder,* 1930 Historical Edition.
[105] Conrad, Yesterdays, 10.
[106] Virginia Lainhart, Feb. 26, 1998.

department, despite the 1934 economy. Hue bought a 1913 Ahrens-Fox pumper with $75 from his own pocket. With it and 500' of hose borrowed from Elsmere, the Florence Volunteer Fire Department began in 1936. The Main Street firehouse was built the following year.

Fire Chief Hue served until 1952 when he died of a heart attack on the way to a fire. In 1970, a second fire building was added near the Industrial Park at Industrial Road and U.S. 25.

Burlington School

After being reincorporated in 1910, Burlington's charter was annulled in 1923. It remains unincorporated, one of only two unincorporated county seats in the Commonwealth. Electricity and street lights came to Burlington in the '20s.[107]

Building a school gymnasium in 1928 at the Burlington school allowed boys and girls to play basketball. Female players were required to wear bloomers until 1934 when shorts were allowed.

Mrs. Elizabeth McMullen Kirtley drove a mule and buggy to school until two parents combined two old trucks into a bus in 1930. Two grades shared a classroom, singing and listening to Bible stories. Eventually a family across the street from the school began offering hot lunches to students. Soup, sandwiches and milk were a nickel each.[108]

Class valedictorian, debate and public speaking team member, as well as yearbook editor, Mrs. Kirtley was given a partial college scholarship, but the $123 annual tuition wasn't affordable for her family.

The P.T.A. began serving lunches at Burlington High School in 1927. A drinking fountain was installed in 1929. A new Burlington High School was built in 1939.

Nelson Poston recalled that Burlington High School was heated with coal when he attended from 1931 until 1943.

By February 1937, students could watch moving pictures at the Gayety Theater in Burlington. Current features were "Big Broadcast of 1937" starring Jack Benny, "The Great Ziegfeld," and a Zane Grey Western "Desert Gold."[109]

Burlington Churches Updated

Burlington Baptist Church gave up kerosene lighting for electricity in 1919. In 1925, they sold the Delco light plant to the Petersburg Baptist Church, which connected a public utility line to the Burlington church. In 1930, Burlington added a choir loft at a cost of $28.

Burlington Methodist Church's oldest member and the town's oldest citizen, Mary Thompson, died on Oct. 20, 1922. Born in Brooklyn, New York, in 1828, she taught at public and private schools for 50 years.

B.W. Campbell, a grateful student and then a wealthy Cincinnati businessman, saw the church's bare floors, oil lamps and coal-burning stoves when he came for Miss Thompson's funeral. So, in memory of Miss Thompson and his mother, Sally Campbell, who had attended the church 50 years before, he remodeled the church. The *Recorder* printed weekly progress reports.

"J.J. Kirkpatrick, the town's expert carpenter, began work in April 1923. In removing a floorboard, Mr. Jess found a razor, took it home, honed it and used it to shave. The Recorder *printed the story, but the mystery of how it got there was never revealed."*[110]

A July 1923 *Recorder* said, *"The new gong for the Burlington Methodist Church was purchased in Yokohama, Japan, by B.W. Campbell who is having the church remodeled – paying for it himself, arrived last week and has been placed in the new belfry. Made of bronze and in the shape of a large kettle, which sits on an iron pedestal –* (it is) *rung by striking with a small hammer, producing sweet melodious sound, which can*

---

[107] Mrs. Elizabeth Kirtley, Jan. 8, 1998 interview.
[108] *A Look At Our Yesterdays: Burlington Hometown.*
[109] *Boone County Recorder*, Feb. 18, 1937, 1.
[110] Walton, 14.
* from Gulley and Pettit store records, Katie Presnell.

The Recorder office in 1928, R.E. Berkshire, publisher; Howard Kirkpatrick, linotype operator; Bell B. Fleeman, printer, and N.E. Riddell.
Boone County Recorder, 1930 Historical Edition, Courtesy of Ruth Green

be heard quite a distance."

Campbell added a stained glass window behind the pulpit in honor of his mother. Sally Campbell's grandsons, John Braxton and Wendel Siebern Campbell, donated a pulpit Bible, bound in Moroccan leather.[111]

Burlington Families

Born in Burlington in 1874, Arthur B. Rouse was the son of Eliza B. and Dudley, who was president of Boone County Deposit Bank. After attending Hanover College and graduating from Louisville Law School in 1900, Arthur became a Burlington attorney and entered politics. He won election to the U.S. House of Representatives in 1910 then married Minnie Elizabeth Kelly in December. They honeymooned in Panama, where they watched construction of the canal, which was opened three years later.

In 1926, Rouse announced he would not run for re-election because he wanted his sons, Robert Kelly Rouse and Arthur Blythe Rouse Jr., educated in Kentucky. He returned to a law practice in Erlanger and became involved in banking, land development and bus lines. A federal court clerk from 1935 to 1953, he retired to Lexington.

One of three surviving heirs from a family of nine boys and four girls, Benjamin Thomas Kelly was a farmer who dabbled in fruit growing. He died after an appendicitis operation in 1930, at the age of 67. His grandfather, Jesse Kelly (who married Jane Porter) moved to Kentucky about 1810. They also had 13 children, eight boys and five girls. The family was remarkable for two reasons: All the children survived to adulthood and all the boys were extremely tall –over six feet.

Burlington jailer Charles A. Fowler had served the county for a dozen years, taking charge of 356 prisoners during that time. The

---
[111] Walton, 16.

prisoners "*caused him very little trouble with the exception of one Ben Sweeney, who thru trickery and taking advantage of Mr. Fowler's goodness struck him over the head with an iron bar, which nearly caused his death. The prisoner and two others left the jailer for dead and made their escape on the night of Nov. 19, 1926. The other two have been captured, but Sweeney never was heard from.*"[112]

Fowler refused to run again in 1929 "*afraid ill health would not permit him to do justice to the position.*"

Dr. Gladys Rouse, one of the region's first female physicians, was born at Limaburg. She married Robert Rouse who chaired the board of Florence Deposit Bank. From the '30s through the '50s, she practiced in Florence in the red brick house that is now Rose Schneider's art studio. Like most doctors of the time, her office was in her home.

Judge Riddell

After serving as county attorney from 1906 until 1919, N.E. Riddell was elected judge. Said to "know every man, woman, child and hound dog in Boone County," Riddell contributed 35 years as a Boone County public servant.

Born on July 17, 1872, Riddell grew up in Burlington. After attending Morgan Academy, he graduated from Cincinnati Law School in 1895. He joined Judge John M. Lassing in law practice before being elected county attorney in 1906 in a hotly contested race against D.E. Castleman. In 1920, when Judge Cason died, Riddell was appointed county judge to fill out the term.

Elected without opposition, he served 28 years in public office. During that time, he was president of Boone County Deposit Bank, a post once held by his father, for 15 years and was re-elected in 1930. Riddell owned and operated the *Boone County Recorder* for two years, first selling a half interest, then the balance to R.E. Berkshire.

During Judge Riddell's tenure in public office, the county went from toll roads to public highways. A new jail was built in 1928. Modern heating and water systems were installed in the infirmary and the courthouse.[113]

As one of a trio who started Consolidated Telephone Co., the judge himself dug some post holes and ran some of the county's first telephone lines.[114]

Newspaper Changes Hands

Riddell's partner in the newspaper business, Robert Ewing Berkshire was also elected without opposition (to circuit clerk in 1921). Chairman of the county Democratic Party, Berkshire was also master commissioner (responsible for selling property if taxes are not paid) and trustee of the jury fund.

Berkshire bought half interest in the *Boone County Recorder* in 1924 with "little or no knowledge of the 'fourth estate,' except a natural talent…" A year later he became the sole owner. Berkshire was re-elected in 1927. "*He accomplished the almost impossible task of running his newspaper and taking care of his clerical duties without aid, other than the mechanical help at the printing plant.*"[115]

Berkshire grew up near Petersburg, attended schools there and graduated from Aurora High School across the river in 1912. After winning several medals as a track star, he decided to run track and study law at the University of Kentucky. At UK he ran the 100-yard dash in 10.2 seconds in a meet against the University of Cincinnati.

But in July 1914, a mule kicked Berkshire so severely that he barely recovered. While he returned to college in the fall, he was unable to continue during the spring term and came back to Boone County to undergo an operation. He recovered and married Leila Thompson of Petersburg. He farmed for a few years, then began clerking for the

---

[112] *Boone County Recorder*, 1930 Historical Edition.

[113] *Boone County Recorder*, 1930 Historical Edition.
[114] Joe W. Johnston, "Boone County's 'Country Jake' Lawyer Wins 6th Term as Judge," *The Kentucky Post*, n.d., n.p.
[115] *Boone County Recorder*, 1930 Historical Edition.

Chapter 11 1920-1939 A Flood Change

Berkshire Company in Petersburg.

Later, he became a marker in the Aurora Loose Leaf Tobacco market. Then he purchased the White Brothers' store and Berkshire Company, combining them into one business. He operated it for several months then resold it to White Brothers. By that time, the father of three daughters, he began a truck line that carried freight from Petersburg to Cincinnati.[116]

Smith's Grocery

Luther and Lucille Smith bought the old brick house behind the Burlington courthouse and remodeled it into a store, building shelves, stocking them and opening for business on their son Raymon's (cq) second birthday, Sept. 23, 1937. Raymon had a brother Bill and a sister Mary. (On the market in 1998, this brick building was most recently one of the Merchants of Historic Burlington, Café Arabesque Restaurant.)

Out of respect for the building's age (it was constructed between 1824 and 1827) the Smiths carefully converted the structure, avoiding damaging any of the woodwork as they made living quarters upstairs and storage down. They changed a window into a door, but replaced it when they moved.

The Smiths spent a total of $380 to open the store – including purchasing the merchandise. Customary store hours were 6 a.m. until 11 p.m. six days a week. By year's end, the Smiths were bringing in $300 a week.

"At that time, a $5 grocery order required more than one person to carry it out." The electric bill for both the apartment and the store ranged from $7 to $8 a month. The Smiths operated a store at that location for eight years before moving. Raymon and his uncle Bob, Luther's brother, continued in the grocery business.

Theirs was Burlington's fourth store: Gulley

1937 Grocery Prices*	
Maxwell Coffee, lb.	$.19
Bread loaf	$.08
Navy beans 6 lb.	$.25
Spices	$.10
Steak , lb.	$.12
Jowl bacon, l b.	$.10
Zesta crackers, box	$.15
Vegetables, can	$.10
Coke/Pepsi bottle	$.05

and Pettit were just south of Smith's. W.L. Kirkpatrick ran another where the Little Place restaurant is now. Wilford Rouse operated a store in Dudley Rouse Blythe's building on the corner.

Blythe began working for E.E. Kelly when he owned Burlington's General Store in 1910. Nine years later Blythe bought the store. He soon doubled the amount of merchandise available.

On Jan. 13, 1921, Dudley moved across the street into the old Rouse store building once owned by his uncle and namesake, then owned by his father, George. Six months later the building burned to the ground. The younger Blythe lost $3,000, which was only partially covered by insurance. He bought the charred lots and in two months had constructed an attractive two-story brick building. Upstairs was a six-room apartment for his family.[117]

In addition to the traditional merchandise, Blythe carried paint, cigarettes, ice cream and cold drinks. Claude Greenup clerked for him. Blythe rearranged his store so he could put a pool table and restaurant in the front. Wilford Rouse continued the pool hall when he took over the building.[118]

Gulley & Pettit Stock Burlington

In the 1920s, Gulley & Pettit's general store in Burlington stocked everything from fresh meat and penny candy to shoes and silverware. The store even arranged for laundry and dry cleaning services for Burlington residents.

Katie, Mary Jane, Laura and Alberta Pettit grew up in the Tousey house on Jefferson Street and worked in the store their father owned in partnership with his brother-in-law.

"We raised our own food in a big garden behind the house, where there was once a

---

[116] *Boone County Recorder*, 1930 Historical Edition.

[117] *Boone County Recorder*, 1930 Historical Edition.
[118] "Smith's Grocery Store First Started in September 1937," *Boone County Recorder*.

large barn with a big well. We had chickens, pigs and a few cows (from which we got milk to sell at the store). We preserved our food and stored it in the cellar, which had a dirt floor and was always cool, even in the summer.

"We slid down the banister, played in the attic and warmed ourselves by the fireplaces (there was one in every room). Mother never turned anyone away from the door, and as long as we lived there as children, we never found the front door locked.

"Cousins found it a refuge in winter when their rural homes were too far away for them to attend school by school bus."[119]

Limaburg

Limaburg's school had been moved to an acre on S.J. Rouse's farm in 1894. In 1923, it was consolidated with Burlington School. The community meeting place was gone.

Depression Prices in Limaburg	
Eggs, dozen	8 cents
Jowl Bacon, lb.	10 cents
Creamery butter	22 cents
Country butter, lb.	20 cents
Chicken, lb.	4 cents
Flour, 25 lbs.	35 cents
Stock feed, 100 lb.	75 cents

Prices for both goods and farm land rose. The Beemon and Quigley store closed and Quigley died soon after. Newport man J. Proctor Brothers and H.R. Leidy of Ludlow bought the store in February 1920. During the depression, Brothers bought out his partner, then married and began living over the store.

Electricity arrived in 1922 and the Brothers store became an agent for Stewart and Warner radio receivers. Automobile tires and accessories joined the assortment of goods the store offered. Two gasoline pumps appeared out front. A smokehouse was built. Then the depression hit.

From 1936 to 1941, the community grew with better roads and new homes. Brothers was making a name for the tiny community by curing and selling about 750 hams a year, shipping them around the country.

"The green meat was rubbed with a mixture of salt, brown sugar, black pepper and salt peter. The hams lay in this for 28 days when they were hung and smoked with sweet hickory wood. They then hung for nearly a year."

World War II's meat rationing interrupted the business. Then Scott Walton's farm, 1½ miles from Limaburg, was the first tract bought for the new airport. The mill closed and eventually Route 18 was widened, sealing the tiny town's demise.[120]

1937 Flood

The '37 flood took much from Constance and Taylorsport. Homes on or near the main highway were ripped from their foundations and swept away by high water. The road was submerged from five to 15'. The displaced moved into the school where they received food and supplies from the Red Cross.[121]

The disaster drove a million Americans from their homes in 11 states and claimed at least 335 lives, but not one in Boone County. For 18 days, from Jan. 18 to Feb. 5, 1937, the Ohio River remained above the 52-foot stage, cresting at 80' on Jan. 25 and 26. Following newspaper reminders, residents voluntarily rationed water and electricity. Telephone employees worked around the clock keeping lines open. Power was out for weeks around the county.

The problem began when northerly storms brought gale-force rain on Jan 2. Meteorologists said the warm, porous ground would absorb the excess rain and prevent the Ohio from overflowing.

The rains continued. Total precipitation set a new record of 13.52 inches from Jan 1 to 24 – almost four times January's historical average of 3.6 inches for 31 days. Forecasters continued underestimating disaster potential, predicting that a sudden cold snap would keep the river in check.

---

[119] Katie Pettit Presnell information.

[120] Mrs. J.P. Brothers, "Limaburg Community Flourishes in Early Days," *Boone County Recorder*, Aug. 10, 1978.
[121] *Boone County Recorder*, Feb. 4, 1937, 1.

Chapter 11 1920-1939 A Flood Change

Water fell slightly Jan. 15 and predictions called for a crest at 58' at Newport in four days. That would submerge 2,000 residents along Newport's frontage and put the steel plants out of work. Relief efforts were organized. On the 21st, the forecast was revised to 66', then to 71' (the record of 1884) the next day. Jan. 23, the expectation was 73.5'. In reality, the Ohio measured 64' on Jan. 21, then surged 7' in 24 hours.

Snow replaced rain the next day, slowing the river's rise and prompting hopes that the ordeal's end seemed near while increasing the misery of the thousands displaced from their homes. On "Black Sunday" Jan. 24, the rain returned pushing water levels to 78' by morning on the 25th.

Leaking oil from Newport petroleum tanks caught fire when a Cincinnati trolley wire fell into the water. Raging flames leaped 300' adding to the hazards of the flood. The mile-wide fire stretched three miles long. A 60,000-gallon gasoline tank exploded, causing $1.5 million in damage. Barrels of oil and sagging gasoline tanks fed the flames. As the flames were coming under control, a 250,000 gasoline tank broke loose and burst into fire floating down the Ohio, setting fire to homes and cars along the way.[122]

Power failures knocked out every electric plant serving southwestern Ohio and northern Kentucky, forcing residents to search for candles.

Since the entire length of the upper Ohio was over its banks, the flood subsided more slowly than previous disasters. Six days after the crest, water had dropped only 6.5'. After the 1884 flood, it dropped 12' over the same time period. The river didn't return to its banks until Feb. 5.[123]

Temperatures fluctuated wildly, setting a record high of 74 degrees on Feb. 8 and falling to 30 degrees the next morning.[124]

Residents were cautioned that the heavy rains *"washed medal* (cq) (gravel) *from the road beds."* Roads along the Ohio and Kentucky rivers and large creeks were most severely damaged. Highway 42 at Warsaw and Carrollton was still underwater on Feb. 4.[125]

Flooded Dam

While floodwaters never topped the banks in February 1937, Lockmaster E.E. Newman said the flood created underground streams that cut through the sandy banks around Lock 38, sending them into the river. All families living near the McVille banks were evacuated, since many lawns and outbuildings had already caved into something that seemed to be quicksand.

"Almost directly in front of the power house, what used to be a beautiful green decline to the water's edge, is approximately half gone, and unless the underground water ceases to flow and the bank stops caving in, all persons occupying the government homes will be forced to move. The paved road leading from the top of this bank to the lock has also collapsed," a *Recorder* article said.

A half-mile away, Grant (Belleview) with its bank of sand and gravel, was facing the same prospects. The tree line was shoved over 100 yards into the riverbed and nearly covered with water. Underground water was creating unseen damage that would take time to discover.[126]

By Feb. 18, Newman reported slippage had stopped and repairs were underway.

Boone County Recorder February 18, 1937	
Summary Estimates of Flood Damage	
Farmers suffering damage	215
Farm dwellings destroyed	30
Dwelling's value	$30,000
Hay destroyed, tons	715
Corn, bushels	14,300
Other feed, tons	1,500
Small grain acreage destroyed	500
Poultry killed	600
Excessive erosion, acres	40,000
Silt & gravel deposit damage	3,000
Other property damage	$75,000
Farmers needing loans	115
Average loan amount	$75,000

---

[122] *Boone County Recorder*, Feb. 4, 1937, 1.
[123] Purvis, 210-213.
[124] *Boone County Recorder*, Feb. 11, 1937, 1.
[125] *Boone County Recorder*, Feb. 4, 1937, 1.
[126] *Boone County Recorder*, Feb. 11, 1937, 1.

Relief Efforts

School buses carried refugees to school houses quickly furnished as temporary living centers. Former Lawrenceburg residents joined Kentuckians at the Burlington school. Walton was prepared to house 75, but proved too distant to be used. Truckloads of clothing and cash appeared, much donated by Union residents and the less affected regions of the county.

C.L. Cropper chaired the county Red Cross. Prof. R.V. Lents reported that several farmers needed feed for their stock. Charles W. Riley said a few farmers needed help repairing their buildings and that their water had been polluted. Lillard Scott of Grant said several tons of hay were lost, but farmers in his area could survive. W.J. Craig and August Trapp of Rabbit Hash said farmers had lost houses, barns and feed. Trapp suggested that equipment to put houses and barns back on their foundations be secured to loan out. M.C. Carroll said many had lost feed and farm buildings in Hamilton and some needed credit to reconstruct.

Otis Readnour, Frank Walton and W.J. Craig, local feed dealers, gave advice and suggestions at meetings about the disaster. W.O. Blackburn of the rural rehabilitation program offered advice on credit matters for farmers.

The rest of the Red Cross committee included Charles W. Riley, H.E. White, J.W. Conley, J.L. Jones Sr., Frank Walton, D.H. Norris, Hubert Conner, assistant county agent Dave Colvill and county extension agent H.R. Forkner.[127]

---

[127] *Boone County Recorder*, Feb. 4, 1937, 1.

Two weeks later, property loss in Boone County was estimated at $250,000. That was $150,000 over earlier predictions. *"The loss of land and damage to property by soil slipping is going to reach figures almost unbelievable. Many of our river bottom farmers are reporting sinking places in their land, even though the water never reached*

In 1934, a flood decimated the Rabbit Hash creamery. The '37 flood destroyed it completely. Courtesy of Elizabeth Craig Stephens

them," said an article in the Feb. 18 *Recorder*.

"Many of them are of the opinion that all the land known as the Belleview bottoms is resting on what used to be the river bed of the Ohio, and for some reason or another the river has changed its course. At points where the slides have caved as far as 50 or 60', it is nothing but white sand and gravel."

Rabbit Hash

The flood washed away half of Rabbit Hash taking the chair factory, cattle pens, creamery, tobacco warehouse and the blacksmith shop. Despite rumors to the contrary, the two general stores and 14 houses were left, but badly damaged.

Water floated another store building off its foundation into the back of Rabbit Hash Ironworks. Residents used ropes to tie the building to trees so it remained when

This horse-powered ferry returned to use after the flood.
Courtesy of Bob Sharpe

floodwaters receded, offering lumber to expand the blacksmith shop.

"The '37 flood that went to 80' knocked the Knights of Pythias Hall off its foundation. Sheenie (Robert Jennings) Craig, who could make a dollar out of a dime, took the lumber apart and sold it. There were literally houses floating down the river," longtime Rabbit Hash resident Lib Stephens said.

At 60', water covered the General Store's front porch. When it crested at 79.9', the General Store was completely submerged. Mud remains in the attic and crawl space from the '37 flood, even after the flood of '97.

Secure anchors with a series of iron rods through the entire framing structure kept the store from being relocated by the record floods of 1884, 1913, and 1937. Rabbit Hash residents pitched in with wagons whenever floodwaters threatened, emptying the store of its stock. Driven to barns on higher ground, the wagons awaited receding waters when they were driven back to the store with their wares. In '37, water rose so rapidly, stock was loaded into rowboats rather than wagons.[128]

The flood washed out Rabbit Hash's tobacco warehouse, where burley was stored waiting shipment up or down the river.

Everything floated down the river during the flood including hundreds of railroad ties and Seagrams whiskey barrels from the Lawrenceburg distillery. Rumor was the distillery would pay to get its barrels back, so Rabbit Hash residents maneuvered barrels to shore and rolled them up the hills, pushing dozens of railroad ties down river.

As the waters receded and those railroad ties floated further away, railroad representatives came by offering to buy salvaged ties. But Seagrams showed no interest in the barrels lying all over the hillsides. Eventually someone pounded a stopper out of an oak barrel, strained the charcoal out of it and began enjoying the pure and well aged whiskey. People around Rabbit Hash were real happy that summer, Miss Stephens recalled.

---

[128] Clare, 47-48.

Chapter 12
1940-1959 Landing An Airport

The majority of residents sweeping out mud in the '37 flood's wake didn't have many, if any, modern conveniences. Four of five rural Kentucky homes still did not have electricity or telephones. By 1940, 96 percent still had no indoor plumbing or running water.

While the rest of Kentucky lost population between 1940 and 1950 as residents moved north for better paying jobs, Boone County's population grew by 2,195. In the two decades from 1940 to 1960, Boone's population more than doubled – reaching 21,940. By the late '50s, Boone was one of the fastest growing counties in the commonwealth – a designation it is likely to hold through the millennium.

Nearly 60 percent of the population still lived on farms, but the number of Boone County farms had decreased by 21 percent from 1920 to 1940. Average farmland acreage decreased by 3 percent. From 1870 to 1940, farm size had declined from a statewide average of 158 to 80 acres. After the depression exodus, average farm size increased to over 100 acres in 1955.

Now that federal agricultural quotas (limits on the amount of a particular crop that could be grown or sold) had stabilized prices, raising tobacco was again lucrative – enabling the average Kentucky farm to succeed on less than one-third the acreage of the typical American farm.[1]

Various citizens' groups tried to gather support to establish a public library, but were consistently defeated. Boone Countians were forced to travel to Cincinnati and Covington to find a library as well as to purchase dress clothes or appliances. General stores remained community hubs.

Florence with a population of 776, and Walton with 923, were the county's two largest communities. Their stores had diversified and specialized. Drugs came from a drug store, bread from a bakery, and milk from a dairy. But labor was not specialized, one handyman could do plumbing, carpentry and even electrical repairs.

In the early 1940s, Boone Countian O.G. Loomis carefully pulled a variety of governmental units together to level a huge woodland on Price Pike near Hebron for a new Cincinnati airport. His effort brought Boone County tremendous economic growth – at the cost of air and noise pollution as well as a decreased county property tax base.

World War II broke out on the heels of its namesake, pulling communities together while their men headed overseas to fight another war.

The war changed the manufacturing and distribution of most American products. Coonie Hubbard bought a six-cylinder Ford on Dec. 6, 1942. When he returned to pick it up

> **WALTON ADVERTISER**
> October 21, 1943
> **BOYS IN SERVICE**
> Two Walton men, John Earl Robinson, 26, husband of Mrs. Mar Lois Robinson; and Nathan Edward Northcutt Jr., 18, son of Mr. & Mrs. Nathan Northcutt, trained at the U.S. Naval Training station.
> Priv. William L. Hoffman, 18, of Verona, is an aviation cadet in the Army Forces Flying Training Command.

---
[1] Harrison & Klotter, 298.

the next day, the dealer offered to buy it back from him at full price. Japan had bombed Pearl Harbor and auto production stopped. The dealer knew he could sell every vehicle on his lot for a much higher price. Autos weren't produced again until 1946. Manufacturers switched to making military equipment and jeeps.

Everything went first to the military. Anything that could be used in the war effort, or shipped overseas to help in war-torn countries, was.

To conserve cloth, short sleeves and above-the-knee skirts became the style. Even bathing suits were smaller.

Scarcity of silk hose encouraged women to break with tradition and wear trousers.[2] To look like they were wearing stockings, women covered their legs with brown pancake make-up. The particularly meticulous even drew "seams" with eyebrow pencils up the backs of each leg. Only nuns were exempt from the "hemline freeze."[3]

Walton's tomato cannery opened. Seen as a boon to the community, everyone around Walton plowed up every scrap of land and planted tomatoes. *"They were all disappointed that they didn't make any money from it,"* recalled Harold Campbell who worked at the cannery next door to his mother's home as a young teen. Under the tin roof's peak, a young Harold ensured the gravity chute was kept full of tin cans. At tables below, women peeled steamed tomatoes and packed them in cans.[4]

At one point, Walton farmers boycotted the cannery in an attempt to raise prices.

The Cooperative Extension Service set up canning facilities at schools to encourage families to bring produce from their "Victory Gardens" to preserve for the winter. With many fearing modern new pressure cookers would explode, home economists demonstrated safe and effective ways to use the time-saving tool.[5]

In March 1945, the Ohio flooded at 69.2' reminding residents that like war – and exploding pressure cookers, it too could wreak destruction and toss lives in turmoil. The war ended mid-summer as a result of atomic bombs dropped on Hiroshima and Nagasaki.

In 1947, the new look arrived from Paris – using yards and yards of now-available fabrics. Poodle skirts, bobby socks and Spaulding oxfords signaled a new era of consumerism.[6]

During the war, anyone who wanted to work

In 1941, two Rabbit Hash brothers, Charlie "Bits" and Jerry Lustenberg, watch a minesweeper pass Rabbit Hash coming down the river to the Mississippi to the ocean from Pittsburgh. Photo courtesy of Rabbit Hash Museum

did so. Labor shortages prompted by the draft and increased demand for products brought more women into the workforce.

With huge income increases, but few goods available, savings soared. By buying bonds, civilians helped finance the war effort. Cashing them in produced a postwar buying

---

[2] Henderson & Klotter, 371.
[3] Martha Daugherty
[4] Harold Campbell, April 2, 1998.

[5] Bruce Ferguson and Martha Daugherty
[6] Martha Daugherty

spree.

Men had scarcely returned from European and Asian Pacific assignments when others were shipped to Korea to fight yet another war on foreign soil.

Airport Lands in Boone

The age of flight had arrived. When Cincinnati's Lunken Airport, in use since 1927, didn't have room to expand its runways, then flooded badly in '37, the Civil Aeronautics Administration began considering a new site.

Northern Kentucky's Democratic Congressman Brent Spence sent a letter to *The Kentucky Post* urging Kentuckians to develop an airport.

Civil Engineer O.G. "Oggie" Loomis (who had grown up at Hamilton Landing and in Walton) selected insurance agent William Steinfort's 100-acre Boone County farm as the best site in the region for an airport because it was elevated and less prone to fog.

Loomis informally handed his report to V.H. "Hub" Logan, editor of *The Kentucky Enquirer* and son of U.S. Sen. M.M. Logan, who gave it to Phil Vondersmith, president of the Covington-Kenton County Industrial Association and Greenline Transit Co.

The 928-acre site Loomis suggested in 1941 was particularly attractive because of its elevation, $40 to $50 an acre cost, minimal need for grading, expansion potential, and location only 12 miles from Cincinnati's Fountain Square.

But Judge N.E. Riddell was reluctant to change Boone County's rural texture and commit to funding such a large project being supported by a Covington-Kenton County group. Riddell finally agreed to the airport on the conditions that Boone County would not contribute money for land, engineering or construction then or in the future. The county's budget for road construction and maintenance then was a meager $9,000 to $10,000.

Pearl Harbor Day

The second week of December 1941, First Sgt. Frank B. Helms sent a telegram to his family from Honolulu saying he was alive, but unable to get home for Christmas. *"This was the first message to reach the family since the outbreak of the American-Japanese war on Dec. 7 when the cowardly Japanese attack on the island of Hawaii claimed the lives of 2,729 American boys,"* said a *Boone County Recorder* article.[7]

About the same time, Mrs. Emma Hempfling received word that her daughter, Adelaide Bravard and her sons Wayne, 7, and Donnie, 5, were safe at their home in Honolulu. Mr. Bravard (no first name given) was a storekeeper on the cruiser U.S.S. Minneapolis at Pearl Harbor.[8]

War Prompts Flight

On Dec. 23, 1941, Logan asked Loomis, who had worked for the Works Progress Administration (WPA), to fly to Washington and present the case for an airport in Northern Kentucky. On Christmas Eve, Fred Rauch, acting administrator for the WPA, said he'd approve the airport proposal within the month.

Then Loomis met with Sen. Alben W. Barkley (D-Ky.) who agreed to the plan and arranged for $108,000 of Civil Aeronautics Administration funds to be combined with

---

> **December 14, 1944**
> ### Burlington Boy in Philippine Invasion
> Bombing and strafing attacks from Japanese planes pinned Private W.L. Stephens of Burlington to the beach for more than a week in his first month of service as his unit worked long hours to help construct a vitally important airstrip.
>
> A typhoon struck the island compounding the hazards, but the strip was completed and "our fighter planes took off to blast scores of the enemy from the sky."
>
> Private W.L. Stephens, a former trucking contractor, enlisted in the Air Force in June 1941. He is a son of Mr. and Mrs. Elijah Stephens of Burlington.
> Paraphrased from the *Kentucky Enquirer* or *Post*

---

[7] *Boone County Recorder*, Dec. 18, 1941.
[8] *Boone County Recorder*, Dec. 18, 1941.

WPA labor to build the airport on ground purchased by the local sponsors. But Barkley suggested the plan not be publicized immediately.

"*The Boone County Airport . . . no doubt became the first major project in history to be approved and become a reality without a dime of local or organized funds*," Loomis said. "*The major local expenditures and engineering, numerous plans, all trips were of my own financing, with Phil Vondersmith or his company spending some on long-distance phone calls*."

Vondersmith was a "*hardworking Dutchman, the never-give-up type who never took no for an answer,*" Loomis said.

The Kentucky legislature passed a bill to permit Kenton County to expend funds in an adjoining county. The next year, President Roosevelt approved a grant for the WPA to develop the site.

William Wehrman, an attorney from Kenton County, bought 757 Boone County acres to build an airport. This was later expanded to 930 acres. Several land parcels were legally condemned to add to the property. County Judge Carroll Cropper assigned the suits and tried them on the same day to speed the process.[9]

Judge Cropper

C.L. Cropper was appointed Boone County Judge on Sept. 8, 1942, after N.E. Riddell's death. The Burlington High School graduate had begun his business career as assistant cashier at Boone County Deposit Bank in 1927. When the two Burlington banks merged, he became assistant cashier, then vice president at People's Deposit before he was pulled into the political scene.

Judge Cropper served from 1942 until 1962, during the time water districts were created and the groundwork was laid for the I-275 bridge to Lawrenceburg. Born in 1897, the Judge grew up on a Boone County farm, attended the University of Kentucky, served in the Army during WWI and returned to his home county as a farmer and banker.

From 1932-'34, Judge Cropper represented Boone and Grant counties in the legislature. Elected vice president of the bank in 1942, he was honored for 50 years of service in 1975. President of the Kentucky Bankers Association, he was active in Burlington Baptist Church and the Burlington Masonic Lodge.

Judge C.L. Cropper makes the first dial phone call from Burlington on May 1, 1960.
Courtesy of Carolyn Van Huss

(The Boone County Businessmen's Association petitioned the fiscal court to name the I-275 bridge for Judge Cropper. The Kentucky Department of Highways granted the request.)[10]

Drawing Together

Just a few weeks after the U.S. entered WWII, physical standards for draftees and enlisted men were relaxed to accept men with "*minor physical deformities*" and at least "*18 natural serviceable teeth.*"[11] More soldiers were needed.

In 1944, the draft classification that had

---

[9] Loomis, 10-11.

[10] *The Kentucky Enquirer,*
[11] *Boone County Recorder*, Dec. 18, 1941, 1.

deferred farm boys under 26 was changed. Any man under 39 who left the farm was automatically declared 1-A, ready for the next induction.

While the airport was not yet completed, soldiers traveled back and forth to various training camps before they were shipped overseas via Boone County's roads, trains and the Ohio River.

Fort Knox's gold vault stored the Declaration of Independence and the U.S. Constitution, so even more military guards were needed south of Louisville, filling rail cars and increasing traffic on U.S. 42 through Union.

Kiger Murder

In the midst of the airport and war turmoil, a cold-blooded murder shocked the region. Joan Kiger, 16, was charged with shooting her father, Covington Vice Mayor Carl Kiger and her brother, six-year-old Jerry, on Aug. 16, 1943. Joan's mother, Jennie Williamson Kiger, had been wounded in the hip by a handgun blast in their Boone County summer home called Rosegate on U.S. 25 near Devon, north of Richwood.

Boone County Sheriff Jake Williams, assisted by police officers from Covington, Grant County and the state, found evidence to put the teen in Boone County Jail. From her hospital bed, Mrs. Kiger declared her daughter innocent.

The controversial trial raised issues that remain unsettled. The *Kentucky Post* suggested the possibility of gambling connections and payoffs. An informant called Covington police to report an overheard conversation. Joan Kiger was released on $25,000 bond and taken for a psychiatric evaluation, then relatives secreted her away from the hospital to avoid the media. Soon the mother, Jennie Kiger also was charged with murder, either participating in, aiding or counseling the crime.

Noted Northern Kentucky criminal attorney Sawyer Smith defended the teen-ager saying she suffered from a nightmare complex inherited from her father that could include firing 15 shots from three guns. In just over four hours, the jury found her not guilty on the grounds she was "*unconscious or nearly so and that she did not comprehend the situation*" and that she "*believed some member of her family was being robbed or attacked*." The jury declared Joan dangerously insane and dropped charges against her mother.[12]

Later, under hypnosis, Joan told details of the crime, saying she'd set out to kill herself too but ran out of bullets. Still later the Superintendent of Kentucky's Central State Hospital said she was not insane.

First Class Electrician Eugene Abernathy of the U.S. Navy served in the Normandy invasion, the South Pacific and Korean military ventures. Courtesy of Dorothy Richie

First Female Sheriff

Glenrose Williams, 23-year-old daughter of Boone County Sheriff J.T. Williams, was named acting deputy sheriff after Deputy William Green entered the Army in February 1942. Then the senior Williams died of a heart attack in his office two years later and Judge C.L. Cropper appointed the Hebron High School graduate the first female sheriff of Boone County.

Adapting to War

War changed daily life dramatically. Red ration stamps allotted specified amounts of meat. Blue stamps were exchanged for canned goods and staple foods. Rationed items included coffee, butter, cheese, shoes, fuel oil, gasoline, tires and more. Most families were allowed three gallons of gasoline a week. Stamps were swapped and bartered to meet particular needs.

---

[12]Reis, *Pieces of the Past 3*, 107-110.

Those with orchards and gardens could sign up for extra allotments of "canning sugar" to preserve their produce. Victory gardens furnished up to a third of the vegetables consumed nationally in 1943. Cooking grease was collected to make glycerin for gunpowder. Scrap drives brought in junk iron and aluminum. Blood donations were constantly solicited. Banks encouraged war bond purchases.

Tire rationing began in January 1942. Shoe rationing began a year later. Each person could have three pairs of shoes a year.

In this national crisis, the government began withholding federal income taxes from paychecks.

Moral support for soldiers came from every direction. Patriotic groups formed to aid the war effort. Churches and civic organizations – the Red Cross, Boy and Girl Scouts, Eastern Star, Rotary, Lions Clubs, Kiwanis, Garden Clubs, Parent Teacher Associations – made special contributions.

Volunteers became air raid wardens, auxiliary fire fighters and policemen, scrap collectors, troop entertainers, hospital assistants, surgical dressing preparers, teachers for aliens, and clerical assistants.[13]

"*People would not even think about saying anything negative about the country*," Wanda Houston said. Living on a Richwood farm, rationing didn't affect her family as much as city dwellers. Even sugar wasn't a problem because her grandfather received extra sugar to feed the bees he raised.

When something was not available due to the war effort, the universal answer was, "*Don't you know there is a war going on?*" Even Campbell's Soup "went to war," converting its plants to make food for the troops.[14]

After the flood of 1945, Patty Stephens McGuire and her brother Ronald "Bugo" Farrell Stephens stand in front of Craig's General Store in Rabbit Hash run by their parent's. Elizabeth and Cliff Stephens and her brother Sheeny Craig ran the store owned by their parents, Emma and C.W. "Charlie" Craig. The Craig and Stephens families ran the store for 70 years.
Courtesy of Elizabeth Craig Stephens

Frightening News

Telegrams brought news from overseas. Mr. and Mrs. Sterling Stewart of Burlington learned their son Thomas J. Stewart was given a combat engineer's citation for extraordinary bravery during the D-Day assault on Normandy on June 6, 1944. Before he was shipped overseas, Stewart was a welder at E.W. Bushmann Co.

Telegrammed news was usually bad. One informed Mrs. Charlotte E. White of Petersburg that her son Sgt. Alfred E. White was a prisoner of the German government.

Mrs. Marie Hodges learned that her husband Orville E. Hodges was wounded in action.

Mrs. Marian Aylor was notified that her 32-year-old husband William E. Aylor, son of the Taylorsport Leslie Aylors, was wounded in action and being cared for in a French hospital.

---

[13] Klotter, *Portrait in Paradox*, 261

[14] Brittany Densley, "Wanda Houston," *A Peek into the Past*, 97.

The airport on Oct. 27, 1946. Courtesy of the Cincinnati/Northern Kentucky International Airport

Pvt. Elmer C. Webster, son of Mr. & Mrs. Roy Webster of Verona, was also wounded in France.

Mrs. Elizabeth R. Brown of Burlington was notified that her son, Pvt. Milton M. Brown, who had attended Belleview school and worked on his father's farm, was missing in action in Belgium.

Letters brought more frightening news, as well as details of the men's lives in Europe.

After being awarded a Purple Heart for his role in the Normandy invasion, Pfc. Franklin Lloyd Hood recovered from his injuries and earned a Sharp Shooters Medal. The son of Mr. and Mrs. Luther Hood of Constance, he was killed in Germany after seven months overseas. Pvt. Hood would have graduated in the Hebron class of '43 had he not entered the armed services.[15]

Carl F. Rudicill of Walton was promoted to Second Lieutenant after helping to move 4.75 million tons of war supplies to the Russian Army through the Persian Corridor. A Walton High School graduate, he lived with his brother William Rudicill in Burlington before joining the Army.[16]

Airport Construction

The WPA suddenly disbanded to allow its men to join the service. With it vanished the commitments for labor to build the airport. Airport supporters including Covington attorney Greg Hughes went to Washington again. Hughes' brother was an Army Air Corps Colonel. Through his contacts, and with the help of Sen. Barkley and U.S. Rep. Spence, Loomis and Hughes got an appointment with the Air Corps Chief of Staff for ferry transportation.

"We walked in his office at 1 p.m. He told

---

[15] *Boone County Recorder*, Dec. 14, 1944.

[16] Newspaper article, Feb. 1, 1945.

us he was a busy man and could only give us two minutes," Loomis said. *"We were still in his office at 6:30 p.m."*

By the time they left, the Air Force Transport Corps had committed to leasing 500 acres of the 930-acre site and had promised to build four runways, each 5,500' x 150' (rather than the meager 4,670' length planned), plus contribute $2 million. Runways were completed Aug. 12, 1944. Three days later Army Air Corps B-17 bomber crews were practicing takeoffs and landings. The first building was constructed of oak lumber so it could be moved with a bulldozer.

Kenton County Fiscal Court passed a resolution outlining airport development plans. Construction began after the May 3, 1943, groundbreaking. Later that year, the airport board convinced American, TWA (Transcontinental and Western) and Delta to sign 20-year leases, moving their operations from Lunken.

Kenton County Fiscal Court compensated Hughes with $2,500 for his expenses and Loomis received $8,100. After a power struggle with the new airport hierarchy, Hughes resigned and left for the war, as a Red Cross volunteer, because he couldn't pass a military physical. The airport board put Loomis on the payroll temporarily for a nominal salary.

Victory in Europe

The news of V.E. (Victory in Europe) Day, May 10, 1945, came *"hurriedly by telephone. By word of mouth the news was spread through the neighborhood and in the evening a crowd poured into Bullittsburg auditorium without previous announcement."* The spontaneous gathering produced *"prayers of thanksgiving, hymns of praise and unbounded joy,"* recalled William Campbell Sr., whose father was minister at Bullittsburg Baptist.[17]

After nearly six years, the war with Hitler's Nazi Germany was over. Boone County churches opened their doors for prayer and worship services, remembering those left overseas and those never to return.[18]

"Our victory is but half won," President Truman warned. *"The west is free, but the east is still in bondage to the treacherous tyranny of the Japanese. When the last Japanese Division has surrendered unconditionally, then only will our fighting job be done."*

A few weeks later, appalled by what he had seen, Col. Edson Maurer, son of Mrs. Josie Maurer of Burlington sent his brother newspaper clippings detailing the Germans' atrocities. *"Wish you would have Pete Stephens to put this in The* Recorder *so the people in our County will realize what their boys are fighting for."*

Edgar Maurer indeed passed on clippings that filled a half page of the local paper.

Chemist Hopes Bomb Brings Peace
Aug. 1, 1945
Missouri Athletic Club, St. Louis, Mo.

It's a big relief and very exciting to have the lid blown off of at least part of the project I've been working on for so long. According to the incomplete reports the results obtained from the first atomic bomb dropped on Japan are up to our expectations. The whole thing is pretty terrible to contemplate and I hope that those in positions of leadership in all the countries will have the courage and wisdom to control this new source of energy so that it will be used for peaceful pursuits which will benefit all mankind.

We must have peace. The alternative is an armament race that would just about end civilization. More than ever before the scientists are thinking about the social and political expectations of their work and will do everything in their power to see that this discovery is used for people and the benefit of mankind.

It's been a thrilling experience with no end in sight. I hope I can keep in contact with the work when I return to Carnegie Tech. I hope to be back after Oct. 1. I believe the Japs will be through before that, especially now that Russia has come into the war. I would not be surprised to see Japan give up any day from now on. . . . "
J.C. Warner*

---

[17] Campbell, 30.
[18] *Boone County Recorder*, May 10, 1945.
* Warner, great uncle of book editor Jennifer Warner, headed the Carnegie Technical Institute chemistry department when he was drafted to work on the top-secret Manhattan Project from 1943-1945. He supervised research on the chemistry and metallurgy of plutonium. This never-before-published letter was written to his older brother, DeMain Warner, Jennifer's grandfather.

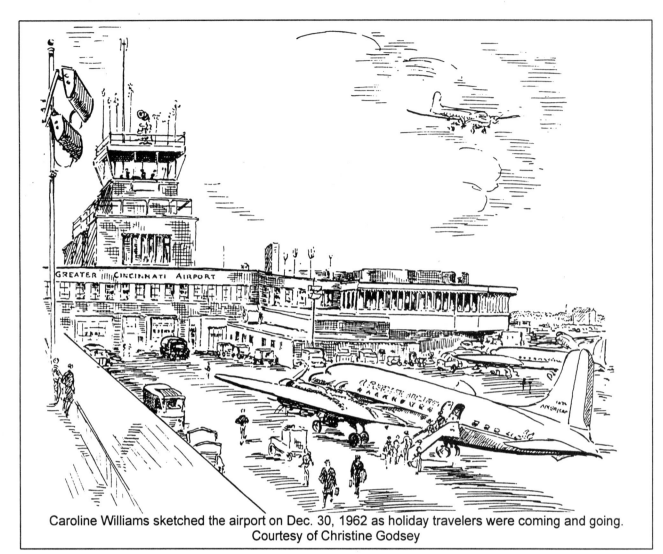
Caroline Williams sketched the airport on Dec. 30, 1962 as holiday travelers were coming and going.
Courtesy of Christine Godsey

Headlines read: *"Nazis' Ornaments Made From Skin of Their Victims, Krauts Made to See, Bury Horror Victims; Civilians Escorted to Scene of the Crime; SS Kills Prisoners Right to the End; Nazi Says It Was Worth It;"* and *"Nazis Massacre 1,000 With Flares, Bullets."*[19]

Truman's wish was met a few months later with the dropping of first one horrifying atomic bomb, and then another on Japan.

Henderson and Klotter said, *"War's end in 1945 returned to the Commonwealth many people with changed attitudes. They joined others who had stayed and evolved as well. The lives of women and blacks would not be the same again."*[20]

Runway Riders

Boone Countian Raymond E. Mattox remembers riding his bicycle to the airport and standing on the runways to watch the bombers practice "touch and goes." A Silver G model taxied up to Mattox and his friend, a door in the back opened and a man began running toward him. The other boy jumped on his bike and pedaled away.

Awed, Mattox waited. The pilot approached him and said, *"'Kid, do you have any idea what would happen while we are practicing landings and takeoffs if one of these things coughed? You'd be a grease spot even if they found some of you, so please get off that runway and tell anyone else to stay off that runway. By the way, do you want a ride?'"*

For the next 90 minutes, Mattox sat between the instructing officer and the pilot as they

---
[19] *Boone County Recorder*, May 24, 1945.
[20] Henderson & Klotter, 372-3.

practiced landings. After that he never went near the runway except in a plane. As a high school student, Mattox landed a job with the fixed base operator, Boone County Aviation. He earned his pilot's license before he could drive a car.

After four years in the Air Force, he worked for American Airlines for 33 years. His collection of American Airlines memorabilia is second only to the airline's own.[21]

New Terminal

The War Production Board approved construction of a $4 million combined administration/terminal building with radio range, weather bureau, post office and control tower. The air corps continued to use the airport until September 1945. In December, the Army declared it surplus property, which allowed commercial use to begin.

Water, electricity, telephones, heating, plumbing, runway and other lighting were added, plus a restaurant, a hangar for the fixed base operator, a fuel system and more. Material shortages delayed some construction temporarily. On June 20, 1946, the three airlines advanced $.25 million to complete construction. Terminal 1 was dedicated on Oct. 27, 1946, attracting a crowd estimated at between 3,500 and 5,000.

The first commercial flights departed from the Greater Cincinnati Airport on Jan. 10, 1947. The first incoming flight, an American Airlines DC-3, touched down at 9:18 a.m. Two minutes later the first Delta plane landed. At 9:32 a.m. the first TWA flight arrived. The first day, there were 51 landings and take-offs, 11 more than Lunken had averaged a day. That year, 147,894 passengers used the facility.

Improvement projects depended largely on federal and state grants combined with airport revenues from landing and parking fees, tenant airlines, government installations, restaurants and lobby shops. In addition to cash outlays by the founders, the only local money spent for the airport was $195,000 from Kenton County for the original land purchases.[22]

In April 1962 there was much speculation about when I-75 would open. It was already open from Florence to Dry Ridge. Courtesy of *Dixie News*.

Aerial Entertainment

Orville and Wilbur Wright's invention remained a great curiosity. In 1944, Mr. and Mrs. Chester Aylor's son Elmo circled above their home, piloting a private plane carrying his wife and daughter from Chicago. The parents didn't know their son had become a pilot more than three years earlier.

For decades, low-cost entertainment included watching planes fly in and out of the new airport. People drove their cars onto the runways to get a closer look, recalled Wanda Houston of Richwood.[23]

While flight was still an adventure, the airport was not above attracting even more attention to itself. In May 1949, it employed a parachute jumper for four consecutive Sundays.

---

[21] Rawe, 32.

[22] Rawe, 40.
[23] Densley, *A Peek Into the Past*, 98.

A 1950s "beauty shop." Photo by Bob Sharpe

part of the national Interstate expressway system: I-75.

The present route was settled upon in the 1950s. Money for the right-of-way purchases between Covington and Lexington was authorized in 1957. The agreement called for property owners to be compensated for replacement cost, not just fair market value. Boone County property purchased for the road was mainly farmland.[24]

First Interstate

About 1946, Northern Kentucky political and business leaders began a push for an "express highway" from Covington to the new airport in Boone County. The new airport was struggling to pull Lunken's air passenger service across the river and there was still talk of a Blue Ash airport.

Determined not to see the Cincinnati airport in the Kentucky "sticks," Ohio businessmen argued that there were no good roads leading to the Boone County site.

Northern Kentucky officials thought if they could provide a better road, Ohio would not be able to undercut the new airport. The new route quickly drew protest when plans showed it would destroy some expensive homes and part of the Ft. Mitchell Country Club. Ft. Mitchell and Park Hills residents sent a delegation to Frankfort to argue against it. The state locating engineer told them the proposed route was the least expensive and best.

Dixie Highway businessmen united with the opposition, fearful a new road paralleling Dixie Highway would kill their businesses. Another route was proposed, but federal officials suggested the new highway become

Tuning in to Television

Progress that improved roads also brought electricity to more and more homes, enabling a new form of entertainment to grow in popularity.

Fuzzy black and white images of Milton Berle, Roy Rogers, and Arthur Godfrey appeared on 12" television screens this decade.

Locals Ruth Lyons, Paul Dixon and newscaster Peter Grant did largely unscripted standup performances on audience participation shows. To watch the shows in person, people wrote for tickets a year in advance.

Cincinnati's experimental TV station, WLWT, began broadcasting in 1948, showing the first: Cincinnati Reds game, University of Cincinnati football and basketball games, religious service, and pro basketball – a Harlem Globetrotters game at Music Hall. Television owners called the stations to receive weekly program lineups.[25]

Early television owners often hosted large groups of neighbors frequently. Women arrived in the mornings for the "soaps." Children stopped in after school for Westerns

---
[24] Reis, *Pieces of the Past*, 199.
[25] John Kiesewetter, "TV's First Days," *The Cincinnati Enquirer*, Feb. 8, 1998.

Florence High School Pep Club in 1952. Cheerleaders in front are Joan Barker (Martin), Alma Clifton (Brown), Barbara Denham (Crume) and Jean Rowland (Stephenson). Courtesy of Virginia Lainhart

and the "Mickey Mouse Club." Some lucky children got to dance the hokey pokey while Uncle Al Lewis played the accordion in his Cincinnati studio. Hopalong Cassidy and Sky King built popularity for Westerns.

And entire families gathered to watch wrestling, Hallmark Hall of Fame, Playhouse 90, Studio One, Red Skelton, Bing Crosby, Ed Sullivan and more in the evenings. Saturday evenings brought "Midwestern Hayride," a popular regional musical variety show.

Inventor Sperti

Meanwhile, Dr. George Speri (cq) Sperti was inventing many advances in science and education. Born in Covington in 1900, Sperti never married but lived with his also unmarried sister Mildred in Boone County. His interest in cancer research contributed significantly to knowledge about the disease and its treatment. While he developed a successful cancer treatment, it never caught on because it took longer than conventional therapies.

Originally trained as an electrical engineer and working for Cincinnati Union Gas & Electric Co., Sperti first invented a more accurate electric meter. Then he founded and directed the Basic Science Research Laboratory at the University of Cincinnati. Working with a group of young researchers, he developed filters to isolate light rays that could kill bacteria or increase the vitamin content in foods.

Sperti turned any money he earned back into research and teaching. He invented Sperti Biodine Burn Ointment, Preparation H, the Sperti sunlamp, cosmetics, aviation instruments and electronic devices.

Sperti held the first patent for fluorescent lights and developed a process for making frozen, concentrated orange juice and another for using ultraviolet light to fortify milk with Vitamin D.

Despite his many successes, he fought for funding during the Depression – beginning a charitable research institute under the Catholic Church called Institutum Divi Thomae. He died in 1991 at 91.[26]

Immunizing Children

In 1952, three employees of the new Boone

---

[26] Crystal Harden, "George Sperti, Scientist and Inventor, Dead at 91," *The Kentucky Post*, April 30, 1991.

Stephen and David Abernathy straddle the horses while Russell Abernathy drives a wagon in about 1942. Courtesy of Dorothy Richie.

County Health Department began setting up immunization clinics for preschool children, visiting schools and inspecting food-handling establishments. Four years later a plumbing code was adopted and a plumbing inspector hired.

In 1962, mass clinics provided polio immunizations. From the mid-'40s to the '50s, the prospect of polio crippling or killing their children terrified parents. In 1953, Jonas Edward Salk developed a vaccine to prevent the brain and spinal cord inflammation, but skepticism and rumors hindered its use. Most Northern Kentucky children had polio vaccinations by 1955. Dr. Albert Sabin of Cincinnati developed an oral vaccine that could be given in a sugar cube in 1961.[27]

Nearly 1,625 children were vaccinated for measles in a 1967 eradication program. The Health Center building was completed with federal money in 1971. The Boone County Board of Health now included the county judge, a fiscal court member, three doctors, a dentist and a nurse. The staff included two nurses, two clerks, two sanitarians, one nutritionist and a plumbing inspector.

Overcrowded Schools

Schools too were changing, from many small schools around the county to larger, more centralized facilities.

By 1950, crowding was a problem at Florence, Burlington, Hebron and New Haven high schools. In 1952, 61 graduated from the four high schools. Total school enrollment was 2,700.

A new two-story school that included a library, auditorium, gym, music rooms, rest rooms, cafeteria and kitchen was built on 20 acres at the edge of Florence on Price Pike. In September 1954, Superintendent Herbert N. Ockerman announced that 2,185 students had enrolled in the elementary schools and the new high school had 515 students.

Ockerman had become Boone County school superintendent in 1947. The namesake of Ockerman Elementary and Middle schools in Florence retired in 1962 as superintendent, but continued to assist Superintendent Rector Jones. Ockerman died in 1981. His wife, Addie, who taught second grade in Florence for 30 years (and also taught in Burlington), died in 1986.

Busing had come to Boone County. Shirley Sutton Woods lived in a four room house with no plumbing, 10 miles from Union on South Fork Church Road. She was bused to New Haven, but after the new Boone County High School in Florence was constructed, she

1947-48 Boone County School Enrollment*	
Burlington High School	76
Burlington Grade School	239
Florence High School	88
Florence Grade School	301
Hebron High School	97
Hebron Grade School	248
New Haven High School	65
New Haven Grade School	161
Constance Grade School	93
Hamilton Grade School	106
Belleview Grade School	77
Petersburg Grade School	86

---
[27] Reis, *Pieces of the Past 2*, 239-241.
*"1,637 Enrolled In Boone Schools," *Boone School News*, September 1947, 1.

transferred there. In 1955, Shirley was one of 74 in the first graduating class.

Nearly everyone wore black and white oxfords. They cost $20 new and were "supposed" to look dirty, so girls stood on the toes to scuff them. Crinoline petticoats made skirts stand out. While school dress codes required girls to wear skirts or dresses, after-school wear included tight "pegged" jeans that were even snug around the ankles.

Integration

While busing and integration were contentious issues in Louisville and other places across the nation, they never became so in Boone County. Rosella Porterfield earned an education degree from Kentucky State University in Frankfort, then in 1944 married Matthew Sleet who farmed 20 acres near Richwood. (Rosella later married Vernon Porterfield.)

In the 1940s, Mrs. Porterfield rode the Lexington-Covington Greyhound Bus to work each day from her Richwood home. Only once did a bus driver ask her to take a seat in the rear. *"I said, 'Sir, I will not go to the rear. I have three brothers fighting for this country.'"* [28] White riders cheered her on, and a white soldier got up and offered her his seat. Later, fearful African-American friends were shocked that she had been so assertive.

Unable to get a teaching job in Boone County, Mrs. Porterfield was hired to teach 33 students in grades 1-3 at a segregated school in Erlanger/Elsmere. It was the first time the school, which included grades 1-8, had more than one teacher. There were no supplies, no running water, nothing to write on the board with, not even toilet paper for the outhouse.

When Mrs. Porterfield asked the superintendent for those basics, she was told the district had never supplied them to the black schools. After she insisted that teaching cleanliness was one of her responsibilities, supplies were provided. Several school board members urged her to continue asking for what she needed.

Rosella Sleet Porterfield at her home. Courtesy of *"A Peek Into the Past"*

"I never took offense," she said. *"I just asked for what I needed and was real happy to get it."* [29] Mrs. Porterfield believed that the oversights weren't intentional, but simply a matter of whites being raised not to think about blacks needing the same things they did.

While some parents had justifiably believed their children were getting an inferior education in the crowded black school, under Mrs. Porterfield's tutelage, students actually learned from each other as they listened to the other lessons. Surprising white administrators, her students earned higher scores on standardized tests than whites.

In the early '50s, white teachers of music, art, gym and band began coming to the "colored" schools once a week. Mrs. Porterfield, a pianist, had been presenting those subjects herself. However, the minority students were not offered any opportunities to participate in extra-curricular activities or sports until after integration.

By 1956, when integration was mandated, Mrs. Porterfield was the Elsmere principal. Her "smooth" integration approach started "colored" and white students sharing a

---

[28] Rosella Porterfield interview, March 4, 1998.
* "Colored Teacher Answers Question With Original Poem," Boone School News, February 1948.

[29] Rosella Porterfield interview, March 4, 1998.
* "Colored Teacher Answers Question With Original Poem," Boone School News, February 1948.

classroom as kindergartners. *Life Magazine* photographed and featured her approach as an alternative to the conflicts taking place elsewhere.[30]

Burlington Colored School

All the "colored" students in Boone County now attended a tiny Burlington public school on Nicholas Street that had been founded in 1891. Next door was the "colored" Baptist Church.

Principal Wallace E. Strader was the only teacher for 34 students in grades 1-8 in 1947. Students wrote an open letter to "Santa Claus" requesting a basketball and enough lumber to build a chalk board. Bullittsburg Baptist Church donated a basketball.

Mr. Strader was a dapper, always soft spoken and meticulously dressed gentleman. Katie Presnell, who lived in the Tousey House on the corner, recalled visiting with Mr. Strader as he walked to the school, always wearing a white shirt, vest, black suit and perfectly shined shoes.

"Colored" students who wished to continue their education boarded at Lincoln Institute in Shelby County. Grant High School in Covington didn't offer convenient transportation, although it was closer.

Boone Colored School operated until the fall of 1956 when schools were integrated.

Did What He Did[*]
By Wallace E. Strader

God bless the name of Lincoln
Who helped to make us free;
Who lit the torch of Freedom,
Which burnt to Liberty.
Who loosed the hand of slav'ry
And helped throw off the lid,
I thank my God that Lincoln
Long ago did what he did.

I'd have a different story
From what I have to-day,
Although I might be singing
It would be another day;
I have sung the song of freedom
Ever since I was a kid,
But I would not, had Lincoln
Long before did what he did.

My folk were bound in slav'ry,
They worked both day and night
On their master's large plantations,
Treated wrong more than right;
But they prayed to God Almighty
For this terrible curse to rid:
And the same God told Abe Lincoln
How to do the thing he did.

I need not tell the story,
It is already old,
Of how they got their freedom,
It so oft' time has been told.
But since the slav'ry evil
From us has been forbid,
I thank my God that Lincoln
Long ago did what he did.

To-day we are advancing,
We do just as we please,
We have most anything we want
We almost live at ease.
The job now for some people
Is to keep the black folk hid;
But they can't because Abe Lincoln
Long ago did what he did.

Three African-American students were transferred to Burlington, two to Hebron, and one to New Haven elementaries. Five went to Boone County High School.[31]

Boone County Jamboree

Extension Agent Joe Claxon, who grew up on a 463-acre tobacco and livestock farm in Owen County, had served in the military before beginning his extension career. During WWII, he was in charge of teaching recruits the infantry rulebook. He revised each chapter into a 45-minute drama, using his 24-man crew as actors.

"When I came to Boone County, I didn't know anything about extension, but I knew about show business," he chuckles. When the 4-H program needed financial support, he asked each school club to create an act.

He pulled the acts together into the "Boone County Jamboree." Knowing families would be a ready audience, they charged a quarter admission fee. Judges selected winning presentations and the clubs received prizes. The program was so successful and popular that the extension service recommended it nationally.[32] Some say the Boone County Jamboree was the precursor to WLW's "Midwestern Hayride" television show. Some 4-Hers went on to perform on the early TV program.

4-H Award Winners

4-H was entering its heyday. County 4-Hers

---

[30] Rosella Porterfield interview, March 4, 1998.
[*] "Colored Teacher Answers Question With Original Poem," *Boone School News*, February 1948.

[31] Jim Reis, "Big Role for Small Church," *The Kentucky Post*, June 30, 1997.
[32] Joe Claxon

received an average of $28.94 a hundred for their tobacco in 1941, assistant county agent Franklin Frazier reported.

James Stephenson, New Haven, had the best tobacco crop, all grades considered, in the district. Best county crop winners were James Stephenson, 1; Clinton Shields, New Haven, 2; David Clore, Grant, 3; Inez Martin, Burlington, 4; Raymond Ashcraft, Hamilton, 5.

Best tobacco record book winners were: Wilston E. Clore, Hebron, 1; Clinton Shields, 2; James Stephenson, 3; Raymond Ashcraft, 4; Sara McNeely, Hamilton, 5; and William Speagel, Florence, 6.[33]

Robert Smith of the New Haven Boosters 4-H Club won the 10-county district swine championship in 1943. Jewell Vice of the Burlington Blue Ribbon 4-H Club took the canning championship. Barbara Lutes of Florence X-LI All 4-H Club won the foods championship.

Other 4-Hers receiving high honors were: Bernice Sebree of Florence in clothing, David King of Verona in gardening, H.R. Fortner Jr. of Burlington in sheep, Robert Rouse and James Tupman of Burlington in dairying.[34]

Kathleen Kenney of Beaverlick modeled pajamas and a robe she made in the County 4-H Style Review. She won the top sewing prize and her garments were sent to the State Fair in Louisville. National 4-H competitions stopped during the war.

Marieta and Dorothy Richie pose on a Farmall tractor.
Courtesy of Dorothy Richie

Tractors Arrive

After WWII, tractor production began again. By '45 small tractors with rubber tires were doing some of the work horse and mule teams had done on Boone County farms. Calvin Cress sold the International Harvester brand at Limaburg. Erlanger Ford's Walton dealership, Kuchle Ford, sold grey Ford tractors.

While the small tractors that worked well on Boone County's hills took the place of two or three horses pulling a one-bottom plow, adapting to their power took some time. Hitting a stone unhooked the plow, hitting it too hard broke the plow point too – meaning a stop for repairs.

After the war, when the University of Kentucky and other colleges were flooded with men taking advantage of the GI Bill's free education benefits, agricultural research began churning out dramatic improvements in hybridized seed, fertilizers and broadening

Average Prices Boone County Farmers Received*							
Year	Tobacco	Soybeans	Corn	Wheat	Beef	Calves	Hogs	Milk
	$./lb.	$/bu.	$/bu.	$/bu.	$/cwt	$/cwt	$/cwt	$/cwt
1935	18.9	1.21	0.85	0.86	5.60	7.70	8.80	1.60
1940	15.8	1.12	0.73	0.81	7.10	9.40	5.50	1.65
1945	39.7	2.02	1.56	1.61	11.60	14.30	14.10	3.25
1950	48.9	2.53	1.48	2.08	22.90	29.00	18.60	3.70
1955	59.4	2.15	1.30	1.95	14.20	20.00	16.00	3.74
1959	61.5	1.95	1.10	1.75	20.90	28.60	14.40	3.85
* Boone County Cooperative Extension Service figures, 1997, prepared by Jerry Brown.								

---

[33] *Boone County Recorder*, Dec. 11, 1941, 1.
[34] *Walton Advertiser*, Oct. 21, 1943, 1.

A roof has been added at the Boone County 4-H and Utopia Fairgrounds since the original grandstand was constructed.   Photo by Jason Dunn

general knowledge of agronomy.

"The majority of farmers would accept the University of Kentucky's recommendations and would seek them out," Agent Claxon said. *"Some came in each year, asking if there were new varieties. Our job was to help the farmer be a better farmer. It was still a rural county in the '50s, I knew most everybody or their family. You didn't say anything about anybody because they were bound to be somebody's cousin."*

John Crigler experimented with growing cotton on his Hebron farm in 1941. Plants grew to 3' tall and had about *"16 mature balls of good cotton."* His greatest difficulty, the *Recorder* reported, was in getting cotton seeds to sprout.[35]

Farming was changing. As soon as the Rural Electric Cooperatives provided electricity, most farmers installed milking machines to take over that time-consuming chore.

For a time, some still relied on milk houses located next to wells or cisterns to cool and preserve the milk. But electricity also brought refrigeration that enabled bulk milk tanks to cool milk quickly after it came out of the cow. Soon buyers would no longer accept the old milk cans that needed to be individually handled and sometimes weren't very sanitary.

The expense of the bulk tank and milking equipment pushed farmers to enlarge their dairy herds to make those purchases cost-effective. Most eliminated milking by hand any more than the single cow that provided the family's dairy foods supply. Some switched to raising beef cattle.

Claxon said in 1952 there were six large dairy farms between Burlington and Florence.[36] (Not one remains there in 1998.)

Hybridized seed dramatically increased farm production. *"It used to be that 35 bushels of grain off an acre was good,"* Claxon said. *"Now they routinely get over 100. For tobacco, 800 pounds to the acre was good at one time. Now due to technology, new varieties and fertilization, they harvest 2,000 pounds and more off an acre."*

The improvements were so dramatic few refused to update their methods. Claxon remembered a couple who refused to admit their crops were riddled with disease and follow proven remedies. One declined, saying he'd put salt on his tobacco last year and he was going to put salt on it this year.

In 1956, Boone County growers harvested

---

[35] *Boone County Recorder*, Dec. 18, 1941, 1.

[36] Joe Claxon interview, March 4, 1998.

Chapter 12 1940-1959 Landing An Airport

15,000 bushels of peaches and 55,000 bushels of apples, principally along northern Route 8.

By '57 a two-row corn picker was available, a sheller could be pulled behind it, then a wagon that held the grain.

Fairgrounds Paid For

County fairs were a gathering event and an opportunity to show off agricultural products. J.G. Pennington organized the first Boone County Fair pony show in 1940, giving $24 in prizes.

On Jan. 16, 1942, donations from 345 individuals paid off the 4-H and Utopia Club Fairgrounds on Burlington-Idlewild Road (KY 338). County attorney Charles W. Riley of the Hebron Bank chaired the committee that raised $3,000 to purchase the 28 acres.

The grounds were deeded to the Boone County Fiscal Court with the agreement the 4-H and Utopia Council could use and improve the grounds.[37]

Superintendent of Schools D.H. Norris was president of the first Burlington fair board. On Saturday, Aug. 22, 1942, the fair opened with poultry, dairy cattle, sheep, tobacco, swine, landscaping, a garden exhibit, 4-H clothing and a draft colt and horse show. Premiums included some merchandise prizes and totaled $150 in value.

In 1947, the fair was increased to two days and admission was charged for the first time. A 79-page catalog detailed activities that paid $906 in premiums. Baby shows began with 15 babies competing for the title of most beautiful. A three-acre lake running parallel to Idlewild Road was completed in 1948.

In 1953, another day was added and premiums were increased to $3,000 plus ribbons. In 1958, 12 more acres were purchased for parking. Another 7.4 acres were added in 1966. R. V. Lents said the 50-acre grounds made Boone County's the largest county fair grounds in the state.

Korean War

Just five years after men had returned from WWII, on June 25, 1950, Communist North Korean troops invaded South Korea. Within three years, more than 33,000 Americans had been killed in a conflict later immortalized by a movie and a television comedy. Both called "M.A.S.H.," they found humor in daily interactions, while illustrating the horror of what the United Nations called a "police action."

> **Boone Countians Killed in the Korean War***
> Army Cpl. James A. Hoelscher, Sept. 24, 1951
> Army Sgt. George Tharp, Nov. 30, 1950
> Marine Sgt. Roy W. Wood, Sept. 23, 1950

The draft, for men between 19 and 25, began the day of the invasion, recruiting about 1,100 Kentuckians a month.

By September, Communists had overtaken most of South Korea. Then Gen. Douglas McArthur took over military strategy for the U.S. and the 15 other United Nations countries allied against North Korea. The tide began to turn. But on Oct. 25, China overwhelmed the United Nations forces with 300,000 soldiers and casualties grew.

President Harry Truman refused to give McArthur permission to move ahead, then fired him in April 1951. In 1952, 2,000 Americans fought their way up Pork Chop Hill – only 100 came back down.

The Korean War finally ended after Gen. Dwight Eisenhower became President and Commander in Chief. A truce was signed on July 27, 1953.[38]

One of Burlington High School's star basketball players, Reynold Todtenbier, was promoted to U.S. Army Sergeant while serving in Korea. He was the son of Mr. and Mrs. E.C. Ruppert of Burlington.

The Korean conflict is yet to end. In 1998,

---

[37] William Conrad, "Conrad chronicles Boone County fair," *Recorder Newspapers*, 1995 Boone County Fair Guide, 24.
*Extensive efforts were made to ensure this list is comprehensive, we regret any inadvertent omissions.

[38] Asa Rouse spent a great deal of time and effort contacting military personnel and veterans from around the nation in an attempt to locate the comprehensive story of Boone Countians' involvement in Korea.

Saucers Sighted

Leery of aerial attack, several Boone County residents reported sighting flat, round objects flying at a high altitude from west to east in early July 1955. Sterling Rouse of Limaburg said the objects were apparently made of metal, but were brighter than any airplane he'd ever seen.

A Cincinnati television station first reported sighting the objects. Rouse's wife, Ernest Gadd, Gadd's granddaughter, and A.W. Weaver of Burlington described similar objects. Mr. Gadd said they were flying in close formation. Mrs. Ralph Bresser of Florence also saw the "bright shining lights."[39]

North Bend Area

Around the county, general stores were beginning to disappear, but churches remained the stalwart centers of their communities.

Up north, the Taylorsport Sand Company began excavating sand to build many Kentucky roads.

On Sept. 19, 1954, the new Sand Run Baptist Church was dedicated before an audience of 500. Frank Estes and Miss Jessie Wilson donated a new piano. Ruth Harvey gave offering plates in honor of her father Rev. C.J. Avery. Franklin Ryle donated all the church wiring labor.

Belleview Baptist Church in 1950.
Courtesy of David and Jeanette Clore

Artist Mary Amanda Moore painted the baptistry scene. Many members donated labor to build and finish the church.

Bullittsburg Baptist

Shortly after war's end, the Bullittsburg Baptist Church decided to build a basement under the 1819 stone foundation. Robert W. "Bobby" Grant, a contractor and congregation member, planned to add an 18" thick retaining wall to the basement's depth. The nature of the building didn't allow modern equipment, so Bobby borrowed "Old George," William Campbell Sr.'s huge 17½-hand tall mule.

After removing the auditorium floor and the original log joists, they dug a ramp to what would become the basement's depth. Big George was harnessed to a dirt scraper, which looked like a giant scoop shovel with two wooden handles for dumping the dirt. When unhitched, the mule roamed the hillside grazing until someone hunted him up and work began again. The project was completed in 1947.

The old saddle house, used to keep saddles dry in inclement weather, was torn down and replaced with a new building behind the church that held the gas-burning motor for recharging batteries to run the Delco lights.[40] (Delco stood for Dayton

---

Belleview Christian Presents 'Star of the East'

Belleview Church of Christ presented the "Star of the East" Christmas drama in 1941.

The cast included Mrs. Leslie Shinkle, Raymond Hightower, Jack Purdy, Leona Kruse, Louis Kelley and brother, Russell Rogers, Allen Rogers, Billy Kruse, Margart Rogers, Gene Purdy, Charles Porter Shinkle, Doodle Kruse and Sam Hamilton. Mrs. Dud Rouse was in charge of music.

"The play, a very fine one, pictures the various incidents surrounding the birth of Christ. There will be eight different changes of scene during the course of the drama." *

---

[39] *Boone County Recorder*, July 7, 1955.
[40] Campbell, 12.
* *Boone County Recorder*, Dec. 18, 1941, 1.

Electric Light Co.)

In 1958, contractors used heavy equipment to excavate the back wall of the auditorium for a Sunday School building. While several parishioners watched, the entire brick wall collapsed into the newly dug basement – doing no damage to the rest of the building. Senior Deacon E. A. Martin oversaw construction of a new concrete wall joining the two buildings.

This advertisement appeared in the 1954 Boone County Telephone Book. Ralph Scotthorn ran the general store at Idlewild through the 1960s. Roy Landrum bought the car dealership and in 1998 customizes and repairs corvettes in Idlewild. Courtesy of Asa Rouse

Petersburg's Chapin Library

While Petersburg's population continued to dwindle, Chattanooga, Tenn. banker E.Y. Chapin built a public library in his hometown. Chapin Memorial Library was dedicated Sept. 10, 1949. Chapin, who loved to read and assumed everyone else did too, directed a furniture factory, a hosiery mill, a spinning mill and a stove works.

Christian Church minister Claude McDonald suggested the library be added when new Sunday School rooms were being built for the church. Mrs. Oleva Delph was named librarian.

Mr. Chapin's grandson, E.Y. Chapin III, manager of Rock City on Lookout Mountain, Chattanooga, Tenn., made the dedication speech. The 6,000 volumes donated included Mr. Chapin's *Harvesting of Green Fields*, and the century-old eight-volume diary of L.A. Loder, a Petersburg tavern keeper who kept a daily account of events from 1857-1905.

Belleview Loses Maurer

At the next little rivertown, Belleview Baptist Church hired its first part-time secretary, Billy Jo Brown, and decided to send *New Testaments* to men serving in Korea. The year after the church's 150th anniversary, it bought a $995 bus to bring young people to church. A Texas minister, a basketball team and a new well came to the church in 1955.[41]

An addition to Belleview Baptist Church, completed in 1949, contained a baptistry, so baptismal services were no longer held in

---
[41] *Belleview Baptist Church*, 8.

More excavations were done at prehistoric sites in Boone County.
Courtesy of Ann Fitzgerald

Middle Creek or the Ohio River. The new addition's materials cost $18,264 and labor was $8,063.[42]

Longtime riverman Capt. Edward Maurer, 75, died in June 1953. The Belleview native became a steamboat pilot in 1900, then moved on to captain the Port of Louisville. After retirement, he filled in as a towboat captain and spoke on riverlore for civic groups. *"He was slow of speech and manner, not easily ruffled in emergency, and had dark, piercing eyes,"* his obituary said. His sister, Mrs. Clara Smith, lived in Burlington.

East Bend Update

The East Bend Baptist Church added new pews, a vestibule and a bell tower in 1952. In 1955, Vernon and Faye Stephens donated land for a parsonage. The house was built by the congregation and is still used.

Reuben Kirtley helped survey electric rights-of-way for lines that came to the East Bend area in 1941 from Owen County Rural Electric. Vernon Stephens, who lived across from the Baptist Church, wired most houses.[43]

Big Bone Baptist Changes

In 1944, Pastor Sam Branham and Everett Jones of the Big Bone Baptist Church sent letters to the governor, senator and congressmen *"regarding the dispersal of strong drinks in our army camps."*[44]

A few months later, the church prepared a bulletin board showing the names of *"our boys in service."* Pastor Sam Hogan's salary was $25 a week. It was increased by $5 a week the next year.

In 1952, Big Bone Baptist Church members voted that pastors must live in the parsonage and that they be allowed to work as long as it didn't interfere with church work. The pastor's salary was then $45 a week. The next year, the janitor's salary was increased from $20 to $40 a week. The church voted to sponsor a radio program. In 1954, it bought a bus for $225.[45]

John Elmer Setters remembered carrying his lunch to Hamilton School in a Karo Syrup bucket. Lunch usually included a jelly or jam-covered biscuit and a fried egg. Children usually owned two outfits and changed clothes as soon as they got home from school. Boys wore long underwear, overalls or blue jeans, a cotton long-sleeved shirt, and buckle shoes.[46]

Hamilton Consolidated School burned June 30, 1953.

Razing Big Bone Hotel

In the late '40s, plans were made to raze the old hotel at Big Bone. *"The hotel stood on a knoll with a steeper, higher hill visible a short distance in the background. The property was*

---

[42] *Belleview Baptist Church*, 8
[43] Mrs. Elizabeth Kirtley, Jan. 8, 1998 interview.
[44] A Brief History of Big Bone Baptist Church, 30.
[45] A Brief History of Big Bone Baptist Church, 34.
[46] B.J. & Stacy Powell, "John Setters," *A Peek into the Past*, 63-64.

fenced with woven wire, as was most of the neighboring farm acreage. . . . A many-posted veranda stretched across the front of the building. Many seekers of a health tonic, a fountain of youth or just simple pleasure, must have swayed back and forth in their rocking chairs on that long front porch."[47]

Double doors at the left end opened to the grand ballroom. Small remains of a plaster medallion in the ceiling's center indicated a chandelier once hung there. Bits of fancy plaster cornice were visible along the ceiling's edge. The second floor included small guest rooms.[48]

Beaverlick

Beaverlick mail carrier Everett Jones did more than deliver mail. He gave rides to Walton and brought groceries for people who left a note in their mailbox asking for a favor. Gifted with an amazing memory, he read the notes then threw them away, delivering the needed items that same afternoon or the next day. In the spring, he carried 3'-square boxes lined with airholes and filled with peeping baby chicks.

When the Walton-Beaver Road was paved, residents asked that their general store – where men gossiped and women shopped for years – be spared from demolition. To this day, the road has an odd jog to dodge that building.

Kathleen Kenney Wiley grew up in a house her family had owned for generations. She played with paper dolls of Swedish ice skater Sonja Henie, child movie star Shirley Temple and England's Princesses Elizabeth (now the Queen) and her sister Margaret. She rode to Walton to roller skate or watch movies featuring Cinderella, Snow White,

Kathleen Kenney Wiley
Courtesy of
"A Peek Into the Past"

Roy Rogers and Gene Autry.

Kathleen and her sister mowed the lawn with a push (non motorized) lawn mower. At five, a great aunt taught Kathleen to sew.

Roy Kenney, Kathleen's father, was a member of the Boone County School board in the '20s and '30s. He supported the family by doing custom farm work, baling hay, combining wheat, filling silo and shearing sheep with a machine he designed and built. He repaired his machinery in the blacksmith shop. A man of many talents, Mr. Kenney even sheared Jack and Asa Rouse's pet billy goat in 1940.

Often 40 men gathered to help chop silage and blow it into silos. The women cooked a big meal and children stayed home from school to "help" and enjoy it all.

Mrs. Sam Hudson of Walton gave piano lessons to the Kenney sisters for 50 cents each. Kathleen played Richwood Presbyterian Church's pump organ, accompanying the youth choir.

New Haven Basketball

In 1948, three girls and eight boys graduated from New Haven High School. They had shared the school's one microscope and completed all the basic classes including Latin. School librarian Miss Cropper traveled to all four county high schools teaching the Dewey Decimal System and how to bind books.

At New Haven, 60 students attended grades 9-12 in three rooms. While school started after Labor Day, the boys didn't start until after tobacco season a month later and they quit early in the spring to set tobacco.

Following in her father's footsteps, Kathleen played high school basketball. Girls' rules required half court play, but Boone County officials ignored the state restrictions and let the girls play on the whole court.

Hebron had the only basketball team that could beat Kathleen's. Her New Haven baseball team was second to Burlington's in

---
[47] Roter.
[48] Roter, 350-353.

Richwood Presbyterian Church Courtesy of *A Peek Into the Past.*

On Sunday evenings, Hop picked up young people, even those who attended other churches, and brought them to Richwood. There Kathleen Kenney Wiley played the pump organ and they sang, played "Alley Alley Over" and volleyball. They held scavenger hunts and treasure hunts on Halloween.

In the summertime, the group put on plays at New Haven School's stage. The 50 cents a patron they collected bought sports equipment or went to the church. The kids cranked freezers by hand for ice cream socials and went to Butler Park on picnics and to swim.

"*Hop took us to summer camp at Kentucky Military Institute near Louisville. The trumpeter played morning wake-up call and evening taps. They had chapel every morning and the kids looked forward to using the swimming pool. We had Indian tribes and competed in all summer sports. The counselors, who were ministers, would tell stories at night,*" Kathleen Wiley said.

On Youth Sunday, young people gave the sermon at Union at 9:30 a.m., Richwood at 11 a.m. and Lebanon at Crittenden in Grant County at 2 p.m. Hop's "*car wouldn't go up*

county standings. Playing at Eastern Kentucky University the next year, she found the half-court rules too dull and quit. After graduating from college, Kathleen began working as a secretary for Sen. Robert Taft's law firm. Because it was such a long way from home, she lived at the Cincinnati YWCA and walked to the office.[49]

Richwood Church Activities

At Christmas, children attending Richwood Presbyterian Church received stockings full of fruit, nuts and candy. Rev. Don "Hop" Hopkins and his wife Bobbye moved from the Louisville Seminary to the old community house in 1944.

---

[49] Melinda Fillmore, "Kathleen Kenney Wiley," A Peek Into the Past, 100-104.

Bally Ache wins again. Courtesy of *A Peek Into the Past*.

the steep hills in Grant County, so we had to walk up the hills while Hop drove," she said. Elizabeth Brady Cox, George Howard (Ann Gullion's brother) and Kathleen wrote and presented the sermons.

After the war through the 1960s, ladies of the Richwood church cooked Thanksgiving dinners as a fund-raiser. As many as 300 paid $2 for turkey and dressing with all the fixings. The price was eventually raised to $4 per person. Girls waitressed and the boys helped with other jobs.[50]

Bally Ache

Brothers Alan H. and Marvin Gaines raised show horses, then began breeding Thoroughbreds at Twin Oak Farm near Richwood. A mare named Celestial Blue foaled a bay colt named Bally Ache on April 23, 1957. His two-year-old earnings set new records.

From January to May of his third year, Bally Ache won many 1960 stakes races: Hibiscus, Bahamas, Flamingo, Florida Derby, Jersey Derby and the Stepping Stone Purse at Churchill Downs. The first three-year-old to win four major stakes races, he was a Kentucky Derby favorite. He led for nearly a mile, coming in second to Venetian Way, a horse he'd defeated six times.

A week before the Preakness, Bally Ache sold for $1.25 million. He won that race by four lengths and was favored for the Belmont. But the day before the big race, his near fore leg was sore. It wasn't broken, but wrenched so severely he couldn't race.

Three months later, he won his first two outings, then headed to Chicago for the Hawthorne Gold Cup. He stumbled at the start, regained his lead, then gave way suddenly in the stretch, finishing fourth – his worst ever. He'd run 1 1/8 miles on three legs with a grotesquely mutilated ankle.

Pain medication led to an intestinal infection and a team of Lexington veterinarians tried in vain to save him. He was buried Oct. 28, 1960 at Bosque Bonita Farm in Versailles. The stable where he was born and the jockey house, now owned by Daryl and Sherrye Hunt, are listed in Kentucky Historical Society books.[51]

Verona Lake Ranch

Boontucky Hoedowners, a local dance team won the National Country Style square dancing contest at the Kentucky State Fair in 1954, taking home a $100 prize.

The team included Burlington residents Mr. and Mrs. Jiggs Scudder and Mr. and Mrs. Ivan Gulley as well as Mr. and Mrs. Irvin Scudder, Hebron, and Mr. and Mrs. Lamar Markesberry, Erlanger.

They also performed at W.D. Scroggins' Verona Lake Ranch recreation center in Verona.[52] Country music lover Bill Scroggins had started the outdoor country music complex in the mid-'50s. A big handsome man, Scroggins always wore a cowboy hat and boots. His wife, Edna Hamilton Scroggins was a highly regarded landowner.

By the late '50s, they sold to Thurston and

---

[50] Kathleen Kenney Wiley, "Richwood Presbyterian Church on the First Sabbath in May," *A Peek Into the Past*, 105-107.
[51] Sherrye Hunt, "Twin Oak Farm and Bally Ache, Richwood, Ky.," *A Peek Into the Past*, 139-140.
[52] *Boone County Recorder*, Sept. 23, 1954.

Georgianna Moore, a hardworking couple with extensive experience in the country western music and entertainment business.

The Moores booked stars including Webb Pierce, Kitty Wells, Ernest Tubb, Hawkshaw Hawkins and others from the Grand Ole Opry cast. Constant rain, nearly every summer weekend, drenched performers and those who braved the downpours to sit in the amphitheater-style seats.

Even with Cincinnati businessman Cyril Elder as a partner, the venture couldn't survive. The Moores moved to New England. Elder now owns the land east of Verona's Star Bank on Verona-Walton Road.

Walton-Verona Schools

Ed Chipman was the principal and teacher at Verona Elementary. Walton and Verona schools had consolidated in 1935 and built a high school on Walton's western edge.

Pat Scott pitches for the Fort Wayne Daisies in 1953. Courtesy of Pat Scott

Walton-Verona High School's junior class presented "Mumbo-Jumbo" as the class play in April 1941. Premised around Haitian voodoo folklore, it included "*murders, murders that turn out to be not murders; a blind man and a hidden fortune – all in three hilarious acts.*"[53]

The Sisters of Saint Benedict taught 29 students at Walton's All Saints Parish Church. The county's other Catholic school, St. Paul Parish in Florence, dedicated a building addition in 1951.[54]

Pat Scott Pitches

Walton native Pat Scott compiled a 48-26 record pitching in the All-American Girls Professional Baseball League in 1951-53. In Scott's first year, 1948, the league drew a million fans.

At eight or 10 years old, she played sandlot baseball with the boys in Burlington. Her parents, Irene and Wilfred Scott, bought a dairy farm, then managed Dr. Sperti's dairy farm on North Bend Road for 22 years. The farm they bought included a baseball field they fixed up and brought semi-pro teams in to play there on weekends.

"*The fellows would let me warm up with them, catching grounders and shagging flys. Sometimes, I would warm up the pitcher until the catcher was ready. They taught me a lot about baseball, which was a great advantage since most girls only had played softball. The baseball field was like the one in the movie, 'Field of Dreams" except that tobacco rather than corn grew around ours.*"

A fast-pitch softball player in Cincinnati, in 1948, Pat's father read a newspaper article about tryouts for the Women's Professional League in Chicago. Although she thought he was kidding, they went to Chicago for the weekend. "*When I got in that big ball field and saw all those people, I was scared to death, but I wasn't going to let that stand in the way of a lifetime dream to play real baseball*," Pat says.

---

[53] *Walton Advertiser*, April 3, 1941, 1.
[54] Conrad, *Boone County Schools*, 22.

"Baseball gave me a chance to travel, meet people from all walks of life, and see what life was like outside a small rural community," she says. Her younger sisters, Gloria Parker, Mary Alice Luce, and Frances W. Staten all became great catchers helping Pat practice.

Pat was one of very few players who pitched overhand. The All-American Girls' Professional League was inducted in the Baseball Hall of Fame in July 1988. She left baseball in 1954 to spend five months living on family farms in Austria as an International Farm Youth Exchange Student in 1954.

After earning a degree in zoology at the University of Kentucky, she worked as a medical technologist for 32½ years. At her farm near Walton, she raised and trained Appaloosa horses where she still lives.

Pat spent three days on the set in Evansville, Ind., during filming of the movie "A League of Our Own" in 1991. The managers never would have been allowed to act like Tom Hanks does in the movie, she says. Every two years the League gathers for a reunion. Pat now photographs wildlife, paints with oils, plays the mountain dulcimer and volunteers full-time.[55]

Cavalryman Huey

A New Haven High School graduate in 1933, J. M. Huey returned to Walton after he attended the University of Kentucky and the University of Louisville Medical School. He graduated Phi Beta Kappa in 1940, interned at St. Elizabeth Hospital, and completed his residency at Booth Memorial.

In March 1942, Dr. Huey became a First Lieutenant in the Medical Battalion's 358th Infantry 90th Division at Camp Barkley, Abilene, Texas. That fall he was transferred to the last horse cavalry where he served along the Mexican border.

Shipped to Burma with the Mars Task Force in July 1944, Dr. Huey was squadron surgeon. He was transferred to China until the war ended, then he worked at an internment camp in Shanghai, returning home on Nov. 18, 1945. Back in Walton, he opened a medical practice in the old Phoenix Hotel.[56]

No doubt unique among medical professionals, Dr. Huey never sent a bill for his medical services, except to estates because he knew the attorneys needed to list one in the records.[57]

The Walton-Nicholson Bridge on Route 16 off U.S. 25. Photo by Bob Sharpe

The Walton Community

In the 1940s, Walton's Main Street included several stores: two hardwares, two dry goods, one drug and six groceries. Businesses included a bank, two hotels, two motels for tourists, a tie factory, a frozen-food locker plant, five restaurants, two taverns, a shoe repair shop, a dry cleaner, a funeral home, a lumber company, a sign shop and a school.

The Civilian Conservation Corps camp, located at the end of Alta Vista Drive in Walton, was being phased out. By March

---

[55] Pat Scott, April 20, 1998.

[56] *150th Anniversary, City of Walton*, 50.
[57] Asa Rouse

1942, most CCC-qualified young men were in the military, filling jobs vacated by service men, or working at new jobs created by the wartime economy. Men who lived in the camp still meet for a reunion the first weekend of October at Cumberland Falls State Park.[58]

City water came from a waterworks fed by two lakes that were rented to a private fishing club with 350 members, one of the largest of its kind in the state. Bottled gas supplemented energy needs. A sewage disposal system wasn't completed until June 1976.

"The town residents are about one-third retired farmers and widowed ladies, a third city folk who came here for low rent and country living, and the rest business people", William Fitzgerald estimated.

Trains were still the heart of the town. In the early '50s, teens spent 47 cents riding to Covington – standing between the cars smoking all the way, laughs Jack Rouse, a longtime Walton resident.[59]

Bishop Mulloy dedicated the All Saints Catholic Church in May 1951. Rev. Henry A. Busemeyer was pastor. The church was moved from Verona where it had been established as a mission in 1854. Rev. Dee Gadd dedicated Walton's Church of God on Sept. 12, 1958.[60]

> **Boone County Recorder**
> July 10, 1941
> **Reeves-Kottmyer Wedding**
>
> The marriage of Miss Bessie Reeves, daughter of Mr. and Mrs. W.B. Reeves, Constance, Ky., to Mr. James Woodford Kottmyer, son of Mr. and Mrs. George Kottmyer, also of Constance, was solemnized at the Constance Christian Church at 8:30 o'clock July 5th with Rev. Orin Erbaugh, Trotwood, Ohio, officiating.
>
> The bride was lovely in white net over white taffeta, with a long train and fingertip veil. She carried a bouquet of white roses and gardenias.
>
> Miss Ester Fryer, Covington, as bridesmaid, looked charming in yellow. She carried a bouquet of yellow roses and blue Delphinium.
>
> Mr. Carl Craven, cousin of the groom, served as best man. The ushers were Messieurs Ben Kottmyer, Richard Kottmyer and Melvin Kenyon.
>
> Mrs. Paul Craven (nee Vivian Hood) gave a program of piano music before the ceremony. Mrs. Gilbert Dolwick sang, "The Sweetest Story Ever Told" and Mrs. Robert Earl Dolwick, "I Love You Truly."
>
> Following the wedding, a reception was held at the groom's parents, with approximately 300 guests present.
>
> After a few days honeymoon trip through southern Kentucky, the groom will return to service in the U.S.A. Air Corps where he has been in training since his enlistment. . . . .
>
> The bride, who is a graduate nurse from St. Elizabeth Hospital, Covington, will continue her services with Dr. C.W. Justice, Ludlow, until circumstances make it possible for her to join her husband in Tampa, Fla.

Entertainment

In the early 1940s, a group of Walton businessmen bought the J.D. Mayhugh Lumber Company across from what is now the Huey Dental Office. They built a modern skating rink. Skating immediately caught on with the young and not-so-young.

Near the war's end, the rink burned to the ground in a spectacular fire seen for miles. Cliff Pruitt, who had become its owner, rebuilt and operated it with his wife Jessie. Later, Wally Wireman converted it to a bowling alley, then sold it.

Stephens Restaurant, where Dewey Mulford's barber shop now stands, directly across Main Street from the intersection of Depot Street, was the most popular gathering place. Mary Stephens' home cooking attracted people for miles around. Jess Hopperton and Helen Gillespie helped Mary.

When the Walton-Verona basketball team won the regional tournament in 1942, the trophy stayed at Stephen's Restaurant with a rabbit's foot around its top, until the boys lost in the Sweet Sixteen in Louisville.

Lewis Shields coached Truitt DeMoisey, Paul Simpson, Russell Groger, Ray Coyle, Stanley Lee McElroy, Leon Pennington, Lawrence Welsh, Cliff Ryan, Harry D. Mayhugh and Charles Holder. Coach

---

[58] *150th Anniversary, City of Walton*, 25.
[59] Jack Rouse, Feb. 18, 1998.
[60] William Fitzgerald, "Walton Established in 1840." *Boone County Recorder*, Jan. 2, 1964.

Shields was killed in the Battle of the Bulge, but his boys all returned safely. DeMoisey became Walton's city attorney in the late 1950s. Simpson became mayor and Groger was fire chief for many years.

In 1956, Walton's population was 1,400. A classic Midwestern small town, everyone knew everyone – especially the telephone operators. The two dentists and one doctor were native sons. Teens enjoyed the James Theater and the town skating rink and feared any interaction that would bring police chief Herman Simmons in contact with their parents.

Louie and Virginia Schwab ran the Phoenix Hotel. The restaurant was a popular gathering place, over morning coffee for adults and after school games for teen-agers and the Schwab daughters' friends.[61]

Walton News
Walton Volunteer Fire Department's first year in service under Fire Chief Jim Bob Allen, 1947, was marred by the accidental death of volunteer Jimmy Isbell. Racing to a fire on Dec. 29, 1947, the old Ford fire engine turned over on a curve on Walton's South Main Street, crushing the 18-year-old.

The Ladies Auxiliary, organized in 1952, provided food for firemen, train crews and other disaster relief personnel. In 1956, emergency squads responded to a tornado. In 1958, they assisted with a train derailment involving a tank of liquid phosphorous. Ambulance service began in 1971.

Martha Wallace succeeded her husband Jim, in operating Walton's weekly newspaper the *Walton Advertiser,* in its old location on High Street.

Mark and Ann Meadows bought the *Advertiser* in 1943. Struggling through the war years, they erected a new facility on North Main. In 1962, after his return from naval service, former employee Malcolm Simpson and his wife Ann bought the paper.

1956 Walton Tornado

On Friday, July 13, 1956, a tornado touched down at M.L. Carey's farm on Beaver Road near Walton and danced through town, out Locust Street, finishing at the Chapman barn. Not a single life was lost, although damage estimates topped $500,000. Five Beaver Road homes were demolished.

Wind stole roofs and broke windows at Walton Feed Mill, the Tie Factory, Walton Skating Rink and other Main Street buildings. Walton Fire Chief Chick Worthington, Deputy Chief Russell Groger and assistant deputy chiefs David Hankinson and Guy Carlisle assisted in the

Union Deposit Bank was built in 1900.
Courtesy of Boone County Historic Preservation

clean-up. Churches collected money for reconstruction. Verona Lake Ranch sponsored a benefit for tornado victims. Many contributed time, labor and money for restoration.[62] Jokesters quipped, *"Walton was totally demolished, damages reached $40."* And, *"it was the first time Verona was swept clean in 40 years."*[63]

---

[61] Asa Rouse

[62] *150th Anniversary, City of Walton*, 48.
[63] Asa Rouse

Union's Pickle-Jar Bandits

While the town was usually quiet, an April 1953 Union robbery became an "open and shut case" – or an "unscrew the lid" case, if you prefer. Union Deposit Bank Cashier Miss Lillian Bristow was robbed of $5,218. Unhurt, she notified authorities.

Sheriff Wendell Easton, Deputy Byron Kinman and State Trooper Chester Henderson began a search for two very nervous men wearing dark glasses and railroad caps and driving a blue sedan with a luggage carrier on top.

They saw the distinctive car, pulled it over and found a Boone County resident who told them the car belonged to friends from Newport. Two nervous men and a shovel with freshly dug earth were found at his house. Following directions from a neighbor boy, the officers unearthed a recently buried pickle jar in the yard. It contained $5,218.[64]

Self-Service Groceries

Pickle jars were plentiful at the Beighle brothers' country store on Walton's Main Street, bought in October 1947 from Harold and Florian Lusby. Like other groceries of the day, items were kept behind the counter and the grocer waited on each customer.

An era ended when the store changed to a self-service grocery. On June 13, 1957, Charles Samuel Beighle and Paul Calvin Beighle, along with nine other greater Cincinnati grocers, became charter members of the Independent Grocers Alliance, creating one of the first IGA stores in the region.

In 1959, growing with the community, the Beighle brothers doubled their business' size and their brothers Truett, Edward and Monty joined them. In 1964, they sold the store to Stan Jones and Dale Dowery and opened the Grant County IGA.[65]

Union

Down at Union, Reuben Kirtley ran the hardware store. Groceries came from Anderson's or Newman's. Newman's included the post office. Men's shirts sold for $1.50.

Benny Zimmerman ran the filling station where gas was 18 cents a gallon. Union Deposit offered banking services. The Baptist Church was at the crossroads and the old Presbyterian Church was where Doll's Dairy Bar now stands.[66]

Samuel Bufford Setters worked for Ed

The new Flicks Grocery Store in Hebron. Photo by Bob Sharpe

Grater, a whiskey salesman and poultry farmer who lived in the big red brick Hick's house on Hathaway Road. Samuel's son, John Elmer Setters, raised 250 turkeys and 200 chickens for the Graters. Grater's wife Eve modeled for Shillitos. Their daughter sang at the Becker Supper Club in Newport.

If John caught a cold, he took a cough syrup his grandmother, Martha Jane Portwood, made of horehound candy sticks and bourbon. After the candy had dissolved, a few spoons full "knocked-out" the cough.

In 1944, Mr. Setters drove his 1935 black Oldsmobile from Union to work at Shillitos in downtown Cincinnati. He earned $18 a week,

---

[64] *Boone County Recorder*, April 2, 1953, 1.

[65] *150th Anniversary, City of Walton*, 78.
[66] Powell, *A Peek Into the Past*, 63.

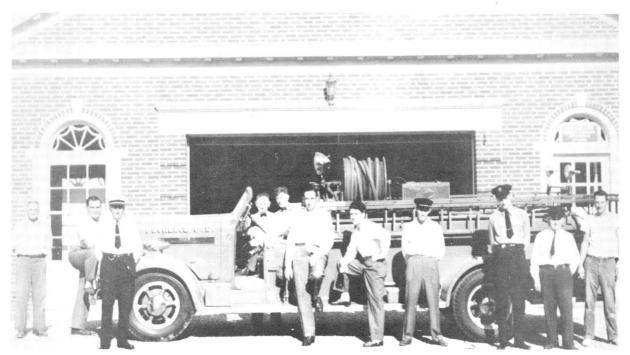

Florence Volunteer Fire Department in the early 1950s. Wilford "Fats" Tanner, Chief Al Hue, possibly Elmer Ruef, Toy Brooks (in front of truck), Vernon Smith, unknown, Al Hue Jr., unknown, and Francis Souther. Courtesy of Tom Utz

paid in cash.[67] (That Shillitos store closed in 1997.)

Dr. Lanter Moves to Union

In 1959, Betty and Kenneth Lanter bought 100 acres with a farm house near Union for $430 per acre. Dr. Lanter's Florence medical practice had opened in the late 1950s, making him one of five physicians in town. Office visits cost $3. House calls were $5. (An Ohio University graduate, the general practitioner returned to school and eventually became a psychiatrist.)

To ensure patient confidentiality, the Lanters paid $500 to run a private phone line from Florence. The Fish and Hunting Commissioner for 17 counties, Dr. Lanter was responsible for regulating hunting and fishing.

Hearing screaming in the night while the doctor was making house calls, Betty was terrified. She contemplated calling the police, but didn't. When the shrieks continued other nights, she finally discovered they came from the neighbor's peacocks.

Another night when she was home alone, honking vehicles alerted her to the fact that her cattle ran through a fence onto U.S. 42. Before the Interstates, 42 was the main road to Louisville.

Halloween Excitement

Around Halloween roads were blocked with trees cut by pranksters on "Cabbage Night." Since children in outlying areas didn't have a ready location for trick-or-treat, the night before Halloween, they made items appear in unusual places – like wagons on top of buildings – or stole hay to barricade roads, sometimes setting it on fire.

Halloween began the night before with cabbage or trick night for "town" kids in Florence. Halloween was treat night. Florence parents traditionally accompanied even older children, so they could walk the streets and visit with neighbors.[68]

Osborn Offers Fireworks

July 4 was another Florence community

---

[67] Powell, *A Peek Into the Past*, 64.

[68] Virginia Lainhart

celebration, spearheaded by "Uncle Ed" Osborn, recalls his niece Virgina Lee Osborn.

The community-oriented storekeeper collected fireworks in a wooden box in his shop all year. At dusk on July 4, everyone gathered, filling the swing and old church bench in the vacant lot next to David and Selma Osborn. He gingerly carried out the box of explosives and began setting them off amidst "oohs" and "ahhhs" of the crowd.

On Mother's Day, the Methodist and Christian churches were decorated with fragrant lily-of-the-valley that ladies picked from Uncle Ed's side yard that bloomed like a white carpet. Weddings also relied on yard flowers. Only funerals required florist flowers.

Osborn's store offered a three-way mix of merchandise, Coney Island hot dogs, and haircuts. At 8, Virginia began watching the store for Uncle Ed while he ate supper, worked in his garden or rested his feet after a long day of haircutting and minding the store. She *"wrote bus tickets, cut lunch meat on the slicer, sold merchandise, dipped ice cream and made Coney Islands."* [69]

Florence Flowers

Fanny and Jane Scott put the mail in boxes at the Post Office on the corner of Girard Street. Mentor Martin ran the grocery. Ann Robinson Conner had the drug store.

John Fisher brought his mules to town each spring to plow gardens. His arrival signaled spring-cleaning time. That included washing windows and laundering the lace curtains. Wet curtains were stretched across wooden frames and pulled until all sides were even. "Fingers would be pierced and sore for days," Mrs. Lainhart recalls.

---

[69] Virginia Lainhart

Warm hearts at Florence Bus Stop
By Virginia Osborn Lainhart, Hebron

During the early 1940s, Florence was a typical country town. On Fridays and Saturdays it was time to buy groceries, maybe get a haircut, buy a few things from Osborn's Department Store. But mainly, people came to visit and have some of Uncle Ed's famous chili or Coney Islands.

When the War came, the townspeople grew even closer and more caring. A large signboard was placed at the corner of Main Street. As each man went off to war, his name was painted on the board along with a star. If he became missing or was killed, the color of his star was changed.

Because of rationing, many things became hard to get. But Uncle Ed couldn't turn down anyone who came to ask for a little sugar to make candy, cookies or cakes for the boxes that were sent to "our boys." And, as there was no mail delivery, people would stop at the store to exchange news.

The Greyhound Bus Station was also in Osborn's store and the buses were stopped using a red light on the building.

One snowy night close to Christmas, the store door opened and in came a tired-looking woman leading two sleepy little children and dragging a large, battered suitcase. She said they had been riding a bus for 48 hours and were put off to change buses.

Uncle Ed told her the bus was due at 2:30 a.m. Suddenly all the worry and frustration of trying to follow her husband all the way across the country became too much and she started to cry. Uncle Ed said she didn't have to worry, he wouldn't put them out in the cold, but would keep the store open.

He asked the hungry-looking children if they would like something to eat. The mother replied she had spent all her money and they had eaten all the food she packed. Without a word, he set bowls of his famous chili in front of them, along with a platter of Coney Islands.

In the meantime, Aunt Eva was growing a bit worried since the hour was late and Uncle Ed wasn't a young man anymore. She got me out of bed to go check on him.

When we walked into the store, there sat two children looking at a book, and Uncle Ed telling the lady all about the town of Florence and the people who lived there.

Aunt Eva took charge and got the lady a new towel from the shelf and a bar of soap and said she could take a bath in the sink bowl of the barber shop where it was warm and there was plenty of hot water.

Not to be outdone, Uncle Ed started putting small toys, some books and candy into a bag for the children. Then I saw him pull out his old, worn, black wallet and take out a $10 bill, which he slipped into the lady's coat pocket.

Right on the dot of 2:30, the bus slid to a stop and after some quick hugs, the children and bag were on the bus. But the young woman stopped halfway up the steps and said, "I'll never forget you and this town of Florence."

I've always wondered what happened to this family and hope they have shared with others what was shared that night. This truly is what friendship is all about, reaching out to help others with what you have, whatever their need may be.

The Greyhound Bus stopped at Osborn's Store, next to the Odd Fellows Hall in Florence. Mentor Martin ran a grocery in the lower level of the Odd Fellows building. This June 1940 photo shows Virginia (Osborn) Lainhart, Mary Roberts, Carrie Martin and Eva Osborn.   Photo contributed by Virginia Lainhart

Before Memorial Day, everyone who was able headed to the old Center Street cemetery with push mowers, grass shears and old scissors. They trimmed around each grave and spruced up the entire cemetery.

Over lunch as they shared sandwiches, *"People would talk of those whose graves we were cleaning. Before we left, every grave would have at least one flower placed on it. This reminded the children of their ties to the past and the reason Decoration Day was founded,"* Mrs. Lainhart said.

As the summer progressed with weeding hoeing, picking off bugs and carrying hundreds of water buckets, garden produce was ready to be canned. In addition to picking, snapping, shelling, washing and preparing vegetables, it meant digging out the canning jars and cleaning everything.

Virginia's small hands were a valuable commodity to ensure as many green beans, lima beans, pickles and tomatoes as would fit were packed into every jar. After helping her family, she assisted the neighbors.

The Methodist Church arranged for the Markesberry brothers' trucks to take children to the Cincinnati Zoo. *"We were wide-eyed looking at Susie the famous gorilla. But the most special trip was going to Cincinnati to board the Island Queen for a trip back into history as we watched the giant paddle wheel carry us to magical Coney Island for the scary rides and cotton candy."*

Some community fishermen went to the Kentucky River. If they caught a lot, they held a fish fry in someone's back yard. Sawhorses topped with planks made tables to hold all the food. As the day passed into evening, the men played cards and the women talked.

In the fall, the huge old woods on Price Pike where the airport now stands was full of color and bittersweet. Both were gathered to decorate homes. Dirt from around fallen logs was collected to repot houseplants that had spent the summer outside.[70]

Winter in Florence

Winter brought snow-covered walks, cleaned by youngsters without a thought of being paid. Mail was picked up for elderly neighbors and extra wood or coal hauled for them as a matter of course. Stove ashes made walking easier on ice. Highway departments spread cinders rather than salt.

The best sledding area in Florence was between Lloyd Avenue and Main, which is now Lynn Street. Metal runners on wooden sleds were kept slick with paraffin or soap. Bonnie Luck, who lived in the only nearby house, always provided warm drinks for sledders.

During the winter, *"Mother would heat flat irons to be used as foot warmers at the bottom of the feather beds each night. Getting dressed for school in the mornings was a teeth chat-tering experience. Nature's necessary trips to the outhouse behind the barn were made in utmost haste and without reading from the Sears and Roebuck catalog,"* Mrs. Lainhart says.

School bus drivers Cliff Tanner and Shelby Beemon traveled the roads regardless of weather. "Snow days" didn't exist.

Christmas meant picking out nutmeats for cookies and cakes, lots of baking and making homemade candy. *"The stores were decorated and everyone seemed to have smiles, even in the midst of the war. We wrote letters to Santa and listened to the radio to see if they had been selected to read over the air,"* she recalled.

Bob Eads, a major Democratic party figure, ran Bob & Gene's Restaurant in Florence in addition to hauling milk for local dairy farmers. The restaurant sold beer, but not hard liquor. For nearly 30 years, teens and adults considered the little building the best place in the county to "hang" out and eat barbecue sandwiches. In the '60s "car hops" delivered meals to people sitting outside in their cars, placing food on trays attached to car windows. Photo by Bob Sharpe

The day after presents were opened was for visiting neighbors and admiring their gifts on display. *"We never seemed envious of what someone had. Our New Year's wishes always included hope of a quick end to the war and good health and happiness for our neighbors."*[71]

Florence in the Forties

In 1943, in an effort to increase business for Main Street companies, the huge trees that formed a green arch over Florence's Main Street were cut down and the street was widened. Development followed.

Bob & Gene's was well know for its barbecue and also served hamburgers, but wasn't fast food.

---

[70] Virginia Lainhart

[71] Virginia Lainhart

Chapter 12 1940-1959 Landing An Airport

Florence's Osborn store in June 1940. Carrie Sine Martin is behind the counter. George Houston, Bob Martin, and Dan Houston are sitting on the soda fountain stools. Standing are Ed Osborn, Hal and Sally Highhouse, Eva Osborn, Elmer Corbin and Mary Roberts. Virginia Osborn is standing in front.
Courtesy of Virginia Osborn Lainhart

Florence Drive In opened and teens flocked to it, staying away from the $.25 movies in theaters. Teens went to the airport to watch planes come in, took hayrides to Cleek Park (off 42 between New Haven and the junction with Rt. 338), watched boats lock through at Belleview, and rode the trolleys in Covington.[72]

Selma Osborn lived on Main Street with her three children. She raised a large garden and had a wash house. When her health bothered her about 1940, she hired Hattie, a tiny little African-American woman who rode the bus from Elsmere to help with the washing.

"Thin as a rail, but quick as a minute, Hattie ruled with an iron hand," Mrs. Lainhart recalled. *"You children better behave or Nigger Hattie is going to give you all a switching,"* she warned. She sang hymns as she hung laundry on the line: *"Shall We Gather At the River, Old Rugged Cross"* and *"In the Garden."*

An old Main Street building that had served many uses, last became the RKO Theater with a big screen and player piano to accompany the silent movies. When interest in movies waned, Mrs. Lainhart's Uncle Ed bought the piano so she could begin music lessons.

Adriene Stith, wife of funeral director Ralph Stith, gave lessons in her home above the funeral parlor at the intersection of 25 and 42. The viewing rooms and piano were on the first floor. *"I was a child not easily intimidated by anything, but it was very scary to smell the funeral flowers and know there was a dead body in a casket close to you,"* Mrs. Lainhart recalled.

Her father bought many music rolls and the old piano became a gathering point for children after school.[73]

Martin Brothers' Garage (on Main Street north of where Florence Baptist Church is now) housed Florence's fire truck. In about 1946, two doors away from the garage, Zeffa Osborn put a kettle on her coal oil stove preparing to do some canning.

---

[72] Marcie & Melinda Fillmore, "Anne Leake," *A Peek Into the Past*, 48-49.

[73] Virginia Lainhart, March 4, 1998.

Heading to the back yard to get something, she turned to see her home on fire. Despite her proximity to the fire station, her home was badly damaged. Someone had parked a locked car in front of the garage door and firefighters couldn't get the truck out![74]

Florence in the Fifties

In the 1950s, uptown Florence had several stores: three groceries – Riddell's, Meyer's and Parkview Market; Florence Hardware, Lucas Hardware and a "five and ten cent store" where Mrs. Louella Houston worked. Ernie's Market thrived on Dixie Highway near where the Turfway Road intersection is now.

Mail was not delivered to each home. Residents either went to the Post Office and asked for it, or rented a box there. At least three houses on a street had to commit to paying for telephone service before a line would be installed. Residents bought gravel to pave their own streets.

Water pressure remained a problem. Some mothers did their laundry at 2 a.m. to ensure they'd have enough water to finish it. During dinner hours, an open spigot produced only a trickle of water. The pipes were too small to accommodate the growing demand.

Many houses still had their own cisterns and outdoor privies. [75]

Florence Department Store on Main Street was the place to shop for styles of the day – poodle, gored and flared skirts; white net crinolines, saddle shoes, cotton print house dresses, men's pleated pants and bow ties.

The Florence Fire Hall and Community Center was completed, featuring colonial architecture, fire department quarters, an auditorium and banquet hall. Another new building housed the Post Office, the Building and Loan Association, a law office and a spacious basement suitable for community meetings.

Clifford Coyle, chairman of Florence's Board of Trustees, signed an ordinance on March 13, 1951, that increased property taxes to 75 cents for each $100 of real property.[76]

Joe Littrell's shoe repair shop earned recognition for 25 years of continuous operation in Florence. Martin Brothers' Garage thrived on a reputation for reliable auto mechanic work.

The 1958 General Assembly changed Florence's designation from a sixth class city to third class, denoting its population increase to 8,000.

Snow surrounded the little Methodist Church in Florence on March 12, 1950 in this sketch by Caroline Williams. Courtesy of Christine Godsey

---

[74] Virginia Lainhart

[75] Brenda Sparks and Martha Daugherty.
[76] Florence Ordinance Book #1, 311.

In 1959, Boone County Historical Society member Lucille W. Jones said, *"Florence is a thriving community of law-abiding citizens. We have no jail and no need of one. It is governed by a Board of Trustees consisting of five men elected by the people every two years."* Professional members were three doctors, a dentist, a chiropractor, and two lawyers.

High School

High school students of the late '50s and early '60s spent a lot of time "hanging out" together, after homework was done, of course. One "hang out" was the Stringtown Bus Stop to watch the Greyhound buses.

"Six of us did everything together," Brenda J. Richie Sparks recalls of her 1957 Boone County High School classmates in Florence. *"We went to the Florence Drive-In, Madison and Liberty Theaters, swimming at Coney Island's Sunlight Pool, parties and anything fun."*

The soda fountain at Denham's Florence Drugs offered phosphates and flavored Cokes and Pepsis for a nickel, served in a real soda fountain glass. Downstairs, Mary Jane's Music Shop sold 45 r.p.m. with one song one each side for 39 cents. Faster playing high fidelity 78 r.p.m. record albums sold for 89 cents.

Active in school clubs, the girls cheered for their favorite high school basketball and football players on Friday nights.

As sophomores, some of the girls could drive. One worked as a "car hop" at a new drive-in restaurant called Zestos' where trays to hold paper-wrapped burgers and fries were hooked over open windows. Zestos, on Dixie Highway at Sanders Drive, introduced creamy whip ice cream to Florence. Cones were 15 cents or a quarter.

More homework and more club activities came in 1959, plus sock hops, parties and the long-awaited Junior Prom. They ventured out of Florence to Covington, Erlanger and Ludlow for movies and shopping. They swam at Pleasure Isle and went to Moonlight Gardens at Coney Island to see famous entertainers like Tommy Sands, who later married Nancy Sinatra.

Brenda's all-time favorite singer is Elvis Presley "The King of Rock and Roll" who made teens across the nation swoon. His suggestive hip-gyrations were considered so obscene that cameramen showed him only from the waist up in his first appearance on the Ed Sullivan Show.

Ritsel Sparks Jr. and Brenda Richie ready to go to Moonlight Gardens at Coney Island in 1961.
Courtesy of Ritsel and Brenda Sparks

"Our senior year was so magical, it was like a dream," Brenda says. *"Everything was so exciting and so much fun. We had a Mother-Daughter Banquet, Senior Christmas Dance, Junior-Senior Prom, Senior Underwater Paradise Dance, a trip to Lexington's IBM plant and on and on."*

Anticipating futures that would separate the classmates at college, jobs and trade schools, all six families gathered at the Caintuckee Grill on Main Street for an evening together before graduation.

Volunteers Fight Fire

On May 6, 1943, A.E. "Tete" Stephens was named the first Burlington volunteer fire department chief at a Boone County Courthouse meeting. A 1938 Ford 1½-ton truck with a 400-gallon pump and 500' of hose cost $700.

In March 1944, the department moved into

the old Boone County Library Association Building on North Jefferson Street. Twenty men were appointed active firemen. They earned money by pumping cisterns and doing other odd jobs.

Newton "Sully" Sullivan, 70, retired after 20 years as Burlington postmaster on Dec. 31, 1953. The Woolper Creek native began teaching school before joining the postal service. He lived in Burlington, behind what is now the administration building. His daughter Nancy Hitzfield lives in Petersburg.

Otis Readnour, chairman of the Boone County Republican executive committee, chose Bert Loomis, a farmer who moved to Burlington after purchasing an apartment building, to succeed Sullivan.[77]

John Uri Lloyd used this house on Florence's Main Street as the setting for his book "Our Willie." Courtesy of Virginia Lainhart

Burlington's Champions

Burlington High School won the State Championship for six-man football, a game created for small schools, in 1949. Team members included: quarterback John Cropper, Robert Walton, Wayne Kelly, Sonny Ockerman, Bill Cave, Sonny Combs, Kay Kelly, Ronnie Jones, Jim Ryle, Jerry Lustenburg, Gayle Rouse, Ray Smith and several others. Bill McBee was team captain and played end.

They didn't lose a game all season, earning the right to play at UK's Stoell Field on Thanksgiving Day. Despite rain and snow, they beat Lebanon Junction, who also hadn't lost a game, 54-0.

Principal Edwin Walton coached. "*About everybody in town went down to watch. By the end of the third quarter, we were so far ahead he took most of the starters out and let everyone play*," McBee recalled. At the big banquet in Lexington that night, the awe-inspiring Adolph Rupp presented McBee with the trophy.

Realtor McBee, whose parents Les and Lois McBee ran a Burlington service station, represented Boone County in the General Assembly from '72-'90.

In the 40s Burlington had a pool hall on the corner and the restaurant where the hardware store is now also had a pool table. Both sold beer. Doc Yelton's practice was near the courthouse.

McBee's grandfather, Bill Cotton, was sheriff in early '30s. For 30 years his uncle, Wilson Stephens, who owned the land where Boone Woods Park now is, collected taxes as the Property Valuation Administrator. Stephens Elementary is named after him.

The Class of 1954 was the last to graduate from Burlington High School before the high schools were consolidated and that building became Burlington Elementary. The new Boone County High School at Florence was large enough to have a regular football team.[78]

Artist Moves to Burlington

Renowned *Cincinnati Enquirer* artist and writer Caroline Williams resigned and bought a log home and 52 acres near Burlington. The two-story log house she lived in with her widowed mother was 100 years old. It included four rooms over a cellar with a

---

[77] *Boone County Recorder*, Jan. 7, 1954.

[78] Bill McBee, April 8, 1998.

kitchen added on in back. She renovated the house herself, taking breaks to dig worms to go fishing with her poodle Letitia.

Early in her career, Williams drew two ink sketches for her friend John Uri Lloyd. After studying art in Cincinnati and New York, she followed her father, art director for the *Cincinnati Enquirer,* in working for the paper. As a staff artist, she sketched old buildings.

After moving to Burlington, she published books she wrote and illustrated under the name PenandHoe Press using her own printing and etching presses. Williams made her living as a freelance artist providing weekly illustrations for the newspaper. Doubleday Publishing Company asked to print her books *Cincinnati Scenes* and *Louisville Scenes.* Her original pen and ink drawings of Cincinnati were reproduced annually in a collectors' series by the British china company, Wedgewood.

Williams printed 750 copies of her book *As Always – Cincinnati* by hand, setting the type, etching each sketch on a copper plate and making the jacket and slipcase. In 1962, she printed her fourth book, *Cincinnati: Steeples, Streets and Steps.* Meanwhile, she completed renovating her house herself, undertaking everything except plumbing. Her interest in genealogy extended to cleaning and restoring a historic cemetery on her property.

As the downtown Cincinnati landmarks she detailed were renovated and changed, she turned to rural inspirations and other communities, last producing *Louisville Scenes.* Five enlargements of her ink drawings decorate the Boone County Public Library in Florence.

The airport in 1957.
Courtesy of the Cincinnati/Northern Kentucky International Airport

Airport Parking

In September 1951, A.T. Bonda and Howard Metzenbaum formed Airport Parking Company of America, which grew to be a nationwide business charging airport parking fees. Metzenbaum eventually became a Democratic senator from northern Ohio.

In 1954, a new airport post office began handling its own mail rather than sending it to Cincinnati.

That fall, the airport began advertising in Cincinnati newspapers to counteract negative ads and media comments placed by proponents of the Blue Ash Airport. Piedmont and Lake Central airlines began using the Boone County airport. Riddle Airlines, a freight handler, began flying out in 1956. Acreage expanded by 150 and a hotel was constructed on the property.

In 1957, ten years after the airport opened, 585,087 passengers – nearly four times the number who flew the first year – departed from Boone County. A contract with Emery Air

Freight was approved and bids were received for terminal expansion and taxiway paving. The remainder of the decade brought more motels and hotels, an Eastern Airlines ticket counter, and runway repairs and renovation.

Boone County's historian Bill Conrad hangs the old Oddfellows stage curtain for a display. Photo by Bob Sharpe

The first major accident was on Jan. 12, 1955, when a TWA Skyline with a crew of three and 10 passengers collided in the sky above Hebron with a DC-3 carrying a crew of two. The Skyline had just taken off for Detroit while the DC-3 was approaching to land. Both planes exploded, killing all 15 on board.[79]

The private plane, owned by a Lexington couple, was not known to be in the area. Both fell on Harold Crigler's and John Boh's farms. McVille Dam lockmaster Ray D. Frost, who was chairman of the Boone County Red Cross, assisted in salvaging the demolished planes.

Stan, Becky and Pa Aylor fix a hotbed for plants in the spring of 1956.
Courtesy of Mrs. Stanley Aylor

---

[79] Reis, *Pieces of the Past 3*, 122.

Chapter 13
1960-1979 Becoming Suburbia

Boone Countians had just become accustomed to airplanes flying around the earth when, on May 25, 1961, President John F. Kennedy asked the nation to work toward putting a man on the moon by the end of the decade.

The Greater Cincinnati Airport's growth and interstates 75 and 71 brought many more to Boone County, increasing the population by about 50 percent in a single decade.

Florence's size doubled to nearly 6,000, surpassing Walton's 1,500 and making it the largest community in the county. Now nearly one-third of the county's 22,000 residents lived in Florence.

Increasingly, the county left more of its agricultural heritage behind to become part of Cincinnati suburbia. By 1960, only 26 percent of the population was classified as rural, while 47 percent lived in the suburbs and 26 percent were considered urban dwellers.[1]

Average farm size remained much the same, 93 acres in 1900 to 102 acres in 1969. By 1960, about 60 percent of Boone County farms used tractors, extension agent Joe Claxon estimated.

Local farmers joined the Kentucky Farm Bureau in protesting anti-smoking television commercials running nationwide on the three major networks.

"The Verona area has seen a significant reduction in the number of farms and farmers since the construction of I-71 and I-75," said local attorney Asa Rouse. *"Subdivisions are springing up left and right."*

Country road construction increased, improving access for commuters and opening more land for subdivision development.

A few reminders of the past could be found, like mill remnants on Limaburg Road. And attitudes, as they always had been in Boone County, were slow to change.

National politics were in great turmoil with Watergate hearings, Henry Kissinger negotiating peace treaties, President Richard Nixon and Spiro Agnew eventually resigning, and George McGovern and George Wallace pushing their own agendas.

Locally, little notice was taken of the Beatles' visit to Cincinnati Gardens. Although nationally, "hippies" and "flower children" were the rage, long-haired teenagers promoting peace and environmentalism weren't common in Boone County.

About 1970, Jerry's Restaurant and Reeves Dairy Cheer opened the first drive-in restaurants in Boone County, introducing the

> **Boone County Recorder**
> July 16, 1970
> **Losing Game**
> *Denton C. Vannarsdall, Editor*
> Once started, the seeds of inflation grow like weeds. . . .
> At the moment, the U.S. worker's average real income is lower than four years ago; his average weekly wages are $117.55, but in terms of 1957-59 dollars, he earns only $77.40 compared with $78.39 four years ago. The trend toward more pay for less work set in a long time ago.
> The man of example, whose income went up $3,000 in 1959 to $4,500 in 1969 gained not $1,500; but only $135 in terms of 1959 dollars. The man who moved from $4,000 to $6,000 gained $235, not $2,000 in purchasing power. The large group who have broken through the $5,000 barrier since 1959 and moved up to $7,500 are not $2,500 ahead – only $290 ahead. . . .

---

[1] 1995 Boone County Comprehensive Plan

Boone County Democrats Nellie McCarty, Virginia Grand, Bruce Ferguson, Bill McBee, and Dan Roberts are sworn into office by Judge Charlie Niblack in 1962.
Photo by Bob Sharpe   Courtesy of Virginia Lainhart

"fast food" concept. Frisch's Big Boy in Erlanger and Reeves in Florence were teenagers' favorite cruising spots.

A hospital was needed, but voters hesitant to pay more taxes defeated a bond issue just as they had defeated road taxes a century earlier.

Boone County and Lloyd high school bands played "Hail to the Chief" to greet President John Fitzgerald Kennedy when he flew into the airport in October 1962.

Also in 1962, downstream in Carroll County near Ghent, Markland Dam raised the Ohio River's depth and widened it, increasing the distance previously crossed with a ferry or skiffs, but improving barge access year-round.

While Markland flooded some little Ohio River islands used for camping and picnicking, the federal government paid farmers for the loss of what had been called the first bottoms or the first terrace. Three smaller dams, including #38 at Belleview, were dynamited.

Dale Appel started the Boone County Water Rescue Team in 1967 to help recover drowning victims and stolen items disposed of in lakes and rivers. In its first six years, the team grew from three to eight members, trained 40 scuba divers and recovered 13 bodies.

The stolen items they recovered helped convict felons. Training includes anticipating the coldest day of the year, cutting a hole in the ice and diving underwater. Team members train monthly to stay ready for emergencies.

True to Kennedy's commitment, Neil A. Armstrong and Edwin "Buzz" Aldrin landed on the moon on Sunday, July 20, 1969. The *Boone County Recorder* said, "*What a wonderful time in history to be living – and what a wonderful place to live – the United States of America – a country that has produced geniuses, who, by their intelligence, can devise machinery that is capable of such feats, and brave men, willing to risk their lives to explore new worlds.*"

After Pete Stephens died, his widow Margaret Stephens continued publishing the *Recorder* with the help of editor Denton Vannarsdall.

Malcolm Simpson's ill health forced him to retire from the *Walton Advertiser* in 1972. He sold the paper to Maynard Meadows, son of previous owners Mark and Ann Meadows.

The *Boone County Recorder* bought the paper in 1978.[2]

One of the worst tornadoes in the region's history cut a swath across northwestern Boone County in April 1974. At least 20 homes were destroyed, 30 more extensively damaged and about 75 barns destroyed.

All around the region, earth was being moved to make scenic hills and forests left by the glaciers easier to reach by car, truck or boat.

On Dec. 22, 1976, I-275 opened westbound to Indiana and eastbound to Cincinnati. Now three major interstate highways – 71, 75 and 275 – were linked through Boone County, making the area easily accessible and within 600 miles of 60 percent of U.S. population.

For the first time in Boone County's voting history, the two principal candidates for President ran a dead heat. In 1976, President Gerald Ford and former Georgia Gov. Jimmy Carter tied with 5,602 votes each.

As it seemed to at least once each decade, the weather created several memorable days. Public Works Director John "Jay" Liver said snowdrifts from the February 1978 blizzard were up to 20 feet deep on Stephenson Mill Road and 15 feet deep on Bullittsville-Burlington Road.

With spring came all kinds of local news.

In May 1978, Walton favorite son Steve Cauthen, the nation's youngest-ever professional jockey, rode a Thoroughbred named Affirmed to victory in the 104th Kentucky Derby.

The May primary election drew only eight percent of registered voters – 1,035 went to the polls, reported County Clerk Jerry Rouse, who chaired the county election commission. After winning the Preakness, June brought a win in the third leg of the Triple Crown for Cauthen and Affirmed.

In July, Mike McKinney, who directed the county parks and recreation department, attempted but failed to get federal matching funds to build a public swimming pool.

Then, nearly 250, including Gov. Julian Carroll, gathered to dedicate the new I-275 bridge over the Ohio in honor of Boone County Judge Carroll Cropper. That same month, the Boone County Fair drew an estimated 30,000, the largest attendance in its 45-year history.

Rapid industrial development in and around the county prompted concerns. In April 1979, Boone County Fiscal Court passed a resolution opposing construction of a power plant across the river in Switzerland County, Ind.

In 1979, the court voted to approve a tax to build a new county administration building with a jail, improve roads, make additions to the parks system and share revenue with the city of Florence.

Judge Executive Bruce Ferguson was one of the politicians who rode in the Hebron Memorial Day parade in the '70s. The parade was an effort to honor war veterans.
Photo by Virginia Lainhart

The population boom continued – totaling 32,812 by 1970 and 45,842 by 1980, overcrowding schools again. Gary Griesser, assistant superintendent of Boone County Schools, announced that 8,226 students attended the first day of classes in 1979.

When Delta began offering nonstop flights to Europe in 1979, the airport was renamed Greater Cincinnati International Airport. Former Boone County attorney William P. McEvoy, Mrs. Hannah Baird of Florence and Paul "Skip" Seltman of Union attended a White House briefing with President Carter.

---
[2] *150th Anniversary, City of Walton*, 28.

Burlington in 1970 before the new administration building was built.
Courtesy of Bruce Ferguson

Cauthen paraded Forego, three-time "Horse of the Year," for charity at Latonia Race Course.[3]

County Politics

Until the '70s, the county fiscal court controlled how money was spent for all county services. Anyone who wanted to be included in the budget presented a proposal annually.

Then the state legislature passed a law allowing for special taxing districts that could support fire service, libraries, extension and soil conservation offices, ambulance districts, and more. Each entity simply had to circulate a petition to establish their own tax to support their cause.

County Judge Executive Bruce Ferguson, responding to citizens' requests for patrol officers, started the county police department with ex-sheriff Melvin Collins, who wasn't allowed to succeed himself in office, Tom Schwartz (now retired) and Don Stamper (now a bailiff).

The sheriff, legally the county's chief law enforcement officer, and his small staff of one or two deputies didn't have the resources to patrol. A Kentucky sheriff's primary responsibility is to collect taxes, and most have hired family members, rather than trained police officers, to help do that.

A payroll tax of ¾ percent with a cap of $125 per person financed an increase in the police force as well as improved county services. Boone was the third county in the state to adopt a payroll tax.

However Boone Countian's legendary reluctance to pay taxes reappeared. County Commissioner Irene Patrick organized a Hebron group that brought suit against the county for collecting the tax. Meanwhile, money was collected but not used.

The airport was buying up more land, a disadvantage to Boone County because it is not required to pay property taxes. However, the airport wasn't immune to the payroll tax, which brought in more than $1 million to Boone's coffers.

Supporting the payroll tax led to Judge Ferguson's defeat in 1982 by fellow Democrat Terry Roberts, who after one term as judge remains on the political scene, running for State Representative in 1998. But Ferguson bested Roberts four years later, regaining the judge executive post.

County Home Renovated for Children

One of Judge Ferguson's early campaign promises was to use available federal and state funds to establish a rest home for the elderly.

---

[3] From Our Files – 1978, The Year in Review, *Boone County Recorder*, Dec. 28, 1978.

Early in the 1960s, the fiscal court appointed a committee to study building a facility for the aging. The Boone County "poor farm" stood behind the fairgrounds on Idlewild Road (KY 338) where the county road department and animal shelter are now.

About a dozen elderly people still lived in the old infirmary built in the 1870s. Indoor plumbing and a furnace had been added in the '30s. Indigent residents raised their own fruits and vegetables there. The property even included a graveyard. The grand jury inspected it annually and reported repair needs to the fiscal court.

County Judge Bruce Ferguson had promised voters a nice nursing home and soon after his election, delegated the task to Walton attorney Asa Rouse. Mr. Rouse served without fee or salary as the first Chairman of the Board of Woodspoint and oversaw site selection, plans and construction.

In 1967, the fiscal court approved a bond issue to finance building Woodspoint, a 100-bed non-profit nursing care facility managed by a 16-member citizens' board called Boone County Kentucky Public Properties Corporation. The property parallels the interstate, next to World of Sports off KY 18 and Houston Road in Florence.

Once the facility was completely furnished and set to open in 1968, Mr. Rouse resigned. Woodspoint is named after the street Judge Ferguson's brother lived on in Lexington.

In January 1969, the first patients were admitted to the Woodspoint Nursing Home, including 13 from the poor farm who were supported with $16,000 annually from the fiscal court, said Nellie McCarty of Florence who chairs the board.

In 1977, Boone County Fiscal Court approved another bond issue to expand Woodspoint by 50 beds. The new wing opened the next year. Brighton Center offers children in day care opportunities to interact with elderly residents. Another addition was completed in 1992, expanding office space, physical therapy facilities and activity room.

A new health department building was added next to Woodspoint, before Boone County consolidated into the Northern Kentucky Health District. That building is now the Northern Kentucky Senior Citizens Center, offering daytime activities for seniors.

What had been the old poor house, then the old folks home, became Maplewood Children's Home in 1970. Photo courtesy of Maplewood

> *"Everything I named has wood in it, because I like wood and work with wood,"*
> Bruce Ferguson, former County Judge Executive

Maplewood Buds

"Youngsters in trouble or with problems should receive proper guidance from qualified personnel instead of the haphazard treatment they now get," Judge Ferguson said in his early campaign literature. After his election the former Boone County School Board president took steps to set up a youth center and add recreation facilities in the county.[4]

---
[4] Bruce Ferguson campaign literature.

In 1970, Mr. and Mrs. Wallace Bates moved into County Home, the old poor farm just outside of Burlington, as caretakers, then approached the juvenile court staff asking to work with young people who needed temporary homes. In January, the first youth was placed in foster care. Within a month, 10 children were living with the Bateses. Fiscal Court reimbursed them $2 per child per day.

Groups from Hebron and Burlington Baptist churches and civic organizations began cleaning and painting. Judge Ferguson suggested the name Maplewood because maple trees surrounded the house. Ferguson and Mrs. Billie Jo Morris, director of Court Services, selected a 13-member citizens' advisory committee to oversee the agency.

To provide additional support and raise funds, the Maplewood Guild began with 60 members and eight associates in 1972. They began sponsoring the Ohio Valley Walking Horse Show in June. It has become an annual fundraising event.[5]

Cross Burning

The '60s were an era of great social change and upheaval, prompting many programs for families and children and creating new phrases and changing attitudes.

While race riots took place in Louisville during the '60s and '70s, those kinds of obvious problems remained far away. In Boone County, crosses burned by an active Ku Klux Klan were quickly and quietly extinguished and removed.

When Walton's Zion Baptist Church hosted a district association meeting, swelling its ranks to four times the Sunday attendance of about 50, a cross was burned in its front yard.

James "Stoney" Ingram who lived across the street from the church saw the cross burning at 5 a.m., rounded up some help, put the fire out and removed the offensive symbol. The experience was hushed so thoroughly that neither the pastor nor the association members ever knew of it.

In connection with the meeting, a quite unrealistic rumor had spread that Rev. Martin Luther King Jr. was coming to Walton to stage a march.

Some of the 150 visiting African American church members attempted to register at local hotels, but were turned away as usual, and stayed with parishioners.[6]

Rev. Don Nunnelley of the Florence Christian Church joined a busload traveling to the Deep South to join a "sit-in" protesting segregation, raising the ire of some church members.[7]

Fleek's Vietnam Heroism

In a tiny country halfway around the world, young American men were fighting another war. High school boys drew a "draft number," went to basic training, and waited to hear if or when those with that number would be shipped to the swamps of Vietnam. Nightly television news blared body counts and showed atrocities committed by both sides.

Charles Fleek of Petersburg, nicknamed "Chalky" because he spent so much time dusting erasers to make up for school pranks, was awarded the Congressional Medal of

---

Dixie News   May 11, 1972

Commentary

The Rise of Mr. Wallace

Mr. George Wallace of Alabama has give politicians of both parties the scare of their lives. When he ran for the Presidency in 1968, he was considered by Republicans and regular Democrats as something of a demagogue. He had a long history of opposing integration, and it was to this segment of the electorate that he made his appeal. He was disavowed by leaders of both parties. . . .

It is very unlikely that Mr. Wallace will become President of the United States. But he has taught the professional politicians something: That people in this country like plain, blunt talk about the things that affect them most closely, that the people are tired of mealy-mouth cliches, and that they admire a man who will stand up and call a spade a spade. It was his sweep of Florida that has finally put the busing issue to sleep. . . .

---

[5] Elizabeth Kirtley, "History of Maplewood," 1998.
[6] Rosella Porterfield, March 4, 1998.
[7] Betsy Conrad, Feb. 25, 1998.

Honor. As a teen, Fleek once attempted to drive his old International truck down the bike path in Petersburg's park. When he left for Vietnam, the Petersburg volunteer firefighter vowed to "*make something of himself or not come back.*"

A squad leader in Binh Duong Province on May 27, 1969, Sgt. Fleek positioned his men for an ambush. When the enemy suspected their position and began to withdraw, he ordered his men to open fire despite their opponent's numbers. A fierce battle ensued.

Realizing his men hadn't seen a grenade thrown in their midst, and although he was in a position to take cover and save himself, Fleek shouted a warning, then threw himself on the exploding shell, saving eight lives.

The son of Wilford and Katherine Fleek was killed on his father's birthday. His cousin, Ronald Lynn Fleek of Hebron who was serving in Germany, escorted the body home. A brass plaque telling the story of the battle, the Congressional Medal and a bust of Charles Fleek are displayed in the courthouse foyer. A historical marker at Boone Woods Park lists the 12 Boone County men killed in the war.

Vietnam Veterans

Marine Corporal Roy G. Harmon of Florence was shipped to Vietnam to serve for 15 months before his daughter's first birthday.[8]

Many were drafted, but weren't sent to Vietnam. Private First Class John E. McHugh, whose parents Mr. and Mrs. John McHugh lived in Walton, received a letter of commendation for capturing an escaped prisoner at Fort Bliss, Texas. McHugh was a security guard with a dog named Mike.[9]

Boone Countians Killed in Vietnam

John Malapelli	'65	Jimmy R. O'Banion	'69
George Roden	'65	Edward A. Barlow	'69
Monty Lyons	'67	Charles Fleek	'69
Arthur Kramer Jr.	'68	William Brewer Jr.	'70
Harlan Secress	'68	Joseph W. Miley	'71
Gary Leslie Moore	'69	John Champlin	'71

Interstates

Back in Boone County, I-75 and 71 were under construction. Getting to the new airport had meant navigating stop and go traffic along Dixie Highway and Donaldson Road.

The Covington to Florence section of I-75 opened in September 1962, making Dixie Highway a local road. The $6 million bridge over the Ohio River, under construction for 3½ years, opened Dec. 2, 1963. Its steel superstructure had been shipped from Pittsburgh by barge.

Northern Kentucky officials wanted a bridge from Boone County to Indiana. In 1956, Congress had passed a bill calling for a new national highway system. In 1961, the idea of a belt-line looping into all three states germinated.

A road that looped around Boston had impressed Commissioner Donald H. Rolf of Hamilton County, Ohio. Thinking it would work for Cincinnati and Northern Kentucky, he located 1925 blueprints for a Cincinnati railroad loop that was never built. Most railroad passenger service had been reduced by the '60s and nearly all was gone by '71.[10]

On Aug. 10, 1962, President Kennedy approved the tri-state Circle Freeway. In 1967, when efforts to purchase property began, opposition and conflict arose.

Although Boone County Surveyor Noel Walton thought the expressway would increase property values, people became concerned about land speculators. Outsiders were buying at modest prices from longtime owners hoping for quick profits even though state highway officials were vague about the road's exact route in an effort to prevent speculative land buying.

---

[8] *Dixie News*, July 3, 1968, 1.
[9] *Dixie News*, July 3, 1968, 1.

[10] Harrison & Klotter, 314.

The airport in 1962. Courtesy of Cincinnati/Northern Kentucky International Airport

In 1970, the airport sold 53 acres to the Commonwealth to construct I-275 and Route 212. On Nov. 10, 1977, I-275 opened from Dixie Highway to Campbell County. A month later the connection to Indiana opened, expanding the belt around Northern Kentucky.

Construction on piers for the Lawrenceburg bridge on I-275 began on April 28, 1968, but funding delays stopped other work. Grading began in 1970, but bridge piers weren't completed for two more years. Then it was two more until the rest of the "bridge to nowhere" was done. Indiana officials were balking at completing the Indiana side because of funding problems. Most of the road opened on Dec. 5, 1977.

Construction took 11 years at a cost of $178 million for the 84.5 mile-long loop. It includes 55.4 miles in Ohio, 26 miles in Northern Kentucky and 3.1 miles in Indiana. Kentucky has 11 interchanges on I-275.[11]

Airport Modernizes

Modern conveniences began arriving at the airport. Dobbs Houses began constructing a building in which to prepare airline food. Valet parking appeared, as did a Walters Fire Truck.

A 1965 agreement with Modern Talking Picture Services allowed travelers to watch movies. A billiard lounge offered another amusement option. Nine land parcels were condemned to build a new runway.

Planes Crash

On Nov. 8, 1965, two miles north of the airport, an American Airlines Boeing 727 coming in from New York City crashed into a steep hillside on John Dolwick's farm as it

---
[11] Reis, *Pieces of the Past 2*, 183-186.

crossed the Ohio River. The site, about two miles west of Constance and about 225 feet below the airport's elevation, was not far from where a Zantop Airlines DC-4 cargo plane had crashed on Nov. 14, 1961.

With thunderstorms impairing the pilot's vision the Boeing 727 came in too low. Fifty-eight passengers died in the crash, three were thrown clear and one crawled out through a hole in the fuselage. Four survivors included two passengers not seriously injured, a flight attendant whose leg was badly hurt and an American pilot who was not part of the crew. Ralph Spague, Gilbert Dolwick, Milton Holt and Rodney McGlasson carried them from the burning wreckage.

Boone and Kenton County emergency personnel responded, finding debris strewn across the wooded site. About 100 rescue workers were forced from the scene by fears leaking fuel would ignite and explode.

Boone County Coroner Jerry Rouse set up a morgue at the airport firehouse. A bulldozer cut a path from Ky. 8 to enable workers to remove the bodies. Only the plane's tail was still intact.[12]

Three other Boeing 727s crashed on approach to other airports during '65 and '66. Less than a year later, the Civil Aeronautics Board ruled that the American Airlines crew was at fault. Rain squalls could have

President Johnson visited the airport on July 23, 1975. On June 12, winds of up to 70 knots blew windows out of the old tower, forcing operations to be handled from a portable radio in a vehicle.
Courtesy of the Kenton County Library

contributed.

On Nov. 6, 1967, a TWA Boeing 707 attempting to abort a take-off, skidded to a fiery crash on a hill at the west end of a runway. Air blasts from a Delta DC-9 mired in mud along the runway hit the TWA plane, causing the crew to think they had collided.

Nearly all 28 passengers escaped serious injury as the eight-member crew evacuated them, but the plane was destroyed in the ensuing fire. A 71-year-old Cincinnati man died a few days later from complications.

Two weeks later, during a light snow, a TWA Convair 880 from Los Angeles crashed into B.S. Wagner's orchard as it was approaching the airport to land. The plane disintegrated when it struck the trees. Sixty-five people were dead at the scene. The Hebron life squad took seven others away. Other ambulances assisted 10 others.

Although many of St. Elizabeth Hospital's nurses had resigned a week earlier over a dispute, most went to work when they learned 14 victims were sent there. Among the 70 dead were Covington attorney Andrew Clark, 53, who represented the airport, and his wife. Ironically, Mr. Clark's law partner, Greg Hughes, had been instrumental in locating the airport in Boone County.

As a result of the accidents, a 36-foot tall T-shaped directional light was installed the next year on the hillside above River Road.[13]

---

[12] Reis, *Pieces of the Past 3*, 123.

[13] Reis, *Pieces of the Past 3*, 125.

The airport in the summer of 1973. Courtesy of Cincinnati/Northern Kentucky International Airport

Just a year later, a TWA flight from Los Angeles clipped trees on a hilltop and crashed into an orchard 1½ miles from the airport. Seventy passengers and crewmembers died, 17 survived as the plane disintegrated and burned. The four-jet Convair 880 had been making an instrument approach to the north-south runway in a light snow, but visibility was deemed sufficient to see the runway in the distance.

The National Transportation Safety Board said the TWA crew visually misjudged their altitude seconds before crashing. An optical illusion caused by lights on the Ohio River 400 feet below contributed to the error.[14]

Airport Crises

By 1967, the airport was 20 years old and carrying more than a million passengers, nearly twice the number as the previous decade.

On June 12, winds of up to 70 knots blew windows out of the old tower, forcing operations to be handled from a portable radio in a vehicle. The next year, President Johnson visited the airport on July 23.

On May 20, 1971, the airport received a bomb threat against the Russian basketball team. Six days later, a Delta DC-9 received a bomb threat.

More revenue bonds financed airport terminal and parking lot expansions in 1972. Murals from Cincinnati's Union Terminal were moved to the airport.

The winter of 1974 brought some minor catastrophes for Delta – a jet blew over a guardhouse with a female officer inside and a

---
[14]Rawe, 58.

Delta L1011 got stuck in the mud off a taxiway. Air Kentucky began flying from Cincinnati in '75. Concourse A was reconstructed, terminal A opened, and the fountain was turned on.

On June 15, 1975, airport firemen Donald Phillips and Thomas Zafaries died fighting a fire in terminal A that damaged airport offices and the Weather Bureau.

The first astronaut to orbit the earth, Neil Armstrong, then a professor of aerospace engineering at the University of Cincinnati, was appointed to the airport's advisory board in 1975. For four years, he brought his 17 years of civilian NASA experience as an engineer, test pilot, astronaut and administrator to the Cincinnati airport board.

COMAIR, an abbreviation of commuter airline, came to the Cincinnati/Northern Kentucky Airport in 1977. The regional carrier is affiliated with Delta, feeding about half its passengers to Delta. With three Piper Navajos, COMAIR connected Cincinnati with Cleveland, Detroit and Akron-Canton in its first scheduled flights

Booth Hospital

The airport's expansion contributed to the county's increasing need for its own hospital. In the early 1970s, Covington was losing population. Boone Countians on the board of Booth Hospital there – Dr. Herbert Booth, Asa Rouse, Judge Ferguson and Dr Leroy "Lee" Hess encouraged the Salvation Army to move their hospital from Covington to Florence.

Booth Hospital was in an antiquated Covington building, the former residence of a wealthy benefactor in the '30s, inadequate to meet rapid increases in population and technology.

Ferguson purchased an option on land off Houston Road in Florence where the Meijer store is now, but the airport opposed the site for a hospital because it is right under a flight path, so Ferguson negotiated for a new plot on Turfway Road.

Ground was broken for the hospital in 1977 on 50 acres of what had been the Walter Scott farm. Dr. Booth, chairman of the board of physicians, became a liaison between the hospital and Boone County officials. Boone County fiscal court provided $24 million in hospital construction bonds in '72 and a new Booth Hospital was built in 18 months.

The facility was dedicated in June 1979. Shortly after the opening, a neighboring doctor's office was built.

Dr. Harry Daugherty's office was on the second floor of the Myers Building in Florence.   Photo contributed by Tom Utz

Doctors Daugherty

When he graduated in 1974, Joseph F. Daugherty III became the first fourth generation of doctors to graduate from the University of Louisville Medical School. The medical family has cared for Boone Countians for a full century.

The great-grandfather of the clan, Dr. Joseph Franklin Daugherty graduated from the Kentucky Medical School in Louisville in 1891 and practiced in Walton. Both his sons became physicians, Dr. Harry R. practicing in Florence, the other Dr. Frank. in

Drs. Daugherty on the side porch of Dr. Harry Daugherty's home in Union in 1974. When young Joe received his medical degree, be became the family's fourth generation of doctors to serve Boone County: Dr. Harry R. Daugherty, Dr. Joseph F. Daugherty III, and Dr. Joseph F. Daugherty II.
Photo by the *Boone County Recorder*

Independence.

Grandfather of the clan, Dr. Harry R. Daugherty began his practice in 1934 in the Myers Building on Florence's Main Street. Before seeing patients, he did a day's work on his 120 acre Angus farm. He raised registered cattle and corn and hay to feed them on the old Townsend farm on U.S. 42 near Union.

Dr. Harry saw patients six days a week and five evenings. Doctors at the time didn't write prescriptions, but dispensed drugs from huge bottles of orange "pain pills" and gallon jugs of stomach medicine kept in the office. In the 1950s, office calls were $3 and house calls were $6 to $10.

His appointments were scheduled on a first-come basis, determined by a sign-up sheet in his Florence office. The list was always long, so people ran up the steep stairs to his second floor office early in the day, signed up and came back when they thought he'd be in. That practice was even more common during hot summer months when the little office was sweltering hot, lacking air conditioning and ventilation. Whatever the complaint, a visit to Dr. Harry was always a complete physical from head to toe.

At 75, Dr. Harry cut back to 6 days a week and three evenings, but he never practiced on UK football Saturdays. During his entire career, Dr. Harry was only away from the practice overnight twice. Once he attended Eisenhower's inauguration. The second time was to visit his newborn grandson in Puerto Rico.

He was gone for a year serving in WWII, but with only Dr. Gladys Rouse left in the county, citizens petitioned to have Dr. Daugherty released early so he could help attend to Boone County's medical needs.

Dr. J.F., who graduated in 1952, practiced with his father and opened what may have been the first medical specialty practice in Boone County in obstetrics and gynecology.

Married to Martha Martin Daugherty of Ludlow, he had four children.

Joe III has a younger brother, James Martin "Macho" Daugherty, C.P.A., who graduated from the University of Kentucky then earned an M.B.A. "Macho" was born in Puerto Rico while his father was in the military service. A Spanish maid who refused to use his English name dubbed him "Macho."

After the family returned to Florence in the 1950s, they built a house on Sweetbriar Avenue. Daughter Mary Katherine "Kate" Daugherty became an attorney, specializing in environmental issues, and lives in Frankfort. The youngest, Sara Daugherty, married Stuart Ferguson of Union, and is now a nurse practitioner midwife.

Martha Daugherty taught art in Boone County schools from '66 to '95. An avid traveler and active in community, she has been president of the Florence Women's Club, Tri-City Church Women United as well as Kentucky Art Education Association and various state curriculum and education committees.

Like his father, Dr. Joseph F. Daugherty, and grandfather Harry Daugherty, young Joe III practices internal medicine in Florence's

Participants in the "Saga of Boone County" play put on for the 175th anniversary celebration.
Photo by Raymond E. Hadorn   Courtesy of Brenda Sparks

Turfway Medical Complex.[15]

Schools Honor Educators

The Daughertys were among the growing numbers of students attending the Boone County school system. In 1972, 10,000 attended two senior high schools, two junior high schools and seven elementaries in the county system; one high school and one elementary in the Walton-Verona district; and three parochial elementary schools.

Conner Junior and Senior High schools near Hebron were dedicated during the '70s. They were named after Hubert Conner, a longtime member of the Boone County Board of Education, who died in the early 1950s. His son, James C. Conner, also served on the school board. The schools were built on part of the Hubert Conner farm. Boone County Vocational School was also established then.[16]

Ritsel Sparks, center, was the winner of the "Brothers of the Brush" contest.
Photo courtesy of Brenda Sparks

A former teacher and administrator, Rector A. Jones, joined Boone County schools in 1941 as a math and commerce teacher at Florence High School. He left to serve in the Air Corps during WWII, then returned to become Florence Elementary Principal. After he became county superintendent in 1962, many new schools were built. He retired in 1976. His widow still lives in Florence. Rector A. Jones Middle School in Florence is

---

[15] Mrs. Martha Daugherty, newspaper accounts, Virginia Lainhart, Ritsel Sparks, etc.
[16] Reis, Pieces of the Past, 26.

named after him.

A.M. Yealey was a teacher and principal in Florence for more than 40 years as well as four-term mayor of Florence. He was chairman of the Boone County Draft Board during WWI. A writer, he was a friend of John Uri Lloyd for whom Lloyd High School in Erlanger was named. Yealey died in November 1962, right before Yealey Elementary was dedicated.[17]

Hebron native Chester Goodridge graduated from Burlington High School in 1920 and began teaching at Hebron Elementary, which is now named after him.

175th Anniversary Celebration

Boone County's 175th anniversary celebration was held in 1973 at the abandoned trotting track on Evergreen Drive on Florence's southwest side. The track opened in the early 1950s and operated until Latonia (Turfway) opened.

The celebration's rocking chair contest *"produced newspaper clippings from every state in the union and overseas from Germany and Japan. Veteran newsmen state that no event in recent memory in Greater Cincinnati has produced such wide publicity. . . ."*

The "Saga of Boone County" employed 300 local costumed actors. The play ran for five nights in September 1973. Prizes recognized the best costumes and beards.

"This week the Brothers of the Brush began shaving off their full beards. It is to be hoped some of them hold on to their brushes as an improvement to the landscape."[18]

The trotting track was sold and made into apartment complexes.

Festivities were *"a fitting prelude"* to the national celebration in 1976. In 1974, a Tri-County Historic Commission was formed to plan Kentucky's bicentennial celebration.

1974 Tornado

Excitement of another kind came from the sky between 4 and 5 p.m. on Wednesday, April 3, 1974. A tornado touched down near Belleview then zigzagged northeast to Taylorsport, leaving a wake of destruction. Spectators said when the whirlwind thundered down the hill and turned toward the Ohio, it divided the water – destroying the Morehead Marina and boats in the river and on shore.[19]

After dropping huge hailstones, the 1974 tornado raced along the river ripping roofs from buildings and wreaking destruction. This photo was taken near North Bend Road in Hebron. Photo by Midge Smith

Belleview residents reported seeing three funnels. Two were spotted from Burlington and Bullittsville. *"One massive twister was seen carving its way through the North Bend and Taylorsport communities.*

"The monster gained force and began its route across the Ohio River. Gladys Jean Maxwell of Belleview saw it swoop up a mass of water then splash it back down again. About 5:30 p.m. all utilities were lost and residents huddled in basements and other areas anticipating the twister's wrath."[20]

Nick Welsh, administrator at the Daniel Boone Treatment Center, lost part of his porch and barn in Belleview. Donn Loomis estimated repairing his barn would cost $15,000 and that his business, D&M Gravel Co., received at least $6,000 in damage. He and another worker ran out of a garage and behind some heavy machinery just as the twister took the roof off.

---

[17] Reis, *Pieces of the Past*, 26.
[18] *Dixie News*, Sept. 20, 1973.

[19] *An Educational & Historical Tour Through Boone County*, 10.
[20] *Boone County Recorder*, April 11, 1974.

"*Back through the fields the monster whirled, demolishing two of Atlee Anderson's barns on Commissary Road, and twisting his frame house beyond repair.*" It ripped the roof off Joseph Kahmann's new brick house across the road. Joe Meyer's barns were destroyed before it moved on to Denton Vannarsdall's farm, ripping off part of the roof and the front porch, then it headed down Idlewild Road, destroying barns, trailers and roofs along the way.[21]

On Feeley Road, Ed Cheslock lost a barn, silo and half a milkhouse. "*The twister ripped the roof off Ed Peel's 152-year-old house, cracking the walls and warping them beyond repair. The monster devoured a house trailer, barns, outbuildings and trucks.*" Mr. Peel was in one of the ruined barns when it hit, and suffered the worst injury reported in the county, a broken leg.

"*Taking a turn and gathering extensive strength, the twister struck and nearly leveled the town of Bullittsville. Some residents claimed they saw two twisters converging on the village at once, joining to form one huge monster.*"

Four suffered minor injuries in Bullittsville. Mr. and Mrs. James Pennington and Oakie Fugate were in Pennington's store when it struck.

"'*I got down almost to the floor,*' Mrs. Pennington recalled. '*Then things began to hit me on the head and back.*' . . . *In just a minute it was over and the Penningtons were covered with the debris of what had been their business.*"

A steel beam protected Mrs. Pennington

Debris cluttered the Lewis Morris home on North Bend Road in Hebron.
Photo by Midge Smith

from the crashing boards, shelves and walls. Hearing her husband's voice when she thought him dead "*was the sweetest voice I'd ever heard,*" she said.

Fugate was standing in the store's doorway when it collapsed. He was still standing after the tornado hit. Surprisingly, he suffered only minor cuts despite the blood streaming down his face.

Next door, the Virgil Stamper family heard "*the howling of the monster*" and ran to the basement – the only part of their home remaining.

Across the road, Mrs. Anna Engle's home was destroyed and her car flipped upside down.

"*Marion Willoughby was on his way to the airport in a van when the twister carved its path through Bullittsville. His van blew up against Pennington's Store, against Virgil Stamper's home and then landed in the Engle yard. He escaped with only slight injuries also.*

"*Then the destructive monster strengthened and broadened its power. When near Belleview it had only snatched up trees here and there, or carved out narrow paths north of Burlington, it widened until it was crushing entire hillsides of homes and trees.*

"*It hit upon the enormous dairy barns on the Helman property off North Bend Road, crunching them right in the center. It crossed North Bend Road, swirling up barns, garages, brick and frame homes in its path. Among the homes it cursed were those of Lewis Morris, Carl Smith, Larry Gouge, Joseph Aylor and others.*"

The Carl Smiths gathered in the basement of their 14-month-old house and listened to it being torn apart. Next door, Mrs. Larry Gouge said the hailstones saved her family. "*She, her children and her parents who lived

---

[21] *Boone County Recorder*, April 11, 1974, 1.

next door were outside picking up the huge hailstones which had fallen previous to the twister.[22]

"'I went around front – thought I'd find bigger ones there.'" Instead, Mrs. Gouge saw the black tornado approaching and rushed her family to the basement. Afterwards, she found boards from a neighbor's barn lying on her living room sofa. While her china cabinet's glass doors were shattered, the dishes in it were unharmed.

The tornado raged onto Tanner's Lane, destroying Jack Terrill's home and their son Ronnie's house while the family hid safely in their basement.

"The monster chose a strange fate for the William Sprague home at the corner of Tanner's Lane and River Road. It was lifted completely off its foundation and set down again at an angle just a few feet away." But the 22-year-old home was impossible to restore, although the contents were not badly damaged.

"Before leaving Kentucky, the pitiless whirling monster brought one last great destruction – the almost total leveling of Taylorsport. Where homes had once looked out on the muddy Ohio River, only concrete foundations, with concrete steps leading up to them, remained. The Cecil Kenyon home was reportedly spun entirely across the river."

Pat Morehead found neither boat dock nor home – instead at least 150 jumbled and smashed boats – the greatest financial loss in the county. Pat's son, Bobby Morehead, only lost the roof of his home.

Hebron Volunteer Firefighters helped patch roofs, cleared debris and distributed food and clothing, and helped salvage whatever they could. The county was declared a federal disaster area, making families eligible for federal funds to rebuild. County road crews stretched their responsibilities to clear any debris *"that could be a health hazard."*[23]

U.S. Army Reservists and the Boone County Jaycees, led by Harold Kohl and Tom Kelly, spearheaded clothing and food collections, as well as worked to clear property and roads.[24]

Jansen Murder

Thinking one of the schoolchildren had dropped them, Mrs. Connie Puckett of Walton stopped to pick up a schoolbook and a child's jacket on Stephenson Mill Road as she went to pick up her niece from Walton-Verona Elementary in April 1978. She called local schools about the name she found inside, but they had no record of it.

Later that morning, Eugene W. Gall Jr., 31, who had been out of prison less than a year, robbed a grocery at gunpoint, shot a Kentucky State Trooper pursing him, caused another to be injured in a collision, then drove up to another trooper and shot him twice.

Trooper Steve Hartman of Florence rammed his car into Gall's in Lanter's Used Auto Sales parking lot, then refused to be taken to the hospital until he assisted in Gall's arrest. (Hartman was released several days later.)

That afternoon, Walton-Verona Elementary Principal Ernest Hahn saw a television broadcast about Lisa Jansen's disappearance from her Cincinnati school, and called Mrs. Puckett, who notified the Hamilton County Police and Kentucky State Police about the

---

> **Dixie News** — April 4, 1974
> *Commentary*
> **Letter Home**
> Recently a first-class postage stamp went from 8 cents to 10 cents. That's too much money to send a letter from New York City to Alaska or Hawaii. At one time we used to be able to do it for 2 cents. Even at that price we never considered it a bargain because we thought Communication was one of the things America was all about. . . .
> Have you any idea how many fine magazines are going to go out of business because of the new postage rates? Life Magazine was the most recent casualty. . .

---

[22] *Boone County Recorder*, April 11, 1974, 1.
[23] *Boone County Recorder*, April 11, 1974, 1.
[24] *Dixie News*, April 4, 1974, 1.

book and jacket. The 12-year-old girl's bullet-riddled body was found the next morning along a creek.

"I must have been right behind him," Mrs. Puckett told a *Kentucky Post* reporter. *"No cars had run over the book or the jacket. I shuddered when I thought about it. If he had seen me pick up the book and the jacket, he might have thought I had seen him."*[25]

Police later speculated that the girl was murdered trying to protect herself from being raped. Additional warrants charged Gall with the rape and kidnapping of a 14-year-old Scott County girl.

Prosecuted by Commonwealth Attorney Willie Mathias, Gall pleaded not guilty at his trial in Burlington before Circuit Court Judge Sam Neace. He has repeatedly appealed the death sentence the jury recommended.

Boone Woods Park

Fufilling a need identified by Judge Ferguson, a federal grant enabled the county to buy 45 acres a mile east of Burlington to develop into Boone Woods Park north off KY 18 between Florence and Burlington. Mrs. Lucile Stephens, vice president and director of People's Deposit Bank, sold the property to the county.

Parks and recreation director Rick Clements' plans for the land included two ball fields, picnic areas, a pond, playground equipment, a soccer field and four tennis courts. Its first building was a 200-year-old log cabin donated by R. C. Durr in 1976.

Two more tennis courts, lights for all six courts, a sewage plant, shelter house, rest rooms and a "Fort Boone" playground were added in 1977. Retiring Kenton County Agriculture Agent William Straw of Independence developed, patented and donated the Aristocrat Pear trees that flower along the entry drive.

Clements, the first county parks director, worked from a courthouse office. The county

Donna R. Centers (now White of Florence) and her sister Barbara A. Centers (now Marks of Burlington) after playing at one of Boone County's new parks. The girls attended Yealey Elementary, Ockerman Junior High and Boone County High School. Courtesy of Donna White

had three other parks. Florence's Lincoln Woods Park was leased to the county for $1 a year for 20 years in 1972, becoming the first Boone County Park. Its 13 acres on Florence's Surfwood Drive include picnic areas, ball fields, tennis courts, mini-bike trails, picnic shelters and playground equipment. Limaburg Park was 50 acres on Limaburg Road with ball fields, soccer fields, picnic areas, garden plots and a storage building. The Maplewood complex owned by the county had two public ball fields.

Blizzards Ground Planes

Temperatures dropped to -25 in January 1977, the coldest ever recorded in Cincinnati. Arctic cold gripped much of the nation and the Ohio River froze. A blizzard hit Jan. 28. A total of 30" of snow fell in January, but crews cleared runways and taxiways so the airport remained open. As the weather eased, the airport bought a high-speed, self-propelled broom and two snow-removal trucks.

The next year matched the cold. Heavy snows canceled many meetings including most of those at the airport. Workmen kept the airfield open, but many flights didn't come in because of the severe weather across the

---

[25] "Lisa Jansen – Girl Found in Walton," *Kentucky Post*, April 13, 1978.

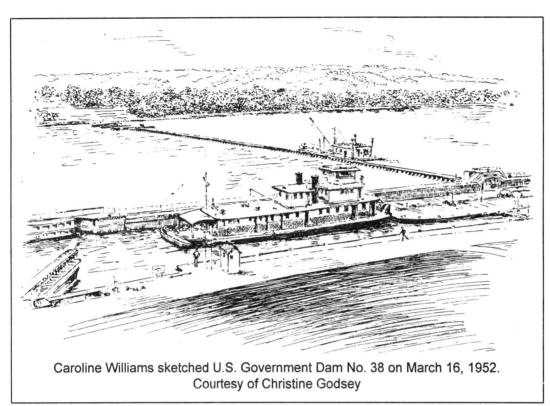
Caroline Williams sketched U.S. Government Dam No. 38 on March 16, 1952. Courtesy of Christine Godsey

nation. A blizzard closed the airport from 6 p.m. on Jan. 26 until 6 a.m. the next day, dumping 6" of snow on top of the 31" that had been there since New Year's. About 250 passengers slept in the terminals that night to avoid the -11 degree temperatures. Most regional highways were closed. People were told to stay home.

In June, a record-setting number of passengers boarded at the Northern Kentucky airport. On July 17, 1978, Flying Tigers began air freight operations. Improvements included a new ambulance, repairs on asphalt surfaces, a new highway advisory radio system, Indiana Airways adding four daily flights, an emergency generator, and parking lot rate increases. On Nov. 20, 1978, the Greater Cincinnati International Airport name was adopted.

Comair flight 444, a Piper Navaho, crashed on takeoff from Runway 18 on Oct. 8, 1979.

The Hebron Volunteer Fire Department raced to the airport many times to assist with aircraft crises. Paid personnel have joined volunteers, since the fire protection district was established in 1979. The department sponsored a Memorial Day parade for many years.

Petersburg Bank Closes

The Kentucky Banking Commission closed Petersburg's Farmers Bank in June 1970 because "*it had reached a state of insolvency beyond any reasonable hope of recovery.*" The bank had extended itself beyond legal lending limits with unsecured loans.

Petersburg Volunteer Fire Department sponsored a fish fry and dance on July 4, 1970. Fish dinners were $1.50 for adults and $.75 for children. Dancing began at 9 with music by "The Drifters."[26]

Belleview-McVille Center

After dam #38 was blown up, the federal government made the grounds available to other governmental agencies. Judge Bruce Ferguson bought the property for $1, then leased it to the state. The dark brick homes built for the lockmaster and his assistants were converted into dormitories for a minimum security prison, Daniel Boone Correctional Center.

About 20-30 women were housed there and looked after by local employees. Other than a couple of runaways through the years, there were no problems, Ferguson said. In fact, Ferguson invited inmates to his farm for

---

[26] *Boone County Recorder*, July 2, 1970, 1.

annual picnics with softball games and hay rides.

In about 1980, the state closed the prison and the property reverted back to the county. County Judge Executive Terry Roberts sold it to a developer who converted it back into private homes.

A Belleview park attracted residents from around the county. A picnic area had an impressive concrete model of dam #38 and the locks.

Irvin Roland was the first chief of the Belleview-McVille volunteer fire department in 1966. The Elsmere department sold them a 1936 Studebaker fire truck. Volunteers met in the Belleview school until the firehouse was built the next year on a lot donated by Will and Laura Rogers and sons.

University of Nebraska hosted an international geology convention focused on the Pleistocene era at Big Bone during their excavation. People from around the world came to Boone County. Photo by Bob Sharpe

Nebraskan Studies Big Bone

With Bruce Ferguson as president and William Fitzgerald as secretary, the Big Bone Lick Historical Association purchased 16 2/3 acres of land and presented it to the Commonwealth in December 1958 to make into a park.

Two years later, the state Department of Parks announced plans to build a shelter house and develop picnic areas. Purchasing additional land parcels brought the total acreage to 175 in 1962.

In 1959, C. Bertrand Schultz, a vertebrate paleontologist, met with Ellis Crawford, a ocal authority on the history of Big Bone Lick, and William S. Webb. Schultz began multi-disciplinary excavations under the auspices of the University of Nebraska.

This time, there was a verbal agreement that while the bones would initially be shipped to Nebraska for evaluation, they would be returned to Kentucky and remain the Commonwealth's property. While the effort exposed many artifacts and remains of Late Pleistocene species, it didn't find the human artifacts they were seeking.

In 1960, Ellis Crawford, director of the Covington William Behringer Memorial Museum, found a mastodon jawbone under an elm tree at the Lick.

Then the Nebraska dig began, bringing national recognition to Big Bone. In 1964, 112,000 visited the new park. The Association's original goal of completing a state of the art museum and research center hasn't yet been met. Other ideas included re-creating Big Bone Springs Hotel and the salt works.

A plan to build a flood control lake at the headwaters of Big Bone Creek was rejected by the U.S. Soil Conservation Service. The locally supported project didn't provide a place for water generated at the head of the creek to go during floods of the Ohio, the report said.[27]

The Fitzgeralds

Edwin Way Teale told of the tour William and Ann Fitzgerald of Florence gave him of Big Bone in his 1958 book, *Wandering Through Winter*.[28]

"We had shown him Big Bone before that," Ann said, *"but he wanted to come in the winter. We had 12" of snow in town that day, but there wasn't a speck at Big Bone. He was fascinated by the songs of the birds living in the weeds that were 10 to 12' tall."*

William Fitzgerald in 1964 at Big Bone with a mammoth vertibra found there. He was secretary-treasurer of Big Bone Lick Historical Association.   Photo courtesy of Ann Fitzgerald

Meeting a nationally renowned author didn't phase the Fitzgeralds, both had been teachers and each had authored two books in their specialties: He was a printer, she was a weaver.

Mr. Fitzgerald taught graphic arts at Holmes High School in Covington for 27 years before becoming director of the Kentucky Historical Society Library in Frankfort.

Mrs. Fitzgerald taught weaving at Berea College for 15 years before marrying William and moving to Northern Kentucky. Both were Peabody College graduates (now Vanderbilt). Mr. Fitzgerald taught English there for 10 years. He did graduate work at Carnegie Institute of Technology in Pittsburgh.

A Florence resident for 30 years, he served as city treasurer in the early 1960s, became a Boone County deputy court clerk and served as judge pro tem of the Boone County Court.

President of the Kentucky Historical Society, Mr. Fitzgerald was an official of the Boone County, Big Bone and Christopher Gist historical societies, and the Kentucky Archives Commission. Mr. Fitzgerald passed away in 1969.[29]

Ann became as avid a historian and genealogist as her husband. Spending time with Bill at the Boone County Courthouse while he was researching books and articles on county history, she began transcribing the original handwritten Court Order Books and eventually had three volumes published, easing research for future generations.

She also indexed assorted old files and records. With Stephen Worrel, Ann Fitzgerald published: *Boone County, Ky., Marriage Records 1798-1850; Boone County, Ky., Court Orders 1799-1815*; and *Boone County, Ky., Cemeteries* (from inscriptions on stones). With her husband William, she wrote *Boone County Index to Marriages* in 1960.

At 95, "Miz Fitz" works every weekday afternoon in the Boone County clerk's office assisting individuals with genealogical research and filing license records – something she has done since the 1940s.

In 1998, she still lives in the Florence home she and William purchased after they decided Covington had too much steel mill smoke and came south looking for property affordable on a teacher's salary.[30]

---

[27] Boone County Recorder, July 2, 1970, 1.
[28] Teale, *243-244*.
[29] "William Fitzgerald, State Historian," *The Post & Times-Star*, March 7, 1969, 10K.
[30] Ann Fitzgerald, March 25, 1998.

Chapter 13 1960-1979 Becoming Suburbia

Verona Community Grows

While the Fitzgeralds were preserving history and attempting to get Big Bone Lick State Park established, Verona was growing. A 1947 Walton-Verona graduate and Verona native, Dr. William M. Waller returned from Navy service to open a medical office on Walton's South Main Street. His wife, Leola Waller, is a Walton School Board member and plays violin in the Northern Kentucky Symphony as well as "fiddles" Blue Grass music.

Walt Ryan chaired the board of the Walton-Verona Independent School District for 15 years. He is still on the board, completing his 35th year of service. A 1955 Walton-Verona graduate, he married Janice Cook, his high school sweetheart, and never left his hometown.

Arthur Doggett, a Virginian who never lost his drawl, also chaired the Board of Education. After returning from WWII, he married another Verona girl, Mildred Leathers.

No Foreclosures at Verona

Verona Bank had been incorporated on July 6, 1903, six years before the town was. In 1921, O.K. Whitson became cashier and Grover Ransom his assistant. Ransom, who was promoted to cashier, became known as "Mr. Verona Bank." The conservative direction he set ensured that while the bank financed many area homes and farms, in its entire 87-year history, it has yet to foreclose on a loan.

Mr. Ransom was always proud of that record and that Verona was the only Boone County bank that did not need to borrow from the federal government to remain open during the Depression.

After Verona Bank was robbed, they kept the door locked. Potential patrons the staff doesn't recognize are quizzed about their business before the door is opened.

In 1966, Verona Bank moved to its 1998 location on the Walton-Verona Road west of the old Verona school. The original bank building became J.D. Risner's dental laboratory.

Cashier Wilma Grant and President Tom Carr spearheaded the effort that resulted in groundbreaking for the new building on July 21, 1965. Directors included Raymond Stephenson, Manford Craft and attorney Asa Rouse.

Fred Hamilton, who built the Hamilton Funeral Home building on the Verona-Walton Road in the 1960s, was vice president and Joyce Vest was assistant cashier. The Hamilton Funeral Home is a multi-generation Verona landmark. Rouse served as a Trial Commissioner, the equivalent to a district judge, during the Ferguson Administration from 1964 to 1973. He retired from actively practicing law in May 1994.

Fire and Water

Raymond Stephenson was also a commissioner of Verona's first water district. Bullock Pen Water District in Crittenden extended its water lines to Verona and built a tower there in the early 1960s, making it one of the first Boone County communities with a public water supply.

In September 1967, residents within five miles of Verona's railroad tracks woke at midnight to explosions. Fourteen L&N tank cars derailed and ignited, shooting searing fireballs as they toppled off the tracks. Fire destroyed the home of Carl and Mary Kathrine Bickers, sending them and two of their three children to the hospital with burns. The explosion ignited Gary Stephenson's barn. Brenda Williams, 18, daughter-in-law of Mr. and Mrs. Boyd Williams, was treated for burns. Joe Perkins also suffered severe burns.

Verona had no fire department. The Walton crew responded, assisted by J.D. Risner, Byron Kent and other Verona volunteers. Kent is credited with saving lives by banging on doors up and down the road rousing people from their sleep. One person said the explosion was like having a miniature A-bomb dropped in their midst. Electric and telephone service were out for a time.

The next year, 25 charter members

Dixie State Bank employees participating in Walton's Old Fashioned Day in September 1976 included Sandy Berkshire, Sylvia Spegal, Helen Renaker, Doris Eisenschmidt, Jean Webb, Richard Robinson, James W. Spencer and Sharon Duncan.
Photo contributed by Jimmy Spencer

organized Verona's volunteer department. The Verona Post Office and Fire House were built in 1978. Rose Yates was postmaster until 1963, when Jean Crouch took over. Tom Hicks remains the fire chief.

Artist Helps Walton Celebrate

Anneliese D. Wahrenburg arrived in the United States in 1954 and soon after began offering painting classes in Walton. Trained at the Art Academy of Hamburg, Germany, she painted with oils, acrylics, watercolors and tempera and drew with pencil, ink and charcoal.

Her paintings hang in homes around the United States and Europe and have been exhibited in galleries, universities and shows throughout the eastern U.S. In addition to wall murals, magazine covers and paintings for public buildings, she created an illustration of the Walton Opera House for the cover of Walton's 150th anniversary book.

Walton Gains Businesses

An old barn-like building next to the Phoenix Hotel was used to show movies in the 1930s. After the picture show moved to the new James Theater, Reamy Simpson turned it into a farm supply store. In the early 1960s it was demolished and replaced with a dental office for Dr. John Maddox and a building for Vic "Doc" Webster who sold and repaired televisions and radios.

The Phoenix was demolished and replaced with Boone County Drugs. With television taking over as primary entertainment, the James Theater closed. Gary Landrum remodeled it into an IGA supermarket.

Walton Emergency

Walton's Life Squad began in 1968 when changing state regulations made it economically unfeasible for funeral directors to provide ambulance service. A 1958 vintage van was converted and equipped as an ambulance. Chambers and Grubbs funeral home donated a wheeled stretcher. Walton Fire Department volunteers, trained in advanced first aid and cardio-pulmonary resuscitation, answered calls.

In 1971, the state licensed a newly purchased commercial ambulance. New regulations required 80 hours of training for ambulance workers. Ed Berkemeier and Jesse Thornton were the first "Registered Emergency Medical Technicians - Ambulance." Jean Thornton, Chick

Chapter 13 1960-1979 Becoming Suburbia

Worthington, Jim Lawrence, John Taylor and Dorothy Still soon earned certification as well. In 1974, a modular ambulance replaced the old van.[31]

Good Friday, April 9, 1971, brought fire to Walton, burning the center of the old business district. Walton Garage, Village Barber Shop and Boone County Drugs were gutted as was the Garnal Glacken home on High Street. Volunteer firemen from all over Northern Kentucky came to fight the flames.

Ab Ryan kept the roof of Ryan Hardware watered down and prevented it from catching fire. James Spencer, vice president of Dixie State Bank saw the fire starting as he was working late. He gathered loose papers and locked them in the vault. Luckily the bank did not catch fire.

In September 1973, Walton began celebrating its heritage with Old Fashion Day, which has become an annual event.

Walton Fire Department volunteers joined others from across the region in assisting with the disastrous Beverly Hills Supper Club fire, which killed 165 John Davidson fans attending a performance on May 28, 1977.

St. Joseph Academy

Four Sisters of St. Joseph the Worker moved to Walton Nov. 1, 1974, to establish a mother house. Soon All Saints parishioners were asking them to reopen the All Saints School, the first Catholic elementary in Walton, which had begun in 1950.

The Sisters of St. Benedict had opened the school, but were transferred after 20 years. The Sisters of Charity sent four nuns, but due to small enrollments, the school closed after three years. St. Joseph Academy opened in August 1976 with 54 students. The enrollment has multiplied rapidly.[32]

William C. Johnson

The first African American elected official in Boone County, Rev. William C. Johnson was elected to the Walton City Council in 1977. A Bourbon County native, he moved here about 1951.

He ran *"during the time Martin Luther King was marching and then was killed. We didn't have any blacks on anything, had roads to be repaired, no one seeing after our interests, so I figured it was time,"* Rev. Johnson said. *"And I didn't want to see policemen beat up on my boy."*

Most people in the small town knew him, he said. He campaigned at laundromats and grocery stores. He didn't have a particular platform – *"I didn't know what I was getting into,"* he says.

He was re-elected, but his responsibilities at Shillitos, where he worked for 18 years, changed. That and preaching at an Ohio church led him to resign in 1985. He recommended Johnnie Ann Johnson, who had just graduated from college, be appointed to serve the rest of his term. She served, then later moved to Florence.[33]

Cauthen Breaks Records at 16

Days after his 16th birthday in 1976, Walton native Steve Cauthen rode his first race as a professional jockey. He rode Red Pipe to victory at River Downs on May 17 and by the end of the year was riding in New York, known as "The Kid."

By the end of 1977, Cauthen had won three Eclipse Awards, was named leading jockey and leading apprentice jockey, broke the New York record for victories in a year (299) and became the first jockey in the world to win $6 million in purses. *Sports Illustrated* named Cauthen Sportsman of the Year and put him on the cover.

In 1978, riding Affirmed at 18, he became the youngest jockey ever to win the Triple Crown, stepping into the Winners Circle at the Kentucky Derby, the Preakness and the Belmont Stakes.

He was England's champion jockey in 1984, 1985 and 1987. Cauthen became the

---

[31] *150th Anniversary, City of Walton*, 46.
[32] *150th Anniversary, City of Walton*, 41.
[33] Rev. William Johnson interview, March 10, 1998.

Steve Cauthen rides Affirmed across the finish line, barely a head of his rival Alydar.
Photo contributed by Brenda Sparks

first jockey to ride the winners of both the Kentucky Derby and the Epsom Derby in 1985. He rode Reference Point to an Epsom Derby win two years later.

The first jockey in the world to win four derbies, he took the French Derby in 1989, the Irish Derby in 1989 and the Italian Derby in 1991. In August 1994, he was inducted into the National Museum of Racing's Hall of Fame. At 34, he was the youngest person ever to receive that honor.

Cauthen retired from riding in 1993 and returned to Northern Kentucky where he is the associate vice president at Florence's Turfway Park and a spokesman for Turfway and the racing industry. He lives on a Verona farm with his wife Amy and their daughters Katelyn Rose and Karlie Stephen.

Walton Writer Published

Dodd, Meade and Co. of New York published Berniece Hiser's book, *Quare Do's in Appalachia*, in 1978. The collection of folk tales and memories of supposedly real events recounted by word of mouth, is one of several books written by the late Walton librarian and teacher.

With a bachelor's degree in English and creative writing from Berea College and a master's in education from the University of Kentucky, she taught in Indiana during the 1970s. Her books include romance, biographies and children's stories that sprout from her Appalachian roots.[34]

Frontier World Rises and Falls

In 1968, Fess Parker of Disney television's popular Daniel Boone show and Gov. Louis B. Nunn announced a $13.5 million Disneyland-type amusement park would be built on 1,500 acres at the junction of I-75 and I-71 near Walton.

---

[34] 150th Anniversary, City of Walton, 57.

The money was to be raised through a state bond issue set up by county attorney William McEvoy and attorney Wilbert Ziegler. Bonds were to be retired from income generated by the theme park.

Scheduled to open in 1970, Frontier World was expected to generate $180 million in tourism over the next decade. It was expected to employ 1,000 and attract millions from around the world.

The entertainment complex was to feel like a step back in time, including an entrance through a replica of the Mayflower.

Combined with the park was to be a manufacturing plant to produce souvenir items like "coonskin" caps. Large segments of the popular television show were to be filmed in Boone County as well.[35]

The Greater Walton Businessmen's Association formed to promote the area. In September 1968, Postmistress Mildred Cleek reported in the *Walton Advertiser* that a new stamp displaying Daniel Boone's Kentucky rifle, powder horn, knife and tomahawk hanging against a roughly hewn board was in high demand.

UK student and Walton-Verona High School graduate, Dale Chapman, son of Marie Blizzard, was chosen ambassador for the group. He left for California with a gold key to the city of Walton to present to Chuck Barry of the "Dating Game." The stunt was part of a plan to link Walton to Frontier World as Anaheim, Calif., was then linked with Disneyland. Dale met Fess Parker and watched filming of the Daniel Boone show.

When plans to develop an amusement park in Kings Mill, Ohio, became public, Fespar Enterprises decided their plan would not be economically feasible and Frontier World

Television's Daniel Boone, Fess Parker with Dan Roberts and Jim Spencer.   Photo contributed by Jimmy Spencer

crumbled before it was built.[36]

Union Fire Department

Robert Doane, Irvin McCormick and Surface Barlow collected money to begin a volunteer fire department in Union. Larry Luebbers was the first chief. McCormick was the first president. They purchased a building for a firehouse on Nov. 4, 1969.

The next month the Ladies Auxiliary began sponsoring fund-raisers, which paid off the $4,500 building debt in two and a half years. Greater Cincinnati Airport donated the first fire engine. Three years later, Harold Bennett donated a 1940 Ford Pumper. A fire department in a Cincinnati suburb called Mack-Groesbeck donated fire-protective gear, hoses and nozzles. A new fire engine was ordered in 1973.

Union's New Barber

As Union's new barber in 1961, Gayle Stewart declined advice from Sheeney Craig, the county dogcatcher. He neither joined the Baptist Church nor drank at the saloon down the road. His signs in his windows brought customers in and they kept coming back.

He opened on the corner of 42 and Mt. Zion Road on Election Day and his building

---

[35] *Dixie News*, July 3, 1968.

[36] *150th Anniversary, City of Walton*, 60.

was a voting spot. Twenty-two years later, he moved down the road to Dr. Senour's building where Family Video and Johnson's Country Ham are located. After his wife Shirley died, Gayle remarried Ruie Collins from Hebron in 1995.[37]

National Tractor Driving Champ

Billy Smith, son of Robert and Jeanette Smith of Union and grandson of Emerson Smith, joined 4-H unofficially at 9 and began competing in the Tractor Safety Project and showing dairy cattle. He never lost a tractor driving contest, winning the county, area, and state levels in the junior division.

As state winner in the senior division at 14, Smith advanced to the national competition. In 1964 it was held at the Virginia State Fair. He placed third. He also won a trip to National 4-H Congress, a week in Chicago with 3,000 4-Hers from around the nation.[38]

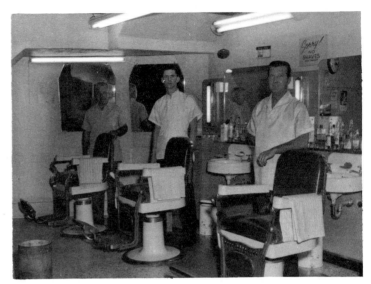

Peck's Barbershop in Florence was located at the corner of Main and Shelby Jim Young is in the center with Jim Peck at the far right. Photo by Bob Sharpe

Average Prices Boone County Farmers Received*								
Year	Tobacco	Soybns	Corn	Wheat	Beef	Calves	Hogs	Milk
	$./lb.	$/bu.	$/bu.	$/bu.	$/cwt	$/cwt	$/cwt	$/cwt
1960	64.1	2.07	1.09	1.74	18.70	25.50	15.50	3.93
1965	69.2	2.48	1.25	1.33	18.50	25.20	19.70	3.96
1970	72.2	2.87	1.52	1.31	26.20	34.80	22.80	5.45
1975	106.7	4.87	2.57	2.96	27.40	27.00	47.20	8.25
1979	145.8	6.42	2.72	4.00	65.10	83.00	41.50	11.80
* Boone County Cooperative Extension Service figures, compiled by Jerry Brown.								

HeeHaw with Price

Towering above fellow country music stars including Minnie Pearl as they hammed it up to open the popular televison show "Hee Haw," Florence's Kenny Price put to use his guitar-, banjo- and harmonica-playing as well as acting and singing talents.

The largest cast member by any comparison, Price used acting talents honed at the Cincinnati Conservatory of Music to bring huge guffaws of laughter from the live crowd as well as television viewers from coast to coast.

A fellow music-writer had dared him to audition at Cincinnati TV station WLW. Taking the dare got Price a new job in June 1954. "Midwestern Hayride," a live country music show, featured Price as a solo artist as well as with his band, a male quartet from Cincinnati called the "Hometowners."

On Arthur Godfrey's Talent Scouts, audiences selected their favorite from three performances. The winning musicians spent a week in New York City then returned to the show. The Hometowners stayed in the Big Apple four weeks by special invitation to reappear on the popular show.

In 1973, a song he wrote, performed and recorded called "Walkin' in New Grass" went to #6 on the Broadcast Music Incorporated (BMI) charts, a national rating determined by radio airplay. Another song Price recorded

---
[37] Melinda Fillmore, "Gayle Stewart," *A Peek Into the Past*, 51.
[38] Bill Smith, March 31, 1998.

soon after, "Sheriff of Boone County," reached the top 20s. Ray Pennington, a Boone County native who now lives in Nashville, wrote that song.

Price made guest appearances on shows including "Love Boat" and the "Orange Blossom Special," where he sang with Loretta Lynn. All during this time, he, his wife Donna and children Chris, Kenny and Jennifer lived in Florence. His parents Bill and Mary Price also lived in Florence.

In association with Gaylord Productions, which produced "Hee Haw," Kenny and Donna filmed their own television show in the Cincinnati region for two years. It ended abruptly when Kenny died of a heart attack after filming a show in Alaska called "Wish You Were Here," which was carried by TNN. It was an interview show featuring highlights on the area.[39]

Hitching a Ride to the Top 40

Disc jockey Jack Reno, an Iowa native and self-taught singer and guitar player, appeared with Kenny Price on "Midwestern Hayride." He also played with Bill Monroe, the great Bluegrass music legend.

Writing and recording country music, he traveled the country before taking a job with WUBE Radio in Cincinnati. After living on Cincinnati's north side for a short time, he moved to Florence in 1972 and flew out of Greater Cincinnati Airport to make appearances. Now he says, *"I'd never leave Boone County."*

"Hitching a Ride," perhaps Reno's best-known song, reached #9 in the top 40 play list in the late '60s. In 1968, "Repeat After Me" went to #5. "I Want One," recorded in 1969, reached #4 on the radio play list. In all, 15 of Reno's songs made the top 20.

In addition to eight appearances on the famous "Grand Ole Opry," Reno performed with Red Foley and Brenda Lee on the "Ozark Jubilee," an ABC TV show recorded in Springfield, Mo. He also recorded songs with Porter Wagoner and Tennessee Ernie Ford.

"I could fly out and make a lot more money performing in Texas", Reno said. *"People here just thought you were local and wanted you to play for free."*

When he was actively recording music, Reno said he could hear a song in a nightclub or while performing in a prison, record it and pay the writer royalties. That is not as common now, when big recording studios hire staff writers.

Reno's family includes wife Beverly, a North Dakota native who is now a nursing professor at Northern Kentucky University, son Randy and daughter Sheila Howe, who

---

The Sheriff of Boone County
Written by Ray Pennington
Performed by Kenny Price

*I don't take no lip
with this cannon on my hip.
Let me tell you boy,
It ain't no toy.
I've got a hat just like a Mounty,
I'm the Sheriff of Boone County.
Be careful, Boy
cause you're in a heap of trouble, Boy.*

*If you're trying to push your Caddy
From Nashville to Cincinnati
You have to come across
the Boone County line.
If you're aimin' on driving through
Better mind your p's and q's
Because this here stretch of interstate
Boy is mine.*

*Might out run my old Chevrolet,
But you can't outrun my old two-way.
Leon's waitin' at the station to hear from me.
Now you're gona be wishin'
I believed in extradition,
I'll chase you all the way back to Tennessee.*

*So far I guess you've been lucky,
But now you're in Boone County, Kentucky.
I don't know how things are in Tennessee.
I'm the roughest you ever saw
Down here I'm the law,
it's been that way since back in '43.*

*I run the grocery store.
I'm the dog catcher,
And the judge, I'm him too.
You might as well just plead guilty.
I'll post your bond for you, if you'd like.
If you wreck your car on the way to the courthouse,
I've got a used car lot down there too.
We're trying to help you
because you're in a heap of trouble boy.
You are guilty just like I thought you was.
Just plead guilty boy.*

---

[39] Donna Price Fancher interview Oct. 7, 1997.

live in Florence with their families. His son Gary lives in Cedar Rapids, Iowa.[40]

Now a Boone County deputy sheriff, Reno says he "*works the court system and doesn't even sing in church.*"

Ewing Becomes Mayor

Another Boone County transplant, Carroll M. "Hop" Ewing, moved his family here in 1953. The former Marine, an 8th and 9th grade math teacher at Ockerman Jr. High School and an insurance salesman, became Florence's mayor in 1961.

Ewing began driving the engine for the Florence Volunteer Fire Department and was appointed to the City Council. Charter president of the Boone County Jaycees, he was also Optimist of the year three times.

While a University of Kentucky student, Ewing had built horse barns. Drawing on his construction skills, he paneled the front wall of the council room himself. Married to Sue Ann Houston, they had five daughters and a son.[41]

Largest Mall

Just west of Florence, a tiny town called Hopeful Heights had incorporated in 1961. Its 500 residents were opposed to being annexed by Florence, but division over a persistent sewer problem led to dissolving the corporation, allowing Florence to annex the

The Florence Y'all water tower at Florence Mall. Photo by Jason Dunn

Mayor C.H. "Hop" Ewing. Photo by Bob Sharpe

land along I-75.

In April 1968, Chelsea Development Co. asked Florence City Council to provide water and sewage service for a regional shopping complex on about 200 acres of what had been Hopeful Heights.

Cincinnati developer Walter "Wally" Seinsheimer and William "Bill" Williams of Western Southern Life Insurance met with Mayor Ewing and County Judge Executive Bruce Ferguson. The developers asked for help in getting a county-maintained road built from 18 to 42 for a new Florence mall.

The foursome visited Lt. Gov. Wendell Ford, who was then running for governor, and his assistant, Walter "Dee" Huddleston, in the lieutenant governor's mansion in Frankfort. They needed a commitment to build the road and an anchor store for the mall.

Ford, a former president of the national Jaycees, called the vice president and head legal council for Sears who had been his vice president in the Jaycees. Assuring him the road would be built if Ford were elected

---

[40] Jack Reno interview, Oct. 2, 1997.
[41] Barbara Fisk, "Florence Mayor Wears Many Hats," *Dixie News*, April 10, 1969.

governor, Sears committed to the new location.

Two doctors' insistence on making their property accessible to the mall nearly derailed the project, the *Dixie News* reported on Dec. 30, 1973. To resolve the stalemate, Mayor Ewing suggested adding another access road for Drs. Ammon and Markesbery.

Touted as the largest shopping center in the southwest, construction began in November 1974 on four anchor stores connected by an interior mall.

Sears opened on March 10, 1976. The rest of the mall opened on Sept. 22, accompanied by the Boone County High School band playing "Bring in the Clowns" and "My Old Kentucky Home." An estimated 53,000 visited the mall that day.

Soon Florence Mall offered 135 shops. Additional shopping complexes opening along Mall Road have made it the largest shopping area in Northern Kentucky. The development has collected millions in state sales taxes, far recouping Mall Road costs.

Reader's Digest Y'All

After a contentious city council meeting, Florence officials voted to accept the higher of two bids to construct a water tower. Following the advice of engineer James Ransom, the city contracted with Pittsburgh-Des Moines Steel Company to build a million-gallon water tower.

They bid $3,430 more than Universal Tank and Ironworks, which also promised an earlier completion date. Ransom's recommendation came because the Pittsburgh company had designed the "hydro pillar" structure.[42]

Visible from I-75, the red and white water tower built to serve the Florence Mall was painted with block letters advertising the mall. But state inspectors from the Bureau of Highways determined the ad was illegal according to its standards.

Rather than paying to repaint the entire sign, Mayor Ewing suggested painting out the legs of the M. His creative approach made the memorable Florence Y'all sign known by I-75 travelers from Canada to Florida.[43] The witty sign amused an Associated Press writer who wrote an article that eventually ran in *Reader's Digest*.

The new tower doubled water pressure in Florence, an improvement gratefully received by those who had scheduled their laundry and dishwashing at odd hours to ensure they would have water.

Boone County Recorder
March 16, 1972
Winner of Art Contest
A watercolor by Teresa Byrd won the Fifth District Women's Clubs Art Contest in 1972.
The daughter of Mr. and Mrs. William L. Byrd of Florence is a junior at Boone County High School and a pupil of Mrs. Martha Daugherty.

Mrs. Beverly Jo Searcy
Courtesy of Dixie News

Ricky Rice at 16
Courtesy of Dixie News

Notable Florence Residents

Eagle Scout Ricky Rice was selected to have lunch with Gov. Edward Breathitt on Feb. 13, 1967, representing the Boy Scouts of Kentucky. The son of Mr. and Mrs. Ward Rice of Florence, Ricky was to report on "Scouting in the Nation" for President Lyndon Johnson. A straight-A student, Ricky earned 22 merit badges and the "God and Country Award."

Mrs. Beverly Jo Searcy of 245 Locust Lane, Florence, prepared "Pineapple Peppermint Ripple Cake" which made her a finalist in the National Pineapple Cooking Classic in Hawaii,

---

[42] *Dixie News*, March 15, 1973.
[43] letter from Hop Ewing.

Aug. 7-14, 1973. She competed with 40 cooks from coast to coast for a top cash award of $25,000.

Industrial Development

The Chamber of Commerce and other business and civic groups incorporated the Northern Kentucky Industrial Foundation on April 1, 1959, to develop 1,000 acres of Boone and Kenton County, south of Florence.

Financed by selling five-year-non-interest-bearing certificates, land (formerly Jerome B. Respess' Highland Stock Farm) was purchased in October.

Great Lakes Carbon Web was the first factory to move in. They made fireproof insulating board from pearlite treated to extreme temperatures that explodes like popcorn. It is shipped all over the country to use in construction.

The park was designed to host fabricators and distributors, not heavy industry that would need smokestacks and large amounts of waste disposal. Intended to look almost like a college campus, it now employs about 10,000. Businesses were given 10 years of tax-free operations as an incentive to relocate there.

With access to rail, truck, river and air and an abundant labor supply, eight years later 20-some industries had built facilities at a cost exceeding $40 million.

American Sign and Manufacturing Service opened in 1964. About 200 employees made illuminated signs, menu boards and advertising clocks. Johnson Controls Inc.'s Battery Group began making plastic battery containers, covers and vents with 280 employees in 1967.

Aristech Chemical Corp.'s Acrylic Sheet Unit opened the next year, making plastic acrylic sheets with 235 employees. Lasco Panel Products manufactured fiberglass wall panels, roofing and siding as well as sanitary wall restaurant panels with 202 employees in 1969.

Florence Expansion

Everything was growing in Florence. A new city building – housing administrative offices, council chambers, police headquarters and a three-cell jail – was built off U.S. 42 on Niblack Drive. Houses were springing up everywhere. Jobs were plentiful – as was noise from the airport and the constant construction.

J. Coldiron Jr. built a new townhouse complex on Turfway road opposite Rinks. Rent started at $140 a month.

The Ramada Inn found a way around a Florence moratorium against further hotel/motel development – a restriction added to protect the city's overtaxed sewer system. It made arrangements for service through the Northern Kentucky Industrial Foundation.[44]

Caintuckee Restaurant in Florence, where Florence Baptist Church parking lot is now,

Florence's Caintuckee Restaurant was a popular gathering place.
Photo contributed by Hannah Baird

---
[44] *Dixie News*, Sept. 30, 1971.

was the gathering place for local politicians and community leaders. John Cain, father of the 1998 Kenton County Judge Executive Rodney "Biz" Cain, owned the restaurant.

When the "Caintuck" closed, locals said the Baptist Church needed to open up a new Sunday School class for all the parents who dropped their children off at Sunday School then went next door to eat Kentucky ham and biscuits.[45]

Uptown Florence merchants saw their business going to the new mall. Many closed their doors for the last time. Doctors Gladys Rouse and Harry Daugherty still visited homes, just like members of the extended family.

Agents from the Alcohol and Tobacco Tax division, assisted by Boone County Sheriff Melvin Collins, arrested three men for distilling moonshine at a farmhouse three miles south of Florence. The illicit still was so heavy the men had reinforced the floor of the second story to hold it. Officials estimated it produced 50 to 60 gallons of moonshine a day. They confiscated 1,900 gallons of mash and 1,200 pounds of sugar as well as the whiskey.[46]

In July 1968, Florence issued revenue bonds to cover the cost of expanding water service in the U.S. 42 area beyond the I-75 interchange. The City Council also awarded a $5,909 contract to L.E. Bergin of Florence to resurface Patricia Street and Shenandoah Drive.[47]

Florence experienced a construction boom in 1968, with 76 one-family, 2 two-family, and 515 multi-family dwelling units constructed. A new tax levy was passed, setting a rate of 29½ cents per $100 valuation.

Patrolman Mack Gaddis was promoted to Sergeant at a salary of $2.70 an hour. The monthly police report included two thefts, two breaking and entering charges, one disorderly conduct, one grand larceny, two auto tamperings and one case of vandalism.[48]

With four years of experience as a police officer, William I. Hiler began on the Florence force working for $2.60 an hour in 1969.[49]

Florence Mayor C.M. Ewing, Fourth District Congressman Frank Chelf and County Attorney William McEvoy cut the ribbon to open the new Florence City building on June 28, 1964.
Courtesy of *Dixie News*

Establishing a Library

In early 1973, the Association for Boone Library Establishment (ABLE) gathered signatures to get a library referendum on the November 1973 ballot. Before Boone County's libraries existed, some paid to use the Kenton County Library and others simply went without.

The group asked Ted Bushelman, the airport public relations director, for promotional help to start a library. "*I was not in the door for three minutes until they nominated me as chairman,*" he says.

---

[45] Martha Daugherty
[46] *Boone County Recorder*, Dec. 12, 1963.
[47] *Dixie News*, July 3, 1968.

[48] *Dixie News*, May 15, 1969, 1
[49] *Dixie News*, April 10, 1969, 1.

"*Women-power got it passed. I'd say I think we ought to do this and it'd be done in five minutes. It was an unbelievable experience for me to see a group who were so dedicated.*"

Don Ravenscraft, the organization's treasurer, accepted a $500 check from Boone County Jaycettes President Sherry Lou Noel to help in the campaign. Former Jaycette President Ginny Kohl was vice chairman of ABLE.

"*The jail was on the ballot at the same time and we knew it would hurt us,*" Bushelman said. Voters turned down the jail, but voted for the 2 percent property tax for the library.[50] (The library is now funded through 2 cents per $100 valuation on property tax bills.)

Bushelman presided at the first meeting of the Boone County Public Library Board of Trustees on Dec. 17, 1973. The board applied for a state library construction grant and began seeking a temporary library location. Then they looked for books and furniture from other libraries and agencies. State grants for $70,000 paid the first year's operating expenses and bought more books.

On Oct. 14, 1974, Jane Smith opened the first library in #2 Girard Street in Florence, an old feed store that volunteers had built a ceiling and floor in. "*That day more than 180 Boone County residents visited the library and walked away with brand new library cards,*" says Cindy Brown, library director.

"*By the end of the year, the library collection had grown from 8,000 books to over 11,000. Customers were checking out an average of 165 books per day. Parents brought their children to the library for programs and films.*"

Ground was broken on July 17, 1975 at 7425 U.S. 42 in Florence. The building designed by architect Robert Hayes was complete nine months later.

"*In June 1976, the new library opened with 18,000 books and 9,000 registered borrowers,*" Ms. Brown says.[51]

'70s Bring More Expansion

By 1973, 35 plants were operating and two more were under construction in the Industrial Park, employing 6,000 with an annual payroll of $50 million. In 1992, 52 plants operated from Boone County's part of the complex, employing 4,000-5,000.

In the spring of 1972, Florence City Council endorsed a plan requested by the Boone County Businessmen's Association to make Burlington Pike four lanes. While that vote was unanimous, a proposal to make Main and Girard streets one way led to contentious debate. Required to break a tie, Mayor Ewing said, "*Anything with this much controversy has no business passing council.*"[52]

Boone State Bank, an outgrowth of Belleview's Citizens Deposit Bank, opened in Florence in 1972. President Warren E. "Gene" Kelly said in its first six months in Florence, the bank's assets had increased by $1 million and the number of new accounts being opened daily amazed board members.

Ben A. Courtney was chief operating officer, vice president and cashier. Mary Sue Rudicill was assistant cashier. Kenneth R. Lucas, chairman of the executive committee, said there were 105 stockholders in addition to a 17-member board representing a large cross-section of the community committed to service.[53]

The city council looked into the problem of Florence's ineffective storm sewers after record rainfall in July 1973. Water backed up in basements, pushed manhole covers up and mixed with raw sewage.

Florence received a safety award for 32 years without a pedestrian death due to automobiles.[54]

Three new businesses came to Florence in 1973. BAWAC Sheltered Workshop opened with 160 employees. Hopple Plastics hired 259 to make package blisters, material handling trays, food and hospital trays. Sweco Inc.'s Finishing Equipment Division began

---

[50] Ted Bushelman interview, March 10, 1998.
[51] Lucinda Brown

[52] *Dixie News*, May 11, 1972.
[53] *Dixie News*, June 20, 1972.
[54] *Dixie News*, July 26, 1973.

making metal finishing and process equipment with 150 employees.

Mazak Corp. relocated here the next year. About 575 employees manufacture metal cutting machinery.

Littleford Day Inc. opened in 1976 with 180 employees building industrial mixing and food processing equipment, chemical and special mixing machinery. The next year brought Owens/Brockway, hiring 250 to manufacture plastic bottles.[55]

Thoroughbreds Come to Turfway

Turfway Road was created in the 1960s to connect U.S. 25 with the new Latonia Race Track, which opened for Thoroughbred racing.

Thoroughbreds race at Latonia before the name was changed to Turfway.
Photo by Bob Sharpe

The original Thoroughbred track in Latonia closed on July 29, 1939. The name was changed to Turfway Park in 1986.

Thoroughbreds began racing at Florence's Latonia Race Track on Aug. 27, 1959. On Sept. 7, 11,415 fans poured through the turnstiles, setting an attendance record. Night racing was introduced in 1968. The opening of I-75 in 1962 simplified travel to and f in 1962rom the track. A new tote board showed win, place and show pools for each horse and the totals bet on each race. The grandstand was enclosed in glass in 1968 when additional barns were added. More barns and modern washroom facilities came in 1973.

A weatherized grandstand and a clubhouse now seat 7,200 fans. Horses, 1,300 of them, can wait in stalls to run on the mile-long, 75-foot wide track. In 1965, the Ohio Valley Harness Racing Association began trotting Standardbreds around Latonia.

On Oct. 4, 1969, Latonia hosted the first pari-mutual Quarter Horse meet east of the Mississippi. Some sort of racing is now offered nine months of the year at Florence track.

On Aug. 27, 1959, the new Latonia opened in Florence, and Gov. Happy Chandler, re-elected to a second term, was back for opening day. In 1983, the New Latonia track owners decided to begin a six-furlong "Wishing Ring Stakes" competition for fillies and mares, but a typing error changed it to Wishing Well Stakes and the name has stuck.[56]

The Wintergreen Stakes recognizes 1909 Kentucky Derby winner Wintergreen, the only Ohio-born horse to win the Derby. Mrs. J.B. "Rome" Respess, who owned Highland Stock Farm south of Florence on Dixie Highway, with her late husband, attended the first running on Sept. 12, 1964. Their famous Dick Welles horse was buried on their farm in a grave marked with purple and white iris, the colors of his racing silks.

On Sept. 24, 1969, a win of $484.40 on a $2 bet set a new track record. Night racing

---

[55] True, 12-13.

[56] Conrad, *The Top of Kentucky*, 30.

began that year. New owners took over in 1985, changing the name to Turfway Park.

The annual "Jim Beam Stakes" race commanded national attention with a $500,000 purse. A major Derby-prep race, a "Call to Post" luncheon added excitement by bringing in celebrity speakers like Bob Hope, Jerry Lewis and President Gerald Ford. In 1992, Jim Beam Stakes winner Lil E. Tee won the Kentucky Derby.[57]

Williams Wins Recognition

In 1962, Burlington's Caroline Williams became the first female recipient of the Rosa F. and Samuel B. Sachs Prize sponsored by the Cincinnati Institute of Fine Arts. The award included a $500 prize and recognized the publication of her fourth and final book about Cincinnati, *Cincinnati Scenes: Steeples, Streets and Steps*. Cited for "*capturing the special charm of Cincinnati in her sketches and accompanying text*" the honor recognized Caroline Williams as a writer as much as an artist.

A year later she was cited by the Ohioana Library Association in Columbus for "distinguished service to Ohio in the cause of the Arts." Then she was honored at the Annual Achievement Tea of the Cincinnati branch of the National Association of Pen Women at the Taft Museum.[58]

Burlington

Burlington Pot Pie factory (now the Antique Emporium on Jefferson Street), that operated under contract to major manufacturers, was closed by health restrictions in the 1970s because they had no sewage or public water.

Cincinnati Telephone Bulletin in February 1969 featured Caroline Williams. Here she stands in front of the Boone County log cabin she restored herself with her faithful poodle.
Courtesy of Christine Godsey

The Petersburg and Burlington Methodist Churches merged in the '70s. When the Petersburg church was razed, the old bell was moved to Burlington.[59] Burlington United Methodist Church made plans to begin constructing a new church on KY 18 the next spring 1979.

---
[57] Conrad, *The Top of Kentucky*, 30.
[58] Dottie L. Lewis, editor, *Caroline Williams: Her Spot in Cincinnati*, The Cincinnati Historical Society, Cincinnati, Ohio, 1990, 11.

[59] 175th Anniversary Historical Book, 13.

Chapter 14
1980 and Beyond – Record Growth Continues

Rosella Porterfield is one of many who watched Boone County change dramatically during the 20th Century. *"There was such poverty when I moved to Boone County and joined the Zion Church in 1944. No one* (in my church) *had good jobs, only about three people owned cars. Now every family has beautiful cars. If there are five in the family, each one has his own car. They are prosperous, you can't help but see that. Our church is installing stained glass windows without going into debt."*

Prosperity

Mrs. Porterfield's observation is reflected in demographic statistics. Boone County has the second highest median income in the Commonwealth, behind Oldham, which borders the eastern edge of Louisville. Neighboring Kenton County was fourth, following Woodford, west of Lexington. Campbell County was sixth in 1990 median income.[1]

U.S. Census figures also show that the number living in a Boone County household is decreasing from 3.07 in 1980 to a projected 2.3 persons in 2020, following national trends toward smaller families and more people living alone.

From 1989 to 1993, Boone County's average per capita income increased 18 percent, from $15,997 to $18,884, slightly surpassing Campbell County and a few hundred dollars below Kenton County.

Nearly $2,000 higher than the Commonwealth's average, Boone's average income is slightly lower than average wages in Indiana and Ohio, by $329 and $812 respectively. It remains, however, $1,916 below the national income average.[2]

The median income went from $34,485 in 1989 to $40,607 in 1993. Boone's poverty rate is estimated at 8.4 percent or 5,688 people in 1993. Of those, 1,365 are children between the ages of five and 17.

Boone County Population Projections*

Year	Population
1980	45,842
1990	57,589
1995	70,097
2000	79,172
2010	94,672
2020	109,372

Housing Boom

The average value of a single-family dwelling in Boone County in 1990 was $74,300. Just 10 years earlier, it was not quite $53,000. These values consistently exceed the state average by $14,000 and more. The average cost for a new home jumped from $75,500 in 1986 to $92,237 for the years 1991-1993 averaged together.[3]

In 1995, the average selling price of a home in Hebron was $150,297. By June 1997, that increased 9 percent to $163,836. Union's figures showing a 21 percent jump are slightly more dramatic – from $155,939 to $188,215. Walton's 1995 average

---

[1] U.S. Census Bureau website.
*U.S. Census Bureau Statistics, Ky. State Dad Center Estimates.

[2] Rene True, program manager, Keith Roberts, research, Kentucky Cabinet for Economic Development, Division of Research in cooperation with Tri-County Economic Development Corp., *Kentucky Resources for Economic Development, Northern Kentucky*, 1996, 4, 8.
* True, 11.
[3] 1995 Boone County Comprehensive Plan.

of $95,575 increased to $129,709 – a 36 percent leap.

The Northern Kentucky Association of Realtors reported the average selling price in every community in Boone, Campbell and Kenton counties had risen between 1995 and June 1997.[4]

Less than 7 percent of Boone's homes were built before 1940. More than 20 percent were constructed between 1984 and 1990.

Countywide, the percentage of single family homes has decreased in proportion to multi-family or apartment units. Florence has more multi-family dwellings than any place else in the county. The vacancy rate in 1990 was 6.3 percent, indicating a high demand for housing.[5]

Population Increases

Between 1980 and 1994, Boone County's population increased 45 percent to 67,491, making it the second-fastest growing county in the Commonwealth. The population is projected to reach 91,500 by 2020.

In 1990, Boone County's population grew by nearly 26 percent.[6] By 1997, 61 percent of the county's population lived in urban areas, 36 percent in the suburbs and slightly over 2 percent remained on working farms.

Florence increased by nearly 20 percent in 1990, Walton by 23 percent, Union by 67 percent and the unincorporated areas by 28 percent.

The population increase comes from younger middle class "whites." The population is relatively youthful, with a median age of 31.4 years in 1990. Most, 76 percent, graduated from high school.

Boone County is not racially diverse. Only 1.5 percent of the population is considered non-white. In 1990, the entire county's population of African-Americans totalled 361. There were almost an equal number of Asians, 355.[7]

From appearances, Boone County's growing minority is Hispanics, as it is across the nation. With increasing numbers of Mexicans traveling north to work in tobacco, many are attracted to the region's prosperity and are moving their families here.

Schools Bulge

Total school enrollment in the fall of 1994 was 11,194 in Boone County schools and 949 in Walton-Verona Independent District. Pupil-teacher ratios were 18-1 and 17-1. Boone County spent an average of $3,578.30 per pupil annually and the independent district spent $4,092.40. About the same numbers, 56 and 57 percent of the high school graduates went on to college after the 1993-1994 school year.[8]

In 1997, Boone County was the sixth largest school district in Kentucky, serving 11,000 students in 16 institutions. That number is down slightly from the 12,271 enrolled during the 1991-92 school year.

Nine elementary schools offered kindergarten through grade five, with the first four years in an ungraded primary format. In the 1980s, Kelly Elementary at Belleview replaced the Hamilton and Petersburg elementary

1995 Population by Age Boone County*

Age group	Percent
17 & under	29.7
18-24	8.1
25-34	16.2
35-49	25.3
50 & over	20.7

1994 Average Weekly Boone County Wages by Industry*

All Industries	$469
Mining & Quarrying	$503
Contract construction	$529
Manufacturing	$582
Transportation, communication, & Public utilities	$692
Wholesale & retail	$321
Finance, Ins. & real estate	$496
Services	$343
State/local gov't	$405

---

[4] Valerie Kincaid, , "Home Boom Raises Prices," *Cincinnati Business Courier*, June 20, 1997, 29.
[5] 1995 Boone County Comprehensive Plan
[6] True, 45.

[7] U.S. Census Bureau statistics.
[8] True, 34.
* Kentucky Agricultural Statistics 1996-1997.

Boone County Democratic Club members and students in the statehouse rotunda in Frankfort.
Photo contributed by Virginia Lainhart

schools. Stephens Elementary opened in 1991. Erpenbeck Elementary was scheduled to open in the fall of 1998. Construction is expected to be completed on yet another elementary in the Hebron area by 1999.

Four middle schools and three high schools, Boone County, Conner and Ryle (which opened in 1992), offer general academics, college preparatory and vocational training through 120 courses.

While sports may not carry quite the following they have in the past, interest and enthusiasm for girls' sports is growing. The Boone County Lady Rebels basketball team from Florence won the 9th Region title, advancing to the state tournament in 1997 and 1998.

Boone County Center of Kentucky Technical School allows students to spend three hours each day there and the remainder at the high school. A tech prep program blends academic and technical subjects leading to an associate degree.

In 1997 teachers earned from $23,977 to $47,636 per year, while top administrative salaries reached $83,363.[9]

The majority of Boone County's public school students ride the bus to school. Buses – 96 of them – leave at 7 a.m. and quit at 4:15 p.m., covering 7,500 miles and consuming 1,309 gallons of gasoline each weekday.

Dropout rates are among the lowest in Kentucky. Sixty percent continued their education after high school. Boone County students consistently score above average on ACT and SAT exams. In the mid-'90s students

---
[9] Annual Performance Report, Local School District, 1996-97.

in grades 4, 8 and 12 exceeded state and national averages in math, reading, science and social studies.

The number of classrooms needed for the expected student increase as the century turns is rapidly outpacing available space. By the 2008 school year, 16,000 students are anticipated in the County school system alone.

Walton-Verona Independent Public Schools operate an elementary for grades K-6 and a junior/senior high school for grades 7-12, with a combined enrollment of 950. The teacher/student ratio is 1-to-14 and four types of diplomas are offered: basic, pre-college, college prep, and academic.

Four Catholic elementary schools in the Diocese of Covington offer private education. Five high schools are available to Boone Countians wishing to earn diplomas from Catholic schools.

More and more parents are home schooling their children, but often dropping them back into the public system after a time or as they get older. Administrators struggle constantly to keep up with the population growth without new taxes to add buildings.

Ralph and Molly Newman Lents donated land for the Hebron library.

Community Education

In 1977, the Board of Education began offering 600 elementary children opportunities for remedial tutoring, enrichment activities and recreation through a combined program with the Parks and Recreation Department. Volunteers lead the programs.

A community education program for all ages offers activities, classes and special projects like organizing a walking tour of historic Petersburg. A countywide Community Education Council represents 14 departments, agencies and organizations to assess needs and interests and develop programs to meet them.[10]

Library Expansion

In 1985, under the direction of new director Lucinda Brown, a grant financed converting the card catalog to computerized records.

A contribution from longtime library supporters, Mr. and Mrs. R.V. Lents enabled construction of a branch in Hebron that opened in 1989. The Walton branch opened in 1994, when new barcoded library cards were used to check out books.

In 1998, the Boone County Public Library District offers more than 150,000 books, videos, audiotapes, and CDs. Reference librarians answer more than 150 questions a day. Special programs attract hundreds each year. The library's Internet services continue to expand.[11]

An architect is now drawing plans for a new Union library, said Ted Bushelman who still chairs the library board.. Administrative services will be consolidated there, which will allow expansion of other libraries within their existing buildings. The board also is looking for property in Belleview Bottoms for another new library.[12]

Teen Activities

Breakdancing was all the rage among teens and preteens in the 1980s. Chuckie Cheese's arcade and pizza place on Mall Road attracted costumed kids from all over the region, offering cash prizes for break dancing.

---

[10] Conrad, *Top of Kentucky*, 42.
[11] Cindy Brown
[12] Ted Bushelman interview, March 10, 1998.

In 1998, William Claiborne Ryle, a sophomore at Conner High School, says he and his friends seldom plan a place to go. *"Recently I got my license and that's made my life a lot more fun,"* says the teen, who will graduate in the Class of 2000. While he says some of his classmates hang out at the mall, he and his friends like outdoor activities, including backpacking, hiking up Gunpowder Creek, biking along the Ohio and hanging out at Rabbit Hash.

Claiborne doesn't see the school spirit he remembers from attending basketball games with his father, Larry Ryle, the superintendent for whom Ryle High School was named. *"Half the bleacher section would be the pep section full of kids screaming and yelling."*

The 16-year-old plans to attend college *"probably out of state,"* study engineering and return to Boone County. He knows his family has lived on Beech Grove Road outside of Burlington for seven generations and owns a watch from his grandfather and a pocketknife from his great-grandfather.

"I'd like to think the rural areas will stay like they are now. It seems like there is another house going up every time I go by," Claiborne says. If his family is any indication, at least some of the youth will return. His sister Sally earned a teaching degree and is now building a home on five-acres of the family farm where she will live with her husband.[13]

Economic Development

The broad diversity of industry, which is at least in part bringing the newcomers, will likely

One of Boone County's longest running businesses is the Kottmyer family ferry at Constance. Photo by Jason Dunn

prevent any major economic downturn or recession. Economists describe the region as almost unusually stable.

About 22,000 commuted into Boone County in 1990, while 14,412 who live here commuted out to work. A nearly equal number, 14,102, work and live in Boone County.

In 1981, Gov. John Y. Brown brought Northern Kentucky business leaders together to pool their efforts to attract new industry here. In 1986, the Tri-County Economic Development Corporation or Tri-ED opened. Ken Lucas, Boone County's judge executive from 1992-98, was one of the founders, a board member and the first president. In 1995 Tri-ED obtained permanent funding from rental car license fees.

Now called one of the top 10 economic development organizations in the U.S., Tri-ED

---

[13] William Claiborne Ryle, April 5, 1998.

claims to have helped bring more than 150 new businesses to Northern Kentucky, creating 16,000 new jobs and stimulating $1.26 billion in new investment.

"We've tried to seek out quality development and have turned down businesses that we didn't think would be beneficial to the area," Lucas said. *"There is a definite plan and design."*

"We're not offering incentives to anyone who comes down the pike. We have plenty of entry-level jobs, we're looking for higher paying jobs, office developments, and higher priced manufacturing jobs that require technical skills."[14]

Big Business in Boone

The local newspaper has gone the route of many closely held businesses in the late 20th century. Gene Clabes bought the *Boone County Recorder* in 1991. In 1995 Press Community, a national conglomerate which is owned by Suburban Communications, purchased it. The chain now owns numerous local papers in the region.

Boone County's largest employers are IRS, Delta Airlines, The Gap/Banana Republic, COMAIR holdings, DHL Airways, St. Luke Hospital, Boone County Board of Education and Fidelity Investments, all employing 1,200 to 5,300.

Duro Bag Manufacturing, Sabatasso Foods and Equitable Paper Bag Company employ more than 600 each. Entex Information Services employs 520 working with computers. Keco Industries has 384 making air conditioning equipment. HK Systems (formerly Western Atlas) makes conveyor systems with 300 workers.

In the 200-300 employee range are: The Nielsen Company, a printer; Sach Automotive of America which makes automotive struts; and Aristech Chemical Corporation the manufacturers acrylic sheet products.

Smaller companies with 175 to 220 workers include: Clarion Manufacturing Corporation that makes automobile radios and stereos; Johnson Controls Battery Group that makes plastic battery containers; Lasco Panel Products that makes fiberglass building panels; Emerald Industries Inc, a cookie and cake baker; The Hennegan Company, a printer, Owens-Brockway Inc. that manufacturers plastic bottles; and Littleford Day Inc. that makes industrial mixing equipment.

The three Northern Kentucky Judge Executives serve on the Tri-County Economic Development Corporation of Northern Kentucky. In 1997 that included Kenneth Paul, Campbell; Kenneth R. Lucas, Boone; and Clyde Middleton, Kenton. Courtesy of Tri-AD

Levi Strauss built a major distribution facility on Limaburg Road that employs 800. The Gap/Banana Republic employs 1,650 at a retail distribution center on Mineola Pike.[15]

In 1996, Toyota Motor Corporation announced plans to locate a $26.5 million manufacturing support headquarters near

---

[14] Ken Lucas, April 4, 1998.

[15] Tri-ED, 14.

Hebron. Toyota moved its various North American support headquarters to Boone County, consolidating them under the name Toyota Motor Manufacturing, North America Inc. By 1998, Toyota had 560 employees in Boone County with average annual salaries of $60,000.[16]

Holland Roofing Group moved its headquarters to Burlington in 1986. Named the 20th largest commercial roofing company in the United States by the national trade magazine, *Roofing, Siding and Insulation (RSI)*, it has offices in Louisville, Indianapolis, Columbus and Nashville as well as a residential roofing company in Burlington. Those six offices employ 150 and have revenues of $24 million. Its 1997 revenues were 83 percent over 1996.[17]

Service businesses – hotels, repair, health, computer, legal, etc. – are also growing phenomenally. In 1970, 84 service businesses employed 720. By 1989, 422 services had hired 6,029 people.[18]

Infrastructure Support

Service business growth has been hampered in older, established communities like Burlington and Hebron by the lack of sewage and water service. Those who live or work in new developments have water and sewer service through the Northern Kentucky Sanitation District.

"A lot of work had to be done to get the main trunk lines in place for the sewer," Judge Executive Ken Lucas said. *"One of our problems is that the county is so affluent, we aren't eligible for federal money"* to assist with water and sewer lines.[19]

The highway infrastructure has expanded to support the growth. The Turfway Road exit off I-75 was added at a cost o $1.6 million. Houston Road and Route 18 were widened and repaved in 1997. Roadwork continues.

Regional Shopping District

Florence Mall's construction established the area as a regional shopping district. After nearly two centuries of traveling to Cincinnati and Covington to shop, Boone County residents could finally find specialty goods within county boundaries.

Mall and Houston roads on Florence's west side have become shopping meccas. In 1970, nine retailers employed 1,213. By 1991, 488 retailers had hired 8,627 employees.

One disadvantage of having a large regional mall is that thieves prey upon the concentrations of people and cars there. The mall and the airport are responsible for a disproportionate percentage of the county's crime.

Small Businesses

Unique retailers and entrepreneurs are finding their niche in Boone County's environment or meeting new and growing needs. Many shops and specialty services, like the majority of businesses in Boone County, are small and family-owned.

In 1995, of the 1,897 companies existing in Boone County, 900 or 40 percent had fewer than four employees. Another 399 had five to nine employees. And, 259 had 10 to 19 workers. That means 75 percent of Boone County's businesses had fewer than 20 employees.

Former corporate executives like Lauren Abel of Abel Associates, are relocating to communities like Burlington for the quality of life offered here as well as the small-town attitudes that encourage government officials to see their jobs as helping, rather than controlling small businesses. Abel serves public and media relations clients around the country through electronic connections and telephone lines from her home office.

---

[16] Rawe, 85.
[17] Hans Philippo, Holland Roofing.
[18] 1995 Boone County Comprehensive Plan
[19] Ken Lucas, April 4, 1998.

"*Since we moved, this sleepy little town has grown, but it's still a great place to live*," says the former radio and television anchor who worked in Cincinnati, St. Louis and Fort Wayne. "*Businesses have a great opportunity to grow and prosper here*," she says. "*Boone County gets a lot of positive press. People and tax rates are friendly, not big bureaucracy like in Cincinnati.*"[20]

Part of Abel's business is helping clients capitalize on opportunities on the World Wide Web.

The *Internet* is enabling more and more Boone Countians to work from home and attracting visitors by showcasing Boone County's scenic and historic nature.

Turning Vocation to Avocation

Boone County seems to inspire entrepreneurs who follow the philosophy embodied in the book title – "do what you love and the money will follow."

"*Falling in love with*" a five-acre lot on Green Road brought Millard and Monica Long and their young daughters to Burlington in 1994. Transplants from Mississippi and Cincinnati, they built a home, then began investing in Millard's dream of owning a honey business.

Katelyn's Shoo Sho Sha Honey Inc. (named by one toddler) is creatively packaged in half-pints as "Kentucky Wildcat Reserve" and in Papa, Mama and Baby Bear containers as well as others. The Longs have trademarked the Beenuts name and roast cashews and pecans that are soaked in unprocessed honey.

While Millard maintains a full-time job in addition to the family businesses, they hope increased awareness of unprocessed locally grown honey's health value will rapidly expand their sales.[21]

Wild Walks Photography

Cincinnati native Bruce Wess completed graduate school in Minnesota and became a school psychologist. But "*politics and paperwork*" eventually left him so discouraged he began seeking an affordable rural getaway, "*a hillbilly crackerbox with an acre*" for his garden.

He found it on Bullittsburg Church Road near Idlewild. In 1994, he started Wild Walks Photography. Now he sells art photo cards at Kentucky's state parks and through specialty retailers. Business is growing every year, he says, since his first four-months of backpacking around the Big South Fork of the Cumberland.[22]

Musician and Playwright

Musician David Kisor moved to Florence in 1997 to join his wife Nancy, a fourth-grade teacher at Florence Elementary. Through their business, KISOR MUSIC, they write, record and publish music and scripts.

"Just for Fun," a tape and cd of interactive children's songs, features David's children and nieces and nephews singing his original songs. He has written scripts and the accompanying music for the Ensemble Theatre of Cincinnati and plays for young actors for the University of Cincinnati College Conservatory of Music preparatory department.

David presents school programs using music to encourage imagination, self-esteem building, and introduce international cultures. He also regularly provides live music for TKR Cable's Northern Kentucky Magazine.[23]

Rabbit Hash Fiber Artist

Another Boone County artist, Jane Burch Cochran makes unique quilts at her Rabbit Hash log home. Her artistry has traveled around the nation in prestigious collections, including Quilt National.

---

[20] Lauren Abel, April 1, 1998.
[21] Monica Long, March 31, 1998.
[22] Bruce Wess, April 1, 1998.
[23] David Kisor, April 6, 1998.

In describing her work, she says, "*In my art quilts, I try to combine my art training in painting, my love of fabric, and the tradition of American Quilting. I unconsciously combine the loose, free feeling of abstract painting with the time consuming and controlled techniques of sewing and beading.*"

Cochran incorporates the nostalgia of Victorian crazy quilts with Native American beadwork, old fashioned women's dress gloves and other materials into her work. "*The gloves (hands) are reaching and searching for both questions and answers about race, the environment, and the human psyche. My quilts are highly embellished with beads, buttons, and paint to enhance the narrative with a unique and personal texture.*"[24]

Cochran's art quilts appear in exhibitions, memorials and corporate collections all over the country and regularly win national awards. Her work can be seen in museums in New York, San Francisco, England and Japan. Cochran is featured in the book *Kentucky Women: Two Centuries of Indomitable Spirit and Vision*, by Genie Potter published in 1997.

Cochran designed the Ace of Spades for a deck of cards featured in the Smithsonian Magazine, illustrating the work of reknowned quilt artists from all over the country.

Cochran designed a quilt featuring 200 noted Kentucky women that will be donated to the Kentucky History Center in Frankfort. Michelle Lustenberg helped Jane with the quilt, which was displayed at Rabbit Hash Old Timer's Day in 1996. Names on it include Wanetta Clause and Carrie Hightower.[25]

A Wall Street Journal writer, Gail King, reviewed "Quilt National," an annual touring exhibition in which Cochran's quilts have appeared. She said Ms Cochran is "*not subtle about anything, and the result is a wonderful, flamboyant exuberance that strangely echoes antique album and crazy quilts.*"[26]

Jane Burch Cochran usually cuts and sews combinations of three cloth strips to make her unique quilts, found in corporate collections around the world. She then "*cuts those apart into smaller pieces and keeps sewing and adding until it grows into large enough patches to use.*"

Racing Summers

Scott Summers, who grew up in Petersburg, turned his expensive childhood hobby into a profitable specialty business that brings him customers from around the world. He holds a number of patents for specialty motorcycle racing products that are marketed internationally through Summers Racing Components, owned with his father who helps with the engineering. He also is under contract with various component manufacturers, like Honda and Pirelli, to assist with development and promotion.

---

[24] Jane Cochran, March 20, 1998.
[25] Barbara Fallis, Rabbit Hash, *Boone County Recorder*, March 12, 1998.
[26] Gail King, "Quilt Art: Breaking Out of the Bedroom," *The Wall Street Journal*, July 3, 1991.

After winning a long series of prestigious national motorcycle races, Scott Summers of Petersburg is a spokesman for Honda and Pirelli and markets internationally specialty motorcycle products he designed and patented. Photo contributed by Scott Summers

A five-time winner of the Grand National Cross Country motorcycle racing series, Scott has won nine off-road championships. For nearly three hours he races 8- to12-mile long laps over natural terrain, dodging hundreds of competitors in the nation's most prestigious motorcycle racing series.

He is the first rider to win the Hare Scrambles title two consecutive years, the first to finish a Cross Country season with a perfect score, winner of both titles twice in the same year, and has been named AMA Cross Country rider of the year six times.

Born March 25, 1967, Scott began riding Honda motorcycles at five and was racing two years later. Out of a desire to ride with his dad on weekends, Scott was *"in the garage all the time, wrenching on my motorcycle."*

The Summers family moved to Boone County in the 1980s, when Scott's father was transferred from Louisville to work at Florence Industrial Park. Scott attended Ockerman Junior High, then graduated from Conner High School.

By the time he was 21, Scott was making a name for himself in American Motorcyclist Association races. Both of Scott's parents have moved out of Boone County, but he bought the more than 100 acres off Snyder Lane where he'd grown up. The three practice tracks he has bulldozed into the rolling Boone County hills may have been the edge that has kept him winning, he says. *"When you do something enough, I guess you get good at it."*

He rides several hours a day, usually between 9 a.m. and 5 p.m. weekdays, out of respect for neighbors who are gone during those hours. He plans to continuing buying property *"to create a buffer zone"* for the motorcycle noise.

In 1995, Summers and his mechanic and manager Fred Bramblett volunteer for the National Youth Project Using Minibikes to help motivate "at risk youth." Many inner city youth *"don't even know places like my ranch exist."*

Scott also works with the National Off Highway Vehicle Conservation Council to secure and promote areas for recreational riding of horses, dirt bikes and off-road vehicles. In addition, he writes a column for *Dirt Bike* magazine and will host a new television show called "OHV (Off-Highway Vehicle) Video Magazine" that showcases sites for off road riding.[27]

---

[27] Scott Summers, March 20, 1998.

Woolper's Arrow Smith

In 1978, John Arrasmith left a corporate job and began selling the American Indian artifacts he had been restoring or making.

The interest had been cultivated decades before. Arrasmith's Uncle Bill was plowing a ridge on the Gunpowder Creek farm he bought in 1936 when his plow snagged on a rock. The open space under the large flat rock reminded him of a grave. He replaced everything but a weathered piece of leather rolled around a muzzleloader and a powderhorn. He eventually gave the gun to his nephew who was infatuated with Daniel Boone, Davey Crockett and other Westerns.

When Arrasmith's parents moved to Boone County to care for his grandparents (who owned a Richwood farm, near Triple Crown that was sold in 1989), John began high school here. After graduation, he attended vocational school to become a mechanical engineer.

"*My father's mother was full-blooded Cherokee, and his father was ¾ Cherokee,*" John says. "*On my mother's side, there is a little bit of Cherokee and Sioux, and we may be related to Daniel Boone,*" he says.

After quitting his job, John raised cattle, hay and tobacco on his 167 acres off Woolper Creek Road. He began recreating artifacts for himself, but people wanted to buy them, so he began selling.

With help from Terry Sawyer, the woodsman of Rabbit Hash, Arrasmith moved a 3,100-square-foot, two-story log cabin from Kenton County to his farm, added a porch and a modern kitchen and moved in.

Meanwhile, his Spotted Horse Reproductions were selling in galleries all over the country.

While mowing hay, he got a call from Kevin Costner's production company asking if he'd make some war shirts, knife sheaths and bows for a movie called "Dances With Wolves."

Arrasmith had appeared in "Mountain Men" with Charleton Heston and Brian Keith in 1979, but being invited to participate in the Costner movie infused his reputation and career. He has also made props for "Teenage

John Arrasmith of Woolper Road crafted $10,000 worth of American Indian arrows for the Oscar-winning movie "Dance with Wolves." He also authenticated and arranged for a pipe owned by Sitting Bull to be placed in a museum.
Photo contributed by John Arrasmith

Average Prices Boone County Farmers Received*								
Year	Tobacco	Soybns	Corn	Wheat	Beef	Calves	Hogs	Milk
	$./lb.	$/bu.	$/bu.	$/bu.	$/cwt	$/cwt	$/cwt	$/cwt
1980	**166.0**	**7.75**	**3.35**	**3.85**	**59.30**	**72.40**	**38.50**	**12.80**
1985	159.9	5.26	2.37	2.90	46.40	57.30	44.80	12.80
1990	**175.5**	**5.86**	**2.48**	**2.77**	**70.80**	**89.60**	**53.70**	**14.30**
1995	185.7	7.01	3.27	3.84	53.30	63.70	39.40	13.50
1996	**192.2**	**6.90**	**2.95**	**4.30**	**43.80**	**46.50**	**51.40**	**15.40**
* Boone County Cooperative Extension Service figures, compiled by Jerry Brown.								

Mutant Ninja Turtles II" and the "Lonesome Dove" television mini-series, among others.

Arrasmith makes objects using processes as similar as possible to the way they were originally made, tanning deer hides with deer brains, then smoking them so creosote saturates the fibers and water runs off. He uses sinew from deer's hind legs to sew and bind items together.

Now a national authority on Native American art, Arrasmith was asked to authenticate a pipe and tobacco pouch that belonged to Sitting Bull. In addition to verifying their authenticity, Arrasmith arranged to have them donated to the Indian Museum of North America in Custer, S.D., near where a mountain is being carved into the image of Crazy Horse astride as a memorial honoring all North American Indian tribes.

Locally, his work appears in the Cincinnati Historical Society Museum and the Richwood interstate rest stop.[28]

Agriculture Holds Ground

Non traditional career paths are bringing Boone Countians far more profit and notoriety than traditional agricultural endeavors. With land values skyrocketing due to residential development potential, it's nearly impossible for farmers to buy or lease enough land to make a living.

Making a profit in crop farming in the 1990s requires specialization and extensive acreage, something no longer available in the county and impractical with the topography of

Silage equipment in 1991

Rachel Aylor feeds a little diary calf.
Courtesy of Mrs. Stanley Aylor

rolling hills. Since 1949, the county has lost 516 farms encompassing 53,241 acres. Average farm size returned to the 101-acre average of the 1800s after peaking at 124 acres in 1978.

As farmland acreage has decreased, livestock numbers have declined. With increased residential development in previously agricultural areas, livestock numbers are likely to continue declining. Most homeowners

---

[28] John Arrasmith, March 16, 1998.

prefer living adjacent to cropland than livestock.

While the U.S. Soil Conservation Service considers 11,704 Boone County acres prime farmland, much of it may be developed by 2020.[29]

The 1992 Agricultural Census said there were 798 farms in Boone County. Nearly 5 million pounds of tobacco were grown on 524 Boone County farms in 1992. Nearly 12,000 acres were devoted to growing hay and alfalfa. Beef and dairy cattle were raised on 375 farms. Hogs, sheep and chickens are also raised here.

Only two African-Americans now own farms in Boone County. William Lewis inherited his parents' farm off Mt. Zion road. Their 136-acres remaining in farmland are managed by a tenant. Subdivisions surround the property, as they do most Boone County farmland now.

Charles and James Baker are the third generation to raise corn, tobacco and dairy cattle on several hundred acres off U.S. 42.[30]

One form of agriculture that fits with Boone County's new suburban look is the "you-pick" farm. In 1998, those included Walton's Benton Farms, McGlasson's Farm in Taylorsport, and Valley Orchards along the river and KY 8 in Hebron.

In late 1997, regional authorities attempted to condemn the McGlasson farm and turn it into a wastewater treatment plant, but a concerted local and family effort convinced the agency to seek a location other than the multi-generation family farm.

County Agricultural Data*

1996 Crops	Acres Harvested	Yield
Corn for grain, bu.	3,000	108
Soybeans, bu.	1,700	35
Burley Tobacco, lbs.	1,220	2,115
Alfalfa hay, tons	2,800	3
Other hay, tons	12,000	2.1

Jan 1, 1997 All Cattle and Calves 13,500
Jan. 1, 1997 Beef cows   7,100
Dec. 1., 1996 All hogs and pigs 1,100
'96 milk production, 1,000 lbs.   5,600

The Cooperative Extension Service also has adapted to their new urban role. In 1987, agent Joe Claxon hosted a gardening show for WLW TV in his own backyard. He was surprised to learn that some of the 65,000 who watched from as far away as West Virginia replicated whatever he did in his garden each week in theirs.[31]

Ellis Donates to Agriculture

The Extension Service moved into a new office at the intersection of KY 18 and Camp Ernst Road, thanks to land donated by Bob and Nellie Ellis. The two-story red brick building housing the Natural Resources & Conservation Office and the Farm Service Agency loan office provides "one-stop shopping" for farmers.

A native of England, Bob Ellis grew up in Latonia. The avid conservationist and his wife Nellie, a teacher, bought the Boone County property in 1941. They obtained a copy of George Washington's plans for Mount Vernon and built a scaled-down replica, using old timbers from a Cincinnati brewery.

After Mr and Mrs. Ellis passed away, their home became the national headquarters for the Extension Homemakers in 1992. The group is now called the National Association of Family and Community Education.

Mrs. Ellis' three maiden aunts lived on one side of their tall columned white house just outside of Burlington. Ellis raised cattle and tobacco, terracing the hillsides so *"the water doesn't run off, it walks,"* as he said.

He had worked for the U.S. Army Corps of Engineers from '37 to '45 when dams were built in the wake of the '37 flood. Trained as a writer, he wrote for the *Post* and *Enquirer*

---

[29] 1995 Boone County Comprehensive Plan.
[30] Rosella Porterfield interview, March 4, 1998.

[31] Joe Claxon

Bob and Nellie Ellis donated their home, patterned after Mount Vernon, to the Cooperative Extension Service.
Photo by Bruce Wess, Wild Walks Photography

before joining the *Cincinnati Enquirer* columnist and reporter in 1951. After 19 years there, he worked for the *Boone County Recorder* for eight years.[32]

"*Committed to be a caretaker of God's earth,*" Ellis was president of the Kentucky Association of Soil Conservation Districts, and won the Kentucky Soil Conservationist of the Year award. He served on the National Association of Conservation Districts Soil Stewardship Committee, the county Farm Bureau, the Boone County Planning Commission and the Northern Kentucky River Port Authority.

Ellis was known for his leadership, enthusiasm and dedication to many endeavors. A founding father of Florence's Grace Episcopal Church, he helped to establish Big Bone State Park, the Northern Kentucky Chamber of Commerce and the Boone County Water Commission, which set up the first county water service.[33]

Ellis also donated land for the church on Camp Ernst Road.

"*If Bob Ellis saw there was a need, he never hesitated to provide the means, whether it was money or property,*" says Bill Smith who has been active in all levels of Cooperative Extension work.[34]

Maplewood Fills

On the other side of Burlington, an old building was coming down. With changes in social services programs, Maplewood Home needed a new facility. By 1984, the 100-year-old building needed to be replaced. It was razed on Nov. 1, 1986 and a new building, with facilities for 12 boys and 12 girls opened July 19, 1987.

Designed to shelter for up to 29 children, Maplewood provides temporary care for children who have been neglected, abandoned, physically or sexually abused, or temporarily removed from their families.

A multi-purpose building was added in 1993 after the Fiscal Court issued $250,000 in municipal bonds. The "W.R. McDavid Building," dedicated on Nov. 21, 1993, was named to honor a childcare worker known for his love for children. The next year, Dave Mosmeier, became the home's administrator

To avoid shuffling children between shelters to meet regulatory guidelines, in August 1996, Maplewood established a treatment program to help youth develop, physically, mentally, emotionally and spiritually.

From 1986 to 1997, more than 3,500 children from newborns to 18-year-olds, lived at Maplewood.[35]

---

[32] Jack Hicks, "Environmentalist, 88, leads rural groups to field of opportunity, *Kentucky Post*, Aug. 25, 1989, 1K, 2K.
[33] information provided by William Smith

[34] Bill Smith, March 31, 1998.

Chapter 14 1980 and Beyond – Record Growth Continues

Boone County Sheriff's Department members pose with marijuana confiscated in a raid. Shown here are Deputy Daren Harris, Sgt. Jim Beach, pilot, Sheriff Michael Helmig, Sheriff Ron Kenner, Sgt. Tony Trimble and Sgt. Richard Spencer.   Photo courtesy of Mike Helmig

Sheriff's Department Grows

Many children come to Maplewood through the courts, police or sheriff's departments.

The first Boone County sheriff allowed to succeed himself, Elmer Wright served a dozen years. Under Sheriff Wright, and then Ron Kenner, the department began offering 24-hour a day, 7-day-a-week law enforcement and patrols.

In '82, all five sheriff's department officers were supplied with cars and equipment for the first time. Mike Helmig, hired at 21 in 1982, was the first deputy Wright sent to Eastern Kentucky University's police training academy. Now all new hires attend the orientation there.

In 1998, under Sheriff Mike Helmig, four office workers plus part-time help during tax season support a patrol staff of 30. In the early '90s, tax records were computerized, speeding collection procedures for some $41 million in property taxes.

In 1995, sheriff's employees began using a national computer system to track parents who didn't pay child support. Working with Steve Dallas of the Child Support Division in the first two years, 400 deadbeat parents were brought to court.

In 1998, Helmig hired retired policemen and troopers for courtroom security and to extradite out-of-state prisoners, so road deputies can keep patrolling the streets.[36]

Marijuana Growing

Strongly committed to fighting the war on drugs, the sheriff's department has used planes and helicopters to spot marijuana growing in isolated locations. *"In '83, we did six raids in one day and cut 507 plants – that was the biggest marijuana bust in the department's history,"* Helmig recalled. Soon, *"it was nothing to find patches with 1,000 plants. One had over 2,000."*

In the '80s, cooperating law enforcement agencies together demolished a wild marijuana patch estimated to contain 290,000 plants on River Road. While it was not cultivated, out-of-county harvesters visited it, he said.

Like everything else, marijuana growing is becoming more sophisticated in the '90s. *"It hasn't stopped, it's just changed,"* Helmig says. *"Smaller plots are now being grown in barns, attics and basements."*

---

[35] Elizabeth Kirtley, "History of Maplewood," 1998.

[36] Mike Helmig

Sheriff's Deputy Gary Peace and K-9 "Consul" pose with seized marijuana. Photo courtesy of Mike Helmig

The sheriff's department works actively with schools and community groups to educate about drug abuse.

"Most of our guys were born and raised in Boone County and have a genuine interest in helping and taking care of people," Helmig says.[37]

In 1998, Helmig seeks re-election to the position he was appointed to after Ron Kenner's death. Jailer John Schickel, a Democrat turned Republican, defeated Mike's father to become jailer. He had previously run for sheriff, but was unable to defeat longtime sheriff Elmer Wright.

Police Mutual Aid Channel

In March 1998, police at the Cincinnati/ Northern Kentucky International Airport began using a new radio frequency that allows officers in Boone, Kenton and Campbell counties to converse with each other from their cars. The three counties planned to divide the $5,000 annual cost, although city officers have access to it as well.

"It's something that law enforcement has recognized as a need for the last 20 years,"

said Boone County Police Chief Ed Ammann. *"As Northern Kentucky continues to grow, the need has become more obvious to communicate with officers in fellow districts."*

The chief hopes Cincinnati law enforcement officers would join the frequency, so Kentucky officers could communicate directly with them.

Now, an officer in pursuit of a suspect must only ask the dispatcher to notify others to tune into the mutual-aid channel, rather than waiting for the dispatcher to tediously relay emergency information that often changed before it was received.[38]

The cities of Florence and Walton and the airport have their own police departments while the Boone County Police Department and the Sheriff's Office provide police protection for the rest of the county.

Florence, Burlington, Hebron, Belleview, Petersburg, Point Pleasant, Union, Hamilton, Walton and airport departments or districts supply fire and emergency medical services. Many have full-time staffs, but most still rely heavily on volunteers.[39]

Actress Tracey Edwards
Courtesy of Brenda Sparks

Edwards Women

In 1979, after Jailer Wilson J. Edwards, a Petersburg native, was killed in an auto accident, his wife Ruth, who had been his deputy, became Boone County's first female jailer. Judge Bruce Ferguson had originally appointed Wilson to fill a vacancy and he was elected later. Ruth had the same experience.

Ruth and Wilson and their three adopted children lived in the jail building next to the bank (now Planning and Zoning) on the corner

---

[37] Mike Helmig, March 20, 1998.

[38] Amy Charley, "Local police to connect over mutual-aid channel," *Boone County Recorder*, March 12, 1998.

[39] 1995 Boone County Comprehensive Plan

in Burlington. Their quarters included two bedrooms, a kitchen and a bath, plus responsibility for 21 jail beds that were *"pretty full most of the time."*

"It was a great opportunity to help people," Mrs. Edwards says. *"A lot who went to jail got their GED* (high school graduation equivalency certificate). *I guess we were just supposed to be in that position to help people. We had escapes and suicide attempts, just like all small jails."* [40]

One of the Edwards children, Tracey Denise, a 1982 Conner High School graduate, attended Northern Kentucky University, then worked at Kings Island. Always interested in acting, she wrote and produced her own show and acted in an NKU production of the "Sound of Music."

In the mid-'80s while in-between New York theater assignments, Tracey visited the Statue of Liberty. Perusing a tribute to WWII veterans, she found the name of her uncle, a bomber pilot who taught her mother to fly in the '40s. While one of Mrs. Edwards' brothers returned, the other was lost when his plane went down in the Atlantic.

In 1998, Tracey appears regularly on "Home Shopping Network" out of Tampa. *"She really sells, they love her down there,"* her mother says proudly. Tracey prefers stage shows with their live audiences, but also enjoys taking her Chihuahuas on the Florida television show to market dog products. [41]

Patrick, First Female Commissioner

Like Ruth Edwards, more and more women were getting into Boone County politics. Many – like many men – got their start through an appointment. In the early '50s, Mary Jane Jones was the first woman appointed to head fiscal court for a short time.

But despite warnings that a woman couldn't be elected in Boone County, Irene

Rabbit Hash named its landing after Irene Patrick in gratitude for her assistance.
Photo by Jennifer Warner, Write to the Point

Patrick ran against incumbent County Commissioner Galen McGlasson in 1977. She became the first female county commissioner elected in Kentucky.

The former PTA President, Extension Homemakers officer, Girl Scout Leader, and farmer credits "knowing a lot of people" with her first election win. Because of her extensive community involvement and her work at the family business – Patrick Auto Parts, people knew she could get things done, she said. Also, her husband, Charles Abraham Patrick, had been a magistrate, the precursor to the county council, so she had his name recognition.

"It was a strain at first," she says of her friendship with Mr. McGlasson, *"but now we are dear friends."* Mrs. Patrick served 17 years, losing one election, but getting back in until she retired in 1998.

Mrs. Patrick's family is from Walton. Her mother was Nora B. Colston Martin. For 48

---
[40] Ruth Edwards, March 26, 1998.
[41] Ruth Edwards, March 26, 1998.

years, the Patricks have lived in the same Hebron house, raising daughters Charlene Tipton and Tracey Beck who both live and work in Boone County.

Rabbit Hash named its dock after Irene Patrick in gratitude for *"helping to move a few rocks with the Corps of Engineers"* and recruiting some volunteers to get it built. The dock allows boats and ferries to stop at the General Store and museum there.

During her public service, Mrs. Patrick is most proud of *"dogs sniffing drugs in schools. We've got to keep working with these children and teaching them about harmful drugs and keep the guns out of the schools. I'm sorry the county has grown so fast that the schools can't keep up with the need."*[42]

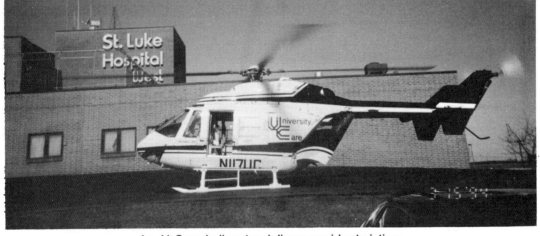

An AirCare helicopter delivers accident victims and emergency patients to St. Luke West.   Photo by Virginia Lainhart

Women Move Up

While Patrick is stepping down, she has endorsed Jean Scheben Kimmich for her county commission seat. Like Patrick, Kimmich's husband Scott preceded her in politics, as an assistant to Judge Ferguson.

Also in 1998, Marilyn Rouse is running for the Boone County Clerk position long held by her father Jerry W. Rouse. One of her opponents is Republican Joyce Wilson Bonar, a lifelong Boone County resident.

Property Valuation Administrator David Turner, like many before him, hired his mother and brother to work with him.

Women took over several Northern Kentucky policy-making positions for the first time in 1997. Bert Huff, president of Jim Huff Realty, became the new Airport Board chairman.

Juanita Mills, who operates THP Limited Consulting Engineers, now heads the Northern Kentucky Chamber of Commerce. Dr. Mary Ann Barnes was appointed to lead the Northern Kentucky Independent District Health Department.[43]

St. Luke Hospital

In 1989, the Salvation Army decided to divest itself of all its Eastern hospitals including Booth in Boone County. St. Luke, the Campbell County Hospital, bought it. By mid-summer, the Boone County hospital was renamed St. Luke West.

In 1998, St. Luke Hospital West is a 177-bed private, non-profit organization without religious affiliations. A "birthing center" was completed in the early 1990s, offering eight rooms where families can participate in childbirth, a neonatal intensive care nursery and a 12-bassinet nursery.[44] Both St. Luke

---

[42] Irene Patrick, April 2, 1998.

[43] Terry Flynn, "Women Take Charge," *The Kentucky Enquirer*, Sept. 21, 1987, B1.
*Tri-County Economic Development Corporation, 1997 Economic Forecast and Community Profile, 17.
[44] Conrad, *Top of Kentucky*, 28.

hospitals joined the Health Alliance of Greater Cincinnati in 1995.

A new 70,000-square-foot emergency department including 24 beds – three times the unit's previous size – and outpatient wing opened in November 1996. The $17.4 million project took a year and a half to complete. The number of outpatients at St. Luke has quadrupled in the last decade.

In January '97, a pediatric urgent care facility opened in the emergency area. In 1995-'96, 27,847 visited St. Luke's emergency room. St. Luke's medical staff includes 750 employees and more than 500 staff physicians.

1997 Flood

No Boone Countians required hospitalization as a result of the 1997 flood. Record rainfall pushed the Ohio over its banks again in February 1997, hitting the 64.7 foot mark in Cincinnati. Fifty-three tri-state cities were declared disaster areas, but Boone County escaped the worst of the problem.

Rabbit Hash General Store was again deluged, but community members pitched in to clean it up and out, and the store was open by late summer.

After an extremely mild '97-'98 winter, when trees and flowers were beginning to flower in early March, record-breaking temperatures closed schools and froze the new growth. Three weeks later, warmth broke records with a week in the 80s.

Airport Growth

The airport's name grew repeatedly in this era, adding the word International in 1978, then becoming Cincinnati /Northern Kentucky International in 1991 to appease local residents. Airport business grew even more significantly. 1982 brought a 33 percent

The '97 flood greeted Alexis and Brandon Scott the first month they owned the historic Rabbit Hash General Store. Photo by Alexis Scott

increase in weekly flights over the year before. Weekly departures of 1,069 were a 57 percent increase over 1981. Service to nine more non-stop markets than the 31 offered before included 27 percent more available seats. COMAIR began constructing a new hangar.

During an airport police pistol match at the airport on Aug. 6-7, 1982, Jim Kavanaugh scored the first perfect 400 score in the match's history. Later in 1983, an automated teller machine was installed in Terminal C. Others were soon added in the other terminals.

On June 2, 1983, Air Canada flight 797, a DC-9 going from Dallas to Toronto made an

The airport. Courtesy of Ted Bushelman

emergency landing here. Passengers and crew members smelled smoke. The airport's fire brigade roared up as the plane rolled to a stop.

Passengers began popping windows out and exiting over the wings and through the front door. The crew shouted instructions and passengers ran from the plane. Although 18 passengers and five crew members escaped, 23 passengers died of smoke inhalation. [45]

DHL Worldwide Express came to the Northern Kentucky airport in 1983. Around the globe, 27 DHL hubs shipped freight direct to 220 countries. From 10 p.m. until 6 a.m., between 40 and 50 DHL flights arrive with roughly 150,000 packages from all over the U.S. which are unloaded and sorted by more than 1,000 employees.

"Seventy percent of the nation's industrial base is within 90 minutes flying time of the Ohio Valley," said Gary Pasborg of DHL. *"That includes New York City, the Eastern seaboard, Detroit, Chicago, and all the major industrial areas."* He notes Boone County's time zone is ideal, the weather good, work ethic is strong, and at night, the company has the airport to itself.[46]

In 1985, the airport acquired more land from private homeowners and began another Delta expansion. As Delta's North American hub, the airport opened a new concourse with 25 gates and began daily service to London in 1987.

In 1987 The Cincinnati/Northern Kentucky International Airport began offering non-stop service to Europe. It now provides non-stop flights to 110 cities from the 6,500-acre property used by 16 airlines. Passengers, 19 million of them, rely on 530 departures daily out of a terminal with 1.6 million square feet. Airport officials envision non-stop international flights to Asia and a transition to smaller, quieter, more fuel efficient planes.

---

[45] Richard L. Rawe, *Creating a World-Class Airport: Cincinnati/Northern Kentucky International 1947-1997*, Cherbo Publishing Group Inc., 1996-1997, 79

[46] Rawe, 76, 156.

In 1993, COMAIR opened its own 53-gate terminal at the Cincinnati airport, the largest air terminal in the U.S. totally dedicated to regional operations. COMAIR employs more than 2,800 who offer 600 flights a day to airports in 27 states, Canada and the Bahamas.[47]

Delta and COMAIR completed a massive $500 million expansion in 1994. The next year, Cincinnati/Northern Kentucky was ranked the world's second-fastest growing major airport. In 1996, the airport served more than 18 million passengers, now carrying about as many people annually as it did in its first 20 years combined.

Celebrating is 50th anniversary on Jan. 10, 1997, the airport's economic impact on the tri-state exceeds $3 billion annually. Now covering 10 square miles, the airport employs 10,000.

The 10 days before Christmas, 1 million pounds of holiday mail floods DHL Airways, Kitty Hawk Air Cargo and the U.S. Postal Service at the airport. Four hundred temporary workers sort and send it on its way.

Travelers have a choice of 14 airlines, including seven major carriers, six commuters and two low-cost airlines, plus charter carriers. There are roughly 550 daily flights to more than 100 non-stop locations. A master plan projecting to 2011 expects the number of passengers to double. Two new concourses will replace terminals 1 and 2, new access roads will be added and more.

The Ohio-Kentucky-Indiana Regional Council of Governments sees a pollution-reducing *light rail link* between the airport, Covington, downtown Cincinnati and Cincinnati's northern suburbs. Delta included plans for it at its new terminal.

Hebron Landmarks Lost

The airport demolished a Hebron landmark in 1994. The Immaculate Heart of Mary Catholic Church off Limaburg Road had surprisingly dramatic architecture for its rural location. An unusual arched roof swooped down to within 6' of the ground. The front, which faced West, was covered with stained glass.

Its elementary school included housing at one end for the parish priest, and at the other for the two nuns who assisted with the school. Later, separate houses were built for the priest and teachers. The lunchroom overlooked a lake. As air traffic increased, the airport offered to soundproof the building, but was too noisy for children to play outdoors, so the church sold the property and moved to its 1998

The airport demolished the Immaculate Heart of Mary Church in 1994 after noise had made it impossible for children to play outside at the school. Photo by Virginia Lainhart

location off KY 18.

A demolition contractor, slamming his wrecker ball into the stained glass with regret, stopped to give a teary-eyed Baptist neighbor a glass memoir of the Catholic landmark.

An old cemetery had been nearby. A previous owner is said to have broken the headstones up and used them as gravel for his driveway.[48]

---

[47] Rawe, 113.

[48] Virginia Lainhart

Ground was broken for the new Hebron Firestation in 1990. Bob Flick, J.A. Doepker, Harvey Pelley, Mickey Conner, Nick Furnish, and in the front Virginia Lainhart and Bill Smith. Photo courtesy of Virginia Lainhart

On Hebron land now owned by the airport, a group called Environment and Archeology LLC is conducting a dig in 1998. Before a two-story log cabin can be demolished, federal regulations require the airport to document its historical value.

The site is unique, says Laura Clifford, president of the environmental consulting company doing the excavation. The same family, the Aylors, owned the home from the time it was built until the 1960s.

Spring excavations had reached levels dating between 1890 and 1919, although researchers already have found small fragments of prehistoric materials. "*It's in a field that rises from a creek, a perfect place for a prehistoric site*," Clifford says.[49]

New Hebron Businesses

Hebron's Volunteer Fire Department was established in 1937, but the first firehouse on KY 20 wasn't built until 1945. A tax district established in 1979 allowed the department to modernize and move to the North Bend Road location in 1990. In 1991, the Hebron fire department began a Boy Scouts of America Explorer Post allowing youth from 14 to 20 an opportunity to pursue fire fighting.

Thompson Co. of Toronto consolidated its U.S. operations into a distribution center in Hebron in a new industrial park called SkyPort on Progress Drive north of the airport. The Discovery Distribution Center will ship college and other school books. The company also owns South-Western Publishing in Cincinnati and 70 daily newspapers. It already had a distribution center on Empire Drive in Florence and a manufacturing and headquarters office in Cincinnati.[50]

Western Atlas Inc.'s material handling systems opened in 1983, paying 560 to construct conveyor systems, industrial control systems, palletizer and epalletizers. In 1994, Lemforder Corp. began making automotive parts with 300 employees.[51]

Belleview/McVille

"*Belleview hasn't changed hardly at all*," says Sebern Stephens who with his wife Agnes has lived along the river near Belleview his whole life. "*This was a general farming area. Used to be nearly everyone had a dairy, now there's not hardly one left in this part of the county. Now farms specialize in grain or hogs*."

Those who farm along the riverfront bottoms, like Stephens who raises truck crops on 24 acres, are constantly asked to sell small tracts for houses. Stephens turns down those requests.

Some of his six children have stayed near the homestead and helped farm the land, while others have ventured further and aren't likely to return. "*Maybe the older generation that wouldn't think about selling lots off will be

---

[49] Laura Clifford, April 2, 1998.

[50] Melissa & Dan Sies, Hebron News, *The Boone County Recorder*, Dec. 18, 1997, B3.
[51] True, 13.

Chapter 14 1980 and Beyond – Record Growth Continues

replaced by a younger generation that wants the money more than the land," he speculates, looking into the future.

While Stephens grew up farming, a growing family combined with little return on long working hours pushed him to buy a coal yard and a fuel-oil truck. Still, he supplemented the new business and the truck patch by working nights or driving a truck, working sunup to sundown as he did on the farm where he grew up.[52]

Rabbit Hash

New businesses like Jane Cochran's combine with the ever-popular General Store to give the Rabbit Hash community a unique personality. The movie Huckleberry Finn was filmed in Rabbit Hash in 1984. The old blacksmith shop became Rabbit Hash Iron Works that sold wood stoves. Rabbit Hash Museum, a restored log cabin, was dedicated in December 1992.

Unable to watch their father Lowell Scott sell the historic Rabbit Hash General Store, Alexis and Brandon Scott, a sister-brother team, bought it just before the '97 flood. After many repairs, they are restocking the store with unique kitchen goods and utensils handmade in Kentucky.

> ***Boone County Recorder***
> July 16, 1970
> Joe Rice reminisced about the closing of John's Truck Stop, a 1937-vintage lunch counter on Dixie Highway in Florence. In his words are some elemental truths.
>
> *"For years I have been telling people that we live in two worlds, sort of in a stretch of Boone County caught between the modern industrial complex and a part of the Old South that I really liked. On the one hand, you can see the world where dollars and cents reign supreme, and on the other hand, a world with a different set of values.*
>
> *"The serenity and peacefulness, the calm country gardens are removed from the work-a-day world, the time-clock slaves, the forced hourly wage scale. Each person does something for the other without regard of dollars in an unhurried scheme of things. . . .*
>
> *"You know, change does not always mean progress either! What was so wrong with resisting the Industrial Age where stop lights so rudely tell us what and when to do as if we can't think for ourselves. . . .*
>
> *"It takes just a fleeting instant to smile, and the tone of voice will do more for a person than all the fancy lighted eating palaces dotting the landscape today where rudeness is to strikingly present. Courtesy is contagious, and nowhere is it more catching than here."*
>
> Rice went on to mention *"the smallness of big business and the greatness of small business."*

"Our goal is to preserve a historic site and for the business to become profitable enough to pay for its expensive repairs. We don't plan to expand, just to use the area we have," Alexis says. *"We would like it to be a successful old fashioned General Store."*[53]

Still the center of communication in the tiny town, the Rabbit Hash General Store remains a post office, voting place and spot to visit, gossip, court, play checkers and horseshoes and argue politics and religion. The General Store's rear porch was removed after several floods eroded the ground beneath it. The back door now opens to a 20-foot drop off.

On Feb. 6, 1989, the store was listed on the National Register of Historic Places.[54] Flooded again in 1997, the entire community turned out as it had several times before, to help clean and salvage the building and its inventory. Visitors can no longer arrive by ferry or steamboat, but come along the narrow winding road on motorcycles and in sportscars or dock at the new landing.

Brandon's and Alexis' father, Lowell Scott lives in the five-room log cabin he created in

---

[52.] Sebern Stephens, March 18, 1998.

[53] Alexis Scott, April 2, 1998.
[54] Clare, 60.

the early 1980s from one built in Campbell County in 1840. The bathroom includes a washbowl made from an Old Grand Dad Distillery whiskey barrel. The shower was once a small, gravity-fed water tower.

One of James Alexander's sons, Samuel C. Wilson, known as "Uncle Sam" in Rabbit Hash, was a popular local historian, as was his son, Robert Hayden Wilson.[55] The later Wilson claimed to be the only person able to throw a softball across the Ohio River.

New and old Rabbit Hash residents and visitors gather for special events like Old Timer's Day on Labor Day Weekend and Christmas in Rabbit Hash in late November.

Dinsmore Foundation Buys Home

Since Julia Dinsmore had died in 1926, the farm had passed to several generations of nieces. The last family owners, Martha Ferguson Breasted, Robert Munro Ferguson and John Selmes Greenway employed a series of housekeepers and farmhands and maintained the house from a distance, though they did not attempt to farm the land.

In June 1988, the Dinsmore Homestead Foundation bought the house and 31 acres from Greenway and Breasted to preserve as a historic landmark. The house, outbuildings and their contents are preserved as if the family was still living there.

Nearly 9,000 pages of family letters, journals and business records have been preserved on microfilm and used to ensure the accuracy of the home's displays. The non-profit corporation's goal is to preserve the site as a living history museum, a research center with hiking trails, and a place that welcomes artists.

Elementary students can become "Pioneers of the Past" during day camps offered each summer at Dinsmore. They churn butter, cook over an open hearth and tend farm animals. Catron Louise Gillette Rose, a seventh-generation Dinsmore, has been visiting the old homestead in the summer to assist with the camp and review her family's history.[56]

In early 1998, the Dinsmore Foundation purchased Caroline William's log cabin with plans to restore it and possibly create an artist's retreat there.[57]

Salt Festival

Former Big Bone State Park Director Bob Lindy has submitted a request to the state annually for funding to create a museum and research center at the park. But the General Assembly has never allocated the funds. A few bones sit in glass cases in a little room while plans for a museum building await funding.

Bones excavated by the University of Nebraska await return to Boone County until a "suitable" museum is available for them.

Big Bone "*is a 12,000 plus year continuum of prehistory and history*," says Don Clare of the Rabbit Hash Historical Society, which has set up a special fund for the Friends of Big Bone to accept donated funds as a tax deduction.[58]

In 1998, the park will host the 12th annual Salt Festival. The third weekend in October each year, people dressed in period costumes boil water down to salt and share samples with visitors.

Ten buffalo graze there year-round, fenced safely away from hikers. Four buffalo calves were expected in May 1998. Park officials sell or trade to keep the herd at about a dozen.

About $500,000 in improvements will be made in 1998. That includes enhancing the walking trail behind the existing museum/gift shop, upgrading water plant building, improving the campground picnic shelter and the footbridge from the playground. In addition, the trail, a shelter house, and the central service building in the campground will be made wheelchair accessible.

---

[55] Clare, 43-44.

[56] Chastang, 31.
[57] Christine Godsey
[58] Friends of Big Bone Newsletter, Vol.1, No. 1, Winter 1998.

Chapter 14 1980 and Beyond – Record Growth Continues

In 1997, two women from Warsaw, Ky., Mrs. Glenna McMichael and Mrs. Alberta Allphin donated a nearly 3'-long shoulder blade of a probiscidian (mastodon or mammoth) their grandfather found on his Gallatin County farm about 90 years ago.

Park manager Clarence Metcalf who has been with the State Park Department for eight years is beginning his fourth season at Big Bone. "*I feel confident we will have a museum some day,*" he says. Community efforts to encourage political support will help push funding for a better museum, he says.[59]

Verona

Further south, Verona spreads itself out at the intersection of KY 14 and 16, or Verona-Walton and Verona-Crittenden roads, or Glencoe and Duckhead roads, depending on your vintage. The community includes an ever-increasing number of homes and people.

"*Verona's always been more about people than geography,*" says Asa Rouse. "*The physical heart of the town may be its landmark intersection, but the real heart of the town and area are its present-day residents.*"

On the southwest corner the intersection once held a white two-story funeral home owned by Jess and Rose Hamilton. It is now Bobby Sturgeon's used car lot. Diagonally across was Allie Chandler Stephens' hardware and dry goods. On the northwest quadrant was Jim Coyle's grocery, now Mr. Herb's Restaurant that brings people in from as far away as Covington to eat fried fish. Clayton Renaker's son Jeff has taken over his garage.[60]

In 1980, another modular ambulance replaced Walton Life Squad's '71 model. On May 1984, both ambulances were damaged in accidents on the same day. A used 1976 ambulance was purchased from Cincinnati Gas & Electric and used until the other two were repaired. Another new ambulance was added in 1988. The '74 model was converted into a rescue salvage truck to carry extrication equipment to free victims trapped in accidents.[61]

Walton's new city building.   Courtesy of Walton City Hall

Walton Dedicates City Hall

On May 5, 1985, Walton dedicated its new $250,000 city hall to volunteer fireman Jimmy Isbell who lost his life on the way to a fire. The old city hall had burned down in August 1983. Dr. William Waller had allowed city employees to work from his property on South Main Street while the new building was planned and constructed. A time capsule was buried near the flag pole to be opened in 2040.

In 1985, Walton had 10 city employees working for five departments. Three full-time police officers answered about 1,500 calls, issued about 400 citations, investigated 30-

---

[59] Claence Metcalf, April 7, 1998.

[60] Asa Rouse
[61] *150th Anniversary, City of Walton*, 47

some accidents, made 60-some arrests and took about 500 reports annually.⁶²

A new firehouse was completed in 1985 – 105 years after Walton's first bucket brigade was organized. It housed five pumpers, two tankers, one rescue truck, a utility truck and three ambulances.

Industry has come to Walton as well. Duro Bag Manufacturing Co. began creating polyethylene and paper bags in Walton in 1986, employing 500. The next year, Clarion Manufacturing Corp. of America hired 288 to make automotive radios, amplifiers and tape players. In 1993, Dynamec began making automotive seat systems with 200 employees. Continental Web Press moved in 1995, hiring 200 to do printing.⁶³

A Utah company opened the Flying J Truck Plaza in Walton on March 26, 1990. More than 200 semi-tractor trailers can park on the 15-acre lot at the intersection of Stephenson Mill Road and Kentucky 14.

In 1990, Walton was the second-largest community in Boone County with a population of 2,034 living in a two-square-mile area.

Inventor Wally Wireman

Walton inventor Wally Wireman created the molecular Adsorber, a device that removes odors, gases, moisture and smoke from the air. It is used around the country to eliminate cigarette smoke, refresh the air at livestock shows, and keep moisture from U.S. Air Force missiles and jets. In 1990 the U.S. Department of Defense and the City of Walton honored Wireman for his contributions as an inventor.

Richwood

In 1998, Richwood is known for its year-round flea market offered in a huge pole barn right off I-75. Vendors offer everything from vegetables to carpet and plumbing supplies.

The Industrial Park directly behind it continues to grow.

Union Annexation Opposed

Union attempted to annex 2,500 acres in 1981 but met with opposition, then deannexed the land and 200 residents. Union's population boomed to 5,000 in the early '90s with assets like Lassing Pointe Golf Course and Central Park, operated by the Boone County Parks Department. A 1993-vintage city building provides offices for the mayor and city clerk and a community meeting room.

In 1990, Union had a population of 1,001 living in a three-square mile area.

In July 1997, a 380-acre Christian youth ranch and family life ministry opened off KY 338, six miles past Big Bone State Park. Potter's Ranch includes a lodge, banquet facilities, retreat center, campgrounds and an authentic teepee village created by John Arrasmith. The non-profit foundation selected the location because of its acreage and natural landscape to provide a wilderness retreat.

Last Smith Family Farm

Many city dwellers see Boone County as a wilderness retreat, yet want the convenience of shopping nearby. That eventually will prompt the sale of the Smith family farm on U.S. 42, where their Virginians settled in 1851. William A. "Bill" Smith says the 60-acre tract is now within a half mile of a Kroger grocery and a strip shopping center.

"We know that property will get more valuable as time goes on. I hate to see it go from farmland, but we must be realistic, so practicality will set in."

Just two years ago, prompted by a broken ankle, his father sold his entire dairy herd.

A new U.S. 42 bypass, with five traffic lanes and a bicycle lane, is scheduled to go around Union in 2000 or 2020, Smith says. That will dramatically change Union – and make it even

---

⁶² *150th Anniversary, City of Walton*, 8-11
⁶³ True, 13.

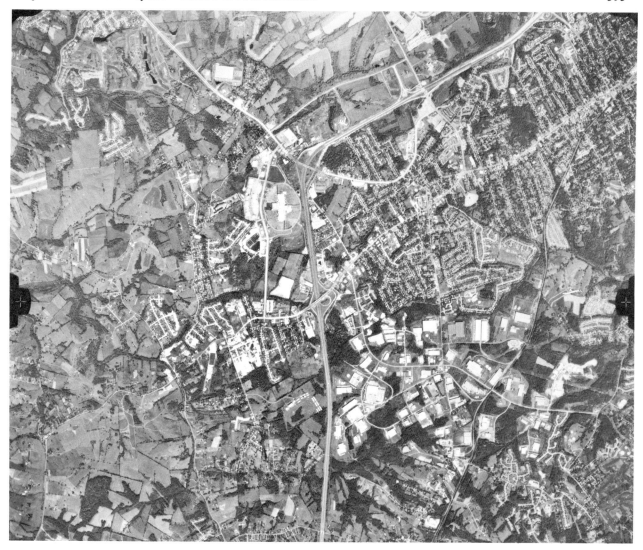

This aerial photo of Florence was taken on Oct. 2, 1984. Courtesy of City of Florence

more accessible to developers and would-be country dwellers.

Smith built a house on 94 acres of his parents' farm on Rice Pike 20 years ago. Now head of the eastern region of a seed company, he raises hay and tobacco there part-time.

Technology has advanced so far that he bales hay in the rain, wrapping the huge bales in a special white plastic coating that prompts a fermentation process leaving fodder much like silage.

Smith doesn't expect his 15-year-old son to farm, but hopes he'll have an interest in an agriculture-related business and return to Boone County after college.[64]

Florence

In 1990, Florence's population was 18,624 living in nine-square miles, making it one of the fastest growing cities in the nation. A 10.4 percent population increase between 1990 and 1992, left it second to Covington in size.

As one might expect of a sizeable city, a wide diversity of change and events take place there regularly.

Television stars Cheryl Ladd, Mickey Rooney and Wayne Rogers came to Turfway Park to film the CBS minseries "Bluegrass" in

---

[64] Bill Smith, March 31, 1998.

October 1987. Seventy local citizens had the opportunity to serve as extras. The horse in the script was modeled after '87 Derby winner Alysheba and wore his silks.[65]

In the fall of 1997, ball fields at Florence's Tri-City YMCA got a face-lift with 300 tons of soil and 1,000 pounds of grass seed as well as improved drainage.

Former Florence resident Rhonda Gowler Greene published two children's books. *"When a Line Begins. . . A Shape Begins"* and *"Barnyard Song."* The daughter of Wanda Gowler and daughter-in-law of Gilby Greene, both of Florence, is an elementary and preschool teacher. She taught a learning disabilities class at Goodridge in Hebron.

Houghton Mifflin and Simon and Schuster/Antheneum published Greene's books. She was in town to do book signings and story times at Barnes and Noble bookstoes.

In 1982, Keco Industries began manufacturing air condition and heat exchange equipment with 375 employees. Two years later, Hoechst Celanese Corp.'s Advanced Materials Group began making specialty resins with 154 employees and Thatcher Tubes employed 165 to make laminate tubes.

Tri-AD announced that three new companies opened in 1985: Ohio Valley Litho Division of The Neilsen Co. began doing lithographic printing with 270 employees; Redken Laboratories, with 200 employees, began making professional hair and skin care products; Sabatasso Food Inc. hired 600 to manufacture frozen specialty foods.

Continental Pet Technologies began manufacturing plastic bottles, using 150 employees in 1987. Emerald Industries came to Florence in 1988, employing 185 to manufacture cookies, snacks and frozen cakes.[66]

Florence city offices were scheduled to move into a new Government Center on Ewing Boulevard in 1998.

New Fellowship

A Florence church called the Fellowship of Believers began a construction project in late 1997 that will triple the size of the 16-year-old church.

The new "family life center" will include an auditorium/gymnasium with basketball and volleyball courts, a large foyer/fellowship hall, expanded parking, children's facilities, an

Celebrating the anniversary of the Florence Y'all Festival in 1989 are Brenda Sparks, general and publicity chairperson; Roger Rolfes, Florence Mayor 1982-'91; Ted Bushelman, festival vice chairman; C.M. "Hop" Ewing, Florence Mayor 1961-81 and Evelyn Kalb, Florence Mayor 1991-98 and festival chairperson. Photo courtesy of Brenda Sparks

auditorium for children and youth and a full kitchen with a coffee and expresso bar. The church attracts up to 650 people in two services each Sunday to hear pastor Bo Weaver. Services include music, drama and videos.[67]

---

[65] *Boone County Recorder*, Oct. 15, 1987, 1

[66] True, 12-13.
[67] Karen Meiman, Believers build, embrace growth, *The Boone County Recorder*, Dec. 18, 1997, A7.

Kelly Killed, Honored

Burlington native Charles Kelly taught physics and math at Boone County High School and the old Daniel Boone Boys' Center in Belleview.

He was a principal at Florence Elementary and Conner Senior High in Hebron and secondary curriculum supervisor for Boone County Schools. Kelly and his wife Barbara were killed in an auto accident near Eaton, Ohio, in 1983. Charles Kelly Elementary was named in his honor.[68]

Kirkpatrick Electrocuted

A freak ice storm hit Boone County in October 1989. Many were without power for several days. Burlington Fire Department responded to a call about an electric line that fell on a cable television line on East Bend Road. When Assistant Fire Chief Donnie Kirkpatrick went to investigate, strong winds blew the line into him, electrocuting him instantly.

Hundreds of friends and firefighters from several states followed the firetruck carrying his body as it passed under crossed aerial ladders to the cemetery on Burlington Pike.

Donnie, 42, had been a volunteer for the Burlington department for 27 years and served as chief for six years. He left his wife Judy, daughter Traci, 13; son Brad, 11 and his mother Marge.

Restoring Historic Burlington

In the county seat, 27 buildings were listed as a National Register of Historic District in 1979. In 1998, a half-dozen rehabilitated structures house "The Merchants of Historic Burlington," small businesses selling antiques, quilts, herbs and home decor.

"Speaking also for my neighbors, Burlington has been, and continues to be, a source of great pride for those of us

A double row of firetrucks made a procession down KY 18 following the Burlington firetruck carrying Donnie Kirkpatrick's body who was electrocuted following up on an emergency call. Photo by Virginia Lainhart

committed to preserving it as one of the last concentrated areas of architectural treasures in Boone County, and for its small community closeness," says Linda Bruce Whittenburg.

After 15 years of teaching art in the Kenton County schools and at Cincinnati's School for Creative and Performing Arts, in 1990 the Florence native opened Cabin Arts, offering fabric and quilting supplies, handcrafted gifts and quilting classes. Her parents, Estill and Ruth Bruce, still live in Florence.

Linda's husband Dan, also a Boone County High School graduate, grew up in Hebron, the son of Marie and Lewis Whittenburg Sr. He opened an auto repair shop called Superior Imports, just off Burlington's Jefferson Street, in 1975. When adjoining property, including the Hogan House, became available they bought it.

A second log cabin, where Cabin Arts classes will be held, is under construction in 1998. It is a combination of an old corncrib from Dry Ridge, and two barns from the early 1800s.

One Saturday night, driving past the Ellis property on KY 18 before Extension Office construction was to begin, the Whittenburgs saw a pile of hand-hewn logs had been

---
[68]Reis, *Pieces of the Past*, 26.

bulldozed into a pile. They made calls first thing Monday morning and managed to negotiate for the contractor to stop work for two hours so they could drag as many logs away as they could, although some were already burning.

The rest of the vintage logs came to them just as accidentally. The Whittenburgs were hiking near the Pebble Creek subdivision off Camp Ernst Road and saw a pile of logs from a barn being demolished by developer George Finke and asked for them.

"While surrounded by a burgeoning number of subdivisions, fast food shops and car dealerships, area residents seek to maintain as much of Burlington's original atmosphere as possible," she says.

"Many feel the 'country setting' is the main drawing point to those moving in large numbers to our section of the county. We can only hope that Historical Burlington can survive the onslaught."

"As a group, the Merchants of Historic Burlington also see how economically important the historic element is to the town and county. It is the initial attraction to commerce and shopping in Burlington. We have found that our customers appreciate the rarity of such a preserved area."

Merged Government?

While each community retains its own personality, the 1980s brought discussion about merging county and Walton, Florence and Union city governments into one more efficient unit, similar to the Lexington-Fayette Urban County Government.

The issue continues to arise, as do discussions of merging various services in the three-county Northern Kentucky area.

The Ohio-Kentucky-Indiana Regional Council of Governments (OKI) is the region's transportation planning authority. Its' long-range plan recommends emission control programs, using alternative fuels, expanding public transit systems, improving highway capacities, deploying highway surveillance systems, promoting bicycle and pedestrian travel and fostering employee commuting programs.[69]

Looking to the Future

"The 21st Century is just around the corner. We need to look at what a population of perhaps 120,000 will do to emergency service delivery, police protection, water, sewage, transportation, economics, communication, finance, congestion, and more," said Dr. Herbert Booth, a member of the Quest governance subcommittee. *"Are we going to have central oversight or a hodgepodge of little municipalities?*

"Some people see the effort as a power grab and a seizing of assets. Most fear change because they've adapted, adjusted or tolerated the current situation, it's the devil they know," he added.

In trying to create a better way rather than relying on century-old routines, the Quest group is considering topics like merging central services to eliminate duplication and reduce problems caused by lack of coordination.

"What happens in the Industrial Park or Airport affects all of the region, we are interdependent," Booth says. The group is exploring alternatives to reduce traffic and pollution, like installing a light rail line to downtown Cincinnati.

"Government change has succeeded best when there has been a crisis", Booth says. *"The merged governments in Lexington and Indianapolis both came out of crises."* But Boone is yet to have a crisis, and economic indicators give no hint of one to come anytime soon.

Many of the issues Quest is attempting to address are uphill battles, like make more efficient use of schools by eliminating summer vacations.

---

[69] 1995 Boone County Comprehensive Plan

Booth says, *"Schools developed around an agrarian model, so they had a summer vacation for the kids to work in the fields. Now we have nine-month employees who job-hunt in the summer because they're underpaid. It's an anachronism. We could increase the functional equivalent of schools by ¼ by using school buildings year-round. Increasing teacher pay by 25 percent would attract and keep better teachers, and we would be paying less to keep school buildings up."*[70]

Artfully renovated log homes or spacious new log or cedar homes are typical in the Rabbit Hash area. This one is owned by Jane and Randy Cochran. Randy is a photographer for the *Kentucky Post*. Photo by Jason Dunn

A Bright Future

Most, like retiring county commissioner Harold Campbell, *"see nothing but great things happening for Boone County."*

His concerns about uncontrolled growth are common: *"I hope the growth will be controlled so that we don't lose our identity in being a real nice small community."*[71]

Controlling the growth, having good schools, good recreational opportunities, low crime and low taxes will keep the quality of life high in Boone County says retiring Judge Executive Ken Lucas.

"Boone County is huge geographically," he says. *"Even though we've had a lot of growth on the eastern side and across the northern quarter, I think a lot of Boone County will stay pristine for decades to come. All kinds of lifestyles are available in Boone County."*

Noting that real estate taxes have decreased for three consecutive years, Lucas notes *"Commerce and industry carry the tax burden."*[72]

In Conclusion

Despite record-breaking development, dramatically increasing population figures, the even-more frequent roar of airplanes overhead, and belching exhaust from bulldozers cutting yet another wooded hillside into carefully shaped lawns for expensive houses, some parts of Boone County remain nearly as they were 200 years ago.

Delicate white Queen Anne's Lace, purple iron-weed, pointed clusters of goldenrod, and wild pink roses still grow in untended fields between the airport and the increasingly dense housing and shopping developments growing out from Florence.

More and more entrepreneurs, retirees and escapees from city life revel in the views and amenities of their Boone County homes.

Outside investors who bought cheap land decades ago let it lie fallow, waiting for developers to multiply its value many times over their original purchase price.

As it was 200 years ago, Boone County remains a place where people come with dreams for a better life, to escape from the pressures others put upon them and live their lives in their own ways.

---

[70] Dr. Herbert Booth
[71] Harold Campbell
[72] Ken Lucas

Boone County Facts and Figures

Judges of Boone County Fiscal Court
Cyrus Riddell
L.H. Dills
E.H. Baker
Ben Stephens
C.C. Roberts
P.E. Cason
N.E. Riddell
C.L. Cropper
C. Niblack
Mary Jane Jones
Bruce Ferguson
Burnham Terry Roberts
Ken Lucas

U.S. Census figures

Boone County Population 1800s

	1800	1810	1820	1830	1840	1850	1860	1870	1880	1890
Total whites.*	1,194	2,924	5,227	7,214	7,824	9,044	9,403	9,684	10,764	11,134
Free colored*	15	28	19	41	27	37	48	1,012	1,232	1,112
Slaves*	325	656	1,296	1,820	2,183	2,104	1,745	emancipation		
Petersburg				503		400	603	400	441	
Walton (inc.1840)						50			280	
Burlington (inc. 1834)				276/350	200	250		277		
Florence (inc. 1830)				63	200	252		374	309	250
Union						50			113	
Hamilton/Big Bone				200				Taylorsport 120		
Grant/Belleview									61	124

*County totals are U.S. Census figures. Unincorporated community populations are from various texts.

Boone County Population 1900s

	1900	1910	1920	1930	1940	1950	1960	1970	1980	1990
Boone Co.*	11,170	9,420	8,942	9,595	10,820	13,015	21,940	32,812	45,842	57,589
Petersburg	559**				350	356				
Walton	538	537		*854	973	1,358	1,530	1,801	1,651	2,034
Verona					165					
Union									601	1,001
Burlington					216		350			
Grant/ Belleview					170					
Florence	258				*450	776	1,325	5,837	11,457	15,586	18,924

**Loders' 1896 census

Boone County Population Projections 2000s

	2000	2010	2020
Boone Co.	79,172	94,672	109,373

Boone County Bicentennial Community Heroes

A Community Hero is a Boone County resident who:
- *Performs outstanding volunteer work*
- *Serves as a community leader, role model or mentor*
- *Performs acts of generosity or kindness*
- *Performs extraordinary feats or accomplishments, locally or nationally*
- *Has overcome some sort of adversity in his/her life*

Eighty Community Heroes were honored at the Bicentennial kickoff ceremony with a certificate signed by Governor Paul Patton, a typed version of the nominator's letter, a silver medal and a T-shirt. These names are on a plaque hanging in the courthouse:

Belleview

Steve Alford - Has a habit of collecting and restoring souls, introducing them to Christ

Luella Burcham - Sunday School teacher and strong family life

Bill Rudicill - Looks out for his friends and neighbors

Agnes Scott - Her door is always open to a friend or stranger in need

Sebe Scott - The unknown saint who does the unnoticed tasks

Burlington

Tom Ginn - Helps with Burlington Christmas and Boone County Fair

Christine Godsey - Tireless organizer and volunteer at Dinsmore

Patrick L. Jones - Watches out for his neighbors and enjoys sharing his farm with children

Gene King – Avid child confidence builder, offering extra pats on the back

Carmen Schulte - Outstanding Boone County Parks Dept. volunteer

Barbara Snow - Quietly participates and gives her all

Debbie K. Stidham - Active in PTA, Scouts, 4-H, Sunday School, Special Olympics

Nancy J. Tretter - A volunteer's volunteer; willingness to volunteer knows few boundaries

Hebron

John T. Alexander - Since his retirement has devoted his time to a variety of volunteer work

Colleen R. Dixon - Just two, has faced many challenges in life, but is generous in her affections

Charles A. Patrick - Serves his community and always willing to help someone in need

Irene F. Patrick - Has great love and concern for the elderly, children and her community

B. T. Pickett - A source of inspiration and leadership to his peers

Florence

Shaun E. Alexander - Positive role model for young people

Justin B. Ashcraft - Trying to lead a normal life after overcoming many major health problems

Hannah Baird - Driving force behind many Boone County nonprofit causes

Gary Bentle - Outstanding community service, high integrity, quick study leader

Sarah S. Blanken - Generous in her community leadership and volunteerism

Lucinda A. Brown - An energetic participant in library cooperation in the tri-state area

Ruth C. Bruce - Very active role in her church and quilting guild

Ed Burcham - Donates legal services and is dedicated to youth education

Bob Chastang - Very involved in his church and Exodus Jail Ministries

Joyce Chastang - Very involved in her church and with marriage encounter

Helen Collins - Deep devotion to her community and to her political party

Betsy Conrad - Lives and breathes Boone County

Bernice Denham - Serves as model for our community, participates in community events

Dave Geohegan - Active in community and church and missionary work

Diane R. Grady - Through many adversities, she maintains a loving smile and positive attitude

Albert T. Hampton - Helps the elderly and disabled and volunteers at church

Lois Y. Hampton - Cooks for shut-ins, visits the sick, volunteers at Burlington Elementary

Jean C. Houston - Active volunteer at Boone County Public Library and DAR

Ray J. Huls - Works with Civitan Club and lives his life in a sharing manner

Evelyn M. Kalb - With unfailing loyalty she upholds her associates with praise and friendship

Betty J. Klette - Undying selflessness and concern for others, the community and the world

David W. Kolb - Coaches childrens' sports and believes in each child

LaVerne L. Lawson - Helped low-income families and seniors

Polly Mynk - Visits friends in nursing homes and tends toddlers at her church

James E. Pitts - Unselfishly puts others first

Gail A. Ruef - Never allowed her SLE disease to keep her down

Cheryl Welch - Dedicated to making life easier for the handicapped children on her bus

Rabbit Hash

Judy Caudill - Quietly caring for elderly neighbors

Duane Doyle - Very giving, an unsung hero and a wonderful friend to all

Vince Fallis - Always pitching in cleaning and volunteering

Barbara Fallis - Cleaned up flood mess and helped clean up local church

Joyce Hansel - Named Mother of the Year and is a wonderful friend and neighbor

Jack H. Mettey - Volunteers time, talents and thoughtfulness

Carleen Stephens - Involved in her church and community

Lin Unterreiner - Volunteers at school and helps her neighbors

Union

Nancy Drews - Even when battling her own adversities, has never lost her spirit or sense of humor

Greg T. Grout - Works hard so Mom can stay home with their children

Brenda Hartman - Exemplary service and dedication to Boone County youth

Jan M. Keene - Never too tired or busy to lend help or encouragement

Richard E. Newman - Exodus Jail Ministry, Habitat houses, youth leader and elder at church

Jay B. Tracy - Active in Boy Scouts

Petersburg

Patty Birkle - Very active in volunteer fire department and in taking care of the elderly

Alice Jarrell - Shares her knowledge and love of her historic community

Katie Shuffett - Volunteers at Dinsmore, good student and athlete

Myra Shuffett - Volunteers at Dinsmore, good student and athlete

Verona

Greg Vest - Helps on his father's farm, is pleasant and polite

Walton

Lloyd Clements - Never too busy to assist any neighbor in need

Truett DeMoisey - Outstanding athlete, wounded in WWII

Bill Dixon - Gives of himself and his resources to his neighbors, friends and church

John Ingram - Helped rescue a child who was swept into a flooded culvert

Helen V. Jones - Good neighbor, organized the Walton Wa Na Club

Bill Kromer - Foster parent to 40 children over the years

Elizabeth Kromer - Foster parent to 40 children over the years

Peggy McClure - Dedicated to making life easier for the handicapped children on her bus

Donald McIntyre - Served on the fire department since he was 15 years old

Robert Ranshaw - Volunteers for the betterment of Walton

Wayne Rice - A big supporter of schools and his church

Daniel Stephens - Rescued a child from a flooded culvert pipe

Jean Thornton - Volunteers on the fire department and life squad

Jesse Thornton - Volunteers on the fire department and life squad

Phillip W. Trzop - Works many hours for the city as well as volunteering at BeCon

Wallace Wireman - Has received patents on many of his inventions

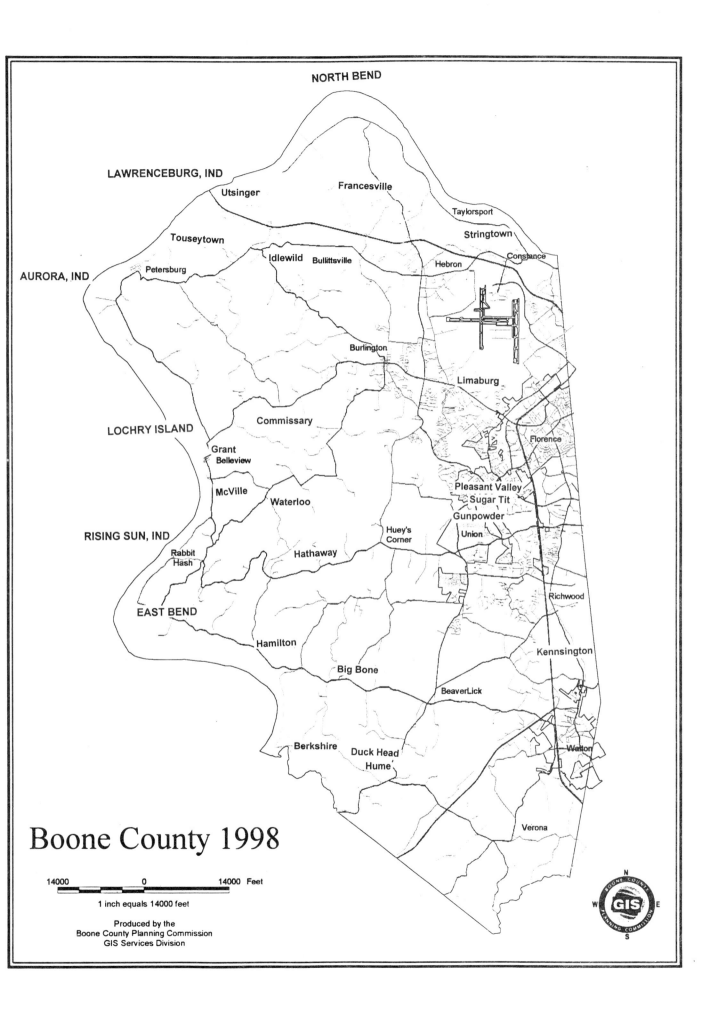

Bibliography

Boone County Recorder, Historical Edition, R.E. Berkshire publisher, Sept. 4, 1930.

Blakely, Margaret J., a paper entitled "The Piatts of Kentucky," May 27, 1952.

Bushelman, Gloria, *Boone County/Florence Magazine,* Boone County Fiscal Court, Burlington, Ky, Florence City Council, Florence, Ky., 1995.

Caldwell, Merrill S, "A Brief History of Slavery in Boone County, Kentucky," a paper presented to the Boone County Historical Society, June 21, 1957.

Campbell, William Bruce Sr., *Bullittsburg's Ministry of Faith, 175 Years,* Bullittsburg Baptist Church, 1969.

Collins, Richard H., updated version of Lewis Collins' *History of Kentucky,* Louisville, Ky. Richard H. Collins & Co. Publishers, originally printed in 1874, 1877 edition.

Collins, Lewis, *History of Kentucky,* Kentucke Imprints, Berea, Ky., originally printed in 1874, 1976 edition.

Conrad, William, *A Story about Florence, Ky. and the Florence Rotary Club,* self published, Florence, Ky. 1989

Conrad, William, *An Educational and Historical Tour Through Northern Boone County, The Top of Kentucky,* Community Education Program, Boone County Schools, 1986.

Conrad, William, *Boone County, The Top of Kentucky, 1792-1992,* Kentucky's 200th Anniversary, Picture This! Books, Ft. Mitchell, Ky., 1992.

Conrad, William, *The History of Boone County Schools,* Boone County Community Educational Council, Boone County, Ky. 1982.

Conrad, William, editor, *The Loder Diary, Part 1, The Ante-bellum Years, Jan. 1, 1857-April 21, 1861; Part 2, The Civil War Years, April 21, 1861-Sept. 30, 1868; Part 3, The Next Ten Years, Oct. 1, 1868-Jan. 24, 1878; Part 4, Jan. 1, 1879-Dec. 31, 1884; Part 5, Jan. 1, 1885-Dec. 31, 1892; Part 6, Jan. 1, 1893-Jan. 29, 1904,* Boone County Schools, Florence, Ky., 1985 & 1988.

Conrad, William, *A Story about Florence, Ky. and the Florence Rotary Club,* self published, Florence, Ky. 1989.

Conrad, William, *Yesterdays, An Enriching Adventure in Boone County's Past,* self published, Florence, Ky. 1987.

Douglas, Lloyd C., *Time to Remember,* Houghton Mifflin Co., Boston, 1951.

Eckert, Allan W., *The Frontiersmen,* Bantam Books, Boston, Mass., 1970.

Fillmore, Ann, *A Peek Into the Past,* A History of the Union and Richwood Areas, Ryle High School PTSA, 1998.

Filson Club, *The Prehistoric Men of Kentucky,* John P. Morton & Co., Printers to the Filson Club, Louisville, Ky. 1910.

Fraser, K.M., *The Prehistory of Man in Kentucky,* The Kentucky Prehistory Curriculum Project, Murray & Golden Pond, Ky. 1986.

Geaslen, Chester, *Strolling Along Memory Lane #1,2, 3, Chronicles of Heritage,* Otto Printing Co. Newport, Ky. est. 1975.

Griffing, B.N., An Atlas, Boone, Kenton and Campbell Counties, Kentucky, D.J. Lake & Co., Philadelphia, 1883, 12.Blaker, Vivian, *Sand Run Baptist Church 1819-1994, self published, 1994.*

Harrison, Lowell H & James C. Klotter, *A New History of Kentucky,* University Press of Kentucky, Lexington, Ky. 1997.

Henderson, A. Gwynn, *Prehistoric Research at Petersburg, Boone County, KY* University of Kentucky, Program for Cultural Resource Assessment, Lexington, Ky. Dec. 1993.

Henderson, A. Gwynn, *Kentuckians Before Boone,* University Press of Kentucky, Lexington, Ky. 1992.

Jillson, Willard Rouse, *Big Bone Lick,* The Standard Printing Co., Louisville, Ky. 1936.

Jones, Lucille; Yealey, A.M.; Aylor, Lawrence; Lutes, Roy C.; *Florence Boone County Kentucky,* papers by the Boone County Historical Society, 1959 est.

Keefe, Robert A. *Chronological History of the Greater Cincinnati International Airport 1941-1985,* February 1986.

Kelly Elementary PTA, *Ancestry - Our Ohio River Heritage*, Windmill Publications, Mt. Vernon, Ind., 1996.

Kirtley, Elizabeth McMullen and Carlene Stephens, *East Bend Baptist Church 175 Years* booklet, 1994.

Kirtley, Elizabeth McMullen, *Burlington Baptist Church 150th Anniversary* booklet, 1992.

Kleber, John E., editor in chief, *The Kentucky Encyclopedia,* Thomas D. Clark, Lowell H. Harrison, James Klotter, a project of the Kentucky Bicentennial Committee, University Press of Kentucky, Lexington, Ky. 1992.

Klotter, James, C., *Kentucky - Portrait in Paradox, 1900-1950*, Kentucky Historical Society, 1996.

Lentz, Rev. H. Max, *A History of the Lutheran Churchs in Boone County, Kentucky*, York, Pa., 1902.

Levin, H., *Lawyers & Lawmakers of Kentucky*, Lewis Publishing Co., Chicago, reprinted by the Filson Club of Louisville, 1982.

Lewis, Dottie L., editor, *Caroline Williams: Her Spot in Cincinnati*, The Cincinnati Historical Society, Cincinnati, Ohio, 1990.

Lewis, R. Barry, editor, *Kentucky Archaeology*, University Press of Kentucky, Lexington, Ky. 1966.

Lloyd, Emma Rouse *Clasping Hands With Generations Past,* Wiesen-Hart Press, Cincinnati, 1932.

Masters, Frank M., *A History of Baptists in Kentucky*, Kentucky Baptist Historical Society, Louisville, Ky. 1953.

Morith, Mrs. Lorie, paper titled "History of the Old South," Jan. 12, 1960.

No Author or Publisher Listed, *150th Anniversary, City of Walton*, Jan. 21, 1990.

No Author or Publisher Listed, *90th Anniversary, The Cincinnati and Suburban Bell Telephone Company 1873-1963.*

No Author or Publisher Listed, *Belleview Baptist Church, 190th Anniversary, "A Look at the Past -- A Vision for the Future,"* 1993 est.

No Author or Publisher Listed, *Boone County 175th Anniversary Historical Book 1798-1973.*

No Author or Publisher Listed, *A Brief History of Big Bone Baptist Church 1843-1968.*

No Author or Publisher Listed, Boone County, a brief history of the much honored land located just 12 miles from Cincinnati, 1940.

No Author Listed, Minutes of Rabbit Hash Telephone Co., 1903-1919.

No Author or Publisher Listed, *Welcome to an Educational & Historical Tour Through Boone County,* sponsored as a community education program by Boone County Schools, no publication date.

Pearce, John Ed & Richard Nugent, *The Ohio River*, University Press of Kentucky, 1989.

Pettit, Eunie, parts of her diary 1906 - 1949

Pollack, David, editor, *The Archaeology of Kentucky: Past Accomplishments and Future Directions*, Vol. 1&2, Kentucky Heritage Council, Frankfort, Ky. 1990.

Purvis, Thomas L, editor with Kenneth M. Clift, Betty Maddox Daniels, Elisabeth Purser Fennell and Michael E. Whitehead, *Newport, Kentucky, A Bicentennial History*, Newport, 1996.

Rawe, Richard L., *Creating a World-Class Airport: Cincinnati/Northern Kentucky International 1947-1997*, Cherbo Publishing Group Inc., 1996-1997.

Rector, Mary Amanda, high school essay on Petersburg history written in May 1928.

Rennick, Robert M., *Kentucky Place Names*, University Press of Kentucky, Lexington, Ky. 1984.

Reis, Jim, *Pieces of the Past,* Kentucky Post, Covington, Ky. 1988.

Reis, Jim, *Pieces of the Past 2,* Kentucky Post, Covington, Ky. 1991.

Reis, Jim, *Pieces of the Past 3,* Kentucky Post, Covington, Ky. 1994.

Roter, Elizabeth Rose "Betty Jo" Weaver, "White Kittens and Four-Leaf Clovers," handwritten manuscript, 1996.

Rouse, Jack, *The Civil War in Boone County, Kentucky*, Boone County Historic Preservation Review Board, Windmill Publications, Mt. Vernon, Ind.. 1996.

Rouse, Frank H., handwritten diary kept from 1906 to 1960.

Shaffer, James F., *Piatt's Landing Eastbend*, Cincinnati Gas & Electric Co., Cincinnati, Ohio, 1978.

Tanner, Paul, *Toll Roads in Kentucky 1817-1917 and Boone County*, self-published 1992.

Taylor, John, *A History of Ten Baptist Churches*, Art Guild Reprints Inc., Cincinnati, Ohio, 1823.

Teale, Edwin Way, Wandering Through Winter, Dodd, Mead & Co., New York, 1957.

True, Rene, program manager, Keith Roberts, research, Kentucky Cabinet for Economic Development, Division of Research in cooperation with Tri-County Economic Development Corp., *Kentucky Resources for Economic Development, Northern Kentucky*, 1996,

Walton, Ivalou H., Historical Study Burlington Methodist Church, May 1975.

Yealey, A.M. (Almer Michael) *History of Boone County, Kentucky*, reprint of newspaper articles, 1960.

Interviews

Arrasmith, John, March 20, 1998, regarding his Indian artifacts and movie career.

Campbell, Harold, April 4, 1998, regarding his experiences.

Claxon, Joe, March 4, 1998, regarding his experiences as county agent.

Cochran, Jane, March 20, 1998, regarding her quilt-making.

Daughtery, Martha, numerous interviews and editing assistance, December through April.

Dye, Barbara, December, 1997, regarding the Lutheran Churches in Boone County.

Edwards, Ruth, March 26, 1998, regarding her experiences as jailer.

Fallis, Barbara, Dec. 9, 1997, regarding Rabbit Hash history.

Fancher, Donna Price, Oct. 7, 1997, regarding Kenny Price and his musical career.

Ferguson, Bruce, repeated conversations regarding his experiences and research.

Kirtley, Mrs. Elizabeth, Jan. 8, 1998, regarding her memories.

Lainhart, Virginia, numerous interviews and editing assistance regarding Florence and Hebron.

Long, Monica, March 31, 1998, regarding the family honey business.

Lucas, Ken, April 4, 1998, regarding involvement in Boone County government and economic development.

McBee, Bill, April 9, 1998, regarding his role on the championship Burlington football team.

Northington, Mary, March, 3, 1998, regarding African Americans in Northern Kentucky.

Patrick, Irene, April 2, 1998, regarding her expereiences.

Porterfield, Rosella, March 3, 1998, regarding her experiences.

Purnell, Katie, numerous interviews and editing assistance, regarding her father's store in Burlington.

Reno, Jack, Oct. 2, 1997, regarding his relocation to Boone County and musical career.

Rouse, Jack, Feb. 18, 1998, regarding Walton and early exploration.

Rouse, Asa, repeated conversations regarding Walton, Verona and more.

Ryle, Claiborne, April 8, 1998, regarding his future plans and perceptions.

Scott, Sebern, March 21, 1998, regarding his memories of Belleview.

Smith, William A., March 31, 1998, regarding agriculture in Boone County and his 4-H experience.

Stephens, Elizabeth "Lib" Craig, December 10, 1997, regarding Rabbit Hash.

Summers, Scott, March 20, 1998, regarding his motorcycle racing and other businesses.

Walton, John, March 5, 1998, regarding his experiences and individual references.

Whittenburg, Linda, March 31, 1998, regarding future of Burlington and restoring log cabins.

And others, as indicated

Other Sources

Boone County Recorder, Historical Edition, R.E. Berkshire publisher, Sept. 4, 1930.

| *Boone County Recorder* | *Kentucky Post* | *Kentucky Enquirer* | *The Dixie News* |

About the Author

Jennifer Warner moved to the old G. Henry Stevens farmhouse in the Idlewild area in 1996 with her husband Dana Kisor and daughter Tatiana Warner Kisor. Choosing Boone County for many of the same reasons others have moved here, they were attracted to the beautiful rolling hills and potential for what has already become a very successful location for a bed and breakfast.

Growing up on a Northern Indiana farm, Jen worked in the garden and orchards with her grandfather. After his father died about 1910, 4th grader DeMain Warner dropped out of school to take over as the "man of the family."

Jen's grandfather, Demain Warner, and father, Phillip Warner, at the Goshen, Indiana, family farm in 1935.

Regrets about not completing his education haunted DeMain to his death, although he put his three younger brothers through college. An avid reader, he educated himself far beyond a college degree, earned a statewide reputation for his orchards and was re-elected president of the Indiana Farm Bureau Co-op for nearly three decades.

His avid reading encouraged Jen to read constantly throughout childhood and prompted her interest in writing at a young age. Jen edited the Goshen High School yearbook, then graduated from Purdue University with a Bachelor of Arts in Mass Communication. She accepted a position working in Lexington.

Several decades and moves later – after writing for the Kentucky departments of education and natural resources, a St. Louis art magazine and then an Illinois utility – she married Dana Kisor from West Portsmouth, Ohio. They experimented with parenthood by hosting Tanja Allenbach, a 15-year-old Swiss exchange student from the Youth for Understanding Program, then Jen gave birth to Tatiana (Russian for Little Tanja) in 1994.

While in St. Louis, Jen had accompanied a friend to a community education class on how to start a bed and breakfast. She soon realized that combining a bed and breakfast with a writing career would be the perfect fit for her interests.

The combination would allow Tatiana to grow up in the country, Dana to try country living, and Jen to return to the lifestyle she preferred and be a stay-at-home Mom. Years of research, house hunting and business plan preparation paid off when Walton realtor Judy Robin located "the perfect place" for their country bed and breakfast in northern Boone County. Defying all financial logic, they left lucrative jobs in the flatlands, packed up several U-Hauls and moved in October 1996.

Meeting Hannah Baird at Dinsmore Homestead's Candlelight Christmas celebration led Jen to the book, an experience that has provided insights into the county's existing politics and problems as well as great historical stories to entertain guests and encourage them to visit Boone County's unique sites.

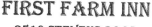

FIRST FARM INN
2510 STEVENS ROAD
BURLINGTON, KY 41005
606-586-0199
FAX 606-586-0299
firstfarm@goodnews.net
http://www.bbonline.com/ky/firstfarm

INDEX

4-H Clubs.. 262, 310, 311, 313
Abel Associates...................375
Abel, Lauren 375, 376
Ackemyer, W....................166
Acra, Albert M. 161
Acra, Corey Slater.............278
Acra, Lark 248
Acra, Lonnie 248
Acra, Otis.........................248
Adams family...................150
Adams, Annie 150
Adams, B.W.............166, 219
Adams, Capt. Robert........283
Adams, Dr. S.M. 180
Adams, Dr. Sam................151
Adams, Elizabeth 206, 209
Adams, Ella......................151
Adams, Etta K. Carpenter..151
Adams, Fannie 150
Adams, Hampton 151, 276
Adams, Harry...................151
Adams, Henry DeCoursey 105, 199, 202, 206, 208, 210, 218
Adams, John P. Hampton..150
Adams, Johnnie 180
Adams, Katie Hance..........151
Adams, Lizzie 150
Adams, Lute.....................212
Adams, Maggie 150
Adams, May.....................151
Adams, Presley 180
Adams, R.G. 118
Adams, Rose 151
Adams, Rose Ann 150
Adams, Sallie Ann Kennedy150
Adams, Sam.....................212
Adams, Wayne 151
Adkins, Virginia................285
Afterkirk, Lee...................226
Ahern, Cornelius 101
Akers, Gary......................277
Alcorn, Mrs. D.C. 141
Alden, Charles O............... 57
Alden, Elihu.....................139
Alexander, James 90
All Saints Catholic Church 102
All Saints Parish Church ...320
All Saints School...............357
Allen, Wilson 44
Allen, Jim Bob 323
Allen, Lyle E....................104
Allen, Nate 101
Allen, William 101
Allin, Thomas 37
Alloway, Arthur "Podge"..176
Alloway, Mrs. 122
Alloway, Orville 176
Allphin, Alberta 393
Allphin, B.B. 189
Allphin, Ben B. 201
Allphin, J.C......................189
Allphin, Pink Edwards 189
Allphin, Sheriff.................213
Amann, Mary Jo...............109
Amann, Steve...................109
American Sign and Manufacturing Service 364
Ammann, Ed 384
Anderson Ferry 130
Anderson, Atlee 349
Anderson, Carl 254
Anderson, Efe 122
Anderson's Ferry..............192
Antique Emporium............368
Appel, Dale 336
Applegate, Col. William....137
Appleton, Col. 117, 118, 120, 122
Appleton, Hute.................120
Appleton, William.............109
Aristech Chemical Corp. 364 374
Armstrong, Neil 345
Arnold, Thomas 81
    William 37
Arnold, A. 154
Arnold, John 77, 154
Arnold, Miss 161

Arrasmith Site.....................17
Arrasmith, John. 379, 380, 394
Arrasmith, Margie.............275
Ashcraft, Raymond 311
Ashe, Thomas 41
Association for Boone Library Establishment (ABLE) 365
Atlas Hotel.......................281
Audubon, John James 53
Aurora, IN...................71, 83
Avery, Rev. C.J..................314
Aydelotte, Will 111
Aylor family 45
Aylor family 390
Aylor, Ada 185
Aylor, Chester..................305
Aylor, Earl 271
Aylor, Elmo 305
Aylor, Jim........................205
Aylor, John J. 182
Aylor, Joseph 349
Aylor, Julia 101
Aylor, L.E. 242
Aylor, Leslie 301
Aylor, Marian 301
Aylor, T.S. 194
Aylor, William E...............301
Bachelor, Roy 275
Bagby, D.Y.......................103
Bagby, Dr. D.M. 154
Bagby, Dr. Daniel M. 116
Bagby, Julia F. O'Neal.......116
Bailey's tollgate 231
Baird, Hannah 174
Baker, Bessie 255
Baker, Charles..........226, 381
Baker, E.H. 142
Baker, G.W. 186
Baker, George 184
Baker, George W. 142
Baker, Henrietta 226
Baker, Herbert..................226
Baker, James............226, 381
Baker, Russell 226
Baker, W.H. 92
Balch, W.P.......................124
Balsley, Irwin...................137
Bank of Petersburg...........139
Bannister, H. 156
Barkley, Sen. Alben 302
Barkley, Sen. Alben W. 298
Barlow, Surface 359
Barnes and Noble.............396
Barnes, Dr. Mary Ann.......386
Barnet, James 174
Bartle, John 54
Barton, John 100, 157
Barton, Mrs. John.............126
Basley, Ada Clore 193
Basley, C.S. 193
Basley, George L. 193
Basley, Kenneth 193
Bassett, Denver 200
Bates, William 35
Bates, Wallace 340
BAWAC Sheltered Workshop366
Beacon Light Motel 255
Beall, John 132
Beasley, Pastor J.W..........237
Beaver.............................226
Beaver Lick......................258
Beaver Lick Baptist Church 256
Beaver Lick School...........277
Beaverlick 36, 117, 126, 150, *225*, 226, 317
Beaverlick Baptist Church.226
Beaverlick Mercantile Co..199
Beck, Sen. J.B...................171
Beck, Tracey Patrick.........386
Beckham, Gov. J.C. Wickliffe187
Beckham, Sen. John 255
Bedgood, Raymond...........273
Bedinger, Dr. B.F. 79
    Oliva Morgan................79
Bedinger, D. 154
Bedinger, D.E. 134
Bedinger, George M..........100

Bedinger, Harriett 201
Bedinger, Mrs. J.C. 256
Beech Grove Debate Society236
Beemon family 45
Beemon and Quigley Store292
Beemon, Clark 185
Beemon, Jeremiah.............103
Beemon, Shelby................328
Beemon, W.P....................219
Behringer-Crawford Museum
    .... 28, 45, 353
Beighle, Charles Samuel...324
Beighle, Edward 324
Beighle, Monty 324
Beighle, Paul Calvin 324
Beighle, Truett 324
Beil, Henry 265
Belleview31, 57, 58, 89, 92, 129, 147, 149, 150, 174, 195, 196, 198, 230, 235, 236, 250, 271, 274, 293
Belleview Bank.................273
Belleview Baptist Church52, 195, 235, 273, 315, 316
Belleview Bottoms.............76
Belleview General Store ...271
Belleview's Citizens Deposit Bank
   366
Belleview-McVille Center 352
Belleview-McVille Volunteer Fire Dept. 353
Bellin, Jacques Nicholas 18
Bennett, Bill.....................117
Bennett, Harold 359
Bent, Rev. Joseph J. 159
Bentham, Anita F. Hempfling270
Bentham, H.W. 270
Benton Farms...................381
Bergin, L.E. 365
Berkemeier, Ed 356
Berkshhire, John William..108
Berkshire family 147, 153
Berkshire, Benjamin H......167
Berkshire, Bob 163
Berkshire, Ethel Norris 167
Berkshire, J.W. 166, 195
Berkshire, Leila Thompson290
Berkshire, Melicent McNeeley108
Berkshire, R.E. ... 32, 240, 290
Berkshire, Robert Ewing...290
Berkshire, W.C. 110, 120
Berkshire, William............177
Berry, John 115
Bess, F.M..........................97
Besterman, Joe................226
Besterman, Mrs. Lee 259
Beverly, Raymond 281
Bickers, Carl 355
Bickers, Mary Kathrine....355
Big Bone 35, 40, 41, 42, 43, 44, 45, 55, 58, 70, 77, 81, 82, 83, 89, 92, 93, 236, 353
Creek.............. 35, 40, 45
Big Bone Baptist Church 81, 82, 89, 93, 151, 178, 199, 204, 226, 245, 247, 256, 274, 316
Big Bone Church 119
Big Bone Creek83, 150, 153, 353
Big Bone Hotel 316
Big Bone Lick9, 12, 18, 19, 20, 21, 22, 24, 40, 41, 42, 43, 44, 70, 72, 77, 151, 152, 200, 205
Big Bone Lick Historical Association
   353
Big Bone Lick State Park
    .... 382, 392, 394
Big Bone Methodist Church151
Big Bone Springs 55, 207
Big Bone Springs Hotel 353
Bingham, Ernest 279
Blackburn, W.O. 294
Blakely, Margaret J............56
Blaker, Vivian60, 89, 131, 270
Blaksly, Clarisse 121
Blankenbaker family...........45
Blankenbaker, Clint 286
Blankenbaker, E.H. 231

Blanton, Dr. 186
Blanton, H.C. 248
Blaum, Captain Ray..........139
Blodgett, James 159
Blythe, Dudley.................221
Blythe, Dudley Rouse 291
Blythe, George.................291
Boh, John........................334
Bolen, John 144
Bonar, Joyce Wilson.........386
Bonda, A.T. 333
Bonner, Robert 146
Book, Alice......................134
Book, Dale.......................134
Boone Daniel.... 27, 31, 37, 46
Boone (or Burlington) Academy 62, 103
Boone Cliffs 11, 19
Boone Colored School......310
Boone Co. Bd. of Education374
Boone Co. Businessmen's Association 366
Boone County Deposit Bank161, 186, 289, 290, 299
Boone County Distilling Co.144
Boone County Fair............337
Boone Co. Health Dept. ...308
Boone County High School 271, 308, 310, 331, 332
Boone Co. Insurance Co. 153
Boone County Jaycettes....366
Boone County Journal, The163
Boone County Library 280
Boone County Parks Dept. 394
Boone County Public Library 333, 366, 372
Boone County Recorder 32, 35, 37, 52, 54, 55, 59, 62, 68, 70, 89, 92, 94, 96, 102, 104, 109, 111, 125, 130, 131, 132, 133, 134, 147, 153, 160, 161, 163, 164, 165, 166, 167, 168, 169, 171, 174, 177, 179, 180, 182, 183, 185, 186, 188, 189, 190, 191, 192, 193, 194, 195, 196, 198, 200, 201, 202, 204, 205, 206, 207, 208, 217, 218, 219, 222, 224, 230, 233, 234, 235, 236, 237, 240, 241, 245, 247, 249, 250, 251, 252, 253, 254, 255, 256, 257, 260, 261, 262, 263, 269, 270, 271, 273, 274, 279, 280, 281, 286, 287, 288, 290, 291, 292, 293, 294, 298, 299, 302, 303, 304, 311, 312, 313, 314, 319, 322, 324, 332, 336, 337, 338, 348, 349, 350, 352, 354, 365, 374, 377, 382, 384, 390, 396
Boone Co. Vocational School 347
Boone Co. Water Commission 382
Boone Co. Water Rescue. 336
Boone Hotel......................245
Boone House 104, 161
Boone Lake 280
Boone State Bank.............366
Boone Woods Park 332, 341, 351
Boone, Daniel....... 11, 20, 152
Booth Hospital.................345
Booth, Dr. Herbert 345, 398, 399
Booth, John Wilkes ... 123, 185
Borders, Artie 240
Borders, Ed 277
Borders, Eunie 240
Borders, Helen 277
Borders, Roseann 240
Borders, William 277
Borglum, Gutzon 149
Bossong, Mrs. Ronald.......282
Botts, H.C........................147
Botts, John M. 140
Botts, M...........................169
Botts, S.G. 142, 143
Boyd, James 162
Boyd, Lee 116
Boyd, Mr. 115
Boyton, Capt. Paul...........138

INDEX

Bradford Bros. 220
Bradford, C.C....................158
Bradford, Carrie 265
Bradford, Charlie 187
Bradford, Irene.........103, 160
Bradford, Lute..................265
Bradford, Robert..............132
Bradley, B.B. 139, 140, 145
Bradley, Capt. B.B. 139
Bradley, Dillon..................122
Bradley, Henry.................122
Bradley, James 141
Bradley, Mrs. James.........175
Bradley, W.O. 142
Bradley, William........122, 124
Brady, R. A. 188
Bramblett, Fred 378
Brames, Bob 104
Brames, Jean 104
Branham, Pastor Sam.......316
Brannum, Mrs..................280
Brasher, Charles L. 57
Brasher, E. 77
Brassle, William................254
Bravard, Adelaide Hempfling 298
Bravard, Donnie................298
Bravard, Wayne 298
Breasted, Martha Ferguson 200, 252, 256, 392
Breathitt, Gov. Edward......363
Breckinridge, John 79
Breckinridge family 58
Breeden, William 237
Brent, Father John J. 101
Bresser, Mrs. Ralph...........314
Bricken, S. 140
Bridges, Silas 77
Briggsen, W.S..................124
Brindel, George 142
Bristow, Annie A. 178
Bristow, Annie Anderson ..240
Bristow, Cum...................166
Bristow, Jule 166
Bristow, Katherine 182
Bristow, Lillian 240, 324
Bristow, Nanie D. 156
Bristow, Napoleon 240
Brittenhelm, William..........167
Brockman, Andrew 60
Brockway, Robert D..........230
Bromback, J.J..................153
Bronson (a barber) 140
Broom, J.H.......................274
Brothers, Ebbs 143
Brothers, J. Proctor............292
Brothers, J.P. (Prock) 185
Brothers, Mrs. J.P..............292
Brown, Capt. John......34, 37
Brown, Billy Jo 315
Brown, Cindy............366, 372
Brown, D.H. 184
Brown, Elizabeth R. 302
Brown, Frances 226
Brown, Gov. John Y..........373
Brown, John.....................226
Brown, Joseph 75
Brown, Milton M. 302
Brown, Prof. John D..........126
Browns, Watt 217
Bruce, Estill 397
Bruce, Ruth 397
Bryan, William Jennings 188, 206
Bryant, Dr. Bill 9, 11
Bryant, J.C. 97
Buchanan, Irene Alloway ..195
Buchanan, S.C..................195
Buckner, Col. H. 101
Buckner, H.M. 100
Buckner, J.C. 184, 207
Buckner, S.B. 142
Bulaney, B.A. 116
Bullitt, Capt. Thomas 32, 34, 40
Bullitt, Thomas 24
Bullitt's Bottom 33
Bullittsburg 31, 32, 33, 34, 39, 50, 131, 132, 177

Bullittsburg Baptist Church 31, 33, 34, 39, 52, 56, 59, 89, 131, 178, 232, 274, 310, 314
Bullittsville 34, 81, 132, 133, 166, 170, 189, 193, 222, 233, 268
Bullittsville Christian Church 132
Bullock Pen Water District 355
Burbridge, Gen. 122
Burbridge, Gen. Stephen ...109
Burdsall, Theodore............280
Burke, Capt. 115
Burke, F.J. 158
Burlington 17, 32, 34, 35, 38, 40, 54, 56, 57, 59, 62, 72, 77, 79, 80, 81, 82, 84, 85, 91, 92, 93, 94, 95, 97, 103, 104, 118, 122, 129, 132, 154, 161, 162, 166, 168, 170, 184, 185, 186, 188, 189, 199, 207, 210, 213, 215, 217, 218, 219, 243, 245, 248, 253, 262
Burlington Advertiser..........83
Burlington Advertiser, The 103
Burlington and Florence Turnpike Company 231
Burlington Baptist Church 34, 40, 51, 60, 82, 104, 186, 210, 218, 274, 288, 299, 340
Burlington Fire Department 397
Burlington High School 226, 246, 271, 288, 299, 313, 332
Burlington Hotel 161, 217
Burlington Masonic Lodge 299
Burlington Methodist Church 81, 104, 134, 288, 368
Burlington Methodist Church, 164
Burlington Presbyterian   104
Burlington Seminary............62
Burlington United Methodist 368
Burlington Vol. Fire Dept. 331
Busby Heights..................205
Busby, L.H.......................205
Busemeyer, Rev. Henry A. 322
Bush, Major John 35
Mary Wright (nee Gaines)...34
Bushelman, Ted 365, 366, 372
Butler, Rev. Thomas R......101
Butts, Doc........................122
Butts, Elizabeth..................77
Cabin Arts...............163, 397
Cain, John........................364
Cain, Rodney "Biz" 365
Caintuckee Grill................331
Caintuckee Restaurant......364
Caldwell, Merrill S.   49, 67
Calendar, Fred..................180
Callender, R.M..................281
Calvert, James............97, 110
Camp Ernst........................67
Camp Michaels 11
Campbell...........................82
Col. John...........................28
William Bruce, Sr. 46
Campbell, B.W. 220, 288
Campbell, Harold....297, 399
Campbell, J.W. 232
Campbell, John Braxton 289
Campbell, June 62
Campbell, Sally.........288, 289
Campbell, Thomas 62
Campbell, Wendel Siebern 289
Campbell, William 232, 235, 267
Campbell, William Bruce Sr. 165
Campbell, William Sr. 314
Campfield, Lodick 49
Canby, Dr. Israel...............123
Canby, Elizabeth Piatt.......123
Canby, Gen. E. R. Spriggs 123
Carey, Hugh....................254
Carey, M.L.......................323
Carey, Mrs. 111
Carlin, Mr. 30
Carlisle, Columbus............163
Carlisle, Guy....................323
Carlisle, John G. 171
Carlton 150
Carpenter family 45
Carpenter, Polly Aylor 61
Carpenter, Rev. William 67

Carpenter, William........45, 60
Carr, Tom 355
Carroll, Gov. Julian............337
Carroll, M.C. 294
Carson, Jack 90, 101, 117, 118, 120
Carson, John 101, 142
Carter, Pres. Jimmy...........337
Cason, Judge P.E. 188
Cason, Ralph....................237
Castleman, Clay 119
Castleman, D.E. 219, 290
Castleman, Grace R. Yeager 207
Castleman, T.B. 207
Cates, A.S. 207
Cauthen, Amy..................358
Cauthen, Karlie Stephen ...358
Cauthen, Katelyn Rose......358
Cauthen, Steve 337, 357
Cave, John 37
  William...........................33
Cave, Bill..........................332
Cave, John 84, 162
Celoron de Bienville, Pierre Joseph
 19
Central House 161
Central Park 394
Chambers and Grubbs.......356
Chambers and Grubbs Funeral Home
  ....201, 202
Chambers, Aleen..............201
Chambers, Alfred 89
Chambers, Alfred E., Sr. 89
Chambers, Alta Terrill 194, 201
Chambers, Amanda............89
Chambers, C.S. 194
Chambers, Charles 218
Chambers, Cleveland Scott 201
Chambers, Jean 201
Chambers, Joseph 162
Chambers, Scott 281
Chambers, Susan F. Whitaker 89
Chamblin, Dr. B.W. 84
Chandler, Gov. A.B. ..257, 367
Chapin Memorial Library .315
Chapin, E.Y. 315
Chapin, E.Y. III 315
Chapin, Ed 138
Chapin, Edward Young.....134
Chapin, Elizabeth................57
Chapin, John 92
Chapin, Mrs. 145
Chapin, William 57
Chapman, Clyde 279
Charley, Amy 384
Cheslock, Ed 349
Chipman, R.....................320
Christian, Col. Wm. 40
Churchill, Gen. 115
Cincinnati Advertiser & Journal
 55
Cincinnati and Lexington Railroad
 153
Cincinnati Chronicle...........55
Cincinnati Enquirer, The 53, 99, 134, 236, 306, 332, 333, 382
Cincinnati Gazette..............55
Cincinnati Republican.........55
Cincinnati Times Star 111
Cincinnati/ Northern Kentucky Airport.................. 11, 388
Citizens Deposit Bank........224
Civilian Conservation Corps 258, 261, 283
Clabes, Gene....................374
Clare, Don 14, 17, 20, 56, 75, 95, 135, 295, 392, 391, 392
Clarion Manufacturing Corp. 394, 374
Clark, George Rogers..........
  28, 29, 42, 43, 44
  William...........................42
Clark, Andrew 343
Clark, Caroline..................176
Clark, Cyrus......................95
Clarkson School 103
Clarkson, Jacob..................67
Clause, Wanetta 377
Claxon, Joseph.. 310, 312, 381

Clay, Cassius 78
Clay family 58
Clayton, W.H. 132
Cleek Park 329
Cleek, Dr. Jacob 258
Cleek, Emily Hughes.........258
Cleek, Ira 78
Cleek, J.W. 199
Cleek, Jessie 240
Cleek, Mildred 359
Cleek, Mrs. M. 281
Cleek-McCabe site 17, 18
Clements, 'Nase' 256
Clements, Della Mae Booth 256
Clements, Ivan.................256
Clements, Nathan..............256
Clements, Rick 351
Clifford, Laura..................390
Clock of Middle Creek 237
Clondas, Pitman.................80
Clore family.......................45
Clore, A. 132
Clore, Bruce 210, 217
Clore, C.E. 194
Clore, Cave 126
Clore, David 311
Clore, Fletcher 111
Clore, James L. 217
Clore, Jim 215
Clore, Joel C. 271
Clore, John Samuel 250
Clore, Jonas 148
Clore, M. 132
Clore, Michael 149
Clore, Mrs. 217
Clore, Wilston E. 311
Cloud, John B. 271
Cloud, Payliss....................60
Clutterbuck Brothers Store 216
Clutterbuck, Anna Garrison 217
Clutterbuck, Charlotte G. 217
Clutterbuck, Homer .. 215, 216
Clutterbuck, James R........215
Clutterbuck, Lawrence......217
Clutterbuck, Rebecca 101
Clutterbuck, Roy....... 215, 216
Clutterbuck, William A. 160
Cobb, O.P. 106
Cochran, Jane Burch. 376, 391
Coffin, Levi 61, 99
Coffman, Elias...................81
Coffman, Alice 201
Coffman, Evelyn...............282
Coldiron, J. Jr. 364
Cole, Eldora 287
Coleman, Lucy Duncan 121
Coleman, Philip 121
Coleman, Ward.................248
Collier, Frank....................169
Collier, Thomas 145
Collin, Capt. 106
Collins family 98
Collins, Andrew 101
Collins, Helen... 285, 286, 287
Collins, Melvin 338, 365
Collins, Richard H. 11
Colquohoun, Mr. 44
Colsher, John N. 122
Colvill, David 294
Colville, David 262
COMAIR.......... 374, 387, 389
Combs, Sonny 332
Comer, George 122
Conley, John W. 32
Conley, Col. John W. 146
Conley, Emily I. 156
Conley, J.W. 294
Conley, John 163
Connely, Nathan................77
Conner, Jacob 80
  John 33, 37
Conner & Utz Store 156
Conner Junior and Senior High Schools 271
Conner, Ann Robinson 326
Conner, Fannie Mae Latham 246
Conner, Harold 245, 246
Conner, Hubert . 194, 294, 347

412 INDEX

Conner, Ida 277
Conner, J.W. 204
Conner, James C. 347
Conner, Lewis Albert 245
Conner, Lillie Goodridge .. 194
Conner, O.P. 191, 219
Conner, R.I. 156
Conner, Will 103
Connersville 80
Conrad, Steve 80
William 30, 31, 45,50, 80
Conrad Hardware 238
Conrad, Betsy R.285, 286, 287, 340
Conrad, Harold "Connie" .. 283
Conrad, Powers 238
Conrad, William 22, 54, 56, 69, 84, 105, 106, 107, 108, 109, 110, 111, 113, 117, 118, 119, 120, 122, 123, 124, 125, 126, 127, 130, 132, 133, 134, 135, 137, 138, 139, 140, 141, 142, 143, 145, 146, 147, 162, 163, 164, 165, 166, 168, 169, 171, 173, 174, 175, 178, 181, 182, 223, 237, 243, 250, 263, 269, 279, 285, 287, 313, 320, 372, 386
Conrad's Hardware 281
Consolidated Telephone Co. 280
Constance39, 56, 87, 92, 125, 130, 132, 165, 192, *224*, 268, 292
Continental Pet Technologies396
Continential Web Press 394
Conway, John L. 96
Coombs, Thomas 151
Cooper, John 120
Cooperative Extension Service 381
Corbin, A. 147
Corbin, A., & Son General Store 196
Corbin, Henry 118
Corbin, J.H. 156
Corbin, M.J. 196
Corbin, Mrs. A. 196
Corbin, Ruby..... 160, 208, 243
Corbin, W.P. 118
Corbin, William 143
Corey, Dr. J.A. 159
Corneliusville 34
Cotton, Bill 332
Courtney, Ben A. 366
Covington Journal, The 100
Cowan, Thomas 174
Cox, Elizabeth Brady 319
Cox, Frank 141
Cox, Ruth Wade 275
Coyle, Clifford 330
Coyle, Jim 393
Coyle, Ray 322
Craft, Manford 355
Craig family 31
John H. 37
Samuel 81
Craig, John Hanson 169
Craig, R. J. "Sheenie" 295, 359
Craig, W.J. 294
Craig's Camp 38
Craven, John Henry 179
Craven, S.L. 246
Crawford, Ellis 353
Cresswell, Nicholas 23
Crigler family 45
Crigler family 157
Crigler, Agnes Walton 234
Crigler, Harold 334
Crigler, John 312
Crigler, John W. 234
Crigler, Mary 184
Crigler, Morgan C. 184
Crigler, Rev. Jacob 67
Crisler family 45
Henry 79
Leonard 47, 79
Crisler family 92
Crisler, C.L. 161, 166
Crisler, Carleton C. 233
Crisler, Col 210
Crisler, Dr. O.S. 185
Crisler, Dr. R.H. 161
Crisler, Gabriel 67
Crisler, John C. 116
Crisler, L.H. 166, 219
Crisler, Otto 206
Crittenden family 58
Crocker, Newlan 61
Croghan (or Groghan), Col George 22
Cropper, C.L. 294
Cropper, John 332
Cropper, Judge C.L. .. 299, 300
Cropper, Judge Carroll 337
Cross, Waite 281
Crossroads 184
Crouch, Dr. M.J. 204
Crouch, Dr. M.T. 231
Crouch, Jean 356
Crow, J.C. 81
Cullom, James 75
Cummins, Samuel P. 81
Curley, T.F. 154
Cutcheon, Sally 257
Cuvier, M. 44
Dahling, H.C. 154
Daily Times 55
Dallas, Steve 383
Daniel Boone Boys' Center 397
Daniel Boone Correctional Ctr 352
Daniel Boone Treatment Ctr 348
Daniels, Robert 98
Daugherty, Martha 28
Daugherty, Dr. Frank 345
Daugherty, Dr. Harry 365
Daugherty, Dr. Harry R.345, 346
Daugherty, Dr. Joseph F. III345
Daugherty, Dr. Joseph Franklin 345
Daugherty, James Martin "Macho" 346
Daugherty, Martha 25, 127, 252, 297, 330, 346, 347, 365
Daugherty, Mary K. "Kate" 346
Daughters, J.J. 140
Daughters, Prof. D.J. 160
Davidson, George 78
Davis, Atheleen 132
Davis, Ben K. 131
Davis, C., & Co. 193
Davis, Chester T. 166
Davis, J.A. 132
Davis, James A. 132
Davis, Morgan S. 147
Davis, W.R. 285
de Lery, M. Chasegros 18
Dean, Aboil 140, 142
Dears, Henry 281
Deck, John 147
Deering, Ben 163
Delaney, Dr. John 159
Delph, Charlie 110, 268
Delph, Oleva 315
Delta Air Lines 374
Dement, John 35
DeMoisey, John 281
DeMoisey, John "Frenchy"281
DeMoisey, Truitt 322
Dempsey, John 102
Densley, Brittany 301
Depew, Capt. Abraham 34
Depew's Mill 34
Deweese, Lewis 33
DHL Airways 374, 389
DHL Worldwide Express .. 388
Dicken, E.N. 149
Dickens, James 49
Dickerson, J.N. 153
Dickerson, Volney 100, 163
Dickey, William Pinkney .. 201
Dickson, Charles 170
Dills, L.H. 162, 163
Dinsmoor, Silas 76, 77
Dinsmore, James 76, 77
Dinsmore family 149, 174, 178, 199, 256
Dinsmore Homestead Foundation 392
Dinsmore, Isabella 77
Dinsmore, James 148, 256
Dinsmore, John 76
Dinsmore, Julia 77, 392
148, 178, 257
Dinsmore, Martha Macomb 76
Dinsmore, Susan 77
Dinsmore, Susanna Bell 76
Discovery Distribution Center 390
Dixie News 341, 348, 350, 359, 362, 363, 364, 365, 366, 341, 348, 350, 359, 362, 363, 364, 365,
Dixie State Bank 280, 283, 357
Dixie Traction Co. 255
Dixon, Harry 239
Doane, Robert 359
Doggett, Arthur 355
Doggett, Mildred Leathers 355
Doll's Dairy Bar 324
Dolwick family 192
Dolwick, Gilbert 343
Dolwick, John 342
Douglas, James 24
Douglas, Lloyd 159
Douglas, Lloyd C. 159
Douglas, Lou 159
Dowery, Dale 324
Chamblin, Dr. Braxton 100
Drane, Geo. C. 142
Drennon, John 35
Dry Creek 37
Dry Ridge Deposit Bank ... 261
Duke, Basil 113
Duke, Basil W. 114
Duke, Col. Basil 112
Dulaney, Benjamin 80
Dulaney, Dr. John 109, 118
Dulaney, J.J. 118
Duncan, Dr. 217
Duncan, Dr. E. W. 247
Duncan, Dr. J.E. 141
Duncan, J.A. 189
Duncan, J.W. 142, 162, 189
Duncan, Willie 217
Dunn, Jason 30
Dunn, Dr. W.H. 141, 169
Durant, George B.114, 115, 116
Duro Bag Manufacturing 374, 394
Durr, R. C. 351
Dwyer, Thomas 101
Dyas, C.Y. 180
Dye, Barbara 70
Dynamec 394
Early, J.N. 90
Early, Judge J.N. 142
Early, Solon 142, 170, 195
Early, William 143
East Bend 150
East Bend Baptist 59, 81, 179, 316
East Bend Bottoms 13, 56
East Bend Methodist Church 168
Easton, Wendell 324
Ebenezer Lutheran Church .. 89
Eckert, Allen W. 29
Edwards, A.M. 239, 281
Edwards, Dr. R. A., Jr. 116
Edwards, Ella Nora Pettit .. 117
Edwards, Ruth 384
Edwards, Samuel Lycurgus117
Edwards, Tracey Denise ... 385
Edwards, Wilson J. 384
Elder, Cyril 320
Elijah Creek 56, 92, 130
Elijah's Creek 56
Ellis, Bob 381
Ellis, James 75
Ellis, Nellie 381
Ellis, Tandy 74
Ellsworth, Mr. 115
Emerald Industries 374, 396
Emerald Industries Inc 374
Engle, Anna 349
Entex Information Services374
Environment and Archeology LLC 390
Equitable Bank and Trust Company 154
Equitable Paper Bag Co. .. 374
Erpenbeck Elementary 371
Estes, Frank 314
Ewing, Carroll M. "Hop" .. 362
Ewing, Sue Ann Houston .. 362
Extension Homemakers 381, 385
Fairfield, John 67
Fall, Jennie 156
Falls, Alva 240
Falls, James 240, 282
Faris, Henry 84
Farmers Bank of Petersburg 195
Farmers' Cooperative Store 196
Farmers' Mutual Insurance Co. of Boone County 206
Feagan, John 281
Federal Hall 56, 72, 147
(or Federal Hill) 38
Feldhaus, James 276
Fellowship of Believers 396
Fenton, Bass 139
Ferguson, Bruce 29
251, 252, 257, 261, 287, 297, 338, 339, 340, 345, 351, 352, 353, 362, 384, 386
Ferguson, Robert "Bobby" M. 200
199, 256, 392
Ferguson, Sara Daugherty. 346
Ferguson, Stuart 346
Fernbank Dam 223
Ferneding, Joseph 101
Ferris, J.J. 169
Ferris, John 177
Ferrise, Joseph J. 145
Fichlie, Dorothy Sullivan .. 285
Fidelity Investments 374
Fillmore, Millard 78
Fillmore, Ann 253
Fillmore, Melinda 226, 318, 329, 360
Filson, John 25, 45
Finch, Louisiana 81
Finch, J.M. 207
Finch, T.W. 162
Findley, John 20
Findsen, Owen 53, 99, 100
Finke, George 398
Finnell, Capt. Benjamin 70
Finnell, Dudley 170
Finnell, John W. 99
Finnell, Weden 123
Finnells, James 60
Fischer, Mary 111
Fish, Ezra 101
Fish, Spencer 109
Fisher, Gilbert 120, 122
Fisher, John 326
Fitzgerald, Lewis 32
Fitzgerald, Ann 354
Fitzgerald, William 70, 104, 111, 237, 255, 280, 281, 286, 322, 353, 354
Flandrau, Charles 148
Flandrau, Isabella Dinsmore148
Flandrau, Martha (Patty) ... 148
Flandrau, Sarah (Sally) 148
Fleek, Charles 340, 341
Fleek, Katherine 341
Fleek, Ronald Lynn 341
Fleek, Wilford 341
Flick's grocery 132
Florence 67, 70, 72, 73, 74, 75, 78, 79, 80, 81, 84, 85, 92, 94, 100, 101, 102, 103, 104, 110, 130, 140, 143, 156, 158, 161, 163, 164, 182, 183, 184, 187, 206, 207, 213, 220, 223, 226, 231, 233, 243, 286, 296
Florence Baptist Church 80, 81, 103, 111, 182, 364
Florence Christian Church 80, 111, 143, 159, 287, 340
Florence Deposit Bank 207, 290
Florence Fair 84, 157, 158, 181, 206, 221, 222, 245
Florence Fairgrounds 255, 285
Florence High School 207, 208, 243, 285
Florence Hotel 158

INDEX

413

Florence Mall............363, 375
Florence Presbyterian Church 159
Florence Vol. Fire Dept. 288, 362
Flournoy, Col. John J. 55
Flournoy, John J..............57
Flying J Truck Plaza..........394
Foley, Red....................361
Ford, Burgess.................281
Ford, Gov. Wendell............362
Ford, Pres. Gerald 337, 368
Ford, Tennessee Ernie.........361
Forest, Ned...................126
Forkner, H.R..................294
Fortner, H.R. Jr..............311
Foster, H.J.............142, 164
Foster, J.....................124
Foster, Jedidiah 75
Foster, Mrs. Susan............141
Foster-Sanford House..........104
Foulks, Thomas D............. 56
Fowler Creek.....240, 241, 259
Fowler House..................241
Fowler, Benjamin Piatt 58, 92, 104, 245
Fowler, Charles............... 92
Fowler, Charles A. 245, 289
Fowler, Charlie 110
Fowler, Ed 54
Fowler, Edward............92, 245
Fowler, Ellen Logan...........245
Fowler, Jacob.................. 58
Fowler, Susan Scott...........245
Fowler, Susan Scott Brown 92
Fowlers Branch 58
Foy, Capt. 108
Francesville 132, 193, 244, 248, 270
Francisville 59
Franklin, Benjamin....9, 19, 24
Fraser, K.M................... 11
Frazee, G.H...................105
Frazier, Franklin.............311
Frazier, J.L..................204
Frazier, James Lynn...........126
Frazier, Lynn.................126
Freiberg & Workum..133, 138
Friends of Big Bone 392
Frohlich, Anthony W. 236
Frost, Ray D..................334
Fugate, Oakie.................349
Fulcher, George...............122
Fullilove, J.H................149
Fulton, John 53
Fulton, Lee M.................106
Fulton, Robert 53
Fuqua, David.................. 59
Fuqua, Drucillah 59
Fuqua, Washington 59
Furnish, Dr. 171, 208, 217 161, 189
Furnish, Jo Revill 209
Gadd, Ernest..................314
Gadd, Rev. Dee................322
Gaddis, Mack..................365
Gaff, James W.................141
Gaff, John 101, 105, 106
Gaines, Abner 78
Abner L....................... 34
Archibald K. 34
Augustus W. 34
Benjamin P.................... 34
Col. Abner 34
Elizabeth Matthews............ 34
George 33
James Matthews 34
John P........................ 34
Major John P............78, 79
Richard M..................... 34
William H. 34
Gaines & Berkshire's store 138
Gaines Crossroads62, 75, 77, 78
Gaines family............78, 147
Gaines Ford Road.............. 62
Gaines X Roads................156
Gaines, A.S...................133
Gaines, A.W................... 77
Gaines, Abner 62, 77, 78
Gaines, Adisson...............106
Gaines, Alan H................319

Gaines, Archibald 99
Gaines, B.R......................144
Gaines, Col. Abner............283
Gaines, Col. Abner Legrand78
Gaines, Edwin..................90
Gaines, Elizabeth..............78
Gaines, Elizabeth Winston 233
Gaines, George 59
Gaines, George W.............233
Gaines, J.G............. 118, 124
Gaines, James..................78
Gaines, John W................143
Gaines, Marvin 319
Gaines, Mrs. Sidney...........256
Gaines, Owen..................163
Gaines, P.B...................262
Gaines, William 161
Gaines, William L.............138
Gaines, William Winston ..233
Gaines, Willie 144
Gainesville 133, 139
Gainesville Store.............170
Galway, Ned 160
Garner, Margaret................99
Garner, Mary....................99
Garner, Samuel 99
Garner, Silla...................99
Garner, Simon, Jr. 99
Garner, Simon, Sr. 99
Garner, Thomas..................99
Garnett, Manlius Thompson 189
Garrard, James 29, 37
Garrard, Gov. James 56
Garrison Creek..................38
Garrison, John................240
Garrison, Susie...............240
Gault, John 283
Gault, Madeline 283
Gaunt, John S.................142
Gedge, W.L....................161
George Rouse Creek Bridge67
Gibbs, Clinton................271
Gibbs, Francis................271
Gibbs, James..................271
Gibson, John A. 139
Gillespie, Helen 282, 322
Girty, Simon 28, 32
Gist, Christopher 19
Gist, Col. Christopher 12
Glacken, Garnal...............357
Glenn, Annie Arnold...........117
Glenn, Herbert 117
Glenn, Jerry 156
Glenn, Joseph.................117
Godsey, Christine.............392
Goebel, Gov. William..........187
Goforth, Dr. Wm...........41, 42
Good Faith Lodge #95 102
Good Faith Lodge No. 95, F&AM 143
Goodrich, B.F..................77
Goodrich, Elmer...............218
Goodrich, Mary Ann.............77
Goodrich, Raymond.............218
Goodrich, W.C.................218
Goodridge, Chester ...271, 348
Goodridge, Holland............193
Gorden, Thos R................142
Gordon, Capt. Harry 24
Gordon, Dr. R.P...............169
Gordon, Francis Lafayette......87
Gordon, J.C..............277, 285
Gordon, Lizzie................173
Gordon, Mark 141, 174
Gordon, W.L., General Store 195
Gouge, Larry..................349
Gowler, Wanda.................396
Grace Episcopal Church........382
Grady, G.C....................189
Grand Lodge of Temperance 145
Grange 235, 244, 245
Granger Order.................196
Grant......... 147, 195, 274, 293
Grant, Squire..................37
Grant & Graves store 142
Grant, Charles L........139, 142
Grant, Charley................138
Grant, Col. John...............57

Grant, Dr. E.L................139
Grant, Dr. Ed 88, 147
Grant, Dr. J.M................161
Grant, Dr. James M............169
Grant, Frank 133, 138
Grant, Gen. Ulysses S........122
Grant, J. Frank139, 140, 145, 171
Grant, John 57
Grant, Mrs. R.V...............158
Grant, Robert W. "Bobby"314
Grant, W. Ed..................139
Grant, W.W....................147
Grant, Wilma..................355
Grant's Lick...................57
Grater, Ed....................324
Grater, Eve...................324
Graves, Absalom................39
Graves family.................147
Graves, Absalom........57, 59
Graves, Absolom................59
Graves, Dr. 106, 111
Graves, Harry 145
Graves, Jonathan..............132
Graves, Reuben.................57
Graves, Templeton.............233
Graves, Thomas C. 100
Graves, Willis 104, 162
Grayson, Frank 111
Great Lakes Carbon Web..364
Greater Walton Businessmen's Association 359
Green family..................150
Green, Dr.....................141
Green, J.N.....................89
Green, John W.................181
Green, R.C....................161
Green, William 300
Green, William R..............143
Greene, Gilby.................396
Greene, Nelson 124
Greene, R.C...................280
Greene, Rhonda Gowler....396
Greenup, Claude...............291
Greenway, Isabella............149
Greenway, Isabella S. F. 256, 257
Greenway, John Campbell 256
Greenway, John Selmes 256, 392
Greenwood, Mary 103
Griffith, Deborah K. R.N. ..104
Griffith, J.O.................199
Grisley, John 170
Groger, Russell 322, 323
Gross, Edward 249
Grubb, Dr. 106
Grubbs family.................202
Grubbs, Jimmy.................201
Grubbs, Mary Scott Chambers201
Grubbs, Wallace K.............201
Gulley & Pettit's General Store 82, 243, 291
Gulley, Ivan..................319
Gulley, L.W...................243
Gulley, Lester 244
Gulley, Lloyd.................265
Gulley, Pearl 243, 244
Gulley, Pearl Pettit..........244
Gullion, Ann..................319
Gum Branch Creek 150
Gunpowder 157, 205, 268
Gunpowder Baptist 32, 59, 245
Gunpowder Creek 11, 17, 58, 67, 92, 93, 102, 104, 156, 162, 182, 184, 198, 209, 240, 245, 273, 373, 379
Hafer, Dr. Lewis C............233
Hafer, George Owen 234
Hafer, Katherine Crigler ...234
Hafer, Owen Clyde.............234
Hafer, Robert.................234
Hafer, W.A....................194
Hahn, Ernest..................350
Hahn, Raymond.................279
Hall, Elizabeth................33
John 33, 37
Halloway, Jasper 106
Hamcrick, J.G.................106
Hamilton..70, 83, 92, 150, 186
Hamilton Consolidated School 316

Hamilton Funeral Home 279, 355
Hamilton Gazette..........48, 55
Hamilton Landing..............298
Hamilton, Fred..........279, 355
Hamilton, George 70
Hamilton, Jess 393
Hamilton, John 150
Hamilton, Nannie E. 153
Hamilton, Rose 393
Hamilton's Landing 274
Hammond, R.C..................247
Hammons, Joseph 224
Hance family..................150
Hankinson, Davis..............323
Hanson, Col. Roger 116
Hardeman, Capt................109
Harden, Crystal...............307
Hardesty, Richard 122
Hardesty, Uriah................57
Harmar, Brig. Gen. Josiah...35
Harmon, Roy G. 341
Harrison, Clarissa (nee Pike)35
Gen. Wm.......................39
John Cleaves Symmes 35
Pres. William Henry 35, 49, 79
Rev. Joseph Cabell 79
Harrison & Klotter 28, 31, 32, 39, 48, 223, 224, 234, 241, 251, 252, 255, 257, 263, 264
Harrison place.................35
Harrison, Amos.................98
Harrison, Ira L. 279
Harrison, Lowell H. 18
Hart, James E. 271
Hart, Sybil 237
Hartman, John 281
Hartman, Steve 350
Harvest Home Association 158
Harvest Home Fair......206
Harvey, Ruth 314
Hathaway.......... 166, 204, 231
Hawkins, J.F..................281
Hayden, William...............146
Hayes, Robert 366
Hayes, Sgt. Will..............113
Hays, H.H.....................166
Hays, Sam K...................100
Hazelton, Robert..............138
Head, Alma....................276
Heath, Brig. Gen. Henry 111, 115
Hebron 39, 45, 46, 87, 93, 112, 130, 132, 170, 175, 193, 194, 199, 222, 233, 270, 271, 296
Hebron Bank...................313
Hebron Baptist Church 340
Hebron Deposit Bank........271
Hebron Elementary School271
Hebron High School 300
Hebron Lodge 222
Hebron Lutheran Church 87, 132
Hebron Vol. Fire Dept. 352, 390 350
Hedges, W.W.................. 121
Helmig, Mike............383, 384
Helms, Frank B................298
Hempfling family 192
Hempfling, C. Liston 270
Hempfling, Charles............125
Hempfling, Charles O.192, 270
Hempfling, Charlie 270
Hempfling, Elizabeth Dolwick 192
Hempfling, Elizabeth M....270
Hempfling, Emma..............298
Hempfling, John 192
Henderson family 121
Henderson, A. Gwynn .. 14, 16
Henderson, Chester 324
Henderson, Mrs. Thomas .. 121
Henderson, Thomas 110
Henman, Mary F. M. 285
Hennegan Company............374
Hensley, H.B. 235
Hensley, Robert 271
Hensley, Sam..................141
Henthorn, Bill................132
Heritage Bank 237
Hess, Dr Leroy "Lee" 345
Hickman, William, Sr. 27

414 INDEX

Hicks, H.A. 156, 163
Hicks, Jack 382
Hicks, Sam 241
Hicks, Tom 356
Hightower, Carrie 377
Hiler, William I. 365
Hillforest 101
Hillis, George 198
Hindman, John 30
Hines, Capt. Thomas 118
Hiser, Berniece 358
Hitzfield, Nancy Sullivan ..332
HK Systems 374
Hodges, Benjamin 59
Hodges, Elizabeth 59
Hodges, John 59
Hodges, Marie 301
Hodges, Orville E. 301
Hodges, William 59
Hoechst Celanese Corp. 396
Hoffman, Elizabeth 46
Hoffman, Adam Jr. 169
Hoffman, Jule 170
Hoffman, Mabel Davis 285
Hoffman, Philip 169
Hogan House 397
Hogan, J. 163
Hogan, Joseph 253
Hogan, Loretta 253
Hogan, Overton P. 77
Hogan, Pastor Sam 316
Hoggins, John S. 142
Hoggins, Wesley 156
Holden, Michael 45
Holden, Denis 141
Holder, Charles 322
Holiday, William 29
Holland Roofing Group 375
Holt, Milton 343
Holton, Elijah 167
Hood, Franklin Lloyd 302
Hood, J.L. 193
Hood, Luther 302
Hood, R.S. 193
Hope, Bob 368
Hopeful Church 46
Hopeful Heights 362
Hopeful Lutheran Church 60, 66, 67, 89, 159, 221
Hopkins, Bobbye 318
Hopkins, Dr. Y. Frank 197
Hopkins, Rev. Don "Hop" .318
Hopper family 68
Hopperton, Jess 282, 322
Hopple Plastics 366
Hornberger, John 101
Horshall, John 163
Houghton Mifflin 396
House, John and Milly 46
House, Russell 285
House, Sim 241
Houston, Louella 330
Houston, Wanda 301, 305
Howard, Fannie Underhill .226
Howard, George 319
Howard, Jack 135
Howe, Sheila Reno 361
Huatt, Ben 171
Hubbard, Coonie 296
Hubbard, Otho "Coonie" ...253
Hubbel, Elizabeth H. (nee Gaines) 34
Huddleston family 136
Huddleston, Walter "Dee" .362
Hudson, Marvin Jr. 282
Hudson, Mattie 226
Hudson, Mrs. Sam 317
Hue, Albert 287
Huey, Samuel 82
Thomas 81
Huey, Dr. J. M. 321
Huey, Lee 205
Huey, Thomas 94
Huey's Corner 231
Huff, Bert 386
Huff, Bertha 274
Huff, Tom 274
Huff, Wood 170
Hughes, Charley 199
Hughes, Greg 302, 343
Hughes, Jack 282
Hughes, Joseph C. 100
Hughes, Mrs. R.P. 282
Hughes, Perry 282
Hughes, Prof. 212
Hume, Benjamin B. 189
Hume, L.J. 153
Humpries, Rev. William 56
Hunt, Daryl 319
Hunt, Sherrye 319
Huston, Archibald 37
Hutchins, Thomas 24
Idlewild133, 139, 199, 201, 206
Immaculate Heart of Mary Catholic Church 389
Independent Order of Odd Fellows 139
Ingles, Mary Draper 21, 22
Ingram, Gladys 204
Ingram, James "Stoney"204, 340
IOOF (International Order of Odd Fellows) Cemetery 248
IRS 374
Irwin, William 96
Isbell, Jimmy 323, 393
J.A. Huey 178
J.A. Riddell Co 177
Jack, Bertha 280
Jack, Daisy 278
Jack, Shirley 280
Jack's Barber Shop 239
Jack's Grocery 225, 226
Jackson, Andrew 48, 50
Jackson, L.F. 144
James Clore Hotel 222
James Theater240, 283, 323, 356
Jamison, Katherine Robinson280
Jansen, Lisa 350
Jarrell, Alice 109
Jarrell, Ben 170
Jarrell, James 170
Jeager, Al 253
Jefferson, Thomas 36, 40, 41, 42, 43, 44, 9, 152
Jenkins, Bill 142
Jenkins, J.C.109, 118, 123, 124, 134, 84, 92, 122, 144
Jenkins, Joseph 87, 169
Jenkins, William 90
Jenner, Edward 106
Jerral, Jim 142
Jillson, Willard Rouse 12
Joe Weaver family 258, 265
Johnson, Cave 33, 37, 49
Robert 37
Johnson Controls Battery Group 374, 364
Johnson, C.A. 124
Johnson, Cave 59
Johnson, Dick 55
Johnson, Don 104
Johnson, J.L. 150
Johnson, Jackie 104
Johnson, Johnnie Ann 357
Johnson, LaFayette "Lafe" 178
Johnson, Omer W. 279
Johnson, Pearl Rouse 201
Johnson, Pete 281
Johnson, Pres. Lyndon344, 363
Johnson, Rev. William C. .357
Johnson, W. L. 230
Johnson, W.C. 199
Jolliffe, John J. 99
Jones, Aaron 126
Jones, Earl C. 269
Jones, Edgar DeWitt 189
Jones, Everett 316, 317
Jones, Frances C. Willis 189
Jones, Harmon Hayes 268
Jones, Ira Huey 269
Jones, J.L. Sr. 294
Jones, Jennie Pearl Aylor ..268
Jones, John 59
Jones, John L. 152
Jones, John L. Jr. 153
Jones, Joseph H. 269
Jones, Lucille W. 331
Jones, Mary Jane 385
Jones, Rector 308
Jones, Rector A. 347
Jones, Robert W. 238
Jones, Ronnie 332
Jones, Sofie C. Reib 153
Jones, Stan 324
Jones, Virginia 275
Jones, Virginia Pearl 269
Jump, James H. 283
Kahmann, Joseph 349
Katelyn's Shoo Sho Sha Honey Inc. 376
Kavanaugh, Jim 387
Keco Industries 374, 396
Keefe, William J. 171
Keen, Elder 145
Keene, W.S. 132
Keim, Peter 140
Kelley, B.W. 221
Kelley, Effie 222
Kelley, Elmer 221, 222
Kelly, Barbara 397
Kelly, Benjamin Thomas ..289
Kelly, Charles 246, 397
Kelly, Cyrus 196
Kelly, E.E. 291
Kelly, Effie 246
Kelly, Jane Porter 289
Kelly, Jesse 289
Kelly, Jessie 218
Kelly, Jodena 104
Kelly, Kay 332
Kelly, Tom 350
Kelly, Warren E. "Gene" ..366
Kelly, Wayne 332
Kemp, Dr. Robert 187
Kendrick, Joseph 67
Kennedy, Thomas 50
Kennedy & Whitson 153
Kennedy, Bettie 179
Kennedy, J.W. 150
Kennedy, James W. 199
Kennedy, Pres. John F. 335
Kennedy, Thomas 62
Kenner, Ron 383, 384
Kenney, Kathleen 311, 317, 318, 319
Kenney, Roy 226, 317
Kennon, Elizabeth C. 150
Kent, Byron 355
Kenton, Simon 11, 24
Kentucky Enquirer, The298, 299
Kentucky Gazette 39
Kentucky Huckster gift shop 274
Kentucky Post 224, 230, 279, 284, 290, 298, 300, 307, 310, 351
Kentucky Post, The 78
Kenyon, Cecil 350
Kiesewetter, John 306
Kiger, Carl 300
Kiger, Jennie Williamson ..300
Kiger, Jerry 300
Kiger, Joan 300
Kilgore, C.G. 116
Kimmich, Jean Scheben 386
Kimmich, Scott 386
King, David 311
King, Gail 377
King, Harry O. 257
Kinman, Byron 324
Kintpuash (Capt. Jack) 123
Kipp, J.J. 154
Kirby, William H. & Co. ...137
Kirk, William 248
Kirkoff, Mrs. 124
Kirkpatrick family 210
Kirkpatrick, Bess 251
Kirkpatrick, Brad 397
Kirkpatrick, Donnie 397
Kirkpatrick, Elmer 163, 222
Kirkpatrick, Herbert 215
Kirkpatrick, J.J. 288
Kirkpatrick, Jesse 210
Kirkpatrick, Judy 397
Kirkpatrick, Katie 210
Kirkpatrick, Marge 397
Kirkpatrick, Maude 161
Kirkpatrick, Olga 215
Kirkpatrick, Roy 210
Kirkpatrick, Traci 397
Kirkpatrick, W.E. 222
Kirkpatrick, W.L. 253, 291
Kirkpatrick, William 222
Kirtley family 147, 82
James A. 39
Jeremiah 37, 39, 81
Louisa Graves 40
Mary 39
Mary Lacy 81
Polly 81
Polly (nee Thompson) 39
Rev. James A. 82
Robert 39, 40, 49, 81
Robert E. 39
Robert Edward 81
Kirtley, Bluford C. 273
Kirtley, Christina Stephens 274
Kirtley, Elizabeth 34, 80, 84, 191, 193, *246*, 273, 316, 340, 383, 59, 121, 288
Kirtley, Howard 274
Kirtley, James 85, 94
Kirtley, James A. Jr. . 179, 199
Kirtley, Marie 274
Kirtley, Missouri 273
Kirtley, Owen 96, 131, 186
Kirtley, Reuben. 274, 316, 324
Kirtley, Rev. 149
Kirtley, Rev. James A. 60, 178
Kirtley, Rev. Robert 178
Kirtley, Robert 55
Kirtley, Robert E. 132
Kirtley, William 273
KISOR MUSIC 376
Kisor, David 376
Kisor, Nancy 376
Kissick, John C. 122
Kite and Purdy Beech Grove Dairy Farm 262
Kite, Elijah 99
Kite, J.W. 196
Kite, Josie Clore 196
Kite, Mary 99
Kizex, John 56
Klotter, James C. 18
Knights of Pythias 175, 274, 295
Knights of Pythias Lodge ..274
Knights of Pythiasis 84
Kohl, Harold 350
Kohl, Virginia Nestor 366
Kottmeyer, Lillie 192
Kottmyer, Charles 124
Kottmyer, George 125
Kottmyer, Henry 125
Kottmyer, Henry Sr. 269
Kottmyer, Henry, Jr. 125
Kottmyer, Ollie 125
Ku Klux Klan 121
Lafferdette, Louie 170, 171
Lail, Mrs. Kate 126
Lainhard, Virginia 206
Lainhart, Virgina Lee Osborn326
Lainhart, Virginia 68, 287
Lampson, Eliza 156
Lampton, James 156
Landrum, Gary 356
Lanter, Betty 325
Lanter, Dr. Kenneth 325
Lasco Panel Products 364, 374
Lassing Pointe Golf Course29, 394
Lassing, Anna 180
Lassing, C.W. 251
Lassing, Dr. H. C.188, 180, 139
Lassing, James Maurice 161
Lassing, Jennie M. Kennedy 204
Lassing, John M. 139, 180, 217, 188, 290
Lassing, L.W. 186, 204
Lassing, Mary Lillard Brady188
Lassing, Theresa 204
Latonia Race Track ... 348, 367
Lawell, Daniel E. 217
Lawrence, Jim 357
Lawrenceburg Ferry .. 133, 138
Lawrenceburg, IN53, 57, 71, 82

INDEX 415

Lawring, Miss....173
Laws, Frank....169, 173
Le Moyne, Capt. Charles.... 19
Leak, Anne Eliza....124
Leake, Anne....329
Leary, Joe....279
Leathers, Benjamin.... 54
Leathers, John W.....100
LeBosquet, John....126
Lee, Brenda....361
Lee, Capt. Hancock.... 23
Lee, Gen. Robert E....122
Leidy, H.R.....292
Lemforder Corp....390
Leming, Merit E....145
Lenard, Andy....141
Lents, Mollie Newman....269
Lents, R.V. 294, 313, 372, 269
Lentz....47, 79
Rev. H. Max.... 45
Leonard, Margaret.... 77
Levi Strauss....374
Lewis, C.D.....153
Lewis, Dottie L.....368
Lewis, Jerry....368
Lewis, R. Barry.... 17
Lewis, William....381
Lightfoot, Mrs.....175
Lillard, J.J.....218
Limaburg 103, 104, 168, 184, 194, 206, 217, 219, 222, 290
Limaburg Park....351
Lincoln Woods Park....351
Lincoln, Pres. Abraham 120, 121, 122, 123, 186
Lindy, Bob....392
Little Place Restaurant....291
Littleford Day Inc....367, 374
Littrell, Joe....330
Liver, John "Jay"....337
Lloyd, Curtis Gates....164
Lloyd, Emma Rouse 60, 83, 85, 86, 93, 96, 126
Lloyd, Jimmy....145
Lloyd, John Uri 32, 85, 102, 108, 111, 126, 164, 208, 285, 333, 348
Lloyd, Nelson....102, 164
Lloyd, Sophia Webster102, 164
Lochry, Col. Archibald.... 29
Lochry Island 57, 77, 138, 139
Locust Grove....218
Locust Grove School 149, 161 235
Loder House 55, 57, 134, 143, 175
Loder, A. Leon.. 171, 174, 175
Loder, Anora....145
Loder, G.R.....143
Loder, George.... 57
Loder, James.... 165, 140, 146
Loder, John. 89, 111, 118, 124
Loder, Julia....57, 169
Loder, Julia Barbara....171
Loder, L.A. 57, 84, 85, 88, 89, 90, 91, 92, 94, 95, 96, 97, 101, 122, 124, 130, 131, 142, 143, 165, 166, 168, 171, 174, 175, 315
Loder, Milton Bryan....171
Logan, Sen. M.M.....298
Logan, V.H. "Hub"....298
Long Branch.... 67
Long, Millard....376
Long, Monica....376
Loomis, Bert....332
Loomis, Donn....348
Loomis, O.G.....296, 298
Louisville and Cincinnati Packet Co., 168
Lowry, Dr. W.M.....154
Lowry, Pat.... 74
Lucas, Judge Kenneth 373, 374, 375, 399, 366
Lucas, Squire....151
Luce, Mary Alice....321
Luck, Bonnie....328
Luebbers, Larry....359
Lusby, D.L.....282
Lusby, Florian....324
Lusby, Harold....324
Lustenberg, Michelle....377
Lustenburg, Jerry....332
Lutes, Barbara....311
Lynn, Samuel....79
Lynn, Loretta....361
Lyon, Harry....141
Lyon, William....29, 90
Lyons, Taylor....111
Macomb family....76
Madden, Thomas....70, 79
Maddentown....80
Maddox, Dr. John....356
Maddox, Grant....262
Major, P.U.....142
Mallory, Henry....94
Mann, Sue Evelyn....282
Maplewood 84, 339, 340, 351, 382, 383
Markesberry, Lamar....319
Marksbery, G.S.....253
Marquiss, Miles....97
Marshall family....58
Marshall, James....99
Marshall, William....99
Martin Brothers' Garage329, 330
Martin, E. A.....232, 315
Martin, Inez....311
Martin, Mentor....326
Martin, Nora B. Colston....385
Martin, Samuel....89
Masonic Lodge....274
Masonic Lodge #95....164
Masons....84, 145
Masters, "Old Father"....75
Mastodon....43
Mathews, Agnes....33
Chichester....33
Mathews, T.B.....170
Mathis, Willie....351
Matthews, Chichester....59
Mattox, Raymond E.....304
Maurer, Edgar....303
Maurer, Edson....303
Maurer, Edward....196, 316
Maurer, Joseph....147
Maurer, Josie....303
Maurer, William....196
Maxwell, Gladys Jean....348
Mayfield Electric Co.....237
Mayfield, Harry....237
Mayhugh, Harry D.....322
Mayhugh, J.D.....280
Mayhugh, J.D. Lumber Co.280
Mazak Corp.....367
McAfee, Robert....40
McAfee, Robert....24
McAllister, Sallie....169
McBee, Bill....332
McBee, J.W.....154
McBee, Les....332
McBee, Lois....332
McCabe, Anna Cleek....17
McCarty, Nellie....339
McClellan, Gen.....122
McClellan, Wayne B.....58
McCool, Mike....126
McCormick, Irvin....359
McCoy's Fork Creek....68
McCrey, Gen.....115
McCrey, T.H.....116
McCubbin, Roy Elmer....68
McDavid, W.R. Building..382
McDonald, Claude....315
McDowell family....58
McElroy, Stanley Lee....322
McEvoy, William....359
McGlasson family.... 130, 192
McGlasson farm....381
McGlasson, Alice Quiggley270
McGlasson, Galen....385
McGlasson, George....70
McGlasson, H.F.....192
McGlasson, Rodney....343
McGlasson, William....75
McGlasson, William T.....270
McGlasson's Farm....381
McGryar, Maria....126
McGuffin, Shan....120
McHugh, John E.....341
McHugh, Patrick....92
McKee, Mrs.....240
McKensie, Dr. J.R.....163
McKim, Frank....214
McKinley, William "Mickey"284
McKinney, Mike....337
McLean, Samuel....77
McMichael, Glenna....393
McMullen, G.B.....148
McMullen, Green (Isaac)..148
McNeeley, P.W.....92
McNeeley, Perry....95
McNeeley, Polus....145
McNeely, Charles Ernest..224
McNeely, Fannie Ryle....273
McNeely, J.D.....273
McNeely, Linn Boyd....106
McNeely, Mrs. P.....140
McNeely, Perry....91, 97
McNeely, Sara....311
McVille....148, 196, 273, 293
McVille Dam....334
McWethy, J.H.....142
McWethy, J.T.....166
McWethy, Katie Weindel..195
McWethy, Mattie Lyons...195
McWethy, Mrs.....141
McWethy, R.A.....174, 195
McWethy, S.S.....133
McWethy, William....165
McWhethy, S.....90
Mead, Sackett....103
Meadows, Ann....323, 336
Meadows, Mark 283, 323, 336
Meadows, Maynard....336
Meeks, Col. Edward....57
Meiman, Karen....396
Menefee, Dr. B.K.....237
Menzie, John W.....117
Menzies, Dr.....70
Merchant, Silas....110
Merchants of Historic Burlington 397, 398
Merriman Sisters....145
Metcalf, Clarence....393
Methodist Episcopal Church161
Metzenbaum, Howard....333
Middle Creek....31, 48, 52
Middle Creek11, 58, 59, 235, 274
Middle Creek Baptist Church 58, 59, 81, 149, 274
Miller, Alta Fogel....285
Miller, Bertha D.....179
Miller, John C.....179
Miller, Lurrel R.....179
Miller, Pastor J.A.....274
Miller, Robert....149
Mills, Juanita....386
Mills, Louise (Cindy)....263
Mills, Nordine....282
Milner, A.F.....247
Milner, Frank....247
Milner, Mrs. A. F.....247
Miss Sebree's School....118
Mitchell, Benjamin....60
Mitchellsville....34, 130
Modern Woodsmen....84
Monfort, Warren....142
Monroe, Bill....361
Moody, John....135
Moore, George R.....124
Moore, Georgianna....320
Moore, J.H.....92
Moore, Mary Amanda....314
Moore, Thurston....319
Morehead Marina....348
Morehead, Bobby....350
Morehead, Pat....350
Morgan, Allen....31, 103
Morgan Academy 62, 103, 143, 160, 162, 185, 186, 222, 235, 271, 290
Morgan, Capt. Samuel....112
Morgan, John Hunt 108, 109, 112, 118
Morith, Lorie 81, 59, 75, 89
Morris, Billie Jo....340
Morris, Lewis....349
Morrison, Agnes Nancy....32
Ephraim....32
Thomas....32
Morrison, Joe....175
Morrison, John B.....177
Mosby, Thomas....30
Mosby, Mary Spangler....55
Mosby, Robert....55
Moses, Felix 85, 108, 143, 165
Mosmeier, Dave....382
Mount Pleasant Church of Predestinarian Baptist..81
Mr. Herb's Restaurant....393
Mt. Vernon....57
Mud Lick....189
Mud Lick Baptist Church60, 150
Mud Lick Creek.... 17, 189
Mudlick Creek....278
Mulford, Dewey.... 282, 322
Mullins, Brenda....104
Murphy, John....154
Murphy, Major....99
Murray, J.F.....184
Mussy, Doc....141
Myers, Jacob....44
Myers Academy....238
Myers, C.W.....207
Myers, Charles Jr. "Winnie"287
Myers, Charles Winfield Sr.287
Myers, Georgia B. Snyder 287
Myers, Scott....180
Neace, Judge Sam....351
Nead, J.W.....183
Neal, Agnes....59
Neal, John....59
Neal, Nancy....59
Neal, Rebecca....59
Neal, William....59
Needmore....184
Nelson, B.W.... 197, 198
Nelson, Beverly....173
New Bethel Cemetery....68
New Haven High School 285, 317, 321
Newberry, Bertha....179
Newman, E.E.....293
Newton, Henry. 161, 185, 271
Newton, Prof. Henry....189
Nipher, Jake....141
Nixon, Ad....126
Nixon, Enos....171
Nixon, Pres. Richard....335
Noel, Reuben....77
Noel, Sherry Lou Denham 366
Norman, Ben....241
Norman, L.N.....77
Norman, M.C.....142
Norman, W.I.....154
Norman, W.L.....154
Norman's Landing....179
Norman's Store....154
Normansville.... 150, 198
Norris, Charles....122
Norris, D.H..... 285, 294, 313
Norris, John109, 118, 145, 232
Norris, Mrs. Joseph....108
North Bend 33, 35, 36, 49, 50, 59, 130, 193
North, Henry....143
Northern Ky. Industrial Foundation 364
Northern Ky Industrial Park 183
Northern Kentucky Sanitation District....375
Nunn, Gov. Louis B.....358
Nunnelley, Rev. Don....340
Oak Woods Baptist Church.60
Ockerman, Addie....308
Ockerman, Herbert N.....308
Ockerman, Sonny....332
Odd Fellows....84
Ogden, Laura Pettit....244
Ohio Valley Litho Division of The Neilsen Co.....396
Olds, Lizzie....145
Olsner, John....207

INDEX

Osborn, "Uncle Ed" 326
Osborn, Ben 206
Osborn, David 326
Osborn, James 287
Osborn, Selma 326, 329
Osborn, W.E. 242
Osborn, Zeffa 329
Osborn's Store 159
Ossman, Bertha Brown 226
Ossman, Jack 226
Ossman, Jennie 226
Owens/Brockway 367
Owens-Brockway Inc. 374
Painter Branch.................. 68
Palmer House Hotel 161
Panborn, Sam 124
Panther Creek.................... 68
Parker, Elijah 123
Parker, Fanny 118
Parker, Fess 358, 359
Parker, Gloria 321
Parker, Henry 137
Parker, Mrs. Sally 141
Parker, Rich 118
Parker, Richard . 110, 123, 141
Parlor Grove125, 130, 145, 164
Pasborg, Gary..................388
Passiers, Joseph................. 23
Patrick, Charles Abraham..385
Patrick, Irene............385, 386
Pearl, Minnie..................360
Peck, D.R.......................118
Peddicord, Dr. 248
Peel, Ed.........................349
Pendleton, George 122
Penn, W.A......................164
Pennington, J.G................313
Pennington, James............349
Pennington, Leon 322
Pennington, Ray...............361
Penniston, Richard 146
Peoples Deposit Bank161, 219, 261, 273, 299, 351
Percival, Tom..................281
Perkins, George Gilpin......162
Perkins, H.A...................220
Perkins, James.................. 84
Perkins, Joe....................355
Perkins, W.S. 220
Perkins-Campbell Co. 220
Petersburg 14, 15, 17, 30, 38, 49, 55, 56, 57, 71, 79, 83, 84, 87, 88, 89, 90, 91, 92, 94, 95, 96, 97, 101, 102, 103, 105, 106, 107, 108, 109, 110, 111, 117, 118, 119, 120, 122, 124, 125, 126, 129, 132, 133, 135, 137, 138, 139, 141, 142, 143, 144, 145, 166, 167, 168, 171, 174, 175, 177, 187, 189, 194, 195, 223, 232, 279
Petersburg Academy 122
Petersburg Baptist Church 234, 288
Petersburg Christian Church 81, 133, 140, 247
Petersburg distillery 90
Petersburg Distillery..........234
Petersburg Distilling Co. ..138
Petersburg Elementary School 173
Petersburg General Store...234
Petersburg Methodist Church 88, 124, 135, 139, 145, 175, 368
Petersburg school 111
Petersburg Vol. Fire Dept..352
Petersburg's Farmers Bank352
Pettit family 82, 244
Pettit, Albert....................243
Pettit, Alberta..................291
Pettit, Eunie B. Adams 224, 244
Pettit, Fannie Elizabeth Horton
..........................243, 244
Pettit, James B..........244, 245
Pettit, Laura....................291
Pettit, Mary Jane 291
Pettit, William Albert........244
Phillips, Donald................345
Phoenix Hotel   281, 282, 321, 323, 356

Piatt, Benjamin 38
    Elizabeth (nee Barnett)..38
    family 56, 71, 82
    Hannah (nee McCullough)
        John 38
Piatt, Abram (Abraham) S...71
Piatt, Adele 147
Piatt, Asael Daniel 118
Piatt, Caroline 72
Piatt, Charles D. 147
Piatt, Daniel 118
Piatt, Jacob.............38, 56, 118
Piatt, Jacob Wycoff.....71, 147
Piatt, Martha Eugenie de Valcourt
.........................72, 147
Piatt, Mary Catherine Nolan147
Piatt, Robert 59
Piatt, Widow 106
Piatt, William Cain...........118
Piatt's landing 56, 71, 123
Pierce, Edna Beall............248
Pierce, George B. 248
Pike, Clara (nee Brown).......35
Lieut. Zebulon Montgomery35
Pinhook..........................157
Piper, W.E. 161
Pitcher, William..................77
Platt, John 241
Pleasant Ridge 156, 208
Pleasant Ridge School #9..157
Pleasant Valley.................277
Pleistocene 24
Plummer, Charlie 278
Point Pleasant....................75
Point Pleasant Christian 75, 189
Polecat.............................79
Pollack, David..............18, 41
Pollard, Mildred (nee Gaines)34
Pope, W.H. 168
Porter, Ellen 150
Porter, Omer 120
Porterfield, Rosella 309, 310, 340, 369, 381
Porterfield, Vernon...........309
Portwood, Martha Jane......324
Poston, Nelson 288
Powers, Burdetta Feagan...239
Powers, G.B. 238
Powers, George................279
Powers, Mary..................159
PowWow..........................79
Presnell, Katie   82, 245, 286, 288, 291, 310
Presser, Clara Ryle............249
Presser, Ora B. 94
Presser, William...............249
Price, Albert....................163
Price, Bill.......................361
Price, Chris 361
Price, Donna 361
Price, Jennifer 361
Price, Kenny 360, 361
Price, Mary 361
Prospect Hill 109
Pruitt, Cliff.....................322
Pruitt, Jessie....................322
Public Ledger...................55
Puckett, Connie 350
Purdy, O.E. 275
Purvis, Thomas L.   28, 47
Quigley, Eva Beemon 185
Quigley, J.W. 185
Rabbit Hash11, 13, 31, 32, 56, 75, 76, 93, 94, 150, 166, 186, 197, 204, 217, 232, 255, 262, 273, 274, 294, 373
Rabbit Hash and Normansville Telephone Co.............198
Rabbit Hash General Store 75, 76, 197, 387, 391
Rabbit Hash Historical Society
............................392
Rabbit Hash Iron Works....391
Rabbit Hash Ironworks 294
Rabbit Hash Museum........391
Rabbit Hash-Rising Sun ferry75
Rachal & Norman's 241
Rachal family..................241

Rachal, Matson 241
Rachal, W.M. 218
Ransler, George 154
Ransom, Francis 279
Ransom, Grover...............355
Ransom, James 363
Rauch, Fred 298
Ravenscraft, Don 366
Ravenscraft, Mr. 114
Raymond, Belle 148
Read, Floyd 254
Readnour, Otis .. 280, 294, 332
Rector, Mary..............30, 31
   84, 90, 91, 106, 108, 232
Redding, Joseph............27, 33
Redkin Laboratories..........396
Reed, "Uncle Joe"..............239
Reich, Fred 158, 207
Reich, Georgia B. Snyder .207
Reid, Archibald..................37
Reid, Archibald..................77
Reif, Henry 143
Reis, Jim 34, 37, 38, 59, 62, 71, 107, 112, 123, 154, 164, 248, 271, 285, 300, 306, 308, 310, 334, 342, 343, 347, 348, 397
Reiss, Benjamin 79
Renaker, A.B. 219
Renaker, Alvin Boyers......261
Renaker, Clayton 393
Renaker, Henrietta E. Riddell 261
Renaker, Jeff...................393
Renaker, Mary Louise.......261
Reno, Beverly..................361
Reno, Gary......................362
Reno, Jack 361, 362
Reno, Randy 361
Repress, Jerome "Rome" B. 182, 364
Respess, Mrs. J.B. "Rome"367
Revill, Mrs......................209
Rice, Fannie A. Crisler......218
Rice, General 106
Rice, Grace M. M. Dudgeon 81
Rice, Jackson....................92
Rice, Ricky.....................363
Rice, T...........................154
Rice, W.J. 218, 221
Rice, Ward............... 281, 363
Rice, Wilford 237, 203, 216, 254, 255, 280, 281, 281
Rice, William Felix...........281
Rich, Gussie....................247
Rich, Melville 77
Rich, W.O. B. 247
Richardson family.............119
Richardson, Philip Todd ...234
Richwood 79, 92, 98, 99, 121, 305, 319
Richwood Presbyterian Church
   79, 126, 156, 201, 275, 317
Richwood Station..... 154, 155
Riddell, Cal G. 197
Riddell, Carrie 213
Riddell, Cy......................213
Riddell, Edison . 199, 215, 216
Riddell, Eliza 101
Riddell, Fountain 180, 189
Riddell, J.M. 161
Riddell, James A. 177
Riddell, John...................126
Riddell, Judge N.E. ... 290, 298
Riddell, Lewis...................57
Riddell, M......................219
Riddell, Mrs. Martha C. 144
Riddell, W.L. 142, 162
Riddell's Run 93
Riddle, Louis 81
Rigg, D..........................143
Riggs, John Sr...................75
Riggs, Mrs. Smith.............198
Riggs, S.N. 198
Riggs, Simpson..................75
Riley, John C. 81
Riley, Charles W.271, 294, 313
Riley, Eugenia 241
Riley, G.M. 132
Riley, Harry 241

Riley, J. L. 189
Riley, John C......................94
Riley, Marietta.................241
Riley, Oma Hankins..........271
Riley, Susie.....................226
Rising Sun Times, The..... 71
Rising Sun, IN 71, 75
Risner, J.D. 355
Robbins Mound 14
Robbins, Ab....................265
Robbins, Robert 160, 208, 243
Roberts, Agnes 275
Roberts, Arthur 200
Roberts, C.C. 179
Roberts, George W. 166
Roberts, Jack 282
Roberts, Judge Terry. 338, 353
Roberts, Lizzie 153
Roberts, Lt. 113
Roberts, Lulu Powers........200
Roberts, Mrs. John............217
Roberts, Rozanna Odell 235
Roberts, Thomas....... 218, 235
   161, 235, 236
Robinson family 98
Robinson, Aaron.................97
Robinson, Alberta Pettit....244
Robinson, Andrew..............97
Robinson, George 97
Robinson, John 91, 97
Robinson, Julius 97
Robinson, Landon..............60
Robinson, Lewis 97
Robinson, Liza 97
Robinson, Peggy Smith........97
Robinson, Red 281
Robinson, Walter and Sons262
Robinson, Webster............122
Roebling, John Augustus .. 125
Rogers, Col. David 28
Rogers, William................52
Rogers, Alpha 271
Rogers, James Edward......273
Rogers, Laura .. 52, 273, 353
Rogers, Viola Huey 271
Rogers, Will 353
Roland, Beverly 84
Roland, Irvin 353
Rolf, Donald H. 341
Roosevelt, Eleanor............199
Roosevelt, Pres. Franklin . 199
Roosevelt, Pres. Franklin D.257
Roosevelt, Pres. Theodore148, 199
Rootes, Edmund 44
Rose, Catron Louise Gillette392
Roseberry family 200
Roseberry, Harry 200
Roseberry, Susan Reily.....200
Ross, David 40, 41, 42, 44
Roter, "Ali" 282
Roter, Betty 73, 110, 224, 225, 226, 228, 229, 230, 240, 241, 242, 110, 203, 224, 255, 256, 258, 260, 264, 265, 267, 268, 274, 275, 276, 277, 279
Roter, Raymond .. 258, 282
Roter's Garage.................225
Rourke, Bill 176
Rouse, Elizabeth 46
   family 45, 93, 98, 157
   George 46
   John 46
   Ludwig 45
   Nancy 46
   Thomas......................83
Rouse Brothers Saw and Grist Mill
............................154
Rouse Store 185
Rouse, A.B. 219
Rouse, A.M. 154, 200, 201
Rouse, Ada Wilhoit 200
Rouse, Arch 265
Rouse, Arthur B......... 255, 289
Rouse, Asa 201, 237, 238, 280, 281, 282, 287, 313, 317, 321, 323, 335, 339, 345, 355, 393
Rouse, B.B. 132
Rouse, Bonnie 222

INDEX 417

Rouse, Charles..........280, 283
Rouse, Dr. Gladys290, 346, 365
Rouse, Dr. W.O.................219
Rouse, Dudley... 161, 219, 289
Rouse, E.E. 205
Rouse, E.O. 205
Rouse, Eliza......................219
Rouse, Eliza B...................289
Rouse, Ella Rogers............201
Rouse, Ezra.......................207
Rouse, F.H. 246
Rouse, Frank H. 220, 246
Rouse, Gayle.....................332
Rouse, Henderson 98
Rouse, Hubert...................163
Rouse, Israel.....................104
Rouse, J.S. 205
Rouse, J.W...............184, 185
Rouse, Jack 109, 116, 119, 201, 287, 317, 322
Rouse, Jerry......283, 337, 343
Rouse, Jerry W..................386
Rouse, John T. 98
Rouse, Julius.....................112
Rouse, Lena.............221, 246
Rouse, Lillie......................179
Rouse, Marce....................246
Rouse, Marilyn..................386
Rouse, Mary......................201
Rouse, Mary Coffman.......201
Rouse, Minnie E. Kelly.....289
Rouse, Nancy A. Henderson 93
Rouse, Robert.... 104, 290, 311
Rouse, Robert Kelly..........289
Rouse, S.J. 185, 292
Rouse, Silas.......................185
Rouse, Silas J....................185
Rouse, Stella.....................163
Rouse, Sterling..................314
Rouse, Thomas 60, 70, 93, 221
Rouse, W.H.......................217
Rouse, W.O.......................185
Rouse, W.R.......................154
Rouse, W.R.......................200
Rouse, Wendell.................287
Rouse, Wilford..................291
Rouse, William O.............201
Royal Airdrome Moving Picture Show..........................239
Royal Neighbors 84
Rucker, Alfred..................144
Rucker, Paschal.................141
Ruddell, Capt. Isaac 45
Rudicill, Carl F. 302
Rudicill, Mary Sue............366
Rudicill, William...............302
Rue, Irvin.................220, 222
Runion, Rev. Harlan..........287
Rupp, Adolph............281, 332
Ruppert, E.C. 313
Rusche, Harvey Herbert....247
Russ, O.R..........................262
Ryan, Ab...........................357
Ryan, Cliff........................322
Ryan, Janice Cook............355
Ryan, Walt........................355
Ryle, Elizabeth.................. 31
James.........31, 51, 52, 81
James Jr. 31
John 31, 51
Mary "Polly".............. 31
Sallie.......................... 31
Ryle High School.............. 29
Ryle, Franklin...................314
Ryle, Helen.......................247
Ryle, J. Mat.......................249
Ryle, Jim...........................332
Ryle, John P......................173
Ryle, Larry........................373
Ryle, Solon.......................174
Ryle, William Claiborne....373
Sabatasso Food Inc...........396
Sabatasso Foods................374
Sachs Automotive of America 374
Salem Creek.................67, 68
Sallee, Betty......................104
Sallee, Charlie...................104
Salt Festival......................392
Sand Run Creek..................32
Sand Run Baptist Church59, 60, 81, 89, 131, 193, 270, 314
Sanders, Ira.......................220
Sanford, Lawrence.............49
Sanford House..................161
Satchwill, W.L..................251
Saunders, W......................150
Sayers, Dr. A. 158
Sayers, Henry......................54
Sayre, Dr. Adolphus...........93
Sayre, Dr. Frank.................93
Sayre, Nannie Lodge...........93
Scales, William.................170
Schickel, John...................384
Schiffer, Thomas...............114
Schmidt, Michael................45
Schneider, Roberta Kenney275
Schneider, Rose................290
Schramm, Catherine...........57
Schramm, Charles.....133, 139
Schramm, John...................57
Schultz, Bertrand..............353
Schwab, Louie..................323
Schwab, Virginia..............323
Schwybold, Cooney..........265
Scopes, John.......................10
Scothorn, Sara..................132
Scott, Chasten.....................81
D.M. 80
Martha..........................81
Mary (nee Ryle)...........51
Moses.............37, 51, 52
Paly 81
Perryander C................82
Squire...........................82
Scott, Alexis......................391
Scott, Brandon..................391
Scott, Dr. Samuel S... 105, 159
Scott, Fanny......................326
Scott, Irene........................320
Scott, Jane........................326
Scott, L.P. 90
Scott, Lillard.....................294
Scott, Lowell.....................391
Scott, Moses.......................59
Scott, Pat..................320, 321
Scott, P.C. 60
Scott, Rev. Walter...............75
Scott, S.S. 54, 70
Scott, Squire G....................60
Scott, Walter.....................345
Scott, Wilfred....................320
Scroggins, Bill..................319
Scroggins, Edna Hamilton.319
Scroggins, W.D.................319
Scudder, Irvin...................319
Scudder, Jiggs...................319
Searcy, Beverly Jo............363
Sears, Hugh.........................29
Sebree, William..................37
Sebree, Bernice.................311
Sebree, Sallee....................119
Sebree, Sarah June..............92
Sechrist, "Moss"..................97
Seft, John............................30
Seinsheimer, Walter "Wally" 362
Selmes, Isabella........174, 199
Selmes, Patty Dinsmore....178
Selmes, Tilden..................178
Senour, Dr. O.E. 241
Setters, John Elmer...316, 324
Setters, Mary.....................275
Setters, Samuel Bufford....324
Sexton, Susie....................167
Shaffer, James F..................71
Shaler, Nathaniel Southgate152
Sharp, George...................281
Shelby, Gov. Isaac..............38
Shepherd, John H................57
Sherrill, B.W.....................117
Shields, Clinton.................311
Shields, Lewis...................322
Siementel..........................141
Simmons, John....................30
Simmons, Herman.............323
Simon and Schuster/Antheneum 396
Simpson, Ann...................323
Simpson, Frank.................142
Simpson, Malcolm....323, 336
Simpson, Paul...................322
Simpson, Reamy...............356
Sisters of Charity...... 107, 357
Sisters of Saint Benedict...320
Sisters of St. Benedict.......357
Sisters of St. Joseph the Worker 357
SkyPort.............................390
Slater, Dr. Charles R.........159
Sleet, Anna Mae...............278
Sleet, Henry.............278, 279
Sleet, Matthew..................309
Smarr, John.......................109
Smarr, Sharon...................109
Smith, Joseph......................33
Leannah.......................33
Smith family.....................394
Smith, Annie.....................241
Smith, Bill .291, 360, 382, 395
Smith, Billy......................360
Smith, Bob........................291
Smith, Carl........................349
Smith, Charles B...............118
Smith, Clara......................316
Smith, Dr. J.F....................161
Smith, Emerson........265, 360
Smith, Eva........................241
Smith, Frank............154, 241
Smith, Gen. Kirby 78, 107, 111, 123
Smith, George...................265
Smith, Hattie.....................241
Smith, Jane.......................366
Smith, Jeanette..................360
Smith, Lucille...................291
Smith, Luther....................291
Smith, Mary......................291
Smith, Pepper...................230
Smith, Ray........................332
Smith, Raymon.................291
Smith, Rev. Will...............262
Smith, Richard..................241
Smith, Robert...... 20, 311, 360
Smith, Sawyer...................300
Smith, Sue........................169
Smith, Tom.......................146
Smith, Will.......................265
Smith, William A. "Bill"...394
Smith, William N..............163
Smith, Zach F. 160
Smither, William.................59
Snelling, Dill.....................141
Snelling, John...................124
Snelling, Pete....................120
Snow, Kirby......................171
Snyder, Henry F..................80
Sally 80
Snyder, D.M. 189
Snyder, J.H. 139
Snyder, James P................287
Snyder, Michael..................77
Snyder, Orlando................173
Snyder, Permulia Chambers 89
Snyder, Sallie Springer.....287
Snyder, Vie.......................169
Snyder, William 57, 89, 96, 109, 133, 145
Sons of Temperance............84
South Fork Christian Church153
Souther, A.........................121
Souther, Alice Gordon......194
Souther, Lula....................173
Souther, Malchus..............194
Souther, Wagoner Otto.....249
Southern Hotel......... 157, 158
Southern Railroad..... 111, 127
Southgate, Richard.............37
South-Western Publishing.390
Sparks, Brenda J. Richie...331
Speagel, William...............311
Speagle, Harold................279
Spence, Brent...........298, 302
Spencer, James..................357
Spencer, Levi....................175
Sperti, Dr..........................320
Sperti, Dr. George.............307
Sperti, Mildred..................307
Spotted Horse Reproductions379
Sprague, Caroline Hafer......56
Sprague, Louis H. 56
Sprague, Ralph.................343
Springer, Reuben..............287
Squirrel Hollow School70, 102
Squirrel Hunter's Brigade...32
St. James Hotel.................161
St. Joseph Academy..........357
St. Luke Hospital...... 374, 386
St. Patrick's Catholic Church101
St. Paul Catholic Church... 101
St. Paul Parish School.......320
St. Paul's Church.............159
Stamler, R. D....................230
Stamler, Roy.....................283
Stamler, Roy D......... 238, 239
Stamper, Amanda Louden. 196
Stamper, Nancy Henderson196
Stamper, Virgil.................349
Stamper, W.H...................196
Stamper, William H..........156
Stanisfer, Henry..................81
Stanley, Gov. A.O.............223
Stansifer, Benjamin H.......163
Star Bank..........................204
Starr, S.F. 12
Staten, Frances W.............321
Steele, Bettie.....................203
Steele, Darkas...................204
Steele, Elvira....................204
Steele, Fannie...................204
Steele, Frisby....................204
Steele, Layton...................203
Steele, Louisa...................204
Steele, Nat........................203
Steele, Sallie.....................204
Steele, Willie.....................204
Steinfort, William.............298
Stephens, Albert.................83
H.P. 82
John 55, 83
Leonard........................80
Rosie............................82
Stephens Elementary.........371
Stephens Elementary School 332
Stephens, A.E. "Tete"........331
Stephens, Agnes...............390
Stephens, Allie Chandler..393
Stephens, Ben...................167
Stephens, Carlene....... 59, 121
Stephens, E.L....................197
Stephens, Faye..................316
Stephens, H.P. 156
Stephens, Leonard...... 55, 182
Stephens, Lib.... 273, 274, 295
Stephens, Lucile...............351
Stephens, Margaret...........336
Stephens, Mary......... 282, 322
Stephens, Pete.......... 303, 336
Stephens, Sebern....... 390, 391
Stephens, Solon................198
Stephens, Vernon.............316
Stephens, Wilson..............332
Stephenson Mill Road.........68
Stephenson Mill School....276
Stephenson, Faye..............280
Stephenson, Gary..............355
Stephenson, James............311
Stephenson, Raymond......355
Stephenson, Raymond A.....68
Stephenson, Warren..........237
Stevens, J. Henry..............195
Stevens, Thomas A.............94
Stevenson, Dr. J.E.............151
Stewart, Gayle.......... 359, 360
Stewart, Ruie Collins........360
Stewart, Shirley................360
Stewart, Sterling...............301
Stewart, Thomas J.............301
Still, Dorothy....................357
Stith, Adriene....................329
Stith, Ralph.......................329
Stockton, Julia..................148
Stott, Allen.........................88

Stott, Billy..................142
Strader, Jacob...............163
Strader, R....................166
Strader, R.S. 124, 163
Straw, William..............351
Stringfellow.............130, 192
Stuard, John................117
Stubbs, Parson................39
Stuffs, Robert.................37
Stumf, Ghetel.................21
Sturgeon, Bobby.............393
Sturgeon, Chester Lee......276
Sturgeon, Clarence..........276
Sturgeon, Hattie Straub....276
Sturgeon, Luther............276
Sturgeon, Sarah.............276
Suburban Communications374
Sugar Grove..............34, 35
Sugar Tit................157, 209
Sullivan, Leland..............37
Sullivan, LaVerne....241, 275
Sullivan, Leslie..............241
Sullivan, Newton "Sully"..332
Sullivan, Susie..............241
Summers Racing Components377
Summers, Caleb...............62
Summers, Scott.........377, 378
Superior Imports......163, 397
Surface, Susie Carpenter...205
Surface, W.N................205
Sutton, Dr...................106
Sutton, W.D.................230
Swartzel, Bob & Nancy.....104
Sweco Inc.'s Finishing Equipment Division.................366
Sweeney, Ben................290
Swetman, F.L................287
Swetnam, John C............100
Swetnam, T L................158
Taggart, John..........155, 240
Taggert, Bessie..............240
Taggert, Hymer..............240
Tanner, Edward...............30
   Ephraim..............46, 44
   family.............30, 31, 45
   Frederick................45
   John.................29, 30, 31
   Paul......................39
   Simeon...................46
   Susanna..................46
Tanner Creek................136
Tanner family..........157, 231
Tanner, Cliff................328
Tanner, Doc..................141
Tanner, Enos..................89
Tanner, Ephraim.............231
Tanner, Ephraim..............54
Tanner, Hank................182
Tanner, Harry....160, 208, 243
Tanner, Harvey S............185
Tanner, Henry...............207
Tanner, J.J..................168
Tanner, James P.............185
Tanner, Mabel...160, 208, 243
Tanner, Paul................231
Tanner, W.A.................205
Tanner, W.H.................158
Tanner's Creek....95, 124, 145
Tanner's Station 29, 30, 31, 32, 33, 57
Tannertown..................231
Taylor, John 27, 33, 50, 51, 52
   Zachary..................78
Taylor Creek.............56, 94
Taylor, Gen. Richard........123
Taylor, Gov. William S.....187
Taylor, Hancock..............24
Taylor, J.S..................199
Taylor, James................56
Taylor, John................357
Taylor, Kittie...............275
Taylor, W.S.................193
Taylorsport 31, 56, 92, 101, 117, 125, 130, 132, 161, 192, 292
Taylorsport Methodist Episcopal Church................56
Teale, Edwin Way....19, 354
Terrell, John.................57

Terrell, William.........141, 173
Terrill, Dr Ed 138, 141, 143
Terrill, Dr. J.D..............141
Terrill, Dr. J.E.........132, 141
Terrill, Dr. Jonas C.........169
Terrill, Dr. L.B.........132, 169
Terrill, Dr. W.H........132, 141
Terrill, G.W............109, 133
Terrill, Henry...............110
Terrill, John...........108, 123
Terrill, Robert..............117
Terrill, W.R.................158
Thatcher Tubes..............396
The Covington Journal......37
The Gap/Banana Republic.374
The Nielsen Company......374
The Waltonian................34
Thom, James Alexander.....22
Thomas, Bill................236
Thomas, David................54
Thomas, Philemon............57
Thomason, James............142
Thompson, Bill..............142
Thompson, Lewis......182, 207
Thompson, Mary.............288
Thompson, Nath..............98
Thornton, Jean..............356
Thornton, Jesse.............356
Thorpe and Lloyd Bros. Drug Mfg. Co. 164
Thumb, Tom............110, 120
Tilley, Dr...................169
Tilley, Dr. R.C..............170
Tilley, Ralph C..............141
Tilly, Ralph.................143
Tipton, Charlene Patrick...386
Todd family..................58
Todtenhahn, Reynold........313
Tolen, S.W..................175
Tolin, Sen. S.W..............56
Tolon, Sen. S.W.............188
Tomlin, J.G.............200, 204
Tou, Henry..................120
Tousey, Catherine (nee Piatt)82
   Erastus..................82
   Thomas..................49
Tousey house...........210, 217
Tousey House217, 243, 244, 291
Tousey, Erastus..............62
Tousey, Moses................56
Touseytown...................56
Townsend, Bill.........275, 276
Townsend, Hubert............275
Toyota Motor Corporation 374
Toyota Motor Manufacturing, North America Inc. 375
Trapp, August...............294
Tri-City YMCA..............396
Tri-County Economic Development Corporation..................373
True, Rene..................369
Truman, Pres. Harry S.304, 313
Tupman, James..............311
Turfway Park358, 367, 368, 395
Turner, David...............386
Turner, William..............87
Turnpikes....................92
Underground Railroad61, 67, 99
Underhill, John..............32
   William..................31
Underhill, Floyd............281
Underwood, Scott............209
Union 14, 58, 79, 81, 84, 92, 93, 103, 104, 110, 118, 156, 166, 178, 180, 182, 186, 189, 204, 218, 224, 226, 231, 240, 241, 253, 256, 258, 268, 269, 274, 275
Union Baptist Church 81, 240, 263, 276
Union Deposit Bank 126, 204, 240, 241, 324
Union Fire Department.....359
Union High School240, 269, 279
Union Presbyterian Church241
Urb's Garage................103
Utopia Clubs................263
Utz family...................45
Utz, A.J....................156
Utz, Alice..................241

Utz, Dick...................206
Utz, F.A....................206
Utz, Fannie.................241
Utz, James..................185
Utz, T.L...............196, 207
Valley Orchards.............381
Vance, Dr. Ap...............209
Vandyke, Henry N............81
Vanhorn, William.............77
Vanlandingham, Stanley....238
Vannarsdall, Denton .336, 349
Vardiman, A.M...............149
Varner, Robert..............102
Vaughn, Larkin..............112
Veerkamp, John..............207
Verona 68, 72, 79, 101, 153, 166, 200, 209
Verona Bank.................355
Verona General Store.......200
Verona Lake Ranch ..319, 323
Verona School...............179
Vest House, The.............153
Vest, Jimmy.................281
Vest, John L................200
Vest, Joyce.................355
Vest, Lizzy.................207
Vest, W.E..............154, 189
Vice, Jewell................311
Vondersmith, Phil.....298, 299
Voshell, Francis M..........271
Voshell, L.H...........189, 191
Voshell, Lon................241
Voshell, Lou................241
Vox, Volintine..............146
Wagner, B.S.................343
Wagoner, Porter.............361
Wahrenburg, Anneliese D. 356
Walden, Ed..................141
Wallace, John S..............35
Wallace, Bruce..............237
Wallace, Gen. Lew ...111, 112
Wallace, James R. "Jim"...238
Wallace, Jim...........283, 323
Wallace, Martha.............323
Waller, Dr. William.........393
Waller, Dr. William M......355
Waller, Leola...............355
Walls family................280
Walton 32, 34, 55, 62, 68, 70, 72, 73, 77, 78, 79, 81, 84, 94, 102, 111, 113, 115, 116, 117, 126, 128, 150, 153, 164, 167, 180, 187, 191, 200, 201, 203, 209, 212, 223, 230, 237, 245, 248, 256, 281, 296
   Ivalou H...................81
Walton Advertiser 238, 239, 252, 253, 257, 258, 262, 264, 280, 281, 282, 283, 230, 283, 311, 320, 323, 336, 359
Walton Bank and Trust.....280
Walton Baptist Church154, 237
Walton Christian Church180, 237, 238
Walton Church of God......322
Walton Deposit Bank.......154
Walton Equitable Bank280, 281
Walton family...............147
Walton Fire Dept. 283, 356, 357
Walton Garage..........238, 281
Walton Graded School......201
Walton High School 226, 269, 280, 281
Walton Life Squad...........393
Walton Methodist Church 200, 280
Walton Opera House 239, 280, 356
Walton Outlook.............238
Walton Roller Mills.........200
Walton school district......237
Walton Volunteer Fire Dept 323
Walton, Edwin..............332
Walton, Frank...............294
Walton, George..............234
Walton, Hubert (or Herbert)232
Walton, Ivalou H. 134, 164
Walton, J.H.................87
Walton, Jack................106
Walton, James H............130

Walton, John C..............100
Walton, John H. 101, 108
Walton, Mary................173
Walton, N.S. 171, 206
Walton, Noel................341
Walton, Park.................75
Walton, Robert..............332
Walton, Scott...............292
Walton, W.B.................130
Walton, W.S.................130
Walton's Life Squad........356
Walton's Opera House......180
Waltonian, The..............78
Walton-Verona High School238, 280, 283
Walton-Verona Independent Public Schools..................372
Walton-Verona Schools....279
Warren, William..............37
Washington, Lawrence......19
Washington, Pres. George. 164
Waterloo......31, 196, 249, 273
Watkins, Solomon...........154
Watson, Eugene.............237
Watts, O.S..................189
Watts, Owen.................219
Watts, W.B..................100
Watts, Wash.................122
Watts, Washington..........100
Wayman, Rev. D.C...........237
Wayne, Gen. Anthony.......33
Weaver family..........45, 241
Weaver, A.W................314
Weaver, Bo..................396
Weaver, Ella Porter Adams205
Weaver, Ephraim............110
Weaver, Hannah.............110
Weaver, Harold..............275
Weaver, J.F.................162
Weaver, Joe...... 265, 268, 279
Weaver, Joseph Ephraim ..204
Weaver, Lewis..............265
Weaver, Sarah 260, 268, 275, 276, 279
Webb, W.S...................14
Webb, William S............353
Webster, Elmer C............302
Webster, Roy................302
Webster, Vic "Doc".........356
Wehrman, William..........299
Weindel, William J..........195
Welsch, Lawrence...........322
Welsh, John.................184
Welsh, Nick.................348
Wess, Bruce..............43, 48
Wess, Bruce.................376
West, William................30
Western Atlas Inc...........390
Western Spy 48, 55, 57
Weyant, Zella Hale..........264
Whipper, A.J................154
Whipps, A.J.................154
Whitaker, Judith Lacy........89
Whitaker, Mark..............141
Whitaker, William............89
White Haven Academy126, 156, 188, 285
White, Alfred E.............301
White, Charlotte E..........301
White, H.E..................294
White, Mary Higgins........285
White, Melva................280
White, Rev. W.G............126
White, Rev. William........126
Whitlock, A.B. 132, 170
Whitson, John...............186
Whitson, O.K...............355
Whitson, Walter.............281
Whittenburg, Dan...163, 397
Whittenburg, Lewis Sr......397
Whittenburg, Linda... 163, 397
Whittenburg, Marie.........397
Wild Walks Photography..376
Wiley, Kathleen Keeney...275
226, 318
Wilhelm family...............79
Wilhoit, Harriet & Melton ..81
Wilhouit, William............47

INDEX

Wilks, Mills 82
Willey, Father Lambert 101
Williams, Boyd 355
Williams, Brenda 355
Williams, Caroline 332, 368, 392
Williams, Carrie 276
Williams, Glenrose............300
Williams, J.T. 300
Williams, Jake...................300
Williams, Lyle 276
Williams, Smith 130
Williams, William "Bill"...362
Williamson, Mamie............ 31
Willis family 147
Willis, Benjamin G. 57
Willis, Eunie B.................260
Willis, Laura 145
Willis, T.G. 221
Willoughby, Marion 349
Wilmington 38
Wilson, Christopher 52
Wilson (or Willson), J.A. ...197
Wilson, Augustus E............191
Wilson, Frances Stevens....279
Wilson, Gov. Augustus 281
Wilson, Harry 265
Wilson, J.C. 105
Wilson, James...................273
Wilson, James Alexander 76, 150
Wilson, Jane K. Stephens....76
Wilson, Jessie 314
Wilson, Joe 265
Wilson, John 163
Wilson, Robert..................265
Wilson, Robert Hayden.....392
Wilson, Robert Mosby 255
Wilson, Samuel C. 392
Wilson, Whitney 98
Wilson, Wilbur 221
Wingait, Calvin.................124
Wingait, Ira......................174
Wingait, M.F............166, 174
Wingait, William 90, 118, 140
Wingate, Gaines................232
Winston, A.G. 194
Winston, Charles A. 177
Winston, Jack.....................94
Winston, Nina Wright 177
Wireman, Wally........322, 394
Wistar, Dr. Caspar 43
Witham, C.E. 247
Woman's Literary Club 256
Wood, Dr. John A. 150
Wood, W.A.M. 234
Woods, Abraham 18
Woods, Shirley Sutton 308
Woodson, Mr. 115
Woodspoint.......................339
Woolper Creek. 30, 33, 37, 49, 94, 140, 169, 332
Woolper's Bottoms 33
Woolpert, John David 30
Workum, Levi J. 145
World of Sports 339
Worrel, Stephen 354
Worth, Angelo J................140
Worthington, Chick .. 323, 357
Worthington, Mary 280
Wright, Elmer 383, 384
Y.M.C.A. 145
Yager family.......................45
Yates, Rose.......................356
Yeager, L. Conner Jr......... 160
Yealey, A.M.19, 31,32,35, 36, 37, 39, 46, 49, 54, 55, 61, 67, 69, 78, 105, 112, 160, 242, 285, 348
Yealey, Almer Michael.....207
Yelton, Doc 332
York, Newton 253
York, Watt........................106
Youell, George 180
Youell, Kirtley....................57
Zafaries, Thomas 345
Zeller, Aaron Slaughter..... 163
Ziegler, Wilbert 359
Zimmerman family 45
    Frederick 46
    Joshua................... 70, 79
    Rose 46
    William 45
Zimmerman School 102
Zimmerman, Benny 324
Zimmerman, Peter 143
Zion Baptist Church.. 154, 340
Zollicoffer, Jacob Christopher 45